BIOLOGICAL ANTHROPOLOGY

Readings from
**SCIENTIFIC
AMERICAN**

BIOLOGICAL
ANTHROPOLOGY

with introductions by
Solomon H. Katz
University of Pennsylvania

▣ W. H. Freeman and Company
San Francisco

Most of the SCIENTIFIC AMERICAN articles in
Biological Anthropology are available as separate
Offprints. For a complete list of more than 900 articles
now available as Offprints, write to W. H. Freeman
and Company, 660 Market Street, San Francisco,
California 94104.

Library of Congress Cataloging in Publication Data
Main entry under title:
Katz, Solomon H   1939-   comp.
    Biological anthropology.

        1. Physical anthropology—Addresses, essays, lectures.
I. Scientific American.   II. Title.
[DNLM: 1. Anthropology, Physical—Collected works.
GN60 K19b]
GN60.K35   573   74-12327
ISBN 0-7167-0896-5
ISBN 0-7167-0895-7 (pbk.)

Printed in the United States of America

9 8 7 6 5 4 3 2

PREFACE

Several features have been incorporated into this book in an attempt to enhance its contribution to our emerging knowledge of biological anthropology and the evolution of our species in the twentieth century. In addition to the introductions and bibliographies, quotations from recent correspondence with many of the authors have been introduced to supplement the articles with the authors' latest ideas and references. The authors' remarks, which appear either in the introductory statements before each section or directly after the original articles, both provide new interpretations of their original work and suggest how this work fits into the broader concerns of biological anthropology. Some of the classic book reviews have also been included here, as well as excerpts from recent Science and the Citizen columns and letters to the editor of *Scientific American* debating highly relevant topics. It is my hope that these supplementary features will help make the scientific issues and controversies come alive for the reader.

I want to thank the panel of graduate and undergraduate students at the University of Pennsylvania whose appraisals of the readability and relevance of potential readings helped me greatly in my selection. They include: David Armstrong, Ira Gerstman, Pamela Gottesman Freedman, John Hartung, Yigu Kwon, Barbara Mattucci, Joan Schall, and Linda Valleroy. In particular, I want to acknowledge the excellent assistance of Mary Hediger, Evelyn Bowers, and Rochelle Prague, whose many hours of effort contributed to the ultimate completion of this book and, finally, Don Miller for his excellent secretarial assistance.

July 1974   *Solomon H. Katz*

CONTENTS

Note on cross-references: References to articles included in this book are noted by the title of the article and the page on which it begins; references to articles that are available as Offprints, but are not included here, are noted by the article's title and Offprint number; references to articles published by SCIENTIFIC AMERICAN, but which are not available as Offprints, are noted by the title of the article and the month and year of its publication.

BIOLOGICAL ANTHROPOLOGY

PROLOGUE

The greatest problem facing humanity as we near the end of the twentieth century may be to determine the potential of the human species for adaptation. If we are to survive the long-range consequences of our technological achievements, with their compounding effects upon our environment and overwhelming effects on our population size, we must discover new ways of integrating our knowledge of human evolution and adaptation to determine the limits and potentials of our species. The process of feeding back new information about our adaptive limits and capabilities into the world planning system could itself prove to have profound evolutionary consequences.

In compiling this book of *Scientific American* readings, I have attempted to show how evolutionary and adaptive theory and evidence might yield answers to vital questions of concern to humanity now and in the near future. With this aim, I have selected what seem to me to be the best current articles in biological anthropology, including summaries and syntheses of significant data and issues, and have incorporated with them a number of milestone articles from other sciences that have shaped or will be shaping the concerns of the whole field of anthropology. I have arranged the articles in such a way that they point toward the types of syntheses our current knowledge and needs demand. Together the readings make up what I hope to be a new kind of catalog of perspectives on the human species. Necessarily incomplete, it should nevertheless provide a beginning resource for the study of biological anthropology and the broad biosocial understanding of contemporary man.

Biological anthropology° encompasses various areas of specialization, which frequently overlap. Human paleontologists, specialists in the morphology or structure of early humans, work with geologists, archeologists, and other specialists to explore the course of human evolution from our primate ancestors to the species *Homo sapiens*. They also work with primatologists to gain new behavioral perspectives by studying our closest living relatives. Primate studies can range from comparative analyses of social behavior in natural habitats to laboratory studies involving biochemical, physiological, and anatomical methods and data. Other biological anthropologists, more interested in later human evolution, attempt to reconstruct our evolution, adaptation, and subspeciation from the viewpoints of genetics, morphology,

---

° "Physical anthropology" was the first term used for studying the physical evidence (fossil and skeletal) of human evolution. Recently this term has been generally supplanted by "human biology" in England and "biological anthropology" in the United States. Rather than attempt to make fine distinctions of questionable value to a book of readings organized around holistic and synthetic concepts, I have chosen to use the term "biological anthropology" throughout.

and paleopathology (the study of early structural and functional changes produced by disease). To do so, they analyze skeletal remains and, working with archeologists, attempt to discover the environmental and social factors that influenced more recent human evolution. Still other biological anthropologists study living populations, including their racial and subracial groupings and individual patterns of growth and change from conception to old age. Their studies make use of behavioral, anatomical, physiological, biochemical and genetic data to evaluate the processes of evolution. Many of these studies focus on the question of how populations adjust to various ecological settings.

Interdisciplinary approaches incorporating the natural, biomedical, and social sciences are being employed more and more by biological anthropologists in their study of human evolution. Although interdisciplinary work produces a diversity of approaches within the field, it helps unify the overall picture. There is serious concern in the field whether to emphasize specialized scientific studies or the integration of important evolutionary findings from these studies. Both approaches must be cultivated, however, if biological anthropology is to have a significant impact on scientific thinking. With the complex problems of biosocial adaptation demanding holistic solutions, the growing sciences of man will all eventually have to integrate their vast findings in ways similar to those biological anthropology is now pioneering.

The first section of this volume explores the evolutionary roots and potentials of the human species. Since our present status is the product of a complex series of evolutionary events leading from our remote primate ancestors, we must see ourselves as primates before we can look at the hominid line—only at the end of that line do we see *Homo sapiens*. By exploiting our scientific knowledge of our closest ancestral and living primate relatives, we can begin to understand the evolutionary significance of our unique combination of physical and mental characteristics. In a sense, this first section deals with the underpinnings of our knowledge of human evolution, both evidence and interpretation. Our knowledge, of course, is far from complete; it changes from one year to the next with exciting new fossil finds, new and broader questions, and surprising answers. A theme is emerging, however, and new syntheses of information about the limits and potentials of our biosocial adaptability are converging, in the historic tradition of Charles Darwin's *The Descent of Man* (1871) and Thomas Huxley's *Evidence as to Man's Place in Nature* (1863).

The second section traces the origin and development of the concept of evolution from its pre-Darwinian roots to its elegant incorporation of genetic discoveries. The discussions of the basic mechanisms of evolution should provide a solid background for interpreting both the broad phylogenetic issues raised in the first section and the details of human variation, adaptability, and evolutionary problems raised in the later sections.

The third section examines the questions of race and individuality. It focuses on the important shift away from the typological concept of subspeciation, based on classification of subspecies, or races, according to averages of morphological features, to the population concept, based on statistical descriptions of variability in whole populations. Central to this whole concept of population variation is that there is variation which occurs in individuals and develops as a result of genetic and environmental interactions over the entire life cycle. Human variation is represented here in articles on growth, maturation, and aging.

The fourth section develops the concepts of human adaptation and adaptability. It begins with a consideration of the genetic bases for the adaptation to disease and the nutritional differences in modern populations. It then shows how biological adaptations are variably supplemented and complicated by sociocultural adaptations, as in the cases of adaptation to cold and altitude. The articles on infectious diseases and the energy flow in hunting and agricultural populations demonstrate the interaction of biological, sociocultural, and environmental variables, and together make a strong case for an integrated approach to the problems of adaptation.

The fifth section is concerned with the challenges of the present. Opening with the question of our evolutionary potential, it probes the significance of our new knowledge of genetics and methods of *in utero* selection of fetuses. Next it discusses the complex agricultural, technological, and biomedical interactions that determine the world's food supply, and the possible effects on the world ecosystem of industrialization and the release of toxic chemicals into the environment. This last section ends with one of the most serious problems facing humanity today—the problem of worldwide population growth and its increasing demands on the collective resources of the world.

I

THE EVOLUTIONARY ROOTS AND POTENTIALS OF THE HUMAN SPECIES

I   THE EVOLUTIONARY ROOTS
AND POTENTIALS
OF THE HUMAN SPECIES

INTRODUCTION

Nowhere in the biosocial sciences are there more intriguing questions than those of how our species evolved to its present state, who our ancient ancestors were, and how our nearest biological relatives function. When we see how our perspectives on the human species have been expanded by discoveries about our earliest direct ancestors and living primate relatives, it is easy to understand why those discoveries have aroused curiosity and serious scientific interest throughout the world. We are fortunate that some of the leading scientists in these fields have agreed to contribute to *Scientific American*, over the last decade, some of the finest summaries available on these subjects. This has made it possible for me to select an excellent representative sample of articles for this section and, through their ordering, to suggest some of the major trends that are emerging in biological anthropology, as well as some of the critical questions that remain to be answered in the future. New aspects of these issues are introduced by the excerpts from the "Science and the Citizen" columns of *Scientific American*.

Several important trends become apparent in this first section. First, there has been a very strong trend in biological anthropology over the last twenty-five years to integrate hominid fossil evidence with the general biological principles of evolution. This trend is evident in the articles that deal with scientific questions concerning the interpretation of fossil evidence, the application of the species concept, and the related concern with population variation, as opposed to the older typological classification of fossils. The development of more precise methods of dating and associating the fossils with environmental, archeological, and geological contexts has greatly affected our understanding of human evolution. Another trend is the increasing emphasis upon the interrelations of morphological structure, function, and behavior in a particular ecosystem. This has led to the realization that a major component in our understanding of hominid evolution lies in the reconstruction of the behavioral adaptations of the genera and species ancestral to *Homo sapiens*. Research has increasingly focused on human cerebral capabilities, especially the highly developed ability to communicate with symbols.

A major approach to the study of behavior has been the observation of free-ranging primates in their natural habitats. Important links have been established between analogous and even homologous behavior of primates, particularly the social primates, and humans. For example, for the first time it has become clear that chimpanzees under natural conditions make a form of tool. (See "Toolmaking Chimpanzees," in Science and the Citizen.) Of course, for a long time tool use among the primates was considered an exclusively human province. Equally important are our new insights into the interrelations of individual and group behavior, and the relations of behavior to the particular ecosystem in which it occurs. Many of the ecological, social, and individual factors observed by social and cultural anthropologists have now also been observed in the patterns of organization and behavior of other primates (see comments by Geza Teleki following his article). Perhaps one of the most exciting lines of inquiry in primate studies has been in the area of communication, particularly symbolic communication. Because communication is precisely the area in which man excels, studies of primate communication can help explain the greater complexity of human society and individual human behavior.

Communication in humans and other primates constitutes a truly important area where scientific findings are converging. Among the important studies of communication are the studies of primate communication in natural and laboratory settings, particularly the use of symbols by chimpanzees demonstrated by the Gardiners (1969) and Premacks (1972); the analyses of the underlying structure of human language (*generative grammars* as Noam Chomsky has called them); the analyses of the structure of myth being carried out by the French anthropologist Levi-Strauss; and the exciting breakthroughs by Geschwind (1972) and others in the study of the neurological structures responsible for different aspects of human thought and communication capabilities. While each of these areas is interesting in and of itself, together they make us increasingly aware that we are on the edge of a scientific breakthrough that will give us whole new insights into both the evolved limits and the adaptive capacities of human thought processes and abstract communication. New insights linking human evolution with the structure and function of the human mind will probably lead us toward new explanations of some of the universal characteristics of individuals and society.

The following section of Science and the Citizen of paleontological finds made over the last 15 years presents us with some fascinating insights into the issues underlying the field. First, we should note the striking paucity of fossil finds. Although there are many scientific teams working to make new discoveries, there are still immense temporal and geographical gaps in our knowledge. For example, in the reconstruction of hominid evolution there is a phenomenal lack of fossils from the Miocene and Pliocene epochs (approximately 22.5 million to 1.8 million years ago); and even when there are fossils available they come from only a few geographic areas. Secondly, we should note the changing concepts and methods used to identify fossils and also note the fact that new methods are continuously being introduced, particularly by scientists from other fields such as geology, oceanography, biochemistry, medicine, and dentistry. Finally, we should be aware of the state of flux that exists in the interpretation of these fossils. In fact, there are a number of controversies concerning the interpretation of nearly all the major fossil finds, which are too numerous and detailed to catalogue adequately in the short space of an introductory book of readings. Nevertheless, the controversies concerning evolutionary interpretation of these fossils do not mean that there is a total lack of agreement at broad levels about the evolution of the genus *Homo*. Rather, they caution against reading too much into the available fossil evidence.

Science and the Citizen
November 1959

Man and Man-Ape Linked

At Olduvai Gorge in Tanganyika, L. S. B. Leakey has uncovered, almost intact, a skull that may furnish "the connecting link between the South African near-man or ape-man—*Australopithecus* and *Paranthropus*—and true man as we know him." Leakey believes that his find is between 600,000 and a million years old. If this estimate is supported by radioactive-dating tests soon to be undertaken at the University of California, the skull is the oldest yet discovered of a tool-making man.

The skull, that of a youth of about 18, was found with "examples of the very primitive stone culture called Oldowan," which Leakey had previously identified in his 27-year investigation of the Gorge [see "Olduvai Gorge," by L. S. B. Leakey; SCIENTIFIC AMERICAN, January, 1954]. The bones of mammals, birds and reptiles indicate that the youth and his contemporaries had begun to diversify a diet that had been composed principally of nuts. According to Leakey, the skull is in some respects (its large teeth and palate) more primitive than that of *Australopithecus*, but in other respects closer to *Homo sapiens*. The lack of fossil evidence had made it difficult to determine whether *Australopithecus* was a well-developed ape or a poorly developed man. Leakey's find suggests that he was definitely a man.

One reason for the scarcity of Lower Paleolithic human fossils was suggested by Leakey in his article for this magazine. The ape-men did not bury their dead but left them exposed to scavengers. The present specimen may be the remnant of a scavenged corpse left in a propitious location and preserved by the flooding of the Gorge.

Science and the Citizen
April 1961

Earliest Man

Fossil remains of a new human species, the earliest yet uncovered, have been found in Olduvai Gorge in Tanganyika. Portions of the skeletons of two individuals, a child and an adult, were dug up by L. S. B. Leakey, who also discovered Zinjanthropus, the "nut-cracker" man-ape, in the same region. The fragments have yet to be precisely dated but Leakey is confident they are considerably older than half a million years. With the remains was found a bone tool, probably used for working leather. Leakey believes that the tool was used by the newly discovered man and not by Zinjanthropus.

The new species—as yet unnamed— is older than Zinjanthropus but more manlike. The more complete remains are those of the child, who was about 11 years old, and include the skull, part of the jaw and a collarbone, and parts of the hands and a foot. The skull lacks the apelike sagittal crest of Zinjanthropus. This suggests, says Leakey, that "we are dealing with a hominid with a larger brain capacity and somewhat less specialized than Zinjanthropus." But the child had canine teeth resembling those of Proconsul, an East African ape of 30 million years ago. The proportions of the collarbone indicate that the newly found hominid had a bigger chest than modern man. Neither the height nor the sex of the child, who appears to have been killed by a blow on the head, has been determined. The remains of the adult are much scantier, consisting only of hand bones, a collarbone and a few teeth.

Science and the Citizen
September 1961

More Time for Evolution

The first known toolmakers now appear to have lived 1,750,000 years ago, more than a million years earlier than was previously believed. Radioactive dating has suggested this age for *Zinjanthropus*, the "Nutcracker Man" of Olduvai Gorge in Tanganyika, and for an unnamed manlike animal discovered in the same place by L. S. B. Leakey of the Coryndon Museum.

The dating was carried out by Jack F. Evernden and Garniss H. Curtis of the University of California. There is no way to date bone more than 50,000 years old, so they analyzed samples of rock from immediately above and below the level where the bones were found. By measuring the content of potassium 40 and its decay product, argon 40, in six samples Evernden and Curtis obtained an average age of 1,750,000 years, plus or minus "a couple of hundred thousand years." The younger samples showed signs of weathering, so the dates yielded by the older rocks may be more reliable and the finds may actually date back more than 1,750,000 years.

The unnamed specimen came from a slightly lower, and therefore older, stratum than did *Zinjanthropus*. The difference in age is not great—according to Curtis no more than 50,000 years—but the older individual is somewhat more highly developed than *Zinjanthropus*. Which of the two men was the maker of the many stone tools found in conjunction with both of them is still an open question.

The new date for the two Olduvai hominids puts the emergence of tool-making back before the date of a million years usually given for the start of the Pleistocene, the era of ice ages and of the history of man. But many early Pleistocene dates are themselves in doubt. In any event, as T. Dale Stewart of the Smithsonian Institution commented, it seems more reasonable to fit human evolution into a span of 1.7 million years than to compress the entire process into little more than 500,000.

Science and the Citizen
May 1962

Toward Man

From a hillside in Kenya has come a new exhibit in the gallery of human ancestry. The creature is represented by a fossilized bony palate with several teeth attached, plus a lower molar. Both teeth and palate place their owner somewhere between Proconsul, a primitive ape of 25 million years ago, and the earliest known tool-making man, who inhabited East Africa about two million years ago.

L. S. B. Leakey and his wife Mary, British prehistorians who have made several major discoveries in East Africa, found the remains in a slope above a river valley 40 miles from Lake Victoria. The site, a former British outpost called Fort Ternan, has long been known for its richness in fossils. In 1959 a farmer from the area sent the Leakeys a sack of bones collected on his farm. They were unusual enough to bring a visit from the prehistorians and, last fall, a digging crew from their permanent camp at Olduvai Gorge in Tanganyika. In addition to the primate fragments the excavators uncovered a wealth of fossils, including the first evidence of a small ancestor of the present-day giraffe.

The Fort Ternan primate, which has not yet been given a name, had low-crowned molars and canine teeth that projected only a fraction of an inch below the incisors—both prominent characteristics of human teeth. A depression in its cheekbone below the eye resembles a feature associated with muscles for control of the lips in man, which are not found in apes. The fossil primate, Leakey said, is not a hominid but "would seem to be heading toward man." It was established as being 14 million years old by Garniss H. Curtis and Jack F. Evernden of the University of California, who carried out radioactive-dating tests on the rock in which the remains were found.

Science and the Citizen
February 1963

Older Man; Longer Pleistocene

A controversy over the age of *Zinjanthropus,* the Australopithecine hominid from Olduvai Gorge in East Africa, has ended with agreement that he and related early Australopithecine hominids from South Africa lived nearly two million years ago. The date not only stretches out the evolution of man but also promises to push back the beginning of the Pleistocene, the geological epoch of the ice ages, to three million years ago.

In 1961 L. S. B. Leakey, the British prehistorian who had found the bones of *Zinjanthropus* two years earlier, and J. F. Evernden and G. H. Curtis of the University of California estimated the age of *Zinjanthropus* at 1.75 million years on the basis of potassium-argon dating tests of volcanic rock from the stratum in which the bones were found. Their date was in conflict with accepted ideas on both human evolution and the duration of the Pleistocene. Man has traditionally been regarded as a child of the Pleistocene, and the Pleistocene (including a preliminary period of cooling before the appearance of the first continental ice sheets) has been considered to have lasted about a million years. A sharp controversy ensued when G. H. R. von Koenigswald, an eminent Dutch authority on human evolution, reported altogether different results from potassium-argon tests on other Olduvai specimens carried out at the Max Planck Institute for Nuclear Physics in Heidelberg. The dispute grew to include the character of the fossil mammals at Olduvai and the over-all geological history of the gorge.

The resolution came in a symposium on the dating of man and the Pleistocene at the December meeting of the American Association for the Advancement of Science in Philadelphia. Evernden and Curtis reported additional potassium-argon studies clarifying and confirming the 1.75-million-year date. The latter was immediately accepted by participants in the symposium, including von Koenigswald. It was also agreed that the fossil mammals in the *Zinjanthropus* stratum belong to a period called the Upper Villafranchian. Similar fossils have been found in association with the earliest South African Australopithecine hominids. Thus the South African hominids also date back almost two million years.

In addition, an earlier period known as the Lower Villafranchian has been regarded as the start of the Pleistocene. As noted separately by Evernden and Curtis, by von Koenigswald and by Cesare Emiliani of the University of Miami, a 1.75-million-year date for the Upper Villafranchian must move the Lower Villafranchian, and the start of the geological era that brought both ice and man, back to at least three million years ago and perhaps earlier.

Science and the Citizen
May 1964

Earlier Man, Earlier Pre-Men

Two developments in recent weeks appear to have pushed far back in time the eras of the first men and of their forebears. The British paleontologist L. S. B. Leakey has discovered in Africa the bones of creatures he regards as the earliest men, for whom he has proposed the name *Homo habilis.* Elwyn L. Simons of Yale University has proposed a classification of pre-men that "increases tenfold the approximate time period during which human origins can now be traced with some confidence."

Previously the first true man had been thought to be *Pithecanthropus,* a creature that lived about 500,000 years ago. The bones Leakey and his colleagues have found appear to date as far back as 1.8 million years. Leakey describes the creatures as walking erect on feet almost identical with modern man's and as having hands of considerable dexterity. Leakey also announced that he has abandoned his earlier opinion that *Zinjanthropus,* a manlike creature whose bones he found in Africa in 1959, was on the line of evolution to man. A more recent find of a specimen about 200,000 years younger indicates, he said, that *Zinjanthropus* did not continue evolving toward man.

Simons' proposal relates to the transition from the dryopithecine apes of the Miocene-Pliocene epochs (25 million to two million years ago) to the first true hominids, or manlike creatures, of the early Pleistocene, which was the epoch following the Pliocene. In the *Proceedings of the National Academy of Sciences* Simons describes his determination that several fossil bones previously classified under such names as *Bramapithecus* and *Kenyapithecus* belong to the genus *Ramapithecus.* Since some of the bones have been dated by several methods as being 14 million to 15 million years old, *Ramapithecus* dates back to the Miocene epoch. In a comment separate from his paper, Simons said: "Since *Ramapithecus* is unlike the apes in dentition, and since it foreshadows in known parts the structure of the same parts in Pliocene relatives of man, it is logical to conclude that *Ramapithecus* is on, or near, our ancestral line. The exciting thing about this proposal is that we now have a forerunner of man nearly 10 times as old as . . . the earliest undoubted relative of man."

Science and the Citizen
August 1964

Hominids and Humans

A British taxonomist has challenged the recent addition of a third human species to the hominid fossil record and a British archaeologist has proposed that the ranks of living hominids be widened to include two of the three species of great apes. The third human species—*Homo habilis*—was proposed this spring by L. S. B. Leakey and applied to a number of hominid bones and skull fragments found in two separate strata at Olduvai Gorge in Tanganyika. Writing in *Discovery,* Bernard Campbell points out that most students of human evolution now see a smooth transition from the hominid australopithecines, by way of *Homo erectus,* to the sole living hominid species: *Homo sapiens.* Campbell is unable to find enough "morphological space" between the australopithecines and *Homo erectus* for the proposed transitional species.

At the heart of Campbell's challenge lies an increasingly troublesome question: Which fossil hominids properly belong within the genus *Homo*? Cultural criteria—for example, the new remains at Olduvai were associated with stone tools—appear invalidated by the fact that stone tools have also been found with australopithecine remains. The basic distinction between *Homo erectus* and *Homo sapiens* is anatomical: the average cranial capacity of the former is a little more than 1,000 cubic centimeters; that of the latter is 1,500 cc. If a similar criterion is applied to *Homo habilis*, Campbell argues, the outcome is doubtful. A cranial capacity between 642 and 742 cc. has been estimated only for the larger and more fragmentary of the two Olduvai skulls. Thus the figure is far from certain, and it is not much above the australopithecine maximum and is about the same as that for living gorillas.

The gorilla and the chimpanzee may soon raise the total of living hominid species from one to three, writes Sonia Cole in the *New Scientist*. Commenting on the important evolutionary position of fossil apes in general and the genus *Proconsul* in particular, she reports that recent work on blood proteins and chromosomes has shown the two great apes of Africa to be related more nearly to man than they are to the orangutan and gibbon of Asia. She suggests that no justification exists any longer for barring the gorilla and the chimpanzee from membership in the family Hominidae.

Science and the Citizen
May 1965

The Problem of Man's Emergence

Dating by means of radioactive isotopes has now shown that the Pleistocene epoch, the geological period during which modern man appeared, began some three million years ago—three times earlier than had been supposed. One would think that the additional two million years would give the builders of hypotheses about human evolution more time to organize their fossil evidence into a coherent scheme, but such is not the case. This was made clear in March at a conference in Chicago of leading paleontologists, anthropologists, prehistorians and geneticists.

The conference, sponsored by the Wenner-Gren Foundation for Anthropological Research, was called by Sol Tax of the University of Chicago to review evidence concerning the origin of man uncovered since a similar conference he had chaired in 1959. The participants in the reconvened meeting agreed as a starting point that the hominoid line of evolution first split into proto-apes and proto-men during Miocene time: from 13 to 25 million years ago (see "The Early Relatives of Man," by Elwyn L. Simons; SCIENTIFIC AMERICAN, July, 1964). After that, however, there is an immense barren period before the first firmly dated hominid remains appear about 1.8 million years ago, or a third of the way through Pleistocene time. These oldest Pleistocene hominids are the various proto-men uncovered by L. S. B. Leakey in the lowest level at Olduvai Gorge in East Africa. The first hominids the majority at the conference considered members of the genus *Homo* are not found until a million years later; these are the earliest examples of the species *Homo erectus*, long known from sites in Java and China and more recently in Africa. Students of early man agree that modern *Homo sapiens* evolved directly from *Homo erectus*, although there is no direct evidence for the transition.

The most controversial subject at the conference was Leakey's new arrangement of fossil hominids from various levels at Olduvai. In addition to the two lowest-level forms, *Zinjanthropus* (first announced in 1959 and now identified as an East African variety of australopithecine proto-man) and *Homo habilis* (first announced in 1964 and of uncertain classification), Leakey presented a restored skull nicknamed "George" (first announced in part in 1964 and then tentatively assigned to *Homo habilis*). "George," Leakey stated, represents still a third hominid species at Olduvai: an East African variety of *Homo erectus*. In support of his view Leakey drew attention to a comparatively recent hominid skull from Olduvai he had uncovered some years ago and named the "Chellean" skull because of its association with stone hand axes similar to French ones of that name; on reexamination, he declared, the "Chellean" skull had now proved to be another *Homo erectus*.

Leakey concludes that three hominid species coexisted at Olduvai for as long as 1.5 million years; in his view both australopithecines and *Homo erectus* became extinct, leaving *Homo habilis* as the sole immediate ancestor of modern man. African specialists at the meeting, notably J. T. Robinson of the University of Wisconsin, were tentatively prepared to welcome both "George" and the ex-Chellean to the ranks of African *Homo erectus.* They were unprepared, however, to accept *Homo habilis* as anything but another variety of australopithecine.

Science and the Citizen
January 1966

Homo erectus in Europe

Homo erectus,* the immediate precursor of modern man, has been represented only by fossils found in China (Peking man, formerly known as *Sinanthropus*), in Java (Java man, formerly known as *Pithecanthropus*) and in Africa. Now for the first time fossils of *H. erectus* have been found in Europe.

The fossils were uncovered in a quarry near Vértesszöllös, some 30 miles west of Budapest, by M. Kretzoi and L. Vértes of the Hungarian National Museum. In 1963 Kretzoi and Vértes had excavated a deeply buried hearth used by Lower Paleolithic hunters; it contained pebble tools similar to those from the caves at Choukoutien in northern China, where the remains of Peking man were found. In addition to the distinctive stone tools, the hearth site contained the split and burned bones of deer, bear, wild ox, horse and dog but—on first examination—no human remains.

During the 1964 season the two investigators washed out and sieved several hundred pounds of the muddy matrix that contained the hearth floor; the washed material was taken to the National Museum for further study. Kretzoi and Vértes now announce in *Nature* that the washings contained one intact canine tooth and two fragmentary molars that unmistakably belong to *Homo erectus.*

Science and the Citizen
June 1969

Old Australopithecines

Ever since the first discovery of "man-ape" fossils in South Africa during the 1920's, students of human evolution have faced a dilemma. The extinct hominid genus, named *Australopithecus,* was an excellent candidate for the role of man's immediate ancestor—except that the fossils were not old enough. Their apparent age made some man-apes contemporary with *Homo erectus,* the primitive but fully human species that first appeared about a million years ago. How then could *Australopithecus* have given rise to *Homo?* This temporal barrier has now been removed by the discovery of *Australopithecus* fossils that are three million years old.

The new finds were made in Ethiopia (in the fossil-rich formations of the valley of the Omo River, a tributary of Lake Rudolf) in 1967 and 1968 by members of a joint U.S.-French expedition. They consist of four incomplete jaws and more than 50 individual teeth. The fossil formations contain volcanic ash; potassium-argon isotope dating shows that its age ranges from less than two million years, fairly early in the Pleistocene epoch, to more than four million years, when the preceding epoch, the Pliocene, was drawing to a close.

Opposition to the acceptance of *Australopithecus* as man's immediate ancestor began to lessen when remains of the genus uncovered at Olduvai Gorge by L. S. B. Leakey in 1959 proved to be some 1.75 million years old. It further diminished when a 2.5-million-year-old fragment of hominid arm bone, discovered by Bryan Patterson of Harvard University in 1965 near Lake Rudolf in Kenya, was identified as another *Australopithecus* fossil.

Announcing the Omo finds recently, one of the discoverers, F. Clark Howell of the University of Chicago, pointed out that the two jaws found by his group evidently belong to *Australopithecus robustus,* the sturdier of the two species that comprise the genus. Both jaws are about two million years old. One is the largest *Australopithecus* mandible yet found. In Howell's opinion, most of the teeth discovered by his group and perhaps the jaws and some of the teeth unearthed by French workers belong to the smaller species, *A. africanus.* Some of the teeth are about three million years old, making them the oldest hominid remains known. In addition to giving *Australopithecus* ample time to fit into man's family tree, the Omo discoveries support the view that the two species had begun to develop along divergent lines long before Olduvai times.

Science and the Citizen
September 1969

Man among Men

Two fragmentary human skulls recently unearthed from a fossil formation in Ethiopia's Omo Valley may upset a generally held belief with respect to man's evolution. They suggest that *Homo erectus,* whose era is usually thought to have ended some 500,000 years ago, may have lived on in Africa for another 450,000 years or so in the presence or even in the company of his eventual successor, *H. sapiens.* The skull fragments were found by a team of investigators led by L. S. B. Leakey's son, Richard Leakey of the Kenya National Museum, in two exposures of the same stratum less than two miles apart on opposite sides of the Omo River. The stratum is at least 35,000 years old, and it may be twice as old, but even at its oldest it is recent in terms of evolutionary history.

The first skull to be found, Omo I, is essentially identical with the skull of modern man. The second, Omo II, is much more rugged and primitive than would be expected of a contemporary of Omo I. Even though it too is representative of *H. sapiens,* the skull has a low forehead, a flat top and a bun-shaped occipital region that are strongly reminiscent of the fossils from Solo in Java and Broken Hill in Rhodesia, both either identical with or only slightly evolved beyond *H. erectus* (see "Homo Erectus," by William W. Howells; SCIENTIFIC AMERICAN, November, 1966). Commenting on the fossils in *Nature,* Michael H. Day of the Middlesex Hospital Medical School observes that until more than preliminary studies have been completed the relation of Omo II to other early representatives of *H. sapiens* and *H. erectus* will remain unclear.

Science and the Citizen
February 1970

Adam and Ape

How long ago did the most progressive line of primate evolution divide into the lineages that led on the one hand to man and on the other to the anthropoid apes? The answer to this question is usually sought through interpretation of the fossil record, but two workers at the University of California at Berkeley have suggested another way. Their method is based on the extent of mutational change in such proteins as blood-serum albumin and hemoglobin. It suggests that the lineages of man and the apes of Africa may have separated much more recently than has been supposed.

Allan C. Wilson and Vincent M. Sarich report in *Proceedings of the National Academy of Sciences* that the rate of mutational change among the hemoglobin lineages of mammals evidently results in one replacement in the sequence of amino acids every 3.5 million years. The "mutational distance" separating the lineage of primates from the lineage of horses, for example, suggests that the two lines separated some 90 million years ago, early in Upper Cretaceous times. The estimate is within 15 percent of agreement with the estimate based on the fossil record.

Wilson and Sarich find that man is as closely related to the gorilla and chimpanzee in terms of the amino acid sequences of their hemoglobins as the donkey is to the horse. Moreover, the serum albumins of man and of the two African apes are some six times more different from the albumins of the macaque, a representative Old World monkey, than they are from one another. The lineage of Old World monkeys separated from the lineage of apes and men some 30 million to 45 million years ago; the separation of man and African ape must therefore have occurred only a sixth as long ago. Dating the separation on this basis places the event from five million to a little more than seven million years ago, in Upper Pliocene times. This is between seven million and 14 million years closer to the present than is suggested by the fossil record.

Science and the Citizen
June 1970

Who's Who at Swartkrans

The limestone quarry at Swartkrans, a fossil-rich site first investigated in 1948 by the late Robert Broom and his colleague John T. Robinson, is one of five sites in South Africa that have yielded remains of the subhuman hominid *Australopithecus.* Renewed work there since 1965 by the staff of the Transvaal Museum and other scholars has yielded a number of fresh glimpses into the nature of the region's ancient population and the question of how the fossil deposit came into being over several thousand years during Pleistocene times. First in importance is the confirmation of Robinson's long-standing belief that a more advanced hominid was present at Swartkrans along with *Australopithecus*.

Until last summer this second hominid, named *Telanthropus capensis* by Robinson on its discovery in 1949, was represented by only five fragments: a lower jaw, a smaller piece of jaw, a single tooth, one end of an arm bone and a piece of palate. Examining the collection of *Australopithecus* fossils from Swartkrans at the Transvaal Museum last July, R. J. Clarke of the Kenya Center for Prehistory and Palaeontology noticed among them some skull fragments, including a cheek bone and the orbit of an eye, that appeared to differ substantially from the rest. Clarke, together with F. Clark Howell of the University of Chicago and Charles K. Brain of the museum staff, found not only that these fossils could be fitted together but also that the fragment of palate found in 1949 matched the assembly perfectly.

The combination represents the left side of a face and most of the upper jaw; when they are joined to the *Telanthropus* lower jaw, the result is the partial image of a hominid with a heavy brow ridge and a face substantially shorter and smaller than the faces of the robust Swartkrans australopithecines. Reporting their conclusions in *Nature*, the three investigators state that the assembled fossil should be regarded as a species of *Homo* and that it resembles *Homo erectus*, an identification Robinson has long suggested for *Telanthropus*. Until further fossil material is recovered, however, they prefer to write it down simply as *Homo* (species indeterminate).

Meanwhile Brain has concluded from his study of the 14,000 fragments of bone thus far obtained from Swartkrans that the deposit represents a typical carnivore's accumulation, in particular the kind that results today from the arboreal feeding and storage habits of leopards. The prey at Swartkrans included antelope, hyrax, baboon and the australopithecines themselves. Brain's identification of leopards as the probable predators is neatly supported by puncture wounds in the skull of one immature *Australopithecus*—wounds that are frequently cited as evidence of man's long record as a killer of his own kind. The punctures are spaced 33 millimeters apart; this is roughly the distance between the tips of a leopard's lower canine teeth. Brain suggests in *Nature* that the holes were made as a leopard dragged the dead australopithecine by the head to its feeding retreat.

Science and the Citizen
March 1971

Humans before Man

When did man start to make tools? A few decades ago it seemed that the oldest tools dated back no more than half a million years, but evidence recently unearthed in northern Kenya clearly indicates that stone tools were being manufactured more than 2.5 million years ago. The toolmaker appears to have been not modern man but his ancestor *Australopithecus*. This has raised the question of whether *Australopithecus* might not better be regarded as being culturally human rather than as being a prehuman hominid.

The remarkably ancient evidence of toolmaking, which consists of the stone flakes struck off in the process of shaping pebble choppers, was discovered by Richard Leakey in the Koobi Fora area, east of Lake Rudolf, where he found the flakes embedded in a stratified deposit of volcanic tuffs. The potassium-argon ratio of the tuffs indicates that the deposit is 2.61 million years old, an age that places the toolmaking late in Pliocene times. Heretofore the oldest pebble tools in Africa, which were also the world's oldest, were dated with some uncertainty around 1.75 million years ago, or early in the Pleistocene period, and a little more than two million years ago, or roughly at the boundary dividing the Pliocene from the Pleistocene. In both instances the tools were found loose on the ground, and there were strong indications that they were associated with the fossil remains of *Australopithecus*.

The significance of the Koobi Fora discovery has now been assessed in *Antiquity* by Kenneth P. Oakley of the British Museum (Natural History), a strong proponent of the view that cultural rather than anatomical considerations provide the best evidence of man's evolution from the other hominids. Oakley notes Leakey's initial concern that the age of the pebble tools he collected at Koobi Fora might be in doubt. Unlike the embedded flakes, the tools were found only on the surface; moreover, they were less primitive in appearance than the 1.75-million-year-old tools his father, L. S. B. Leakey, had found in Olduvai Gorge in Tanzania.

After some study Oakley has concluded that the Koobi Fora tools and flakes conform to the Olduvai pebble-tool tradition. He attributes their more sophisticated appearance to their being made from stone that flakes more readily than the stones used at Olduvai. Noting Richard Leakey's recovery of several *Australopithecus* craniums from other parts of the Koobi Fora deposit, Oakley concludes that, in spite of their subhuman anatomical status, these Pliocene artisans should be classed as men.

Science and the Citizen
October 1972

Last Adam

There are only two members of the genus *Homo: Homo sapiens* and the extinct *Homo erectus*. (Neanderthal man, who was once regarded as being a separate species, is now generally classified as *Homo sapiens neanderthalensis*.) The heavy-boned *Homo erectus* flourished in Java at least 700,000 years ago (where it was named Pithecanthropus when it was first discovered in 1891); the fossil remains unearthed since then both in China ("Sinanthropus" and "Lantian man") and in Africa ("Swartkrans man" and "Olduvai Bed II hominid") are of almost equal age. Skulls that were buried a scant 10,000 years ago now suggest that at a time when elsewhere in the Old World the successor species *Homo sapiens* was turning from hunting and gathering to agriculture, some *Homo erectus* genes lingered on in Australia.

The place of burial is Kow Swamp, a reservoir in the state of Victoria some 120 miles north of Melbourne. Since 1968 the heavily mineralized bones of some 40 adult, juvenile and infant human beings have been unearthed there along with grave goods that include stone tools, animal teeth, shells and lumps of ocher. Writing in *Nature*, A. G. Thorne of the Australian National University and P. G. Macumber of the Geological Survey of Victoria note that 15 of the adult skulls were sufficiently preserved to allow detailed study.

The bones of the skulls are thick, the browridges are massive and prominent and the back of the skull is bun-shaped and marked by a clearly defined horizontal ridge for the attachment of neck muscles. The lower jaws are unusually large and the teeth are severely worn. Similar features are rarely seen in the skulls of other prehistoric inhabitants of Australia. Thorne and Macumber suggest that the overall skull form includes archaic features that preserve almost unmodified the morphology typical of *Homo erectus* fossils from Java, combined with elements reminiscent of early representatives of *Homo sapiens*. Because later *Homo sapiens* strains were present in Australia some 15,000 years before the time of the Kow Swamp burials, the two investigators conclude that the archaic skulls represent isolated remnants of an even earlier population.

Science and the Citizen
June 1973

Man among the Man-Apes

When did man arise? In recent years serious estimates for the first appearance of the genus *Homo* have ranged from 750,000 years ago to nearly two million years ago. Now it seems that the genus may be a million years older. If that is the case, a species of *Homo* lived contemporaneously with "man-apes" of the genus *Australopithecus* three million years ago.

The evidence for the greater antiquity of *Homo* is some 150 fragments of a single skull found near Lake Rudolf in Kenya last year by workers under the direction of Richard E. F. Leakey of the National Museum of Kenya. The fragments are from a stratum of sandy soil that lies 35 meters below a layer of volcanic rock known, on the basis of potassium-argon dating, to be 2.6 million years old. Leakey believes the age of the deeper stratum is 2.9 million years.

When the fragments were assembled, they made up much of the skull of a hominid with a cranial capacity of some 810 cubic centimeters. There are two species of *Australopithecus;* the smaller one has a cranial capacity of about 420 cc. and the larger a capacity of about 530 cc. The cranial capacity of *Homo sapiens* averages 1,400 cc.; the capacity of his fossil relative *Homo erectus* ranges from 900 to 1,100 cc. Leakey notes that the cranial capacity of the Lake Rudolf skull is too large for *Australopithecus*, and that the skull is quite unlike the skull of *Homo erectus*. He therefore proposes classifying the fossil as *Homo* sp. indet. (species indeterminate).

The oldest *Australopithecus* fossils date back 5.5 million years; the youngest, less than a million years. Leakey's father, the late L. S. B. Leakey, believed that a hominid contemporary of *Australopithecus* he had found at Olduvai Gorge in Tanzania was a member of the genus *Homo,* and he classified it *Homo habilis.* Moreover, at Swartkrans in South Africa, J. T. Robinson found among plentiful *Australopithecus* fossils fragmentary remains that were later classified as belonging to the genus *Homo.* The big-brained hominid of Lake Rudolf, however, is at least a million years older than any known so far.

Science and the Citizen
July 1964

Toolmaking Chimpanzees

The use of "tools" is uncommon but not unknown in the animal kingdom: solitary wasps tamp the soil over nest entrances with pebbles; short-billed finches probe for bark-concealed insects with thorns; sea otters have a hammer-and-anvil technique for opening shellfish. Toolmaking, however, appears to be confined to the primates and, except in the case of man, the behavior is known for the most part only among caged apes and monkeys. Jane Goodall of the University of Cambridge has now reported in *Nature* her observations of toolmaking and tool-using among wild chimpanzees over a three-year period in a Tanganyika reserve. The most frequently observed behavior (91 occasions) involved the chimpanzees' making probes out of twigs six inches to a foot long by stripping off leaves with their hands or lips. The probes were then pushed into holes in termite nests. When a probe was withdrawn, a few termites that had seized it were eaten.

Some chimpanzees prepared their "tools" before visiting termite nests, and immature animals frequently watched their elders at work and imitated their actions. Because the termites extend their passages to the surface of the nest only during three months of the year, this form of tool-using is unrewarding most of the time. Nonetheless, Miss Goodall saw one mature chimpanzee and one immature one make, and attempt to use, a tool out of season. She concludes that the chimpanzee population of the reserve is transmitting a series of primitive cultural traditions from one generation to the next.

Science and the Citizen
January 1964

The Smiles of Men and Monkeys

"When men are amused, they draw back the corners of their mouth and emit a series of quavering grunts. Why should they make this quite arbitrary gesture, rather than some other one, to show friendliness and pleasure?" With these words R. J. Andrew, a Yale University biologist, begins an article in *Science* inquiring into the evolution of facial expression.

Andrew finds that man's basic repertory of facial displays is clearly related to that of the apes and that its evolution has been parallel to the evolution of similar displays in other primates. Whereas expressions do communicate information about an animal's motivations and intentions, expressions did not originate as reflections of drives or emotions. They stem rather from such simple responses as those associated with the protection of vulnerable areas of the head, preparation for biting, vigorous respiration, grooming and so on. In the course of evolution increased facial mobility due to changes in musculature, coupled with an increased need among social animals for displays conveying information, has "facilitated" these responses; they seem to have become less tied to a physical response and to have acquired more generalized meanings. Parting the lips and flicking out the tongue, for example, is a preliminary to grooming in social primates; in some advanced primates lip-smacking may become a generalized form of greeting.

Tracing the "grin," or retraction of the corners of the mouth, Andrew notes its occurrence in various primates and man. Originally it was apparently a protective response to a threat to the animal's head or a preparation for biting. In more advanced primates it becomes a generalized "startle" response. A man, Andrew writes, may grin while he is being criticized by a superior, while he is fighting or engaged in other physical exertion and even "during periods when some undesirable event seems likely to occur suddenly"—as when he is making fine adjustments in a delicate mechanism. Speculating on the connection between smiles and feelings of pleasure, Andrew reports that a large change in stimulation is generally considered unpleasant and evokes a protective response. With "facilitation" the grin—now a smile—may have come to be evoked by a small change in stimulation. Such a change, he points out, is considered pleasurable and is, indeed, one of the conditions of a successful joke.

Science and the Citizen
August 1961

Two-minded Monkeys

Monkeys that behave as though they had two separate and independent brains are opening "promising new approaches to the study of cerebral organization." So says R. W. Sperry, psychobiologist at the California Institute of Technology, in a recent article in *Science*. Sperry and his associates produce the unusual behavior by severing the nerves that connect the hemispheres of the monkeys' brains and then giving the animals special training.

The "twin brain" technique is a product of an investigation, begun by Sperry nearly 10 years ago, into the functions of the corpus callosum, a large bundle of nerve fibers joining the right and left hemispheres of the brain. From its structure and location, the callosal bundle (particularly prominent in man) was assumed to integrate the activities of the cerebral hemispheres, each of which can carry out most of the functions of the brain on its own. Strangely, however, cutting the callosal fibers, as was occasionally done in epilepsy patients, seemed to make little difference in behavior.

Working with cats and monkeys, Sperry and his students finally proved that the corpus callosum ties the hemispheres together, functionally as well as structurally, by cutting not only the corpus callosum but also the optic chiasm (where the optic fibers cross over) in such a way that the left hemisphere receives visual information from the left eye only and the right hemisphere only from the right. A normal animal taught through one eye to perform a task involving visual discrimination can perform it using the other eye. Treated animals retain the ability for tasks learned before surgery but not for those learned afterward. Moreover, the split-brain animal can be taught contradictory discrimination tasks with each eye.

In one series of experiments C. B. Trevarthen, a member of Sperry's group, placed the monkeys in a training box equipped with polarized light filters to make a stimulus object look different to the two eyes. Thus while the animal learned in one hemisphere that it could get a reward by pushing a lever marked with a circle but not one marked with a cross, it learned the reverse in the other hemisphere. Many split-brain monkeys were taught the two tasks during the same training period by switching back and forth between the two eyes. They learned both tasks as quickly as an ordinary monkey learns just one.

The behavior of divided-brain monkeys is otherwise quite normal. They encounter no special difficulties because of having two "masters," partly because both halves of the brain receive much the same visual and auditory stimulation when the animal is outside the training box. When the animal is made to choose between two tasks—one learned by the right hemisphere and the other by the left—there is only slight hesitancy over which to do. First one hemisphere takes command and does what it learned; then the other gets a turn.

The first paper in this section, "The Earliest Apes" by Elwyn L. Simons, represents years of study of the fossils leading from the early hominoids (apes) toward the Hominidae (the line leading directly to *Homo sapiens*, of which the human species is the only survivor). For a clearer picture of both the current diversity of the primates and their early ancestors from the Paleocene to the present, two diagrams are presented from one of Simons' earlier works (see "The Early Relatives of Man," *Scientific American* Offprint 622). What makes "The Earliest Apes" so useful, aside from the interesting facts, fossil finds, and interpretations that it offers, are the insights that it provides into the kinds of evidence available and the kinds of logic used by a paleoprimatologist in constructing a meaningful pattern. It is also evident in reading Simons' article that the scarcity and fragmentary nature of the fossil evidence for hominid evolution have led inevitably to considerable controversy surrounding its interpretation.

For example, one such controversy surrounds the fossil called *Ramapithecus*, first found in India in the 1930's by G. E. Lewis and dated to the Late Miocene. As can be seen from Simons' second diagram, he considers *Ramapithecus* to be a form that lies directly on the line between the earlier *Aegyptopithecus* and dryopithecines and the later genus *Homo*. The fossil evidence from the Miocene epoch on the whole, as stated earlier, is scanty, and, therefore, *Ramapithecus* is perhaps the only and the best candidate for a human ancestor. A later discovery by Louis Leakey at Fort Ternan in East Africa, which was named *Kenyapithecus*, was also reinterpreted by Simons as being a species of *Ramapithecus* (see "Toward Man" in Science and the Citizen, p. 9). However, more recent evidence cited by William W. Howells (1973) interprets these fragmentary fossils of *Ramapithecus* as not being as close to modern humans as previously suspected, that is, directly ancestral, although they are still probably of hominid status.

In light of Simons' article, Richard Leakey's recent find of crania and other material, reported in the Science and the Citizen column "Man among Man-Apes" appears to represent a hominid that is separate from the well-known australopithecine line and may be related to the earlier *Ramapithecus* fossil remains. This suggests that the genus *Australopithecus* may not have led to the genus *Homo*, a possibility calls for some reconsideration of the phylogenetic status of the so-called *Homo habilis* fossil evidence, discovered by Richard's father, the late Louis Leakey, since it too may not be part of the genus *Homo* (see "Hominids and Humans," in Science and the Citizen, p. 10, and the communication from Napier, p. 23). Moreover, the evidence has also been disputed from another direction. The famous paleontologist and anatomist Sir Wilfrid E. LeGros Clark has suggested that the cranial capacity of *Homo habilis* of about 680 cubic centimeters is too small for *Homo habilis* to be considered part of the genus *Homo*. If this newest find by Richard Leakey ("ER 1470") is as fully verified in the future as it now appears to be, it will mean that the hominid line diverged from some ape ancestor much earlier than was generally supposed on the basis of fossil evidence and structural studies of the differences of various serum and other proteins and of the DNA of living primates (see "Adam and Ape," in Science and the Citizen, p. 13).

In considering other methods of dealing with the fossil evidence of human evolution, no discussion would be complete without including the multidisciplinary approach developed by Sherwood L. Washburn. Perhaps more than any other anthropologist in recent years, Washburn has integrated the study of the physical evidence of human origins with reconstructions of their behavioral potentials. This approach is illustrated in his article "Tools and Human Evolution." By examining the potential range of behavior necessary for tool-making, upright posture, speech, and culture, Washburn has suggested important new ways of approaching human evolution. Although we should always be wary of overstepping the limits of new approaches, this

TAXONOMY of the living primates ranks the order's 52 genera (*scientific and common names at far right*) according to divisions of higher grade. There is no universal agreement on how this should be done. For example, the two infraorders of anthropoids in this system are held by many investigators to be suborders and thus equal in rank with the Prosimii. It is generally agreed, however, that man belongs among the catarrhines and, within that group, is a member of the hominoid superfamily (as are all the apes) and the hominid family, in which he is the only living species of the genus *Homo*. (From E. L. Simons, "The Early Relatives of Man." Copyright © 1964 by Scientific American, Inc. All rights reserved.)

ORDER	SUBORDER	INFRAORDER
PRIMATES	PROSIMII	LEMURIFORMES
		LORISIFORMES
		TARSIIFORMES
	ANTHROPOIDEA	PLATYRRHINI
		CATARRHINI

SUPERFAMILY	FAMILY	SUBFAMILY	*GENUS*	COMMON NAME
TUPAIOIDEA	TUPAIIDAE	TUPAIINAE	*TUPAIA* *DENDROGALE* *UROGALE*	COMMON TREE SHREW SMOOTH-TAILED TREE SHREW PHILIPPINE TREE SHREW
		PTILOCERCINAE	*PTILOCERCUS*	PEN-TAILED TREE SHREW
LEMUROIDEA	LEMURIDAE	LEMURINAE	*LEMUR* *HAPALEMUR* *LEPILEMUR*	COMMON LEMUR GENTLE LEMUR SPORTIVE LEMUR
		CHEIROGALEINAE	*CHEIROGALEUS* *MICROCEBUS*	MOUSE LEMUR DWARF LEMUR
	INDRIDAE		*INDRI* *LICHANOTUS* *PROPITHECUS*	INDRIS AVAHI SIFAKA
	DAUBENTONIIDAE		*DAUBENTONIA*	AYE-AYE
LORISOIDEA	LORISIDAE		*LORIS* *NYCTICEBUS* *ARCTOCEBUS* *PERODICTICUS*	SLENDER LORIS SLOW LORIS ANGWANTIBO POTTO
	GALAGIDAE		*GALAGO*	BUSH BABY
TARSIOIDEA	TARSIIDAE		*TARSIUS*	TARSIER
CEBOIDEA	CALLITHRICIDAE		*CALLITHRIX* *LEONTOCEBUS*	PLUMED AND PYGMY MARMOSETS TAMARIN
	CEBIDAE	CALLIMICONINAE	*CALLIMICO*	GOELDI'S MARMOSET
		AOTINAE	*AOTES* *CALLICEBUS*	DOUROUCOULI TITI
		PITHECINAE	*PITHECIA* *CHIROPOTES* *CACAJAO*	SAKI SAKI UAKARI
		ALOUATTINAE	*ALOUATTA*	HOWLER
		CEBINAE	*CEBUS* *SAIMIRI*	CAPUCHIN SQUIRREL MONKEY
		ATELINAE	*ATELES* *BRACHYTELES* *LAGOTHRIX*	SPIDER MONKEY WOOLLY SPIDER MONKEY WOOLLY MONKEY
CERCOPITHECOIDEA	CERCOPITHECIDAE	CERCOPITHECINAE	*MACACA* *CYNOPITHECUS* *CERCOCEBUS* *PAPIO* *THEROPITHECUS* *CERCOPITHECUS* *ERYTHROCEBUS*	MACAQUE BLACK APE MANGABEY BABOON, DRILL GELADA GUENON PATAS MONKEY
		COLOBINAE	*PRESBYTIS* *PYGATHRIX* *RHINOPITHECUS* *SIMIAS* *NASALIS* *COLOBUS*	COMMON LANGUR DOUC LANGUR SNUB-NOSED LANGUR PAGI ISLAND LANGUR PROBOSCIS MONKEY GUERAZA
HOMINOIDEA	HYLOBATIDAE		*HYLOBATES* *SYMPHALANGUS*	GIBBON SIAMANG
	PONGIDAE		*PONGO* *PAN* *GORILLA*	ORANGUTAN CHIMPANZEE GORILLA
	HOMINIDAE		*HOMO*	MAN

expanded perspective nevertheless allows us to use the neurological, anatomical, ethological, and anthropological sciences in various combinations to expand our theories about the necessary concomitants of human evolution. The fact that humans use symbolic communication, cooperative behavior, and multipurpose tools raises important questions, which can only be answered by attempting to reconstruct how the morphology, behavior, ecology, and social priorities all interacted to produce effective adaptation for our human ancestors. This expanded view prompts considerations of, for example, the origins of tools and their possible relations to speech; the concept of culture as it applies to the behavior of the social primates and to human evolution; and the significance of bipedalism for potential local adaptations to a particular ecosystem. Raising these issues is only the first step toward the holistic theories and explanations of human nature offered by these new frameworks for research.

In the following note, Washburn gives his current view of the relationship between tool use and human evolution. In the same communication, he points out that the theory that in monkeys and apes year-round sexual activity holds the society together was included erroneously in the original article. As his article "The Social Life of Baboons" notes, this is not the case.

Since this paper was written more than a dozen years ago, there have been great advances in the discovery of fossil humans, the techniques of determining dates, and the knowledge of the behaviors of the nonhuman primates. Fossils of *Australopithecus* (in the broadest possible sense) go back more than 4 million years. Forms intermediate between *Australopithecus* and traditional *Homo erectus* date between 3 and 1 million years. Living sites with stone tools and bones date back at least to 2.6 million years. In general the theory that tool-using, bipedalism, and hunting constitute the human way of life still seems probable. But the idea that events went rapidly after the discovery of tools is clearly wrong. This notion was based on the short time scale of the guess dates prior to the radiometric date and the belief that tool-using was so important that it would have changed the course of evolution rapidly. But chimpanzees make considerable use of objects for a variety of purposes, showing that object use does not necessarily make a great change in the way of life. [See the Science

PHYLOGENY of all the primates traces the evolution of the order from its beginnings sometime before the middle of the Paleocene (*see time scale in illustration at right*). The first to appear were prosimian families that stemmed from a basic stock of small and sometimes arboreal mammals called Insectivora (whose living kin include the shrews and moles). The chart's broken lines show hypothetical evolutionary relations. In the interval between Eocene and Miocene times these relations are particularly uncertain. Solid lines (*color*) show the periods when species of the groups named (*black type*) are known to have flourished. The names of two prosimian and two anthropoid genera appear in color. Subsequent to the completion of this diagram in 1963, further details were incorporated by Simons in 1967 (see "The Earliest Apes"). As expected some of the new finds have clarified the details of this basic scheme. Nevertheless it has generally stood the test of time.

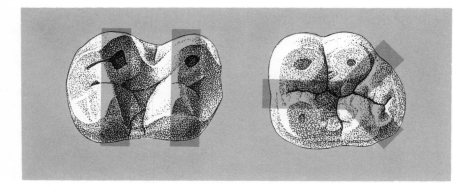

SHAPE OF MOLAR TEETH serves to split the catarrhines into two groups. The crowns of Old World monkeys' molars have a cusp at each corner (*baboon, left*): both front and rear pairs of cusps are connected by ridges (*color*). The crowns of apes' and man's lower molars normally have five cusps (*chimpanzee, right*), and the "valleys" between the cusps resemble the letter Y (*color*). This Y-5 pattern first appeared some 24 million years ago. It serves to identify the abundance of hominoid fossil teeth, and, because of its consistency, it has provided paleontologists with a constant guide to the identification of these fossils.

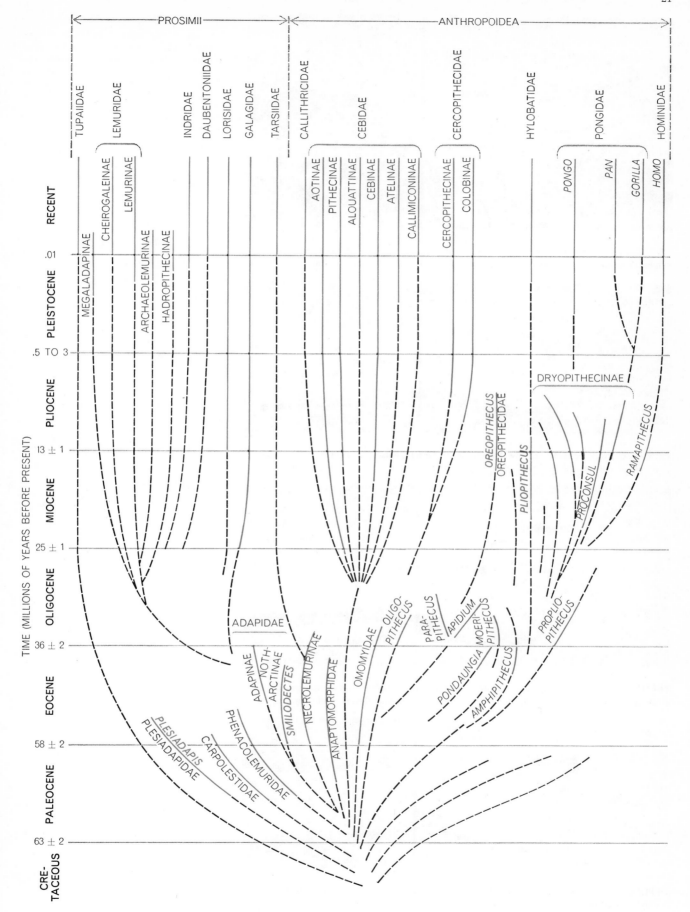

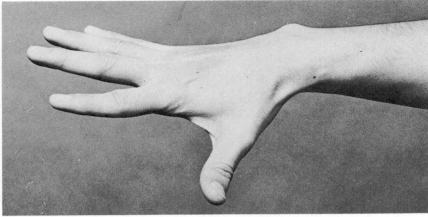

(1)

DIVERGENCE, generally associated with weight-bearing function of hand, is achieved by extension at the metacarpophalangeal joints. All mammalian paws are capable of this action.

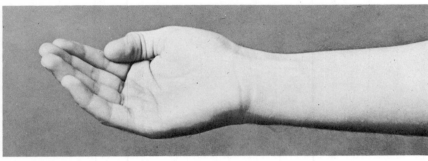

(2)

CONVERGENCE is achieved by flexion at metacarpophalangeal joints. Two convergent paws equal one prehensile hand; many mammals hold food in two convergent paws to eat.

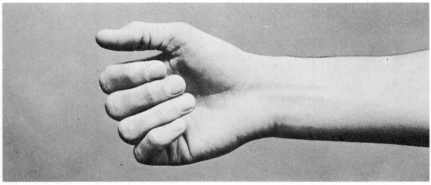

(3)

PREHENSILITY, the ability to wrap the fingers around an object, is a special primate characteristic, related to the emergence of the specialized thumb during evolutionary process.

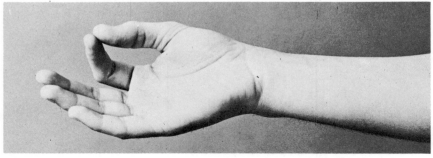

(4)

OPPOSABILITY is ability to sweep thumb across palm while rotating it around its longitudinal axis. Many primates can do this, but underlying structures are best developed in man.

Photographs by Robert Saracco

and the Citizen column "Toolmaking Chimpanzees."] Further, the early tools were there for hundreds of thousands of years without indications of great changes. There must have been a very long formative period after the separation of humans and apes. The origin of the human way of life lies back in that period, possibly 5 to 10 million years ago.

Sherwood L. Washburn, November 1973

John Napier, author of "The Antiquity of Human Walking," has studied in great detail the anatomical concomitants of tool use, upright posture, and walking. Napier has demonstrated some very important physical characteristics that distinguish human evolution from the evolution of other primates. Besides those characteristics associated with the enlarged cranium and small facial structure of humans, upright posture and manual dexterity are probably the most important. Napier has devoted considerable study to the opposability of the thumb with the fingers, and suggests that of the four mammalian possibilities, two basic hand grips are uniquely developed in the living primates. The first is called the *power grip* (Picture 3) and is common to all primates. It allows the grasping of heavy objects or the supporting of one's body on a limb, and it is thought to be very important in the locomotions of many arboreal primates. The second grip—the most developed in humans (Picture 4)—is the one with which we write. It is called the *precision grip* and is associated with fine motor control and ability for delicate manipulation. Its use shows an important dependence on fine eye-hand coordination, which requires complex associations involving integrated feedback between the occipital visual areas and the motor and cerebellar areas of the brain. Most of these same skills involved in writing were also used in early tool-making and hence are intimately associated with what is thought to be one of the most significant selective advantages of the early hominids. It might be interesting to question how language and the specialized use of the hands in tool-making and writing are related to various lateralized functions of the cerebral cortex (see "Two Minded Monkeys," in Science and the Citizen, p. 17).

In reference to the other major human physical adaptation, Napier has supplied us with a classic study of the significance of human walking. His detailed analysis of walking and posture suggests the potential of structural and functional anatomical studies in biological anthropology. Nevertheless, the analyses made in Napier's article were carried out without the benefit of the electromyographic methods, which measure the electrical changes in muscle in response to normal movements. Using evidence from these new techniques and biomechanical analyses of *Homo sapiens* and australopithecine skeletal material, C. Owen Lovejoy and his associates (1973) reasoned that australopithecines do not, as Napier thought, have a different locomotor pattern; apparently, the striding gait was already present in the early hominids. This work exemplifies the ways in which the newly emerging methods help to reshape our models of human evolution.

In a recent letter Napier comments on two new findings that bear on the study of bipedalism:

> One rather surprising additional piece of evidence suggests that the bipedalism of *Homo habilis* was not necessarily antecedent to that of *Homo erectus* and, thus, to modern man. A study by Day and Wood (1968) of the talus (astragalus) of *Homo habilis* by a multivariate statistical technique indicates that it was very different both from the modern human and from the gorilla and chimpanzee pattern. Its nearest counterpart is the talus of *Australopithecus* from Kromdraai in South Africa. This and other evidence (unrelated to bipedalism as such) point to the possibility of *Homo habilis* being an advanced australopithecine rather than an early *Homo*.

> The recent discovery of a skull from the East Rudolf area of East Africa by Richard Leakey gives further credence to this revised view of the taxonomic

status of *Homo habilis*. The skull, which has not yet been officially named and is known by its site number, KNM-ER 1470, has been dated at nearly 3 million years old. The skull is very advanced in many features, including a large cranial capacity, and is distinctly reminiscent of *Homo erectus*. Associated with this find were the parts of three femora which have a very "human" look about them. We must await the full analysis of this most important fossil material which may represent the earliest evidence of true man. In functional terms the anatomy of the femora argues the existence of quite advanced bipedalism at least 3 million years ago.

John R. Napier, January 1974

As we proceed in our study of the evolution of *Homo sapiens*, we should be aware that the recent finds of Richard Leakey will unquestionably influence not only the interpretations of what species were present contemporaneously with the Australopithecines, but also the interpretation of *Homo erectus*, the species of humans preceding *Homo sapiens*. The line represented by these new finds might continue right into *Homo erectus* from some intermediate form, but this remains to be determined. In his article entitled "*Homo erectus*," William W. Howells describes some of the reasoning and methods required for the incorporation of these new finds into our interpretation of human evolution. As Howells' article illustrates so well, it is important to remember, especially in the midst of this excitement over "ER 1970" (see "Man among Man-Apes" in Science and the Citizen, p. 15), that the fossil record of the hominids is really quite incomplete. This being the case, reinterpretations of our ancient ancestors will continue to appear until the number of finds grows large enough to constitute valid samples from which definite conclusions about their origins and interrelationships can be drawn. What this means is that we must keep an open mind about the paradigm used to explain the origins of the hominids and even some of the less remote ancestors of modern humans. Howells' recent comments on *Homo erectus* show how the picture of that species has been altered by recent findings.

The idea of *Homo erectus*, as a chronospecies of the Middle Pleistocene lasting about half a million years, remains useful. However, on the principle that interpretations and family trees are simplest when fossil finds are fewest, it was predictable that so clear an outline would erode with new finds and more secure dating. At the early end of the time zone postulated for *Homo erectus*, "Telanthropus" of Swartkrans (shown in Campbell's (1965) chart as *Homo erectus capensis*) has been corroborated as early *Homo*, coeval with robust australopithecines, by the detection of further parts which can be fitted to one of the original fragments to form half a skull. Dates here remain uncertain, but recent finds by Richard Leakey in East Africa give strong evidence of emerging *Homo* (much more acceptable as such than *H. erectus habilis* shown in Campbell's grade 1) at a date of more than 2.6 million years, and thus far earlier than the 1 million years suggested in the article. It would appear that progressive and conservative subspecies of australopithecines overlapped for a long stretch of the Lower Pleistocene.

The other end of the time zone postulated for *Homo erectus* is likewise extended, since *H. erectus pekinensis* now appears to be dated (by amino acid racemization techniques) at more like 300,000 than 500,000 years. Javanese crania found in 1969 and 1973 resemble the Solo skulls (never securely dated, though doubtless Upper Pleistocene); but they were recovered from the Trinil zone, of the Middle Pleistocene, at least one of them being early in the zone. This tends to establish continuity (corresponding to Franz Weidenreich's (1947) ideas) more strongly between *H. erectus erectus* and *H. erectus soloensis* in Java, which had previously been believed to be well separated in time. In Europe, closer consideration of the well-preserved Petralona skull, found in 1959 in Greece, suggests that it is like Vértesszöllös in stage of development, and at least as early in time. (Thoma (1966) eventually placed Vértesszöllös on the borderline between *erectus and sapiens*; that is, the line between grades 4 and 5, which would be a fair position for Petralona). The two fossils appear more progressive than contemporary *Homo erectus* of the Far East. Remembering the Lower Paleolithic cultural distinctions noted long ago by H. L. Movius (1944), perhaps we should pay more attention to possible generalized east-west differences in *erectus* populations. T. D. Steward has done so with respect to mandibles.

Thus time and morphology of *erectus* have become somewhat blurred. Other nicks and dents in the 1966 article might be repaired; for example, the original Java skull and thigh bone may be from a redeposited river bed containing fossils of different age, so that the Trinil thigh bone might be younger than the skull. The Rhodesian skull is probably older than previously thought, perhaps Middle Pleistocene. But the general framework of *Homo erectus*, in the morphological sense, certainly represents a framework of agreement, or at least of nondisagreement, which should serve for the immediate future.

William W. Howells, January 1974

In one of the latest articles in this book, Ralph Holloway brings us several steps further in the trend toward the analysis of the potentials of our early hominid ancestors for humanlike behavior. In his article on "The Casts of Fossil Hominid Brains," Professor Holloway has synthesized much of his previous work with hominid endocasts (casts made of the inside of the skull, which have the general topographic features of the brain) with the endocast of the most recent "ER 1470" skull discovered by Richard Leakey. From this approach of studying the endocasts, he was able to make qualitative inferences about neural organization and quantitative inferences about the relations between cranial capacity (brain volume) and body weight of several hominid species including the Australopithecines and the "ER 1470" skull. Among his conclusions on the regular and close relations between brain volume and body weight are that Australopithecines are clearly more hominid than pongid. Perhaps even more striking in the context of all the discussion of "ER 1470" in the recent correspondence with various paleontologists included in this book was his conclusion that the endocast of this three-million-year-old fossil was essentially human in neural organization and had an even larger cranial capacity than the Australopithecines. Hence, if the dating of "ER 1470" is as old as the initial datings would indicate, then it appears to push back considerably the time dimension for the evolution of the hominid brain and to open up whole new areas of inquiry about the selective factors associated with its evolution.

One of the best phylogenetic mirrors for viewing our species is the study of our nearest primate relatives. The observation of free-ranging social primates in their natural habitats has been particularly beneficial to our understanding of human evolution and social organization. This approach has taught us, for example, that primates do solve rather complex problems as a group and that it is the group which is the integral evolutionary unit. It has also led us to suggest that many of the observed phenomena in human groups, such as age, sex, hierarchical, and mother-infant interactions, are at least observable to some degree at the level of other social primates. The study of primates has the further advantage of avoiding the issue of ethnocentricity, which may arise when anthropologists study other human cultures. Of course, there is still the danger of anthropomorphizing the behavior of social primates. However, it is difficult to do so when the social primates being studied are very different from humans, as are the baboons described by S. L. Washburn and Irven DeVore in their article "The Social Life of Baboons." Their historic study in primatology should be looked at as one of the earliest of a series of important breakthroughs that have come about as a result of the testing and rejecting of a variety of hypotheses about the so-called distinguishing evolutionary characteristics of humans, including hunting behavior, tool use, and symbolic communication. In the following note, Washburn offers some new observations about the social life of baboons.

Since this paper was written more than a dozen years ago, there have been some twenty major studies of the behavior of baboons. There is much more variation in behavior than we originally supposed, and it is now clear that groups will have to be studied for some years before group dynamics can be understood, and that experiments will have to be performed before differing interpretations can be resolved. Perhaps the greatest mistake in the early study was thinking that the local groups were inbreeding. Probably most, if not all, males change groups, especially in the late juvenile-young adult period. In some localities there is considerable, deliberate hunting. The one-male groups of Geladas and Hamadryas offer a sharp contrast to the many-male groups of the common baboons. Both species may form temporary, very large aggregations, especially when safe sleeping locations are limited to cliffs.

In comparing the behaviors of baboons and humans it is easy to stress the great success of human language, social adaptation, and technical skills. But, prior to agriculture, these successes did not lead to great numbers of human beings. The human species was widely dispersed, but in most localities monkeys far outnumbered human beings. Probably, the requirements of hunting which was so important in the human adaptation, kept local human populations smaller than those of the vegetarian primates.

Sherwood L. Washburn, November 1973

Soon after this study by Washburn and DeVore, Jane van Lawick-Goodall began her now-famous studies of the chimpanzees of the Gombe Stream Preserve. At this site some of the first observations of tool use by chimpanzees was observed (see Science and the Citizen, p. 16) and some of the first careful studies of hunting and important group interactions were made. More recently, Geza Teleki has been working with Jane Goodall in carrying out very careful field studies of the nutrition of the chimpanzee. Teleki's article "The Omnivorous Chimpanzee" presents the results of his studies. These unexpected findings cause us to question our long-held belief that man was the only hunter among the primates that could have killed other primates for meat. In a recent note printed on page 101 after the original article, Teleki brings us up to date on the field research and suggests its implications for the study of human prehistory.

Another type of primate study of particular interest to students of human evolution is the experimental investigation of chimpanzees' ability to learn to use symbols for communication. To the surprise of nearly everyone, the Premacks have taught their chimpanzee Sarah to "read" and "write" with symbols, and the Gardiners have taught Washoe to use American Sign Language for the deaf. (Washoe has recently been teaching other chimpanzees to use sign language.) Ann James Premack and David Premack discuss their experiment in the article "Teaching Language to an Ape." The results of these experiments with chimpanzees have sent deep and far-reaching shock waves through the fields of linguistics, anthropology, psychology, and even philosophy. Currently there is a flurry of synthetic scientific inquiry going on in these fields and in the neurological sciences to try to bridge the new gaps created by these findings.

Two basic perspectives on human language are provided by Norman Geschwind's article "Language and the Brain" and Charles F. Hockett's review of Eric H. Lenneberg's book *Biological Foundations of Language*. Reading these articles on language and communication with the other supplementary materials should elicit some new and exciting insights into the adaptive capacities of the human central nervous system, which is clearly the most significant human evolutionary adaptation. Geschwind, in a recent letter, suggests how this capacity may have developed.

It seems likely, on the basis of recent studies, that some capacity for language exists in the higher nonhuman primates. Despite this fact, it also seems likely that the degree of development of language in man is his most striking biological attribute. Furthermore, this capacity for language must depend primarily on evolutionary changes in the brain. The most striking of these is the anatomical asymmetry, which Levitsky and I described, although the existence of such asymmetries had long been denied. The planum temporale is larger in the left hemisphere where it makes up part of the speech area. This finding has now been confirmed by Wada, Teszner, and Witelson and Pallie, and it has been demonstrated that this asymmetry is present at birth. It is therefore almost certainly not the result of environmental effects but is genetically determined. No such asymmetries have yet been demonstrated in any other mammalian brain.

Marjorie Lemay and Antonio Culebras (1972) demonstrated further asymmetries, including the tendency of the right Sylvian fissure to rise higher than the one on the left. Lemay, furthermore, showed the presence of this asymmetry in the cast of the Neanderthal La Chapelle-aux-Saints skull dating back 30,000 years.

Several authors have agreed recently that the evolution of language could not have been based on the auditory system, but rather developed through gestures. Lieberman and Crelin (1971) have argued that Neanderthal man could not have had articulate speech because the bony structure of his skull and mandible would have made it impossible for his larynx to have the proper form. Lemay (1973) has, however, cast serious doubt on this argument by showing that there are modern men with normal speech who have exactly the same skeletal features. My own theory is that the evolution of language depended on the evolution of the angular gyrus region.

Norman Geshwind, January 1974

What we will do with these cerebral capacities is a question worthy of our most serious consideration. The question of whether the species is capable of destroying itself, either by war or by outstripping its ecosystem, is difficult to answer. However, if we consider the evolutionary roots and potentials of the human species and our nearest relatives among the primates, we can begin to integrate these concepts and use evolutionary theory as a method of attaining a more holistic picture of human attributes. Toward this end, the reader should consult Section V where several reviews have been included of books, written by authors and scientists both within and outside the field of bioanthropology, that over the years have sparked considerable controversy over their interpretations of the basic nature of our species.

1

The Earliest Apes

by Elwyn L. Simons
December 1967

What kind of animal gave rise to modern apes and man? The answer has been brought considerably closer by the unearthing in Egypt of the skull of an ancestral ape that dates back 28 million years

When it was that the early primates of the Old World first gave rise to the hominoid line from which the modern apes and man evolved is a question that has not had a satisfactory answer since it was first asked a century ago. Just where hominoid primates first evolved and why they evolved at all are rather more recent questions, but they too have lacked generally accepted answers. All three questions now appear to be answerable on the basis of evidence provided by fossil discoveries made during a recent series of Yale University expeditions to the Fayum region of Egypt. Our most exciting discovery, an almost complete primate cranium dating back between 26 and 28 million years, is the oldest ape skull ever found. It belongs to an individual of the newly established genus *Aegyptopithecus*. Studies of the skull, of abundant jawbones and teeth, of scarcer limb bones and of a few other skull fragments that represent this genus and five more genera of Fayum primates have added substance and precision to what was formerly a scant and hazy chapter in the record of primate evolution.

Only 60 miles southwest of Cairo, the Fayum is an area in which fertile fields gradually give way to desert badlands surrounding a large, brackish body of water called Lake Qârûn. (The name of the region is derived from the ancient Egyptian word for lake: *pa-yom*.) The desert buttes and escarpments have been a fossil-hunter's paradise since late in the 19th century, when a few commercial collectors and professional paleontologists first explored the area. The Mediterranean coast is 120 miles away, but during Oligocene times it cut across the Fayum. There large rivers entered the sea and gradually built up layers of sand and mud that reach a total thickness of more than 600 feet. What is desert today

was then a well-watered landscape in which forest was interspersed with open glades. Many fossilized tree trunks have been found; some are nearly 100 feet long. In trying to reconstruct the appearance of the Fayum during the Oligocene one gains the overall impression of a

tropical forest along the banks of meandering rivers.

The fossil remains show that fishes, turtles, dugongs, crocodiles and their narrow-snouted cousins, false gavials, lived in the rivers. In the open areas there were carnivores the size of weasels,

EARLIEST APE SKULL, found in the Fayum region of Egypt last year, comes from a stratum of later Oligocene age. The front and side photographs show it one-half larger than life size. The lower jaw is a restoration based on jaw fragments not found in association

small and large cousins of the modern elephant and a four-horned herbivore as big as a modern rhinoceros. The forest was inhabited by bats, perhaps by tiny rodents and by several species of primates. The fossilized bones of the primates are found in the sands of the former riverbeds. Of the scores of primate jaws we have uncovered in these deposits, only one, judging by the eruption and wear of the teeth, belonged to an individual that had lived to a ripe old age. These fossils apparently originated with a young animal's misjudged leap through the trees beside the river or its carelessness while drinking.

Hunting for fossil primates in the Fayum is largely a matter of examining two specific sedimentary layers called the upper and lower fossil-wood zones. The upper zone lies some 300 feet above the lower, and the fossil-rich sites are found on slopes adjacent to an escarpment of volcanic rock above Lake Qârûn. The volcanic rock, which lies some 250 feet above the upper fossil-wood zone,

has been dated by the potassium-argon method. Actually there have been two age determinations; one made at the University of California at Berkeley gives a figure of 24.7 ± .4 million years, and one made at Yale 27 ± 2 million years. Either date approximates the end of the Oligocene period, placing the upper fossil-wood zone in the later Oligocene. Comparisons with fossils in Europe suggest that the lower fossil-wood zone is perhaps six million years older and thus belongs to the early Oligocene.

The search for fossils is aided by the fact that in many places the desert winds have blown away the sand and soil and laid bare the upper surfaces of buried bones [*see lower illustration on page 31*]. The winds had plagued earlier Fayum fossil-hunters, but to us they have been a blessing in more ways than one. When we have quarried for fossils, our crews have been able simply to remove overlying rock or to sweep away the "desert pavement," or surface stones; the wind has then scoured tons of uncon-

solidated sediments out of the quarries, leaving the fragile fossils still in place. Once the wind has done its work it is still necessary to clear the fossils further and to protect and remove them. Apparently there has been little percolation of groundwater through the Fayum sandstones, with the result that the bones have little or none of the mineral content characteristic of most vertebrate fossils. We have found, however, that modern synthetic resins make excellent "instant" fossilizers.

Until the Yale expeditions to the Fayum were inaugurated under my direction in 1961 the entire inventory of primate fossils from the area was seven fragments of bone and teeth. These fragments nonetheless played a major role in the development of modern theories about primate evolution. The greatest service the Fayum expeditions may have performed is that they have uncovered enough new fossils to correct several misconceptions arising from the fact that the

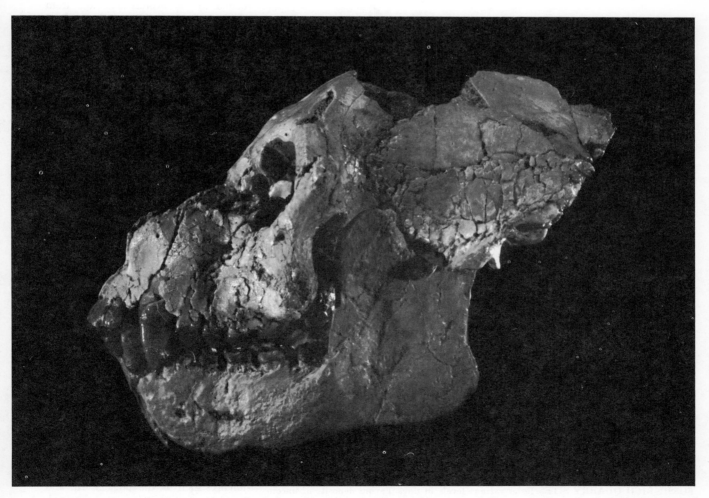

with the cranium; the four incisor teeth of the upper jaw are also restorations. Generally monkey-like, the skull belongs to a species of ape recently named *Aegyptopithecus zeusix* by the author. The species was probably ancestral to the dryopithecine apes of the Miocene (*see illustration on page 35*). The latter, once abundant in Africa and Eurasia, apparently gave rise to modern apes and man.

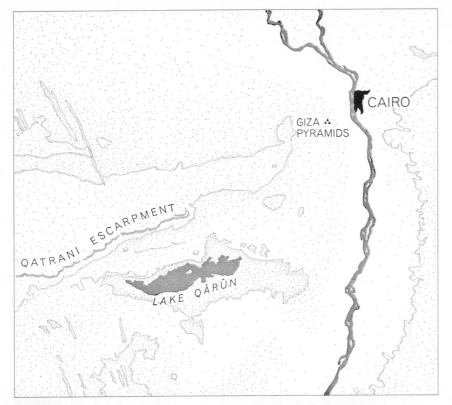

FAYUM REGION, 60 miles southwest of Cairo, is noted for its Oligocene fossils, which are found along the slope that rises from Lake Qârûn, 150 feet below sea level, to the top of the 1,000-foot-high Qatrani escarpment, which is capped with post-Oligocene volcanic rock.

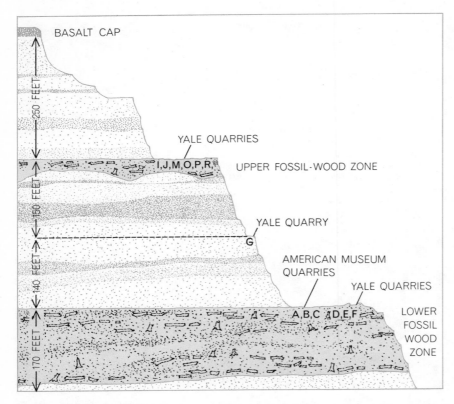

FOSSIL-RICH QUARRY SITES lie at various levels in thick Fayum deposits of unconsolidated sandstones and mudstones, seen here in a schematic cross section. Most of the animal remains have been found in two strata that also contain fossilized wood. The bones of primates are quite scarce; they have been found only in the four quarries E, G, I and M.

original sample of fossils was so small.

The recent discoveries are seen most clearly against a background of the earlier interpretations that our findings have confirmed or modified. I shall begin my review of these earlier interpretations with two Fayum primate genera that are *not* apes. They belong to the family Parapithecidae, a group that may be ancestral to the Old World monkeys.

One genus of this family accounts for more fossils than any other primate found in the Fayum beds. It is the genus *Apidium*, represented by two species: *Apidium phiomense* and *A. moustafai*. The first fossil of the genus—a lower jaw—was discovered early in this century by the German fossil-hunter Richard Markgraf, who was working for the American Museum of Natural History. The generic name, proposed in 1908, is derived from Apis, the sacred bull of Egypt. This odd choice was made because at first the specimen was not clearly recognized as belonging to a primate. Paleontologists have gradually come to agree, however, that *Apidium* may be related to the evolutionary line from which the Old World monkeys evolved or to *Oreopithecus*, an apelike fossil primate found in Italy. As a result of our six seasons of work, *Apidium* is now represented by parts of more than 50 lower jaws and four upper jaws. *Apidium* had a short face and was evidently about the size of a squirrel monkey. Like this monkey of the New World, it had 36 teeth arranged according to the "dental formula" that is written in anatomical shorthand as 2 : 1 : 3 : 3. This is to say that on each side of the upper and lower jaw there were two incisors, one canine, three premolars and three molars [*see illustration on page 34*].

The other member of the family Parapithecidae found in the Fayum is the species that gave the family its name: *Parapithecus fraasi*. This fossil primate was also discovered by Markgraf; it was described and named in 1910 by the German paleontologist Max Schlosser, who had become acquainted with fossil primates while studying specimens from North America in a collection at Yale that had been assembled by Othniel Marsh. What Markgraf found was both sides of a lower jaw, cracked at the midline but otherwise apparently complete except for one tooth. Counting the specimen's teeth, Schlosser concluded that the animal had the same dental formula—1 : 1 : 3 : 3—as certain living "prosimians" such as the tarsiers. He and most later students interpreted the crack at the midline of the jaw as further evidence supporting this view; among prosimians the suture between the two halves of the lower jaw rarely fuses as it does early in life among the higher primates. Together with the specimen's small size—about the same as the jaw of a tarsier or a squirrel monkey—these were clues enough for Schlosser. He concluded that *Parapithecus* represented a transition between the early prosimians and the higher primates. Later, counting the teeth in a different way, Schlosser and others decided that the animal had affinities with man.

With the advantage of hindsight and many more specimens to study, it is easy to see how Schlosser's findings were in error. In fact, his conclusions exemplify the difficulties inherent in reaching wide-ranging evolutionary conclusions on the basis of a single fragmentary specimen. One can scarcely blame Schlosser for expressing his opinion before other specimens had been found, but if he had been able to wait, he would never have been deceived. For example, additional *Parapithecus* jaws we have found show that both sides of the jaws are solidly fused in front, even among the juvenile specimens, as they are in the higher primates. Moreover, the *Parapithecus* dental formula is like that of *Apidium*: 2 : 1 : 3 : 3. The jaw discovered by Markgraf had evidently broken apart at the front suture at the time of burial or of discovery. Somehow the two side incisors and their supporting bone were lost, leaving posterity with the false impression that the specimen had only one pair of front teeth.

The fact that both of these Oligocene primates have the same tooth count as New World monkeys should not be considered evidence of any particularly close relation with such monkeys. There is no theoretical reason why the ancestors of Old World monkeys should not once have had an extra premolar all around. Indeed, it is the exception rather than the rule for all members of a mammalian suborder to have the same dental formula. Actually the formula of *Parapithecus* and *Apidium* is the same as that of an even earlier forebear of the Old World primates: *Amphipithecus*, found in an Eocene formation of Burma [see "The Early Relatives of Man," by Elwyn L. Simons; SCIENTIFIC AMERICAN Offprint 622].

Almost certainly the oldest of all the Fayum primates is *Oligopithecus savagei*, an animal that was unknown until our first season of work in 1961. *Oligopithecus* is represented by the left half of a lower jaw from which both incisors and the rear molar have been lost;

the jaw was found in the lower fossil-wood zone. Unlike *Parapithecus* and *Apidium*, this animal apparently had the same advanced dental formula as the Old World monkeys, the apes and man (2 : 1 : 2 : 3). *Oligopithecus* appears to be the descendant of a primate that had arrived in the region in the Eocene period. Its molars, although they clearly can be classified as belonging to an advanced primate, are related in form to the molars of the primitive prosimian family Omomyidae, whose fossil remains are found in Eocene formations of Europe, Asia and North America. Such a generalized tooth structure agrees well with the antiquity of the strata that contain the remains of *Oligopithecus,* which were probably laid down more than 32 million years ago.

Perhaps the best-known Oligocene primate is *Propliopithecus haeckeli,*

another of Markgraf's discoveries. In giving it this name Schlosser was expressing his belief that the animal, then represented by two nearly complete halves of a lower jaw, could have been ancestral to the fossil gibbon *Pliopithecus,* found in younger formations of the Miocene and Pliocene in France. Later workers agreed with this assessment, and *Propliopithecus* was generally accepted as an early ape, ancestral to the modern gibbons. As we shall see, this is a position it should probably not occupy.

As a result of our fossil collecting, the remains of *Propliopithecus* now include two more lower jaws and about a dozen teeth. The site of Markgraf's discovery cannot be located with certainty today. Some of our *Propliopithecus* specimens, however, come from the site we call Quarry G. In terms of stratigraphy Quarry G lies about halfway between the

REMOVAL OF STONES that form a protective layer of "desert pavement" on the surface of a quarry lets the Fayum windstorms blow the loose grains of sand away, laying fossils bare.

FOSSIL JAWBONES exposed by the wind are those of a fish-eating crocodilian, the false gavial. Reptiles, fishes and mammals lived in the rivers of the Fayum in Oligocene times.

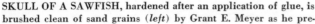

SKULL OF A SAWFISH, hardened after an application of glue, is brushed clean of sand grains (*left*) by Grant E. Meyer as he pre-

pares to remove the fossil from the rock that surrounds it. Next (*center*) Meyer pours water on the fossil as Thomas F. Walsh holds

lower and the upper fossil-wood zone. The *Propliopithecus* fossils from this location must therefore be younger than *Oligopithecus* from the lower zone. The same may be true of Markgraf's find.

In any case, the teeth of the proposed ancestral gibbon show few exclusively apelike characteristics. Among the apes the front premolars are elongated and the canines are large. In the fossil apes of the Miocene, and in the modern gorilla and orangutan, the three molars at the rear of the jaw usually increase in size from front to back. None of these characteristics is evident in *Propliopithecus*. Moreover, to judge from the tooth sockets and the adjacent bone, the animal's incisors appear to be placed vertically rather than jutting forward as they usually do in apes and monkeys.

These and a few other details of *Propliopithecus'* dentition make the animal seem more closely related to man's family, the Hominidae, than to either of the two families of apes: the Hylobatidae (which include the gibbon and the siamang) and the Pongidae (which include the chimpanzee, the gorilla and the orangutan). Indeed, some students have taken this hominid trait in *Propliopithecus* to mean that apes ancestral to the human line had branched off the main line of ape evolution as early as Oligocene times. I would prefer an alternative

interpretation, at least for the present.

Still another of Markgraf's discoveries was described by Schlosser; it was named *Moeripithecus markgrafi* in honor of the indefatigable fossil-hunter. The original specimen, preserved in the paleontological collection at Stuttgart, consists of a juvenile jaw fragment in which only the first and second molars are in place. In 1963 I visited Stuttgart to compare the original with several of the individual teeth attributable to *Propliopithecus* that we had found in Quarry G. This comparison and later study of other specimens convinces me that almost every consideration on which Schlosser based his designation of *Moeripithecus* as a genus is attributable to the fact that the original jaw fragment came from a young animal whose molars had not been much worn down. The jaw appears to belong to a species of the genus *Propliopithecus*, although not the species *P. haeckeli*. Consequently *Moeripithecus* should be dropped as a genus and the fossil assigned to the genus *Propliopithecus*.

During our third season in the Fayum, one of the best fossils to be collected from Quarry I in the upper fossil-wood zone was a full lower jaw, fused at the front suture and containing almost a full complement of teeth. The incisors were gone, but fortunately the bony sockets

that had held them were still intact. The jaw differs from the jaws of most of the other Fayum primates in having elongated first premolars and relatively massive canines with thick roots. These are apelike characteristics. Still other characteristics, including a quite small third molar and a decrease in the depth of the jaw from front to back, are reminiscent of the gibbons. I have named this species, which was about half the size of a modern gibbon, *Aeolopithecus chirobates*. It is possible that this animal, rather than *Propliopithecus*, was the Oligocene forebear of the full-fledged gibbons that are found as fossils in Miocene formations of East Africa and Europe dated eight to 10 million years later. Both *Aeolopithecus* and *Propliopithecus*, however, may have been diminutive early apes that left no descendants.

The largest Fayum primate, to which I have given the name *Aegyptopithecus zeuxis*, was known until recently only from four incomplete lower jaws and half a dozen individual upper teeth that were also found at Quarry I in the upper fossil-wood zone. The size of the animal's lower jaw is about equal to that of a gibbon; it is nearly a third larger than the jaw of *Propliopithecus*. Several characteristics of the teeth make it clear that this new genus of upper Oligocene

a basin for mixing plaster. Finally (*right*) layers of paper cover the damp specimen. They will keep the plaster, which protects the fossil during transit, from adhering to its surface.

primate could have evolved from a species of *Propliopithecus* during the several million years or so separating it from the fossil remains of the earlier genus. The evolution had been in a direction that gives the younger animal a close resemblance to the still later apes of the genus *Dryopithecus,* which were a major element of the Old World primate population in Miocene times.

Students of primate evolution today generally agree that it was from the dryopithecine apes of the Miocene period that the lines of development arose leading on the one hand to the great apes and on the other, by way of *Ramapithecus* and *Australopithecus,* to modern man's immediate precursor *Homo erectus.* It is therefore of great interest to discover an ape with teeth particularly like those of the earliest species of *Dryopithecus* but that is something between eight and 12 million years older. The earliest dryopithecine is another fossil from Africa, *Dryopithecus africanus* ("Proconsul"), a skull of which was discovered in a Miocene formation of Kenya by Mary Leakey in 1948. Until recently this was the only known skull of a fossil ape.

Aegyptopithecus, although no larger than a gibbon, has teeth much like a gorilla's; the canines are large and the front premolars are elongated. From front to back the three lower molars in-

crease markedly in size; the entire jaw is more apelike than the jaw of *Propliopithecus* and is much deeper under the canines. It quickly became apparent to us that, however useful our other fossil discoveries might be in disposing of old misconceptions and clarifying the picture of Oligocene primate life in the Fayum, our discovery of *Aegyptopithecus* could provide a major contribution to the understanding of early primate evolution. Here was an animal of the right form and the right age to be ancestral to the dryopithecine apes of the following epoch. It could thus occupy an early position in man's lineage and even perhaps be the direct forebear of apes such as the modern gorilla as well.

Late in the 1966 season my research associate Grant E. Meyer was making a surface reconnaissance of Quarry M in the upper fossil-wood zone. He came on the frontal bone and both parietal bones of a skull—an exciting find because six seasons of work had yielded only a few fragments of cranial bone. Meyer at once soaked the bones and the surrounding matrix with glue so that a sizable chunk of quarry floor could be safely dug out, covered with plaster and burlap and shipped to our laboratory at Yale for the delicate job of cleaning. It would be hard to say whether our surprise or our delight was the greater when

the cleaning process revealed that Meyer had found not just a few skull fragments but a nearly whole skull of *Aegyptopithecus* from which only portions of the top and bottom of the skull and the four incisor teeth proved to be missing [*see illustrations on pages 28 and 29*].

With the world's oldest-known ape skull added to the rest of the fossils available for analysis, we return to the three questions raised at the beginning. As to when it was that the hominoid line leading to modern apes and man first evolved from a more generalized Old World primate, the almost inescapable answer today is during the Oligocene epoch. At least with respect to the great apes and man, the specific primate involved in the branching is *Aegyptopithecus,* although *Aeolopithecus* is perhaps a twig pointing toward the lesser apes. In turn, the primate stock from which the main branch grew could be the earlier fossil form *Propliopithecus.* An even earlier connecting link could be *Oligopithecus* of the early Oligocene, with its teeth that bear resemblances to Eocene primates as well as to most later monkeys and apes.

Obviously the second question, as to where these events took place, has already been answered. They certainly occurred in this one area of forest and glade where nameless rivers entered the sea. Presumably they were also taking place elsewhere to the west and south in Africa as boisterous populations of proto-monkeys and near-apes flourished and evolved over a span of some 12 million years. An accident of fossil preservation requires that, if we are asked, "Exactly where?" we must reply, "In the Fayum." Someday the answer may be much more wide-ranging.

It is well to remember in this connection that almost nothing is known of the Paleocene and Eocene animals of Africa, although together the two epochs comprise nearly half of the length of the Age of Mammals. Africa's fossil fauna in Oligocene and Miocene times, although better known, remain painfully scanty. The evolutionary scheme I have proposed here and the fossil genera on which it is founded represent a rationale based on chance fossil preservation and discovery. The evidence is still susceptible to a number of alternative interpretations. Many early African primates must have existed about which we now know nothing. No one can say if some of them were more directly related to living man and the apes than any we now know.

There remains the question of why it

is that hominoid primates evolved. The answer, it seems to me, is that the Oligocene primates' arboreal way of life, involving feeding on leaf buds and fruits near the end of branches, gave survival value to certain kinds of dexterity. If this suggestion regarding the arboreal life is to be useful in assessing the Fayum fossils, it is necessary to digress briefly and examine some surprising parallels between the behavior of some modern apes and that of certain lower primates, specifically the large lemurs *Indri* and *Propithecus.*

These large lemurs, familiarly known as indris and sifakas, are specialized in various quite distinct ways for a life of arboreal foraging; the same is true of the lesser apes, in particular the gibbon and the siamang of Asia. The gibbon and the siamang are exclusively tree-dwellers and primarily eaters of insects and fruit. Their ability to move out among small branches in order to feed while in a suspended position, as well as their dexterity in swinging by their arms, is extraordinary. Among the apes of Africa the arboreal way of life is less extreme; the gorilla spends more time on the ground than in the trees, although in evolutionary terms this is a recent adaptation. The chimpanzee is mainly terrestrial in locomotion. Its dexterity when feeding in the branches of trees, however, is exceeded only by that of the Asian apes. Nor is large size an absolute barrier to arboreal life: the orangutan spends all its years as a tree-dwelling forager, although the male may weigh 160 pounds at maturity.

The dexterity of the large lemurs in tree-climbing, clinging and leaping is equal to that of their more advanced primate kin. These animals' snouts are somewhat flattened, and their eyes are far enough forward in the skull to add depth perception to their manual dexterity and locomotor versatility. Yet no one could anatomically confuse the indris and sifakas with the apes. Their dental formula is different, and so are many other details of skull, limb and hand. Moreover, one of them—the sifaka—has a long tail. The resemblances are in behavior and in locomotion, not in anatomy. Like the gibbons, the two large lemurs form small social groups and

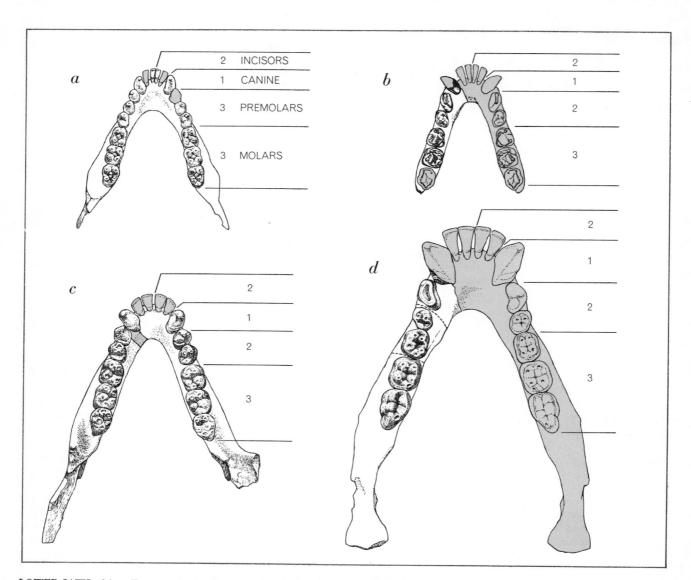

LOWER JAWS of four Fayum primates illustrate the relative size of the fossils and the difference between the New World and Old World "dental formula." *Apidium* (*a*) is a small parapithecid and the most abundant Fayum fossil primate; the number of its teeth is the same as that of New World monkeys. *Oligopithecus* (*b*) is probably the oldest Fayum primate. Like *Propliopithecus* (*c*) and the largest Fayum primate, *Aegyptopithecus* (*d*), its tooth count is the same as that of all Old World monkeys, the apes and man. The teeth and jawbones shown in detail are based on fossil specimens; where teeth or bones are in color they represent reconstructions.

communicate with loud, hooting cries. Seeing them in the trees, clinging with their torsos erect, or on the ground moving on their hind limbs (the sifaka curls its tail neatly out of the way on such occasions), one is struck by the similarity between these prosimians and the fossil apes of the Fayum, whose pattern of life was apparently much like theirs. The large lemurs demonstrate that, even at the quite primitive prosimian level of primate evolution, striking behavioral advances and locomotor adaptations are possible. It seems evident that the apes first arose from one such adaptive shift; the Fayum apes are apparently not far from that point.

It should come as no surprise, then, to learn that among the fossil discoveries in Quarry I are a number of tailbones, almost certainly assignable to *Aegyptopithecus*. Speaking anatomically, it was to be expected that some ancestral primate would cross the threshold separating monkey from ape and still bring its monkey tail along. The successful tree life of the tailed lemur, however, helps us to realize that possession of a tail was not necessarily a handicap to *Aegyptopithecus'* adaptation as an arboreal ape.

The skull of *Aegyptopithecus*, and also three fragments of frontal bone we have found (belonging to at least two different species), show that the Fayum primates' eyes had shifted forward, with a consequent enhancement of depth perception. *Aegyptopithecus* has a narrow snout (still long by ape standards), some expansion of the forebrain and a related reduction in the dimensions of the brain's olfactory lobes [*see illustrations on pages 28 and 29*]. These are changes in form that are correlated with a greater predominance of the visual sense over the olfactory, and they are typical adaptations with survival value for arboreal life. The foot bones and many other limb bones we have found, which probably belong mainly to *Apidium*, are suggestive of adaptation to life in the trees. The few that appear to belong to *Aegyptopithecus* suggest the same habitat.

To me it seems probable that the selective pressures of millions of years in the trees forced a comparatively primitive population of the kind represented by the anatomically generalized early *Oligopithecus*—with its echoes of even more primitive Eocene forebears—along the road to apehood. That the pressures were effective is shown by the evolution en route of several anatomically intermediate species of *Propliopithecus*. When the pressures culminated near the

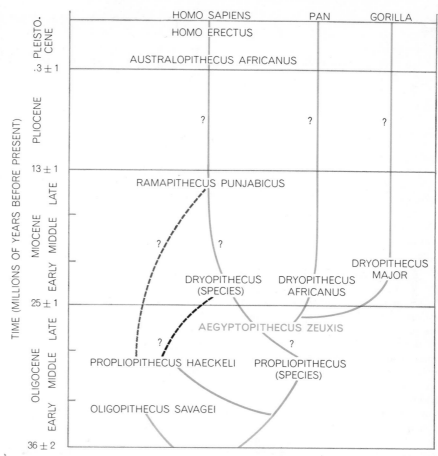

TENTATIVE FAMILY TREE prepared by the author shows alternate ways in which the Oligocene primates of the Fayum may be connected with the main lines of ape and human evolution. The ancestral position of *Oligopithecus*, the earliest in the group to have an advanced dental formula, is uncertain; the animal therefore is put to one side of the main line that leads to various species of *Propliopithecus* in the mid-Oligocene. These are shown to be most probably ancestral to *Aegyptopithecus* of the later Oligocene, the genus that in turn is proposed as the most probable forebear of the dryopithecine apes of the next geological epoch, the Miocene. Lesser probabilities are that one species of *Propliopithecus*, *P. haeckeli*, gave rise to those dryopithecines from which *Ramapithecus* and the hominid line arose (**broken black line**) or was directly ancestral to *Ramapithecus* (**broken gray line**). In either event, *Aegyptopithecus* remains ancestral to the two dryopithecine species, *D. africanus* and *D. major*, the apparent forebears of the chimpanzees and gorillas respectively.

end of the Oligocene, the evolutionary process had brought forth an anatomically ideal prototype for the dryopithecines in the form of *Aegyptopithecus*.

The primitiveness of such hand, foot and limb bones of dryopithecines as are now known has allowed scholars to characterize the dryopithecines somewhat flippantly as animals with the heads of apes attached to the bodies of monkeys. If I were to characterize *Aegyptopithecus* in the same fashion, I would have to speak of the skull of a monkey equipped with the teeth of an ape. Why not? If my analyses, both of the evolutionary sequence and of the skull's anatomy, are correct, this animal was an oversized tree-dweller, still carrying a tail in spite of anatomical advances such as suture-closing and hominoid teeth. The animal's

braincase, in relation to its face, was smaller than that of any subsequent hominoid. The bone behind the eyes formed a less complete closure than it does in hominoids or in Old World and New World monkeys. The auditory canals are not enclosed in an external tube, as they are in all the later Old World monkeys, the apes and man, and the tympanic ring is fused in a manner resembling the prosimian lorises and the New World monkeys. But what is more important than the primitive anatomical traits of *Aegyptopithecus* is the clear stamp of the higher primates to be seen in it. The animal was evidently pursuing an arboreal pattern of life directing it along the evolutionary path leading from lemur-like and monkey-like forms to apes and perhaps ultimately to man.

2

The Antiquity of Human Walking

by John Napier
April 1967

*Man's unique striding gait may be the most significant
ability that sets him apart from his ancestors. A big-toe
bone found in Tanzania is evidence that his ability dates
back more than a million years*

Human walking is a unique activity during which the body, step by step, teeters on the edge of catastrophe. The fact that man has used this form of locomotion for more than a million years has only recently been demonstrated by fossil evidence. The antiquity of this human trait is particularly noteworthy because walking with a striding gait is probably the most significant of the many evolved capacities that separate men from more primitive hominids. The fossil evidence—the terminal bone of a right big toe discovered in 1961 in Olduvai Gorge in Tanzania—sets up a new signpost that not only clarifies the course of human evolution but also helps to guide those who speculate on the forces that converted predominantly quadrupedal animals into habitual bipeds.

Man's bipedal mode of walking seems potentially catastrophic because only the rhythmic forward movement of first one leg and then the other keeps him from falling flat on his face. Consider the sequence of events whenever a man sets out in pursuit of his center of gravity. A stride begins when the muscles of the calf relax and the walker's body sways forward (gravity supplying the energy needed to overcome the body's inertia). The sway places the center of body weight in front of the supporting pedestal normally formed by the two feet. As a result one or the other of the walker's legs must swing forward so that when his foot makes contact with the ground, the area of the supporting pedestal has been widened and the center of body weight once again rests safely within it. The pelvis plays an important role in this action: its degree of rotation determines the distance the swinging leg can move forward, and its muscles help to keep the body balanced while the leg is swinging.

At this point the "stance" leg—the leg still to the rear of the body's center of gravity—provides the propulsive force that drives the body forward. The walker applies this force by using muscular energy, pushing against the ground first with the ball of his foot and then with his big toe. The action constitutes the "push-off," which terminates the stance phase of the walking cycle. Once the stance foot leaves the ground, the walker's leg enters the starting, or "swing," phase of the cycle. As the leg swings forward it is able to clear the ground because it is bent at the hip, knee and ankle. This high-stepping action substantially reduces the leg's moment of inertia. Before making contact with the ground and ending the swing phase the leg straightens at the knee but remains bent at the ankle. As a result it is the heel that strikes the ground first. The "heel strike" concludes the swing phase; as the body continues to move forward the leg once again enters the stance phase, during which the point of contact between foot and ground moves progressively nearer the toes. At the extreme end of the stance phase, as before, all the walker's propulsive thrust is delivered by the robust terminal bone of his big toe.

A complete walking cycle is considered to extend from the heel strike of one leg to the next heel strike of the same leg; it consists of the stance phase followed by the swing phase. The relative duration of the two phases depends on the cadence or speed of the walk. During normal walking the stance phase constitutes about 60 percent of the cycle and the swing phase 40 percent. Although

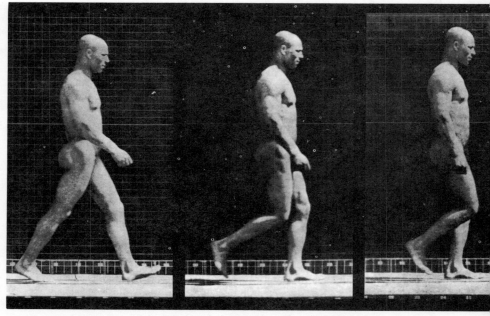

**WALKING MAN, photographed by Eadweard Muybridge in 1884 during his studies of
human and animal motion, exhibits the characteristic striding gait of the modern human.**

the action of only one leg has been described in this account, the opposite leg obviously moves in a reciprocal fashion; when one leg is moving in the swing phase, the other leg is in its stance phase and keeps the body poised. Actually during normal walking the two phases overlap, so that both feet are on the ground at the same time for about 25 percent of the cycle. As walking speed increases, this period of double leg-support shortens.

Anyone who has watched other people walking and reflected a little on the process has noticed that the human stride demands both an up-and-down and a side-to-side displacement of the body. When two people walk side by side but out of step, the alternate bobbing of their heads makes it evident that the bodies undergo a vertical displacement with each stride. When two people walk in step but with opposite feet leading, they will sway first toward each other and then away in an equally graphic demonstration of the lateral displacement at each stride. When both displacements are plotted sequentially, a pair of low-amplitude sinusoidal curves appear, one in the vertical plane and the other in the horizontal [see illustrations on next page]. General observations of this kind were reduced to precise measurements during World War II when a group at the University of California at Berkeley led by H. D. Eberhart conducted a fundamental investigation of human walking in connection with requirements for the design of artificial legs. Eberhart and his colleagues found that a number of functional determinants interacted to move the human body's center of gravity through space with a minimum expenditure of energy. In all they isolated six major elements related to hip, knee and foot movement that, working together, reduced both the amplitude of the two sine curves and the abruptness with which vertical and lateral changes in direction took place. If any one of these six elements was disturbed, an irregularity was injected into the normally smooth, undulating flow of walking, thereby producing a limp. What is more important, the irregularity brought about a measurable increase in the body's energy output during each step.

The Evidence of the Bones

What I have described in general and Eberhart's group studied in detail is the form of walking known as striding. It is characterized by the heel strike at the start of the stance phase and the push-off at its conclusion. Not all human walking is striding; when a man moves about slowly or walks on a slippery surface, he may take short steps in which both push-off and heel strike are absent. The foot is simply lifted from the ground at the end of the stance phase and set down flat at the end of the swing phase. The stride, however, is the essence of human bipedalism and the criterion by which the evolutionary status of a hominid walker must be judged. This being the case, it is illuminating to consider how the act of striding leaves its distinctive marks on the bones of the strider.

To take the pelvis first, there is a well-known clinical manifestation called Trendelenburg's sign that is regarded as evidence of hip disease in children. When a normal child stands on one leg, two muscles connecting that leg and the pelvis—the gluteus medius and the gluteus minimus—contract; this contraction, pulling on the pelvis, tilts it and holds it poised over the stance leg. When the hip is diseased, this mechanism fails to operate and the child shows a positive Trendelenburg's sign: the body tends to fall toward the unsupported side.

The same mechanism operates in walking, although not to the same degree. During the stance phase of the walking cycle, the same two gluteal muscles on the stance side brace the pelvis by cantilever action. Although actual tilting toward the stance side does not occur in normal walking, the action of the muscles in stabilizing the walker's hip is an essential component of the striding gait. Without this action the stride would become a slow, ungainly shuffle.

At the same time that the pelvis is stabilized in relation to the stance leg it also rotates to the unsupported side. This rotation, although small, has the effect of increasing the length of the stride. A familiar feature of the way women walk arises from this bit of anatomical mechanics. The difference in the proportions of the male and the female pelvis has the effect of slightly diminishing the range through which the female hip can move forward and back. Thus for a given length of stride women are obliged to rotate the pelvis through a greater

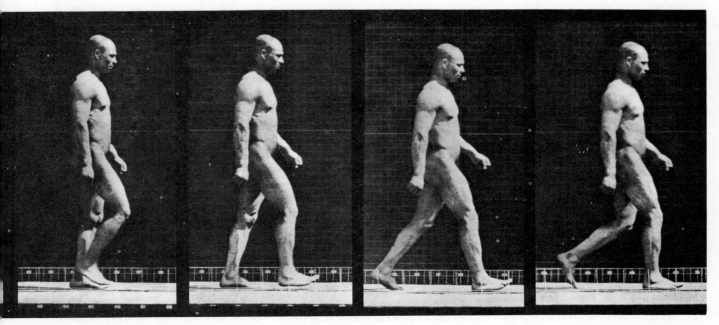

The free foot strikes the ground heel first and the body's weight is gradually transferred from heel to ball of foot as the opposite leg lifts and swings forward. Finally the heel of the stance foot rises and the leg's last contact with the ground is made with the big toe.

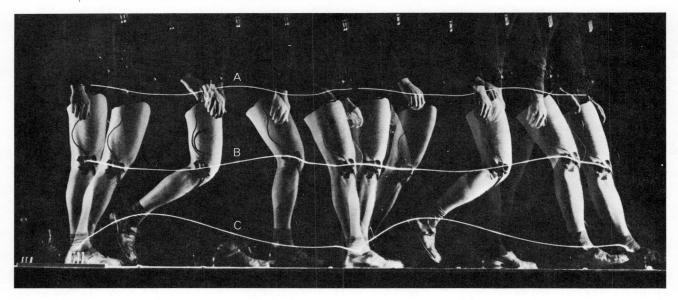

WALKING CYCLE extends from the heel strike of one leg to the next heel strike by the same leg. In the photograph, made by Gjon Mili in the course of a study aimed at improvement of artificial legs that he conducted for the U.S. Army, multiple exposures trace the progress of the right leg in the course of two strides. The ribbons of light allow analysis of the movement (*see illustration below*).

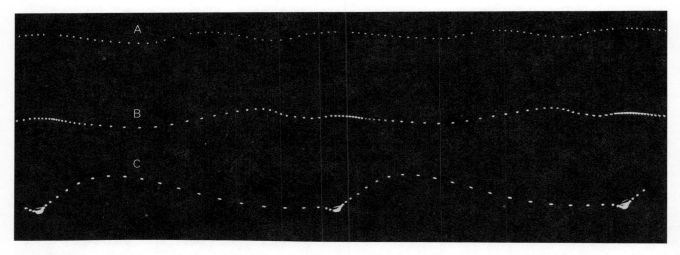

SINE CURVE described by the hip of a walking man was recorded on film by means of the experimental system illustrated above. An interrupter blade, passing in front of the camera lens at constant speed, broke the light from lamps attached to the walker into the three rows of dots. The speed of hip (*a*), knee (*b*) or ankle (*c*) during the stride is determined by measuring between the dots.

angle than men do. This secondary sexual characteristic has not lacked exploitation; at least in our culture female pelvic rotation has considerable erotogenic significance. What is more to the point in terms of human evolution is that both the rotation and the balancing of the pelvis leave unmistakable signs on the pelvic bone and on the femur: the leg bone that is joined to it. It is by a study of such signs that the walking capability of a fossil hominid can be judged.

Similar considerations apply to the foot. One way the role of the foot in walking can be studied is to record the vertical forces acting on each part of the foot while it is in contact with the ground during the stance phase of the walking cycle. Many devices have been built for this purpose; one of them is the plastic pedograph. When the subject walks across the surface of the pedograph, a motion-picture camera simultaneously records the exact position of the foot in profile and the pattern of pressures on the surface. Pedograph analyses show that the initial contact between the striding leg and the ground is the heel strike. Because the foot is normally turned out slightly at the end of the swing phase of the walking cycle, the outer side of the back of the heel takes the brunt of the initial contact [*see illustration on opposite page*]. The outer side of the foot continues to support most of the pressure of the stance until a point about three-fifths of the way along the sole is reached. The weight of the body is then transferred to the ball of the foot and then to the big toe. In the penultimate stage of push-off the brunt of the pressure is under the toes, particularly the big toe. Finally, at the end of the stance phase, only the big toe is involved; it progressively loses contact with the ground and the final push-off is applied through its broad terminal bone.

The use of pedographs and similar apparatus provides precise evidence about the function of the foot in walking, but every physician knows that much the same information is recorded on the soles of everyone's shoes. Assuming that the shoes fit, their pattern of wear is a true record of the individual's habitual gait. The wear pattern will reveal a limp that one man is trying to hide, or unmask one that another man is trying to feign, perhaps to provide evidence for an insurance claim. In any case, just as the form of the pelvis and the femur can disclose the presence or absence of a striding gait, so can the form of the foot bones, particularly the form and proportions of the big-toe bones.

The Origins of Primate Bipedalism

Almost all primates can stand on their hind limbs, and many occasionally walk in this way. But our primate relatives are all, in a manner of speaking, amateurs; only man has taken up the business of bipedalism intensively. This raises two major questions. First, how did the basic postural adaptations that permit walking—occasional or habitual—arise among the primates? Second, what advantages did habitual bipedalism bestow on early man?

With regard to the first question, I have been concerned for some time with the anatomical proportions of all primates, not only man and the apes but also the monkeys and lower primate forms. Such consideration makes it possible to place the primates in natural groups according to their mode of locomotion. Not long ago I suggested a new group, and it is the only one that will concern us here. The group comprises primates with very long hind limbs and very short forelimbs. At about the same time my colleague Alan C. Walker, now at Makerere University College in Uganda, had begun a special study of the locomotion of living and fossil lemurs. Lemurs are among the most primitive offshoots of the basic primate stock. Early in Walker's studies he was struck by the frequency with which a posture best described as "vertical clinging" appeared in the day-to-day behavior of living lemurs. All the animals whose propensity for vertical clinging had been observed by Walker showed the same proportions—that is, long hind limbs and short forelimbs—I had proposed as forming a distinct locomotor group.

When Walker and I compared notes, we decided to define a hitherto unrecognized locomotor category among the primates that we named "vertical clinging and leaping," a term that includes both the animal's typical resting posture and the essential leaping component

in its locomotion. Since proposing this category a most interesting and important extension of the hypothesis has become apparent to us. Some of the earliest primate fossils known, preserved in sediments laid down during Eocene times and therefore as much as 50 million years old, are represented not only by skulls and jaws but also by a few limb bones. In their proportions and details most of these limb bones show the same characteristics that are displayed by the living members of our vertical-clinging-and-leaping group today. Not long ago Elwyn L. Simons of Yale University presented a reconstruction of the lemur-

like North American Eocene primate *Smilodectes* walking along a tree branch in a quadrupedal position [see "The Early Relatives of Man," by Elwyn L. Simons; SCIENTIFIC AMERICAN Offprint 622]. Walker and I would prefer to see *Smilodectes* portrayed in the vertical clinging posture its anatomy unequivocally indicates. The fossil evidence, as far as it goes, suggests to us that vertical clinging and leaping was a major primate locomotor adaptation that took place some 50 million years ago. It may even have been the initial dynamic adaptation to tree life from which the subsequent locomotor patterns of all the living pri-

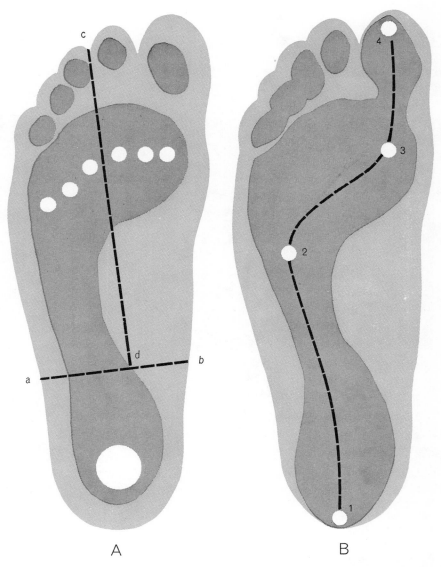

A   B

DISTRIBUTION OF WEIGHT in the human foot alters radically as action takes the place of rest. When motionless (*A*), the foot divides its static load (half of the body's total weight) between its heel and its ball along the axis *a–b*. The load on the ball of the foot is further divided equally on each side of the axis *c–d*. When striding (*B*), the load (all of the body's weight during part of each stride) is distributed dynamically from the first point of contact (*1, heel strike*) in a smooth flow via the first and fifth metatarsal bones (*2, 3*) that ends with a propulsive thrust (*4, push-off*) delivered by the terminal bone of the big toe.

mates, including man, have stemmed.

Walker and I are not alone in this view. In 1962 W. L. Straus, Jr., of Johns Hopkins University declared: "It can safely be assumed that primates early developed the mechanisms permitting maintenance of the trunk in the upright position.... Indeed, this tendency toward truncal erectness can be regarded as an essentially basic primate character." The central adaptations for erectness of the body, which have been retained in the majority of living primates, seem to have provided the necessary anatomical basis for the occasional bipedal behavior exhibited by today's monkeys and apes.

What we are concerned with here is the transition from a distant, hypothetical vertical-clinging ancestor to modern, bipedal man. The transition was almost

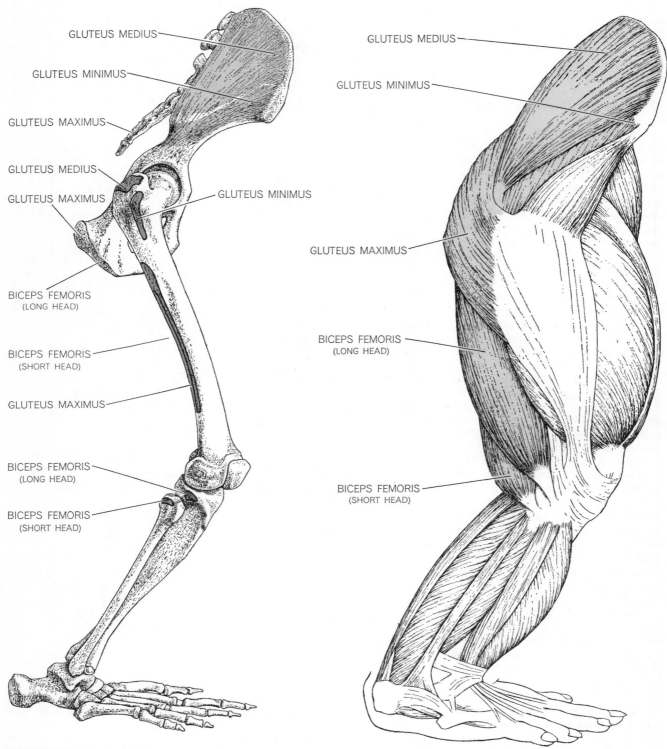

QUADRUPEDAL POSTURE needs two sets of muscles to act as the principal extensors of the hip. These are the gluteal group (the gluteus medius and minimus in particular), which connects the pelvis to the upper part of the femur, and the hamstring group. which connects the femur and the lower leg bones. Of these only the biceps femoris is shown in the gorilla musculature at right. The skeletal regions to which these muscles attach are shown in color at left. In most primates the gluteus maximus is quite small.

certainly marked by an intermediate quadrupedal stage. Possibly such Miocene fossil forms as *Proconsul*, a chimpanzee-like early primate from East Africa, represent such a stage. The structural adaptations necessary to convert a quadrupedal ape into a bipedal hominid are centered on the pelvis, the femur, the foot and the musculature associated with these bones. Among the nonhuman primates living today the pelvis and femur are adapted for four-footed walking; the functional relations between hipbones and thigh muscles are such that, when the animal attempts to assume a bipedal stance, the hip joint is subjected to a stress and the hip must be bent. To compensate for the resulting forward shift of the center of gravity, the knees must also be bent. In order to alter a bent-hip, bent-knee gait into

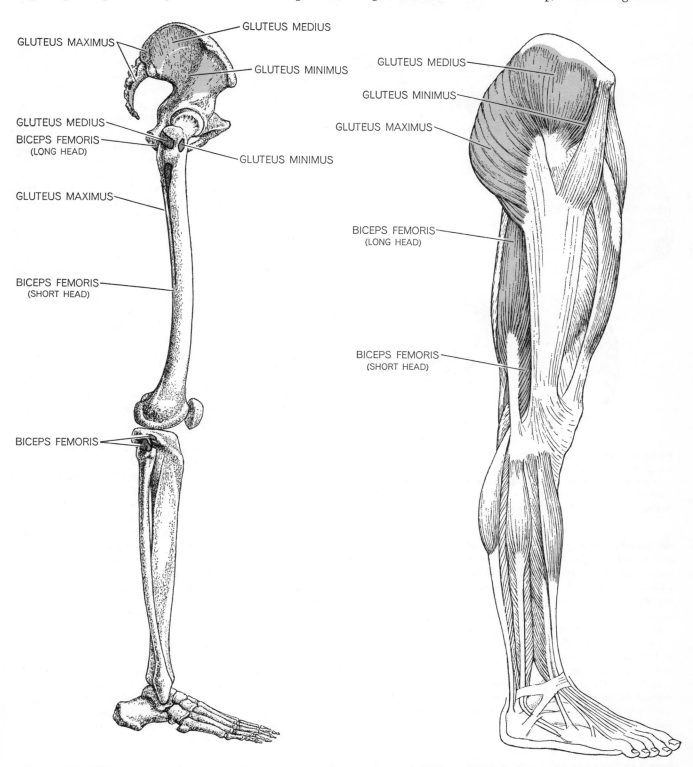

BIPEDAL POSTURE brings a reversal in the roles played by the same pelvic and femoral muscles. Gluteus medius and gluteus minimus have changed from extensors to abductors and the function of extending the trunk, required when a biped runs or climbs, has been assumed by the gluteus maximus. The hamstring muscles, in turn, now act mainly as stabilizers and extensors of the hip. At right are the muscles as they appear in man; the skeletal regions to which their upper and lower ends attach are shown in color at left.

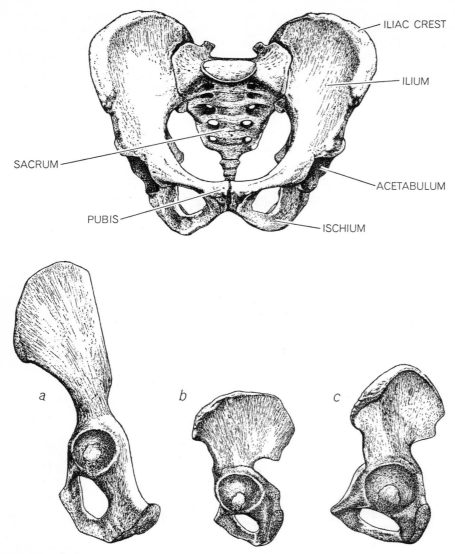

ILIAC CREST

ILIUM

SACRUM

ACETABULUM

PUBIS

ISCHIUM

a

b

c

COMPONENTS OF THE PELVIS are identified at top; the bones are those of the human pelvis. Below, ilium and ischium of a gorilla (a), of *Australopithecus* (b) and of modern man (c) are seen from the side (the front is to the left in each instance). The ischium of *Australopithecus* is longer than man's; this almost certainly kept the early hominid from striding in the manner of *Homo sapiens*. Instead the gait was probably a kind of jog trot.

man's erect, striding walk, a number of anatomical changes must occur. These include an elongation of the hind limbs with respect to the forelimbs, a shortening and broadening of the pelvis, adjustments of the musculature of the hip (in order to stabilize the trunk during the act of walking upright), a straightening of both hip and knee and considerable reshaping of the foot.

Which of these changes can be considered to be primary and which secondary is still a matter that needs elucidation. Sherwood L. Washburn of the University of California at Berkeley has expressed the view that the change from four-footed to two-footed posture was initiated by a modification in the form and function of the gluteus maximus, a thigh muscle that is powerfully

developed in man but weakly developed in monkeys and apes [*see illustrations on preceding two pages*]. In a quadrupedal primate the principal extensors of the trunk are the "hamstring" muscles and the two upper-leg muscles I have already mentioned: the gluteus medius and gluteus minimus. In man these two muscles bear a different relation to the pelvis, in terms of both position and function. In technical terms they have become abductor muscles of the trunk rather than extensor muscles of the leg. It is this that enables them to play a critical part in stabilizing the pelvis in the course of striding. In man the extensor function of these two gluteal muscles has been taken over by a third, the gluteus maximus. This muscle, insignificant in other primates, plays a sur-

prisingly unimportant role in man's ability to stand, or even to walk on a level surface. In standing, for example, the principal stabilizing and extending agents are the muscles of the hamstring group. In walking on the level the gluteus maximus is so little involved that even when it is paralyzed a man's stride is virtually unimpaired. The gluteus maximus comes into its own in man when power is needed to give the hip joint more play for such activities as running, walking up a steep slope or climbing stairs [*see illustration on page 44*]. Its chief function in these circumstances is to correct any tendency for the human trunk to jackknife on the legs.

Because the gluteus maximus has such a specialized role I believe, in contrast to Washburn's view, that it did not assume its present form until late in the evolution of the striding gait. Rather than being the initial adaptation, this muscle's enlargement and present function appear to me far more likely to have been one of the ultimate refinements of human walking. I am in agreement with Washburn, however, when he states that changes in the ilium, or upper pelvis, would have preceded changes in the ischium, or lower pelvis [see the article "Tools and Human Evolution," by Sherwood L. Washburn beginning on page 47]. The primary adaptation would probably have involved a forward curvature of the vertebral column in the lumbar region. Accompanying this change would have been a broadening and a forward rotation of the iliac portions of the pelvis. Together these early adaptations provide the structural basis for improving the posture of the trunk.

Assuming that we have now given at least a tentative answer to the question of how man's bipedal posture evolved, there remains to be answered the question of why. What were the advantages of habitual bipedalism? Noting the comparative energy demands of various gaits, Washburn points out that human walking is primarily an adaptation for covering long distances economically. To go a long way with a minimum of effort is an asset to a hunter; it seems plausible that evolutionary selection for hunting behavior in man was responsible for the rapid development of striding anatomy. Gordon W. Hewes of the University of Colorado suggests a possible incentive that, acting as an agent of natural selection, could have prompted the quadrupedal ancestors of man to adopt a two-footed gait. In Hewes's view the principal advantage of bipedalism over quadrupedalism would be the free-

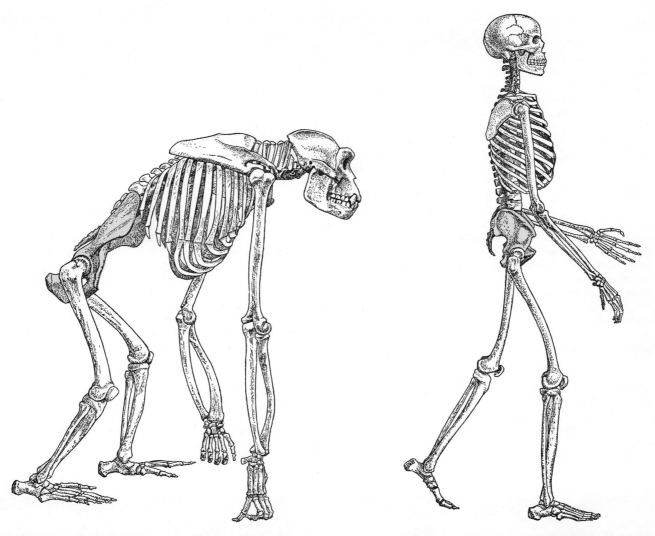

SHAPE AND ORIENTATION of the pelvis in the gorilla and in man reflect the postural differences between quadrupedal and bipedal locomotion. The ischium in the gorilla is long, the ilium extends to the side and the whole pelvis is tilted toward the horizontal (*see illustration on opposite page*). In man the ischium is much shorter, the broad ilium extends forward and the pelvis is vertical.

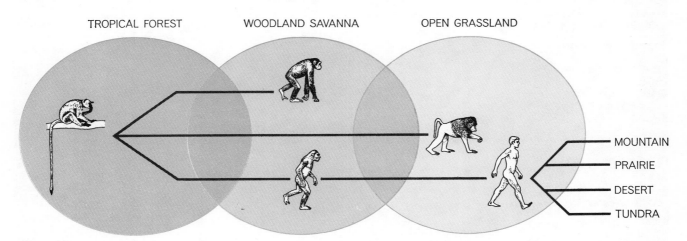

TROPICAL FOREST   WOODLAND SAVANNA   OPEN GRASSLAND

MOUNTAIN
PRAIRIE
DESERT
TUNDRA

ECOLOGICAL PATHWAY to man's eventual mastery of all environments begins (*left*) with a quadrupedal primate ancestor living in tropical forest more than 20 million years ago. During Miocene times mountain-building produced new environments. One, a transition zone between forest and grassland, has been exploited by three groups of primates. Some, for example the chimpanzees, have only recently entered this woodland savanna. Both the newly bipedal hominids and some ground-living quadrupedal monkeys, however, moved beyond the transition zone into open grassland. The quadrupeds, for example the baboons, remained there. On the other hand, the forces of natural selection in the new setting favored the bipedal hominid hunters' adaptation of the striding gait typical of man. Once this adaptation developed, man went on to conquer most of the earth's environments.

ing of the hands, so that food could be carried readily from one place to another for later consumption. To assess the significance of such factors as survival mechanisms it behooves us to review briefly the ecological situation in which our prehuman ancestors found themselves in Miocene times, between 15 and 25 million years ago.

The Miocene Environment

During the Miocene epoch the world-wide mountain-building activity of middle Tertiary times was in full swing. Many parts of the earth, including the region of East Africa where primates of the genus *Proconsul* were living, were being faulted and uplifted to form such mountain zones as the Alps, the Himalayas, the Andes and the Rockies. Massive faulting in Africa gave rise to one of the earth's major geological features: the Rift Valley, which extends 5,000 miles from Tanzania across East Africa to Israel and the Dead Sea. A string of lakes lies along the floor of the Rift Valley like giant stepping-stones. On their shores in Miocene times lived a fantastically rich fauna, inhabitants of the forest and of a new ecological niche—the grassy savanna.

These grasslands of the Miocene were the domain of new forms of vegetation that in many parts of the world had taken the place of rain forest, the dominant form of vegetation in the Eocene and the Oligocene. The savanna offered new evolutionary opportunities to a variety of mammals, including the expanding population of primates in the rapidly shrinking forest. A few primates—the ancestors of man and probably also the ancestors of the living baboons—evidently reacted to the challenge of the new environment.

The savanna, however, was no Eldorado. The problems facing the early hominids in the open grassland were immense. The forest foods to which they were accustomed were hard to come by; the danger of attack by predators was immeasurably increased. If, on top of everything else, the ancestral hominids of Miocene times were in the process of converting from quadrupedalism to bipedalism, it is difficult to conceive of any advantage in bipedalism that could have compensated for the added hazards of life in the open grassland. Consideration of the drawbacks of savanna living has led me to a conclusion contrary to the one generally accepted: I doubt that the advent of bipedalism took place in this environment. An environment neglected by scholars but one far better suited for the origin of man is the woodland-savanna, which is neither high forest nor open grassland. Today this halfway-house niche is occupied by many primates, for example the vervet monkey and some chimpanzees. It has enough trees to provide forest foods and ready escape from predators. At the same time its open grassy spaces are arenas in which new locomotor adaptations can be practiced and new foods can be sampled. In short, the woodland-savanna provides an ideal nursery for evolving hominids, combining the challenge and incentive of the open grassland with much of the security of the forest. It was probably in this transitional environment that man's ancestors learned to walk on two legs. In all likelihood, however, they only learned to stride when they later moved into the open savanna.

Moving forward many millions of years from Miocene to Pleistocene times, we come to man's most immediate hominid precursor: *Australopithecus*. A large consortium of authorities agrees that the shape of the pelvis in *Australopithecus* fossils indicates that these hominids were habitually bipedal, although not to the degree of perfection exhibited by modern man. A few anatomists, fighting a rearguard action, contend that on the contrary the pelvis of *Australopithecus*

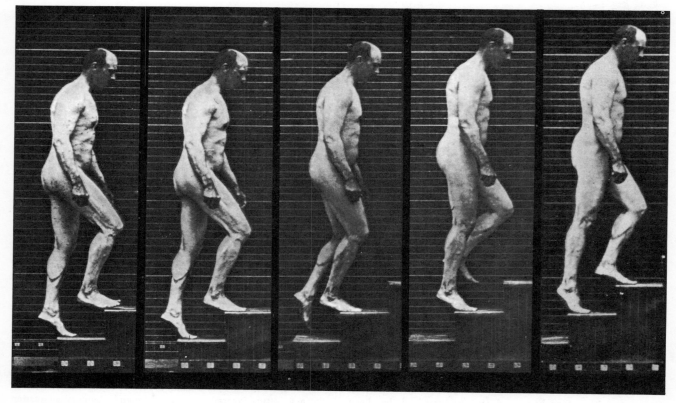

STAIR-CLIMBING, like running, is a movement that brings the human gluteus maximus into play. Acting as an extensor of the trunk, the muscle counteracts any tendency for the body to jack-knife over the legs. Photographs are from Muybridge's collection.

shows that these hominids were predominantly quadrupedal. I belong to the first school but, as I have been at some pains to emphasize in the past, the kind of upright walking practiced by *Australopithecus* should not be equated with man's heel-and-toe, striding gait.

From Bipedalist to Strider

The stride, although it was not necessarily habitual among the earliest true men, is nevertheless the quintessence of the human locomotor achievement. Among other things, striding involves extension of the leg to a position behind the vertical axis of the spinal column. The degree of extension needed can only be achieved if the ischium of the pelvis is short. But the ischium of *Australopithecus* is long, almost as long as the ischium of an ape [*see illustration on page 42*]. Moreover, it has been shown that in man the gluteus medius and the gluteus minimus are prime movers in stabilizing the pelvis during each stride; in *Australopithecus* this stabilizing mechanism is imperfectly evolved. The combination of both deficiencies almost entirely precludes the possibility that these hominids possessed a striding gait. For *Australopithecus* walking was something of a jog trot. These hominids must have covered the ground with quick, rather short steps, with their knees and hips slightly bent; the prolonged stance phase of the fully human gait must surely have been absent.

Compared with man's stride, therefore, the gait of *Australopithecus* is physiologically inefficient. It calls for a disproportionately high output of energy; indeed, *Australopithecus* probably found long-distance bipedal travel impossible. A natural question arises in this connection. Could the greater energy requirement have led these early representatives of the human family to alter their diet in the direction of an increased reliance on high-energy foodstuffs, such as the flesh of other animals?

The pelvis of *Australopithecus* bears evidence that this hominid walker could scarcely have been a strider. Let us now turn to the foot of what many of us believe is a more advanced hominid. In 1960 L. S. B. Leakey and his wife Mary unearthed most of the bones of this foot in the lower strata at Olduvai Gorge known collectively as Bed I, which are about 1.75 million years old. The bones formed part of a fossil assemblage that has been designated by the Leakeys, by Philip Tobias of the University of the Witwatersrand and by me as possibly the earliest-known species of man: *Homo*

habilis. The foot was complete except for the back of the heel and the terminal bones of the toes; its surviving components were assembled and studied by me and Michael Day, one of my colleagues at the Unit of Primatology and Human Evolution of the Royal Free Hospital School of Medicine in London. On the basis of functional analysis the resem-

blance to the foot of modern man is close, although differing in a few minor particulars. Perhaps the most significant point of resemblance is that the stout basal bone of the big toe lies alongside the other toes [*see upper illustration on next page*]. This is an essentially human characteristic; in apes and monkeys the big toe is not exceptionally robust and

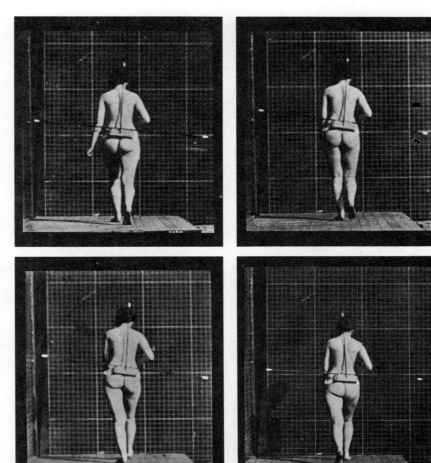
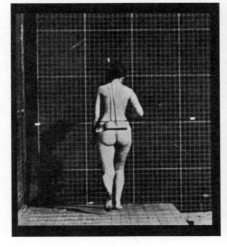
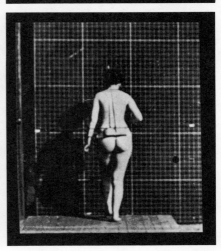

PELVIC ROTATION of the human female is exaggerated compared with that of a male taking a stride of equal length because the two sexes differ in pelvic anatomy. Muybridge noted the phenomenon, using a pole with whitened ends to record the pelvic oscillations.

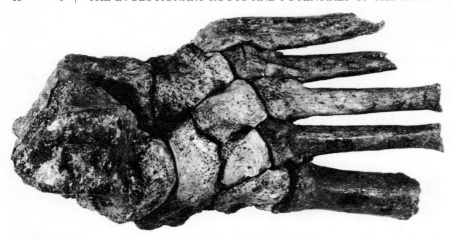

PRIMITIVE FOOT, complete except for the back of the heel and the tips of the toes, was unearthed from the lower level at Olduvai Gorge in Tanzania. Attributed to a very early hominid, *Homo habilis,* by its discoverer, L. S. B. Leakey, it is about 1.75 million years old. Its appearance suggests that the possessor was a habitual biped. Absence of the terminal bones of the toes, however, leaves open the question of whether the possessor walked with a stride.

BIG-TOE BONE, also discovered at Olduvai Gorge, is considerably younger than the foot bones in the top illustration but still probably more than a million years old. It is the toe's terminal bone (*bottom view at left, top view at right*) and bore the thrust of its possessor's push-off with each swing of the right leg. The tilting and twisting of the head of the bone in relation to the shaft is unequivocal evidence that its possessor walked with a modern stride.

diverges widely from the other toes. The foot bones, therefore, give evidence that this early hominid species was habitually bipedal. In the absence of the terminal bones of the toes, however, there was no certainty that *Homo habilis* walked with a striding gait.

Then in 1961, in a somewhat higher stratum at Olduvai Gorge (and thus in a slightly younger geological formation), a single bone came to light in an area otherwise barren of human bones. This fossil is the big-toe bone I mentioned at the beginning of this article [*see lower illustration at left*]. Its head is both tilted and twisted with respect to its shaft, characteristics that are found only in modern man and that can with assurance be correlated with a striding gait. Day has recently completed a dimensional analysis of the bone, using a multivariate statistical technique. He is able to show that the fossil is unquestionably human in form.

There is no evidence to link the big-toe bone specifically to either of the two recognized hominids whose fossil remains have been recovered from Bed I at Olduvai: *Homo habilis* and *Zinjanthropus boisei*. Thus the owner of the toe remains unknown, at least for the present. Nonetheless, one thing is made certain by the discovery. We now know that in East Africa more than a million years ago there existed a creature whose mode of locomotion was essentially human.

Tools and Human Evolution

3

by Sherwood L. Washburn
September 1960

*It is now clear that tools antedate man, and that their
use by prehuman primates gave rise to Homo sapiens*

A series of recent discoveries has linked prehuman primates of half a million years ago with stone tools. For some years investigators had been uncovering tools of the simplest kind from ancient deposits in Africa. At first they assumed that these tools constituted evidence of the existence of large-brained, fully bipedal men. Now the tools have been found in association with much more primitive creatures, the not-fully bipedal, small-brained near-men, or man-apes. Prior to these finds the prevailing view held that man evolved nearly to his present structural state and then discovered tools and the new ways of life that they made possible. Now it appears that man-apes—creatures able to run but not yet walk on two legs, and with brains no larger than those of apes now living—had already learned to make and to use tools. It follows that the structure of modern man must be the result of the change in the terms of natural selection that came with the tool-using way of life.

The earliest stone tools are chips or simple pebbles, usually from river gravels. Many of them have not been shaped at all, and they can be identified as tools only because they appear in concentrations, along with a few worked pieces, in caves or other locations where no such stones naturally occur. The huge advantage that a stone tool gives to its user must be tried to be appreciated. Held in the hand, it can be used for pounding, digging or scraping. Flesh and bone can be cut with a flaked chip,

and what would be a mild blow with the fist becomes lethal with a rock in the hand. Stone tools can be employed, moreover, to make tools of other materials. Naturally occurring sticks are nearly all rotten, too large, or of inconvenient shape; some tool for fabrication is essential for the efficient use of wood. The utility of a mere pebble seems so limited to the user of modern tools that it is not easy to comprehend the vast difference that separates the tool-user from the ape which relies on hands and teeth alone. Ground-living monkeys dig out roots for food, and if they could use a stone or a stick, they might easily double their food supply. It was the success of the simplest tools that started the whole trend of human evolution and led to the civilizations of today.

From the short-term point of view, human structure makes human behavior possible. From the evolutionary point of view, behavior and structure form an interacting complex, with each change in one affecting the other. Man began when populations of apes, about a million years ago, started the bipedal, tool-using way of life that gave rise to the man-apes of the genus *Australopithecus*. Most of the obvious differences that distinguish man from ape came after the use of tools.

The primary evidence for the new view of human evolution is teeth, bones and tools. But our ancestors were not fossils; they were striving creatures,

full of rage, dominance and the will to live. What evolved was the pattern of life of intelligent, exploratory, playful, vigorous primates; the evolving reality was a succession of social systems based upon the motor abilities, emotions and intelligence of their members. Selection produced new systems of child care, maturation and sex, just as it did alterations in the skull and the teeth. Tools, hunting, fire, complex social life, speech, the human way and the brain evolved together to produce ancient man of the genus *Homo* about half a million years ago. Then the brain evolved under the pressures of more complex social life until the species *Homo sapiens* appeared perhaps as recently as 50,000 years ago.

With the advent of *Homo sapiens* the tempo of technical-social evolution quickened. Some of the early types of tool had lasted for hundreds of thousands of years and were essentially the same throughout vast areas of the African and Eurasian land masses. Now the tool forms multiplied and became regionally diversified. Man invented the

———→

STENCILED HANDS in the cave of Gargas in the Pyrenees date back to the Upper, Paleolithic of perhaps 30,000 years ago. Aurignacian man made the images by placing hand against wall and spattering it with paint. Hands stenciled in black (*top*) are more distinct and apparently more recent than those done in other colors (*center*).

OLDUVAI GORGE in Tanganyika is the site where the skull of the largest known man-ape was discovered in 1959 by L. S. B. Leakey and his wife Mary. Stratigraphic evidence indicates that skull dates back to Lower Pleistocene, more than **500,000** years ago.

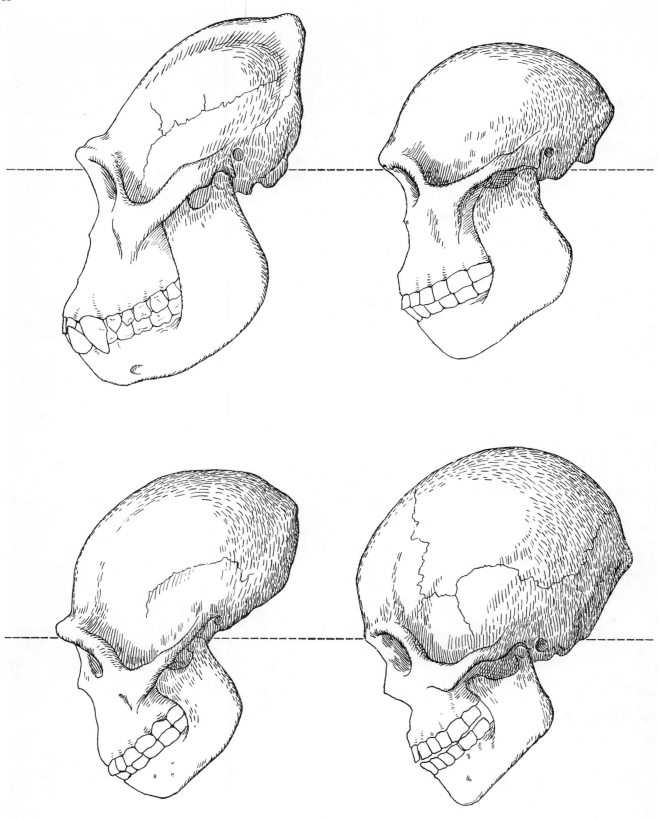

EVOLUTION OF SKULL from ape (*upper left*) to man-ape (*upper right*) to ancient man (*lower left*) to modern man (*lower right*) involves an increase in size of brain case (*part of skull above broken lines*) and a corresponding decrease in size of face (*part of skull below broken lines*). Apes also possess canine teeth that are much larger than those found in either man-apes or man.

bow, boats, clothing; conquered the Arctic; invaded the New World; domesticated plants and animals; discovered metals, writing and civilization. Today, in the midst of the latest tool-making revolution, man has achieved the capacity to adapt his environment to his need and impulse, and his numbers have begun to crowd the planet.

The later events in the evolution of the human species are treated in other articles in the September 1960 issue of SCIENTIFIC AMERICAN. This article is concerned with the beginnings of the process by which, as Theodosius Dobzhansky says in the concluding article of the issue, biological evolution has transcended itself. From the rapidly accumulating evidence it is now possible to speculate with some confidence on the manner in which the way of life made possible by tools changed the pressures of natural selection and so changed the structure of man.

Tools have been found, along with the bones of their makers, at Sterkfontein, Swartkrans and Kromdraai in South Africa and at Olduvai in Tanganyika. Many of the tools from Sterkfontein are merely unworked river pebbles, but someone had to carry them from the gravels some miles away and bring them to the deposit in which they are found. Nothing like them occurs naturally in the local limestone caves. Of course the association of the stone tools with man-ape bones in one or two localities does not prove that these animals made the tools. It has been argued that a more advanced form of man, already present, was the toolmaker. This argument has a familiar ring to students of human evolution. Peking man was thought too primitive to be a toolmaker; when the first manlike pelvis was found with man-ape bones, some argued that it must have fallen into the deposit because it was too human to be associated with the skull. In every case, however, the repeated discovery of the same unanticipated association has ultimately settled the controversy.

This is why the discovery by L. S. B. and Mary Leakey in the summer of 1959 is so important. In Olduvai Gorge in Tanganyika they came upon traces of an old living site, and found stone tools in clear association with the largest man-ape skull known. With the stone tools were a hammer stone and waste flakes from the manufacture of the tools. The deposit also contained the bones of rats, mice, frogs and some bones of juvenile pig and antelope, showing that even the largest and latest of the

SKULL IS EXAMINED *in situ* by Mary Leakey, who first noticed fragments of it protruding from the cliff face at left. Pebble tools were found at the same level as the skull.

SKULL IS EXCAVATED from surrounding rock with dental picks. Although skull was badly fragmented, almost all of it was recovered. Fragment visible here is part of upper jaw.

52

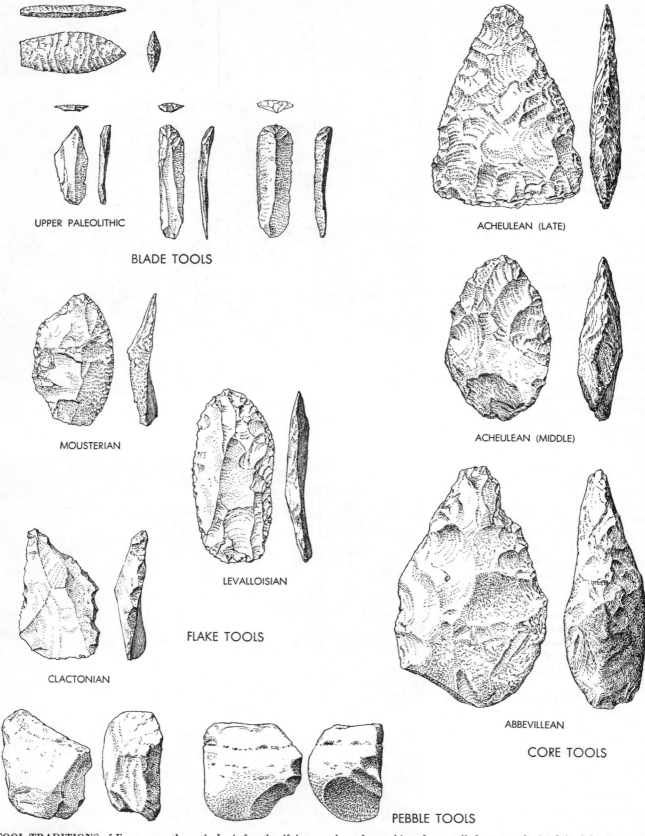

UPPER PALEOLITHIC

BLADE TOOLS

ACHEULEAN (LATE)

MOUSTERIAN

ACHEULEAN (MIDDLE)

LEVALLOISIAN

FLAKE TOOLS

CLACTONIAN

ABBEVILLEAN

CORE TOOLS

PEBBLE TOOLS

TOOL TRADITIONS of Europe are the main basis for classifying Paleolithic cultures. The earliest tools are shown at bottom of page; later ones, at top. The tools are shown from both the side and the edge, except for blade tools, which are shown in three views. Tools consisting of a piece of stone from which a few flakes have been chipped are called core tools (*right*). Other types of tool were made from flakes (*center and left*); blade tools were made from flakes with almost parallel sides. Tool traditions are named for site where tools of a given type were discovered; Acheulean tools, for example, are named for St. Acheul in France.

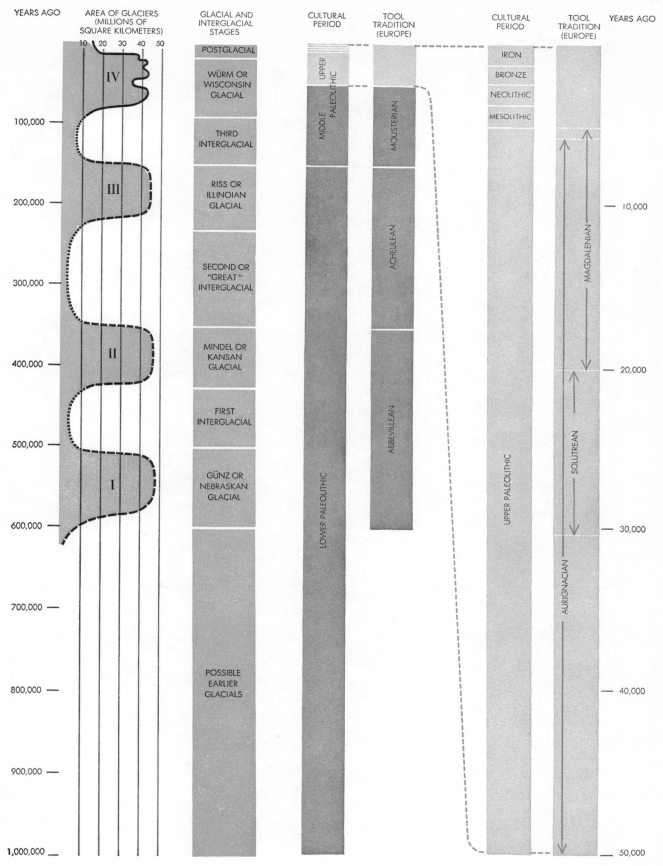

TIME-SCALE correlates cultural periods and tool traditions with the four great glaciations of the Pleistocene epoch. Glacial advances and retreats shown by solid black curve are accurately known; those shown by broken curve are less certain; those shown by dotted curve are uncertain. Light gray bars at far right show an expanded view of last 50,000 years on two darker bars at center. Scale was prepared with the assistance of William R. Farrand of the Lamont Geological Observatory of Columbia University.

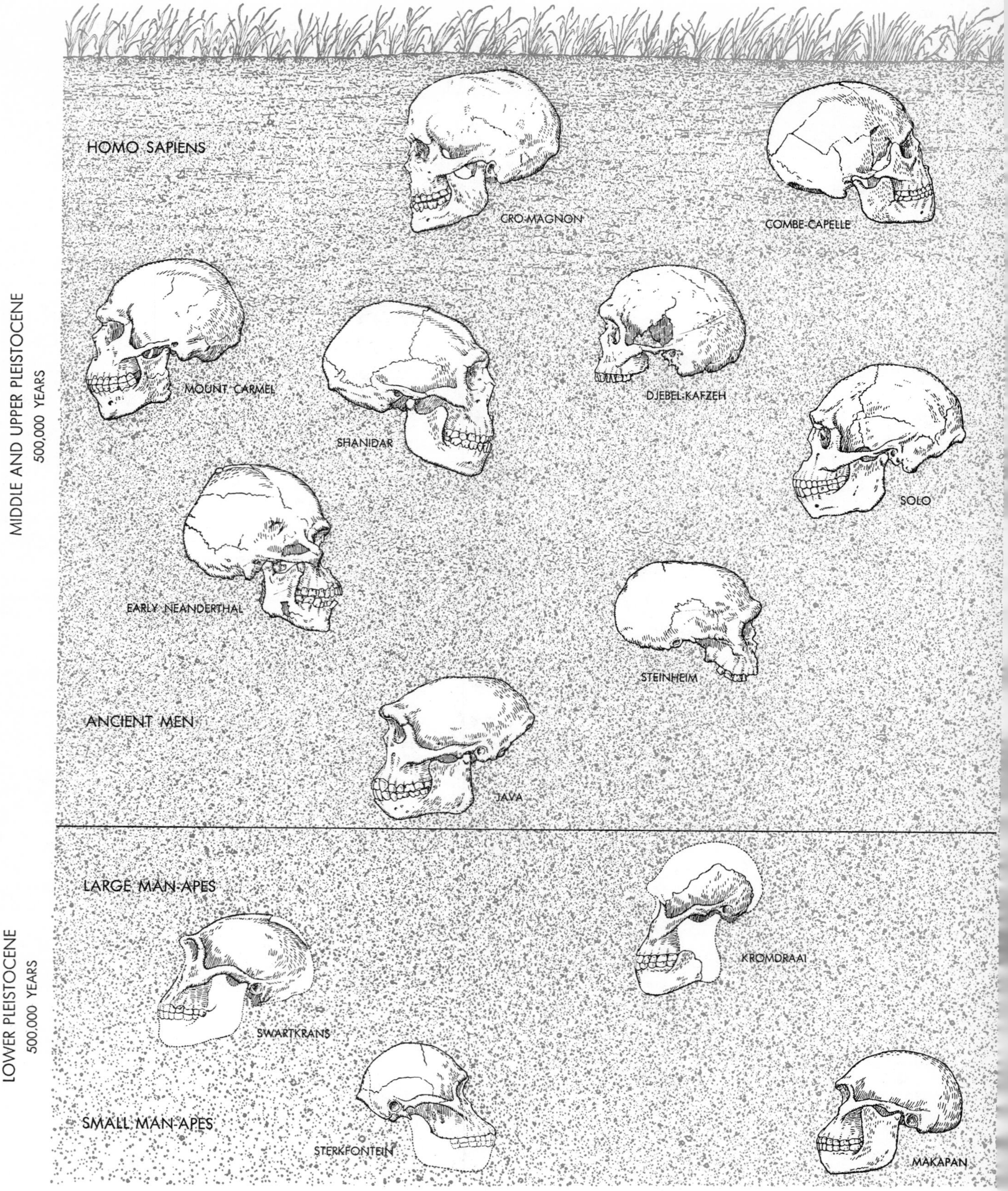

MIDDLE AND UPPER PLEISTOCENE
500,000 YEARS

LOWER PLEISTOCENE
500,000 YEARS

HOMO SAPIENS

CRO-MAGNON

COMBE-CAPELLE

MOUNT CARMEL

SHANIDAR

DJEBEL-KAFZEH

SOLO

EARLY NEANDERTHAL

STEINHEIM

ANCIENT MEN

JAVA

LARGE MAN-APES

SWARTKRANS

KROMDRAAI

SMALL MAN-APES

STERKFONTEIN

MAKAPAN

FOSSIL SKULLS of Pleistocene epoch reflect transition from man-apes (*below black line*) to *Homo sapiens* (*top*). Relative age of intermediate specimens is indicated schematically by their posi- tion on page. Java man (*middle left*) and Solo man (*upper center*) are members of the genus *Pithecanthropus*, and are related to Peking man (*middle right*). The Shanidar skull (*upper left*) be-

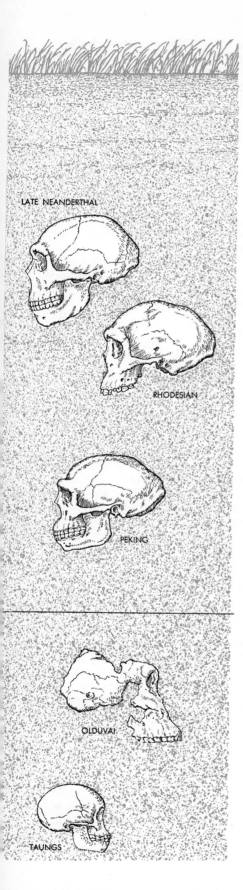

LATE NEANDERTHAL

RHODESIAN

PEKING

OLDUVAI

TAUNGS

longs to the Neanderthal family, while Mount Carmel skull shows characteristics of Neanderthal and modern man.

man-apes could kill only the smallest animals and must have been largely vegetarian. The Leakeys' discovery confirms the association of the man-ape with pebble tools, and adds the evidence of manufacture to that of mere association. Moreover, the stratigraphic evidence at Olduvai now for the first time securely dates the man-apes, placing them in the lower Pleistocene, earlier than 500,000 years ago and earlier than the first skeletal and cultural evidence for the existence of the genus Homo [*see illustration on these two pages*]. Before the discovery at Olduvai these points had been in doubt.

The man-apes themselves are known from several skulls and a large number of teeth and jaws, but only fragments of the rest of the skeleton have been preserved. There were two kinds of man-ape, a small early one that may have weighed 50 or 60 pounds and a later and larger one that weighed at least twice as much. The differences in size and form between the two types are quite comparable to the differences between the contemporary pygmy chimpanzee and the common chimpanzee.

Pelvic remains from both forms of man-ape show that these animals were bipedal. From a comparison of the pelvis of ape, man-ape and man it can be seen that the upper part of the pelvis is much wider and shorter in man than in the ape, and that the pelvis of the man-ape corresponds closely, though not precisely, to that of modern man [*see top illustration on page 57*]. The long upper pelvis of the ape is characteristic of most mammals, and it is the highly specialized, short, wide bone in man that makes possible the human kind of bipedal locomotion. Although the man-ape pelvis is apelike in its lower part, it approaches that of man in just those features that distinguish man from all other animals. More work must be done before this combination of features is fully understood. My belief is that bipedal running, made possible by the changes in the upper pelvis, came before efficient bipedal walking, made possible by the changes in the lower pelvis. In the man-ape, therefore, the adaptation to bipedal locomotion is not yet complete. Here, then, is a phase of human evolution characterized by forms that are mostly bipedal, small-brained, plains-living, tool-making hunters of small animals.

The capacity for bipedal walking is primarily an adaptation for covering long distances. Even the arboreal chimpanzee can run faster than a man, and any monkey can easily outdistance him.

A man, on the other hand, can walk for many miles, and this is essential for efficient hunting. According to skeletal evidence, fully developed walkers first appeared in the ancient men who inhabited the Old World from 500,000 years ago to the middle of the last glaciation. These men were competent hunters, as is shown by the bones of the large animals they killed. But they also used fire and made complicated tools according to clearly defined traditions. Along with the change in the structure of the pelvis, the brain had doubled in size since the time of the man-apes.

The fossil record thus substantiates the suggestion, first made by Charles Darwin, that tool use is both the cause and the effect of bipedal locomotion. Some very limited bipedalism left the hands sufficiently free from locomotor functions so that stones or sticks could be carried, played with and used. The advantage that these objects gave to their users led both to more bipedalism and to more efficient tool use. English lacks any neat expression for this sort of situation, forcing us to speak of cause and effect as if they were separated, whereas in natural selection cause and effect are interrelated. Selection is based on successful behavior, and in the man-apes the beginnings of the human way of life depended on both inherited locomotor capacity and on the learned skills of tool-using. The success of the new way of life based on the use of tools changed the selection pressures on many parts of the body, notably the teeth, hands and brain, as well as on the pelvis. But it must be remembered that selection was for the whole way of life.

In all the apes and monkeys the males have large canine teeth. The long upper canine cuts against the first lower premolar, and the lower canine passes in front of the upper canine. This is an efficient fighting mechanism, backed by very large jaw muscles. I have seen male baboons drive off cheetahs and dogs, and according to reliable reports male baboons have even put leopards to flight. The females have small canines, and they hurry away with the young under the very conditions in which the males turn to fight. All the evidence from living monkeys and apes suggests that the male's large canines are of the greatest importance to the survival of the group, and that they are particularly important in ground-living forms that may not be able to climb to safety in the trees. The small, early man-apes lived in open plains country, and yet

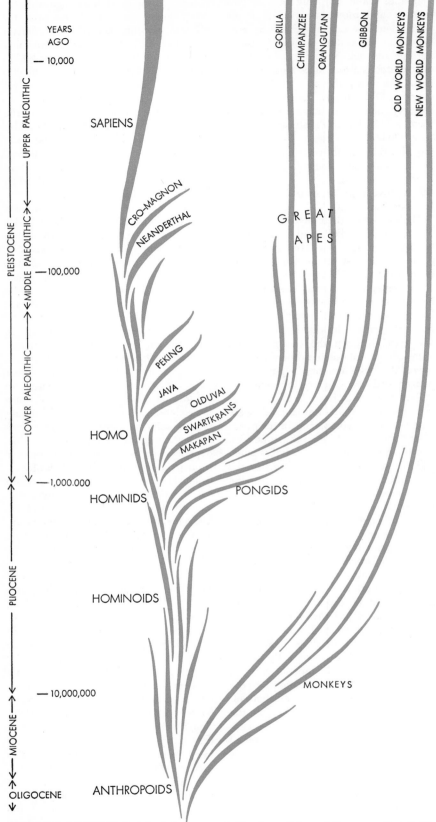

LINES OF DESCENT that lead to man and his closer living relatives are charted. The hominoid superfamily diverged from the anthropoid line in the Miocene period some 20 million years ago. From the hominoid line came the tool-using hominids at the beginning of the Pleistocene. The genus *Homo* appeared in the hominid line during the first interglacial (*see the chart on page 53*); the species *Homo sapiens*, around 50,000 years ago.

none of them had large canine teeth. It would appear that the protection of the group must have shifted from teeth to tools early in the evolution of the man-apes, and long before the appearance of the forms that have been found in association with stone tools. The tools of Sterkfontein and Olduvai represent not the beginnings of tool use, but a choice of material and knowledge in manufacture which, as is shown by the small canines of the man-apes that deposited them there, derived from a long history of tool use.

Reduction in the canine teeth is not a simple matter, but involves changes in the muscles, face, jaws and other parts of the skull. Selection builds powerful neck muscles in animals that fight with their canines, and adapts the skull to the action of these muscles. Fighting is not a matter of teeth alone, but also of seizing, shaking and hurling an enemy's body with the jaws, head and neck. Reduction in the canines is therefore accompanied by a shortening in the jaws, reduction in the ridges of bone over the eyes and a decrease in the shelf of bone in the neck area [*see illustration on page 50*]. The reason that the skulls of the females and young of the apes look more like man-apes than those of adult males is that, along with small canines, they have smaller muscles and all the numerous structural features that go along with them. The skull of the man-ape is that of an ape that has lost the structure for effective fighting with its teeth. Moreover, the man-ape has transferred to its hands the functions of seizing and pulling, and this has been attended by reduction of its incisors. Small canines and incisors are biological symbols of a changed way of life; their primitive functions are replaced by hand and tool.

The history of the grinding teeth—the molars—is different from that of the seizing and fighting teeth. Large size in any anatomical structure must be maintained by positive selection; the selection pressure changed first on the canine teeth and, much later, on the molars. In the man-apes the molars were very large, larger than in either ape or man. They were heavily worn, possibly because food dug from the ground with the aid of tools was very abrasive. With the men of the Middle Pleistocene, molars of human size appear along with complicated tools, hunting and fire.

The disappearance of brow ridges and the refinement of the human face may involve still another factor. One of the essential conditions for the organization of men in co-operative societies was the suppression of rage and of the uncontrolled drive to first place in the hierarchy of dominance. Curt P. Richter of Johns Hopkins University has shown that domestic animals, chosen over the generations for willingness to adjust and for lack of rage, have relatively small adrenal glands. But the breeders who selected for this hormonal, physiological, temperamental type also picked, without realizing it, animals with small brow ridges and small faces. The skull structure of the wild rat bears the same relation to that of the tame rat as does the skull of Neanderthal man to that of *Homo sapiens*. The same is true for the cat, dog, pig, horse and cow; in each case the wild form has the larger face and muscular ridges. In the later stages of human evolution, it appears, the self-domestication of man has been exerting the same effects upon temperament, glands and skull that are seen in the domestic animals.

Of course from man-ape to man the brain-containing part of the skull has also increased greatly in size. This change is directly due to the increase in the size of the brain: as the brain grows, so grow the bones that cover it. Since there is this close correlation between brain size and bony brain-case, the brain size of the fossils can be estimated. On the scale of brain size the man-apes are scarcely distinguishable from the living apes, although their brains may have been larger with respect to body size. The brain seems to have evolved rapidly, doubling in size between man-ape and man. It then appears to have increased much more slowly; there is no substantial change in gross size during the last 100,000 years. One must remember, however, that size alone is a very crude indicator, and that brains of equal size may vary greatly in function. My belief is that although the brain of *Homo sapiens* is no larger than that of Neanderthal man, the indirect evidence strongly suggests that the first *Homo sapiens* was a much more intelligent creature.

The great increase in brain size is important because many functions of the brain seem to depend on the number of cells, and the number increases with volume. But certain parts of the brain have increased in size much more than others. As functional maps of the cortex of the brain show, the human sensory-motor cortex is not just an enlargement of that of an ape [*see illustrations on last three pages of this article*]. The areas for the hand, especially the thumb, in

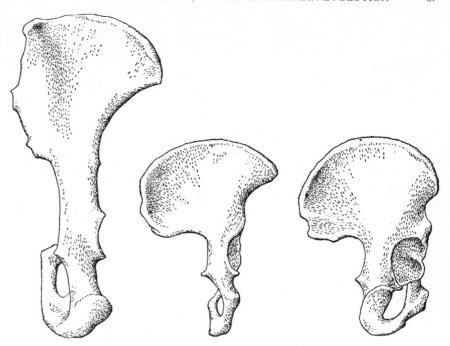

HIP BONES of ape (*left*), man-ape (*center*) and man (*right*) reflect differences between quadruped and biped. Upper part of human pelvis is wider and shorter than that of apes. Lower part of man-ape pelvis resembles that of ape; upper part resembles that of man.

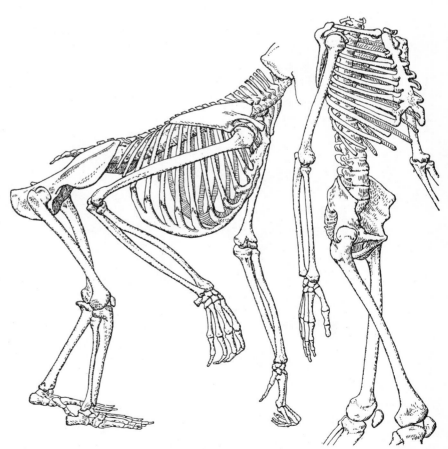

POSTURE of gorilla (*left*) and man (*right*) is related to size, shape and orientation of pelvis. Long, straight pelvis of ape provides support for quadrupedal locomotion; short, broad pelvis of man curves backward, carrying spine and torso in bipedal position.

man are tremendously enlarged, and this is an integral part of the structural base that makes the skillful use of the hand possible. The selection pressures that favored a large thumb also favored a large cortical area to receive sensations from the thumb and to control its motor activity. Evolution favored the development of a sensitive, powerful, skillful thumb, and in all these ways —as well as in structure—a human thumb differs from that of an ape.

The same is true for other cortical areas. Much of the cortex in a monkey is still engaged in the motor and sensory functions. In man it is the areas adjacent to the primary centers that are most expanded. These areas are concerned with skills, memory, foresight and language; that is, with the mental faculties that make human social life possible. This is easiest to illustrate in the field of language. Many apes and monkeys can make a wide variety of sounds. These sounds do not, however, develop into language [see "The Origin of Speech," by Charles F. Hockett; SCIENTIFIC AMERICAN Offprint 603]. Some workers have devoted great efforts, with minimum results, to trying to teach chimpanzees to talk. The reason is that there is little in the brain to teach. A human child learns to speak with the greatest ease, but the storage of thousands of words takes a great deal of cortex. Even the simplest language must have given great advantage to those first men who had it. One is tempted to think that language may have appeared together with the fine tools, fire and complex hunting of the large-brained men of the Middle Pleistocene, but there is no direct proof of this.

The main point is that the kind of animal that can learn to adjust to

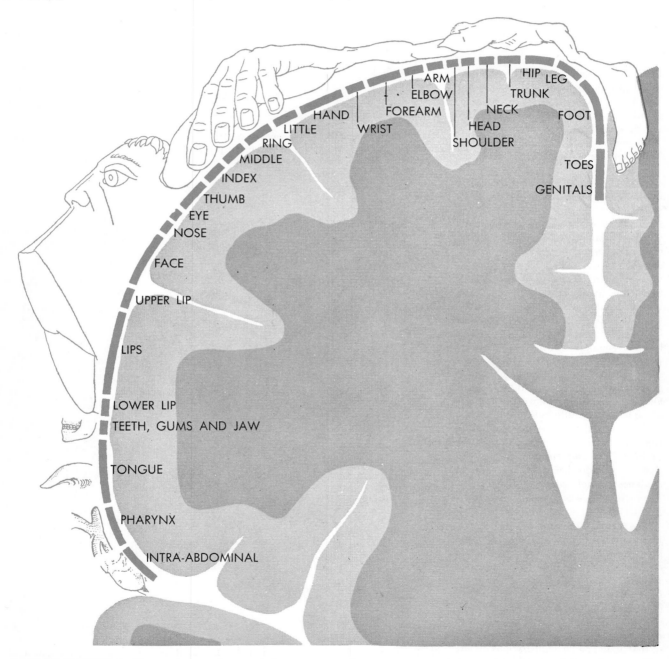

SENSORY HOMUNCULUS is a functional map of the sensory cortex of the human brain worked out by Wilder Penfield and his associates at the Montreal Neurological Institute. As in the map of the sensory cortex of the monkey that appears on the preceding page, the distorted anatomical drawing (*color*) indicates the areas of the sensory cortex associated with the various parts of the body.

complex, human, technical society is a very different creature from a tree-living ape, and the differences between the two are rooted in the evolutionary process. The reason that the human brain makes the human way of life possible is that it is the result of that way of life. Great masses of the tissue in the human brain are devoted to memory, planning, language and skills, because these are the abilities favored by the human way of life.

The emergence of man's large brain occasioned a profound change in the plan of human reproduction. The human mother-child relationship is unique among the primates as is the use of tools. In all the apes and monkeys the baby clings to the mother; to be able to do so, the baby must be born with its central nervous system in an advanced state of development. But the brain of the fetus must be small enough so that birth may take place. In man adaptation to bipedal locomotion decreased the size of the bony birth-canal at the same time that the exigencies of tool use selected for larger brains. This obstetrical dilemma was solved by delivery of the fetus at a much earlier stage of development. But this was possible only because the mother, already bipedal and with hands free of locomotor necessities, could hold the helpless, immature infant. The small-brained man-ape probably developed in the uterus as much as the ape does; the human type of mother-child relation must have evolved by the time of the large-brained, fully bipedal humans of the Middle Pleistocene. Bipedalism, tool use and selection for large brains thus slowed human development and invoked far greater maternal responsibility. The slow-moving mother, carrying the baby, could not

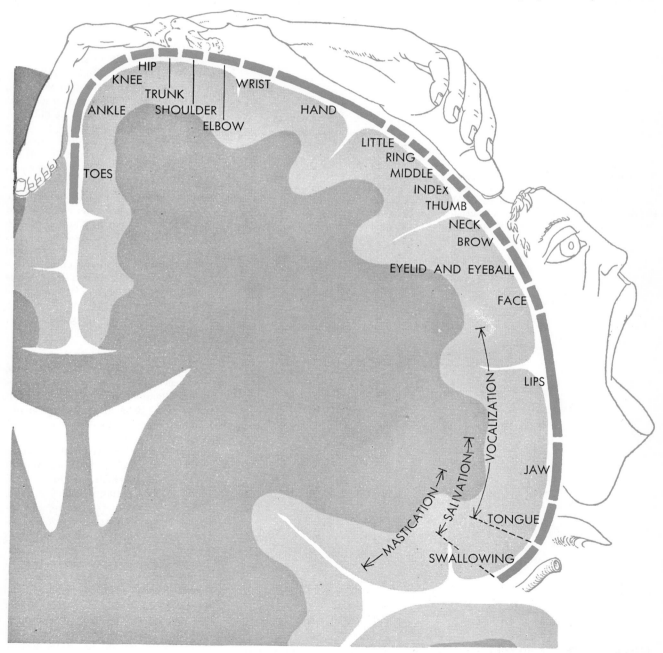

MOTOR HOMUNCULUS depicts parts of body and areas of motor cortex that control their functions. Human brain is shown here in coronal (ear-to-ear) cross section. Speech and hand areas of both motor and sensory cortex in man are proportionately much larger than corresponding areas in apes and monkeys, as can be seen by comparing homunculi with diagram of monkey cortex.

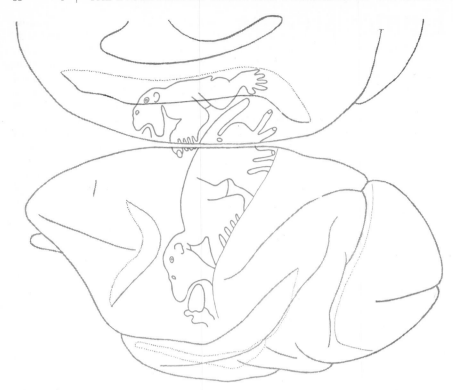

MOTOR CORTEX OF MONKEY controls the movements of the body parts outlined by the superimposed drawing of the animal (*color*). Gray lines trace the surface features of the left half of the brain (*bottom*) and part of the right half (*top*). Colored drawing is distorted in proportion to amount of cortex associated with functions of various parts of the body. Smaller animal in right half of brain indicates location of secondary motor cortex.

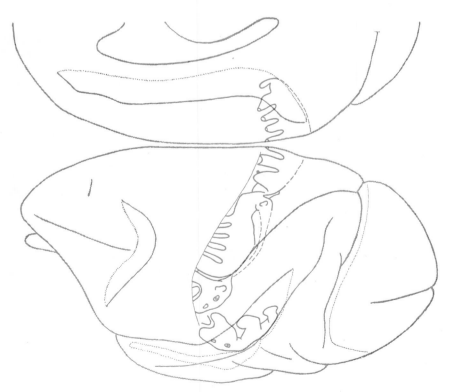

SENSORY CORTEX OF MONKEY is mapped in same way as motor cortex (*above*). As in motor cortex, a large area is associated with hands and feet. Smaller animal at bottom of left half of brain indicates location of secondary sensory cortex. Drawings are based on work of Clinton N. Woolsey and his colleagues at the University of Wisconsin Medical School.

hunt, and the combination of the woman's obligation to care for slow-developing babies and the man's occupation of hunting imposed a fundamental pattern on the social organization of the human species.

As Marshall D. Sahlins suggests ["The Origin of Society," SCIENTIFIC AMERICAN Offprint 602], human society was heavily conditioned at the outset by still other significant aspects of man's sexual adaptation. In the monkeys and apes year-round sexual activity supplies the social bond that unites the primate horde. But sex in these species is still subject to physiological—especially glandular—controls. In man these controls are gone, and are replaced by a bewildering variety of social customs. In no other primate does a family exist that controls sexual activity by custom, that takes care of slow-growing young, and in which—as in the case of primitive human societies—the male and female provide different foods for the family members.

All these family functions are ultimately related to tools, hunting and the enlargement of the brain. Complex and technical society evolved from the sporadic tool-using of an ape, through the simple pebble tools of the man-ape and the complex toolmaking traditions of ancient men to the hugely complicated culture of modern man. Each behavioral stage was both cause and effect of biological change in bones and brain. These concomitant changes can be seen in the scanty fossil record and can be inferred from the study of the living forms.

Surely as more fossils are found these ideas will be tested. New techniques of investigation, from planned experiments in the behavior of lower primates to more refined methods of dating, will extract wholly new information from the past. It is my belief that, as these events come to pass, tool use will be found to have been a major factor, beginning with the initial differentiation of man and ape. In ourselves we see a structure, physiology and behavior that is the result of the fact that some populations of apes started to use tools a million years ago. The pebble tools constituted man's principal technical adaptation for a period at least 50 times as long as recorded history. As we contemplate man's present eminence, it is well to remember that, from the point of view of evolution, the events of the last 50,000 years occupy but a moment in time. Ancient man endured at least 10 times as long and the man-apes for an even longer time.

Homo Erectus

4

By William W. Howells
November 1966

*This species, until recently known by a multiplicity
of other names, was probably the immediate
predecessor of modern man. It now seems possible
that the transition took place some 500,000 years ago*

In 1891 Eugène Dubois, a young Dutch anatomist bent on discovering early man, was examining a fossil-rich layer of gravels beside the Solo River in Java. He found what he was after: an ancient human skull. The next year he discovered in the same formation a human thighbone. These two fossils, now known to be more than 700,000 years old, were the first remains to be found of the prehistoric human species known today as *Homo erectus*. It is appropriate on the 75th anniversary of Dubois's discovery to review how our understanding of this early man has been broadened and clarified by more recent discoveries of fossil men of similar antiquity and the same general characteristics, so that *Homo erectus* is now viewed as representing a major stage in the evolution of man. Also of interest, although of less consequence, is the way in which the name *Homo erectus*, now accepted by many scholars, has been chosen after a long period during which "scientific" names for human fossils were bestowed rather capriciously.

Man first received his formal name in 1758, when Carolus Linnaeus called him *Homo sapiens*. Linnaeus was trying simply to bring order to the world of living things by distinguishing each species of plant and animal from every other and by arranging them all in a hierarchical system. Considering living men, he recognized them quite correctly as one species in the system. The two centuries that followed Linnaeus saw first the establishment of evolutionary theory and then the realization of its genetic foundations; as a result ideas on the relations of species as units of plant and animal life have become considerably more complex. For example, a species can form two or more new species, which Linnaeus originally thought was impossible. By today's definition a spe-

cies typically consists of a series of local or regional populations that may exhibit minor differences of form or color but that otherwise share a common genetic structure and pool of genes and are thus able to interbreed across population lines. Only when two such populations have gradually undergone so many different changes in their genetic makeup that the likelihood of their interbreeding falls below a critical point are they genetically cut off from each other and do they become separate species. Alternatively, over a great many generations an equivalent amount of change will take place in the same population, so that its later form will be recognized as a species different from the earlier. This kind of difference, of course, cannot be put to the test of interbreeding and can only be judged by the physical form of the fossils involved.

In the case of living man there is no reason to revise Linnaeus' assignment: *Homo sapiens* is a good, typical species. Evolution, however, was not in Linnaeus' ken. He never saw a human fossil, much less conceived of men different from living men. Between his time and ours the use of the Linnaean system of classification as applied to man and his relatives past and present became almost a game. On grasping the concept of evolution, scholars saw that modern man must have had ancestors. They were prepared to anticipate the actual discovery of these ancestral forms, and perhaps the greatest anticipator was the German biologist Ernst Haeckel. Working on the basis of fragmentary information in 1889, when the only well-known fossil human remains were the comparatively recent bones discovered 25 years earlier in the Neander Valley of Germany, Haeckel drew up a theoretical ancestral line for man. The line began among some postu-

lated extinct apes of the Miocene epoch and reached *Homo sapiens* by way of an imagined group of "ape-men" (Pithecanthropi) and a group of more advanced but still speechless early men (Alali) whom he visualized as the worldwide stock from which modern men had evolved [*see illustration on page 63*]. A creature combining these various presapient attributes took form in the pooled imagination of Haeckel and his compatriots August Schleicher and Gabriel Max. Max produced a family portrait, and the still-to-be-discovered ancestor was given the respectable Linnaean name *Pithecanthropus alalus*.

Were he living today Haeckel would never do such a thing. It is now the requirement of the International Code of Zoological Nomenclature that the naming of any new genus or species be supported by publication of the specimen's particulars together with a description showing it to be recognizably different from any genus or species previously known. Haeckel was rescued from retroactive embarrassment, however, by Dubois, who gave Haeckel's genus name to Java man. The skull was too large to be an ape's and apparently too small to be a man's; the name *Pithecanthropus* seemed perfectly appropriate. On the other hand, the thighbone from the same formation was essentially modern; its possessor had evidently walked upright. Dubois therefore gave his discovery the species name *erectus*. Since Dubois's time the legitimacy of his finds has been confirmed by the discovery in Java (by G. H. R. von Koenigswald between 1936 and 1939 and by Indonesian workers within the past three years) of equally old and older fossils of the same population.

In the 50 years between Dubois's discovery and the beginning of World

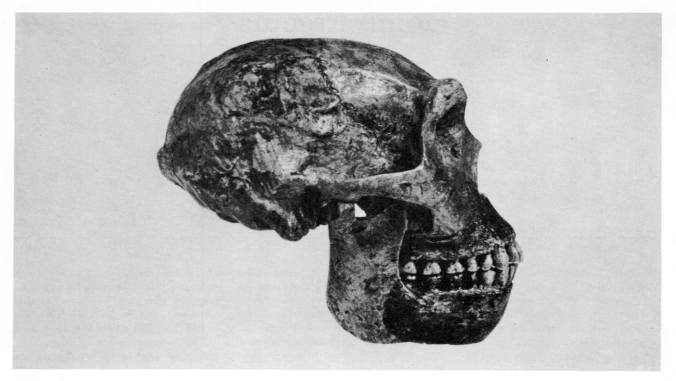

JAVA MAN, whose 700,000-year-old remains were unearthed in 1891 by Eugène Dubois, is representative of the earliest *Homo erectus* population so far discovered. This reconstruction was made recently by G. H. R. von Koenigswald and combines the features of the more primitive members of this species of man that he found in the lowest (Djetis) fossil strata at Sangiran in central Java during the 1930's. The characteristics that are typical of *Homo erectus* include the smallness and flatness of the cranium, the heavy browridge and both the sharp bend and the ridge for muscle attachment at the rear of the skull. The robustness of the jaws adds to the species' primitive appearance. In most respects except size, however, the teeth of *Homo erectus* resemble those of modern man.

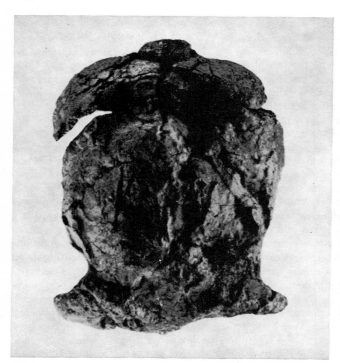

LANTIAN MAN is the most recently found *Homo erectus* fossil. The discovery consists of a jawbone and this skullcap (*top view, browridge at bottom*) from which the occipital bone (*top*) is partially detached. Woo Ju-kang of the Chinese Academy of Sciences in Peking provided the photograph; this fossil man from Shensi may be as old as the earliest specimens of *Homo erectus* from Java.

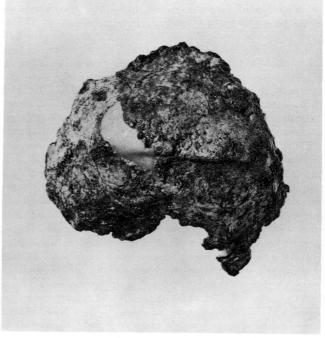

OCCIPITAL BONE found at Vértesszöllös in Hungary in 1965 is 500,000 or more years old. The only older human fossil in Europe is the Heidelberg jaw. The bone forms the rear of a skull; the ridge for muscle attachment (*horizontal line*) is readily apparent. In spite of this primitive feature and its great age, the skull fragment from Vértesszöllös has been assigned to the species *Homo sapiens*.

War II various other important new kinds of human fossil came into view. For our purposes the principal ones (with some of the Linnaean names thrust on them) were (1) the lower jaw found at Mauer in Germany in 1907 (*Homo heidelbergensis* or *Palaeanthropus*), (2) the nearly complete skull found at Broken Hill in Rhodesia in 1921 (*Homo rhodesiensis* or *Cyphanthropus*), (3) various remains uncovered near Peking in China, beginning with one tooth in 1923 and finally comprising a collection representing more than 40 men, women and children by the end of 1937 (*Sinanthropus pekinensis*), and (4) several skulls found in 1931 and 1932 near

Ngandong on the Solo River not far from where Dubois had worked (*Homo soloensis* or *Javanthropus*). This is a fair number of fossils, but they were threatened with being outnumbered by the names assigned to them. The British student of early man Bernard G. Campbell has recorded the following variants in the case of the Mauer jawbone alone: *Palaeanthropus heidelbergensis, Pseudhomo heidelbergensis, Protanthropus heidelbergensis, Praehomo heidelbergensis, Praehomo europaeus, Anthropus heidelbergensis, Maueranthropus heidelbergensis, Europanthropus heidelbergensis* and *Euranthropus*.

Often the men responsible for these

redundant christenings were guilty merely of innocent grandiloquence. They were not formally declaring their conviction that each fossil hominid belonged to a separate genus, distinct from *Homo*, which would imply an enormous diversity in the human stock. Nonetheless, the multiplicity of names has interfered with an understanding of the evolutionary significance of the fossils that bore them. Moreover, the human family trees drawn during this period showed a fundamental resemblance to Haeckel's original venture; the rather isolated specimens of early man were stuck on here and there like Christmas-tree ornaments. Although the arrangements evinced a vague consciousness of evolution, no scheme was presented that intelligibly interpreted the fossil record.

At last two questions came to the fore. First, to what degree did the fossils really differ? Second, what was the difference among them over a period of time? The fossil men of the most recent period—those who had lived between roughly 100,000 and 30,000 years ago—were Neanderthal man, Rhodesian man and Solo man. They have been known traditionally as *Homo neanderthalensis, Homo rhodesiensis* and *Homo soloensis*, names that declare each of the three to be a separate species, distinct from one another and from *Homo sapiens*. This in turn suggests that if Neanderthal and Rhodesian populations had come in contact, they would probably not have interbred. Such a conclusion is difficult to establish on the basis of fossils, particularly when they are few and tell very little about the geographical range of the species. Today's general view is a contrary one. These comparatively recent fossil men, it is now believed, did not constitute separate species. They were at most incipient species, that is, subspecies or variant populations that had developed in widely separated parts of the world but were still probably able to breed with one another or with *Homo sapiens*.

It was also soon recognized that the older Java and Peking fossils were not very different from one another. The suggestion followed that both populations be placed in a single genus (*Pithecanthropus*) and that the junior name (*Sinanthropus*) be dropped. Even this, however, was one genus too many for Ernst Mayr of Harvard University. Mayr, whose specialty is the evolutionary basis of biological classification, declared that ordinary zoological standards would not permit Java and Peking man to occupy

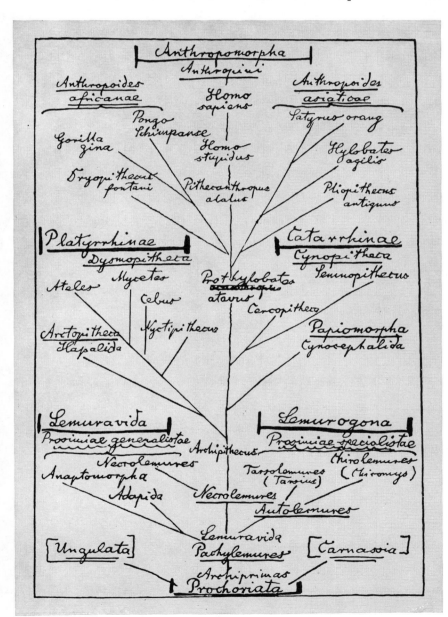

THE NAME "PITHECANTHROPUS," or ape-man, was coined by the German biologist Ernst Haeckel in 1889 for a postulated precursor of *Homo sapiens*. Haeckel placed the ape-man genus two steps below modern man on his "tree" of primate evolution, adding the species name *alalus*, or "speechless," because he deemed speech an exclusively human trait.

a genus separate from modern man. In his opinion the amount of evolutionary progress that separates *Pithecanthropus* from ourselves is a step that allows the recognition only of a different species. After all, Java and Peking man apparently had bodies just like our own; that is to say, they were attacking the problem of survival with exactly the same adaptations, although with smaller brains. On this view Java man is placed in the genus *Homo* but according to the rules retains his original species name and so becomes *Homo erectus*. Under the circumstances Peking man can be distinguished from him only as a subspecies: *Homo erectus pekinensis*.

The simplification is something more than sweeping out a clutter of old names to please the International Commission on Zoological Nomenclature. The reduction of fossil hominids to not more than two species and the recognition of *Homo erectus* has become increasingly useful as a way of looking at a stage of human evolution. This has been increasingly evident in recent years, as human fossils have continued to come to light and as new and improved methods of dating them have been developed. It is now possible to place both the old discoveries and the new ones much more precisely in time, and that is basic to establishing the entire pattern of human evolution in the past few million years.

To consider dating first, the period during which *Homo erectus* flourished occupies the early middle part of the Pleistocene epoch. The evidence that now enables us to subdivide the Pleistocene with some degree of confidence is of several kinds. For example, the fossil animals found in association with fossil men often indicate whether the climate of the time was cold or warm. The comparison of animal communities is also helpful in correlating intervals of time on one continent with intervals on another. The ability to determine absolute dates, which makes possible the correlation of the relative dates derived from sequences of strata in widely separated localities, is another significant development. Foremost among the methods of absolute dating at the moment is one based on the rate of decay of radioactive potassium into argon. A second method showing much promise is the analysis of deep-sea sediments; changes in the forms of planktonic life embedded in samples of the bottom reflect worldwide temperature changes. When the absolute ages of key points in sediment sequences are determined by physical or chemical methods, it ought to be possible to assign dates to

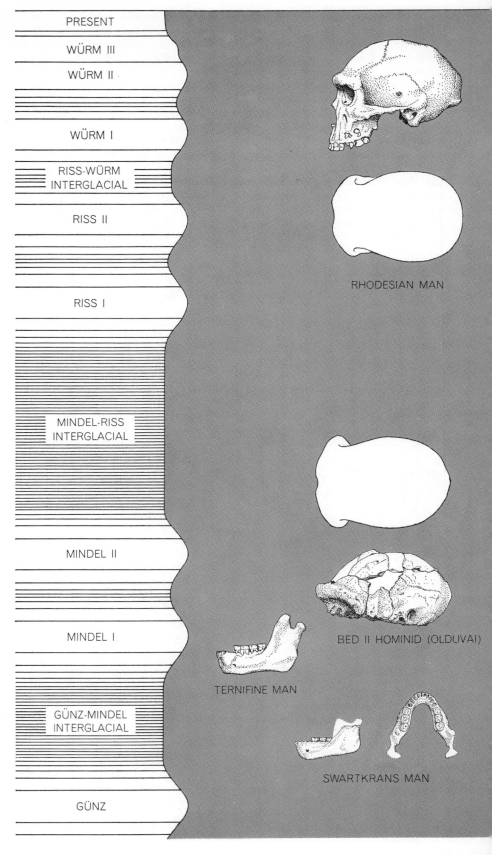

PRESENT
WÜRM III
WÜRM II
WÜRM I
RISS-WÜRM INTERGLACIAL
RISS II
RISS I
MINDEL-RISS INTERGLACIAL
MINDEL II
MINDEL I
GÜNZ-MINDEL INTERGLACIAL
GÜNZ

RHODESIAN MAN

BED II HOMINID (OLDUVAI)

TERNIFINE MAN

SWARTKRANS MAN

FOSSIL EVIDENCE for the existence of a single species of early man instead of several species and genera of forerunners of *Homo sapiens* is presented in this array of individual remains whose age places them in the interval of approximately 500,000 years that separates the first Pleistocene interglacial period from the end of the second glacial period (*see scale at left*). The earliest *Homo erectus* fossils known, from Java and China, belong to the first interglacial period; the earliest *Homo erectus* remains from South Africa may be equally

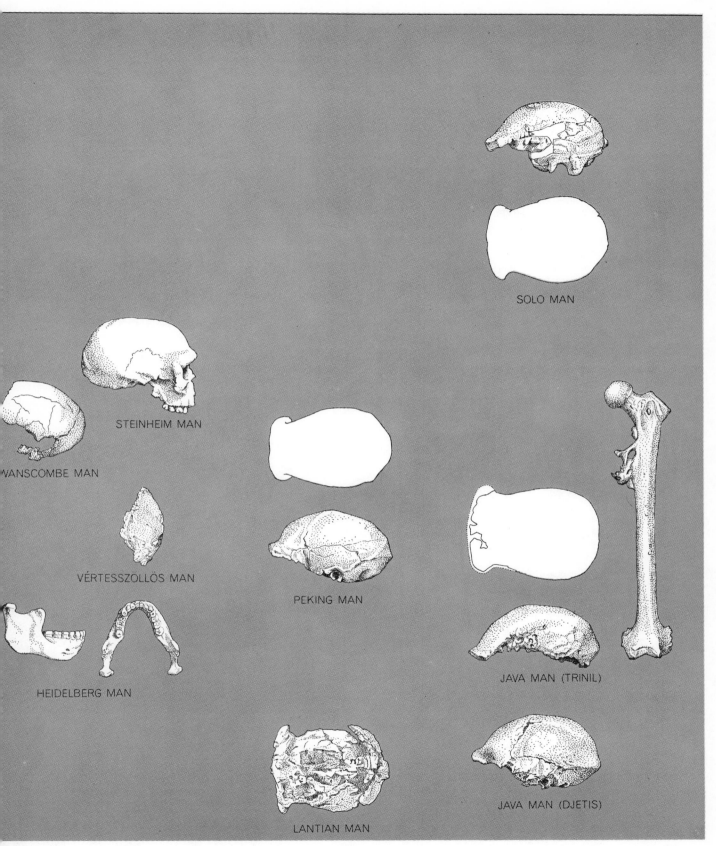

SOLO MAN

STEINHEIM MAN

WANSCOMBE MAN

VÉRTESSZÖLLÖS MAN

PEKING MAN

JAVA MAN (TRINIL)

HEIDELBERG MAN

LANTIAN MAN

JAVA MAN (DJETIS)

old. Half a million years later *Homo erectus* continued to be represented in China by the remains of Peking man and in Africa by the
skull from Olduvai Gorge. In the intervening period this small-
brained precursor of modern man was not the only human species
inhabiting the earth, nor did *Homo erectus* become extinct when
the 500,000-year period ended. One kind of man who had apparent-

ly reached the grade of *Homo sapiens* in Europe by the middle or
later part of the second Pleistocene glacial period was unearthed
recently at Vértesszöllös in Hungary. In the following interglacial period *Homo sapiens* is represented by the Steinheim
and Swanscombe females. Solo man's remains indicate that *Homo
erectus* survived for several hundred thousand years after that.

all the major events of the Pleistocene. Such methods have already suggested that the epoch began more than three million years ago and that its first major cold phase (corresponding to the Günz glaciation of the Alps) may date back to as much as 1.5 million years ago. The period of time occupied by *Homo erectus* now appears to extend from about a million years ago to 500,000 years ago in terms of absolute dates, or from some time during the first interglacial period in the Northern Hemisphere to about the end of the second major cold phase (corresponding to the Mindel glaciation of the Alps).

On the basis of the fossils found before World War II, with the exception of the isolated and somewhat peculiar Heidelberg jaw, *Homo erectus* would have appeared to be a human population of the Far East. The Java skulls, particularly those that come from the lowest fossil strata (known as the Djetis beds), are unsurpassed within the entire

group in primitiveness. Even the skulls from the strata above them (the Trinil beds), in which Dubois made his original discovery, have very thick walls and room for only a small brain. Their cranial capacity probably averages less than 900 cubic centimeters, compared with an average of 500 c.c. for gorillas and about 1,400 c.c. for modern man. The later representatives of Java man must be more than 710,000 years old, because potassium-argon analysis has shown that tektites (glassy stones formed by or from meteorites) in higher strata of the same formation are of that age.

The Peking fossils are younger, probably dating to the middle of the second Pleistocene cold phase, and are physically somewhat less crude than the Java ones. The braincase is higher, the face shorter and the cranial capacity approaches 1,100 c.c., but the general construction of skull and jaw is similar. The teeth of both Java man and Peking man are somewhat larger than modern man's

and are distinguished by traces of an enamel collar, called a cingulum, around some of the crowns. The latter is an ancient and primitive trait in man and apes.

Discoveries of human fossils after World War II have added significantly to the picture of man's distribution at this period. The pertinent finds are the following:

1949: Swartkrans, South Africa. Jaw and facial fragments, originally given the name *Telanthropus capensis*. These were found among the copious remains at this site of the primitive subhumans known as australopithecines. The fossils were recognized at once by the late Robert Broom and his colleague John T. Robinson as more advanced than the australopithecines both in size and in traits of jaw and teeth. Robinson has now assigned *Telanthropus* to *Homo erectus*, since that is where he evidently belongs.

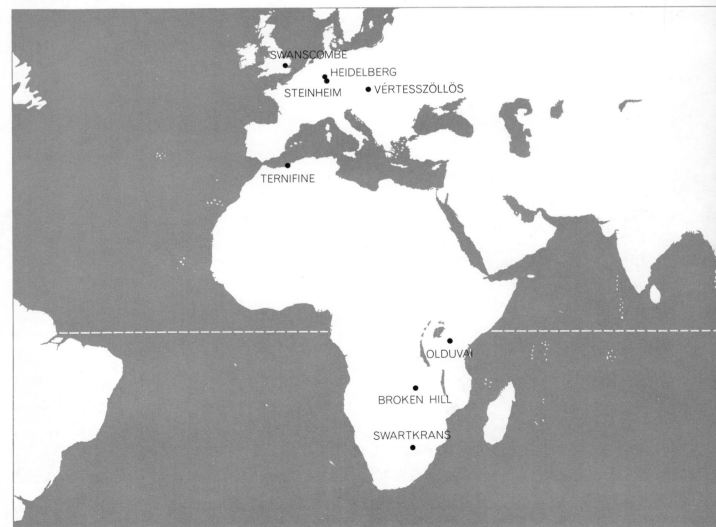

DISTRIBUTION of *Homo erectus* seemed to be confined mainly to the Far East and Southeast Asia on the basis of fossils unearthed

before World War II; the sole exception was the Heidelberg jaw. Postwar findings in South, East and North Africa, as well as dis-

1955: Ternifine, Algeria. Three jaws and a parietal bone, given the name *Atlanthropus mauritanicus*, were found under a deep covering of sand on the clay floor of an ancient pond by Camille Arambourg. The teeth and jaws show a strong likeness to the Peking remains.

1961: Olduvai Gorge, Tanzania. A skullcap, not formally named but identified as the Bed II Hominid, was discovered by L. S. B. Leakey. Found in a context with a provisional potassium-argon date of 500,000 years ago, the skull's estimated cranial capacity is 1,000 c.c. Although differing somewhat in detail, it has the general characteristics of the two Far Eastern subspecies of *Homo erectus*. At lower levels in this same important site were found the remains of a number of individuals with small skulls, now collectively referred to as "Homo habilis."

1963–1964: Lantian district, Shensi, China. A lower jaw and a skullcap were found by Chinese workers at two separate localities in the district and given the name *Sinanthropus lantianensis*. Animal fossils indicate that the Lantian sites are older than the one that yielded Peking man and roughly as old as the lowest formation in Java. The form of the skull and jaw accords well with this dating; both are distinctly more primitive than the Peking fossils. Both differ somewhat in detail from the Java subspecies of *Homo erectus,* but the estimated capacity of this otherwise large skull (780 c.c.) is small and close to that of the earliest fossil cranium unearthed in Java.

1965: Vértesszöllös, Hungary. An isolated occipital bone (in the back of the skull) was found by L. Vértes. This skull fragment is the first human fossil from the early middle Pleistocene to be unearthed in Europe since the Heidelberg jaw. It evidently dates to the middle or later part of the Mindel glaciation and thus falls clearly within the *Homo erectus* time zone as defined here. The bone is moderately thick and shows a well-defined ridge for the attachment of neck muscles such as is seen in all the *erectus* skulls. It is unlike *erectus* occipital bones, however, in that it is both large and definitely less angled; these features indicate a more advanced skull.

In addition to these five discoveries, something else of considerable importance happened during this period. The Piltdown fraud, perpetrated sometime before 1912, was finally exposed in 1953. The detective work of J. S. Weiner, Sir Wilfrid Le Gros Clark and Kenneth Oakley removed from the fossil record a supposed hominid with a fully apelike jaw and manlike skull that could scarcely be fitted into any sensible evolutionary scheme.

From this accumulation of finds, many of them made so recently, there emerges a picture of men with skeletons like ours but with brains much smaller, skulls much thicker and flatter and furnished with protruding brows in front and a marked angle in the rear, and with teeth somewhat larger and exhibiting a few slightly more primitive traits. This picture suggests an evolutionary level, or grade, occupying half a million years of human history and now seen to prevail all over the inhabited Old World. This is the meaning of *Homo erectus*. It gives us a new foundation for ideas as to the pace and the pattern of human evolution over a critical span of time.

Quite possibly this summary is too tidy; before the 100th anniversary of the resurrection of *Homo erectus* is celebrated complications may appear that we cannot perceive at present. Even today there are a number of fringe problems we cannot neglect. Here are some of them.

What was the amount of evolution taking place within the *erectus* grade? There is probably a good deal of accident of discovery involved in defining *Homo erectus*. Chance, in other words, may have isolated a segment of a continuum, since finds from the time immediately following this 500,000-year period are almost lacking. It seems likely, in fact practically certain, that real evolutionary progress was taking place, but the tools made by man during this period reveal little of it. As for the fossils themselves, the oldest skulls—from Java and Lantian—are the crudest and have the smallest brains. In Java, one region with some discernible stratigraphy, the later skulls show signs of evolutionary advance compared with the earlier ones. The Peking skulls, which are almost certainly later still, are even more progressive. Bernard Campbell, who has recently suggested that all the known forms of *Homo erectus* be formally recognized as named subspecies, has arranged the names in the order of their relative progressiveness. I have added some names to Campbell's list; they appear in parentheses in the illustration on page 68. As the illustration indicates, the advances in grade seem indeed to correspond fairly well with the passage of time.

What are the relations of *Homo erectus* to Rhodesian and Solo man? This is a point of particular importance, because both the African and the Javanese fossils are much younger than the date we have set as the general upward boundary for *Homo erectus*. Rhodesian man may have been alive as recently as 30,000 years ago and may have actually overlapped with modern man. Solo man probably existed during the last Pleistocene cold phase; this is still very recent compared with the time zone of the other *erectus* fossils described here. Carleton S. Coon of the University of Pennsylvania deems both late fossil men to be *Homo erectus* on the basis of tooth size and skull flatness. His placing of Rhodesian man is arguable, but Solo man is so primitive, so like Java man in many aspects of his skull form and so close to Peking man in brain size that his classification as *Homo erectus* seems almost inevitable. The meaning of his survival hundreds of thousands of years after the period I have suggested, and his relation to the modern men who

covery of a new *Homo erectus* site in northern China, have extended the species' range.

GRADE	EUROPE	NORTH AFRICA	EAST AFRICA	SOUTH AFRICA	EAST ASIA	SOUTHEAST ASIA
(5)	*HOMO SAPIENS (VERTESSZOLLOS)*					
(4)						*(HOMO ERECTUS SOLOENSIS)*
3	*HOMO ERECTUS HEIDELBERGENSIS*	*HOMO ERECTUS MAURITANICUS*	*HOMO ERECTUS LEAKEYI*		*HOMO ERECTUS PEKINENSIS*	
2						*HOMO ERECTUS ERECTUS*
1			*HOMO ERECTUS HABILIS*	*HOMO ERECTUS CAPENSIS*	*(HOMO ERECTUS LANTIANENSIS)*	*HOMO ERECTUS MODJOKERTENSIS*

EIGHT SUBSPECIES of *Homo erectus* that are generally accepted today have been given appropriate names and ranked in order of evolutionary progress by the British scholar Bernard G. Campbell. The author has added Lantian man to Campbell's lowest *Homo erectus* grade and provided a fourth grade to accommodate Solo man, a late but primitive survival. The author has also added a fifth grade for the *Homo sapiens* fossil from Vértesszöllös (*color*). Colored area suggests that Heidelberg man is its possible forebear.

succeeded him in Southeast Asia in recent times, are unanswered questions of considerable importance.

Where did *Homo erectus* come from? The Swartkrans discovery makes it clear that he arose before the last representatives of the australopithecines had died out at that site. The best present evidence of his origin is also from Africa; it consists of the series of fossils unearthed at Olduvai Gorge by Leakey and his wife and called Homo habilis. These remains seem to reflect a transition from an australopithecine level to an *erectus* level about a million years ago. This date seems almost too late, however, when one considers the age of *Homo erectus* finds elsewhere in the world, particularly in Java.

Where did *Homo erectus* go? The paths are simply untraced, both those that presumably lead to the Swanscombe and Steinheim people of Europe during the Pleistocene's second interglacial period and those leading to the much later Rhodesian and Neanderthal men. This is a period lacking useful evidence. Above all, the nature of the line leading to living man—*Homo sapiens* in the Linnaean sense—remains a matter of pure theory.

We may, however, have a clue. Here it is necessary to face a final problem. What was the real variation in physical type during the time period of *Homo erectus?* On the whole, considering the time and space involved, it does not appear to be very large; the similarity of the North African jaws to those of Peking man, for example, is striking in spite of the thousands of miles that separated the two populations. The Heidelberg jaw, however, has always seemed to be somewhat different from all the others and a little closer to modern man in the nature of its teeth. The only other European fossil approaching the Heidelberg jaw in antiquity is the occipital bone recently found at Vértesszöllös. This piece of skull likewise appears to be progressive in form and may have belonged to the same general kind of man as the Heidelberg jaw, although it is somewhat more recent in date.

Andor Thoma of Hungary's Kossuth University at Debrecen in Hungary, who has kindly given me information concerning the Vértesszöllös fossil, will publish a formal description soon in the French journal *L'Anthropologie.* He estimates that the cranial capacity was about 1,400 c.c., close to the average for modern man and well above that of the known specimens of *Homo erectus.* Although the occipital bone is thick, it is larger and less sharply angled than the matching skull area of Rhodesian man. It is certainly more modern-looking than the Solo skulls. I see no reason at this point to dispute Thoma's estimate of brain volume. He concludes that Vértesszöllös man had in fact reached the *sapiens* grade in skull form and brain size and accordingly has named him a subspecies of *Homo sapiens.*

Thoma's finding therefore places a population of more progressive, *sapiens* humanity contemporary with the populations of *Homo erectus* 500,000 years ago or more. From the succeeding interglacial period in Europe have come the Swanscombe and Steinheim skulls, generally recognized as *sapiens* in grade. They are less heavy than the Hungarian fossil, more curved in occipital profile and smaller in size; they are also apparently both female, which would account for part of these differences.

The trail of evidence is of course faint, but there are no present signs of contradiction; what we may be seeing is a line that follows *Homo sapiens* back from Swanscombe and Steinheim to Vértesszöllös and finally to Heidelberg man at the root. This is something like the Solo case in reverse, a *Homo sapiens* population surprisingly early in time, in contrast to a possible *Homo erectus* population surprisingly late. In fact, we are seeing only the outlines of what we must still discover. It is easy to perceive how badly we need more fossils; for example, we cannot relate Heidelberg man to any later Europeans until we find some skull parts to add to his solitary jaw.

5

The Casts of Fossil Hominid Brains

by Ralph L. Holloway
July 1974

The skulls of man and his precursors can be used as molds to make replicas of the brain. These casts indicate that man's brain began to differ from that of other primates some three million years ago

Man is not the largest of the primates (the gorilla is larger), but he has the largest brain. How did this come about? The question is hardly a new one, but a considerable amount of new evidence is now available to those in search of the answer. In brief the evidence suggests that, contrary to what is widely believed, the human brain was not among the last human organs to evolve but among the first. Neurologically speaking, brains whose organization was essentially human were already in existence some three million years ago.

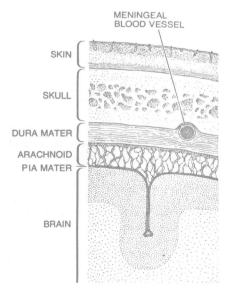

LAYERS OF TISSUE lie between the surface of the brain and the cranium. They include the pia mater, the arachnoid tissue that contains the cerebrospinal fluid, and the thick dura mater. Meningeal blood vessels (*color*) often leave a clear imprint on the inner surface of the cranium. The sutures of the cranial bones may also show, but among higher primates the convolutions of the cerebral cortex are not often apparent.

The brain is the most complex organ in the primate body or, if one prefers, the most complex set of interacting organs. It consists of a very large number of interconnected nuclei and fiber systems, and its cells number in the billions. With certain exceptions, however, the cortex, or upper layer, of one primate brain exhibits much the same gross morphology as the cortex of another, regardless of the animals' relative taxonomic status. Whether the animal is a prosimian (for example a lemur), a monkey, a pongid (an ape) or a hominid (a member of the family that includes the genus *Homo*), what varies from one primate brain to another is not so much the appearance of the cortex as the fraction of its total area that is devoted to each of the major cortical subdivisions. For instance, whereas the chimpanzee is taxonomically man's closest living primate relative and the brains of both look much alike superficially, the chimpanzee brain is significantly different from the human brain in the relative size and shape of its frontal, temporal, parietal and occipital lobes. The differences are reflected in the different position of the sulci, or furrows, that mark the boundaries between lobes, and in the differently shaped gyri, or convolutions, of the lobes themselves.

The comparative neurology of living primates can of course cast only the most indirect light on human brain evolution. After all, the living representatives of each primate line have reached their own separate evolutionary pinnacle; their brains do not "recapitulate" the evolutionary pathway that man has followed. The neurological evidence is nonetheless invaluable in another respect. It is the only source of information linking aspects of gross brain morphology with aspects of behavior. The results of a great many primate studies allow some valid generalizations on this subject. For example, it is well established that the occipital lobe of the cortex, at the back of the brain, is involved in vision. The parietal lobe is involved in sensory integration and association, the frontal lobe in motor behavior and the more complex aspects of adaptive behavior, and the temporal lobe in memory. It is the interactions among these gross cortical divisions, and also among the subcortical nuclei and fiber tracts, that organize coordinated behavior.

It is also a valid generalization to say that a gross brain morphology which emphasizes relatively small temporal and parietal lobes and a relatively large area of occipital cortex is neurologically organized in the pongid mode and is thus representative of the apes' line of evolutionary advance. Conversely, a gross morphology that emphasizes a reduced area of occipital cortex, particularly toward the sides of the brain, and an enlarged parietal and temporal cortex is hominid in its neurological organization. It follows that any evidence on the neurological organization of early primates, including hominids and putative hominids, is of much importance in tracing the evolution of the human brain.

Such evidence is of three kinds: direct, indirect and inferential. The only direct evidence comes from the study of endocranial casts, that is, either a chance impression of a skull interior that is preserved in fossil form or a contemporary man-made replica of the interior of a fossil skull. The indirect evidence is of two kinds. The first is a by-product of endocranial studies; it consists of the conclusions that can be drawn from a comparison of brain sizes. To draw conclusions of this kind, however, can involve some degree of acceptance of the

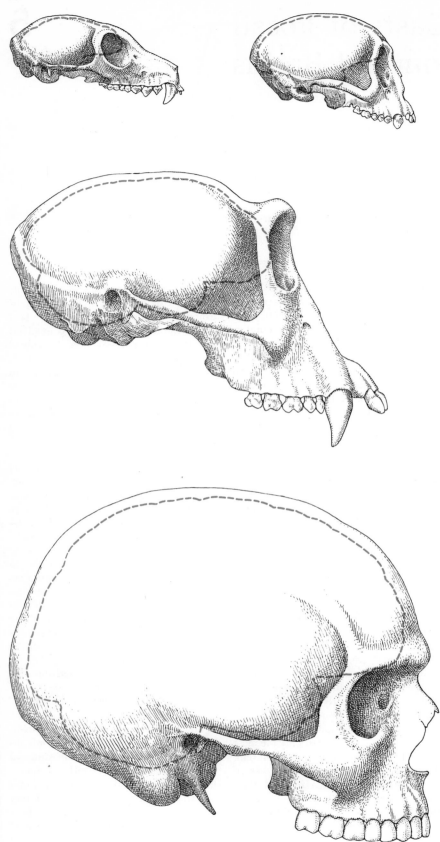

INCREASE IN BRAIN SIZE among primates is apparent in the different dimensions of the skull of a prosimian (*top left*), a New World monkey (*top right*), a great ape (*second from bottom*) and modern man (*bottom*). The brains (*color*) of the latter three are illustrated on the opposite page; skulls are reproduced at approximately half actual size.

questionable premise that there is a correlation between brain size and behavioral capacity. The second kind of indirect evidence comes from the study of other fossil remains: primate hand and foot bones, limb bones, pelvises, vertebral components, jaws and teeth. From these noncranial parts conclusions can be drawn about body size and behavioral capabilities such as bipedal locomotion, upright posture, manual dexterity and even mastication. Various patterns of musculoskeletal organization, of course, reflect matching variations in neurological organization.

Finally there is inferential evidence, particularly with respect to early hominid evolution. This can be described as fossilized behavior. The inferential evidence includes stone tools that exhibit various degrees of standardization (suggesting "cultural norms") and bone debris that reveals what animals the hominids selected as their prey. Any evidence of activity provides some grounds for inference about the general state of the individuals' neurological organization. Our concern here, however, will be with the direct endocranial evidence and with a part of the indirect evidence.

The convolutions of the cerebral cortex and its boundary furrows are kept from leaving precise impressions on the internal bony table of the skull by the brain's surrounding bath of cerebrospinal fluid and by such protective tissues as the pia mater, the arachnoid tissue and the dura mater, or outer envelope. In mammals the extent of masking varies from species to species and with the size and age of the individual. The skull interiors of apes and men, both living and fossil, are notable for bearing only a minimal impression of the brain surface. In virtually all cases the only detailed features that can be traced on the endocranial cast of a higher primate are the paths of the meningeal blood vessels. Depending on the fossil's state of preservation, however, even a relatively featureless cast will reveal at least the general proportions and shape of the brain. This kind of information can be indicative of a pongid neurological organization or a hominid one.

Just how far back in time can the distinction between pongid and hominid brains be pursued? There is a barrier represented by the key Miocene primate fossil *Ramapithecus:* no skull of the animal has been discovered. *Ramapithecus* flourished some 12 million to 15 million years ago both in Africa and in Asia. Elwyn L. Simons and David Pilbeam of Yale University have proposed that it is a hominid, but its only known remains are teeth and fragments of jaws. For the present we must make do with more numerous, although still rare, primate skulls that are many millions of years more recent.

The first of these skulls became known in 1925, when Raymond A. Dart of the University of Witwatersrand described the fossilized remains of a subadult primate that had been discovered in a limestone quarry at Taung in South Africa. The find consisted of a broken lower jaw, an upper jaw, facial bones, a partial cranium and a natural endocranial cast [*see illustrations on page 75*]. In the half-century since Dart named the specimen *Australopithecus,* or "southern ape," seven other skulls of *Australopithecus* (six of them internally measurable) have been found in South Africa and from three to six more in East Africa.

"Three to six" refers not to any uncertainty about how many skulls have been found but to how they are to be assigned to one or another genus or species of hominid. For example, the genus *Australopithecus* consists of two species: *A. africanus,* the "gracile," or lightly built, form to which the Taung fossils belong, and *A. robustus,* a larger, more heavily built species [*see illustration on page 76*]. Of the eight South African skulls, six are gracile, one is robust and the eighth (a specimen from Makapansgat designated MLD 1) is not definitely assigned to either species. In the same way three of the East African skulls are unanimously assigned to the robust species of *Australopithecus.* The other three, designated *Homo habilis* by their discoverers, Louis and Mary Leakey, are classed with the gracile species by some students of the subject, but they are still generally known by the name the Leakeys gave them. As will become apparent, there are grounds for preserving the distinction.

Fortunately, no matter what controversy may surround the question of how these early African hominids are related to one another, it has very little bearing on the question of their neurological development. The reason is that in each instance where an endocast is available, whether the skull is less than a million years old or more than two million years old, the brain shows the distinctive pattern of hominid neurological organization. Let us review the cortical landmarks that distinguish between the pongids and the hominids. Starting with the frontal lobe, the *Australopithecus* endocasts show a more hominid pattern in the third inferior frontal gyrus, being larger and more convoluted than endo-

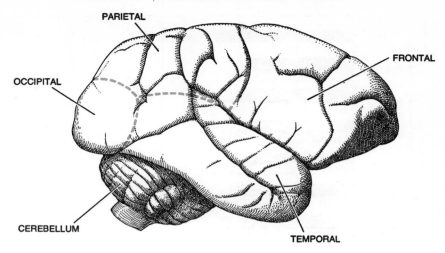

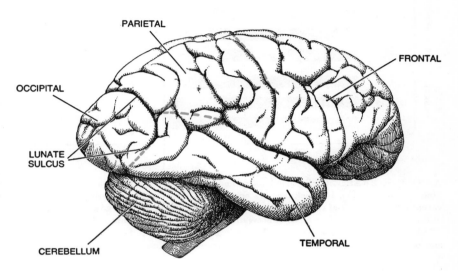

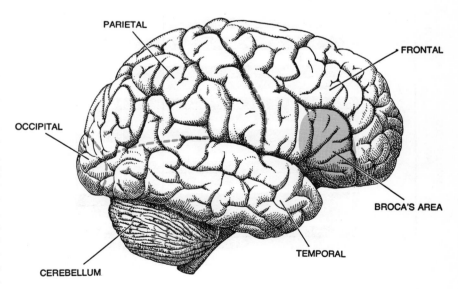

GROSS DIFFERENCES in the neurological organization of three primate brains are apparent in the size of the cerebral components of a ceboid monkey (*top*), a chimpanzee (*middle*) and modern man (*bottom*). The small occipital lobe and the large parietal and temporal lobes in man, compared with the other primates, typify the hominid pattern. Lunate sulcus, or furrow (*color*), on the chimpanzee's brain bounds its large occipital lobe.

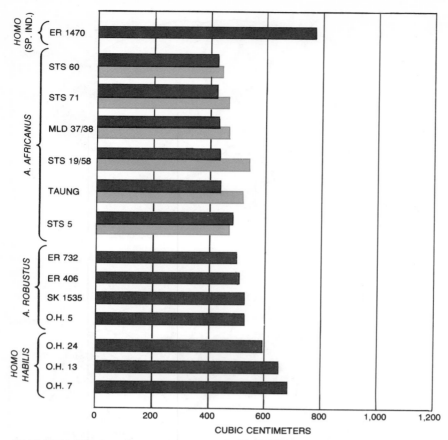

ABSOLUTE BRAIN SIZES varied both among and between the four earliest African hominid species. The 14 specimens are shown here in order of increasing brain volume, except for the earliest of all: the three-million-year-old specimen from East Rudolf, ER 1470, at the head of the list. The other abbreviations stand for Sterkfontein (STS), Makapansgat (MLD), Olduvai hominid (O.H.) and Swartkrans (SK). Double bars show former (*color*) and present calculated brain sizes of six specimens; the Taung volumes are adult values.

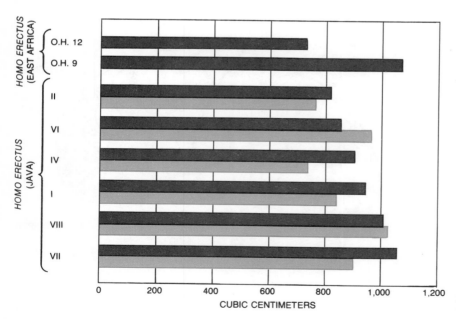

LATER HOMINID'S BRAINS were larger both on the average and absolutely, with the exception of one doubtful specimen from Olduvai Gorge. Shown here are the brain volumes for the seven certain specimens and one doubtful specimen of *Homo erectus*; two are from East Africa and six are from Java. Double bars show former (*color*) and present calculated brain sizes of the Java specimens. Casts of other *H. erectus* brains are not available.

casts of pongid brains of the same size. The orbital surface of their frontal lobes displays a typically human morphology rather than being marked by the slender, forward-pointing olfactory rostrum of the pongid. The height of the brain, from the anterior tips of the temporal lobes to the summit of the cerebral cortex, is proportionately greater than it is in pongids, suggesting an expansion of the parietal and temporal lobes and a more "flexed" cranium. Moreover, the temporal lobes and particularly their anterior tips show the hominid configuration and not the pongid one.

Another landmark of neurological organization provides further evidence, in part negative. This is the lunate sulcus, the furrow that defines the boundary between the occipital cortex and the adjacent parietal cortex. In all ape brains the lunate sulcus lies relatively far forward on the ascending curve of the back of the brain. The position is indicative of an enlarged occipital lobe. In modern man, when the lunate sulcus appears at all (which is in fewer than 10 percent of cases), it lies much closer to the far end of the occipital pole. On those *Australopithecus* endocasts where the feature can be located, the lunate sulcus is found in the human position, which indicates that the (perhaps associative) parietal lobes of the *Australopithecus* brain were enlarged far beyond what is the pongid norm.

It may seem surprising that *Australopithecus*, a genus that has only in recent years been granted hominid status on other anatomical grounds, should have an essentially human brain. It has certainly been a surprise to those who view the human brain as a comparatively recent product of evolution. The finding is not, however, the only surprise of this kind. The most remarkable new fossil primate discovery in Africa is the skull known formally as ER 1470, found by Richard Leakey and his colleagues in the region east of Lake Rudolf in Kenya in 1972. The fossil is nearly three million years old.

Through the courtesy of its discoverer I recently made an endocranial cast of ER 1470. Two facts were immediately apparent. Not only had the skull contained a brain substantially larger than the brain of either the gracile or the robust species of *Australopithecus* (and that of *Homo habilis* too) but also this very ancient and relatively large brain was essentially human in neurological organization. Leakey's find pushes the history of hominid brain evolution back in time at least as far as the shadowy

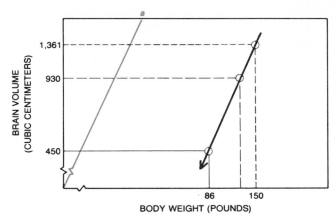

ALLOMETRIC GROWTH EQUATIONS with different exponential slopes are tested against known data in this group of graphs. A known average body weight of 150 pounds for modern man, combined with a known average brain volume of 1,361 cubic centimeters, is tested against a slope of 1.9 (*a, color*); the slope appears as a straight line on the double-log plot. At a brain volume of 450 c.c., the *Australopithecus* average, a projected body weight of 86 pounds is heavier than estimates of *Australopithecus* weight allow.

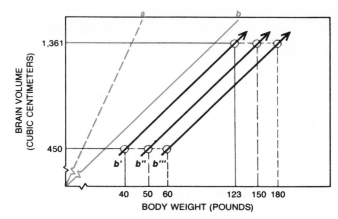

LESS RADICAL SLOPE, 1.0 (*b, color*), is tested in this graph against three different estimates of the average body weight of *Australopithecus*: 40 pounds, 50 pounds and 60 pounds. Where the parallel exponential slopes intersect the average cranial capacity for modern man (*b', b", b'''*) only the 50-pound body weight estimated for *Australopithecus* yields a projected body weight for man that agrees with the known average. An *Australopithecus* body weight much above or below 50 pounds thus appears improbable.

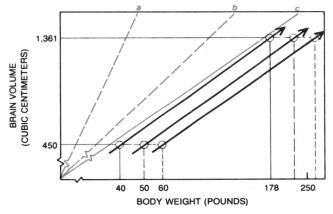

STILL A THIRD SLOPE, .66 (*c, color*), which is usually the most favorable allometric rate for mammals, is tested against the same three *Australopithecus* body-weight estimates. The .66 slope proves clearly unsuited to hominids. When even the minimum weight for *Australopithecus* is projected, the predicted weight for modern man is excessive; added weight yields even more grotesque results.

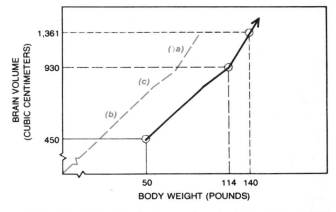

COMBINATION OF SLOPES tests the assumption that hominid rates of growth differed at different times. The zigzag predicts a plausible 114-pound body weight for *Homo erectus* with an average-size brain (930 c.c.) and a body weight for modern man not far below average. The implication is that rates of growth probably did vary, thereby varying selection pressures for changes in brain size.

boundary between the Pliocene and Pleistocene eras.

To summarize the direct evidence of the endocasts, it is now clear that primates with essentially human brains existed some three million years ago. Let us go on to see what details, if any, the indirect evidence of brain size can add to this finding. Here it is necessary, however, to state an important qualification. So far as modern man is concerned, at least, no discernible association between brain size and behavior can be demonstrated. On the average, to be sure, *Homo sapiens* is a big-brained primate. What is sometimes forgotten, however, is that the human average embraces

some remarkable extremes. The "normal" sapient range is from 1,200 cubic centimeters to 1,800, but nonpathological brains that measure below 1,000 c.c. and above 2,000 are not uncommon. Moreover, this range of more than 1,000 c.c. is in itself greater than the average difference in brain size between *Australopithecus* and *H. sapiens*.

As to how such variations may affect behavior, it is probably sufficient to note that the brains of Jonathan Swift and Ivan Turgenev exceeded 2,000 c.c. in volume, whereas Anatole France made do with 1,000 c.c. Clearly the size of the human brain is of less importance than its neurological organization. This con-

clusion is supported by studies of pathology. For example, microcephaly is a disease characterized by the association of a body of normal size with an abnormally small brain. The brain may have a volume of 600 c.c., which is smaller than some gorilla brains. (The gorilla average is 498 c.c., and brains almost 200 c.c. larger have been measured.) Humans with microcephaly are quite subnormal in intelligence, but they still show specifically human behavioral patterns, including the capacity to learn language symbols and to utilize them.

I have recently made complete or partial endocasts of 15 early fossil hominids from South and East Africa. These

SQUIRREL MONKEY	1:12
PORPOISE	1:38
HOUSE MOUSE	1:40
TREE SHREW	1:40
MODERN MAN	1:45
MACAQUE	1:170
GORILLA	1:200
ELEPHANT	1:600
BLUE WHALE	1:10,000

WEIGHT OF THE BRAIN, expressed as a proportion of the total body weight, varies widely among mammals. In spite of his large brain modern man is far from showing the highest proportional brain weight. The proportional weight for man, however, is greater than that of other higher primates. So too, it appears, was the proportional weight for the hominid predecessors of modern man.

endocasts, together with natural ones, have allowed me to calculate the specimens' brain size [see top illustration on page 72]. Leaving aside for the moment two specimens from Olduvai Gorge (one of them certainly Homo erectus and the other possibly so), my findings are as follows. First, the brains of most of the South African specimens were substantially smaller than had previously been calculated. Of the six gracile specimens of Australopithecus from South Africa none had brains that exceeded 500 c.c. in volume, and most were well below 450 c.c. In contrast, none of the four specimens of the robust Australopithecus species had a brain volume of less than 500 c.c. Moreover, two of the four, the one from South Africa and one from East Africa, had brains measuring 530 c.c. Of the three representatives of Homo habilis, all from Olduvai, the one with the smallest brain was hominid No. 24, with a possibly overestimated cranial capacity of 590 c.c. The brains of the other two respectively measured 650 c.c. and 687 c.c.

Now, one reason—perhaps the main reason—students of human evolution were so slow to accept Australopithecus africanus as a hominid, even though Dart had emphasized the manlike appearance of the Taung endocast from the first, was that its estimated cranial capacities were so small. The brains of some apes, particularly the brains of gorillas, were known to be larger. In fact, as we now know, the brains of the gracile species of Australopithecus are even smaller than was originally thought. Since it is now also evident that the Australopithecus brains were essentially

human in neurological organization, what are we to make of their surprisingly small size? The answer, it seems to me, is that in all likelihood the size of Australopithecus' brain bore the same proportional relation to the size of its body that modern man's brain does to his body.

This contention cannot be proved beyond doubt on the basis of the Australopithecus fossils known today. One can estimate body weight on the basis of known height, but the height of both the gracile and the robust species must also be estimated, on the basis of an imperfect sample of limb bones. Even though guesswork is involved, however, it is still possible to estimate various body weights and relate each of these guesses to the species' known brain size. One can then see how the results compare with the known brain-to-body ratio among the other mammals, particularly the primates.

The exponential relation between variations in overall body size and in the size of a specific organ, known technically as allometry, has been studied for nearly a century, so that the brain-to-body ratio is well known for a number of animals [see illustration on this page]. The brain-to-body ratio of modern man is not first among mammals; various marine mammals, led by the porpoise Tursiops, rank higher than man. So does one small primate, the ceboid squirrel monkey. However, among the hominoids, that is, the subdivision of primates that includes both the apes and man, modern man's brain-to-body ratio does rank first. Depending to some extent on what weight estimate one accepts for Australopithecus, this early hominid appears to have enjoyed a position similar to modern man's.

Thanks to Heinz Stephan and his colleagues at the Max Planck Institute for Brain Research in Frankfurt, an assessment of the relation between brain size and body size has become available that is subtler than simple allometry. Stephan's group has been collecting quantitative data with respect to animal brains for many years. The size and weight of various parts of the brain are measured, and these measurements are related to similar measurements of the animals' entire brain and body. One outcome of the work has been the development of what Stephan calls a progression index. It is the ratio between an animal's brain weight and what the brain weight would have been if the animal had belonged to another species with the same body dimensions. As their standard in this com-

parison Stephan and his colleagues use the brain-to-body ratio of "basal insectivores" such as the tree shrew, which are representative of the original stock from which all the primates evolved.

When the progression index is calculated for modern man, assuming an average body weight of 150 pounds and an average cranial capacity of 1,361 c.c., the resulting index value is 28.8. If different body weights are used with the same average cranial capacity and vice versa, the range of progression indexes for modern man extends from a minimum of 19.0 to a maximum of 53.0. It is interesting to compare the range of the human progression indexes with the indexes of other primates, including those based on estimated brain-to-body ratios for the two species of Australopithecus. For example, the maximum progression index for chimpanzees is 12.0. If one works the formula backward and assumes a chimpanzeelike progression index for the gracile species of Australopithecus, using an average cranial capacity of 442 c.c., the required body weight turns out to be about 100 pounds. That is nearly twice the maximum estimated weight for the species.

If one uses the same average cranial capacity and assumes that the body weight of the gracile species was only 40 pounds, the progression index is 21.4, which is well within the human range and comfortably close to the human average. When the body weight of the gracile species is estimated at 50 and 60 pounds and the body weight of the robust species is estimated at 60 and 75 pounds, the resulting progression indexes also fall close to or within the human range.

To recapitulate, both the direct evidence of neurological organization and the indirect evidence of comparative brain size appear to indicate that Australopithecus and at least one other African primate of the period from three million to one million years ago had brains that were essentially human in organization and that Australopithecus was also probably within the human range of sizes with respect to the proportion of the brain to the body. That the brain was small in absolute size, particularly in the gracile species of Australopithecus, therefore seems to be without significance. The ratio of brain size to body was appropriate. So far as the subsequent absolute cranial enlargement is concerned, the major mechanism involved, although surely not the only one, appears to have been that as hominids grew larger in body their brains enlarged proportionately. Quite possibly this ex-

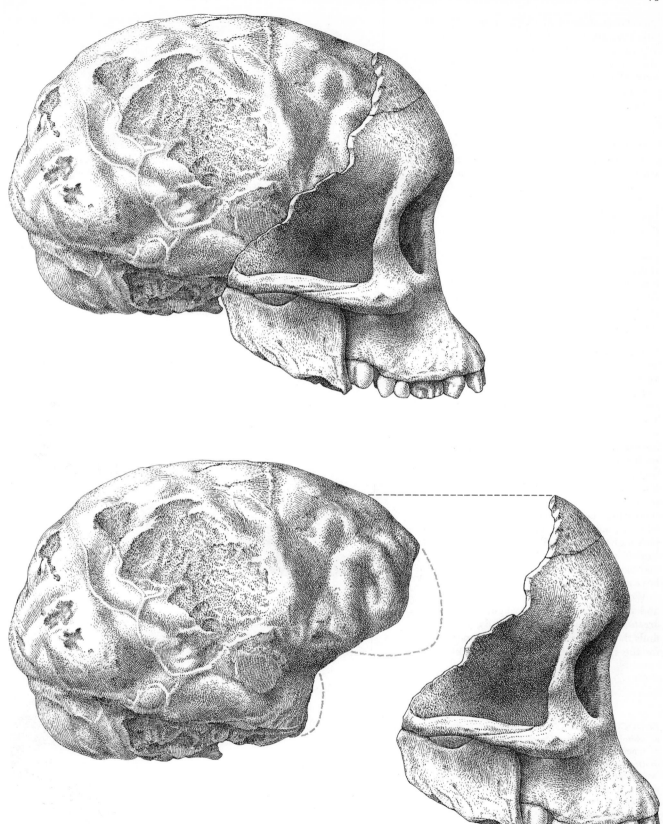

TAUNG JUVENILE, the first specimen of *Australopithecus* to be unearthed, is shown in the top drawing with a portion of the fossilized skull (including the facial bones, the upper jaw and a part of the lower jaw) in place on the natural cast of its brain. The cast is seen separately in the bottom drawing; parts of the frontal and temporal lobes that were not preserved are indicated. The estimated brain volume of an adult of this lineage, once calculated at about 525 cubic centimeters, has now been scaled down to 440 c.c.

pansion progressed at different rates at different times [see illustrations on page 73]. In any event, for at least the past three million years there has been no kind of cranial Rubicon waiting to be crossed.

Considering the gaps in the primate fossil record, it is remarkable that so many specimens of a hominid intermediate between the earliest African fossil forms and modern man have been unearthed. The intermediate form is *Homo erectus*. The skulls and fragmentary postcranial remains of that species have been found at various sites in China and in Java, and more fossils are steadily being turned up in both areas. There is also one specimen (and possibly a second) from Olduvai and, depending on one's choice of authorities, one from southern Africa, one from eastern Europe and perhaps two from northern Africa. With the possible exception of the Olduvai and Java fossils, no *H. erectus* specimen is much more than 500,000 years old, and one or more may be a great deal younger.

I have made endocasts of five of the six available *H. erectus* specimens from Java and of both the certain Olduvai specimen and the doubtful one. The *erectus* fossil with the largest cranial capacity is Olduvai hominid No. 9; its brain measures 1,067 c.c. Omitting the doubtful Olduvai specimen, the *erectus* fossil with the smallest brain is one of those from Java. Its cranial capacity is 815 c.c., only 40 c.c. larger than the capacity of the three-million-year-old East Rudolf skull. The average *erectus* cranial capacity, based on the endocasts I have made, is 930 c.c.

Working with this average brain size and estimating the body weight of *H. erectus* to have been 92 pounds, one finds that the Stephan progression index for the species is 26.6. That is remark-

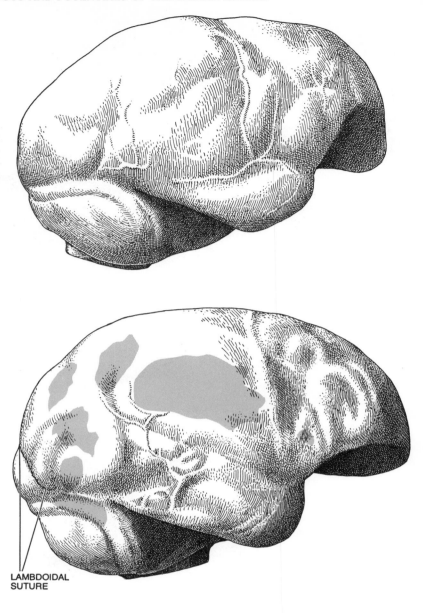

LAMBDOIDAL
SUTURE

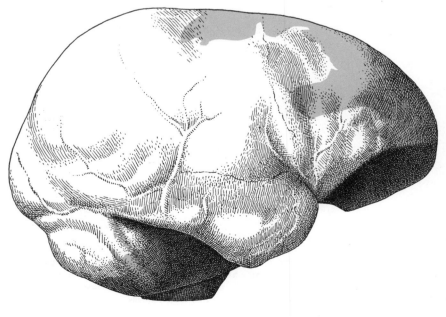

ENDOCRANIAL CASTS are those of (*top*) a chimpanzee, *Pan troglodytes*, (*middle*) a gracile *Australopithecus africanus*, and (*bottom*) the other species, *A. robustus* (*color indicates restored areas*). In all three casts details of the gyral and sulcal markings of the cerebral cortex are minimal. A differing neurological organization, however, ·can be seen. Both of the hominid brains are higher, particularly in the parietal region. Orbital surface of their frontal lobes is displaced downward in contrast to chimpanzee's forward-thrusting olfactory rostrum. The location of the hominids lunate sulcus, indicated (*middle*) by suture markings, implies a far smaller occipital lobe than the ape's.

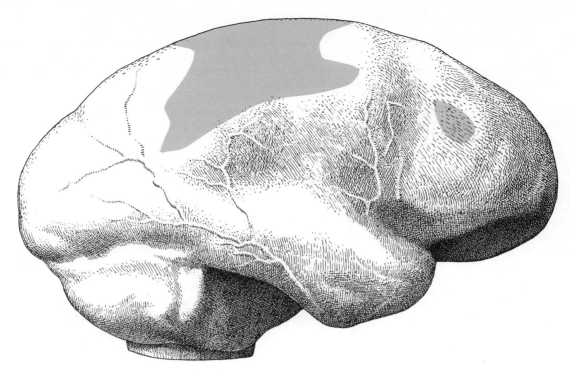

BRAIN CAST OF HOMO ERECTUS shows similar evidence of human neurological organization. As is true of most human cranial casts, the position of the lunate sulcus cannot be determined but the expansion of the temporal lobe and the human shape of the frontal lobe are evident. This is a cast of Java specimen VIII (1969); it reflects the flat-topped skull conformation typical of the fossil forms of *H. erectus* found in Indonesia. Like endocranial casts on preceding page and below it is shown 90 percent actual size.

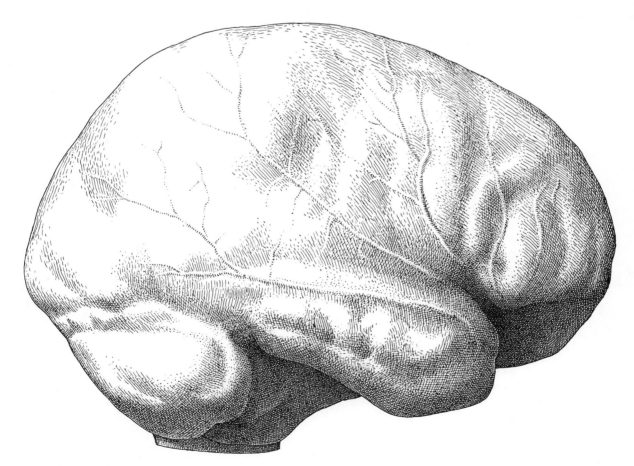

BRAIN CAST OF HOMO SAPIENS was made from a cranium in the collection at Columbia University. The height of the cerebral cortex, measured from its summit to the tip of the temporal lobe, and the fully rounded, expanded frontal lobe, showing a strong development of Broca's area (*see illustration on page 71*), typify the characteristic *H. sapiens* pattern of neurological organization.

ably close to modern man's average of 28.8. Even if the body-weight estimate is raised by some 30 pounds, the progression index falls only to 22.0. This being the case, it is difficult to escape the conclusion that, like *Australopithecus*, *H. erectus* possessed a brain that had become enlarged in proportion to the enlargement of the body. Although the average *erectus* brain is smaller than the average brain of modern man, it nonetheless conforms in gross morphology to the species' status as a recognized member of the genus *Homo* [*see top illustration on preceding page*].

I am not suggesting that any simple, straight-line progression connects the earliest African hominids, by way of *Homo erectus*, to modern man. As others have noted, it is the investigator's mind, and not the evidence, that tends to follow straight lines. The data are still far too scanty to trace the detailed progress of the human brain during the course of hominid evolution. For example, it would not even be safe to assume that, after attaining the stage represented by the earliest-known hominid endocasts, the brain thereafter consistently increased in size. Perhaps there were times when on the average brain sizes decreased simply because body sizes also decreased. One might even go so far as to speculate, and it would be pure speculation, that we are seeing something like this when we observe that the specimens of *Homo habilis* at Olduvai had substantially smaller brains than the far older East Rudolf hominid did.

Some generalizations are nonetheless possible. First, both the direct evidence of the endocasts and the indirect evidence of comparative cranial capacities indicate that the human brain appeared very much earlier than the time when *H. erectus* emerged, perhaps 500,000 years ago. Second, it can be inferred that the emergence of the human brain was paralleled by the initiation of human social behavior. It is not appropriate here to review the evidence of relations between nutrition and behavioral development or of those between the endocrine system and brain growth. Still, it is obvious that brains do **not operate in** a vacuum and that a part of the nourishment the brain requires is social as well as dietary. Much of the humanness of man's brain is the result of social evolution. The weight of the inferential evidence today suggests that the genesis has been long in the making. It may well predate such elements of fossil behavior as the systematic use of stone tools and the large-scale practice of hunting.

6

The Social Life of Baboons

by S. L. Washburn and Irven DeVore
June 1961

*A study of "troops" of baboons in their natural
environment in East Africa has revealed patterns of
interdependence that may shed light on the evolution
of the human species*

The behavior of monkeys and apes has always held great fascination for men. In recent years plain curiosity about their behavior has been reinforced by the desire to understand human behavior. Anthropologists have come to understand that the evolution of man's behavior, particularly his social behavior, has played an integral role in his biological evolution. In the attempt to reconstruct the life of man as it was shaped through the ages, many studies of primate behavior are now under way in the laboratory and in the field. As the contrasts and similarities between the behavior of primates and man—especially preagricultural, primitive man—become clearer, they should give useful insights into the kind of social behavior that characterized the ancestors of man a million years ago.

With these objectives in mind we decided to undertake a study of the baboon. We chose this animal because it is a ground-living primate and as such is confronted with the same kind of problem that faced our ancestors when they left the trees. Our observations of some 30 troops of baboons, ranging in average membership from 40 to 80 individuals, in their natural setting in Africa show that the social behavior of the baboon is one of the species' principal adaptations for survival. Most of a baboon's life is spent within a few feet of other baboons. The troop affords protection from predators and an intimate group knowledge of the territory it occupies. Viewed from the inside, the troop is composed not of neutral creatures but of strongly emotional, highly motivated members. Our data offer little support for the theory that sexuality provides the primary bond of the primate troop. It is the intensely social nature of the baboon, expressed in a diversity of inter-

individual relationships, that keeps the troop together. This conclusion calls for further observation and experimental investigation of the different social bonds. It is clear, however, that these bonds are essential to compact group living and that for a baboon life in the troop is the only way of life that is feasible.

Many game reserves in Africa support baboon populations but not all were suited to our purpose. We had to be able to locate and recognize particular troops and their individual members

GROOMING to remove dirt and parasites from the hair is a major social activity among baboons. Here one adult female grooms another while the second suckles a year-old infant.

and to follow them in their peregrinations day after day. In some reserves the brush is so thick that such systematic observation is impossible. A small park near Nairobi, in Kenya, offered most of the conditions we needed. Here 12 troops of baboons, consisting of more than 450 members, ranged the open savanna. The animals were quite tame; they clambered onto our car and even allowed us to walk beside them. In only 10 months of study, one of us (DeVore) was able to recognize most of the members of four troops and to become moderately familiar with many more. The Nairobi park, however, is small and so close to the city that the pattern of baboon life is somewhat altered. To carry on our work in an area less disturbed by humans and large enough to contain elephants, rhinoceroses, buffaloes and other ungulates as well as larger and less tame troops of baboons, we went to the Amboseli game reserve and spent two months camped at the foot of Mount Kilimanjaro. In the small part of Am-

boseli that we studied intensively there were 15 troops with a total of 1,200 members, the troops ranging in size from 13 to 185 members. The fact that the average size of the troops in Amboseli (80) is twice that of the troops in Nairobi shows the need to study the animals in several localities before generalizing.

A baboon troop may range an area of three to six square miles but it utilizes only parts of its range intensively. When water and food are widely distributed, troops rarely come within sight of each other. The ranges of neighboring troops overlap nonetheless, often extensively. This could be seen best in Amboseli at the end of the dry season. Water was concentrated in certain areas, and several troops often came to the same water hole, both to drink and to eat the lush vegetation near the water. We spent many days near these water holes, watching the baboons and the numerous other animals that came there.

On one occasion we counted more

than 400 baboons around a single water hole at one time. To the casual observer they would have appeared to be one troop, but actually three large troops were feeding side by side. The troops came and went without mixing, even though members of different troops sat or foraged within a few feet of each other. Once we saw a juvenile baboon cross over to the next troop, play briefly and return to his own troop. But such behavior is rare, even in troops that come together at the same water hole day after day. At the water hole we saw no fighting between troops, but small troops slowly gave way before large ones. Troops that did not see each other frequently showed great interest in each other.

When one first sees a troop of baboons, it appears to have little order, but this is a superficial impression. The basic structure of the troop is most apparent when a large troop moves away from the safety of trees and out onto open plains. As the troop moves the less dominant

MARCHING baboon troop has a definite structure, with females and their young protected by dominant males in the center of the formation. This group in the Amboseli reserve in Kenya includes a female (*left*), followed by two males and a female with juvenile.

adult males and perhaps a large juvenile or two occupy the van. Females and more of the older juveniles follow, and in the center of the troop are the females with infants, the young juveniles and the most dominant males. The back of the troop is a mirror image of its front, with less dominant males at the rear. Thus, without any fixed or formal order, the arrangement of the troop is such that the females and young are protected at the center. No matter from what direction a predator approaches the troop, it must first encounter the adult males.

When a predator is sighted, the adult males play an even more active role in defense of the troop. One day we saw two dogs run barking at a troop. The females and juveniles hurried, but the males continued to walk slowly. In a moment an irregular group of some 20 adult males was interposed between the dogs and the rest of the troop. When a male turned on the dogs, they ran off. We saw baboons close to hyenas, cheetahs and jackals, and usually the baboons seemed unconcerned—the other animals kept their distance. Lions were the only animals we saw putting a troop of baboons to flight. Twice we saw lions near baboons, whereupon the baboons climbed trees. From the safety of the trees the baboons barked and threatened the lions, but they offered no resistance to them on the ground.

With nonpredators the baboons' relations are largely neutral. It is common to see baboons walking among topi, eland, sable and roan antelopes, gazelles, zebras, hartebeests, gnus, giraffes and buffaloes, depending on which ungulates are common locally. When elephants or rhinoceroses walk through an area where the baboons are feeding, the baboons move out of the way at the last moment. We have seen wart hogs chasing each other, and a running rhinoceros go right through a troop, with the baboons merely stepping out of the way. We have seen male impalas fighting while baboons fed beside them. Once we saw a baboon chase a giraffe, but it seemed to be more in play than aggression.

Only rarely did we see baboons engage in hostilities against other species. On one occasion, however, we saw a baboon kill a small vervet monkey and eat it. The vervets frequented the same water holes as the baboons and usually they moved near them or even among them without incident. But one troop of baboons we observed at Victoria Falls pursued vervets on sight and attempted, without success, to keep

BABOON EATS A POTATO tossed to him by a member of the authors' party. Baboons are primarily herbivores but occasionally they will eat birds' eggs and even other animals.

INFANT BABOON rides on its mother's back through a park outside Nairobi. A newborn infant first travels by clinging to its mother's chest, but soon learns to ride pickaback.

BABOONS AND THREE OTHER SPECIES gather near a water hole (*out of picture to right*). Water holes and the relatively lush vegetation that surrounds them are common meeting places for a wide variety of herbivores. In this scene of the open savanna of

them out of certain fruit trees. The vervets easily escaped in the small branches of the trees.

The baboons' food is almost entirely vegetable, although they do eat meat on rare occasions. We saw dominant males kill and eat two newborn Thomson's gazelles. Baboons are said to be fond of fledglings and birds' eggs and have even been reported digging up crocodile eggs. They also eat insects. But their diet consists principally of grass, fruit, buds and plant shoots of many kinds; in the Nairobi area alone they consume more than 50 species of plant.

For baboons, as for many herbivores, association with other species on the range often provides mutual protection. In open country their closest relations are with impalas, while in forest areas the bushbucks play a similar role. The ungulates have a keen sense of smell, and baboons have keen eyesight. Baboons are visually alert, constantly looking in all directions as they feed. If they see predators, they utter warning barks that alert not only the other baboons but also any other animals that may be in the vicinity. Similarly, a warning bark by a bushbuck or an impala will put a baboon troop to flight. A mixed herd of impalas and baboons is almost impossible to take by surprise.

Impalas are a favorite prey of cheetahs. Yet once we saw impalas, grazing in the company of baboons, make no effort to escape from a trio of approaching cheetahs. The impalas just watched as an adult male baboon stepped toward the cheetahs, uttered a cry of defiance and sent them trotting away.

The interdependence of the different species is plainly evident at a water hole, particularly where the bush is thick and visibility poor. If giraffes are drinking, zebras will run to the water. But the first animals to arrive at the water hole approach with extreme caution. In the Wankie reserve, where we also observed baboons, there are large water holes

the Amboseli reserve there are baboons in the foreground and middle distance. An impala moves across the foreground just left of center. A number of zebras are present; groups of gnus graze together at right center and move off toward the water hole (*right*).

surrounded by wide areas of open sand between the water and the bushes. The baboons approached the water with great care, often resting and playing for some time in the bushes before making a hurried trip for a drink. Clearly, many animals know each other's behavior and alarm signals.

A baboon troop finds its ultimate safety, however, in the trees. It is no exaggeration to say that trees limit the distribution of baboons as much as the availability of food and water. We observed an area by a marsh in Amboseli where there was water and plenty of food. But there were lions and no trees

and so there were no baboons. Only a quarter of a mile away, where lions were seen even more frequently, there were trees. Here baboons were numerous; three large troops frequented the area.

At night, when the carnivores and snakes are most active, baboons sleep high up in big trees. This is one of the baboon's primary behavioral adaptations. Diurnal living, together with an arboreal refuge at night, is an extremely effective way for them to avoid danger. The callused areas on a baboon's haunches allow it to sleep sitting up, even on small branches; a large troop can thus find sleeping places in a few trees. It is known that Colobus monkeys

have a cycle of sleeping and waking throughout the night; baboons probably have a similar pattern. In any case, baboons are terrified of the dark. They arrive at the trees before night falls and stay in the branches until it is fully light. Fear of the dark, fear of falling and fear of snakes seem to be basic parts of the primate heritage.

Whether by day or night, individual baboons do not wander away from the troop, even for a few hours. The importance of the troop in ensuring the survival of its members is dramatized by the fate of those that are badly injured or too sick to keep up with their fellows. Each day the troop travels on a circuit

83

LIONESS LEAPS AT A THORN TREE into which a group of baboons has fled for safety. Lions appear to be among the few animals that successfully prey on baboons. The car in the background drove up as the authors' party was observing the scene.

of two to four miles; it moves from the sleeping trees to a feeding area, feeds, rests and moves again. The pace is not rapid, but the troop does not wait for sick or injured members. A baby baboon rides its mother, but all other members of the troop must keep up on their own. Once an animal is separated from the troop the chances of death are high. Sickness and injuries severe enough to be easily seen are frequent. For example, we saw a baboon with a broken forearm. The hand swung uselessly, and blood showed that the injury was recent. This baboon was gone the next morning and was not seen again. A sickness was widespread in the Amboseli troops, and we saw individuals dragging themselves along, making tremendous efforts to stay with the troop but falling behind. Some of these may have rejoined their troops; we are sure that at least five did not. One sick little juvenile lagged for four days and then apparently recovered. In the somewhat less natural setting of Nairobi park we saw some baboons that

had lost a leg. So even severe injury does not mean inevitable death. Nonetheless, it must greatly decrease the chance of survival.

Thus, viewed from the outside, the troop is seen to be an effective way of life and one that is essential to the survival of its individual members. What do the internal events of troop life reveal about the drives and motivations that cause individual baboons to "seek safety in numbers"? One of the best ways to approach an understanding of the behavior patterns within the troop is to watch the baboons when they are resting and feeding quietly.

Most of the troop will be gathered in small groups, grooming each other's fur or simply sitting. A typical group will contain two females with their young offspring, or an adult male with one or more females and juveniles grooming him. Many of these groups tend to persist, with the same animals that have been grooming each other walking together when the troop moves. The nucleus of

such a "grooming cluster" is most often a dominant male or a mother with a very young infant. The most powerful males are highly attractive to the other troop members and are actively sought by them. In marked contrast, the males in many ungulate species, such as impalas, must constantly herd the members of their group together. But baboon males have no need to force the other troop members to stay with them. On the contrary, their presence alone ensures that the troop will stay with them at all times.

Young infants are equally important in the formation of grooming clusters. The newborn infant is the center of social attraction. The most dominant adult males sit by the mother and walk close beside her. When the troop is resting, adult females and juveniles come to the mother, groom her and attempt to groom the infant. Other members of the troop are drawn toward the center thus formed, both by the presence of the pro-

BABOONS AND IMPALAS cluster together around a water hole. The two species form a mutual alarm system. The baboons have keen eyesight and the impalas a good sense of smell. Between them they quickly sense the presence of predators and take flight.

tective adult males and by their intense interest in the young infants.

In addition, many baboons, especially adult females, form preference pairs, and juvenile baboons come together in play groups that persist for several years. The general desire to stay in the troop is strengthened by these "friendships," which express themselves in the daily pattern of troop activity.

Our field observations, which so strongly suggest a high social motivation, are backed up by controlled experiment in the laboratory. Robert A. Butler of Walter Reed Army Hospital has shown that an isolated monkey will work hard when the only reward for his labor is the sight of another monkey [see "Curiosity in Monkeys," by Robert A. Butler; SCIENTIFIC AMERICAN Offprint 426]. In the troop this social drive is expressed in strong individual prefer-

ences, by "friendship," by interest in the infant members of the troop and by the attraction of the dominant males. Field studies show the adaptive value of these social ties. Solitary animals are far more likely to be killed, and over the generations natural selection must have favored all those factors which make learning to be sociable easy.

The learning that brings the individual baboon into full identity and participation in the baboon social system begins with the mother-child relationship. The newborn baboon rides by clinging to the hair on its mother's chest. The mother may scoop the infant on with her hand, but the infant must cling to its mother, even when she runs, from the day it is born. There is no time for this behavior to be learned. Harry F. Harlow of the University of Wisconsin has shown that an infant monkey will auto-

matically cling to an object and much prefers objects with texture more like that of a real mother [see "Love in Infant Monkeys," by Harry F. Harlow; SCIENTIFIC AMERICAN Offprint 429]. Experimental studies deomonstrate this clinging reflex; field observations show why it is so important.

In the beginning the baboon mother and infant are in contact 24 hours a day. The attractiveness of the young infant, moreover, assures that he and his mother will always be surrounded by attentive troop members. Experiments show that an isolated infant brought up in a laboratory does not develop normal social patterns. Beyond the first reflexive clinging, the development of social behavior requires learning. Behavior characteristic of the species depends therefore both on the baboon's biology and on the social situations that are present in the troop.

As the infant matures it learns to ride on its mother's back, first clinging and then sitting upright. It begins to eat solid foods and to leave the mother for longer and longer periods to play with other infants. Eventually it plays with the other juveniles many hours a day, and its orientation shifts from the mother to this play group. It is in these play groups that the skills and behavior patterns of adult life are learned and practiced. Adult gestures, such as mounting, are frequent, but most play is a mixture of chasing, tail-pulling and mock fighting. If a juvenile is hurt and cries out, adults come running and stop the play. The presence of an adult male prevents small juveniles from being hurt. In the protected atmosphere of the play group the social bonds of the infant are widely extended.

Grooming, a significant biological function in itself, helps greatly to establish social bonds. The mother begins grooming her infant the day it is born, and the infant will be occupied with grooming for several hours a day for the rest of its life. All the older baboons do a certain amount of grooming, but it is the adult females who do most. They groom the infants, juveniles, adult males and other females. The baboons go to each other and "present" themselves for grooming. The grooming animal picks through the hair, parting it with its hands, removing dirt and parasites, usually by nibbling. Grooming is most often reciprocal, with one animal doing it for a while and then presenting itself for grooming. The animal being groomed relaxes, closes its eyes and gives every indication of complete pleasure. In addition to being pleasurable, grooming serves the important function of keeping the fur clean. Ticks are common in this area and can be seen on many animals such as dogs and lions; a baboon's skin, however, is free of them. Seen in this light, the enormous amount of time baboons spend in grooming each other is understandable. Grooming is pleasurable to the individual, it is the most important expression of close social bonds and it is biologically adaptive.

The adults in a troop are arranged in a dominance hierarchy, explicitly revealed in their relations with other members of the troop. The most dominant males will be more frequently groomed and they occupy feeding and resting positions of their choice. When a dominant animal approaches a subordinate one, the lesser animal moves out of the way. The observer can determine the order of dominance simply by watching the reactions of the baboons as they move past each other. In the tamer troops these observations can be tested by feeding. If food is tossed between two baboons, the more dominant one will take it, whereas the other may not even look at it directly.

The status of a baboon male in the dominance hierarchy depends not only on his physical condition and fighting ability but also on his relationships with other males. Some adult males in every large troop stay together much of the time, and if one of them is threatened, the others are likely to back him up. A group of such males outranks any individual, even though another male outside the group might be able to defeat any member of it separately. The hierarchy has considerable stability and this is due in large part to its dependence on clusters of males rather than the fighting ability of individuals. In troops where the rank order is clearly defined, fighting is rare. We observed frequent bickering or severe fighting in only about 15 per cent of the troops. The usual effect of the hierarchy, once relations among the males are settled, is to decrease disruptions in the troop. The dominant animals, the males in particular, will not let others fight. When bickering breaks out, they usually run to the scene and stop it. Dominant males thus protect the weaker animals against harm from inside as well as outside. Females and juveniles come to the males to groom them or just to sit beside them. So although dominance depends ultimately on force, it leads to peace, order and popularity.

	ECOLOGY			ECONOMIC SYSTEM	
	GROUP SIZE, DENSITY AND RANGE	HOME BASE	POPULATION STRUCTURE	FOOD HABITS	ECONOMIC DEPENDENCE
	GROUPS OF 50–60 COMMON BUT VARY WIDELY. ONE INDIVIDUAL PER 5–10 SQUARE MILES. RANGE 200–600 SQUARE MILES. TERRITORIAL RIGHTS; DEFEND BOUNDARIES AGAINST STRANGERS.	OCCUPY IMPROVED SITES FOR VARIABLE TIMES WHERE SICK ARE CARED FOR AND STORES KEPT.	TRIBAL ORGANIZATION OF LOCAL, EXOGAMOUS GROUPS.	OMNIVOROUS. FOOD SHARING. MEN SPECIALIZE IN HUNTING, WOMEN AND CHILDREN IN GATHERING.	INFANTS ARE DEPENDENT ON ADULTS FOR MANY YEARS. MATURITY OF MALE DELAYED BIOLOGICALLY AND CULTURALLY. HUNTING, STORAGE AND SHARING OF FOOD.
	10–200 IN GROUP. 10 INDIVIDUALS PER SQUARE MILE. RANGE 3–6 SQUARE MILES; NO TERRITORIAL DEFENSE.	NONE: SICK AND INJURED MUST KEEP UP WITH TROOP.	SMALL, INBREEDING GROUPS.	ALMOST ENTIRELY VEGETARIAN. NO FOOD SHARING, NO DIVISION OF LABOR.	INFANT ECONOMICALLY INDEPENDENT AFTER WEANING. FULL MATURITY BIOLOGICALLY DELAYED. NO HUNTING, STORAGE OR SHARING OF FOOD.

APES AND MEN are contrasted in this chart, which indicates that although apes often seem remarkably "human," there are fundamental differences in behavior. Baboon characteristics, which may be taken as representative of ape and monkey behavior in

Much has been written about the importance of sex in uniting the troop, it has been said, for example, that "the powerful social magnet of sex was the major impetus to subhuman primate sociability" [see "The Origin of Society," by Marshall D. Sahlins; SCIENTIFIC AMERICAN Offprint 602]. Our observations lead us to assign to sexuality a much lesser, and even at times a contrary, role. The sexual behavior of baboons depends on the biological cycle of the female. She is receptive for approximately one week out of every month, when she is in estrus. When first receptive, she leaves her infant and her friendship group and goes to the males, mating first with the subordinate males and older juveniles. Later in the period of receptivity she goes to the dominant males and "presents." If a male is not interested, the female is likely to groom him and then present again. Near the end of estrus the dominant males become very interested, and the female and a male form a consort pair. They may stay together for as little as an hour or for as long as several days. Estrus disrupts all other social relationships, and consort pairs usually move to the edge of the troop. It is at this time that fighting may take place, if the dominance order is not clearly established among the males. Normally there is no fighting over females, and a male, no matter how dominant, does not monopolize a female

for long. No male is ever associated with more than one estrus female; there is nothing resembling a family or a harem among baboons.

Much the same seems to be true of other species of monkey. Sexual behavior appears to contribute little to the cohesion of the troop. Some monkeys have breeding seasons, with all mating taking place within less than half the year. But even in these species the troop continues its normal existence during the months when there is no mating. It must be remembered that among baboons a female is not sexually receptive for most of her life. She is juvenile, pregnant or lactating; estrus is a rare event in her life. Yet she does not leave the troop even for a few minutes. In baboon troops, particularly small ones, many months may pass when no female member comes into estrus; yet no animals leave the troop, and the highly structured relationships within it continue without disorganization.

The sociableness of baboons is expressed in a wide variety of behavior patterns that reinforce each other and give the troop cohesion. As the infant matures the nature of the social bonds changes continually, but the bonds are always strong. The ties between mother and infant, between a juvenile and its peers in a play group, and between a mother and an adult male are quite different from one another. Similarly, the

bond between two females in a friendship group, between the male and female in a consort pair or among the members of a cluster of males in the dominance hierarchy is based on diverse biological and behavioral factors, which offer a rich field for experimental investigation.

In addition, the troop shares a considerable social tradition. Each troop has its own range and a secure familiarity with the food and water sources, escape routes, safe refuges and sleeping places inside it. The counterpart of the intensely social life within the troop is the coordination of the activities of all the troop's members throughout their lives. Seen against the background of evolution, it is clear that in the long run only the social baboons have survived.

When comparing the social behavior of baboons with that of man, there is little to be gained from laboring the obvious differences between modern civilization and the society of baboons. The comparison must be drawn against the fundamental social behavior patterns that lie behind the vast variety of human ways of life. For this purpose we have charted the salient features of baboon life in a native habitat alongside those of human life in preagricultural society [see chart below]. Cursory inspection shows that the differences are more numerous and significant than are the

SOCIAL SYSTEM					COMMUNICATION
ORGANIZATION	SOCIAL CONTROL	SEXUAL BEHAVIOR	MOTHER-CHILD RELATIONSHIP	PLAY	
BANDS ARE DEPENDENT ON AND AFFILIATED WITH ONE ANOTHER IN A SEMIOPEN SYSTEM. SUBGROUPS BASED ON KINSHIP.	BASED ON CUSTOM.	FEMALE CONTINUOUSLY RECEPTIVE. FAMILY BASED ON PROLONGED MALE-FEMALE RELATIONSHIP AND INCEST TABOOS.	PROLONGED; INFANT HELPLESS AND ENTIRELY DEPENDENT ON ADULTS.	INTERPERSONAL BUT ALSO CONSIDERABLE USE OF INANIMATE OBJECTS.	LINGUISTIC COMMUNITY. LANGUAGE CRUCIAL IN THE EVOLUTION OF RELIGION, ART, TECHNOLOGY AND THE CO-OPERATION OF MANY INDIVIDUALS.
TROOP SELF-SUFFICIENT, CLOSED TO OUTSIDERS. TEMPORARY SUBGROUPS ARE FORMED BASED ON AGE AND INDIVIDUAL PREFERENCES.	BASED ON PHYSICAL DOMINANCE.	FEMALE ESTRUS. MULTIPLE MATES. NO PROLONGED MALE-FEMALE RELATIONSHIP.	INTENSE BUT BRIEF; INFANT WELL DEVELOPED AND IN PARTIAL CONTROL.	MAINLY INTERPERSONAL AND EXPLORATORY.	SPECIES-SPECIFIC, LARGELY GESTURAL AND CONCERNED WITH IMMEDIATE SITUATIONS.

general, are based on laboratory and field studies; human characteristics are what is known of preagricultural Homo sapiens. The chart suggests that there was a considerable gap between primate behavior and the behavior of the most primitive men known.

BABOONS AND ELEPHANTS have a relationship that is neutral rather than co-operative, as in the case of baboons and impalas. If an elephant or another large herbivore such as a rhinoceros moves through a troop, the baboons merely step out of the way.

similarities.

The size of the local group is the only category in which there is not a major contrast. The degree to which these contrasts are helpful in understanding the evolution of human behavior depends, of course, on the degree to which baboon behavior is characteristic of monkeys and apes in general and therefore probably characteristic of the apes that evolved into men. Different kinds of monkey do behave differently, and many more field studies will have to be made before the precise degree of difference can be understood.

For example, many arboreal monkeys have a much smaller geographical range than baboons do. In fact, there are important differences between the size and type of range for many monkey species. But there is no suggestion that a troop of any species of monkey or ape occupies the hundreds of square miles ordinarily occupied by preagricultural human societies. Some kinds of monkey may resent intruders in their range more than baboons do, but there is no evidence that any species fights for complete control of a territory. Baboons are certainly less vocal than some other monkeys, but no nonhuman primate has even the most rudimentary language. We believe that the fundamental contrasts in our chart would hold for the vast majority of monkeys and apes as compared with the ancestors of man. Further study of primate behavior will sharpen these contrasts and define more clearly the gap that had to be traversed from ape to human behavior. But already we can see that man is as unique in his sharing, co-operation and play patterns as he is in his locomotion, brain and language.

The basis for most of these differences may lie in hunting. Certainly the hunting of large animals must have involved co-operation among the hunters and sharing of the food within the tribe. Similarly, hunting requires an enormous extension of range and the protection of a hunting territory. If this speculation proves to be correct, much of the evolution of human behavior can be reconstructed, because the men of 500,000 years ago were skilled hunters. In locations such as Choukoutien in China and Olduvai Gorge in Africa there is evidence of both the hunters and their campsites [see "Olduvai Gorge," by L. S. B. Leakey; SCIENTIFIC AMERICAN, January, 1954]. We are confident that the study of the living primates, together with the archaeological record, will eventually make possible a much richer understanding of the evolution of human behavior.

LETTER TO THE EDITOR

Sirs:

I read with interest the article "The Social Life of Baboons," by S. L. Washburn and Irven DeVore, in the June issue of SCIENTIFIC AMERICAN.

I have spent a number of years hunting this fascinating animal in the heavily populated area due north of the Kavirondo Gulf of Lake Victoria in Kenya, where baboons have become a significant problem to the local peasant farmers, taking grain and livestock in ever increasing quantities to meet the needs of their expanding troops. At the same time the human population grows at an alarming pace and the extent of arable land decreases annually because it is overworked and poorly maintained. The two species find themselves in direct competition.

As an antisocial counterpoint to the theme of this fine article I recall one enormous old male I hunted for months and never did get. He no longer lived with the troop but batched it alone and did very well for himself. In the game of hunting and being hunted he was far superior to any animal, including man, I have ever encountered. As I depleted a number of the troops by fair percentages, he is not being idly praised. There were also a number of leopards in this area, and they are particularly fond of baboon. This is one animal that the baboon cannot escape by tree-climbing.

I did not observe the following point to verify it. However, the locals told me that this particular chap, when corn came into season, would bind a rope or vine about his middle and as he raided a field or storage bin would insert corn under the belt and make a far larger haul than he could with his two hands—particularly as he would usually have to leave in a rather big hurry.

I did see him on one occasion ambush two women on their way to market with baskets of grain on their heads. He confronted them in the path making terrifying noises and gestures at them. This immediately had what appeared to be the desired effect on the two women; they panicked and fled, leaving their produce scattered along the path. The old gent ate well that day.

CHARLES P. SKODA

Headquarters
First Cavalry
New York, N.Y.   *October 1961*

7

The Omnivorous Chimpanzee

by Geza Teleki
January 1973

*Observation of chimpanzees in the wild indicates
that they not only eat plant foods but also hunt, kill
and eat other mammals. Moreover, they display a
well-developed pattern of sharing meat*

It is widely believed that apes and monkeys are vegetarians, and that man is alone among the primates in preying on other animals. The assumption has influenced a number of hypotheses about human evolution that were framed in the days when scarcely any of man's primate relatives had been studied in the wild. For example, it has been suggested that the pursuit of game and the consequent social sharing both of the hunt and of the kill were key factors in the divergence of the earliest hominids from the rest of the primate line.

Today, after some 40 years of field observations of ape and monkey behavior, it is quite clear that man is not the only primate that hunts and eats meat. Many other primates are omnivorous. One in particular—the chimpanzee —not only cooperates in the work of the chase but also engages in a remarkably socialized distribution of the prey after the kill. The chimpanzees whose predatory behavior has been most closely observed are semi-isolated residents of the Gombe National Park in western Tanzania. The area, formerly known as the Gombe Stream Chimpanzee Reserve, is where Jane van Lawick-Goodall began her notable long-term field study of chimpanzees in 1960. I myself spent 12 months watching the predatory behavior of these apes in 1968–1969.

Gombe Park covers some 30 square miles and has an estimated population of 150 chimpanzees. All belong to the eastern chimpanzee subspecies *Pan troglodytes schweinfurthii*. Goodall and

her colleagues quickly came to know on sight some 50 individual apes that lived in a 10-square-mile zone centered on Kakombe Valley. This zone became the main study area, and its chimpanzees were made the subjects of daily records that now cover more than a decade of observation.

It was soon apparent to the observers that the chimpanzee population was organized in a social hierarchy headed by a single adult male that was senior to all the other males, adult and subadult. Most adult males and even some of the subadults, in turn, usually outranked the female chimpanzees, regardless of the females' age. The females' behavior in many situations showed, however, that there was an independent hierarchy among them as well. Between 1960 and 1970 the position of senior male, or "alpha," was occupied successively by two different adults. During my 12 months of observation the position was held by a chimpanzee Goodall had named Mike.

Sherwood L. Washburn and Irven DeVore of the University of California at Berkeley were among the first to observe primates eating meat. Studying olive baboons and yellow baboons in Kenya in 1959, they saw these ground-dwelling primates kill and eat newborn antelopes [see the article "The Social Life of Baboons," by S. L. Washburn and Irven DeVore, beginning on page 79]. Not long afterward Goodall found that the Gombe chimpanzees were omnivorous. Their diet included insects, lizards, birds' eggs and fledgling

birds, young bushbucks and bushpigs, blue monkeys, redtail monkeys, colobus monkeys and infant and juvenile baboons. Meanwhile observations of primates in the wild around the world revealed that an omnivorous diet was far from unusual. By the end of the 1960's the list of primates that feed on animals larger than insects had grown to include two chimpanzee populations outside Gombe Park, two species of baboons in addition to the olive baboon and the yellow baboon, vervet monkeys in Africa, macaques in Japan and even woolly monkeys and capuchin monkeys in the New World. Only baboons and chimpanzees, however, are known to actively seek out and pursue their prey.

In the decade between 1960 and 1970 Goodall and others, myself included, were able to note that the 50-odd chimpanzees in the vicinity of the Kakombe Valley field station killed and ate no fewer than 95 individual mammals and attempted to capture another 37 that escaped. In 46 of the predatory incidents the kills were actually witnessed. Another 38 kills were known through examination of the chimpanzees' feces, and recognizable fragments of 11 additional prey animals were carried by the chimpanzees to within sight of an observer.

During my year at Gombe Park I witnessed 30 episodes of predation, 12 of them successful. Kills during the decade, including those I observed, averaged a little more than nine mammals per year. The fact that I witnessed 30 episodes and 12 kills in a 12-month period is less likely to mean that the period was an above-average one for predation than that in the other years some kills and many episodes probably went unnoticed. In terms of predation on baboons, however, the period of my observations was

MEAT-EATING CHIMPANZEES in Tanzania, seen in the photograph on the opposite page, are engaged in the socially structured sharing behavior that follows a successful hunt. The prey animal is a young baboon. Its captor is reacting negatively to the "requesting" behavior of the second chimpanzee, higher in the tree, by starting to move away. Most of the requesters that join a "sharing cluster" after a kill eventually receive a little meat.

clearly not average. Goodall's records for the decade include identifications of 56 of the 95 prey animals. Primates were in the majority: 14 colobus monkeys, 21 baboons, one blue monkey and one redtail monkey. Of the 19 other mammals identified 10 were young bushpigs and the rest were young bushbucks. In contrast, of the kills I observed in 1968–1969 the prey animal on 10 out of 12 occasions was a baboon. Moreover, all 18 unsuccessful episodes I witnessed involved baboons as prey animals.

The prey species I have mentioned are very nearly the only mammals available to the Gombe chimpanzees, so that what might appear to be preference in reality demonstrates the diversity of the apes' predatory efforts. Indeed, the only limit to chimpanzee predation that I observed was the size of the prey animal. There is no evidence that chimpanzees capture or even pursue an animal that weighs more than about 20 pounds. For example, most captured baboons were infants or juveniles with an estimated weight of 10 pounds or less. Similarly, the bushbucks and bush-

pigs that the chimpanzees kill are either newborn or very young. Few of the adult mammals killed by the Gombe chimpanzees (colobus monkeys, blue monkeys and redtail monkeys) weighed as much as 20 pounds.

The prevalence of baboons as prey in Gombe Park must be due to the fact that baboons are the primates the chimpanzees most frequently encounter. Both species live mainly on the ground, both travel the same trails through grassland and forest and both eat many of the same foods and visit the same foraging areas. Each species may displace the other from special feeding sites, such as trees bearing fruit, and may even interact competitively over access to favored foods. At the same time baboons and chimpanzees engage in amicable interactions such as grooming and play. During my 12 months at Gombe I saw play groups made up of young chimpanzees and baboons at the field station almost daily. On two occasions I saw adult male chimpanzees suddenly pursue and capture a young baboon that until shortly before had participated in a mixed play

group that was being tolerantly observed by female chimpanzees and baboons sitting a short distance away.

The coexistence of both social and predatory interactions between chimpanzees and baboons at Gombe may be anomalous. Elsewhere in Africa adult male baboons are reported to defend their troop against threatening carnivores, even to the extent of seriously injuring such formidable adversaries as large leopards. Indeed, I observed the baboons of one Gombe troop kill a 35-pound African wildcat that appeared to have threatened them.

The Gombe baboons' response to predatory chimpanzees appears to be far more ambivalent. I have seen an adult male baboon sit unchallenged shoulder to shoulder with three adult male chimpanzees that were dividing the carcass of a bushbuck, while other baboons and chimpanzees searched together through the underbrush for fallen pieces of meat. At the opposite extreme I have seen a single chimpanzee stand upright and run into the midst of

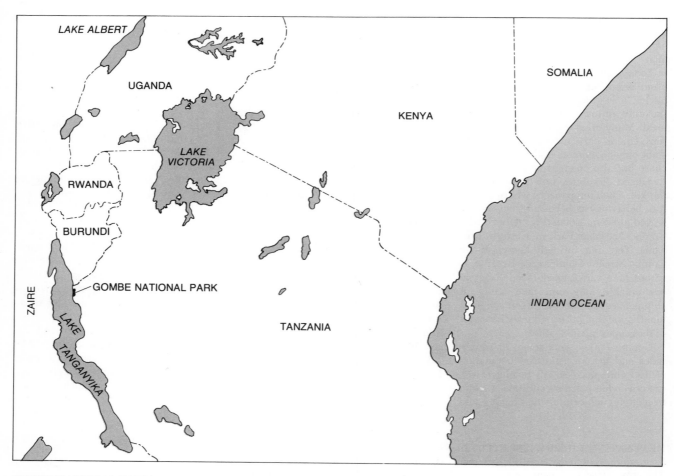

GOMBE NATIONAL PARK, a former game reserve in Tanzania where the hunting behavior of chimpanzees was studied, is on the shore of Lake Tanganyika. Jane van Lawick-Goodall's work in the area since 1960 has made the apes accustomed to human observers.

a baboon troop, where it selected, pursued and captured a young baboon while exhibiting complete indifference to the numerous adult male baboons that "mobbed" it, threatening it, slapping it and even leaping on its back. Nor was this an unusual event. The Gombe records show that predatory chimpanzees are rarely more than scratched by the baboons that undertake the defense of a troop member. A severe injury to a chimpanzee predator has never been reported.

Perhaps it is both the frequency and the variety of social interactions between the Gombe chimpanzees and baboons that are responsible for the ambivalence of the baboons' response. The use of the same trails and foraging areas, the mutual recognition of many communicative signals and the grooming and play among the young of both species may have resulted in the development of an interspecific "communal" atmosphere, so that the baboons respond to the chimpanzees much as they might respond to other baboons. That something of this kind is possible, at least in reverse, is apparent from the following observation. An adult baboon was fatally injured by another member of the troop; the fight was witnessed by several chimpanzees. Instead of considering the dead baboon fair prey, some of the chimpanzees inspected the carcass, touched it and finally groomed it. The same kind of curiosity has been observed when chimpanzees are confronted with a dead chimpanzee.

Insofar as it has been observed among the Gombe chimpanzees, hunting behavior is an exclusively adult activity and is almost exclusively a male one. Adult females have occasionally been observed pursuing and even capturing prey, but in every instance no adult males were in the vicinity at the time. The males may hunt alone, or two or more males may coordinate their actions. I once witnessed five males working together to surround three baboons that had taken shelter in trees; the movements of the chimpanzees were plainly cooperative.

A predatory episode that results in a kill consists of a sequence of three events, each marked by its own characteristic activities. The first of the three I shall call "pursuit," even though the distance covered is sometimes only a few feet and the time elapsed is seconds. The second event, "capture," is a brief period that ends with the initial dismemberment of the prey. The third and longest event, "consumption," involves highly structured activities. On one occasion I observed a consumption period that lasted nine hours and involved 15 chimpanzees.

The mean duration of the 12 successful predatory episodes I witnessed was a little less than four hours; the shortest episode lasted an hour and 45 minutes. An unsuccessful episode is of course much briefer. The mean duration of the 18 I witnessed was 12 minutes. The Gombe chimpanzees spend more than 90 percent of the total time they devote to predation in sharing and eating the prey.

I did not always have the prey animal under observation at the start of a predatory episode, so that it was not always clear to me what had initiated the pursuit. When both the prey and the predator were in view, it was apparent that the chimpanzees perceived and often selected their prey before starting the pursuit. The indicative changes in the hunter's posture and expression were so subtle, however, that it is difficult to specify them.

Many episodes began when the male chimpanzees were relaxed, for example dozing or grooming or resting after they had eaten large quantities of fruit. When the chimpanzees were either interacting intensively among themselves or interacting aggressively with some other species of primate, predatory episodes were uncommon. When a baboon was the prey animal, one apparent stimulus to predation was the vocalization of infant or juvenile baboons. Associated with both aggression and distress, these sounds frequently occurred during the young baboons' play sessions or when a young baboon sought to return to its mother. In more than half of the 28 episodes involving baboons that I witnessed, the crying of young baboons preceded any evidence of predatory interest on the part of the chimpanzees.

As I have indicated, one form of pursuit is simple seizure, an explosive act that lacks obvious preliminaries. The chimpanzee takes advantage of a fortuitous situation to make a sudden lunge and grab the prey animal. In this respect seizure is a kind of instantaneous capture that resembles "opportunistic" feeding on immobile prey (for example a fledgling bird or a "frozen" newborn antelope), the kind of meat-eating frequently noted among lower primates. I was able to witness this form of pursuit in 22 of the 30 predatory episodes I observed; seven involved simple seizure, and three of the lunges were successful.

Two other forms of pursuit are practiced by the Gombe chimpanzees. One

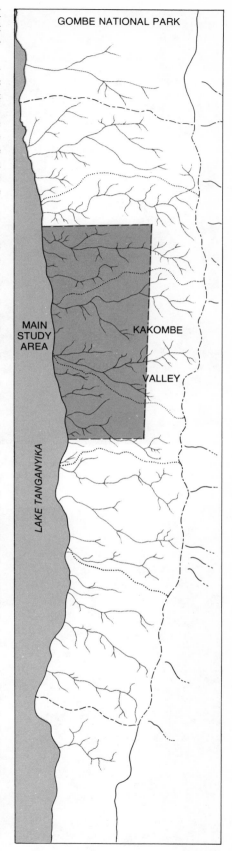

MAIN STUDY AREA at Gombe Park is a 10-square-mile zone (*color*) in and around Kakombe Valley. Of some 150 chimpanzees in the park, about 50 forage in this zone.

SUCCESSFUL HUNTER begins to dismantle the portion of the prey animal it has retained, the forequarters of a baboon. Almost all the Gombe chimpanzee hunters are adults and most of them are males. On the average one in every three hunts is successful.

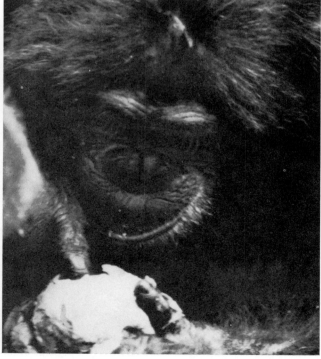

BREAKING INTO A SKULL, a Gombe chimpanzee uses its teeth to crush the frontal bone of a baboon (left) and gain access to the brain. With a finger (right) it then scoops out this prized portion of the prey. Other portions are often shared but the brain is not.

is chasing, which may involve a dash of 100 yards or more. The other is stalking, a cautious and painstaking process that can last more than an hour. Both have the appearance of being more premeditated and controlled than simple seizure. Moreover, on occasion both clearly involve a strategy and maneuvers aimed at isolating or cornering the selected prey. Eleven of the episodes that I observed involved chasing and four involved stalking. Six of the chases were successful but all the stalking efforts failed.

At times, particularly in the early morning and in the evening, the Gombe chimpanzees are quite vociferous. That is not the case when they are in pursuit of prey. Regardless of the time of day or the number of chimpanzees involved in the chase, all remain silent until the prey is captured or the attempt is broken off. This means, of course, that the hunters do not coordinate their efforts by means of vocal signals. Neither did I observe any obvious signaling gestures, although cooperation in movement and positioning was evident. It is noteworthy that the leading position during the chase frequently shifted from one hunter to another regardless of the chimpanzees' relative social rank. Evidently individual chimpanzees do not compete with one another for the most advantageous position during the pursuit of prey.

After the prey animal has been maneuvered within reach begins the central event in the predatory sequence: capture. It usually lasts less than five minutes and exhibits three consecutive stages: acquisition, killing and initial division. The first stage is very much like simple seizure; it consists of a final lunge and grab when the distance between the predator and the prey has been reduced to a yard or less. If the chase has been a cooperative venture, more than one chimpanzee may catch the prey. The instant of acquisition is usually signaled by a sudden outburst of vocalization; the cries not only end the silence of the hunt but their volume and pitch serve to draw other chimpanzees from distances of a mile or more.

The killing stage is normally brief. If the prey is in the grasp of a single chimpanzee, the chimpanzee may bite the back of the prey's neck or twist its neck in both hands. Alternatively the chimpanzee may stand upright, grasping the prey by its legs, and strike its head and body against the ground or a tree trunk. If the prey is caught by more than one

FRAGMENTATION OF PREY ANIMAL proceeds as members of a sharing cluster take pieces from a portion in the hands of the possessor, part of a colobus monkey's rib cage.

SUCCESSFUL REQUESTER (*left*) grasps between thumb and forefinger a sliver of meat proffered by its possessor (*lower right*). Another requester (*upper right*) watches closely.

	LANGUR	MACAQUE	BABOON	CHIMPANZEE
LEAVES, FRUITS, BERRIES, BLOSSOMS, BUDS, SHOOTS, BARK, PITH, GRASSES, RHIZOMES, BAMBOO	■	■	■	■
NUTS, SEEDS, PODS, GRAINS		■	■	■
ROOTS, BULBS		■	■	
MUSHROOMS			■	■
HONEY				■
INSECTS	■	■	■	■
SCORPIONS			■	
MOLLUSKS		■		
FISHES, CRABS		■		
REPTILES			■	■
BIRDS, EGGS			■	■
PRIMATES			■	■
ANTELOPES			■	■
RODENTS			■	
BUSHPIGS				■

OMNIVOROUS DIETS of chimpanzees and of three Old World monkeys include several of the same plant foods, but only one class of animals is eaten by all: insects. Of the four species only the baboons and chimpanzees hunt and eat mammals, including other primates.

chimpanzee, it may be torn apart as each captor tugs on a different limb; in this way killing and dividing are accomplished simultaneously.

The final stage of capture, initial division of the carcass, is an activity that is unrelated to the "meat-sharing" that comes later. For at least a brief period after the killing the carcass appears to be "common property." If chimpanzees other than the captor or captors have arrived within reach of the prey, they are free to try to grab a part of the carcass without risk of retaliation from the similarly occupied captors. For example, I have seen six chimpanzees, four of them postkill arrivals at the scene, divide among them the arms, legs and trunk of a young baboon. Even under these conditions aggressive interactions are rare during the time of initial division. The few incidents I witnessed tended to be mild, and even male chimpanzees of high social status showed nearly complete tolerance for others.

If the captor is able to hoard the prey for several minutes by moving away from the kill site, the common-property character of the prey animal lapses. Chimpanzees that have been attracted to the site are no longer likely to try to tear off a part of the carcass. In the event of a capture by more than one chimpanzee, the same "hoarders' rights" apply equally to the major portions of the carcass. The chimpanzees that share in the initial division then move off, usually no more than a dozen yards apart, each hoarding its piece of the carcass; those that did not participate in the initial division begin to congregate in "sharing clusters" around each possessor of a major fragment. Formation of the sharing clusters initiates the third, and socially the most significant, event in the predation sequence: the consumption period.

The Gombe chimpanzees do not move about their home range in fixed social units. The composition of their small bands is subject to constant change. As a result attendance during consumption periods varies a good deal from one predatory episode to another. It was rare, however, for fewer than five males and females of various ages to be within range of a kill site. At the other extreme, the number of chimpanzees gathered in different sharing clusters around a single kill once reached 15. Even when the number of chimpanzees in the clusters was this large, most of the participants usually obtained a piece of the prey.

Considering the length of time devot-

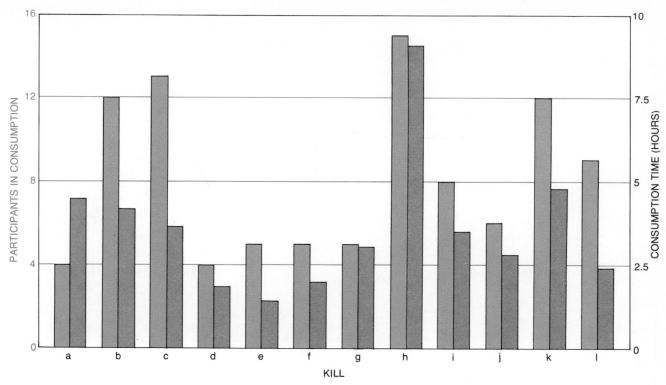

CONSUMPTION OF PREY occupies most of the time devoted to predation. Gray bars show the duration of 12 predatory episodes; colored bars show the number of chimpanzees that joined sharing clusters after the kill. The shortest consumption period was one hour 40 minutes (*e*); five apes participated. The longest was more than nine hours (*h*); the prey animal was a colobus monkey and 15 apes participated. The prey animal in the 12th episode was a bushbuck. In the other 10 episodes the prey animals were baboons.

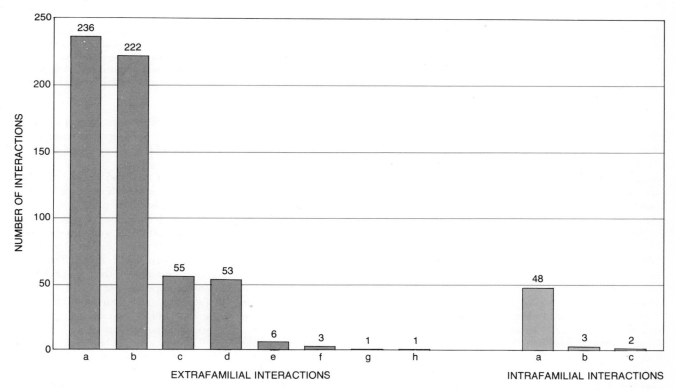

MEAT-SHARING INTERACTIONS in the sharing clusters are most frequent among the adult chimpanzees present. Female-to-male approaches, taking or requesting meat (*a*), are slightly more frequent than male-to-male approaches (*b*). Subadult approaches both to adult males (*c*) and to adult females (*d*), although far fewer, outnumber other nonfamily interactions: female-to-female (*e*), male-to-female (*f*), female-to-subadult (*g*) and subadult-to-subadult (*h*). No male-to-subadult approach occurred. Offspring-to-mother approaches (*a*) were the principal family actions (*color*). The mother-to-offspring (*b*) and intersibling (*c*) approaches were few.

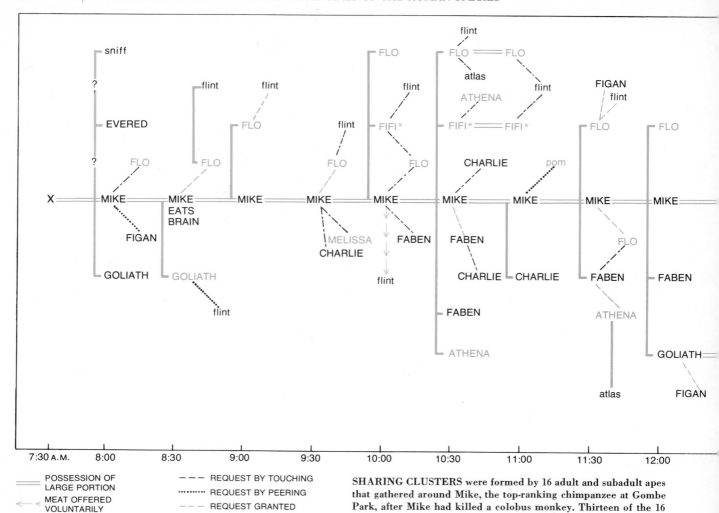

SHARING CLUSTERS were formed by 16 adult and subadult apes that gathered around Mike, the top-ranking chimpanzee at Gombe Park, after Mike had killed a colobus monkey. Thirteen of the 16 received some meat, and the sharing continued from 8:00 A.M. to 5:30 P.M. Names of adults are shown in capital letters; black indi-

Legend:
═══ POSSESSION OF LARGE PORTION
←< MEAT OFFERED VOLUNTARILY
━━━ LARGE PORTION SHARED
X X MEAT SNATCHED
– – – REQUEST BY TOUCHING
········· REQUEST BY PEERING
– – – REQUEST GRANTED
–·–·– REQUEST REFUSED
* RECEPTIVE FEMALE

ed to consumption, the small size of the prey animals and the number of chimpanzees that congregate in sharing clusters, the conclusion is almost inescapable that social considerations and not merely nutritional ones underlie the Gombe apes' predatory behavior. For one thing, many predatory episodes are initiated soon after the chimpanzees have consumed large quantities of vegetable foods. For another, no chimpanzee at Gombe has ever been observed to capture and privately consume a mammal, however small, if other adult chimpanzees were present to form a sharing cluster. In the decade covered by the Gombe records exactly two unshared kills were observed. The events were simultaneous: two adult female chimpanzees happened to encounter two small bushpigs and each ate one of them. No other adult chimpanzees were present at the dual kill.

Before a sharing cluster disperses, all the prey animal's carcass will have been consumed: skin and hair, bones, bone

marrow, eyeballs and even teeth. The brain is evidently the preferred portion. Although I observed frequent sharing of other parts of the carcass, not once in 12 months did I see one ape yield the brain or any part of it to another. A chimpanzee sometimes removes the brain tissue by pushing a finger into the natural opening where the skull joins the backbone. More often it opens a hole in the prey's forehead with its fingers and teeth and then scoops and sucks the cranial cavity clean.

When the Gombe chimpanzees are eating soft foods, they often put leaves in their mouth to form a kind of chewing wad. The procedure prolongs mastication and may also extend the savor of the food. The apes often use a leaf wad when they are eating meat, and they invariably do so when they are eating brains. After several minutes of chewing the eater usually discards the leaf wad, often giving it to one of the other chimpanzees in the cluster, so that brain tissue actually is shared to some extent, if

only indirectly. Three or four chimpanzees in succession may chew on a wad before it is finally swallowed or shredded.

A wad of this kind was the only "implement" I saw a chimpanzee use during any episode of predation. A male that was feeding on a prey animal's brain pushed a leaf wad into the nearly empty skull cavity to soak up the remaining tissue and fluids. The tactic closely resembles other Gombe chimpanzees' repeated use of leaf "sponges" to soak up water from a natural bowl in the crotch of a tree, an action witnessed by Goodall some years ago.

The prey animal's brain may be eaten first or last. Otherwise when a single chimpanzee captor deals with its prey, the dismantling sequence usually begins with the removal and consumption of the viscera. Next the rib cage is cleaned and sectioned, the chimpanzee using its teeth, hands and feet to tear the skin and break the bones. The prey's limbs are consumed last. The process is thorough;

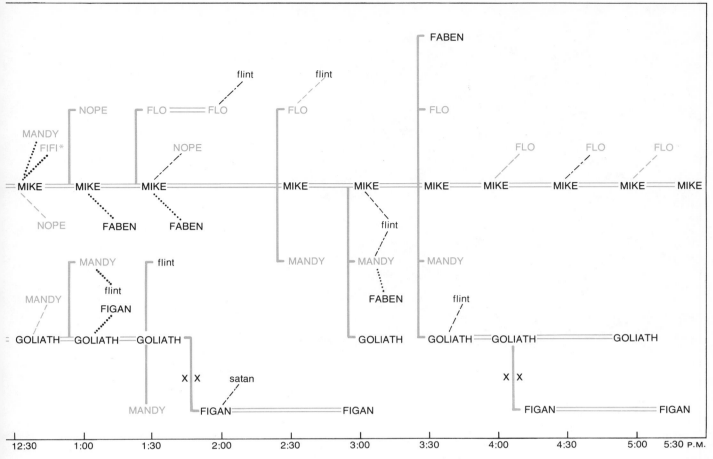

cates a male and color a female. Receipt or possession of meat is indicated by colored lines; a double line shows that the individual holds a sizable piece of the carcass. Unsuccessful requests for meat are shown in black. By keeping the largest portion Mike remained the center of attention all day. Twice Mike gave a big portion of the prey to Goliath, a mature male somewhat past its prime. Both times a younger adult male, Figan, subsequently rushed at Goliath and snatched away some or all of the portion. Mike's most favored sharing partner was Flo. This female successfully requested or was given meat 12 times; twice the portion received was a sizable one.

a careful inspection of a kill site following the chimpanzees' departure yields nothing but a few tiny fragments of the prey.

I have seen chimpanzees in a sharing cluster make use of three methods of getting meat. One that involves a minimum of interaction with the possessor of the meat is to retrieve dropped or discarded bits of the prey that fall to the ground. Such retrieval is usually the activity of subadult chimpanzees and adult females that evidently prefer not to approach the possessor directly.

The second method is simple taking: tearing off a portion of the prey or even seizing bits of meat from the possessor's hands or mouth. This direct approach is often used when the possessor is a female and the taker is one of its offspring. Male possessors are most likely to tolerate meat-taking by another adult male, particularly a sibling, by a female who is sexually receptive or by a female of high social status. The direct approach often finds taker and possessor calmly chewing on the same piece of meat, and I have seen as many as three sharing-cluster apes so engaged without discouragement from the possessor. Subadults rarely attempt the direct approach.

The third course of action, which involves specific behavioral patterns, I call requesting. Meat can be requested in the following ways. The requester can approach the possessor closely, face to face, and peer intently at the possessor or at the meat. Alternatively the requester can extend a hand and touch the possessor's chin or lips or touch the meat. The requester can also extend a hand, open and palm up, holding it under the possessor's chin. The requester may accompany each of the gestures with soft "whimper" or "hoo" sounds. Chimpanzees of virtually any age and of either sex request meat with this repertory of gestures. The youngest I observed doing so was an 18-month-old infant; the most important socially was "alpha" Mike, the top-ranking chimpanzee at Gombe Park.

If the possessor's response to a request is negative, the denial is indicated by ignoring the requester or turning away, by pulling the meat out of reach, by moving to a less accessible place, by vocalizing, by gesturing and occasionally by pushing the requester away. The possessor responds in the affirmative by allowing the requester to chew on the meat or tear off a portion, or by dropping a piece of meat into the requester's upturned hand. Of the 395 requests I observed, 114 were rewarded. Occasionally the possessor will detach a considerable portion of meat and with outstretched hand offer it to the requester. I saw this done only four times during my year at Gombe. On one of those occasions the possessor was holding an entire carcass. An adult male in the sharing cluster had been requesting meat persistently and the possessor at last divided the carcass in two and handed half to the requester.

When chimpanzees are sharing meat,

GESTURE OF REQUEST, arm outstretched with open hand palm upward, is used by a subadult chimpanzee to seek from its mother some of the leaf wad the mother is chewing.

their behavior is generally relaxed and uncompetitive. The pieces of the prey animal are consumed in a leisurely fashion and are evidently relished. I saw very few hostile interactions between apes with meat and apes with none. Individuals in a sharing cluster that had waited in vain for a long time would sometimes threaten or chase other chimpanzees that were also waiting, but they never made such a move against the chimpanzee with the meat.

High social rank is apparently no guarantee of success in requesting meat. Even though the possessor may be a relatively low-ranking adult, a high-ranking adult in the sharing cluster will approach the possessor with the same repertory of gestures that the other requesters use and will make no effort to assert superior social status aggressively. I once observed "alpha" Mike request meat for several hours from a subordinate male; Mike received nothing for his pains. Twice during my year of observing I saw meat seized from a possessor by a surprise dash-and-grab maneuver that may have had hostile overtones; the possessor's only retaliation was to scream and wave its arms. In the total of 43 hours of meat-sharing that I observed not once did two chimpanzees fight over possession of meat.

To what extent do the Gombe findings and similar observations elsewhere suggest a modification of present views concerning human evolution? The theme of hunting as a way of life has been central to many of the hypotheses that attempt to trace the evolution of human behavior and human social organization. For example, it is suggested that the evolution of erect posture left the evolving hominids' hands free to hold weapons and other tools and cleared the way for the pursuit of game on the open savanna. This development is often pictured as the crucial point in primate evolution: the time when "ape-men" (later to become "man-apes") expanded their range from the forests of Africa to the grasslands. As this environmental expansion took place, the hypotheses suggest, the evolving hominids acquired both the technology and the cooperative social organization, including the sharing of labor and food within some kind of nuclear family, that enabled them to survive as nomadic, omnivorous hunter-gatherers.

It seems possible to me that predation developed among primates long before the advent of ape-men. Many primate species have evidently shared a number of adaptive features for some millions of years. Might not the practice of preying on mammals, and on other primates in particular, be one of these features? To an omnivorous primate that enjoys complete mobility in a three-dimensional habitat other primates are perhaps the most readily ac-

cessible prey. Let us briefly test this concept against the record.

Most of the mammals the Gombe chimpanzees kill and eat are primates. Chimpanzees elsewhere in Tanzania and in Uganda have also been observed hunting and eating monkeys. In several other parts of Africa baboons are known to kill fellow primates. Turning to the distant past, the fossil remains of *Australopithecus* in South Africa have been found in association with the damaged skulls of baboons. The association at least suggests the possibility that *Australopithecus* occasionally preyed on the primates that shared its range.

Suppose that predation, cooperative hunting and socially structured food-sharing did become habitual among certain primates long before the first hominids arose. If that were the case, it would throw doubt on a number of current evolutionary hypotheses. For example, the sequence of erect posture, free hands and tool use as prerequisites to the emergence of hunting behavior would no longer appear to be valid. The same is true of the hypothesis that the open savanna is the habitat where hunting most probably developed. Moreover, whether or not predation is a far more ancient primate behavior pattern than has been supposed, at least one hypothesis must be abandoned altogether. As the actions of the Gombe chimpanzees demonstrate, socially organized hunting by primates is by no means confined to man.

The Gombe chimpanzees can be described in summary as omnivorous forager-predators that supplement a basically vegetarian diet in various ways, including the optional practice of hunting other mammals, with fellow primates being their most favored prey. The fact that the chimpanzees' meat-eating is optional means that in terms of meat consumption they do better than purely opportunistic omnivores that "collect" and eat an immobile prey animal now and then. At the same time the Gombe chimpanzees are free of the exclusive dependence on a meat diet that is characteristic of most carnivores.

The primary significance of the Gombe chimpanzees' predatory behavior is not, however, dietary. What is far more important is the behavior that accompanies the predatory episodes: cooperation in the chase and the sharing of the prey. The more we learn about primate behavior, the smaller the differences between human and nonhuman primates appear to be. The observations at Gombe do much to reinforce this conclusion.

Commentary by Teleki

Much new information about the predatory behavior of primates, and notably of chimpanzees and baboons in eastern Africa, has accumulated since I wrote "The Omnivorous Chimpanzee" in December of 1971. This new material serves to further expand and refine our knowledge of a primate behavior pattern vital to the reconstruction of the early stages of human evolution.

At the Gombe Stream Research Centre, where students working under the direction of Jane van Lawick-Goodall continue the long-term observation of some 50 chimpanzees, an additional 36 predatory episodes have been observed since March, 1969, when my first year of field work there was completed. This brings the grand total to 168 cases of predation recorded over 12 years of continuous study. No doubt many facets of this behavior will be brought into sharper focus in the years to come. Richard Wrangham, a Cambridge University student currently working on the general dietary habits of the Gombe chimpanzee, has already informed me that the sharing of brain tissue between three chimpanzees has now been observed on one occasion, and that prey pursuit by subadults (the youngest being 5 years of age) has been seen at least 5 times. Although successful capture remains the domain of adult chimpanzees, hunting by subadults suggests that a predatory tradition may be spreading through the group by means of learning. Similarly interesting speculations will, I am sure, continue to emerge from the data being gathered by the Gombe research team.

In addition to the Gombe data, nearly 20 cases of predation have now been observed among chimpanzees living in the Kasakati Basin area of western Tanzania and the Budongo Forest of Uganda. The behavior observed at these sites by A. Suzuki, T. Nishida, and other Japanese primatologists does not differ significantly from the predatory behavior of Gombe chimpanzees, and thus shows that the Gombe situation is not unique. The point is particularly significant because Budongo is a forest habitat, Gombe a mixed forest–woodland–grassland habitat, and Kasakati a predominantly woodland habitat. This diversity indicates that chimpanzee predation is not linked to a single habitat type, and thereby introduces questions about the popular theory that hunting originated among early men *after* their populations expanded into the savannas of Africa. Once a basic issue of this nature is reopened by new evidence, other features which have been linked with a uniquely human set of evolutionary steps taken in a savanna environment—ranging from tool and weapon making through nuclear family social organization and division of labor by sex to complex verbal communication—become susceptible to collapse.

That predation is not an incidental behavior pattern but one which is deeply rooted in the social behavior of wild chimpanzees is further demonstrated by the broad range of 14 mammalian species preyed upon at several sites: black-and-white colobus, red colobus, redtail, vervet and blue monkey, olive baboon, lesser and great galago, bush pig, bushbuck, suni, klipspringer, white-tailed mongoose, and giant forest squirrel have all been killed and eaten by chimpanzees. It is significant that most of these prey are other primates, for the chimpanzee is thus shown to be more diverse than certain predators that cannot exploit both the arboreal and terrestrial portions of a habitat.

Similarly, great strides have recently been taken in field work on the predatory behavior of baboons, mostly notably at a site called Gilgi in Kenya. Robert Harding, Shirley Strum, and Timothy Ransom, all associated with the University of California at Berkeley, have recorded 112 predatory episodes among the Gilgil baboons in 2 years of study. Including this material, fully 156 authenticated events have been observed among baboon populations living as far south as South Africa and as far north as Ethiopia. The 12 prey species of baboons include vervet monkey and lesser galago, impala, bushbuck, Thomson's and Grant's gazelles, dikdik, klipspringer, steenbok, duiker, the naked mole rat, and African hare. In contrast to the heavy predation on primates by chimpanzees, baboons prey most heavily on ungulates which inhabit savanna regions.

Field research on wild primates is rapidly adding new dimensions to the reconstruction of human origins and evolution, a task which has until now been undertaken mainly by specialists from such disciplines as anatomy, archeology, and geology. There are bound to be fresh facets in the interpretation of prehistory when fossil and artifactual remains found at sites once inhabited by early hominids can be effectively juxtaposed with behavioral and ecological evidence from field studies of living monkeys and apes, as well as from studies of human groups which currently practice hunter-gatherer subsistence patterns. The merit of unravelling the fabric of past events can be aptly illustrated by comparing the predatory habits of extinct australopithecines and living chimpanzees. In a series of publications spanning nearly 5 decades, Raymond Dart has determined that the South African australopithecines killed many species of small game, including such prey as antelopes, baboons, tortoises, hares, rodents, and birds, in addition to some large game; that a majority of the 58 fossil baboon skulls and jaws recovered from cave deposits had been fractured by bludgeon blows; that small, nearly circular holes had been opened in skulls by using hands or tools; and that 4 australopithecines skulls had been fractured by blows, indicating either aggressive or cannibalistic behavior. In the Gombe chimpanzees we can today see similar behavioral features much more directly: they kill and eat mostly the young of other mammals, the prey rarely exceeding 20 pounds in size; they smash the bones of prey not by using sophisticated tools but simply by bashing their prey against solid objects such as rocks and trees; they make small, circular holes with fingers and teeth in the skulls of prey prior to extracting the brain tissue; and they occasionally practice a form of "cannibalism," in that two infant chimpanzees have been partly eaten at the Budongo and Gombe areas.

These and other known parallels in the behavior of various primates, including humans demonstrate the value of a comparative approach which can lead to a more thorough and accurate sketch of human prehistory. This is especially true when an assumption is made that the basic parallels between fossil hominids and living primates indicate further parallels in complex behavior which cannot otherwise be retrieved from archeological sites. It seems reasonable to postulate, for example, that the general matrix of hominid hunting behavior is today reflected, though not precisely duplicated, by the matrix of chimpanzee predatory behavior observed at Gombe National Park. Both apparently pursued, captured, and consumed prey of varied sizes and kinds on a regular basis; in both the group members probably cooperated in pursuing and capturing prey; both probably shared voluntarily the meat proceeds of hunting episodes along lines not always determined by general social rank and status; and in both the predominance of adult male participation in prey pursuit and capture may have set the stage for further "division of labor by sex."

Geza Teleki, November 1973

8

Teaching Language to an Ape

by Ann James Premack and David Premack
October 1972

Sarah, a young chimpanzee, has a reading and writing vocabulary of about 130 "words." Her understanding goes beyond the meaning of words and includes the concepts of class and sentence structure

Over the past 40 years several efforts have been made to teach a chimpanzee human language. In the early 1930's Winthrop and Luella Kellogg raised a female chimpanzee named Gua along with their infant son; at the age of 16 months Gua could understand about 100 words, but she never did try to speak them. In the 1940's Keith and Cathy Hayes raised a chimpanzee named Vicki in their home; she learned a large number of words and with some difficulty could mouth the words "mama," "papa" and "cup." More recently Allen and Beatrice Gardner have taught their chimpanzee Washoe to communicate in the American Sign Language with her fingers and hands. Since 1966 in our laboratory at the University of California at Santa Barbara we have been teaching Sarah to read and write with variously shaped and colored pieces of plastic, each representing a word; Sarah has a vocabulary of about 130 terms that she uses with a reliability of between 75 and 80 percent.

Why try to teach human language to an ape? In our own case the motive was to better define the fundamental nature of language. It is often said that language is unique to the human species. Yet it is now well known that many other animals have elaborate communication systems of their own. It seems clear that language is a general system of which human language is a particular, albeit remarkably refined, form. Indeed, it is possible that certain features of human language that are considered to be uniquely human belong to the more general system, and that these features can be distinguished from those that are unique to the human information-processing regime. If, for example, an ape can be taught the rudiments of human language, it should clarify the dividing line between the general system and the human one.

There was much evidence that the chimpanzee was a good candidate for the acquisition of language before we began our project. In their natural environment chimpanzees have an extensive vocal "call system." In captivity the chimpanzee has been taught to sort pictures into classes: animate and inanimate, old and young, male and female. Moreover, the animal can classify the same item in different ways depending

SARAH, after reading the message "Sarah insert apple pail banana dish" on the magnetic board, performed the appropriate actions. To be able to make the correct interpretation that she should put the apple in the pail and the banana in the dish (not the apple, pail and banana in the dish) the chimpanzee had to understand sentence structure rather than just word order. In actual tests most symbols were colored (*see illustration on following page*).

104

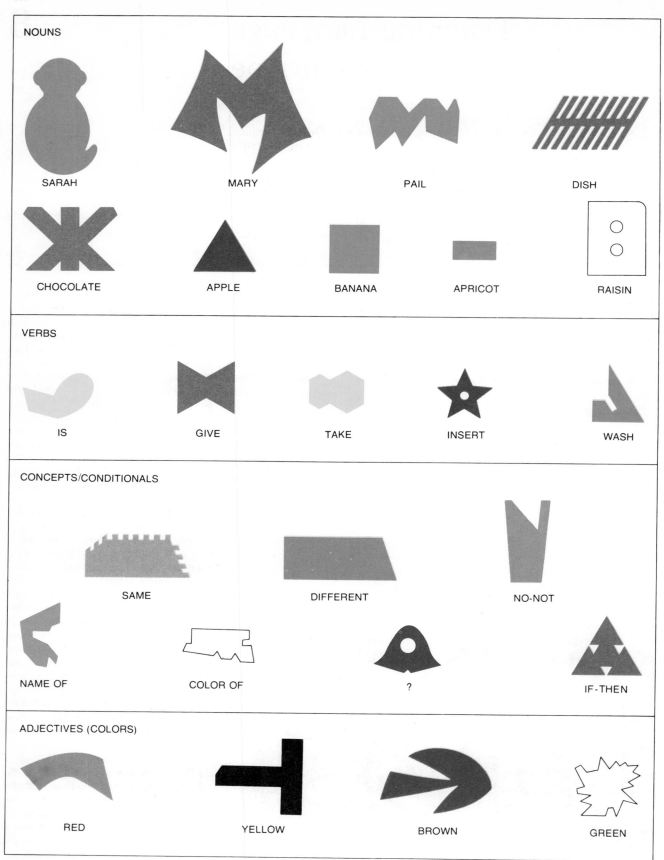

PLASTIC SYMBOLS that varied in color, shape and size were chosen as the language units to be taught to Sarah. The plastic pieces were backed with metal so that they would adhere to a magnetic board. Each plastic symbol stood for a specific word or concept. A "Chinese" convention of writing sentences vertically from top to bottom was adopted because at the beginning of her training Sarah seemed to prefer it. Sarah had to put the words in proper sequence but the orientation of the word symbols was not important.

on the alternatives offered. Watermelon is classified as fruit in one set of alternatives, as food in another set and as big in a third set. On the basis of these demonstrated conceptual abilities we made the assumption that the chimpanzee could be taught not only the names of specific members of a class but also the names for the classes themselves.

It is not necessary for the names to be vocal. They can just as well be based on gestures, written letters or colored stones. The important thing is to shape the language to fit the information-processing capacities of the chimpanzee. To a large extent teaching language to an animal is simply mapping out the conceptual structures the animal already possesses. By using a system of naming that suits the chimpanzee we hope to find out more about its conceptual world. Ultimately the benefit of language experiments with animals will be realized in an understanding of intelligence in terms not of scores on tests but of the underlying brain mechanisms. Only then can cognitive mechanisms for classifying stimuli, for storing and retrieving information and for problem-solving be studied in a comparative way.

The first step in teaching language is to exploit knowledge that is already present. In teaching Sarah we first mapped the simple social transaction of giving, which is something the chimpanzee does both in nature and in the laboratory. Considered in terms of cognitive and perceptual elements, the verb "give" involves a relation between two individuals and one object, that is, between the donor, the recipient and the object being transferred. In order to carry out the act of giving an animal must recognize the difference between individuals (between "Mary" and "Randy") and must perceive the difference between donors and recipients (between "Mary gives Randy" and "Randy gives Mary"). In order to be able to map out the entire transaction of giving the animal has to distinguish agents from objects, agents from one another, objects from one another and itself from others.

The trainer began the process of mapping the social transaction by placing a slice of banana between himself and Sarah. The chimpanzee, which was then about five years old, was allowed to eat the tasty morsel while the trainer looked on affectionately. After the transaction had become routine, a language element consisting of a pink plastic square was placed close to Sarah while the slice of banana was moved beyond her reach. To obtain the fruit Sarah now had to put the plastic piece on a "language board" on the side of her cage. (The board was magnetic and the plastic square was backed with a thin piece of steel so that it would stick.) After Sarah had learned this routine the fruit was changed to an apple and she had to place a blue plastic word for apple on the board. Later several other fruits, the verb "give" and the plastic words that named each of them were introduced.

To be certain that Sarah knew the meaning of "give" it was necessary to contrast "give" with other verbs, such as "wash," "cut" and "insert." When Sarah indicated "Give apple," she was given a piece of apple. When she put "Wash apple" on the board, the apple was placed in a bowl of water and washed. In that way Sarah learned what action went with what verb.

In the first stage Sarah was required to put only one word on the board; the name of the fruit was a sufficient indicator of the social transaction. When names for different actions—verbs—were introduced, Sarah had to place two words on the board in vertical sequence. In order to be given an apple she had to write "Give apple." When recipients were named, two-word sentences were not accepted by the trainer; Sarah had to use three words. There were several trainers, and Sarah had to learn the name of each one. To facilitate the teaching of personal names, both the chimpanzees and the trainers wore their plastic-word names on a string necklace. Sarah learned the names of some of the recipients the hard way. Once she wrote "Give apple Gussie," and the trainer promptly gave the apple to another chimpanzee named Gussie. Sarah never repeated the sentence. At every stage she was required to observe the proper word sequence. "Give apple" was accepted but "Apple give" was not. When donors were to be named, Sarah had to identify all the members of the social transaction: "Mary give apple Sarah."

The interrogative was introduced with the help of the concepts "same" and "different." Sarah was given a cup and a spoon. When another cup was added, she was taught to put the two cups together. Other sets of three objects were given to her, and she had to pair the two objects that were alike. Then she was taught to place the plastic word for "same" between any two similar objects and the plastic word for "different" between unlike objects. Next what amounted to a question mark was placed between pairs of objects. This plastic shape (which bore no resemblance to the usual kind of question mark) made the question explicit rather than implicit, as it had been in the simple matching tests. When the interrogative element was placed between a pair of cups, it meant: "What is the relation between cup A and cup B?" The choices provided Sarah were the plastic words "same" and "different." She learned to remove the interrogative particle and substitute the correct word [see top illustration on page 109]. Sarah was able to transfer what she had learned and apply the word "same" or "different" to numerous pairs of objects that had not been used in her training.

Any construction is potentially a question. From the viewpoint of structural linguistics any construction where one or more elements are deleted becomes a question. The constructions we used with Sarah were "A same A" and "A different B." Elements in these constructions were removed and the deletion was marked with the interrogative symbol; Sarah was then supplied with a choice of missing elements with which she could restore the construction to its familiar form. In principle interrogation can be taught either by removing an element from a familiar situation in the animal's world or by removing the element from a language that maps the animal's world. It is probable that one can induce questions by purposively removing key elements from a familiar situation. Suppose a chimpanzee received its daily ration of food at a specific time and place, and then one day the food was not there. A chimpanzee trained in the interrogative might inquire "Where is my food?" or, in Sarah's case, "My food is?" Sarah was never put in a situation that might induce such interrogation because for our purposes it was easier to teach Sarah to answer questions.

At first Sarah learned all her words in the context of social exchange. Later, when she had learned the concepts "name of" and "not name of," it was possible to introduce new words in a more direct way. To teach her that objects had names, the plastic word for "apple" and a real apple were placed on the table and Sarah was required to put the plastic word for "name of" between them. The same procedure was repeated for banana. After she had responded correctly several times, the symbol for "apple" and a real banana were placed on the table and Sarah had to put "not

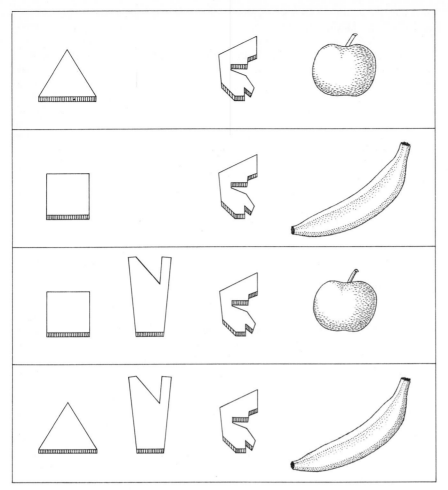

TEACHING LANGUAGE WITH LANGUAGE was the next step. Sarah was taught to put the symbol for "name of" between the word for "apple" and an apple and also between the word for "banana" and a banana. She learned the concept "not name of" in the same way. Thereafter Sarah could be taught new nouns by introducing them with "name of."

name of" between them. After she was able to perform both operations correctly new nouns could be taught quickly and explicitly. The plastic words for "raisin" and "name of" could be placed next to a real raisin and Sarah would learn the noun. Evidence of such learning came when Sarah subsequently requested "Mary give raisin Sarah" or set down "Raisin different apple."

An equally interesting linguistic leap occurred when Sarah learned the predicate adjective and could write such sentences as "Red color of apple," "Round shape of apple" and "Large size of apple." When asked for the relation between "Apple is red ? Red color of apple" and given "same" and "different" as choices, she judged the sentences to be the same. When given "Apple is red ? Apple is round," she judged the sentences to be different. The distinctions between similar and different, first learned with actual objects, was later applied by Sarah in linguistic constructions.

In English the conditional consists of the discontinuous elements "if-then," which are inconvenient and conceptually unnecessary. In symbolic logic the conditional consists of the single sign ⊃, and we taught Sarah the conditional relation with the use of a single plastic word. Before being given language training in the conditional, she was given contingency training in which she was rewarded for doing one thing but not another. For example, she was given a choice between an apple and a banana, and only when she chose the apple was she given chocolate (which she dearly loved). "If apple, then chocolate, if banana, then no chocolate" were the relations she learned; the same relations were subsequently used in sentences to teach her the name for the conditional relation.

The subject was introduced with the written construction: "Sarah take apple ? Mary give chocolate Sarah." Sarah was provided with only one plastic word: the conditional particle. She had to remove the question mark and substitute the conditional in its place to earn the apple and the chocolate. Now she was presented with: "Sarah take banana ? Mary no give chocolate Sarah." Again only the conditional symbol was provided. When Sarah replaced the question mark with the conditional symbol, she received a banana but no chocolate. After several such tests she was given a series of trials on each of the following pairs of sentences: "Sarah take apple if-then Mary give chocolate Sarah" coupled with "Sarah take banana if-then Mary no give chocolate Sarah," or "Sarah take apple if-then Mary no give chocolate Sarah" coupled with "Sarah take banana if-then Mary give chocolate Sarah."

At first Sarah made many errors, taking the wrong fruit and failing to get her beloved chocolate. After several of her strategies had failed she paid closer attention to the sentences and began choosing the fruit that gave her the chocolate. Once the conditional relation had been learned she was able to apply it to other types of sentence, for example "Mary take red if-then Sarah take apple" and "Mary take green if-then Sarah take banana." Here Sarah had to watch Mary's choice closely in order to take the correct action. With the paired sentences "Red is on green if-then Sarah take apple" and "Green is on red if-then Sarah take banana," which involved a change in the position of two colored cards, Sarah was not confused and performed well.

As a preliminary to learning the class concepts of color, shape and size Sarah was taught to identify members of the classes red and yellow, round and square and large and small. Objects that varied in most dimensions but had a particular property in common were used. Thus for teaching the word "red" a set of dissimilar, unnamed objects (a ball, a toy car, a Life Saver and so on) that had no property in common except redness were put before the chimpanzee. The only plastic word available to her was "red." After several trials on identifying red with a set of red objects and yellow with a set of yellow objects, Sarah was shifted to trials where she had to choose between "red" and "yellow" when she was shown a colored object. Finally completely new red and yellow objects were presented to her, including small cards that were identical except for their color.

Again she performed at her usual level of accuracy.

Sarah was subsequently taught the names of shapes, "round" and "square," as well as the size names "large" and "small." These words formed the basis for teaching her the names of the class concepts "color of," "shape of" and "size of." Given the interrogative "Red ? apple" or "Yellow ? banana," Sarah was required to substitute the plastic word for "color of" for the question mark. In teaching class names a good many sentences were not written on the board but were presented as hybrids. The hybrid sentences consisted of a combination of plastic words and real objects arranged in the proper sentence sequence on Sarah's worktable. Typical sentences were "Yellow ?" beside a real yellow balloon or "Red ?" beside a red wood block.

The hybrid sentences did not deter Sarah in the least. Her good performance showed that she was able to move with facility from symbols for objects to actual objects. Her behavior with hybrid constructions recalls the activity of young children, who sometimes combine spoken words with real objects they are unable to name by pointing at the objects.

Was Sarah able to think in the plastic-word language? Could she store information using the plastic words or use them to solve certain kinds of problem that she could not solve otherwise? Additional research is needed before we shall have definitive answers, but Sarah's performance suggests that the answers to both questions may be a qualified yes. To think with language requires being able to generate the meaning of words in the absence of their external representation. For Sarah to be able to match "apple" to an actual apple or "Mary" to a picture of Mary indicates that she knows the meaning of these words. It does not prove, however, that when she is given the word "apple" and no apple is present, she can think "apple," that is, mentally represent the meaning of the word to herself. The ability to achieve such mental representation is of major importance because it frees language from simple dependence on the outside world. It involves displacement: the ability to talk about things that are not actually there. That is a critical feature of language.

The hint that Sarah was able to understand words in the absence of their external referents came early in her language training. When she was given

a piece of fruit and two plastic words, she was required to put the correct word for the fruit on the board before she was allowed to eat it. Surprisingly often, however, she chose the wrong word. It then dawned on us that her poor performance might be due not to errors but to her trying to express her preferences in fruit. We conducted a series of tests to determine her fruit preferences,

using actual fruits in one test and only fruit names in the other. Sarah's choices between the words were much the same as her choices between the actual fruits. This result strongly suggests that she could generate the meaning of the fruit names from the plastic symbols alone.

We obtained clearer evidence at a later stage of Sarah's language training. In the same way that she could use

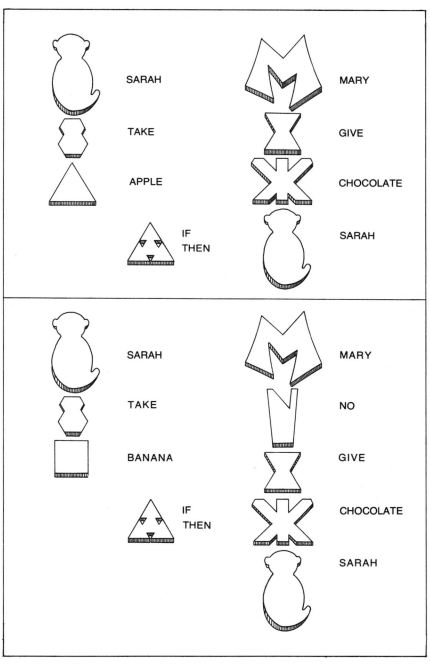

CONDITIONAL RELATION, which in English is expressed "if...then," was taught to Sarah as a single word. The plastic symbol for the conditional relation was placed between two sentences. Sarah had to pay attention to the meaning of both sentences very closely in order to make the choice that would give her a reward. Once the conditional relation was learned by means of this procedure, the chimpanzee was able to apply it to other situations.

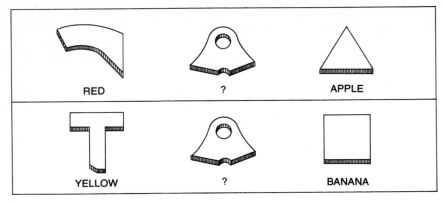

CLASS CONCEPT OF COLOR was taught with the aid of sentences such as "Red ? apple" and "Yellow ? banana." Sarah had to replace the interrogative symbol with "color of."

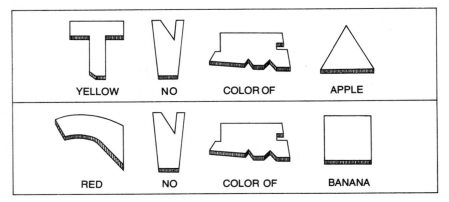

NEGATIVE CONCEPT was introduced with "no-not." When asked "Yellow ? apple" or "Red ? banana," Sarah had to replace interrogative symbol with "color of" or "not color of."

ALTERNATIVE FEATURES			
RED	GREEN	RED	RED
○	□	○	○
⌂	□	⌂	⌂
⌂	○	○	○

FEATURE ANALYSIS of an actual apple and the plastic word for "apple" was conducted. Sarah was shown an apple or the word and made to choose from alternative features: red or green, round or square, square with stem or plain square and square with stem or round. Sarah gave plastic word for "apple" same attributes she had earlier assigned to apple.

"name of" to learn new nouns, she was able to use "color of" to learn the names of new colors. For instance, the names "brown" and "green" were introduced in the sentences "Brown color of chocolate" and "Green color of grape." The only new words at this point were "brown" and "green." Later Sarah was confronted with four disks, only one of which was brown, and when she was instructed with the plastic symbols "Take brown," she took the brown disk. Since chocolate was not present at any time during the introduction of the color name "brown," the word "chocolate" in the definition must have been sufficient to have Sarah generate or picture the property brown.

What form does Sarah's supposed internal representation take? Some indication is provided by the results of a test of ability to analyze the features of an object. First Sarah was shown an actual apple and was given a series of paired comparisons that described the features of the apple, such as red v. green, round v. square and so on. She had to pick the descriptive feature that belonged to the apple. Her feature analysis of a real apple agreed nicely with our own, which is evidence of the interesting fact that a chimpanzee is capable of decomposing a complex object into features. Next the apple was removed and the blue plastic triangle that was the word for "apple" was placed before her and again she was given a paired-comparison test. She assigned the same features to the word that she had earlier assigned to the object. Her feature analysis revealed that it was not the physical properties of the word (blue and triangle) that she was describing but rather the object that was represented by the word [*see bottom illustration at left*].

To test Sarah's sentence comprehension she was taught to correctly follow these written instructions: "Sarah insert apple pail," "Sarah insert banana pail," "Sarah insert apple dish" and "Sarah insert banana dish." Next instructions were combined in a one-line vertical sequence ("Sarah insert apple pail Sarah insert banana dish"). The chimpanzee responded appropriately. Then the second "Sarah" and the second verb "insert" were deleted to yield the compound sentence: "Sarah insert apple pail banana dish." Sarah followed the complicated instructions at her usual level of accuracy.

The test with the compound sentence is of considerable importance, because it provides the answer to whether or not

CONCEPTS "SAME" AND "DIFFERENT" were introduced into Sarah's vocabulary by teaching her to pair objects that were alike (*top illustration*). Then two identical objects, for example apples, were placed before her and she was given plastic word for "same" and induced to place word between the two objects. She was also taught to place the word for "different" between unlike objects.

THE INTERROGATIVE was introduced with the help of the concepts "same" and "different." A plastic piece that meant "question mark" was placed between two objects and Sarah had to replace it with either the word for "same" or the word for "different."

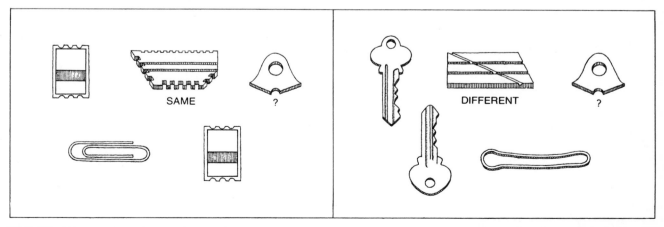

NEW VERSION OF THE INTERROGATIVE was taught by arranging an object and plastic symbols to form questions: "What is [Object A] the same as?" or "What is [Object A] different from?" Sarah had to replace question marker with the appropriate object.

Sarah could understand the notion of constituent structure: the hierarchical organization of a sentence. The correct interpretation of the compound sentence was "Sarah put the apple in the pail and the banana in the dish." To take the correct actions Sarah must understand that "apple" and "pail" go together but not "pail" and "banana," even though the terms appear side by side. Moreover, she must understand that the verb "insert" is at a higher level of organization and refers to both "apple" and "banana." Finally, Sarah must understand that she, as the head noun, must carry out all the actions. If Sarah were capable only of linking words in a simple chain, she would never be able to interpret the compound sentence with its deletions. The fact is that she interprets them correctly. If a child were to carry out the instructions in the same way, we would not hesitate to say that he recognizes the various levels of sentence organization: that the subject dominates the predicate and the verb in the predicate dominates the objects.

Sarah had managed to learn a code, a simple language that nevertheless included some of the characteristic features of natural language. Each step of the training program was made as simple as possible. The objective was to reduce complex notions to a series of simple and highly learnable steps. The same program that was used to teach Sarah to communicate has been successfully applied with people who have language difficulties caused by brain damage. It may also be of benefit to the autistic child.

In assessing the results of the experiment with Sarah one must be careful not to require of Sarah what one would require of a human adult. Compared with a two-year-old child, however, Sarah holds her own in language ability. In fact, language demands were made of Sarah that would never be made of a child. Man is understandably prejudiced in favor of his own species, and members of other species must perform Herculean feats before they are recognized as having similar abilities, particularly language abilities. Linguists and others who study the development of language tend to exaggerate the child's understanding of language and to be extremely skeptical of the experimentally demonstrated language abilities of the chimpanzee. It is our hope that our findings will dispel such prejudices and lead to new attempts to teach suitable languages to animals other than man.

Biological Foundations of Language

by Eric H. Lenneberg

Reviewed by Charles F. Hockett
November 1967

*The foundations of language in man, the
small-mouthed animal*

Some 30 years ago Leonard Bloomfield published his book *Language,* ostensibly an elementary text but in fact a masterly synthesis and compendium of all that had been learned about the subject in the century and a half since scientific linguistics first emerged from the mists of medieval philosophical speculation. In spite of some errors of detail and one major theoretical discrepancy, Bloomfield had sifted the work of his predecessors so carefully, and had himself built so well, that his presentation has still not been superseded.

This is not because Bloomfield's successors have been lazy or incompetent. In fact, they have been very busy. The generalizations Bloomfield ventured on the basis of a small and rather biased sample of the world's languages have been checked on several hundred more, and in the main they have held up; a few about which he was hesitant have been rendered firm. In a more theoretical vein some investigators have tested his frame of reference by suppressing one or another of its features to see if the omission really matters (always to find that it does) or by adding some new twist (only to find that it gets in the way).

Bloomfield was largely or wholly silent on certain issues, not because they are unimportant but because no reliable information was yet available. He not only noted but also insisted that language is an exclusively human prerogative, and that its possession is in turn responsible for much else that is specifically human. He says nothing, however, as to how this may have come about in biological evolution. He makes no comment on the possible ways in which human genes, and the anatomy and physiology that stem from them, differ from those of other animals so that we have language and they do not. Certain directions of research that might in

time shed light on these problems receive short shrift. He offers no systematic comparison of human language with the communicative behavior of other species; he covers the child's acquisition of language only in the briefest outline, and he condenses to a single page the then available reports on the speech behavior of people suffering from aphasia.

It is to just such matters as these that Eric Lenneberg refers by the phrase "biological foundations" in the title of the book reviewed here. Much has been done along these lines in the past three decades. Lenneberg has himself made extensive observations on the communicative behavior of the deaf, of mentally retarded or defective children, and of patients suffering from brain injuries. For this report he draws on his own experience but combines it with a careful combing of an enormous literature that presents the findings of others: psychologists, psychiatrists, brain surgeons, pathologists, primatologists and even a few linguists. The reader's expectations should not be unrealistic. Obviously one will not find in this book a map showing the chromosome loci responsible for our power of speech. Reasonable expectations are that the book be a progress report, explaining which lines of research and speculation have proved fruitless, which have shown promise and should be followed up, and perhaps venturing a few tentative generalizations.

Except in one important respect, these expectations are fulfilled. Several topics that Lenneberg handles in a very interesting way will be omitted here, but I shall give a summary of what to me are his most important positive findings.

The first point is mentioned only in passing, but it was new to me and caught my fancy. For vocal-auditory communication *Homo sapiens* has an advantage over the other hominoids in the relatively small external opening of

his oral cavity. This is a matter of physical acoustics that can be tested in any kitchen. Allowing for differences of material and shape, a container with a small mouth, such as a beer bottle, resonates better than one with a large mouth, such as a jelly glass.

Was the selection for small mouths among our remote ancestors favored because it promoted vocal-auditory communication, or did it come about for other reasons and merely set the stage for the development of language? Lenneberg does not discuss this, but the tenor of his writing shows that he would insist, as I do, that questions in this simple either-or form are misleading. What happens in evolution is always the result of the most complicated interweaving of many factors, no one of which can be singled out as "the" cause. The reduction of mouth size must be related to the slow switch to upright posture, the transfer of grasping and manipulating from mouth to hands, the enlargement of the skull and advancement of the forehead, the recession of the jaw and reduction in size of the teeth, the changing mechanics of supporting the head implied by all of these, and changes of diet, perhaps even the invention of cooking. At present we have only vague notions of the relative timetable of all these developments.

The second finding is that there is no convincing evidence for any extreme localization of brain function, either for language in its various aspects or for any other facet of behavior. Behaviorally equivalent activities may be governed by different parts of different human brains. There is equally no reason to believe the cerebral cortex begins as a homogeneous mass any part of which can equally well come to be involved in any function. Rather there seem to be genetically monitored structural reasons (little understood as yet) why certain functions are most likely to be developed in certain portions of the brain, yet enough flexibility that if something such as a brain injury interferes, other regions are able to take over. This flexibility decreases with age. As far as language is concerned, the evidence from efforts to retrain aphasics suggests that by the age of 14 or 15 it is gone.

Lenneberg warns us, however, that the ways in which we classify and categorize behavior as viewed from the outside may be entirely different from the ways in which it is broken up into bits and pieces for internal storage. It is obviously meaningful to speak of the vocabulary of a language, as against its phonology and its grammar. But this does not imply that a speaker's brain tucks away the words he learns in some particular bank of adjacent cells or synapses, nor even that each individual vocabulary item must be stored as a unit in a cell or synapse somewhere. Of course, unless we are going to abandon altogether the notion that the brain plays a role in behavior (perhaps restoring the classical Greek proposal that its function is to cool the blood), then all the information for behavior must be stored somehow, somewhere. It is simply that behavioral units may not be storage units.

One suggestion of importance emerges. If anything recognizable in behavioral terms is in fact localized within the cerebral cortex, it is most likely to be the triggers for setting off whole complex behavioral routines: scratching, starting to walk, suckling, a cat's twisting of its body into upright position as it falls. The details of such a routine are then provided for elsewhere, probably in a diffuse way. Certain aspects of language behavior may constitute such routines.

The third conclusion is related to the foregoing. It is a proposal for which Lenneberg marshals a good deal of evidence: that lateral dominance, apparently a human universal, is also exclusively human. In other animals the functions of one cerebral hemisphere (whatever they may be) are virtually duplicated by the other. In humans certain things are assigned to one hemisphere alone, leaving the other free for other functions and thus increasing the total effective cerebral capacity without the need for additional biologically expensive tissue. For example, Broca's area, whatever its exact significance, exists (or functions) only on one side. In this connection it might be better to speak not of lateral dominance but of hemispheric asymmetry.

To Lenneberg's evidence one can add the tentative results of some experiments performed recently at the Haskins Laboratories but not yet published, which suggest that the two ears of a normal adult do not transmit the same information. One ear is better for music, the other for other kinds of sounds; one ear may be the chief channel for the recognition of vowel color in the speech signal, the other for the noise bursts that help to identify consonants. Of course, these differences—if they are genuine—do not reside in the ears as end organs but in the peripheral parts of the brain to which the ears feed their data.

If all of this is really true, one is tempted to speculate as follows. The use of tools may be much older than language. The effective manipulation of tools demands different patterns of motion by the two sides of the body. This may have selected for brains with hemispheric asymmetry, which were then available for exploitation by the various developments that in time gave rise to language.

The fourth and last of Lenneberg's findings I shall mention has to do with the timetable of language acquisition by the normal child. In reviewing this timetable Lenneberg makes only the mistake made by almost all nonlinguists in the same connection: he speaks of the child's utterances as consisting of "words" at a stage considerably earlier than that at which the use of this technical term can be justified, and therefore wrongly identifies some of the important transitions from one stage to the next. Luckily this error does not bear seriously on his conclusions, which are these:

The development of language does not begin in the human infant until the age of 18 to 24 months, but then it is almost impossible to prevent. No *formal* teaching is required. Peripheral impairments—for example deafness—force a resort to substitute channels, just as a congenital brain defect or early brain injury may require the involvement of other than the most usual regions of the cortex, but within very wide limits such difficulties are overcome. Eventually the child comes to speak whatever language is in use by surrounding adults. At the earliest childhood stages the language-like behavior of children in different speech communities is remarkably uniform. This suggests that all human languages are, and for a long time have been, erected on a single ground plan, a view amply supported by the results of linguistic research over the past two centuries. It suggests also that this basic plan is genetic and species-specific. Language acquisition does not begin earlier because the genetically monitored maturation of the nervous system (and perhaps of other parts of the body) has not yet reached the right stage. That it begins when and how it does, however, is not merely allowed but forced by maturation. It is as inevitable as menarche or the appearance of axillary hair, and genetically more stable than either. If the environment is so unusual as to keep the child alive until early puberty and yet frustrate his acquisition of language, it is then too late, again for maturational reasons. The adult's learning of a second language, however successful, is in process very different from the child's acquisition of his first, and the kinds of defective language behavior manifested by aphasics do not in any way resemble early stages in the development of language in the child.

One must allow for the fact that the particular elaboration on the ground plan for a given child depends on the language used by those around him. For this Lenneberg does not want to use the familiar term "learning," perhaps because the multitude of conflicting technical senses given that term by our two and seventy jarring sects of psychologists have spoiled it. Instead he proposes that the child's language behavior comes to "resonate" with that of his mentors. This is harmless, provided that we remember it is merely a new label, not an explanation.

These conclusions strike me as well reasoned and in some respects a genuine improvement over our earlier views, although in no sense revolutionary. But in order to dig this positive content out of Lenneberg's discussion I have had to apply more exegesis than should be required. Anyone doing multidisciplinary research is under the obligation to incorporate only the best and most carefully tested results of each discipline. Insofar as I can judge, Lenneberg does this for all the technical fields involved except the most important one: linguistics. This is an old, tiresome story. Time and again researchers without linguistic training have carefully drawn their chemistry from chemists, their physiology from physiologists, and so on, but have assumed that since language is the common possession of all human beings anyone can be his own expert. In this vein Lenneberg does a number of foolish things. Two examples will suffice: his handling of articulatory phonetics and of phonetic notation is amateurish, and he expresses at one point the peculiar opinion that proper names are not part of vocabulary. The results in cases such as these are merely laughable.

What is truly tragic is that, when he sets aside the notion that anyone can invent linguistics for himself and seeks expert guidance, he turns not to our calm and quietly growing tradition of scientific linguistics (Bloomfield's name does not appear in the book!) but to the speculations of the neomedieval philosopher Noam Chomsky.

Chomsky thinks of a language as an ideal rational schema hidden deep inside a human being and reflected only with great distortion in actual speech. Furthermore, this hidden schema is a system in the same sense as any well-defined algorithmic system of mathematics or mathematical logic. He is thus led to ignore empirical evidence, which is necessarily the observation of actual speech and of responses to it, and to reject, one by one, the various simple inferences that have been made from the empirical evidence by generations of linguists. The result is something like what would happen if a chemist should suddenly conclude that the electronic theory of valence cannot possibly be valid and that some totally different theory must be developed to explain how matter behaves. This is all we need say about Chomsky here. I have recently devoted a monograph to the dissection of his weird notions, and anyone really interested can read it. It seems more constructive to devote the final paragraphs of this review to a capsule summary of the design of human language as understood so far by science. What I shall say is at bottom what Bloomfield said. Some of the words (for instance "association" and "habit") have been claimed by various psychologists in various special senses, but I claim them back as part of everyday vocabulary—there is no psychological theory in this summary.

Any speaker of any human language, at any given time, speaks and understands in terms of a set of habits of articulation and hearing that constitute the *phonology* of his language. In speaking he aims his articulatory motions at a series of articulatory targets, although usually the aim is careless. In hearing the speech of others he identifies what is linguistically relevant in the incoming speech signal, when he needs to, in terms of the articulatory targets at which he himself would aim in order to match the signal. (The occasional individual who has been mute from birth but who understands the speech of others obviously cannot do this; we do not know how he manages.) The actual sound of speech in any language shows the widest and wildest variation, but the targets are discrete and finite in number. Func-tionally there is no such thing in any language as an "indefinitely small difference of sound." The number and location of the targets for any one language are specific to the language, as are the sequences in which they are aimed at and the relative timings of the aims. This is consonant with the fact that as time passes the phonology of any language changes, in ways and by mechanisms that are well understood.

Certain arrangements of targets are associated, sometimes precisely and sometimes very vaguely, with certain things or situations, or kinds of things or situations, in the experience of the speaker. Any such recurrent arrangement of targets is a linguistic *form,* and that with which it is associated is the *meaning* of the form.

People imitate each other, so that a form may spread from one speaker, or from one dialect, or even from one language, to another. When language habits are changed or enlarged in this way, the traditional term for the mechanism is "borrowing." Of course, this term is no more explanatory than "imitation" or Lenneberg's "resonance" is, but we are here merely stating facts, not accounting for them. The mechanism plays a constant role in the development of any one speaker's language habits, from their earliest appearance to his death.

Any speaker constantly faces situations, real or imagined, at least a little different from any he has encountered before. If he responds with speech (even silently, to himself), he may use a form already in his repertory, or he may coin a new linguistic form on the *analogy* of those he already knows. He may even follow two or more analogies at once. This creation of new forms goes on all the time: most of our utterances are new. It cannot in any way be distinguished from the mere use of language, although some coinages, it is true, are more strikingly novel than others. The longer and more complex a coinage, the more likely it is to be used just once and then forgotten. Nonetheless, a speaker may remember a new coinage—even a long one, say a poem—and utter it again, and others may borrow it, whereupon it may survive indefinitely. Contrariwise, any form may fall into disuse, forgotten by those who once knew it and never learned by others, and thus disappear.

The stock of forms a speaker controls at any one moment is his *vocabulary* (or *lexicon*). The order of magnitude of the vocabulary of any adult speaker of any language is in the tens of thousands; a more precise measurement is difficult because of constant change. The analo-gies by which new forms are coined are *grammar*. This too is constantly changing. In part these changes are kaleidoscopic, but for the most part they are sufficiently slow that the members of a speech community can usually understand one another, given a little trial and error, and that an investigator can prepare a description of a language that is not seriously out of date by the time it is published.

This is just about all we can say that is true of all human languages. There may be some universal features of a more specific nature. For example, it may be that all languages have something like the Latin or English contrast between noun and verb. Such a feature, however, could be universal without necessarily being part of the genetically controlled, species-specific ground plan. After all, if all the languages of the world except one were to die out, thereafter anything true of that one language would be a language "universal," but that would not change our genes.

Most of the foregoing is straightforward, but some people have trouble with analogy. There is nothing mysterious about it, and it is manifested in all phases of human behavior, not just in language. An exchange student from India went to lunch with an American friend and ordered tea. When the fixings arrived, he carefully tore open the bag and poured the tea leaves into his cup. The American explained that the whole bag could be immersed and that the water would filter through. Grateful for the counsel, the Indian took a paper packet of sugar and dropped it into the cup.

An analogical act may thus be a mistake. In one sense all analogical innovations could be characterized as errors of computation—breakdowns in what would otherwise be mechanically algorithmic, as so much of the communicative behavior of other animals seems to be. Some analogical coinages in speech, like most mutations in genetics, are failures; those that are successful differ from the failures not at all in what brings them about, only in their consequences.

Lenneberg's search for the biological foundations of language would have been easier, and his results a great deal more straightforward, if he had understood the foregoing rather simple facts about language itself. The reader who does not understand them can be badly misled by the book. It would be ungracious, however, to end on this note. My principal attitude is one of sincere appreciation to Lenneberg for the hard work he has done and for what he has taught us.

10

Language and the Brain

by Norman Geschwind
April 1972

*Aphasias are speech disorders caused by brain damage.
The relations between these disorders and specific kinds
of brain damage suggest a model of how the language
areas of the human brain are organized*

Virtually everything we know of how the functions of language are organized in the human brain has been learned from abnormal conditions or under abnormal circumstances: brain damage, brain surgery, electrical stimulation of brains exposed during surgery and the effects of drugs on the brain. Of these the most fruitful has been the study of language disorders, followed by postmortem analysis of the brain, in patients who have suffered brain damage. From these studies has emerged a model of how the language areas of the brain are interconnected and what each area does.

A disturbance of language resulting from damage to the brain is called aphasia. Such disorders are not rare. Aphasia is a common aftereffect of the obstruction or rupture of blood vessels in the brain, which is the third leading cause of death in the U.S. Although loss of speech from damage to the brain had been described occasionally before the 19th century, the medical study of such cases was begun by a remarkable Frenchman, Paul Broca, who in 1861 published the first of a series of papers on language and the brain. Broca was the first to point out that damage to a specific portion of the brain results in disturbance of language output. The portion he identified, lying in the third frontal gyrus of the cerebral cortex, is now called Broca's area [*see illustration on page 116*].

Broca's area lies immediately in front of the portion of the motor cortex that controls the muscles of the face, the jaw, the tongue, the palate and the larynx, in other words, the muscles involved in speech production. The region is often called the "motor face area." It might therefore seem that loss of speech from damage to Broca's area is the result of paralysis of these muscles. This explana-tion, however, is not the correct one. Direct damage to the area that controls these muscles often produces only mild weakness of the lower facial muscles on the side opposite the damage and no permanent weakness of the jaw, the tongue, the palate or the vocal cords. The reason is that most of these muscles can be controlled by either side of the brain. Damage to the motor face area on one side of the brain can be compensated by the control center on the opposite side. Broca named the lesion-produced language disorder "aphemia," but this term was soon replaced by "aphasia," which was suggested by Armand Trousseau.

In 1865 Broca made a second major contribution to the study of language and the brain. He reported that damage to specific areas of the left half of the brain led to disorder of spoken language but that destruction of corresponding areas in the right side of the brain left language abilities intact. Broca based his conclusion on eight consecutive cases of aphasia, and in the century since his report his observation has been amply confirmed. Only rarely does damage to the right hemisphere of the brain lead to language disorder; out of 100 people with permanent language disorder caused by brain lesions approximately 97 will have damage on the left side. This unilateral control of certain functions is called cerebral dominance. As far as we know man is the only mammal in which learned behavior is controlled by one half of the brain. Fernando Nottebohm of Rockefeller University has found unilateral neural control of birdsong. It is an interesting fact that a person with aphasia of the Broca type who can utter at most only one or two slurred words may be able to sing a melody rapidly, correctly and even with elegance. This is another proof that aphasia is not the result of muscle paralysis.

In the decade following Broca's first report on brain lesions and language there was a profusion of papers on aphasias of the Broca type. In fact, there was a tendency to believe all aphasias were the result of damage to Broca's area. At this point another great pioneer of the brain appeared on the scene. Unlike Broca, who already had a reputation at the time of his first paper on aphasia, Carl Wernicke was an unknown with no previous publications; he was only 26 years old and a junior assistant in the neurological service in Breslau. In spite of his youth and obscurity his paper on aphasia, published in 1874, gained immediate attention. Wernicke described damage at a site in the left hemisphere outside Broca's area that results in a language disorder differing from Broca's aphasia.

In Broca's aphasia speech is slow and labored. Articulation is crude. Characteristically, small grammatical words and the endings of nouns and verbs are

LOCATION OF SOME LESIONS in the brain can be determined by injecting into the bloodstream a radioactive isotope of mercury, which is taken up by damaged brain tissue. The damaged region is identified by scanning the head for areas of high radioactivity. The top scan on the opposite page was made from the back of the head; the white area on the left shows that the damage is in the left hemisphere. The bottom scan is of the left side of the head and shows that the uptake of mercury was predominantly in the first temporal gyrus, indicating damage to Wernicke's speech area by occlusion of blood vessels. David Patten and Martin Albert of the Boston Veterans Administration Hospital supplied the scans.

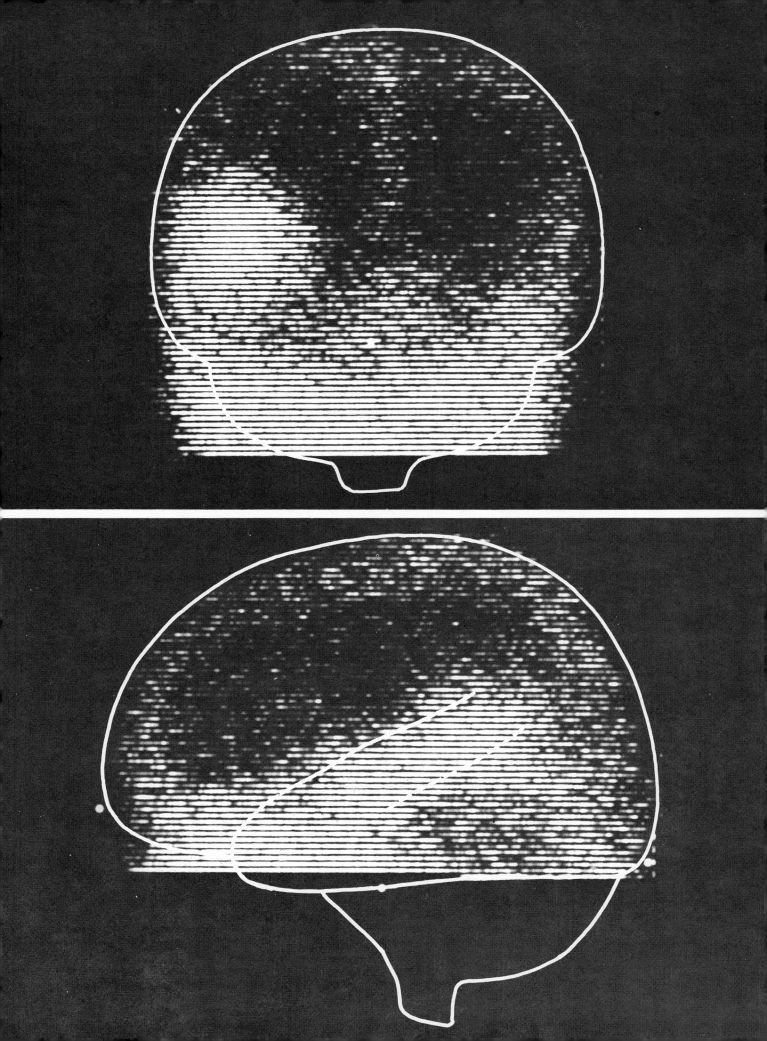

omitted, so that the speech has a telegraphic style. Asked to describe a trip he has taken, the patient may say "New York." When urged to produce a sentence, he may do no better than "Go . . . New York." This difficulty is not simply a desire to economize effort, as some have suggested. Even when the patient does his best to cooperate in repeating words, he has difficulty with certain grammatical words and phrases. "If he were here, I would go" is more difficult than "The general commands the army." The hardest phrase for such patients to repeat is "No ifs, ands or buts."

The aphasia described by Wernicke is quite different. The patient may speak very rapidly, preserving rhythm, grammar and articulation. The speech, if not listened to closely, may almost sound normal. For example, the patient may say: "Before I was in the one here, I was over in the other one. My sister had the department in the other one." It is abnormal in that it is remarkably devoid of content. The patient fails to use the correct word and substitutes for it by

circumlocutory phrases ("what you use to cut with" for "knife") and empty words ("thing"). He also suffers from paraphasia, which is of two kinds. Verbal paraphasia is the substitution of one word or phrase for another, sometimes related in meaning ("knife" for "fork") and sometimes unrelated ("hammer" for "paper"). Literal or phonemic paraphasia is the substitution of incorrect sounds in otherwise correct words ("kench" for "wrench"). If there are several incorrect sounds in a word, it becomes a neologism, for example "pluver" or "flieber."

Wernicke also noted another difference between these aphasic patients and those with Broca's aphasia. A person with Broca's aphasia may have an essentially normal comprehension of language. Indeed, Broca had argued that no single lesion in the brain could cause a loss of comprehension. He was wrong. A lesion in Wernicke's area can produce a severe loss of understanding, even though hearing of nonverbal sounds and music may be fully normal.

Perhaps the most important contribu-

tion made by Wernicke was his model of how the language areas in the brain are connected. Wernicke modestly stated that his ideas were based on the teachings of Theodor Meynert, a Viennese neuroanatomist who had attempted to correlate the nervous system's structure with its function. Since Broca's area was adjacent to the cortical region of the brain that controlled the muscles of speech, it was reasonable to assume, Wernicke argued, that Broca's area incorporated the programs for complex coordination of these muscles. In addition Wernicke's area lay adjacent to the cortical region that received auditory stimuli [see *illustration below*]. Wernicke made the natural assumption that Broca's area and Wernicke's area must be connected. We now know that the two areas are indeed connected, by a bundle of nerve fibers known as the arcuate fasciculus. One can hypothesize that in the repetition of a heard word the auditory patterns are relayed from Wernicke's area to Broca's area.

Comprehension of written language

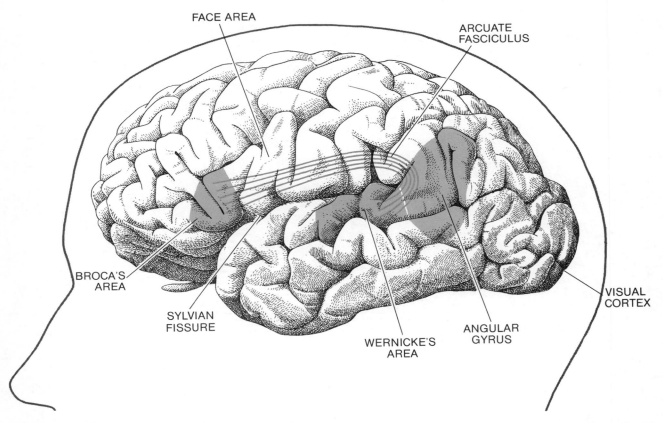

FACE AREA

ARCUATE FASCICULUS

BROCA'S AREA

SYLVIAN FISSURE

WERNICKE'S AREA

ANGULAR GYRUS

VISUAL CORTEX

PRIMARY LANGUAGE AREAS of the human brain are thought to be located in the left hemisphere, because only rarely does damage to the right hemisphere cause language disorders. Broca's area, which is adjacent to the region of the motor cortex that controls the movement of the muscles of the lips, the jaw, the tongue, the soft palate and the vocal cords, apparently incorporates programs for the coordination of these muscles in speech. Damage to Broca's area results in slow and labored speech, but comprehension of language remains intact. Wernicke's area lies between Heschl's gyrus, which is the primary receiver of auditory stimuli, and the angular gyrus, which acts as a way station between the auditory and the visual regions. When Wernicke's area is damaged, speech is fluent but has little content and comprehension is usually lost. Wernicke and Broca areas are joined by a nerve bundle called the arcuate fasciculus. When it is damaged, speech is fluent but abnormal, and patient can comprehend words but cannot repeat them.

would require connections from the visual regions to the speech regions. This function is served by the angular gyrus, a cortical region just behind Wernicke's area. It acts in some way to convert a visual stimulus into the appropriate auditory form.

We can now deduce from the model what happens in the brain during the production of language. When a word is heard, the output from the primary auditory area of the cortex is received by Wernicke's area. If the word is to be spoken, the pattern is transmitted from Wernicke's area to Broca's area, where the articulatory form is aroused and passed on to the motor area that controls the movement of the muscles of speech. If the spoken word is to be spelled, the auditory pattern is passed to the angular gyrus, where it elicits the visual pattern. When a word is read, the output from the primary visual areas passes to the angular gyrus, which in turn arouses the corresponding auditory form of the word in Wernicke's area. It should be noted that in most people comprehension of a written word involves arousal of the auditory form in Wernicke's area. Wernicke argued that this was the result of the way most people learn written language. He thought, however, that in people who were born deaf, but had learned to read, Wernicke's area would not be in the circuit.

According to this model, if Wernicke's area is damaged, the person would have difficulty comprehending both spoken and written language. He should be unable to speak, repeat and write correctly. The fact that in such cases speech is fluent and well articulated suggests that Broca's area is intact but receiving inadequate information. If the damage were in Broca's area, the effect of the lesion would be to disrupt articulation. Speech would be slow and labored but comprehension should remain intact.

This model may appear to be rather simple, but it has shown itself to be remarkably fruitful. It is possible to use it to predict the sites of brain lesions on the basis of the type of language disorder. Moreover, it gave rise to some definite predictions that lesions in certain sites should produce types of aphasia not previously described. For example, if a lesion disconnected Wernicke's area from Broca's area while leaving the two areas intact, a special type of aphasia should be the result. Since Broca's area is preserved, speech should be fluent but abnormal. On the other hand, comprehension should be intact because Wernicke's area is still functioning. Rep-

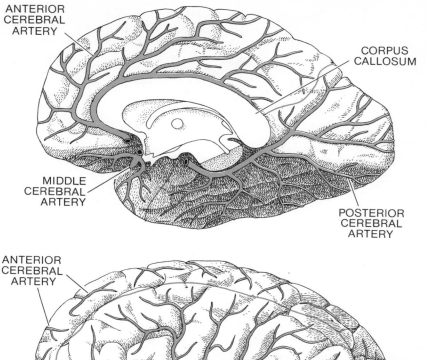

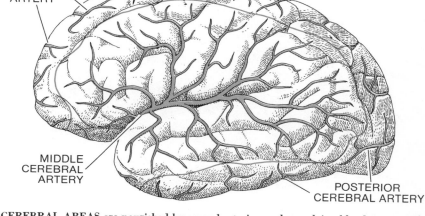

CEREBRAL AREAS are nourished by several arteries, each supplying blood to a specific region. The speech and auditory region is nourished by the middle cerebral artery. The visual areas at the rear are supplied by the posterior cerebral artery. In patients who suffer from inadequate oxygen supply to the brain the damage is often not within the area of a single blood vessel but rather in the "border zones" (*colored lines*). These are the regions between the areas served by the major arteries where the blood supply is marginal.

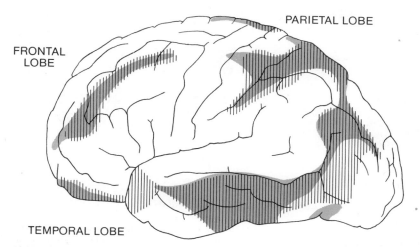

ISOLATION OF SPEECH AREA by a large C-shaped lesion produced a remarkable syndrome in a woman who suffered from severe carbon monoxide poisoning. She could repeat words and learn new songs but could not comprehend the meaning of words. Postmortem examination of her brain revealed that in the regions surrounding the speech areas of the left hemisphere, either the cortex (*colored areas*) or the underlying white matter (*hatched areas*) was destroyed but that the cortical structures related to the production of language (Broca's area and Wernicke's area) and the connections between them were left intact.

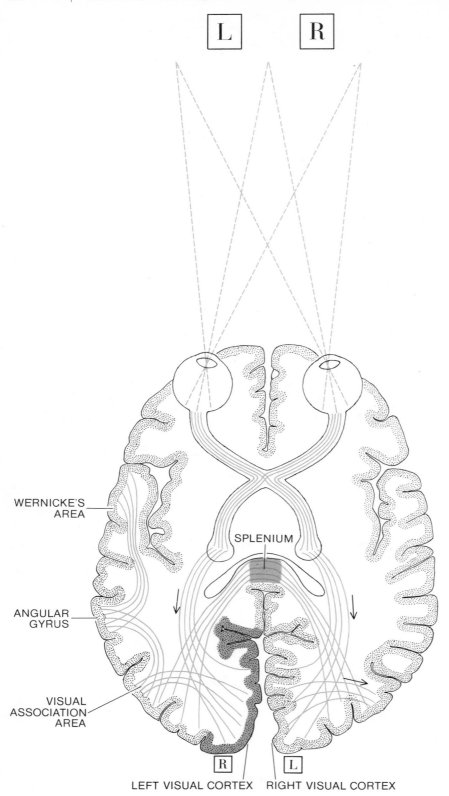

CLASSIC CASE of a man who lost the ability to read even though he had normal visual acuity and could copy written words was described in 1892 by Joseph Jules Dejerine. Post-mortem analysis of the man's brain showed that the left visual cortex and the splenium (*dark colored areas*) were destroyed as a result of an occlusion of the left posterior cerebral artery. The splenium is the section of the corpus callosum that transfers visual information between the two hemispheres. The man's left visual cortex was inoperative, making him blind in his right visual field. Words in his left visual field were properly received by the right visual cortex, but could not cross over to the language areas in the left hemisphere because of the damaged splenium. Thus words seen by the man remained as meaningless patterns.

etition of spoken language, however, should be grossly impaired. This syndrome has in fact been found. It is termed conduction aphasia.

The basic pattern of speech localization in the brain has been supported by the work of many investigators. A. R. Luria of the U.S.S.R. studied a large number of patients who suffered brain wounds during World War II [see "The Functional Organization of the Brain," by A. R. Luria; SCIENTIFIC AMERICAN Offprint 526]. When the wound site lay over Wernicke's or Broca's area, Luria found that the result was almost always severe and permanent aphasia. When the wounds were in other areas, aphasia was less frequent and less severe.

A remarkable case of aphasia has provided striking confirmation of Wernicke's model. The case, described by Fred Quadfasel, Jose Segarra and myself, involved a woman who had suffered from accidental carbon monoxide poisoning. During the nine years we studied her she was totally helpless and required complete nursing care. She never uttered speech spontaneously and showed no evidence of comprehending words. She could, however, repeat perfectly sentences that had just been said to her. In addition she would complete certain phrases. For example, if she heard "Roses are red," she would say "Roses are red, violets are blue, sugar is sweet and so are you." Even more surprising was her ability to learn songs. A song that had been written after her illness would be played to her and after a few repetitions she would begin to sing along with it. Eventually she would begin to sing as soon as the song started. If the song was stopped after a few bars, she would continue singing the song through to the end, making no errors in either words or melody.

On the basis of Wernicke's model we predicted that the lesions caused by the carbon monoxide poisoning lay outside the speech and auditory regions, and that both Broca's area and Wernicke's area were intact. Postmortem examination revealed a remarkable lesion that isolated the speech area from the rest of the cortex. The lesion fitted the prediction. Broca's area, Wernicke's area and the connection between them were intact. Also intact were the auditory pathways and the motor pathways to the speech organs. Around the speech area, however, either the cortex or the underlying white matter was destroyed [*see bottom illustration on preceding page*]. The woman could not comprehend speech because the words did not arouse associations in other portions of the cortex. She could repeat speech correctly because the internal connections of the speech region were intact. Presumably well-learned word sequences stored in Broca's area could be triggered by the beginning phrases. This syndrome is called isolation of the speech area.

Two important extensions of the Wernicke model were advanced by a French neurologist, Joseph Jules Dejerine. In 1891 he described a disorder called alexia with agraphia: the loss of the ability to read and write. The patient could, however, speak and understand spoken language. Postmortem examination showed that there was a lesion in the angular gyrus of the left hemisphere, the area of the brain that acts as a way station between the visual and the auditory region. A lesion here would separate the visual and auditory language areas. Although words and letters would be seen correctly, they would be meaningless visual patterns, since the visual pattern must first be converted to the auditory form before the word can be comprehended. Conversely, the auditory pattern for a word must be transformed into the visual pattern before the word can be spelled. Patients suffering from alexia with agraphia cannot recognize words spelled aloud to them nor can they themselves spell aloud a spoken word.

Dejerine's second contribution was showing the importance of information transfer between the hemispheres. His patient was an intelligent businessman who had awakened one morning to discover that he could no longer read. It was found that the man was blind in the right half of the visual field. Since the right half of the field is projected to the left cerebral hemisphere, it was obvious that the man suffered damage to the visual pathways on the left side of the brain [see illustration on opposite page]. He could speak and comprehend spoken language and could write, but he could not read even though he had normal visual acuity. In fact, although he could not comprehend written words, he could copy them correctly. Postmortem examination of the man's brain by Dejerine revealed two lesions that were the result of the occlusion of the left posterior cerebral artery. The visual cortex of the left hemisphere was totally destroyed. Also destroyed was a portion of the corpus callosum: the mass of nerve fibers that interconnect the two cerebral hemispheres. That portion was the splenium, which carries the visual information between the hemispheres. The destruction of the splenium prevented stimuli from the visual cortex of the right hemisphere

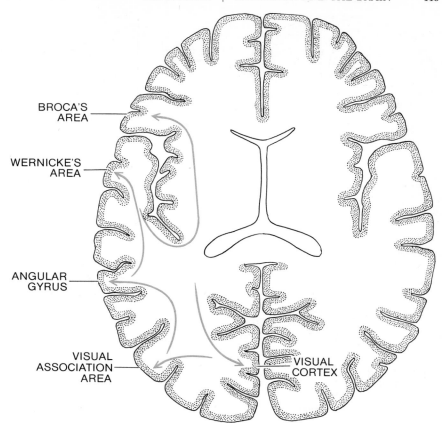

SAYING THE NAME of a seen object, according to Wernicke's model, involves the transfer of the visual pattern to the angular gyrus, which contains the "rules" for arousing the auditory form of the pattern in Wernicke's area. From here the auditory form is transmitted by way of the arcuate fasciculus to Broca's area. There the articulatory form is aroused, is passed on to the face area of the motor cortex and the word then is spoken.

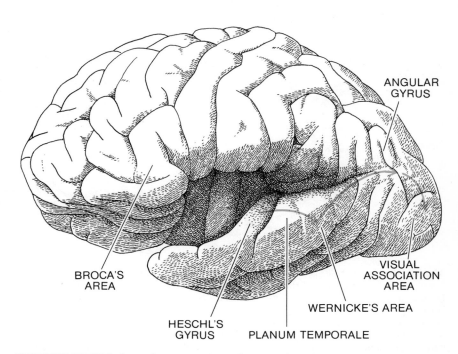

UNDERSTANDING the spoken name of an object involves the transfer of the auditory stimuli from Heschl's gyrus (the primary auditory cortex) to Wernicke's area and then to the angular gyrus, which arouses the comparable visual pattern in the visual association cortex. Here the Sylvian fissure has been spread apart to show the pathway more clearly.

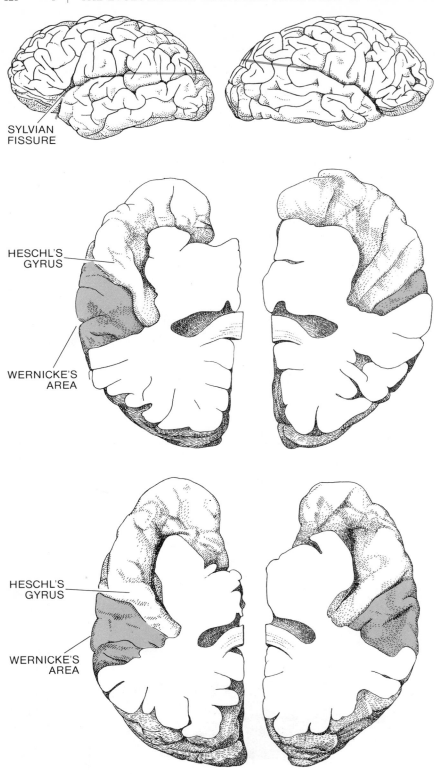

ANATOMICAL DIFFERENCES between the two hemispheres of the human brain are found on the upper surface of the temporal lobe, which cannot be seen in an intact brain because it lies within the Sylvian fissure. Typically the Sylvian fissure in the left hemisphere appears to be pushed down compared with the Sylvian fissure on the right side (*top illustration*). In order to expose the surface of the temporal lobe a knife is moved along the fissure (*broken line*) and then through the brain, cutting away the top portion (*solid line*). The region studied was the planum temporale (*colored areas*), an extension of Wernicke's area. The middle illustration shows a brain with a larger left planum; the bottom illustration shows left and right planums of about the same size. In a study of 100 normal human brains planum temporale was larger on the left side in 65 percent of the cases, equal on both sides in 24 percent of the cases and larger on the right side in 11 percent.

from reaching the angular gyrus of the left hemisphere. According to Wernicke's model, it is the left angular gyrus that converts the visual pattern of a word into the auditory pattern; without such conversion a seen word cannot be comprehended. Other workers have since shown that when a person is blind in the right half of the visual field but is still capable of reading, the portion of the corpus callosum that transfers visual information between the hemispheres is not damaged.

In 1937 the first case in which surgical section of the corpus callosum stopped the transfer of information between the hemispheres was reported by John Trescher and Frank Ford. The patient had the rear portion of his corpus callosum severed during an operation to remove a brain tumor. According to Wernicke's model, this should have resulted in the loss of reading ability in the left half of the visual field. Trescher and Ford found that the patient could read normally when words appeared in his right visual field but could not read at all in his left visual field.

Hugo Liepmann, who was one of Wernicke's assistants in Breslau, made an extensive study of syndromes of the corpus callosum, and descriptions of these disorders were a standard part of German neurology before World War I. Much of this work was neglected, and only recently has its full importance been appreciated. Liepmann's analysis of corpus callosum syndromes was based on Wernicke's model. In cases such as those described by Liepmann the front four-fifths of the corpus callosum is destroyed by occlusion of the cerebral artery that nourishes it. Since the splenium is preserved the patient can read in either visual field. Such a lesion, however, gives rise to three characteristic disorders. The patient writes correctly with his right hand but incorrectly with the left. He carries out commands with his right arm but not with the left; although the left hemisphere can understand the command, it cannot transmit the message to the right hemisphere. Finally, the patient cannot name objects held in his left hand because the somesthetic sensations cannot reach the verbal centers in the left hemisphere.

The problem of cerebral dominance in humans has intrigued investigators since Broca first discovered it. Many early neurologists claimed that there were anatomical differences between the hemispheres, but in the past few decades there has been a tendency to assume that the left and right hemispheres are

MEANING	BROCA'S APHASIA				WERNICKE'S APHASIA
	KANA		KANJI		
	PATIENT'S	CORRECT	PATIENT'S	CORRECT	
INK	キンス (KINSU)	インキ (INKI)	墨 (SUMI)	墨	参 答 (characters) (LONG TIME)
UNIVERSITY	タイ (TAI)	ダイガク (DAIGAKU)	大學	大学 (GREAT LEARNING)	(SOLDIER)
TOKYO	トウ (TOU)	トウキヨウ (TOKYO)	東京	東京 (EAST CAPITAL)	

JAPANESE APHASICS display some characteristics rarely found in Western patients because of the unique writing system used in Japan. There are two separate forms of such writing. One is Kana, which is syllabic. The other is Kanji, which is ideographic. Kana words are articulated syllable by syllable and are not easily identified at a glance, whereas each Kanji character simultaneously represents both a sound and a meaning. A patient with Broca's aphasia, studied by Tsuneo Imura and his colleagues at the Nihon University College of Medicine, was able to write a dictated word correctly in Kanji but not in Kana (*top left*). When the patient was asked to write the word "ink," even though there is no Kanji character for the word, his first effort was the Kanji character "sumi," which means india ink. When required to write in Kana, the symbols he produced were correct but the word was wrong. Another patient who had Wernicke's aphasia wrote Kanji quickly and without hesitation. He was completely unaware that he was producing meaningless ideograms, as are patients who exhibit paraphasias in speech. Only two of characters had meaning (*top right*).

symmetrical. It has been thought that cerebral dominance is based on undetected subtle physiological differences not reflected in gross structure. Walter Levitsky and I decided to look again into the possibility that the human brain is anatomically asymmetrical. We studied 100 normal human brains, and we were surprised to find that striking asymmetries were readily visible. The area we studied was the upper surface of the temporal lobe, which is not seen in the intact brain because it lies within the depths of the Sylvian fissure. The asymmetrical area we found and measured was the planum temporale, an extension of Wernicke's area [see illustration on opposite page]. This region was larger on the left side of the brain in 65 percent of the cases, equal in 24 percent and larger on the right side in 11 percent. In absolute terms the left planum was nine millimeters longer on the average than the right planum. In relative terms the left planum was one-third longer than the right. Statistically all the differences were highly significant. Juhn A. Wada of the University of British Columbia subsequently reported a study that confirmed our results. In addition Wada studied a series of brains from infants who had died soon after birth and found that the planum asymmetry was present. It seems likely that the asymmetries of the brain are genetically determined.

It is sometimes asserted that the anatomical approach neglects the plasticity of the nervous system and makes the likelihood of therapy for language disorders rather hopeless. This is not the case. Even the earliest investigators of aphasia were aware that some patients developed symptoms that were much milder than expected. Other patients recovered completely from a lesion that normally would have produced permanent aphasia. There is recovery or partial recovery of language functions in some cases, as Luria's large-scale study of the war wounded has shown. Of all the patients with wounds in the primary speech area of the left hemisphere, 97.2 percent were aphasic when Luria first examined them. A follow-up examination found that 93.3 percent were still aphasic, although in most cases they were aphasic to a lesser degree.

How does one account for the apparent recovery of language function in some cases? Some partial answers are available. Children have been known to make a much better recovery than adults with the same type of lesion. This suggests that at least in childhood the right hemisphere has some capacity to take over speech functions. Some cases of adult recovery are patients who had suffered brain damage in childhood. A number of patients who have undergone surgical removal of portions of the speech area for the control of epileptic seizures often show milder language disorders than had been expected. This probably is owing to the fact that the patients had suffered from left temporal epilepsy involving the left side of the brain from childhood and had been using the right hemisphere for language functions to a considerable degree.

Left-handed people also show on the average milder disorders than expected when the speech regions are damaged, even though for most left-handers the left hemisphere is dominant for speech just as it is for right-handers. It is an interesting fact that right-handers with a strong family history of left-handedness show better speech recovery than people without left-handed inheritance.

Effective and safe methods for studying cerebral dominance and localization of language function in the intact, normal human brain have begun to appear. Doreen Kimura of the University of Western Ontario has adapted the technique of dichotic listening to investigate the auditory asymmetries of the brain. More recently several investigators have found increased electrical activity over the speech areas of the left hemisphere during the production or perception of speech. Refinement of these techniques could lead to a better understanding of how the normal human brain is organized for language. A deeper understanding of the neural mechanisms of speech should lead in turn to more precise methods of dealing with disorders of man's most characteristic attribute, language.

II

EVOLUTIONARY THEORY: ITS DEVELOPMENT AND APPLICATION TO MAN

EVOLUTIONARY THEORY: ITS DEVELOPMENT AND APPLICATION TO MAN

INTRODUCTION

Modern evolutionary theory emphasizes genetic variation and natural selection as the basic mechanisms underlying the origins, development, and diversity of the human species. Yet, it took over one hundred years for the theory to reach its current level of development. If we look backward to its beginnings at the time of Charles Darwin, we will find that a series of issues related to the biblical interpretation of creation and catastrophe were discarded by the scientific world as a result of accepting Darwin's evolutionary model. Nevertheless, it is perhaps testimony to the bitter controversies that raged over this new explanation involving all of life, and especially humans, that this issue remains unsettled in the minds of some people even today.

Science and the Citizen
July 1967

End of the "Monkey Law"

Tennessee's "monkey law" prohibiting the teaching of evolution in the state's public schools has been repealed. The law was adopted in 1925 and led later that year to the celebrated test case involving John T. Scopes, William Jennings Bryan and Clarence Darrow. The 11-day trial became a bitter contest between religious fundamentalism and biological theory; the judge held, however, that only evidence on whether or not Scopes had taught evolution was admissible, and Scopes was convicted. The conviction was reversed on a technicality but the law was permitted to stand.

In April of this year the lower house of the Tennessee legislature voted to repeal the statute; in May the Senate agreed and the governor approved the repeal. While the repeal bill was before the legislature a high school science teacher, Gary L. Scott, was dismissed— apparently by coincidence—for teaching evolution. He was reinstated, but he filed suit challenging the constitutionality of the statute. The suit is now expected to be withdrawn. Anti-evolution laws are still on the books in Mississippi and Arkansas, and the Arkansas law has just been upheld by the state Supreme Court.

Science and the Citizen
January 1965

Textbooks Victorious

A fundamentalist campaign has failed to prevent adoption in Texas of three high school biology textbooks on the ground that they discuss the theory of evolution (see "Science and the Citizen," October, 1964). In October of last year the 15-member state Textbook Committee voted overwhelmingly to adopt all three books. The group opposing adoption appealed this decision to the 21-member State Board of Education, an elective body. On November 9, after a day of deliberation, the Board of Education voted by a margin of two to one to support the Textbook Committee's decision. In consequence the textbooks—products of a five-year, $5 million project, supported by the National Science Foundation, to raise the level of high school biology teaching—may now be legally used in Texas schools. The three books, known familiarly as the "blue," "yellow" and "green" texts, are respectively *Biological Science: Molecules to Man* (Houghton Mifflin), *Biological Science: An Inquiry into Life* (Harcourt, Brace and World) and *High School Biology* (Rand McNally).

Science and the Citizen
May 1970

The Monkey War Resumes

The classic controversy about evolution has resumed once again in California. The State Board of Education has held that Darwin's theory of evolution through natural selection is just one of a number of possible theories on the origin of life and of man and must be presented as such in the public schools. Several school boards and other groups in the state are threatening lawsuits to block the board's action, which took the form of new guidelines for science teaching that were approved last fall and are now being promulgated. The board inserted into the guidelines, which had been prepared by a committee of science teachers, a statement that "scientific evidence concerning the origin of life implies at least a dualism or the necessity to use several theories." This will presumably require that such competing theories as the story given in Genesis and Aristotle's theory of spontaneous generation be taught along with Darwinism. Textbooks that do not do so will not be bought by the state for the elementary schools or put on the approved list for local purchase by secondary schools. The decision could affect the teaching of biology throughout the country, since California accounts for some 10 percent of all textbook sales and publishers are not likely to give up the California market or to publish special versions tailored to one state's requirements.

The board's decision was reached, according to the *San Francisco Chronicle*, after a seven-year campaign by Fundamentalists who argued that evolution contradicts the Bible and that its teaching therefore undermines religious training. They first sought to have Darwinism eliminated from the curriculum, but they were unsuccessful and settled for the competing-theories approach. Opponents of the board's action maintain that to present fundamentalist Biblical doctrine on the same basis as the findings of scientific investigation is to teach a religious belief in public schools and is therefore unconstitutional. Moreover, they urge that a doctrine of "equal validity" for various theories would lead to chaos in science teaching.

Science and the Citizen
February 1971

Last of the "Monkey Laws"

Mississippi's law against the teaching of evolution, which was the last of several such state laws, has been overturned by the state's Supreme Court. The statute made it unlawful "to teach that mankind ascended or descended from a lower order of animals." The state court, citing a decision by the U.S. Supreme Court in 1968 holding unconstitutional the antievolution law in Arkansas, said that "for all practical purposes" the decision also applied to Mississippi. Tennessee's antievolution law, which had led to the celebrated Scopes trial, was repealed in 1967.

Removal of the antievolution laws does not end efforts to legally limit the teaching of evolution. Such teaching is now under attack from another direction by the Creation Research Society. The society is pressing in a number of states for action to give the doctrine of divine creation equal status with other explanations of the origin of man. . . .

Science and the Citizen
January 1971

Creationism

In recent months the teaching of evolution has come under attack in a number of states. The revival of fundamentalism in biology takes a somewhat new form: the emphasis is on opposition to current theories of the origin of life and the diversity of species not by theologians but by scientists. The movement is led by the Creation Research Society, whose members have appeared before state boards of education and textbook committees in California, Texas, Arkansas and Tennessee. The society's credo says that it is "committed to full belief in the Biblical record of creation and early history" and that its goal is "the realignment of science based on theistic creation concepts." The society's 300 or so members have master's degrees or doctorates in various fields of natural science. Its current president is Henry Morris of Christian Heritage College in San Diego, Calif.

The society's major success to date has been the inclusion of language it favored in a new "science framework," or guidelines, adopted in late 1969 by the California State Board of Education. What the board did was to substitute new wording for two paragraphs in the proposed guidelines prepared by the state advisory committee on science education. The proposed paragraphs had indicated that life probably arose from "a soup of amino-acid-like molecules" some three billion years ago and that the diversity among present species is the result of evolution through natural selection from effective adaptation to changing environments. That language was attacked by representatives of the creationist point of view, led by members of the Creation Research Society, according to an article in *BioScience* by Walter G. Peter III. They argued that the doctrine of special divine creation deserves equal status with other explanations of the origin of man since it is not only a theistic belief but also a scientifically valid doctrine, defensible by the society's professional members; that it is illegal to present merely a humanistic viewpoint, as in the proposed guidelines, and that the rights of Christian children would be violated by what would be in effect the teaching of the absence of God.

Several members of the society testified against the original guideline language. George F. Howe of Los Angeles Baptist College in Newhall, Calif., held that creationism is no less "scientific" and no more "religious" than the general theory of evolution. Indeed, creationism

solves what he called a problem for evolutionists: the large odds that a living protocell—or even a specific protein molecule—could have formed merely through the accretion of various substances in an ancient ocean. The evolutionist's reliance on mutation as the mechanism for evolution, he said, is contradicted by evidence that the vast majority of mutations are harmful; creationists maintain that cells of each living "kind" were formed rapidly by the Creator. Moreover, the manner in which species appear in the fossil record in a "now you don't see them, now you do" manner fits the creationist—not the evolutionist—view. Dennis S. McCurdie, a geologist, argued that wrong conclusions have been drawn from carbon-14 dating of fossil-bearing materials and that carbon-14 studies actually demonstrate that the earth was created recently—perhaps 10,000 years ago.

The board removed the two disputed paragraphs. It substituted a statement that "all scientific evidence to date concerning the origin of life implies at least a dualism or the necessity to use several theories.... Creation in scientific terms is not a religious or philosophic belief.... Creation and evolutionary theories are not necessarily mutual exclusives.... Aristotle proposed a theory of spontaneous generation. In the nineteenth century, a concept of natural selection was proposed.... More recently efforts have been made to explain the origin of life in biochemical terms."

The effect of the new science framework is still not clear. California's state board does not actually adopt textbooks beyond the eighth-grade level; local boards are free to adopt their own high school texts. As for elementary and junior high school science books, the first call for new adoptions since the 1969 guidelines were approved is not due until March. At that time the new point of view will presumably have to be taken into account.

Granted that the nineteenth century Darwinian theory of evolution produced nothing short of a scientific revolution in the biological sciences, it is evident that the developments in this century will undoubtedly have a tremendous impact on our understanding, further elaboration and modification of this theory. When we consider, for instance, the highly significant contribution of population genetics to our understanding of evolution, and the specific roles of gene mutation, drift, and flow within this process, or the concepts underlying genetic adaptation and its expression at various biochemical, physiological, and behavioral levels, we come to the full realization of just how much has been added to our knowledge since the turn of the century. Of course, perhaps the most revolutionary development of this century has to be the development of molecular biology. With the discovery of the structure and function of macromolecules by such scientists as Linus Pauling in the late 1940's and the application of similar methods and concepts to the analysis of the structure and function of the deoxyribonucleic acid (DNA) by James D. Watson, Francis H. C. Crick and Maurice Wilkins in the middle 1950's, a whole new science of molecular biology was generated. In turn, the highly significant findings that led to the development of the concept of an elaborate ribonucleic acid (RNA) mediated system for synthesizing the structural and functional proteins of the body cells provided the necessary link between genes at the level of DNA and the environment of the cell. (For a more complete listing of the research see the Science and the Citizen columns in this section.) These discoveries were associated with others that demonstrate the almost universal structure and function of DNA in living organisms and the unusual properties of the genetic code which together provide real challenges to our attempts at unraveling the evolutionary sequences underlying life on earth.

Thus, the combination of a very general nineteenth century principle of evolution which offered connections among the variables of time, phylogenetic history, and the diversity of species with the modern biological concepts of the molecular structure and function of the gene, and its place as the evolutionary unit within a population, has yielded a new synthetic theory of evolution. However, our understanding of evolution, particularly how it applies to humans, is also changing. Under these conditions, it is reasonable to expect that the theory, like any other scientific theory, will continue to add new dimensions, particularly as findings from the molecular and population genetic approaches begin to be integrated.

When it comes to the human species, we are just beginning to grapple with questions, for example, on the feedback effect of our knowledge upon our own evolution. This is not necessarily a novel idea. Most anthropologists would acknowledge a feedback relationship between cultural adaptation and biological adaptations in human populations, but we still lack the precise ways to estimate the overall effects of these mutual interactions. We do know these interactions occur on a variety of levels, and there are examples in this book all the way from the relatively simple interactions which probably occur in small groups of social primates using simple tools to the more complex interrelationships implicit in genetic screening and counseling for various chronic genetically based illnesses in the United States and other populations of the world. New orders of complexity can be expected from the real and potential interactions involving birth control, artificial insemination, genetic "engineering," and possibly even the cloning of the cell of an individual into groups of humans with identical genetic constitutions.

This is a multifaceted issue, and all we can do at this time is to suggest some of the factors that must be part of a new theory that will combine and integrate biological and sociocultural dimensions in the same model of human evolution. We have seen in Section I of this book the important changes introduced when social behavior and communication links are considered in a new paradigm. Articles in the other sections suggest additional factors that must be considered. Certainly the development of a new theory accounting for the processes underlying our continued biocultural evolution is one of the great challenges that lie before the field of biological anthropology.

Science and the Citizen
July 1961

Genetic Messenger

The communication system that carries instructions from the genes to the protein assembly lines in the living cell has apparently been discovered. Recent papers in *Nature* from the California Institute of Technology and Harvard University report evidence that the job is performed by an unstable "messenger" form of ribonucleic acid (RNA).

In the past few years it has become almost certain that the blueprints for proteins are recorded in the genetic material proper: deoxyribonucleic acid (DNA). The actual templates on which the amino acid units of proteins are assembled consist of stable RNA and are located in small cellular particles known as ribosomes. (A third type of RNA— "transfer RNA"—brings the amino acid units to the ribosomes.)

The link between blueprint and template, however, is not clear. It has been generally supposed that each gene—*i.e.*, each complete coding sequence in the genetic material—acts as a template in making ribosomes that are specialized for the production of a particular protein. But recently this idea has run into a number of difficulties, chiefly the fact that RNA samples from different ribosomes seem remarkably alike and therefore are not adapted to the manufacture of widely different proteins. Accordingly François Jacob and Jacques Monod of the Pasteur Institute in Paris have suggested that ribosomes are general-purpose factory buildings, so to speak, which can house templates for various proteins. The templates are unstable molecules of RNA, made by the genes, and are used perhaps only once before disintegrating.

While visiting Cal Tech, Jacob, together with Sidney Brenner of the University of Cambridge and Matthew Meselson of Cal Tech, found direct support for this picture in experiments on the colon bacillus (*Escherichia coli*) and a virus that infects it. When *E. coli* cells are infected with virus, the cells stop making their normal protein and begin to manufacture virus protein. According to the old view, they would need new ribosomes to do this; on the messenger hypothesis, however, they would require only a new kind of unstable RNA.

Jacob and his colleagues grew *E. coli* in a medium containing heavy isotopes of carbon, nitrogen and phosphorus. Then they infected the bacteria with virus and transferred them to a "light" medium containing a radioactive tracer. Thus RNA formed by the uninfected cells before transfer would be "heavy," whereas RNA formed by the infected cells would be light and radioactively labeled.

Analysis showed that no new stable RNA or ribosomes formed after infection; the virus made use of pre-existing bacterial ribosomes. What was formed after infection was a new and unstable RNA. The new RNA was found, furthermore, to migrate to the ribosomes, which thereupon began manufacturing a new protein—virus protein.

At Harvard, François Gros and H. Hiatt, visiting from the Pasteur Institute, together with the Harvard workers Walter Gilbert, C. G. Kurland, R. W. Risebrough and James D. Watson, performed a similar trick with uninfected colon bacilli. They exposed growing cells to a brief labeling "pulse" (10 to 20 seconds long) in a medium containing radioactive precursors of RNA and found that the radioactivity was incorporated first in unstable RNA molecules and not in ribosomes.

Science and the Citizen
February 1962

Breaking the Code

Further progress has been made in understanding the process that enables RNA (ribonucleic acid) to direct the synthesis of proteins within the cell. Evidence that a special form of RNA, called messenger RNA, represents a one-to-one recoding of information carried by the genes is presented in the article by Jerard Hurwitz and J. J. Furth beginning on page 41 of this issue of SCIENTIFIC AMERICAN. The next transcription of the code, from RNA to protein, is more complicated. The code in RNA is carried by four nitrogenous bases: adenine (A), uracil (U), guanine (G) and cytosine (C). Proteins, in contrast, are codelike chains of molecular subunits, comparable to letters, that can be any of 20-odd different amino acids. In some way the four-letter RNA code is transcribed into a 20-letter protein code.

Last August, at the Fifth International Congress of Biochemistry in Moscow, Marshall W. Nirenberg reported how he and J. Heinrich Matthaei had found that a synthetic RNA molecule made of repeating units of a single base, uracil, stimulated the formation of a synthetic protein composed of repeating units of a single amino acid, phenylalanine. The work, done at the National Institute of Arthritis and Metabolic Diseases, marked the first major break in the coding problem. . . .

Nirenberg and Matthaei have found evidence, however, that the code is "degenerate," meaning that a single amino acid can be designated by two or more code units. Thus leucine is incorporated by molecules containing either U and C or U and G.

Science and the Citizen
July 1962

Universal Genetic Code?

Unquestionably the most exciting development in biology in the past year has been the breaking of the genetic code. The code is embodied in the hereditary molecule deoxyribonucleic acid (DNA), which carries the plans for the thousands of proteins manufactured by the living cell. These plans are expressed in a "four-letter alphabet" in which the letters are the four molecular units called bases contained in DNA. The break came originally from experiments in which extracts of colon bacilli were combined with synthetic ribonucleic acid (RNA) containing known amounts of the four bases. This RNA substituted for "messenger RNA," which normally carries the genetic message from DNA to the ribosomes, the cellular particles where proteins are assembled. With the code for one species of bacteria deciphered, the question arose whether or not the same genetic language would apply to all living cells.

Striking evidence that the code may indeed be universal is reported in the May issue of the *Proceedings of the National Academy of Sciences.* It has been found that when the ribosomes of the colon bacillus are supplied with RNA extracted from the tobacco mosaic virus, the ribosomes synthesize a protein that is almost precisely like the protein units that compose the jacket of the virus. Evidently the bacterial system is able to "read" correctly the hereditary message embodied in the RNA of a virus that normally functions in a totally different biological environment, that provided by cells of the tobacco plant.

The experiment represented a collaboration between Akira Tsugita and Heinz L. Fraenkel-Conrat of the Virus Laboratory at the University of California and Marshall W. Nirenberg and J. Heinrich Matthaei of the National Institute of Arthritis and Metabolic Diseases. Nirenberg and Matthaei were leaders in breaking the genetic code.

Science and the Citizen
September 1962

Genetic Lock

How are the genes turned on and off? Every living cell contains in its chromosomes, coded in molecules of DNA (deoxyribonucleic acid), all the genetic information needed for its replication. Yet even in single-celled organisms such as bacteria not all the information is utilized at all times in the life cycle, and in multicellular organisms most cells become specialized and therefore need very little of the total amount of information. A possible mechanism for turning off the information flow has been suggested by Ru-chih C. Huang and James Bonner of the California Institute of Technology, who had set out to solve another puzzle: the role of the protein that also forms part of chromosomes. Writing in *Proceedings of the National Academy of Sciences,* they propose that the protein serves to lock and unlock the genes.

Huang and Bonner extracted the chromatin (chromosomal substance) from embryo pea plants and found that it is about one-third DNA, one-third a protein called histone, one-sixth protein other than histone and one-sixth RNA (ribonucleic acid). The nonhistone protein includes the enzyme RNA polymerase, which facilitates the synthesis of "messenger" RNA. This substance is the direct product of genetic activity; its role is to transfer from DNA to other parts of the cell the instructions for the synthesis of specific proteins.

When suitable "building blocks" (riboside triphosphates) are added to isolated chromatin, messenger RNA is synthesized, but at a slow rate. If the histone fraction is removed from the chromatin, however, the rate of RNA synthesis increases fivefold. From this and other observations Huang and Bonner have concluded that the function of histone is to bind DNA and block the expression of particular genes, depending on the needs of a particular cell at a particular time.

Science and the Citizen
January 1963

Curb on Degeneracy

In recent discussions of the genetic code the term "degeneracy" frequently appears. Since it implies ambiguity in the meaning of code words, it suggests a certain looseness, or nonspecificity, in the process used by the cell to construct proteins. Recent work by Seymour Benzer, Bernard Weisblum and Robert W. Holley at Purdue University has uncovered features of this process that may limit some of the ambiguity.

The genetic code resides in the DNA (deoxyribonucleic acid) that constitutes the genes of a cell. The code is transmitted to the sites of protein synthesis by "messenger" RNA (ribonucleic acid), which uses as code letters four bases: A, U, G and C (adenine, uracil, guanine and cytosine). It appears that some combination of three of these letters supplies the code word for each of the 20 amino acids, the subunits that link together to form polypeptide chains, or proteins. A doublet code would provide only 16 code words; a triplet code yields $4 \times 4 \times 4$, or 64, words. Since 64 are more than the 20 needed, it was predicted that more than one word might specify a given amino acid. This is one possible type of degeneracy, and it was subsequently found experimentally. For example, the amino acid leucine is coded by either of two triplets: GUU or CUU (the actual sequence is not yet known).

Benzer and his associates looked for the physical mechanism behind this degeneracy. Inside the cell the amino acids are conveyed to the site of protein synthesis by a special soluble form of RNA designated sRNA. For each of the 20 amino acids there is at least one specific sRNA. It had been known that leucine can be recognized and transported by two kinds of sRNA, which have slight molecular differences. Benzer and his colleagues conjectured that one of the leucine sRNA's may respond to the GUU code and the other to the CUU code. They found that in the colon bacillus, at least, this is the case. In other words, coding specificity in the sRNA may compensate for lack of specificity in the messenger RNA.

There is, however, a second form of degeneracy wherein a given triplet codes for two or more amino acids. For example, the triplet UUU codes primarily for phenylalanine, but it seems also to code to a lesser degree for leucine. The Pur-

due workers found that the form of leucine sRNA that responds to GUU also responds somewhat to UUU. The implications of this ambiguity are still being studied.

Writing in the *Proceedings of the National Academy of Sciences*, Benzer and his colleagues speculate that "some degree of degeneracy may confer increased survival value upon a cell, by reducing the number of nonsense coding units, i.e., those that correspond to no amino acid. A mutation that changes one amino acid in a polypeptide chain to another amino acid is less likely to be deleterious than one which completely impedes the completion of the growing chain."

Science and the Citizen
August 1963

Nongenetic Genetic Code?

Evidence is rapidly accumulating that all living organisms use the same "language" in making protein molecules from instructions coded in the giant molecules of DNA (deoxyribonucleic acid). This in turn introduces the surprising possibility that the translation of the genetic code may not be genetically determined. The possibility was put forward by I. Bernard Weinstein of the Columbia University College of Physicians and Surgeons at the recent Symposium on Quantitative Biology in Cold Spring Harbor, N.Y. . . .

From the outset of the coding work it was a matter of great interest to discover whether or not a given codon would have the same meaning in an organism other than the colon bacillus. It was generally thought that the dictionaries would differ among species and that the difference would be greater the greater the evolutionary gap between organisms.

At Cold Spring Harbor, Weinstein reported results in protein-synthesizing systems obtained from several kinds of cells, including the protozoon *Chlamydomonas*, rat liver cells and mouse tumor cells. All the amino acids tested so far (six) are identified by the same groups of codons in all the systems.

If the code is indeed universal, as these and other results suggest, it implies that it has been fixed throughout most of organic evolution, in other words, that it is not subject to mutation. This may mean either that no change can produce an improvement, which seems rather unlikely, or that transfer RNA's can make only certain fixed associations. It had been thought, for example, that a transfer RNA that delivers amino acid A to codon A in the colon bacillus might in another species, as a result of genetic modification in the transfer RNA, deliver amino acid A to some other codon, say codon D. If such a modification cannot take place, the pairing of amino acid and codon must be subject to constraints for which there is no provision in present theory.

Science and the Citizen
May 1965

Structure of a Genetic Molecule

For the first time the complete sequence of nucleotide subunits in a nucleic acid has been determined. The nucleic acid is the ribonucleic acid alanine transfer RNA, a long-chain molecule that has 77 nucleotide subunits. Each nucleotide consists of a "base" (a small group of atoms including atoms of nitrogen), a ribose sugar and a phosphate group. The role of alanine transfer RNA is to combine with the amino acid alanine and deliver it to the site in the living cell where it can be linked up with other amino acids—each transported by its own specific transfer RNA—to form a protein molecule. The determination of the sequence of nucleotides in alanine transfer RNA was accomplished after six years of work by a team of Cornell University and Department of Agriculture investigators headed by Robert W. Holley of Cornell. Holley's co-workers were Jean Apgar, George A. Everett, James T. Madison, Mark Marquisee, Susan H. Merrill, John Robert Penswick and Ada Zamir.

Determination of the nucleotide sequence in alanine transfer RNA opens the way to the analysis of the other transfer RNA's, and of the still longer molecules of "messenger" RNA, which comprise from a few hundred to a few thousand nucleotides. Messenger RNA transcribes from the cell's repository of genetic information—coded in deoxyribonucleic acid (DNA)—the code-word sequence for each protein manufactured by the cell.

Science and the Citizen
April 1967

Common Code

The cells of the colon bacillus, the cells of the South African clawed toad

and the cells of the guinea pig all translate the genetic code in essentially the same way. There are, however, slight differences in emphasis, which might be regarded as "dialects" in a common genetic language. These findings, representing the most comprehensive evidence yet published that the genetic code is the same in all organisms, are reported in *Science* by Richard E. Marshall, C. Thomas Caskey and Marshall Nirenberg of the National Institutes of Health. . . .

A typical finding of the new report from Nirenberg's laboratory is that cells of the South African clawed toad (*Xenopus laevis*) and of the guinea pig also translate GCU, GCC, GCA and GCG as alanine, but with different levels of response. *Xenopus* responds almost equally well to the first three codons but only very weakly to GCG, the codon to which *E. coli* responds most strongly. Guinea pig cells respond about equally well to GCU and GCA, less well to GCC and resemble *Xenopus* cells in responding least well to GCG.

Xenopus, an amphibian, was selected for this investigation because of the possibility that the striking physical changes that occur in an amphibian organism during its life cycle may be related to changes in the response to different codons at different times or in different organs. This possibility was given a limited test by comparing skeletal-muscle cells of *Xenopus* with liver cells. Nirenberg and his co-workers found no difference in the response of the two types of cell to RNA codons.

The hypothesis supported by these experiments is "that the [genetic] code became frozen by the time that organisms as complex as bacteria had evolved," which may have been more than three billion years ago. Nirenberg and his colleagues suggest that the differences found in the way bacterial, amphibian and mammalian cells respond to various codons "may reflect changes in the codon recognition apparatus, acquired after cells had evolved, which may enable cells to store additional genetic information and become more highly differentiated."

Science and the Citizen
November 1969

The Genetic Code (Reconfirmed)

Investigators at the University of Cambridge have reached the long-sought goal of associating a specific sequence of amino acid units in a protein with the sequence of "letters" in the genetic message—a molecule of RNA—that supplies the instructions for the protein's manufacture. The experiment confirms the correctness of the genetic code dictionary, which was compiled by using the four RNA bases—adenine (A), uracil (U), guanine (G) and cytosine (C)—in the various triplet combinations called codons, to see which of the 20 amino acids they would direct into protein-like molecules in a cell-free system. In this way a specific "meaning," or amino acid equivalent, was assigned to 61 of the 64 possible codons from AAA to UUU. Three of the codons have noncoding functions.

The Cambridge workers (J. M. Adams, P. G. N. Jeppesen, Frederick Sanger and B. G. Barrell) identified a sequence of 57 bases out of a total of 3,300 found in the RNA that carries the hereditary message in the bacterial virus designated R17. The 57-base sequence was found to be part of the cistron, or gene, that specifies one of the three proteins synthesized by the virus: the coat protein. The amino acid sequence of this protein had previously been worked out by Klaus Weber of Harvard University. If one knows this sequence, one can, with the aid of the genetic code dictionary, write down all the sequences of codons that will code it. There is more than one possible sequence because nearly every amino acid can be represented by more than one codon.

Particular interest centers on the six amino acids that appear twice in the sequence of 57. Would the virus use the same codon for each repeated amino acid or a different one? It turns out that two of the six are specified both times by the same codon. The other four, however, are each specified by two different codons. Thus the amino acid serine is coded for by UCC and UCG; asparagine is represented by CAU and AAC, threonine by CCU and ACG, and alanine by ACU and GCG. . . .

Science and the Citizen
April 1968

The Genetic Code (Concluded)

The quest to assign a meaning to all 64 triplet "words" in the genetic code is apparently ended with the finding that the triplet UGA is a "period" that results in the termination of a protein chain. Thus UGA plays the same role as two other triplets, UAG and UAA, that had previously been found to terminate protein synthesis. The other 61 triplets, or codons, designate one or more of the 20 amino acids the living cell links in various sequences to make protein molecules.

The letters U, G and A stand respectively for the nitrogenous bases uracil, guanine and adenine; another base, cytosine (C), is the fourth in the set of four "letters" that can be assembled into 64 different triplet sequences. When they are attached to a backbone consisting of alternating units of ribose sugar and phosphate, the four bases, in various triplet sequences, form molecules of messenger ribonucleic acid (messenger RNA). These molecules transcribe the genetic message of the genes and convey it to the site of protein synthesis. A single molecule of messenger RNA, however, usually carries the information needed for making more than one kind of protein molecule. The question therefore arose: What is the signal, presumably embodied in a codon, that tells the cell machinery when one protein molecule is finished and another is to be started?

A study of mutants of the bacterium *Escherichia coli*, conducted in many laboratories, finally supplied the answer. It was found that after mutation the messenger RNA for a particular protein sometimes formed two short protein chains instead of one long chain. This happened when one of the codons in the messenger RNA mutated to become UAG or UAA. Prior to mutation the codon might have been any other triplet differing in the first, second or third position, for example GAG, UGG or UAU. Before mutation these triplets specified a particular amino acid; after mutation to UAG or UAA they no longer specified any amino acid and thus the protein chain terminated. UAG and UAA were termed nonsense codons.

Last year workers at the Laboratory of Molecular Biology at the University of Cambridge found evidence that the unassigned triplet UGA also acted as a nonsense codon, but they were not quite sure that it was fully equivalent to UAG or UAA as a chain-terminator. This was subsequently demonstrated by David Zipser of Columbia University. He produced *E. coli* mutants in which the change of one letter in a particular codon led to the formation of a single long protein chain instead of two short ones. By analyzing his results Zipser could show that the mutation had changed UGA into UGG (the codon for the amino acid tryptophan) and that UGA therefore must have acted as a chain-terminator.

Science and the Citizen
January 1970

Isolated Gene

The goal of isolating a single gene from the 3,000 to 5,000 genes that embody the complete genetic message in a bacterial cell has been accomplished at the Harvard Medical School. The isolated gene, designated *z*, is one of three genes in a sequence (known as an operon) that specifies the synthesis of three enzymes that enable the bacterium *Escherichia coli* to metabolize the sugar lactose. The sequence is called the β-galactosidase operon or the *lac* operon.

When an operon is translated into the protein molecules of enzymes, the translation of the last gene in the series is dependent on the translation of the preceding genes. The *z* gene is the first of three genes in the *lac* operon. Each gene is closely associated with two smaller genetic units, an operator and a promoter, that regulate the expression of the gene. The Harvard workers have determined that the helix of DNA constituting the *z* gene incorporates 3,700 pairs of bases, and that the operator and promoter region attached to it embodies only 410 base pairs. For purposes of comparison, all the genes of *E. coli* form a DNA molecule some three million base pairs long.

To separate the *lac* operon from all the others in the DNA of *E. coli*, the Harvard group employed the services of two "transducing" bacteriophages: bacterial viruses that multiply inside the *E. coli* cell and attach a portion of the cell's DNA to their own much smaller molecule of DNA as they replicate. Two phages, called λ*plac*5 and φ80*plac*1, routinely incorporate the *lac* operon in their DNA. (The *p* indicates that they form clearly visible plaques, or clear areas, when they grow on a culture of *E. coli*.)

The DNA normally present in phages as well as in bacteria is a double-strand helix. One strand is the "sense" strand that is transcribed into messenger RNA and ultimately translated into proteins; the other, or "nonsense," strand is not transcribed. It had been discovered earlier that the two phages λ*plac*5 and φ80*plac*1 insert the *lac* operon into their DNA molecules in opposite orientations. It also happens that because of differing base composition one strand of the DNA in each phage is distinctly heavier than the other, so that the two strands can be separated by centrifugation. When this is done, the heavy strand of one phage contains the sequence of "sensible" bases in the *lac* operon whereas the heavy strand of the other phage contains the complementary, or nonsense, sequence. To reconstitute a stretch of DNA containing both strands of the *lac* operon it is necessary only to bring the heavy strands of the two phages together; the complementary bases then spontaneously pair up. The remaining bases in the two strands, not being complementary, remain separated. The experiment was undertaken on the hypothesis that there would be no complementary stretches in the two heavy strands of the two phages except those provided by the sense and nonsense bases of the *lac* operon. The hypothesis was confirmed.

Electron micrographs of the reconstituted DNA molecule show a double-strand structure whose length (1.4 millimicrons) corresponds to that of the *z* gene of the *lac* operon together with its promoter and operator. At each end of the reconstituted gene the unattached strands form bushy tails. In other micrographs the tails have been chopped off by enzymes that attack single strands of DNA but not double strands, leaving the isolated gene standing alone.

The way is now clear to study in cell-free systems how individual genes are transcribed into messenger RNA and then translated into proteins. With the help of other transducing phages it should soon be possible to isolate a variety of other operons. The Harvard group that achieved the first isolation of a gene was headed by Jon Beckwith; his associates were Jim Shapiro, Larry Eron, Lorne MacHattie, Garret Ihler and Karin Ippen.

Science and the Citizen
January 1971

Two Genes, One Enzyme

Two bacterial enzymes that normally occur in the form of independent protein molecules have been fused into one large protein molecule by mutations that have the effect of erasing the chemical "punctuation mark" that ordinarily separates the two genes directing the synthesis of the enzymes. The fused molecule combines the distinctive chemical functions of the two original enzymes, both of which participate in the synthesis of histidine, one of the 20 amino acids found in proteins. The laboratory demonstration that gene fusion can lead to the fusion of separate protein molecules suggests how large enzymes with several functions may have arisen in the course of evolution.

The gene-fusion experiment, which is described in *Nature,* was performed by John R. Roth of the University of California at Berkeley in collaboration with Joseph Yourno and Tadahiko Kohno of the Brookhaven National Laboratory. The two genes fused in the experiment were the second and third genes ("*hisD*" and "*hisC*") in a sequence of nine genes whose enzyme products enable *Salmonella typhimurium* to synthesize histidine. The nine-gene sequence is known as the histidine operon. Each gene is specified by a particular sequence of bases in the linear molecule of deoxyribonucleic acid (DNA) that embodies the total genetic message of the bacterium. The message contains instructions for synthesizing the more than 4,000 enzymes the cell requires in order to survive and replicate.

The genetic message can be parsed into the sequences of three bases called codons, the great majority of which stand for a particular amino acid when the gene is subsequently translated into a protein. A few codons, however, provide the punctuation that divides the genetic message into separate genes, thus informing the cell's machinery for making proteins where one molecule ends and another begins.

It appears that the *hisD* and *hisC* genes were fused as a consequence of two closely spaced mutations, one on each side of the punctuation mark separating the two genes. The first mutation was a deletion that removed a "letter" from the genetic message; the second mutation inserted an extraneous letter. Such mutations are called "frame-shift" mutations since they cause succeeding bases to be "read" in incorrect groups of three.

In this case the first mutation caused the punctuation mark to be misread and thus to go unrecognized. The second mutation restored the proper reading frame immediately after the unrecognized punctuation mark. As a result all of the *hisD* gene up to the first mutation was read correctly, as was all of the *hisC* gene beyond the second mutation. The intervening codons were evidently translated into a short sequence of amino acids capable of acting as a bridge to join the two enzymes, each essentially complete and therefore still functionally active.

Among the articles selected for this section, "Charles Lyell" by Loren Eiseley offers a most enlightening description of historical processes in science. By introducing us to the ideas, events, and personalities that influenced Darwin's thinking, it gives us an unusual insight into the nature of his discovery. What is particularly useful about this article is that it not only provides an historical model for understanding and interpreting the origins of evolutionary theory, but also gives valuable insights into current issues of human evolution.

Several themes in Eiseley's article also appear in "The Origin of Darwinism" by C. D. Darlington, notably the concept of a *Scala Naturae,* or as Arthur Lovejoy (1936) has called it, "The Great Chain of Being," in which every living organism is assumed to have a fixed place within the natural order. The concept of "The Great Chain of Being" is the supposed logical extension of the biblical explanation of creation, which suggests that since all groups of non-human organisms were created in one day, they must all bear fixed relationships to each other, and the groups must be unchanging. Within this framework, useful taxonomic methods for the classification of species were developed in the eighteenth century by Carolus Linnaeus and John Ray. Geological and faunal discontinuities were explained as evidence of catastrophes, such as the great flood recorded in the Bible. Together the Eiseley and Darlington articles explain both the bases of these biblical concepts and how the scientific world eventually discredited them.

During the years between the early 1930's and the early 1950's, the concept of evolution was reshaped by a variety of important discoveries in population genetics. Particularly important in these advances was the use of *Drosophila,* the common fruit fly, and other ordinary organisms whose short life cycles permitted the breeding and cross-breeding of many generations in a relatively short period. Many of the principles mentioned in Theodosius Dobzhansky's excellent and perceptive article "The Genetic Basis of Evolution" were involved in the development of the synthetic theory of evolution in which all of the mechanisms including gene drift, flows, mutation, and selection were qualitatively and quantitatively described. This theory led many physical anthropologists to investigate the possibility that various simple Mendelian traits could be used to distinguish quantitatively the evolved differences among human populations. For example, William Boyd's book (1950) on human blood groups (such as ABO and Rh) suggested a new method of evaluating serological differences for which the genetic modes of inheritance were understood. This biochemical approach to human variation is still very important methodologically and theoretically in the interpretation of similarities and differences among various human populations. (See Cavalli-Sforza's "Genetic Drift in an Italian Population.")

The development of this synthetic theory of evolution produced a rapid movement in physical anthropology away from concepts of typology, based on the study of modal types or averages, toward concepts utilizing statistical evaluation of the actual variation in naturally occurring human populations. This transition marked the change from scientific dependence on "ideal" types and average types to a dependence on more sophisticated statistical approaches that take into account all the variation that is naturally present in a breeding, or Mendelian, population. In other words, emphasis was shifted from the descriptive approach to human variation, in which average morphology and natural selection are the dominant modes of explanation, to a population approach, in which quantitative data on gene frequencies in Mendelian populations are analyzed according to the mathematical rules describing gene mutation, drift, flow, and selection. The application of a population approach to problems of morphology and genetics prepared the way for the modern use of statistical analyses of biochemical, physiological, and morphological variations to detect the course, conditions, and rates of human evolution.

In reading F. H. C. Crick's article "The Genetic Code: III" we should be aware of the tremendous strides that preceded this now classic work on molecular biology since the initial discovery of the structure of DNA and RNA in the last two decades. Perhaps one of the most exciting periods in this new science occurred between 1960 and 1970 when we saw the elucidation of the genetic code as well as of the structure and function of messenger, transfer, and ribosomal RNA in the operation of protein synthesis of a cell. It was also during this time that the first genes were isolated. Now it is possible, for example, to isolate the exact DNA base substitution responsible for human diseases, such as sickle cell anemia. Victor A. McKusick's article "The Mapping of Human Chromosomes" relates how we have been able to begin to integrate the knowledge of molecular biology with our knowledge of the structural organization and function of the human chromosomes. The bridges between our knowledge of genetics and evolution are partly completed. A recent lecture by McKusick informs us of the latest developments.

As is apparent in the Science and the Citizen sections, our knowledge about the genetic code and the structure and function of the cell poses crucial questions for our concept of evolution. For example, in a controversial article in *Science*, Jukes and King (1968) suggested that given the large variation in hemoglobin structure found throughout human populations, and that only a few of these aberrant hemoglobin molecules seem to have any selective advantages, the rest could be accounted for by a model of non-Darwinian genetic change without natural selection. Other questions raised by the new findings are of an even more profound nature. For example, what is the meaning for life on earth of a genetic code that is apparently universal in all organisms? What does it tell us about the age and origins of life? Is the "degeneracy of the code" really ambiguous or in terms of information theory is it highly redundant, resulting in a reduction in the unstable effects of random error in transcription? Can we use the differential structure of DNA among the primates to map the exact genetic differences between man and his nearest living relatives? What are the relationships between the information stored in the memory of each individual's central nervous system and the genetic information transferred at conception? In human populations what are the adaptive and evolutionary effects of sharing linguistic codes, and how are they analogous or even supplementary to genetic codes? Clearly, we have the potential, now more than ever, to ask new and exciting questions about the knowledge we have already accumulated.

When our knowledge of genetics is applied to the human species, as Christopher Wills has done in "Genetic Load," the immense advantages of human diversity become clear. In taxonomic terms the human species is both *panmictic*, meaning that breeding takes place between individuals of different populations, and *polytypic*, meaning that the species has a series of subspecies. The combination of these two factors has produced an unusually wide range of human variation, and the potential variation of the different combinations of genes present in the human population is astronomical. If all mutation were to stop, the current genetic variation present in the genomes (genetic constitutions) of the human species could probably provide enough phenotypic variation for several hundred generations before further mutations would be needed to provide new variations for natural selection and evolution to occur. Wills, in a recent letter, comments on genetic diversity and offers new evidence of its importance.

> The nature of man's genetic endowment cannot be understood by looking at one or a few humans. Rather, the pool of genes possessed by the entire species must be examined and compared with the gene pools of other species. This article attempts to deal with this diversity of genetic information, and to give some understanding of how natural selection operates. Selection removes harmful genes, more or less rapidly according to how harmful they are and whether or not they are dominant. Useful genes and combinations of genes are selected for. The article concentrates on the nature of these useful genes.
>
> Since the publication of the article, we have been able to use the computer program mentioned briefly in it to predict the behavior of one particular pair of alleles which just happens to be the pair illustrated in the color picture at the beginning of the article. This prediction led to experiments in which we inbred flies carrying these alleles. The result was the removal of other variants, making most of the flies' genomes homozygous *except* for the alleles in question. It was then possible to enhance the selective forces acting on these alleles to the point where they could be detected. *Heterozygotes* for these alleles in the otherwise inbred population were fitter than *homozygotes*—but only when the substrate for the enzyme was added to the medium, causing a specific stress. We now have preliminary evidence that another enzyme system also acts in this way. If this phenomenon should prove to be widespread, it would explain the occurrence of such large numbers of alternative forms of enzymes in natural populations, and how they can be held there without adding greatly to the genetic load.

> *Christopher Wills, November 1973*

James F. Crow's article "Ionizing Radiation and Evolution" discusses several important issues relevant to genetic variation. Particularly important is the clear danger of radiation as a potential mutagen and the complexity of calculating its effects on the individual and the population. For example, in humans we should calculate both its genetic effects on the gonads and its effects on the somatic cells. The latter may effect the individual's rate of aging and adaptability to various environmental threats, including his susceptibility to certain malignancies and various other diseases. Finally, we must consider the relative role of mutation as a source of evolutionary change in the evolution of man and the effects of human evolution on the ecology of other species of organisms both in the past and the present.

Traditionally, biological anthropologists have relied on the concept of natural selection to describe the phylogenetic evolution of the hominids. When it came to explaining differences in blood group frequencies, however, questions arose concerning the role of natural selection. Biological anthropologists like William Laughlin (1963) demonstrated that genetic drift could account for some variation, particularly in the Aleutian Islands off Alaska where clear geographic factors separated populations and small population size was the rule. Moreover, it has become increasingly apparent that much of human evolution occurred during periods in which human populations were small enough to be influenced by genetic drift. In the article entitled "Genetic Drift in an Italian Population" Luigi Luca Cavalli-Sforza demonstrates that genetic drift can account for a significant evolutionary change in a series of small village populations in the Puma Valley that are isolated by mountains. At least two important elements emerge from the approach developed by Cavalli-Sforza's group. First, the use of demographic data demonstrates the critical role of migration in this evolutionary process, which in turn is largely determined by sociocultural factors. Secondly, the use of computer simulation methods, which permit experimentation based on real data, offer an important means of calculating the possible outcomes of genetic change attributable to gene drift as well as opening up the field to new ways of using computer models for simulating the evolution of human populations. The results of this approach strongly suggest that with the application of more sophisticated demographic methods and new computer simulation models incorporating our increasing knowledge about human genetics, we could begin to ask new questions about the role of genetic drift in human evolution.

Science and the Citizen
July 1965

Intelligent Mongoloid

Down's syndrome, or mongolism, is a congenital malformation characterized by mental retardation and certain physical signs; it has been associated since 1959 with specific anomalies of the chromosomes, the structures in the cell nucleus that contain the genetic material. Now investigators at the University of Alabama Medical Center have discovered a patient with the physical but not the mental stigmata of mongolism and with a partial form of one of the typical chromosomal anomalies. Further study of this case and similar ones might locate the genes responsible for the various aspects of mongolism.

The error most commonly seen in the cells of mongoloids is "trisomy": a small chromosome, No. 21 of the 46 in the normal human cell, is present in three copies instead of the usual two (one from each parent). The extra No. 21 material thus implicated in mongolism can also be present in the form of a "translocation": one chromosome No. 21 is attached to a different chromosome, ordinarily one of the group numbered 13 to 15. A "carrier" parent of a translocation mongoloid has only 45 chromosomes, the translocated material being compensated for by the absence of one No. 21 chromosome. When the random sorting of genetic material during germ-cell formation brings two normal No. 21 chromosomes into the fertilized egg along with a translocation chromosome, however, there is an "essential trisomy" of No. 21, and mongolism results.

The patient described (in *The New England Journal of Medicine*) by Sara C. Finley, Wayne H. Finley, Clarence J. Rosecrans and Carey Phillips is a six-year-old boy with the special hand and finger anatomy and facial characteristics of Down's syndrome. Nevertheless, he is alert and articulate, and his IQ—variously scored as 86, 82 and 85—is substantially above the highest previously reported for mongoloid children. Chromosome analysis showed a translocation of what appeared to be the 21st chromosome to a member of the 13-to-15 group. Analysis of cells taken from the patient's normal mother, grandmother and sister, however, showed 46 chromosomes, not 45. There was a tiny fragment, a "partial 21," in addition to the normal No. 21. In other words, only a part of chromosome No. 21 is translocated in this patient and in his carrier relatives; he is therefore trisomic for only a part of the chromosome. If the Alabama workers could be sure just what part of the chromosome is present in excess, they would know what part of the chromosome is responsible for the physical—as distinct from the mental—signs of Down's syndrome.

11 The Origin of Darwinism

by C. D. Darlington
May 1959

Who were the pioneers of the modern concept of evolution? Charles Darwin did not give them the credit they deserved, but his failure to do so ironically paved the way for the acceptance of the concept

In November, 1859, there appeared a book which within a few days convinced quite a large number of those who read it that the ideas they had cherished of the origin and nature of man were false. The book—Charles Darwin's *Origin of Species*—was an unpretentious account of all aspects of life, which could be understood by educated laymen. It attempted to show that all living things were derived by descent and gradual transformation from common origins many millions of years ago. Hence, to the dismay of serious Christians, the Biblical story of Creation seemed in danger of falling to the ground.

The partisans of Creation, both professors and bishops, counterattacked with vigor, and a bitter struggle ensued. In about 10 years' time, however, the educated world was effectively converted to Darwin's view of what had come to be called evolution and was now called Darwinism. The defeated party retired to lick its wounds in quiet places.

Not all the wounds, however, were suffered on one side. Two shafts of criticism struck Darwin more directly than the outside world was allowed to know. They touched his particular theory that evolution took place by natural selection, a process analogous to the artificial selection which plant and animal breeders were practicing with such great success at that time. The first criticism asserted that Darwin's thesis was not true; the second, that it was not new. Such criticisms are raised against all revolutionary hypotheses, but both of these were serious and well informed.

As to the second criticism, it is often said that it matters little whether the theory was truly Darwin's invention. We owe it to him that the world was brought to believe in evolution; we ought to be duly grateful and leave it at that. If a centenary is an occasion merely for acknowledging a debt, the matter could be allowed to stand. But I think it is an occasion for a more useful exercise. Here is a theory that released thinking men from the spell of a superstition, one of the most overpowering that has ever enslaved mankind. We should have no superstition about how such a spell came to be broken.

The assertion that natural selection was not true, or rather would not work, came from several sources. It came most cogently from one Fleeming Jenkin, professor of engineering at Edinburgh University. In 1867 Jenkin pointed out that if all hereditary differences blended on crossing, as Darwin assumed, then any variation that arose would diminish in importance in each succeeding generation and no new variation could persist long enough to be selected by the process that Darwin proposed. Now this was not a criticism of natural selection. It was a criticism of Darwin's notions of heredity. And it was a perfectly sound one for, as Gregor Mendel showed, differences do not blend on crossing. They remain intact and reappear in full strength in later generations. Yet Darwin took it as a criticism of natural selection. Accordingly, in succeeding editions of the *Origin of Species*, he shifted his ground. He began to suggest that direct adaptation of the organism to its environment brought changes in heredity, and that this direct action played a part, along with natural selection, in the transformation of species.

This shift of ground was noticed by Darwin's critics. Darwin responded by calling their attention to something they had overlooked. In the first edition of the *Origin of Species* he had mentioned twice that the effects of the "external conditions of life"—both the direct effects of climate and food and such indirect effects as the use and disuse of organs—were perhaps in some extremely small degree inherited. Change was partly directed before it took place as well as partly selected after it took place. In other words, Darwin had prepared a line of retreat against the possibility that natural selection might be found untenable. He now prudently took this line.

As time went on Darwin relied more and more on a double or mixed theory of evolution: selection plus direction. When he came to write *The Descent of Man* 10 years after the appearance of the *Origin of Species*, the full advantages of this mixed hypothesis began to be felt.

The critical question in *The Descent of Man* was that of the evolution of man's moral, spiritual or religious character. By this time there was nothing in man's physical or intellectual character that could not follow the principles of animal evolution. But on the moral question Darwin had to weigh a risk. The memory of Joseph Priestley's experience was still fresh. Priestley had made incautious statements on religion, and in 1794 his library had been burned and he had been forced to emigrate to the U. S. Darwin also had to consider the feelings of his wife, a doubly devoted woman, who took her religion quite as seriously as she took his work. He was saved by his mixed theory of evolution.

On the one hand, Darwin argued, any intelligent animal with social instincts could by selection come to develop a moral sense, a feeling of duty, a conscience. Selection by itself is enough to produce the moral sense. A dog, he points out, can be bred and trained so that it has a feeling of guilt when it fails to do what it "ought" to have done. So much for the dog. But when Darwin sums up his views and comes to man, he hedges. "Social qualities," he suggests, "were no doubt acquired by the progenitors of man . . . through natural selection aided by inherited habit." And later: "It is not improbable that virtuous tendencies may through long practice be inherited." Finally he concludes that social instincts, which afford the basis for the development of the moral sense, may be "safely attributed" to natural selection. But "the moral qualities are advanced either directly or indirectly, much more through the effects of habit, the reasoning powers, religion, etc."

Here we see the most dangerous passage in all of Darwin's works. For at first glance it seems to mean so much. But when you have read it two or three times you see that it means just what you want it to mean. If you are a rationalist, you will suppose that the blind forces of nature—even an element of chance—working through natural selection produced the moral qualities of man. And if you are devout, you will suppose that man has acquired his spiritual gifts under divine guidance, inspired teachers having instructed him in the principles of religion most pleasing to his Creator. Was it an accident that Darwin's conclusion meant just what every reader wanted it to mean? I think not. Darwin used the same ambiguity in his private letters.

Darwinism, therefore, began as a theory that evolution could be explained by natural selection. It ended as a theory that evolution could be explained just as you would like it to be explained. This brings us back again to the second criticism: that Darwin's theory was not new; that it was not even his own.

The story of the slow growth of evolutionary theory has been told often. The best account that is friendly to Darwin was written by Henry Fairfield Osborn of the American Museum of Natural History in *From the Greeks to Darwin*, published in many editions beginning in 1894. The best unfriendly account was written by Samuel Butler, the author of *Erewhon*, in four books published between 1877 and 1885. The most unreliable account that ever will be written is undoubtedly the "Historical Sketch" which Darwin himself wrote and appended to the third edition of the *Origin of Species* in response to the appeals of his friends and the challenge of his enemies. This reads like the confession of an unhappy man, written under fearful stress. The story of the origin of Darwinism has not been written in the 20th century. It has not yet been written in the cooler, clearer light of what genetics has taught us and of what each evolutionist in turn has said and done. When the evidence is reviewed in this light, it takes on a living continuity that has not been noticed before.

Much of the story must remain in dispute. But the important steps, as they now appear, can be briefly made out.

During the 18th century a cleavage of opinion developed between those who held to the Biblical story of Creation and those who assumed some kind of evolution. In general the idea of evolution was familiar to students of what was already called natural history, but the evolutionary point of view had to be expressed with caution. Governments almost everywhere wished to maintain the religious beliefs of the uneducated masses. This was particularly true outside France after 1789. But it was possible for Benjamin Franklin in the U. S. to refer to man as "a tool-making animal," and it was possible for Lord Monboddo at the same time in Scotland to suppose that man had formerly walked on all fours and was to be reckoned as belonging to the same species as the orangutan.

It was in these circumstances, between 1789 and 1803, that Erasmus Darwin wrote a series of works, in prose and verse, in which he included statements of his view of evolution. These statements attempt to answer the two obvious questions. First, are all living things in truth descended by transformation from a single ancestor? Second, how could they have been transformed?

In favor of the evolution of animals

ERASMUS DARWIN, grandfather of Charles, originated many central ideas in evolutionary theory. Of him Charles said merely: "He anticipated the erroneous ideas of Lamarck."

from "one living filament" Erasmus Darwin assembled the evidence of embryology, comparative anatomy, systematics, geographical distribution and, so far as man is concerned, the facts of history and of medicine. He particularly noted the difference between the fauna of the Old World and the New, which was to become an increasingly prominent debating point in the future. These arguments about the fact of transformation were all of them already familiar. As to the means of transformation, however, Erasmus Darwin originated almost every important idea that has since appeared in evolutionary theory. He supposed that competition and selection were means of change; that overpopulation was a continual agent in enhancing competition; that this was true in plants as well as in animals; that in animals another important kind of selection arose from competition between males in pursuit of the female; that fertility and susceptibility to disease, being hereditary, were fields of selection. He took the Comte de Buffon's notion of the inheritance of acquired characteristics and suggested that this inheritance might be not only direct but also indirect; that the effects of use and disuse might be inherited.

Erasmus Darwin, physician, philosopher and poet, was one of the most celebrated personalities in the England of his time. His writings on evolution enjoyed enormous popularity. Two years after his death the word "Darwinian" was first attached to his ideas. This was five years before the birth of his grandson Charles. His *Zoonomia* was translated into French, German and Italian. Four years after it appeared Thomas Malthus developed one of its ideas into his *Essay on Population*. Nine years later the Chevalier de Lamarck expounded a theory of evolution based on the Darwinian inheritance of the effects of use and disuse. Seventy years later Charles Darwin wrote a book on sexual selection. At the same time another of Erasmus Darwin's grandsons, Francis Galton, began to develop his ideas on human breeding and invented the study of eugenics.

Not one of these works acknowledges their undoubted precursor. But it is not the multiplicity of Erasmus Darwin's intellectual heirs that concerns us here. More important is the fact that his influence upon the immediately ensuing history of evolutionary thought was largely negative. This came about through Lamarck's elaboration upon Erasmus Darwin's idea of the inheritance of acquired

characteristics. By making the notion explicit and giving examples, Lamarck unintentionally revealed its absurdity. After reading about how the race of giraffes had grown a longer neck simply by stretching for the higher branches, the whole world laughed. It seemed, indeed, to have laughed not only Lamarck but the whole idea of evolution off the stage.

Something more than laughter, however, followed from Lamarck's work. In England three Fellows of the Royal Society seem to have been moved independently to retort to Lamarck and to add an appendix to Erasmus Darwin. I say "seem" because, following the custom of the time and of the subject, they did not mention either Darwin or Lamarck. But they all repudiated the inheritance of acquired characteristics. The three men were William C. Wells, James C. Prichard and William Lawrence. Their views, announced at the same time in 1813, were emphatic and almost identical; since they were all physicians they dealt chiefly with man. As Prichard said: "All acquired conditions of the body end with the life of the individual in whom they are produced. But for this salutary law the universe would be filled with monstrous shapes." All three men advanced explicitly and in detail the alternative theory of natural selection foreshadowed by Erasmus Darwin. These three communications were the first clear statements of such an idea—in opposition to notions of evolution guided by design and purpose —since classical times.

What happened to these three men, these precursors of Charles Darwin? Wells died before his essay was published. Prichard lived many years to publish revised editions of his work. And as he revised them he did exactly what Darwin did later: He mixed his theory to include directed variation. The reason why Prichard, and also Darwin, retreated from their positions is revealed by the case of the third man, William Lawrence.

Lawrence's book bore as its subtitle the significant phrase: "Natural History of Man." His argument was that physical, medical, intellectual and moral differences among the races of man and among individuals were hereditary. The races had arisen by such distinct and identifiable mutations as are observed among members of the same litter of kittens or of rabbits. This is perhaps the first time the idea of genetic segregation and recombination appears in modern

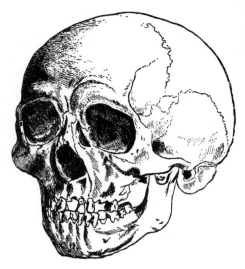

SKULLS appear in William Lawrence's *Lectures on Physiology, Zoology, and the*

times. The characteristics that distinguish the races of men are maintained by barriers against their interbreeding like those that maintain the distinguishing characteristics of species of animals and plants. "Selections and exclusions" are the basis of all adaptation. Differences, either physical or intellectual, between races of men can never be related to the direct action of food, climate or government. Men could be improved or ruined by selection in breeding just as domesticated animals may be improved or ruined. Drawing a political moral, Lawrence noted that the European royal families and aristocracies had mostly followed the second course. Zoology, he concluded—the study of man as an animal—is the only proper approach to the study of either medicine or morals, politics or social science.

Lawrence's book on the natural history of man had the same position in England after the war of 1815 that Marie Stopes's works on sexual relations and birth control had after the war of 1918. It was outspoken and revolutionary. It released personal, sexual, religious and political inhibitions. Lawrence's suggestion that a corrupt and mentally deficient aristocracy and monarchy might be replaced by applying the proper processes of stockbreeding to man was shocking but also extremely readable. His discussion of the orangutan theory of the origin of man was learned but intelligible, and it was relieved by vivid references to the buttocks of Hottentot women and what he called "the rites of Venus."

The clergy read it, enjoyed it and denounced it. The laity read it and enjoyed it. From Lawrence they learned about the principle of sexual selection and the

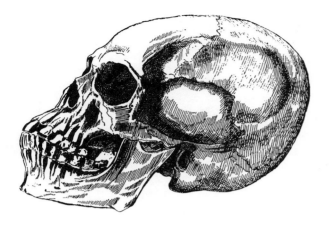

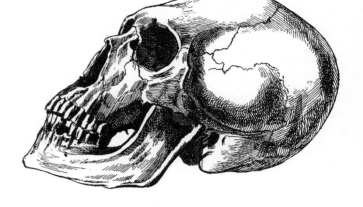

Natural History of Man, published in 1822. In this work Lawrence advanced the idea that men evolved by natural selection, and re-jected the inheritance of acquired characteristics. At left is the skull of a Kalmuck; in center, of a Negro; at right, of a Carib.

analogy with animal breeding that Charles Darwin was later to expound as his own; about the action of mutation and segregation which Darwin was to dismiss; about the comparative study of skulls, to be improved on by Thomas H. Huxley; and about the idea of eugenics, later invented by Galton. All these things were expounded in 500 pages by Lawrence.

Now in those days no one could study or teach at either Oxford or Cambridge who was not approved by the Church of England. Almost all of the teachers had to be ordained ministers of religion. Through the universities the intellectual life of the country was controlled by the Church. The Church itself and the government were both controlled by the landed aristocracy. The whole country, however, was seething with political discontent, and the government faced the imminent danger of revolution. Lawrence's book made it clear that the theory of evolution was bound up with ideas that would destroy both the Church and the governing class.

The government's reaction was inevitable. The book was examined by the Lord Chancellor, who pronounced it contrary to Scripture and refused it copyright. Meanwhile pamphlets, mostly by anonymous Oxford dons, were denouncing the folly and wickedness of "Surgeon Lawrence." His name was linked to that of "Infidel Paine," that is, Thomas Paine. Lawrence, now 36 years of age, had to decide whether to abandon his profession and to become a martyr to science or to enjoy the lawful fruits of his profession and renounce his scientific opinions. He took the second course. He suppressed his book and

made his career. Twice he became president of the Royal College of Surgeons. Later he was appointed Sergeant Surgeon to Queen Victoria, from whom, after more than one offer, he accepted a baronetcy.

So much for Lawrence. His book had a different career. One publisher after another took the risk of reprinting it illicitly. Nine editions had appeared in 1848. Its fame or infamy was enormous. It continued to be extolled by radicals and denounced by tories. Everybody who wrote about evolution in England referred to it. Darwin, Huxley and Alfred Russel Wallace all mentioned it, but not one of them noted its general significance. In their hasty glances at this disfavored book, they had found in it only what they wanted to find: facts but not theories.

Nevertheless, through all these years, evolution was very much alive, even though Charles Darwin, working and waiting at Down, thought that it was dead. Young naturalists were eagerly studying Lawrence and Prichard as well as Erasmus Darwin. Among these were Patrick Mathew, whose priority was later acknowledged by Charles Darwin, and Edward Blyth, whose importance in developing the idea of natural selection has only recently been fully revealed by Loren Eiseley of the University of Pennsylvania. Poets like Browning and Tennyson were well aware of the growing theory, and they could phrase their ideas in such a way as to inform the educated reader without shocking a larger audience.

At almost the same time, on a more scientific level, Charles Naudin in Paris

advanced the view that evolution had taken place by a process of natural selection analogous to what man had done in improving his domesticated crops and stock. Naudin had a good reason for reaching this conclusion because he had for some years been engaged in experiments on the crossing of horticultural plants. These experiments had led him to the conclusion that first-generation crosses are uniform in character but exhibit the characteristics of both progenitors. The dissimilar "essences" derived from the parent strains disjoin in the second generation to give different germ cells and hence a wide range of types of plant. This was the same conclusion that Mendel reached independently at about the same time. Naudin's argument was less well reasoned than Mendel's and his experiments less well designed. His conclusion, however, provided a more defensible explanation of the mutations that heredity supplied to the process of selection than Darwin was ever able to devise. It is therefore significant that Darwin dismissed Naudin and his experiments on heredity as unsound.

Having thrown open the shutters in these forgotten attics, we can see in a clearer light the problem that Darwin faced in 1844 when he put aside his first essay on natural selection and proceeded to devote eight years to the description of barnacles. The idea of evolution, popular as it was with the uneducated masses, was far from respectable in academic circles. It was contrary to the prevailing belief of naturalists, who liked to think that their species were fixed for all time. It was identified with the absurdities of Lamarck or with rubbishy works that adapted Lamarckism to the idea of Cre-

ZOONOMIA;

OR

THE LAWS

OF

ORGANIC LIFE.

VOL. I.

By ERASMUS DARWIN, M. D. F. R. S.

AUTHOR OF THE BOTANIC GARDEN.

Principio cœlum, ac terras, camposque liquentes,
Lucentemque globum lunæ, titaniaque astra,
Spiritus intùs alit, totamque infusa per artus
Mens agitat molem, et magno se corpore miscet.
                                    VIRG. Æn. vi.

Earth, on whose lap a thousand nations tread,
And Ocean, brooding his prolific bed,
Night's changeful orb, blue pole, and silvery zones,
Where other worlds encircle other suns,
One Mind inhabits, one diffusive Soul
Wields the large limbs, and mingles with the whole.

NEW-YORK:

Printed by T. & J. SWORDS, Printers to the Faculty of Physic of
Columbia College, No. 99 Pearl-Street.
—1796.—

AN

ESSAY

ON THE

PRINCIPLE OF POPULATION,

AS IT AFFECTS

THE FUTURE IMPROVEMENT OF SOCIETY.

WITH REMARKS

ON THE SPECULATIONS OF MR. GODWIN,

M. CONDORCET,

AND OTHER WRITERS.

LONDON:

PRINTED FOR J. JOHNSON, IN ST. PAUL'S
CHURCH-YARD.

1798.

TITLE PAGES of four early evolutionary works are reproduced. At left is the title page of an edition of Erasmus Darwin's *Zoono-* mia published in New York. Second from left is the title page of Thomas Malthus's famous *Essay*, which developed one of Erasmus

ation and the phrases of piety. Worse yet, it was associated with revolutionary propaganda such as that in Lawrence's book. In Darwin's own family the idea of evolution was associated with a grandfather whose 18th-century views and conduct were judged to be immoral. In his "Historical Sketch" Charles Darwin refers to the works of Erasmus Darwin as merely having "anticipated the erroneous opinions of Lamarck." Evidently, although he had been allowed to read them when he was young, he had been warned not to believe them. He never returned later to study them and to take them into proper account.

Darwin's attitude toward his precursors now becomes clear. It also explains to us something we otherwise have great difficulty in understanding: the secret of his success in converting the world to evolution.

No doubt Darwin was able to cut himself off so completely from his historical forerunners because he succeeded so well in separating science from history in his own mind. The science of evolution was real; the history of the idea of evolution was unreal. The kindest interpretation we can put on his attitude is that he was looking forward all of the time, wrapped up in his own ideas and his own inquiries. He could not spare the time to look back. Deep in his unconscious he must have known that the past contained the origins of his ideas and that his predecessors were not quite so cheap as he made them out to be. But he wanted to think out his ideas for himself.

This is the kindest interpretation. But we have to record that Samuel Butler advanced a less kind interpretation. He pointed out that the first edition of the *Origin of Species* contained 45 refer-

ences to "my theory." But no one could quite tell what "my theory" might be. Was it the theory that evolution had taken place? Was it the theory of natural selection? Or was it the shifting combination of selection and direction? The British geologist Charles Lyell and the German zoologist Ernst Haeckel made it quite clear that in their opinion justice had not been done to Lamarck by the man who was adopting his theory. Consequently (this is Butler's argument) Darwin gradually cut out the references to "my theory" in successive editions of the *Origin of Species*. Gradually it became "the theory." But by that time the public all over the world had begun to think of it as Darwin's theory.

Whatever the cause, the effect served Darwin splendidly. That he appeared to come suddenly out of nothing, without herald or harbinger, was one of the factors that contributed principally to his

HISTOIRE NATURELLE

DES

ANIMAUX SANS VERTÈBRES,

PRÉSENTANT

LES CARACTÈRES GÉNÉRAUX ET PARTICULIERS DE CES
ANIMAUX, LEUR DISTRIBUTION, LEURS CLASSES, LEURS
FAMILLES, LEURS GENRES, ET LA CITATION DES PRIN-
CIPALES ESPÈCES QUI S'Y RAPPORTENT;

PRÉCÉDÉE

D'UNE INTRODUCTION offrant la Détermination des caractères
essentiels de l'Animal, sa distinction du végétal et des
autres corps naturels, enfin, l'Exposition des Principes
fondamentaux de la Zoologie.

PAR M. LE CHEVALIER DE LAMARCK,

Membre de l'Institut Royal de France, de la Légion d'Honneur,
et de plusieurs Sociétés savantes de l'Europe; Professeur de Zoologie
au Muséum d'Histoire naturelle.

Nihil extrà naturam observatione notum

TOME PREMIER.

PARIS,

VERDIERE, LIBRAIRE, QUAI DES AUGUSTINS, N.° 27.

Mars. — 1815.

LECTURES

ON

PHYSIOLOGY, ZOOLOGY,

AND THE

Natural History of Man,

DELIVERED AT

THE ROYAL COLLEGE OF SURGEONS,

BY

W. LAWRENCE, F.R.S.

PROFESSOR OF ANATOMY AND SURGERY TO THE COLLEGE,
ASSISTANT SURGEON TO ST. BARTHOLOMEW'S HOSPITAL, SURGEON
TO BRIDEWELL AND BETHLEM HOSPITALS,
AND TO THE LONDON INFIRMARY FOR DISEASES OF THE EYE.

WITH TWELVE ENGRAVINGS.

LONDON:

BENBOW, PRINTER AND PUBLISHER, AT THE BYRON'S HEAD, CASTLE STREET,
LEICESTER SQUARE.

1822.

Darwin's ideas. Third from left is the title page of one of the volumes in which the Chevalier de Lamarck advanced his concept of the inheritance of acquired characteristics. At right is the title page of Lawrence's book. Lawrence announced his ideas in 1813.

success. The enemies of evolution liked to believe that Darwin represented a form of infidelity entirely novel in its folly and wickedness, one that no decent Christian could entertain or ever had entertained. On the other hand, the friends of evolution were delighted to discover that Darwin had put it on entirely new grounds, quite unlike those of Lamarck which they had found unacceptable; natural selection now justified a belief in evolution.

It was not without reason, therefore, that Huxley and Wallace and Galton unobtrusively failed to follow Darwin in his retreat from natural selection. Their dislike for Lamarckism was genuine and consistent. It carried them over to the day of their vindication.

The challenge of Lamarckism was taken up at last just a year before Darwin's death. The German zoologist August Weismann asked the question:

What is the evidence for the inheritance of acquired characteristics? He showed that there is indeed none but a collection of old wives' tales. Weismann did not know, of course, any more than Darwin knew, that Lawrence and Prichard had made the matter pretty clear 60 years earlier. Nor, indeed, did the Russian agriculturist Trofim Lysenko, a recent proponent of Lamarckism, realize that the question had been settled long ago.

Another, and equally important, explanation for Darwin's success as the propounder of evolution is to be found in his equivocation on the central issue of selection versus direction. The issue had long been recognized as cardinal in any theory. Those who had taken either side unequivocally, whether that of Lamarck or of his opponents, had failed, though their failure was political. But Darwin confused the alternatives

on all possible occasions. The confusion helped greatly in dealing with untrained opponents who did not notice the blurring of the issue. Darwin's success makes his choice in this dilemma seem deliberate and disingenuous. But it was no doubt unconscious, like most of his more important reasonings.

Thus in his 1858 publication he refers to "changes of external conditions," and once merely to "external conditions," as causing variation. But in 1859 these conditions, through the effects of use and disuse, were already directing variation, and cooperating with natural selection in directing it. The directive component in the theory grew stronger year by year. But his contemptuous references to the authors of the idea—Erasmus Darwin and Lamarck—were sealed off in the prefatory "Historical Sketch," away from the main line of discussion.

A third ground for Darwin's success

THE

NATURAL HISTORY

OF

MAN;

COMPRISING

INQUIRIES INTO THE MODIFYING INFLUENCE OF
PHYSICAL AND MORAL AGENCIES
ON THE DIFFERENT TRIBES OF THE HUMAN FAMILY.

BY

JAMES COWLES PRICHARD, M.D. F.R.S. M.R.I.A.

CORRESPONDING MEMBER OF THE NATIONAL INSTITUTE,
AND OF THE ROYAL ACADEMY OF MEDICINE, AND OF THE STATISTICAL SOCIETY, OF FRANCE;
MEMBER OF THE AMERICAN PHILOSOPHICAL SOCIETY,
AND OF THE ACADEMY OF NATURAL SCIENCES OF PHILADELPHIA;
HONORARY FELLOW OF THE KING'S AND QUEEN'S COLLEGE OF PHYSICIANS IN IRELAND; ETC.

WITH

Thirty-six Coloured and Four Plain Illustrations

ENGRAVED ON STEEL,

AND NINETY ENGRAVINGS ON WOOD.

LONDON:

H. BAILLIERE, 219 REGENT STREET;

FOREIGN BOOKSELLER TO THE ROYAL SOCIETY, TO THE ROYAL COLLEGE OF SURGEONS,
AND TO THE ROYAL MEDICO-CHIRURGICAL SOCIETY.

PARIS: J. B. BAILLIERE, LIBRAIRE, RUE DE L'ECOLE DE MEDECINE.
LEIPSIC: T. O. WEIGEL.

1843.

ON

THE ORIGIN OF SPECIES

BY MEANS OF NATURAL SELECTION,

OR THE

PRESERVATION OF FAVOURED RACES IN THE STRUGGLE
FOR LIFE.

BY CHARLES DARWIN, M.A.,

FELLOW OF THE ROYAL, GEOLOGICAL, LINNÆAN, ETC., SOCIETIES;
AUTHOR OF 'JOURNAL OF RESEARCHES DURING H. M. S. BEAGLE'S VOYAGE
ROUND THE WORLD.'

LONDON:

JOHN MURRAY, ALBEMARLE STREET.

1859.

The right of Translation is reserved.

LATER WORKS are an 1843 edition of James C. Prichard's *The Natural History of Man,* in which he modified some of his earlier ideas on evolution by means of natural selection. At right is the title page of the first edition of Darwin's *Origin of Species.*

is to be found in a perfectly conscious and acknowledged stratagem. He avoided man's origins and relations, the one problem that every one who read his book was thinking about. Mark the words he uses. In the *Origin of Species* he observed: "Much light will be thrown on the origin of man and his history." He was careful not to enlarge upon this statement until he published *The Descent of Man* a decade later. This was a stroke of genius. It turned the flank of the Church party and made it possible to keep at least a part of the argument on a scientific plane. A year after the publication of the *Origin of Species,* as we know, Bishop Wilberforce brought the question down to his own intellectual level. When he asked Huxley at Oxford whether he was descended from an ape through his grandfather or his grandmother, Wilberforce moved the conflict onto the ground that Darwin had earn-

estly wished to avoid. But by this time it was already too late. The Church had lost its battle.

In short, it is clear that Darwin's success was due to several common vices as well as to several uncommon virtues. His gifts as an observer in all fields concerned with the needs of a theory of evolution were extraordinary. His industry and patience in collecting and editing his own observations as well as other people's were hardly less remarkable. On the other hand, his ideas were not, as he imagined, unusually original. He was able to put his ideas across not so much because of his scientific integrity, but because of his opportunism, his equivocation and his lack of historical sense. Though his admirers will not like to believe it, he accomplished his revolution by personal weakness and strategic talent more than by scientific virtue.

We owe to the *Origin of Species* the

overthrow of the myth of Creation, especially the dramatic character of that overthrow. Yet the overthrow itself has led to the growth of a smaller myth with lesser danger of its own: the myth of Darwinism, which obscures what happened. It is important for us to know as clearly as possible what happened, to understand its small deceptions and its larger paradoxes, to grasp how much of the struggle takes place within the mind of the discoverer. We must realize that a man who liberates the whole world may never quite succeed in liberating himself.

These things show that scientific discovery is not purely a matter of science. It is not a purely intellectual process. This is a lesson that we shall need to bear in mind when Darwinian ideas—the ideas he foreshadowed but did not venture to develop—come to be applied to man and society.

Charles Lyell

12

by Loren C. Eiseley
August 1959

He founded modern historical geology and set the stage for the achievement of Charles Darwin. Until late in his career, however, he was reluctant to accept the idea of evolution

---

"I feel as if my books," Charles Darwin once confessed, "came half out of Sir Charles Lyell's brain." The great biologist was admitting to no more than the simple truth. Sir Charles Lyell, who remained until late in his career a reluctant evolutionist, was paradoxically the ground-breaker for the triumph of the *Origin of Species*.

Lyell is remembered chiefly as a founder of modern historical geology. But he was also a biologist whose studies form the backbone of the achievement of Darwin and Alfred Russel Wallace. In his day he addressed tabernacles in both England and America full of people eager to hear the world-shaking views of the new geology. Today the man in the street has forgotten him. By a curious twist of history, Darwin replaced Lyell as a popular idol. Yet this gaunt-faced man who ended his days in near-blindness was one of the greatest scientists in a century of distinguished men.

A generation before Darwin he took a world of cataclysms, supernatural violence and mystery, and made of it something plain, expected and natural. If today we look upon our planet as familiar even when its bowels shake and its volcanoes grumble, it is because Lyell taught us long ago the simple powers in the earth.

It was as though we had been unable to see the earth until we observed it through the eyes of Lyell. Ralph Waldo Emerson wrote at mid-century: "Geology, a science of forty or fifty summers, has had the effect to throw an air of novelty and mushroom speed over entire history. The oldest empires—what we called venerable antiquity—now that we have true measures of duration, show like creations of yesterday. . . . The old six thousand years of chronology becomes a kitchen clock."

To Darwin and Wallace, Lyell gave the gift of time. Without that gift there would have been no *Origin of Species*. Geologic time is now so commonplace that the public forgets it once had to be fought for with something of the vigor that was later to be transferred to the evolutionary debates of the 1860's.

Lyell was, in modern terms, both zoologist and geologist. Indeed, he defined geology as that science "which investigates the successive changes that have taken place in the organic and inorganic kingdoms of nature." Today the splitting-up of science into numerous special disciplines has left Lyell one of the founders of historical geology. The world has tended to forget that he also wrote extensively upon zoological subjects, and that he exerted, as an older friend and influential scholar, a profound effect upon the career of Charles Darwin. "Lyell," remarked the great U. S. evolutionist Asa Gray in the year of Darwin's death "is as much the father of the new mode of thought which now prevails as is Darwin."

Yet in the first years of evolutionary controversy, beginning with Jean Baptiste de Lamarck and extending into the time of Robert Chambers and Charles Darwin, Lyell found himself popularly arrayed with the resistance to evolution. He was not to alter his public position until the autumn of his life. To us it may seem an almost willful rejection of the new age of science. Oddly enough we are wrong. Reading history backward is almost worse than not reading history at all. One must live both in a given time and beyond it to appreciate at once its complexities and its half-veiled insights.

Lyell's rejection of evolution was one of the first rational products of the new geology. A hint as to the nature of the situation is to be found in a passage in Lyell's *The Antiquity of Man*, published in 1863. The issue, to our modern eyes, is obscured by the terms in which it was argued. Lyell wrote: "It may be thought almost paradoxical that writers who are most in favor of transmutation (Mr. C. Darwin and Dr. J. Hooker, for example) are nevertheless among those who are most cautious, and one would say timid, in their mode of espousing the doctrine of progression; while on the other hand, the most zealous advocates of progress are, oftener than not, very vehement opponents of transmutation. We might have expected a contrary leaning on the part of both."

It is in the words "transmutation" and "progression," now unfamiliar, that the key to this mystery lies. When we come to know their significance, we will have learned that the road to the acceptance of evolution had unexpected turnings which, as we look backward, seem to have vanished, but which were real enough to the men of the 19th century. Before we can understand Lyell's position, this queer order of events has to be explored and comprehended.

Charles Lyell was born, the first of 10 children, to well-to-do parents in Scotland in 1797. His father possessed a strong interest in natural history and may have helped unconsciously to guide his son's interests in that direction. As Charles Darwin and Alfred Russel Wallace were later to do, the young Lyell collected insects in his boyhood. Absent-minded but versatile, tree-climber and chess player, he matriculated at Exeter College, Oxford, in 1816. Having early stumbled upon a copy of Robert Bakewell's *Introduction to Geology* in his father's library, he sought out Dean Buckland's geological lectures at Oxford, and from then on was a haunter of chalk pits, rock quarries, caves and river terraces.

In 1818 he made the usual continental tour with his parents and sisters. The slow carriage travel of that day promoted leisurely observation, and Charles made the most of it. He saw the red snow and glaciers of the high Alps as well as the treasures that lie open to the observant in the flints of the common road. Lyell had not as yet settled upon a career in geology. He was destined for the law, and shortly after his graduation from Oxford he came to London to prepare himself for the bar.

Even in London, however, Lyell was soon elected a Fellow of the Geological Society and joined the Linnean Society. Two handicaps tended to retard his

legal career. His eyes were weak and troublesome, and he suffered from a slight speech difficulty, with which he was to contend bravely in his years as a lecturer on the natural sciences. When he was called to the bar in 1825 he was already contributing articles on scientific subjects to the *Quarterly Review*.

It has sometimes been intimated that Charles Lyell was "only an armchair geologist," that he was scientifically timid, a rich man's son who happened to dabble his way to success in a new science. But in those days there was little in the way of public support for science. Even the great schools were still largely concentrated upon the classical education of gentlemen. Only the man of independent means, like Lyell or

Darwin, could afford to indulge his interest in science. With occasional struggling exceptions such as Wallace, it was the amateur who laid the foundations of the science of today. The whole philosophy of modern biology was established by such a "dabbler" as Charles Darwin, who never at any time held a professional position in the field. Charles Lyell and his great precursor, the Scotsman James Hutton, similarly laid the foundations of modern geology without claiming much in the way of formal institutional connections. Important though institutional and government support has come to be, it has led to a certain latent snobbery in professional circles. The amateur has had his day. But his was the sunrise of science, and it was a sunrise it ill becomes us to forget.

The charge that Lyell was an armchair worker will not stand against the facts. But even if the accusation held, the whole question would turn on what came out of the armchair. In actuality Lyell in his younger years made numerous trips to the continent to examine the evidence of geology at firsthand. Later, in the 1840's, he visited America, where he made similar ventures into the field, even though he was by then lecturing to thousands. As his biographer T. G. Bonney remarks: "Whenever there was hope of securing any geological information or of seeing some remarkable aspect of nature, Lyell was almost insensible either to heat or to fatigue." It is hard to see how a man suffering from bad eyes could have done more.

In support of the charge of scientific timidity, it is observed that Lyell opposed himself for many years to evolutionary views; it is said that his public and his private statements upon this score were vacillating. "How could Sir Charles Lyell," wrote one of Darwin's contemporaries, "for thirty years read, write and think on the subject of species and their succession, and yet constantly look down the wrong road?" From the vantage point of a hundred years this question can be answered. A whole new theory of life and time is not built by one man, however able. It is the product of multitudinous minds, and as a consequence it is also compounded of the compromises and hesitations of those same minds. Later, when the new world view comes to be ascribed, as it generally is, to a single individual such as Darwin the precursors of the discoverer begin to seem incredibly slow-witted.

Whatever men may think on this score, however, the record shows that

LYELL was born in Scotland in 1797 and died in 1875. He prepared for a legal career, but turned to geology. This photograph is in *Portraits of Men of Eminence*, published in 1863.

Lyell was a man of intellectual courage. He entered the geological domain when it was a weird, half-lit landscape of gigantic convulsions, floods and supernatural creations and extinctions of life. Distinguished men had lent the power of their names to these theological fantasies. Of the young Lyell, the "timid" Lyell who later strained Darwin's patience, a contemporary geologist wrote: "He stood up as a reformer, a radical reformer, denouncing all the old notions about paroxysms and solving every geological question by reference to the action of constant and existing physical causes. Never had a revolutionist harder work to get a sober hearing, or less prospect of overturning the works and conclusions of other men."

Geology at the beginning of the 19th century was known to many in England as a dangerous science. As such it both attracted and repelled the public. A body of fact and interpretation had arisen that could only be kept in accord with the Scriptural interpretation of earth's history by the exercise of considerable ingenuity. Theological author-ity was strong, and there was the greatest pressure upon geologists to avoid direct conflict with the church. Moreover, some of the early geologists were primarily theologians themselves, and were understandably anxious to reconcile geology with their religious beliefs. By degrees there had thus arisen a widely accepted view of geological history known as catastrophism.

This orthodox geological creed was an uneasy amalgam of the new scientific facts seen in the flickering, unreal light of mythological and romantic fantasy. Unlike the slow evolutionary successions that we recognize today, the record of geology was held to contain sudden catastrophic breaks. Mountain ranges were thought to be heaved up overnight; gigantic tidal waves, floods, paroxysms of the earth's crust, were thought to mark the end of periods of calm. At such hours life vanished only to be restored through renewed divine creation, taking in the new period a more advanced form, and pointing steadily on toward the eventual emergence of man. It may thus be observed that the students of catastrophism had become aware of organic change in the rocks, but they saw the planet as having been molded by forces seemingly more powerful than those at work in the present day, and thus by implication supernatural.

Awareness of a succession of life-forms in the strata of the earth had been slowly increasing since the close of the 18th century. Furthermore, it was seen that these extinct forms of life showed an increasing complexity as one approached the present. Since the record of the land vertebrates is particularly incomplete and broken, there arose the idea that, instead of a genuine continuity of life from age to age, the breaks in the geological record were real breaks. There had been a genuine interruption between the life of one age and that of another; each geological period had its own flora and fauna largely distinct from that which preceded and followed it. The slow, grand progression of life was seen as through a jerky, discontinuous, ill-run motion picture.

Men still did not understand the real age of the earth, nor the fact that the

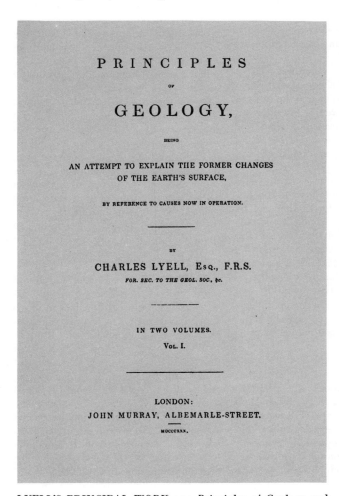

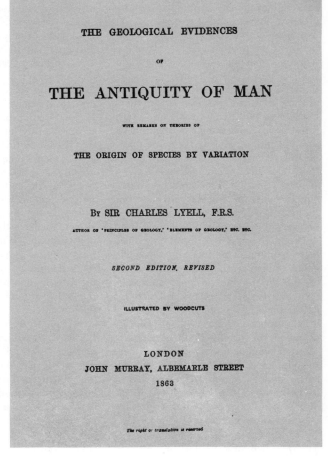

LYELL'S PRINCIPAL WORK was *Principles of Geology*, published in 1830. Although the title page reproduced at left states that the book has two volumes, Lyell later wrote a third. At right is the title page of *The Antiquity of Man*, which was published in 1863.

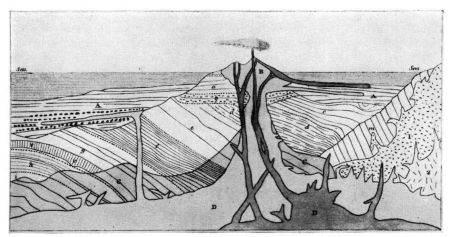

EARTH'S CRUST is depicted in Lyell's *Elements of Geology*. It is captioned: "Ideal section of . . . the Earth's crust explaining the theory of the . . . origin of the four great clafses of rocks." The classes were: aqueous (A), volcanic (B), metamorphic (C) and plutonic (D).

breaks they found in the records of the rocks were not world-wide, but rather only local discontinuities. The imperfections of the geological record, or the passages between the discontinuities, could only be learned through the piling-up of empirical evidence, a task that had only begun.

The catastrophic school had a powerful religious appeal. It retained both the creative excess and fury of an Old Testament Jehovah. "At succeeding periods," wrote Adam Sedgwick, one of Darwin's geological teachers at Cambridge, "new tribes of beings were called into existence, not merely as the progeny of those that had appeared before them, but as new and living proofs of creative interference; and though formed on the same plan, and bearing the same marks of wise contrivance, oftentimes unlike those creatures which preceded them, as if they had been matured in a different portion of the universe and cast upon the earth by the collision of another planet."

People thought in terms of a geotheological drama, a prologue to the emergence of man on the planet, after which no further organic developments were contemplated. The theory predicted a finished world which, in some eyes at least, could be compressed into the figurative week of the Book of Genesis. "Never," commented Lyell, "was there a dogma more calculated to foster indolence, and to blunt the keen edge of curiosity, than this assumption of the discordance between the former and the existing causes of change."

In this half-supernatural atmosphere Sir Charles Lyell in 1830 published the first volume of his *Principles of Geology*. Like most great ideas it was not totally original with its author. But to Sir Charles belongs the unquestioned credit of documenting a then unpalatable truth so effectively and formidably that it could no longer be ignored. In this respect again his career supplies a surprising parallel to that of Darwin. For Darwin too, at a later time, was the resurrector and documenter of forgotten and ill-used truths.

Lyell's principal precursor, James Hutton, died in intellectual eclipse in 1797, the very year that saw the birth of the man who was to revive his views—so tenuous and yet so persistent is the slow growth of scientific ideas. In the 1780's Hutton made the first organized and comprehensive attempt to demonstrate that the forces that had shaped the planet—its mountains, boulders and continents—are the same forces that can be observed in action around us today. Hutton had an ear for the work of raindrops, an eye for frost crystals splitting stones, a feel for the leaf fall of innumerable autumns. Wind and frost and running water, given time enough, can erode continents, ran his argument. Peering into the depths of the past, he could see "no vestige of a beginning, no prospect of an end."

Hutton, though not the first to suspect the earth's antiquity, nor the work that perfectly natural forces can perform, was the first to write learnedly and extensively upon the subject. His work fell, however, into undeserved neglect. He was criticized as irreligious. In England, particularly in the conservative reaction following the French Revolution, the catastrophism theory, with its grander scenery and stage effects, had a more popular appeal. The world of Hutton by contrast was an unfinished world still unrolling into an indeterminate future. Its time depths were immeasurable, and the public had recoiled from its first glimpses into that abyss.

Yet this was the domain, and this the philosophy, upon which Sir Charles Lyell was to force his colleagues to take a long second look. He was a more eloquent and able writer than Hutton. But beyond this he had the advantage of almost 50 years of additional data, including his own personal study of the continental deposits. "Lyell," remarks one of his contemporaries, "was deficient of power in oral discourse, and was opposed by men who were his equals in knowledge, his superiors in the free delivery of their opinions. But in resolute combats, yielding not an inch to his adversaries, he slowly advanced upon the ground they abandoned, and became a conqueror without ever being acknowledged as a leader."

By degrees the idea of gradual change (uniformitarianism, as it came to be called) succeeded the picture of worldwide catastrophes. Supposition and quasi-theological imaginings gave place to a recognition of the work of natural forces still active and available for study in the world about us. The disjoined periods of the catastrophists began to be seen as one continuous world extending into a past of awe-inspiring dimensions. The uniformitarian school began to dominate the geological horizon. With the success of the *Principles* Lyell became one of two or three leading figures in English natural science until the peak of Darwin's fame was achieved with the publication of the *Origin of Species* in 1859. It is no wonder that the young Darwin, just returned from the voyage of the *Beagle* in 1836, gravitated so quickly to Lyell. It was Lyell's revision of geology that was to make Darwin's triumph possible.

Sir Charles Lyell had been raised in a more orthodox home than Charles Darwin. In fact, he was to confess in after-years that it cost him a severe struggle to renounce his old beliefs. Nevertheless, in reviving the conception of limitless time, and in abandoning the notion of world-wide breaks in the geological record as urged by the catastrophists, Lyell was inevitably forced to confront the problem of life itself in all its varied appearances. His great predecessor, Hutton, had been largely able to avoid the issue because of the lack of paleontological information. In Lyell's time, however, the questions pressed for answer.

The catastrophist doctrine had given birth to a kind of romantic evolutionism to explain the increasing complexity of life. This was the doctrine of "progression" which Lyell opposed in many of his writings from the time of the *Principles* onward. Progressionism was the product of the new paleontology which had discovered differences among the life-forms of successive geological eras. The theory can be said to have borrowed from Lamarck the conception of a necessary advance in the complexity of life as we ascend through the geological strata to the present. Instead of establishing biological continuity (the actual physical relationship between one set of forms and their descendants) the progressionists sought to show only a continuity or an organic plan in the mind of God between one age and another. There was, in other words, no phylogenetic relationship on the material plane between the animals of one era and those of a succeeding one.

Progressionism thus implied a kind of miraculous spiritual evolution which ceases only when the human level has been attained. The idea is confusing to the modern thinker because he tends to read back into this literature true evolutionary connotations that frequently were not intended by these early writers. The doctrine is interesting as a sign of the compromises being sought between an advancing science and a still-powerful religious orthodoxy.

"I shall adopt a different course," the young Lyell had written when he was contending for the uniformitarian view in geology. "We are not authorized in the infancy of our science to recur to extraordinary agents." The same point of view led him, in company with T. H. Huxley, Joseph Hooker and, later, Darwin, to reject the claims of progressionism. All of these men, Lyell foremost among them, were uniformitarians in geology. They believed in the play of purely natural forces upon the earth. They refused or were reluctant to accept the notion of divine interposition of creative power at various stages of the geological record. They felt in their bones that there must be a natural explanation for organic as well as geological change, but the method was not easily to be had. Since Lyell was the immediate parent of the new geology, and since he was committed to natural processes, he was continually embarrassed by those who said: "You cannot show how nor why life has altered. Why then should we not believe that geological changes are equally the product of mysterious and unknown forces?"

We are now at the crux of the reason why Lyell was dubious about notions of

"transmutation"—the term then reserved for ideas implying true physical connection among the successions of species or, as we would say, "evolution" from one form to another. Lyell's attitude toward evolution was influenced by the antipathy that he felt toward progression, toward the unexplainable. In bracketing the two together he in effect was indicating the need of a scientific explanation of organic change, if change indeed was demonstrable.

Beginning with the *Principles of Geology*, in which the second volume and part of the third are devoted to

biological matters, Lyell had sought to examine the biological realm with an eye to answering the challenge of the catastrophist progressionists. As a consequence he came close to, but missed the significance of, the natural-selection hypothesis which was to establish the fame of Charles Darwin. It was here that he took the wrong turning that led him away from evolution. Yet ironically enough, though Lyell failed to comprehend the creative importance of natural selection, he did not miss its existence. In fact, through a strange series of circumstances just discovered in the literature, it is likely that he was fundamentally in-

Synoptical Table of Recent and Tertiary Formations.

PERIODS.		Character of Formations.	Localities of the different Formations.
I. RECENT.		Marine.	Coral formations of Pacific. Delta of Po, Ganges, &c.
		Freshwater.	Modern deposits in Lake Superior—Lake of Geneva—Marl lakes of Scotland—Italian travertin, &c.
		Volcanic.	Jorullo — Monte Nuovo — Modern lavas of Iceland, Etna, Vesuvius, &c.
II. TERTIARY.	1. Newer Pliocene.	Marine.	Strata of the Val di Noto in Sicily. Ischia, Morea? Uddevalla.
		Freshwater.	Valley of the Elsa around Colle in Tuscany.
		Volcanic.	Older parts of Vesuvius, Etna, and Ischia—Volcanic rocks of the Val di Noto in Sicily.
	2. Older Pliocene.	Marine.	Northern Subapennine formations, as at Parma, Asti, Sienna, Perpignan, Nice—English Crag.
		Freshwater.	Alternating with marine beds near the town of Sienna.
		Volcanic.	Volcanos of Tuscany and Campagna di Roma.
	3. Miocene.	Marine.	Strata of Touraine, Bordeaux, Valley of the Bormida, and the Superga near Turin—Basin of Vienna.
		Freshwater.	Alternating with marine at Saucats, twelve miles south of Bordeaux.
		Volcanic.	Hungarian and Transylvanian volcanic rocks. Part of the volcanos of Auvergne, Cantal, and Velay?
	4. Eocene.	Marine.	Paris and London Basins.
		Freshwater.	Alternating with marine in Paris basin—Isle of Wight—purely lacustrine in Auvergne, Cantal, and Velay.
		Volcanic.	Oldest part of volcanic rocks of Auvergne.

ROCK FORMATIONS of Recent and Tertiary periods were tabulated in first volume of *Principles of Geology*. Such tabulations showed the continuity of formations over a large area. Before the rise of historical geology local breaks in the continuity of rock formations had been taken as evidence that the history of the earth was a series of catastrophic events.

strumental in presenting Darwin with the key to the new biology. He was so concerned, however, to array the evidence against the doctrine of progression that he missed the support that the same evidence gave for a rational explanation of the origin of species.

Against the progressionists' idea of mass extinction at each break in the geological record he cited the imperfections in that record. "There must," he contended, "be a perpetual dying out of animals and plants, not suddenly and by whole groups at once, but one after another." Although not solving the problem of the emergence of new forms of life, Lyell by arguing for geological continuity was bringing the question of extinction and of the origin of new species within the domain of scientific investigation.

He countered the progressionist hypothesis with a short-lived "nonprogressionism" in which he argued that the discovery of higher forms of life in older strata would demonstrate that the progressionist doctrine was based solely upon the fallible geological record. This retreat from straight evolution on the part of Lyell was somewhat wavering, but it continued into the 1850's. There is no doubt that it was an attempt philosophically to evade a problem which threatened to interpose into his system something miraculous and unexplainable that savored of the catastrophist doctrines he had struggled for so long to defeat. Only with the triumph of Darwin would a uniformitarian, a "naturalistic," explanation for the mutability of life be available to the uniformitarian followers of Lyell. It was only then that Huxley, Hooker and finally Lyell himself became converts to evolution, at a time when it was still being resisted by such men as Sir Richard Owen and Louis Agassiz—old-style catastrophists and progressionists who at first glance one might think would have eagerly embraced the new doctrine of genuine physical evolution.

Although the question has been obscured by hazy difficulties of terminology, Sir Charles Lyell had already described before Darwin the struggle for existence and, up to a certain point, natural selection. He had not, however, visualized its creative aspect. Lyell made the first systematic attempt to treat the factors affecting the extinction of species and the effects of climatic change upon animal life throughout the long course of ages. "Every species," Lyell contended, "which has spread itself from a small point over a wide area must have marked its progress by the diminution or the entire extirpation of some other, and must maintain its ground by a successful struggle against the encroachments of other plants and animals." He goes on to speak of "the tendency of population to increase in a limited district beyond the means of subsistence." Nor was Lyell unaware of plant and animal variation, although he believed such variation to be limited. "The best-authenticated examples of the extent to which species can be made to vary may be looked for in the history of domesticated animals and cultivated plants," he wrote, long before Darwin's investigations.

But Lyell did more than this. In the *Principles of Geology* he marshaled a powerful attack on the possibility that new evolutionary forms might be able thus to maintain or perfect themselves. Lyell advanced what he called his principle of "preoccupancy." In essence this principle simply assumes that creatures or plants already well fitted for occupying a given ecological zone will keep any other forms from establishing themselves in the new habitat, even assuming that the competitors are capable of evolving. "It is idle," said Lyell, "to dispute about the abstract possibility of the conversion of one species into another, when there are known causes so much more active in their nature which must always intervene and prevent the actual accomplishment of such conversions." Using a number of present-day examples Lyell sought to show that local alterations, say that from marsh to dry land, or fresh to brackish water, would never permit of slow organic change, because long before the organisms of the older environment could alter they would die out in competition with already adapted forms intruding to take advantage of the new conditions.

Lyell, in other words, could see how time and changing conditions might alter the percentages of living forms in given localities or change the whole nature of a flora. He understood that "the successive destruction of species must now be part of the regular and constant order of nature." What he still failed to grasp was that he was observing the cutting edge of the natural-selection process in terms of its normal, short-time effects. The struggle in nature that had so impressed him he had seen, if anything, too vividly. There was left no refuge, no nursing ground, by which the new could come into existence. The already created, the already fit, dominated every niche and corner of the living world. Lyell understood ecology before Darwin. He saw the web of life, but he saw it so tightly drawn that nothing new could emerge from it. As geographical or climatic conditions altered in the course of geological time, already existing forms moved from one area to another; he could see no evidence for a mechanism to explain the emergence of new forms.

His vision of the history of life was not wrong; it was simply incomplete. Lyell himself realized the complexities of the problem that beset him: There was a going-out without an equivalent coming-in, an attrition without a compensating creation.

"The reader will immediately perceive," Lyell wrote, "that amidst the vicissitudes of the earth's surface, species cannot be immortal, but must perish one after the other, like the individuals which compose them. There is no possibility of escaping this conclusion without resorting to some hypothesis as violent as that of Lamarck." Drawing back from this gulf, Lyell returns again and again to nonprogressionism. Nevertheless, like many naturalists of his day, he was willing to recognize "a capacity in all species to accommodate themselves, to a certain extent, to a change of external circumstances, this extent varying greatly, according to the species." Lyell recognized minor varietal differences of a seemingly genetic character in some animals. Beyond this he did not venture.

The term natural selection, introduced by Darwin and now everywhere regarded as the leading mechanism in evolutionary change, has a peculiar history. Under other names it was known earlier within the century, but this is little realized. Darwin introduced the principle to his readers under a new term and with new implications so that it has been widely assumed that it originated in his mind. One might say, without minimizing Darwin's achievement, that this widespread impression is not quite accurate. Charles Darwin in reality took a previously recognized biological device and gave it a new and quite different interpretation. In doing so he opened the doorway to unlimited organic change and provided that empirical evolutionary mechanism which had driven Lyell and other objective scientists away from the progressionists, even though the latter had been correct, in a general sense, about the ascending complexity of life. Darwin's achievement was an apt illustration of what can sometimes be done with old principles when someone looks at them in a new way and sees some unexpected possibility within them. Darwin altered our whole conception of the nature of the world in which we live. He did so by making use of a principle already known to Charles Lyell and one other man, a young zoologist by the name of Edward Blyth. Essentially it was the principle that Lyell advanced against the evolutionary arguments of Lamarck in the 1830's.

"Of all forms of mental activity," the historian Herbert Butterfield once wrote, "the most difficult to induce is the act of handling the same bundle of data as before, but placing them in a new system of relations with one another by giving them a different framework, all of which virtually means putting on a different kind of thinking cap for the moment." This is precisely what Charles Darwin did when he took the older conception of natural selection and by altering it a hairbreadth created that region of perpetual change, of toothed birds, footless serpents and upright walking apes in which we find ourselves. Yet difficult as Darwin's feat proved to be, he received a hint, a nudge as it were, which began with Lyell, was elaborated by young Edward Blyth and from him was apparently transferred to Darwin. No clearer sequence in the evolution of ideas can be perceived anywhere in the domain of science.

Edward Blyth was a man of 25 when he read Lyell and, impressed by his ideas, carried them a little further. In the British *Magazine of Natural History* in 1835 and again in 1837, the very year that Darwin opened his first notebook upon the species question, Blyth discussed what today we would call both natural and sexual selection.

"Among animals which procure their food by means of their agility, strength or delicacy of sense, the one best organized must always obtain the greatest quantity; and must, therefore, become physically the strongest and be thus enabled, by routing its opponents, to transmit its superior qualities to a greater number of offspring. The same law, therefore, which was intended by Providence to keep up the typical qualities of a species can be easily converted by man, into a means of raising different varieties."

This idea young Blyth referred to as his "localizing principle." Like Lyell he saw the conservative aspect of selection, but he saw it more clearly. He actually discussed its genetic aspects. As the above quotation indicates, however, he interpreted natural selection as a providential device eliminating the variant and unfit and holding each organism to its divinely appointed place in nature. Nevertheless in the course of his speculations he draws up short before a startling thought. "A variety of important considerations here crowd upon the mind," he confesses, "foremost of which is the enquiry, that, as man, by removing species from their appropriate haunts, superinduces changes on their physical constitution and adaptations, to what extent may not the same take place in wild nature, so that, in a few generations distinctive characters may be acquired, such as are recognized as indicative of specific diversity. . . ? May not then a large proportion of what are considered species have descended from a common parentage?"

The great question had been asked again, but this time more definitively, more perspicaciously, than it had ever been asked before. Sadly, timidly young Blyth in the end rejects his own question: Like Lyell, from whom he had drawn much, he found the new world he had glimpsed too dim, too distant, too awe-inspiringly new to be quite real. One rubbed one's eyes and it was gone. The safe, constricted world of the English hedgerows remained—the world in which everything held its place.

But the year was 1837. Charles Darwin was home from the Galápagos, home from the five-year voyage of the *Beagle*, home with turtles and coral,

CATASTROPHIC VIEW of the earth's history is reflected in this engraving by Albrecht Dürer. The engraving illustrates the passage in the Bible (*The Revelations of Saint John the Divine*, Chapter 6, Verse 13) beginning: "And the stars of heaven fell unto the earth. . . ."

bird beaks and pampas thistles in his head. He read the *Magazine of Natural History* consistently in this time. We know it from recently discovered evidence. In fact, Darwin, in a somewhat cryptic early letter, tells us so: "In such foreign periodicals as I have seen, there are no such papers as White or Waterton, or some few other naturalists in Loudon's and Charlesworth's Journal would have written; and a great loss it has always appeared to me." Loudon's and Charlesworth's Journal is the *Magazine of Natural History*. There, to lie undiscovered for a century, reposed the hint that seemingly started Darwin along the road to the *Origin*. There at last is the reason for the sudden burgeoning of his ideas after the return from the voyage. Interior evidence in Darwin's early essays strongly suggests the relationship.

Later on in the century the two men became friends. As to whether Edward Blyth ever saw or grasped the connection between his youthful thoughts and the intellectual revolution that came in 1859, we do not know. After many years in India, where he devoted himself largely to ornithology, he was invalided home and died in 1873.

Passing from Lyell to Blyth to Darwin, the world faintly glimpsed by a few thinkers before them—that marred, imperfect and yet forever changing world which brings equally into being butterflies and men—dawns fully in our minds. If there is revealed to us the dark shadow of tooth and club by which we have arisen, we are taught also the utter novelty of life, its unguessed potentialities. The lost Eden which, as Francis Bacon had dreamed, might be repossessed by knowledge lies ahead of us,

but it waits upon moral powers that may be as necessary to man as learning.

"Man is an ape and a beast," writes the pessimist. The true evolutionist will only say: "Man is a changeling. He is making himself blindly now, and dragging the dead past forward like a snake's cast-off skin whose fragments still bind him. He is a very young creature, a tick on Emerson's kitchen clock. Do not define him. Let the clock tick once more. Then we will know."

Already in Sir Charles Lyell's mind man's next hour was striking. As one surveys the long record of his life, as one sees his influence upon Edward Blyth, upon Darwin and upon Alfred Russel Wallace, as well as upon many other aspiring workers, one comes to recognize that to a major degree he set the scientific tone of the Victorian age. He brought to bear upon scientific thought and speculation a mind trained to the value of legal evidence. He was, on the whole, dispassionate, clear-headed and objective. By precept and example he transmitted that heritage to Darwin. He emphasized synthesis and logical generalization from facts. Both men eschewed small works and both amassed great bodies of material to carry their points. Lyell warned Darwin away from petty scientific bickering as a waste of time and nerves. At almost every step of Darwin's youthful career Lyell was an indefatigable guide and counselor. Then at that critical hour when Darwin was appalled by the reception of the news of Wallace's independent discovery of natural selection, it was Lyell and Hooker who counseled the simultaneous publication of the papers of both men.

Darwin and Wallace were Lyell's in-

tellectual children. Both would have failed to be what they were without the *Principles of Geology* to guide them. In science there is no such thing as total independence from one's forerunners. It is an illusion we sometimes like to foster, but it does not bear close examination. Even our boasted discoveries are often in reality a construct of many minds. We are fortunate if we sometimes succeed in fitting the last brick into such an edifice. Lyell himself knew this and tasted its irony.

He died in 1875 at the end of a long, outwardly uneventful life spent largely in the company of a beautiful, gracious and intelligent woman. After his wife's death in 1873 the light began to pass away from Lyell; he did not long survive her. A few years before, he had written to Ernst Haeckel: "Most of the zoologists forget that anything was written between the time of Lamarck and the publication of our friend's *Origin of Species*."

Much indeed had been forgotten. In this little sigh of regret Lyell was even then resigning his hold upon the public which had once idolized him. To the true historian of science, however, he remains the kingmaker whose giant progeny, whether acknowledging their master by direct word or through the lines of their books, continue today to influence those who have never heard his name.

Of Charles Lyell, Darwin himself said what is so often remarked in our day of Darwin: "The great merit of the *Principles* was that it altered the whole tone of one's mind and, therefore, that when seeing a thing never seen by Lyell, one yet saw it partially through his eyes."

The Genetic Basis of Evolution

13

January 1950

*The rich variety of living and dead species of plants
and animals is the result of subtle interplay between
the hereditary mechanism and a diversified environment*

THE living beings on our planet come in an incredibly rich diversity of forms. Biologists have identified about a million species of animals and some 267,000 species of plants, and the number of species actually in existence may be more than twice as large as the number known. In addition the earth has been inhabited in the past by huge numbers of other species that are now extinct, though some are preserved as fossils. The organisms of the earth range in size from viruses so minute that they are barely visible in electron microscopes to giants like elephants and sequoia trees. In appearance, body structure and ways of life they exhibit an endlessly fascinating variety.

What is the meaning of this bewildering diversity? Superficially considered, it may seem to reflect nothing more than the whims of some playful deity, but one soon finds that it is not fortuitous. The more one studies living beings the more one is impressed by the wonderfully effective adjustment of their multifarious body structures and functions to their varying ways of life. From the simplest to the most complex, all organisms are constructed to function efficiently in the environments in which they live. The body of a green plant can build itself from food consisting merely of water, certain gases in the air and some mineral salts taken from the soil. A fish is a highly efficient machine for exploiting the organic food resources of water, and a bird is built to get the most from its air en-

vironment. The human body is a complex, finely coordinated machine of marvelously precise engineering, and through the inventive abilities of his brain man is able to control his environment. Every species, even the most humble, occupies a certain place in the economy of nature, a certain adaptive niche which it exploits to stay alive.

The diversity and adaptedness of living beings were so difficult to explain that during most of his history man took the easy way out of assuming that every species was created by God, who contrived the body structures and functions of each kind of organism to fit it to a predestined place in nature. This idea has now been generally replaced by the less easy but intellectually more satisfying explanation that the living things we see around us were not always what they are now, but evolved gradually from very different-looking ancestors; that these ancestors were in general less complex, less perfect and less diversified than the organisms now living; that the evolutionary process is still under way, and that its causes can therefore be studied by observation and experiment in the field and in the laboratory.

The origins and development of this theory, and the facts that finally convinced most people of its truth beyond reasonable doubt, are too long a story to be presented here. After Charles Darwin published his convincing exposition and proof of the theory of evolution in 1859, two main currents developed in evolu-

tionary thought. Like any historical process, organic evolution may be studied in two ways. One may attempt to infer the general features and the direction of the process from comparative studies of the sequence of events in the past; this is the method of paleontologists, comparative anatomists and others. Or one may attempt to reconstruct the causes of evolution, primarily through a study of the causes and mechanisms that operate in the world at present; this approach, which uses experimental rather than observational methods, is that of the geneticist and the ecologist. This article will consider what has been learned about the causes of organic evolution through the second approach.

Darwin attempted to describe the causes of evolution in his theory of natural selection. The work of later biologists has borne out most of his basic contentions. Nevertheless, the modern theory of evolution, developed by a century of new discoveries in biology, differs greatly from Darwin's. His theory has not been overthrown; it has evolved. The authorship of the modern theory can be credited to no single person. Next to Darwin, Gregor Mendel of Austria, who first stated the laws of heredity, made the greatest contribution. Within the past two decades the study of evolutionary genetics has developed very rapidly on the basis of the work of Thomas Hunt Morgan and Hermann J. Muller of the U. S. In these developments the principal contributors have been C. D.

CONTROLLED ENVIRONMENT for the study of fruit-fly populations is a glass-covered box. In bottom of the box are cups of food that are filled in rotation to keep food a constant factor in environment.

Darlington, R. A. Fisher, J. B. S. Haldane, J. S. Huxley and R. Mather in England; B. Rensch and N. W. Timofeeff-Ressovsky in Germany; S. S. Chetverikov, N. P. Dubinin and I. I. Schmalhausen in the U.S.S.R.; E. Mayr, J. T. Patterson, C. G. Simpson, G. L. Stebbins and Sewall Wright in the U. S., and some others.

Evolution in the Laboratory

Evolution is generally so slow a process that during the few centuries of recorded observations man has been able to detect very few evolutionary changes among animals and plants in their natural habitats. Darwin had to deduce the theory of evolution mostly from indirect evidence, for he had no means of observing the process in action. Today, however, we can study and even produce evolutionary changes at will in the laboratory. The experimental subjects of these studies are bacteria and other low forms of life which come to birth, mature and yield a new generation within a matter of minutes or hours, instead of months or years as in most higher beings. Like a greatly speeded-up motion picture, these observations compress into a few days evolutionary events that would take thousands of years in the higher animals.

One of the most useful bacteria for this study is an organism that grows, usually harmlessly, in the intestines of practically every human being: *Escherichia coli*, or colon bacteria. These organisms can easily be cultured on a nutritive broth or nutritive agar. At about 98 degrees Fahrenheit, bacterial cells placed in a fresh culture medium divide about every 20 minutes. Their numbers increase rapidly until the nutrients in the culture medium are exhausted; a single cell may yield billions of progeny in a day. If a few cells are placed on a plate covered with nutritive agar, each cell by the end of the day produces a whitish speck representing a colony of its offspring.

Now most colon bacteria are easily killed by the antibiotic drug streptomycin. It takes only a tiny amount of streptomycin, 25 milligrams in a liter of a nutrient medium, to stop the growth of the bacteria. Recently, however, the geneticist Milislav Demerec and his collaborators at the Carnegie Institution in Cold Spring Harbor, N. Y., have shown that if several billion colon bacteria are placed on the streptomycin-containing medium, a few cells will survive and form colonies on the plate. The offspring of these hardy survivors are able to multiply freely on a medium containing streptomycin. A mutation has evidently taken place in the bacteria; they have now become resistant to the streptomycin that was poisonous to their sensitive ancestors.

How do the bacteria acquire their

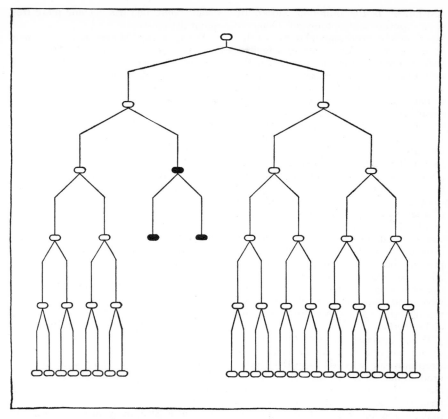

IN NORMAL ENVIRONMENT the common strain of the bacterium *Escherichia coli* (*white bacteria*) multiplies. A mutant strain resistant to streptomycin (*black bacteria*) remains rare because the mutation is not useful.

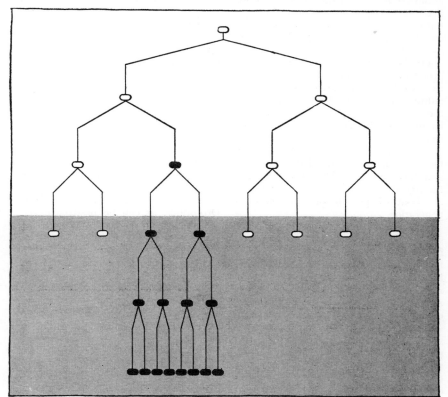

IN CHANGED ENVIRONMENT produced by the addition of streptomycin (*gray area*) the streptomycin-resistant strain is better adapted than the common strain. The mutant strain then multiplies and the common one dies.

resistance? Is the mutation caused by their exposure to streptomycin? Demerec has shown by experimental tests that this is not so; in any large culture a few resistant mutants appear even when the culture has not been exposed to streptomycin. Some cells in the culture undergo mutations from sensitivity to resistance regardless of the presence or absence of streptomycin in the medium. Demerec found that the frequency of mutation was about one per billion; *i.e.*, one cell in a billion becomes resistant in every generation. Streptomycin does not induce the mutations; its role in the production of resistant strains is merely that of a selecting agent. When streptomycin is added to the culture, all the normal sensitive cells are killed, and only the few resistant mutants that happened to be present before the streptomycin was added survive and reproduce. Evolutionary changes are controlled by the environment, but the control is indirect, through the agency of natural or artificial selection.

What governs the selection? If resistant bacteria arise in the absence of streptomycin, why do sensitive forms predominate in all normal cultures; why has not the whole species of colon bacteria become resistant? The answer is that the mutants resistant to streptomycin are at a disadvantage on media free from this drug. Indeed, Demerec has discovered the remarkable fact that about 60 per cent of the bacterial strains derived from streptomycin-resistant mutants become dependent on streptomycin; they are unable to grow on media free from it!

On the other hand one can reverse the process and obtain strains of bacteria that can live without streptomycin from cultures predominantly dependent on the drug. If some billions of dependent bacteria are plated on nutrient media free of the drug, all dependent cells cease to multiply and only the few mutants independent of the drug reproduce and form colonies. Demerec estimates the frequency of this "reverse" mutation at about 37 per billion cells in each generation.

Evolutionary changes of the type described in colon bacteria have been found in recent years in many other bacterial species. The increasing use of antibiotic drugs in medical practice has made such changes a matter of considerable concern in public health. As penicillin, for example, is used on a large scale against bacterial infections, the strains of bacteria that are resistant to penicillin survive and multiply, and the probability that they will infect new victims is increased. The mass application of antibiotic drugs may lead in the long run to increased incidence of cases refractory to treatment. Indications exist that this has already happened in some instances: in certain cities penicillin-resistant gonorrhea has become more frequent than it was.

The same type of evolutionary change has also been noted in some larger organisms. A good example is the case of DDT and the common housefly, *Musca domestica*. DDT was a remarkably effective poison for houseflies when first introduced less than 10 years ago. But already reports have come from places as widely separated as New Hampshire, New York, Florida, Texas, Italy and Sweden that DDT sprays in certain localities have lost their effectiveness. What has happened, of course, is that strains of houseflies relatively resistant to DDT have become established in these localities. Man has unwittingly become an agent of a selection process which has led to evolutionary changes in housefly populations. Similar changes are known to have occurred in other insects; *e.g.*, in some orchards of California where hydrocyanic gas has long been used as a fumigant to control scale insects that prey on citrus fruits, strains of these insects that are resistant to hydrocyanic gas have developed.

Obviously evolutionary selection can take place only if nature provides a supply of mutants to choose from. Thus no bacteria will survive to start a new strain resistant to streptomycin in a culture in which no resistant mutant cells were present in the first place, and housefly races resistant to DDT have not appeared everywhere that DDT is used. Adaptive changes are not mechanically forced upon the organism by the environment. Many species of past geological epochs died out because they did not have a supply of mutants which fitted changing environments. The process of mutation furnishes the raw materials from which evolutionary changes are built.

Mutations

Mutations arise from time to time in all organisms, from viruses to man. Perhaps the best organism for the study of mutations is the now-famous fruit fly, Drosophila. It can be bred easily and rapidly in laboratories, and it has a large number of bodily traits and functions that are easy to observe. Mutations affect the color of its eyes and body, the size and shape of the body and of its parts, its internal anatomical structures, its fecundity, its rate of growth, its behavior, and so on. Some mutations produce differences so minute that they can be detected only by careful measurements; others are easily seen even by beginners; still others produce changes so drastic that death occurs before the development is completed. The latter are called lethal mutations.

The frequency of any specific mutation is usually low. We have seen that in colon bacteria a mutation to resistance to streptomycin occurs in only about one cell per billion in every generation, and the reverse mutation to independence of streptomycin is about 37 times more frequent. In Drosophila and in the corn plant mutations have been found to range in frequency from one in 100,000 to one in a million per generation. In man, according to estimates by Haldane in England and James Neel in the U. S., mutations that produce certain hereditary diseases, such as hemophilia and Cooley's anemia, arise in one in 2,500 to one in 100,000 sex cells in each generation. From this it may appear that man is more mutable than flies and bacteria, but it should be remembered that a generation in man takes some 25 years, in flies two weeks, and in bacteria 25 minutes. The frequency of mutations per unit of time is actually greater in bacteria than in man.

A single organism may of course produce several mutations, affecting different features of the body. How frequent are all mutations combined? For technical reasons, this is difficult to determine; for example, most mutants produce small changes that are not detected unless especially looked for. In Drosophila it is estimated that new mutants affecting one part of the body or another are present in between one and 10 per cent of the sex cells in every generation.

In all organisms the majority of mutations are more or less harmful. This may seem a very serious objection against the theory which regards them as the mainspring of evolution. If mutations produce incapacitating changes, how can adaptive evolution be compounded of them? The answer is: a mutation that is harmful in the environment in which the species or race lives may become useful, even essential, if the environment changes. Actually it would be strange if we found mutations that improve the adaptation of the organism in the environment in which it normally lives. Every kind of mutation that we observe has occurred numerous times under natural conditions, and the useful ones have become incorporated into what we call the "normal" constitution of the species. But when the environment changes, some of the previously rejected mutations become advantageous and produce an evolutionary change in the species. The writer and B. A. Spassky have carried out certain experiments in which we intentionally disturbed the harmony between an artificial environment and the fruit flies living in it. At first the change in environment killed most of the flies, but during 50 consecutive generations most strains showed a gradual improvement of viability, evidently owing to the environment's selection of the better-adapted variants.

This is not to say that every mutation will be found useful in some environment somewhere. It would be difficult to

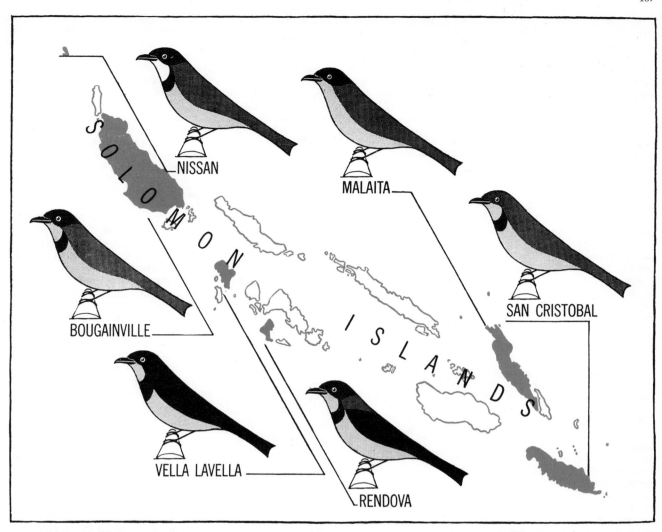

CONCEPT OF RACE is illustrated by the varieties of the golden whistler (*Pachycephala pectoralis*) of the Solomon Islands. The races are kept distinct principally by geographical isolation. They differ in their black and white and colored markings. Dark gray areas are symbol for green markings; light gray for yellow.

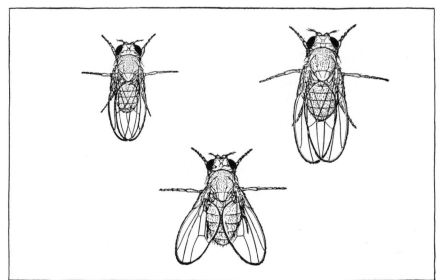

SPECIES OF DROSOPHILA and some other organisms tend to remain separate because their hybrid offspring are often weak and sterile. At left is *D. pseudoobscura*; at right *D. miranda*. Their hybrid descendant is at bottom.

RITUALS OF MATING in *D. nebulosa* (*top*) and *D. willistoni* are example of factor that separates species.

imagine environments in which such human mutants as hemophilia or the absence of hands and feet might be useful. Most mutants that arise in any species are, in effect, degenerative changes; but some, perhaps a small minority, may be beneficial in some environments. If the environment were forever constant, a species might conceivably reach a summit of adaptedness and ultimately suppress the mutation process. But the environment is never constant; it varies not only from place to place but from time to time. If no mutations occur in a species, it can no longer become adapted to changes and is headed for eventual extinction. Mutation is the price that organisms pay for survival. They do not possess a miraculous ability to produce only useful mutations where and when needed. Mutations arise at random, regardless of whether they will be useful at the moment, or ever; nevertheless, they make the species rich in adaptive possibilities.

The Genes

To understand the nature of the mutation process we must inquire into the nature of heredity. A man begins his individual existence when an egg cell is fertilized by a spermatozoon. From an egg cell weighing only about a 20-millionth of an ounce, he grows to an average weight at maturity of some 150 pounds—a 48-billionfold increase. The material for this stupendous increase in mass evidently comes from the food consumed, first by the mother and then by the individual himself. But the food becomes a constituent part of the body only after it is digested and assimilated, *i.e.*, transformed into a likeness of the assimilating body. This body, in turn, is a likeness of the bodies of the individual's ancestors. Heredity is, then, a process whereby the organism reproduces itself in its progeny from food materials taken in from the environment. In short, heredity is self-reproduction.

The units of self-reproduction are called genes. The genes are borne chiefly in chromosomes of the cell nucleus, but certain types of genes called plasmagenes are present in the cytoplasm, the part of the cell outside the nucleus. The chemical details of the process of self-reproduction are unknown. Apparently a gene enters into some set of chemical reactions with materials in its surroundings; the outcome of these reactions is the appearance of two genes in the place of one. In other words, a gene synthesizes a copy of itself from nongenic materials. The genes are considered to be stable because the copy is a true likeness of the original in the overwhelming majority of cases; but occasionally the copying process is faulty, and the new gene that emerges differs from its model. This is a mutation. We can increase the

frequency of mutations in experimental animals by treating the genes with X-rays, ultraviolet rays, high temperature or certain chemical substances.

Can a gene be changed by the environment? Assuredly it can. But the important point is the kind of change produced. The change that is easiest to make is to treat the gene with poisons or heat in such a way that it no longer reproduces itself. But a gene that cannot produce a copy of itself from other materials is no longer a gene; it is dead. A mutation is a change of a very special kind: the altered gene can reproduce itself, and the copy produced is like the changed structure, not like the original. Changes of this kind are relatively rare. Their rarity is not due to any imperviousness of the genes to influences of the environment, for genic materials are probably the most active chemical constituents of the body; it is due to the fact that genes are by nature self-reproducing, and only the rare changes that preserve the genes' ability to reproduce can effect a lasting alteration of the organism.

Changes in heredity should not be confused, as they often are, with changes in the manifestations of heredity. Such expressions as "gene for eye color" or "inheritance of musical ability" are figures of speech. The sex cells that transmit heredity have no eyes and no musical ability. What genes determine are patterns of development which result in the emergence of eyes of a certain color and of individuals with some musical abilities. When genes reproduce themselves from different food materials and in different environments, they engender the development of different "characters" or "traits" in the body. The outcome of the development is influenced both by heredity and by environment.

In the popular imagination, heredity is transmitted from parents to offspring through "blood." The heredity of a child is supposed to be a kind of alloy or solution, resulting from the mixture of the paternal and maternal "bloods." This blood theory became scientifically untenable as long ago as Mendel's discovery of the laws of heredity in 1865. Heredity is transmitted not through miscible bloods but through genes. When different variants of a gene are brought together in a single organism, a hybrid, they do not fuse or contaminate one another; the genes keep their integrity and separate when the hybrid forms sex cells.

Genetics and Mathematics

Although the number of genes in a single organism is not known with precision, it is certainly in the thousands, at least in the higher organisms. For Drosophila, 5,000 to 12,000 seems a reasonable estimate, and for man the figure is, if anything, higher. Since most or all genes

suffer mutational changes from time to time, populations of virtually every species must contain mutant variants of many genes. For example, in the human species there are variations in the skin, hair and eye colors, in the shape and distribution of hair, in the form of the head, nose and lips, in stature, in body proportions, in the chemical composition of the blood, in psychological traits, and so on. Each of these traits is influenced by several or by many genes. To be conservative, let us assume that the human species has only 1,000 genes and that each gene has only two variants. Even on this conservative basis, Mendelian segregation and recombination would be capable of producing 2^{1000} different gene combinations in human beings.

The number 2^{1000} is easy to write but is utterly beyond comprehension. Compared with it, the total number of electrons and protons estimated by physicists to exist in the universe is negligibly small! It means that except in the case of identical twins no two persons now living, dead, or to live in the future are at all likely to carry the same complement of genes. Dogs, mice and flies are as individual and unrepeatable as men are. The mechanism of sexual reproduction, of which the recombination of genes is a part, creates ever new genetic constitutions on a prodigious scale.

One might object that the number of possible combinations does not greatly matter; after all, they will still be combinations of the same thousand gene variants, and the way they are combined is not significant. Actually it is: the same gene may have different effects in combinations with different genes. Thus Timofeeff-Ressovsky showed that two mutants in Drosophila, each of which reduced the viability of the fly when it was present alone, were harmless when combined in the same individual by hybridization. Natural selection tests the fitness in certain environments not of single genes but of constellations of genes present in living individuals.

Sexual reproduction generates, therefore, an immense diversity of genetic constitutions, some of which, perhaps a small minority, may prove well attuned to the demands of certain environments. The biological function of sexual reproduction consists in providing a highly efficient trial-and-error mechanism for the operation of natural selection. It is a reasonable conjecture that sex became established as the prevalent method of reproduction because it gave organisms the greatest potentialities for adaptive and progressive evolution.

Let us try to imagine a world providing a completely uniform environment. Suppose that the surface of our planet were absolutely flat, covered everywhere with the same soil; that instead of summer and winter seasons we had eternally constant temperature and humidity; that instead of the existing diversity of foods there was only one kind of energy-yielding substance to serve as nourishment. The Russian biologist Gause has pointed out that only a single kind of organism could inhabit such a tedious world. If two or more kinds appeared in it, the most efficient form would gradually crowd out and finally eliminate the less efficient ones, remaining the sole inhabitant. In the world of reality, however, the environment changes at every step. Oceans, plains, hills, mountain ranges, regions where summer heat alternates with winter cold, lands that are permanently warm, dry deserts, humid jungles —these diverse environments have engendered a multitude of responses by protoplasm and a vast proliferation of distinct species of life through the evolutionary process.

Some Adaptations

Many animal and plant species are polymorphic, *i.e.*, represented in nature by two or more clearly distinguishable kinds of individuals. For example, some individuals of the ladybird beetle *Adalia bipunctata* are red with black spots while others are black with red spots. The color difference is hereditary, the black color behaving as a Mendelian dominant and red as a recessive. The red and black forms live side by side and interbreed freely. Timofeeff-Ressovsky observed that near Berlin, Germany, the black form predominates from spring to autumn, and the red form is more numerous during the winter. What is the origin of these changes? It is quite improbable that the genes for color are transformed by the seasonal variations in temperature; that would mean epidemics of directed mutations on a scale never observed. A much more plausible view is that the changes are produced by natural selection. The black form is, for some reason, more successful than the red in survival and reproduction during summer, but the red is superior to the black under winter conditions. Since the beetles produce several generations during a single season, the species undergoes cyclic changes in its genetic composition in response to the seasonal alterations in the environment. This hypothesis was confirmed by the discovery that black individuals are more frequent among the beetles that die during the rigors of winter than among those that survive.

The writer has observed seasonal changes in some localities in California in the fly *Drosophila pseudoobscura*. Flies of this species in nature are rather uniform in coloration and other external traits, but they are very variable in the structure of their chromosomes, which can be seen in microscopic preparations. In the locality called Piñon Flats, on Mount San Jacinto in southern Califor-

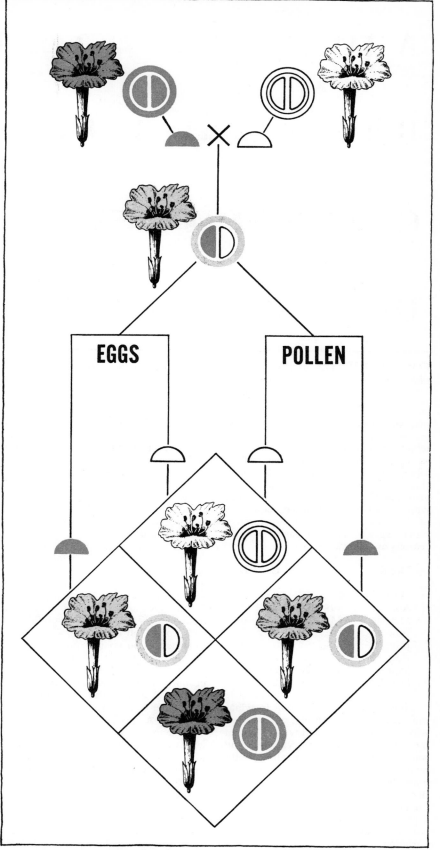

MENDELIAN SEGREGATION is illustrated by the four o'clock (*Mirabilis jalapa*). The genes of red and white flowers combine in a pink hybrid. Genes are segregated in the cross-fertilized descendants of pink flowers.

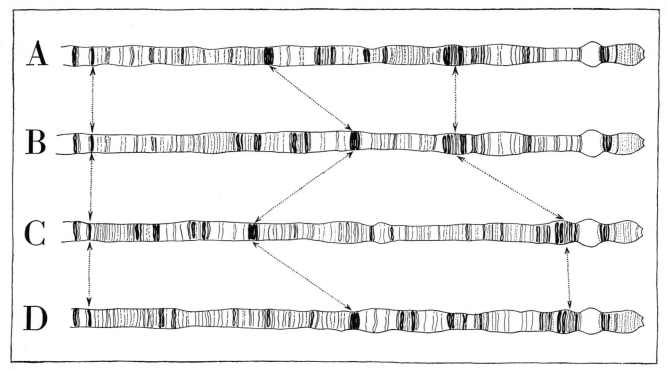

FOUR VARIETIES of the species *Drosophila pseudo-obscura* are revealed by differences in the structure of their chromosomes. Under the microscope similar markings may be observed at different locations (*arrows*).

nia, the fruit-fly population has four common types of chromosome structure, which we may, for simplicity, designate as types A, B, C and D. From 1939 to 1946, samples of flies were taken from this population in various months of the year, and the chromosomes of these flies were examined. The relative frequencies of the chromosomal types, expressed in percentages of the total, varied with the seasons as follows:

Month	A	B	C	D
March	52	18	23	7
April	40	28	28	4
May	34	29	31	6
June	28	28	39	5
July	42	22	31	5
Aug.	42	28	26	4
Sept.	48	23	26	3
Oct.-Dec.	50	26	20	4

Thus type A was common in winter but declined in the spring, while type C waxed in the spring and waned in summer. Evidently flies carrying chromosomes of type C are somehow better adapted than type A to the spring climate; hence from March to June, type A decreases and type C increases in frequency. Contrariwise, in the summer type A is superior to type C. Types B and D show little consistent seasonal variation.

Similar changes can be observed under controlled laboratory conditions. Populations of Drosophila flies were kept in a very simple apparatus consisting of a wood and glass box, with openings in the bottom for replenishing the nutrient medium on which the flies lived—a kind of pudding made of Cream of Wheat, molasses and yeast. A mixture of flies of which 33 per cent were type A and 67 per cent type C was introduced into the apparatus and left to multiply freely, up to the limit imposed by the quantity of food given. If one of the types was better adapted to the environment than the other, it was to be expected that the better-adapted type would increase and the other decrease in relative numbers. This is exactly what happened. During the first six months the type A flies rose from 33 to 77 per cent of the population, and type C fell from 67 to 23 per cent. But then came an unexpected leveling off: during the next seven months there was no further change in the relative proportions of the flies, the frequencies of types A and C oscillating around 75 and 25 per cent respectively.

If type A was better than type C under the conditions of the experiment, why were not the flies with C chromosomes crowded out completely by the carriers of A? Sewall Wright of the University of Chicago solved the puzzle by mathematical analysis. The flies of these types interbreed freely, in natural as well as in experimental populations. The populations therefore consist of three kinds of individuals: 1) those that obtained chromosome A from father as well as from mother, and thus carry two A chromosomes (AA); 2) those with two C chromosomes (CC); 3) those that re-ceived chromosomes of different types from their parents (AC). The mixed type, AC, possesses the highest adaptive value; it has what is called "hybrid vigor." As for the pure types, under the conditions that obtain in nature AA is superior to CC in the summer. Natural selection then increases the frequency of A chromosomes in the population and diminishes the C chromosomes. In the spring, when CC is better than AA, the reverse is true. But note now that in a population of mixed types neither the A nor the C chromosomes can ever be entirely eliminated from the population, even if the flies are kept in a constant environment where type AA is definitely superior to type CC. This, of course, is highly favorable to the flies as a species, for the loss of one of the chromosome types, though it might be temporarily advantageous, would be prejudicial in the long run, when conditions favoring the lost type would return. Thus a polymorphic population is better able than a uniform one to adjust itself to environmental changes and to exploit a variety of habitats.

Races

Populations of the same species which inhabit different environments become genetically different. This is what a geneticist means when he speaks of races. Races are populations within a species that differ in the frequencies of some genes. According to the old concept of race, which is based on the notion that

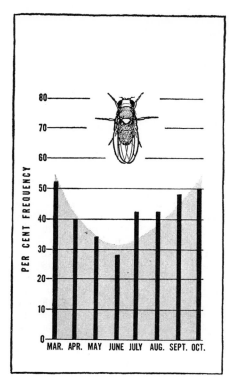

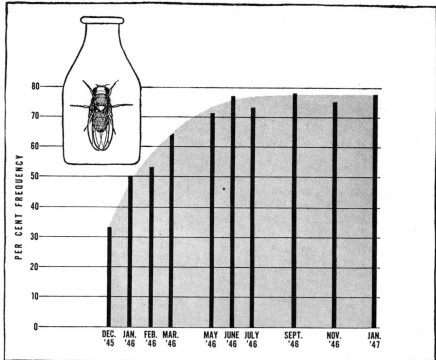

NUMBER OF FLIES of one chromosomal type varies in nature (*left*) and in the laboratory. In seasonal environment of nature the type increases and decreases regularly; in constant environment of laboratory it levels off.

heredity is transmitted through "blood" and which still prevails among those ignorant of modern biology, the hereditary endowment of an isolated population would become more and more uniform with each generation, provided there was no interbreeding with other tribes or populations. The tribe would eventually become a "pure" race, all members of which would be genetically uniform. Scientists misled by this notion used to think that at some time in the past the human species consisted of an unspecified number of "pure" races, and that intermarriage between them gave rise to the present "mixed" populations.

In reality, "pure" races never existed, nor can they possibly exist in any species, such as man, that reproduces by sexual combination. We have seen that all human beings except identical twins differ in heredity. In widely differing climatic environments the genetic differences may be substantial. Thus populations native in central Africa have much higher frequencies of genes that produce dark skin than do European populations. The frequency of the gene for blue eye color progressively diminishes southward from Scandinavia through central Europe to the Mediterranean and Africa. Nonetheless some blue-eyed individuals occur in the Mediterranean region and even in Africa, and some brown-eyed ones in Norway and Sweden.

It is important to keep in mind that races are populations, not individuals. Race differences are relative and not absolute, since only in very remote races

do all members of one population possess a set of genes that is lacking in all members of another population. It is often difficult to tell how many races exist in a species. For example, some anthropologists recognize only two human races while others list more than 100. The difficulty is to know where to draw the line. If, for example, the Norwegians are a "Nordic race" and the southern Italians a "Mediterranean race," to what race do the inhabitants of Denmark, northern Germany, southern Germany, Switzerland and northern Italy belong? The frequencies of most differentiating traits change rather gradually from Norway to southern Italy. Calling the intermediate populations separate races may be technically correct, but this confuses the race classification even more, because nowhere can sharp lines of demarcation between these "races" be drawn. It is quite arbitrary whether we recognize 2, 4, 10, or more than 100 races—or finally refuse to make any rigid racial labels at all.

The differences between human races are, after all, rather small, since the geographic separation between them is nowhere very marked. When a species is distributed over diversified territories, the process of adaptation to the different environments leads to the gradual accumulation of more numerous and biologically more and more important differences between races. The races gradually diverge. There is, of course, nothing fatal about this divergence, and under some circumstances the divergence may

stop or even be turned into convergence. This is particularly true of the human species. The human races were somewhat more sharply separated in the past than they are today. Although the species inhabits almost every variety of environment on earth, the development of communications and the increase of mobility, especially in modern times, has led to much intermarriage and to some genetic convergence of the human races.

The diverging races become more and more distinct with time, and the process of divergence may finally culminate in transformation of races into species. Although the splitting of species is a gradual process, and it is often impossible to tell exactly when races cease to be races and become species, there exist some important differences between race and species which make the process of species formation one of the most important biological processes. Indeed, Darwin called his chief work *The Origin of Species*.

Races of sexually reproducing organisms are fully capable of intercrossing; they maintain their distinction as races only by geographical isolation. As a rule in most organisms no more than a single race of any one species inhabits the same territory. If representatives of two or more races come to live in the same territory, they interbreed, exchange genes, and eventually become fused into a single population. The human species, however, is an exception. Marriages are influenced by linguistic, religious, social, economic and other cultural factors.

Hence cultural isolation may keep populations apart for a time and slow down the exchange of genes even though the populations live in the same country. Nevertheless, the biological relationship proves stronger than cultural isolation, and interbreeding is everywhere in the process of breaking down such barriers. Unrestricted interbreeding would not mean, as often supposed, that all people would become alike. Mankind would continue to include at least as great a diversity of hereditary endowments as it contains today. However, the same types could be found anywhere in the world, and races as more or less discrete populations would cease to exist.

The Isolationism of Species

Species, on the contrary, can live in the same territory without losing their identity. F. Lutz of the American Museum of Natural History found 1,402 species of insects in the 75-by-200-foot yard of his home in a New Jersey suburb. This does not mean that representatives of distinct species never cross. Closely related species occasionally do interbreed in nature, especially among plants, but these cases are so rare that the discovery of one usually merits a note in a scientific journal.

The reason distinct species do not interbreed is that they are more or less completely kept apart by isolating mechanisms connected with reproduction, which exist in great variety. For example, the botanist Carl C. Epling of the University of California found that two species of sage which are common in southern California are generally separated by ecological factors, one preferring a dry site, the other a more humid one. When the two sages do grow side by side, they occasionally produce hybrids. The hybrids are quite vigorous, but their seed set amounts to less than two per cent of normal; i.e., they are partially sterile. Hybrid sterility is a very common and effective isolating mechanism. A classic example is the mule, hybrid of the horse and donkey. Male mules are always sterile, females usually so. There are, however, some species, notably certain ducks, that produce quite fertile hybrids, not in nature but in captivity.

Two species of Drosophila, *pseudoobscura* and *persimilis*, are so close together biologically that they cannot be distinguished by inspection of their external characteristics. They differ, however, in the structure of their chromosomes and in many physiological traits. If a mixed group of females of the two species is exposed to a group of males of one species, copulations occur much more frequently between members of the same species than between those of different species, though some of the latter do take place. Among plants, the flowers of related species may differ so much in structure that they cannot be pollinated by the same insects, or they may have such differences in smell, color and shape that they attract different insects. Finally, even when cross-copulation or cross-pollination can occur, the union may fail to result in fertilization or may produce offspring that cannot live. Often several isolating mechanisms, no one of which is effective separately, combine to prevent interbreeding. In the case of the two fruit-fly species, at least three such mechanisms are at work: 1) the above-mentioned disposition to mate only with their own kind, even when they are together; 2) different preferences in climate, one preferring warmer and drier places than the other; 3) the fact that when they do interbreed the hybrid males that result are completely sterile and the hybrid females, though fertile, produce offspring that are poorly viable. There is good evidence that no gene exchange occurs between these species in nature.

The fact that distinct species can coexist in the same territory, while races generally cannot, is highly significant. It permits the formation of communities of diversified living beings which exploit the variety of habitats present in a territory more fully than any single species, no matter how polymorphic, could. It is responsible for the richness and colorfulness of life that is so impressive to biologists and non-biologists alike.

Evolution v. Predestination

Our discussion of the essentials of the modern theory of evolution may be concluded with a consideration of the objections raised against it. The most serious objection is that since mutations occur by "chance" and are undirected, and since selection is a "blind" force, it is difficult to see how mutation and selection can add up to the formation of such complex and beautifully balanced organs as, for example, the human eye. This, say critics of the theory, is like believing that a monkey pounding a typewriter might accidentally type out Dante's *Divine Comedy*. Some biologists have preferred to suppose that evolution is directed by an "inner urge toward perfection," or by a "combining power which amounts to intentionality," or by "telefinalism" or the like. The fatal weakness of these alternative "explanations" of evolution is that they do not explain anything. To say that evolution is directed by an urge, a combining power, or a telefinalism is like saying that a railroad engine is moved by a "locomotive power."

The objection that the modern theory of evolution makes undue demands on chance is based on a failure to appreciate the historical character of the evolutionary process. It would indeed strain credulity to suppose that a lucky sudden combination of chance mutations produced the eye in all its perfection. But the eye did not appear suddenly in the offspring of an eyeless creature; it is the result of an evolutionary development that took many millions of years. Along the way the evolving rudiments of the eye passed through innumerable stages, all of which were useful to their possessors, and therefore all adjusted to the demands of the environment by natural selection. Amphioxus, the primitive fishlike darling of comparative anatomists, has no eyes, but it has certain pigment cells in its brain by means of which it perceives light. Such pigment cells may have been the starting point of the development of eyes in our ancestors.

We have seen that the "combining power" of the sexual process is staggering, that on the most conservative estimate the number of possible gene combinations in the human species alone is far greater than that of the electrons and protons in the universe. When life developed sex, it acquired a trial-and-error mechanism of prodigious efficiency. This mechanism is not called upon to produce a completely new creature in one spectacular burst of creation; it is sufficient that it produces slight changes that improve the organism's chances of survival or reproduction in some habitat. In terms of the monkey-and-typewriter analogy, the theory does not require that the monkey sit down and compose the *Divine Comedy* from beginning to end by a lucky series of hits. All we need is that the monkey occasionally form a single word, or a single line; over the course of eons of time the environment shapes this growing text into the eventual masterpiece. Mutations occur by "chance" only in the sense that they appear regardless of their usefulness at the time and place of their origin. It should be kept in mind that the structure of a gene, like that of the whole organism, is the outcome of a long evolutionary development; the ways in which the genes can mutate are, consequently, by no means indeterminate.

Theories that ascribe evolution to "urges" and "telefinalisms" imply that there is some kind of predestination about the whole business, that evolution has produced nothing more than was potentially present at the beginning of life. The modern evolutionists believe that, on the contrary, evolution is a creative response of the living matter to the challenges of the environment. The role of the environment is to provide opportunities for biological inventions. Evolution is due neither to chance nor to design; it is due to a natural creative process.

The Genetic Code: III

14

by F. H. C. Crick
October 1966

The central theme of molecular biology is confirmed by detailed knowledge of how the four-letter language embodied in molecules of nucleic acid controls the 20-letter language of the proteins

The hypothesis that the genes of the living cell contain all the information needed for the cell to reproduce itself is now more than 50 years old. Implicit in the hypothesis is the idea that the genes bear in coded form the detailed specifications for the thousands of kinds of protein molecules the cell requires for its moment-to-moment existence: for extracting energy from molecules assimilated as food and for repairing itself as well as for replication. It is only within the past 15 years, however, that insight has been gained into the chemical nature of the genetic material and how its molecular structure can embody coded instructions that can be "read" by the machinery in the cell responsible for synthesizing protein molecules. As the result of intensive work by many investigators the story

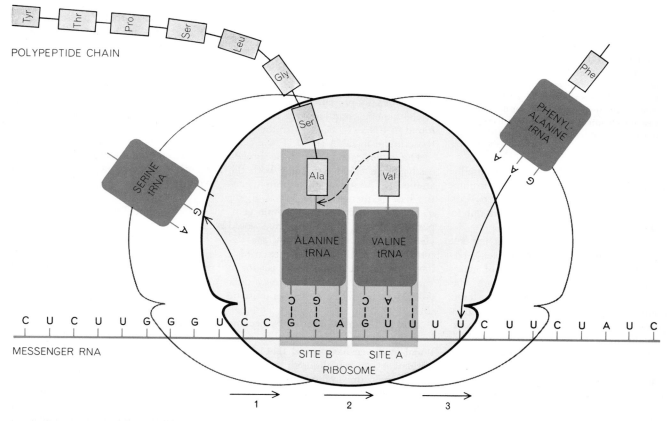

SYNTHESIS OF PROTEIN MOLECULES is accomplished by the intracellular particles called ribosomes. The coded instructions for making the protein molecule are carried to the ribosome by a form of ribonucleic acid (RNA) known as "messenger" RNA. The RNA code "letters" are four bases: uracil (U), cytosine (C), adenine (A) and guanine (G). A sequence of three bases, called a codon, is required to specify each of the 20 kinds of amino acid, identified here by their abbreviations. (A list of the 20 amino acids and their abbreviations appears on the next page.) When linked end to end, these amino acids form the polypeptide chains of which proteins are composed. Each type of amino acid is transported to the ribosome by a particular form of "transfer" RNA (tRNA), which carries an anticodon that can form a temporary bond with one of the codons in messenger RNA. Here the ribosome is shown moving along the chain of messenger RNA, "reading off" the codons in sequence. It appears that the ribosome has two binding sites for molecules of tRNA: one site (A) for positioning a newly arrived tRNA molecule and another (B) for holding the growing polypeptide chain.

AMINO ACID	ABBREVIATION
ALANINE	Ala
ARGININE	Arg
ASPARAGINE	AspN
ASPARTIC ACID	Asp
CYSTEINE	Cys
GLUTAMIC ACID	Glu
GLUTAMINE	GluN
GLYCINE	Gly
HISTIDINE	His
ISOLEUCINE	Ileu
LEUCINE	Leu
LYSINE	Lys
METHIONINE	Met
PHENYLALANINE	Phe
PROLINE	Pro
SERINE	Ser
THREONINE	Thr
TRYPTOPHAN	Tryp
TYROSINE	Tyr
VALINE	Val

TWENTY AMINO ACIDS constitute the standard set found in all proteins. A few other amino acids occur infrequently in proteins but it is suspected in each case that they originate as one of the standard set and become chemically modified after they have been incorporated into a polypeptide chain.

of the genetic code is now essentially complete. One can trace the transmission of the coded message from its original site in the genetic material to the finished protein molecule.

The genetic material of the living cell is the chainlike molecule of deoxyribonucleic acid (DNA). The cells of many bacteria have only a single chain; the cells of mammals have dozens clustered together in chromosomes. The DNA molecules have a very long backbone made up of repeating groups of phosphate and a five-carbon sugar. To this backbone the side groups called bases are attached at regular intervals. There are four standard bases: adenine (A), guanine (G), thymine (T) and cytosine (C). They are the four "letters" used to spell out the genetic message. The exact sequence of bases along a length of the DNA molecule determines the structure of a particular protein molecule.

Proteins are synthesized from a standard set of 20 amino acids, uniform throughout nature, that are joined end to end to form the long polypeptide

chains of protein molecules [see illustration at left]. Each protein has its own characteristic sequence of amino acids. The number of amino acids in a polypeptide chain ranges typically from 100 to 300 or more.

The genetic code is not the message itself but the "dictionary" used by the cell to translate from the four-letter language of nucleic acid to the 20-letter language of protein. The machinery of the cell can translate in one direction only: from nucleic acid to protein but not from protein to nucleic acid. In making this translation the cell employs a variety of accessory molecules and mechanisms. The message contained in DNA is first transcribed into the similar molecule called "messenger" ribonucleic acid—messenger RNA. (In many viruses—the tobacco mosaic virus, for example—the genetic material is simply RNA.) RNA too has four kinds of bases as side groups; three are identical with those found in DNA (adenine, guanine and cytosine) but the fourth is uracil (U) instead of thymine. In this first transcription of the genetic message the code letters A, G, T and C in DNA give rise respectively to U, C, A and G. In other words, wherever A appears in DNA, U appears in the RNA transcription; wherever G appears in DNA, C appears in the transcription, and so on. As it is usually presented the dictionary of the genetic code employs the letters found in RNA (U, C, A, G) rather than those found in DNA (A, G, T, C).

The genetic code could be broken easily if one could determine both the amino acid sequence of a protein and the base sequence of the piece of nucleic acid that codes it. A simple comparison of the two sequences would yield the code. Unfortunately the determination of the base sequence of a long nucleic acid molecule is, for a variety of reasons, still extremely difficult. More indirect approaches must be used.

Most of the genetic code first became known early in 1965. Since then additional evidence has proved that almost all of it is correct, although a few features remain uncertain. This article describes how the code was discovered and some of the work that supports it.

Scientific American has already presented a number of articles on the genetic code. In one of them [" The Genetic Code," Offprint 123] I explained that the experimental evidence (mainly indirect) suggested that the code was a triplet code: that the bases on the messenger RNA were read three at a time and that each group corresponded to a

particular amino acid. Such a group is called a codon. Using four symbols in groups of three, one can form 64 distinct triplets. The evidence indicated that most of these stood for one amino acid or another, implying that an amino acid was usually represented by several codons. Adjacent amino acids were coded by adjacent codons, which did not overlap.

In a sequel to that article ["The Genetic Code: II," Offprint 153]. Marshall W. Nirenberg of the National Institutes of Health explained how the composition of many of the 64 triplets had been determined by actual experiment. The technique was to synthesize polypeptide chains in a cell-free system, which was made by breaking open cells of the colon bacillus (*Escherichia coli*) and extracting from them the machinery for protein synthesis. Then the system was provided with an energy supply, 20 amino acids and one or another of several types of synthetic RNA. Although the exact sequence of bases in each type was random, the proportion of bases was known. It was found that each type of synthetic messenger RNA directed the incorporation of certain amino acids only.

By means of this method, used in a quantitative way, the *composition* of many of the codons was obtained, but the *order* of bases in any triplet could not be determined. Codons rich in G were difficult to study, and in addition a few mistakes crept in. Of the 40 codon compositions listed by Nirenberg in his article we now know that 35 were correct.

The Triplet Code

The main outlines of the genetic code were elucidated by another technique invented by Nirenberg and Philip Leder. In this method no protein synthesis occurs. Instead one triplet at a time is used to bind together parts of the machinery of protein synthesis.

Protein synthesis takes place on the comparatively large intracellular structures known as ribosomes. These bodies travel along the chain of messenger RNA, reading off its triplets one after another and synthesizing the polypeptide chain of the protein, starting at the amino end (NH_2). The amino acids do not diffuse to the ribosomes by themselves. Each amino acid is joined chemically by a special enzyme to one of the codon-recognizing molecules known both as soluble RNA (sRNA) and transfer RNA (tRNA). (I prefer the latter designation.) Each tRNA molecule has its own triplet of bases, called an anticodon, that recognizes the relevant codon on the messenger RNA by pairing bases with it [see illustration on page 163].

Leder and Nirenberg studied which amino acid, joined to its tRNA molecules, was bound to the ribosomes in the presence of a particular triplet, that is, by a "message" with just three letters. They did so by the neat trick of passing the mixture over a nitrocellulose filter that retained the ribosomes. All the tRNA molecules passed through the filter except the ones specifically bound to the ribosomes by the triplet. Which they were could easily be decided by using mixtures of amino acids

in which one kind of amino acid had been made artificially radioactive, and determining the amount of radioactivity absorbed by the filter.

For example, the triplet GUU retained the tRNA for the amino acid valine, whereas the triplets UGU and UUG did not. (Here GUU actually stands for the trinucleoside diphosphate GpUpU.) Further experiments showed that UGU coded for cysteine and UUG for leucine.

Nirenberg and his colleagues synthesized all 64 triplets and tested them for their coding properties. Similar results have been obtained by H. Gobind Khorana and his co-workers at the University of Wisconsin. Various other

groups have checked a smaller number of codon assignments.

Close to 50 of the 64 triplets give a clearly unambiguous answer in the binding test. Of the remainder some evince only weak binding and some bind more than one kind of amino acid. Other results I shall describe later suggest that the multiple binding is often an artifact of the binding method. In short, the binding test gives the meaning of the majority of the triplets but it does not firmly establish all of them.

The genetic code obtained in this way, with a few additions secured by other methods, is shown in the table below. The 64 possible triplets are set out in a regular array, following a plan

SECOND LETTER

FIRST LETTER	U	C	A	G	THIRD LETTER
U	UUU, UUC } Phe; UUA, UUG } Leu	UCU, UCC, UCA, UCG } Ser	UAU, UAC } Tyr; UAA OCHRE; UAG AMBER	UGU, UGC } Cys; UGA ?; UGG Tryp	U C A G
C	CUU, CUC, CUA, CUG } Leu	CCU, CCC, CCA, CCG } Pro	CAU, CAC } His; CAA, CAG } GluN	CGU, CGC, CGA, CGG } Arg	U C A G
A	AUU, AUC } Ileu; AUA; AUG Met	ACU, ACC, ACA, ACG } Thr	AAU, AAC } AspN; AAA, AAG } Lys	AGU, AGC } Ser; AGA, AGG } Arg	U C A G
G	GUU, GUC, GUA, GUG } Val	GCU, GCC, GCA, GCG } Ala	GAU, GAC } Asp; GAA, GAG } Glu	GGU, GGC, GGA, GGG } Gly	U C A G

GENETIC CODE, consisting of 64 triplet combinations and their corresponding amino acids, is shown in its most likely version. The importance of the first two letters in each triplet is readily apparent. Some of the allocations are still not completely certain, particularly for organisms other than the colon bacillus (*Escherichia coli*). "Amber" and "ochre" are terms that referred originally to certain mutant strains of bacteria. They designate two triplets, UAA and UAG, that may act as signals for terminating polypeptide chains.

that clarifies the relations between them.

Inspection of the table will show that the triplets coding for the same amino acid are often rather similar. For example, all four of the triplets starting with the doublet AC code for threonine. This pattern also holds for seven of the other amino acids. In every case the triplets XYU and XYC code for the same amino acid, and in many cases XYA and XYG are the same (methionine and tryptophan may be exceptions). Thus an amino acid is largely selected by the first two bases of the triplet. Given that a triplet codes for, say, valine, we know that the first two bases are GU, whatever the third may be. This pattern is true for all but three of the amino acids. Leucine can start with UU or CU, serine with UC or AG and arginine with CG or AG. In all other cases the amino acid is uniquely related to the first two bases of the triplet. Of course, the converse is often not true. Given that a triplet starts with, say, CA, it may code for either histidine or glutamine.

Synthetic Messenger RNA's

Probably the most direct way to confirm the genetic code is to synthesize a messenger RNA molecule with a strictly defined base sequence and then find the amino acid sequence of the polypeptide produced under its influence. The most extensive work of this nature has been done by Khorana and his colleagues. By a brilliant combination of ordinary chemical synthesis and synthesis catalyzed by enzymes, they have made long RNA molecules with various repeating sequences of bases. As an example, one RNA molecule they have synthesized has the sequence UGUG-UGUGUGUG.... When the biochemical machinery reads this as triplets the message is UGU–GUG–UGU–GUG.... Thus we expect that a polypeptide will be produced with an alternating sequence of two amino acids. In fact, it was found that the product is Cys–Val–Cys–Val.... This evidence alone would not tell us which triplet goes with which amino acid, but given the results of the binding test one has no hesitation in concluding that UGU codes for cysteine and GUG for valine.

In the same way Khorana has made chains with repeating sequences of the type $XYZ...$ and also $XXYZ....$ The type $XYZ...$ would be expected to give a "homopolypeptide" containing one amino acid corresponding to the triplet XYZ. Because the starting point is not clearly defined, however, the homopolypeptides corresponding to $YZX...$ and $ZXY...$ will also be produced. Thus poly-AUC makes polyisoleucine, polyserine and polyhistidine. This confirms that AUC codes for isoleucine, UCA for serine and CAU for histidine. A repeating sequence of four bases will yield a single type of polypeptide with a repeating sequence of four amino acids. The general patterns to be expected in each case are set forth in the table on this page. The results to date have amply demonstrated by a direct biochemical method that the code is indeed a triplet code.

Khorana and his colleagues have so far confirmed about 25 triplets by this method, including several that were quite doubtful on the basis of the binding test. They plan to synthesize other sequences, so that eventually most of the triplets will be checked in this way.

The Use of Mutations

The two methods described so far are open to the objection that since they do not involve intact cells there may be some danger of false results. This objection can be met by two other methods of checking the code in which the act of protein synthesis takes place inside the cell. Both involve the effects of genetic mutations on the amino acid sequence of a protein.

It is now known that small mutations are normally of two types: "base substitution" mutants and "phase shift" mutants. In the first type one base is changed into another base but the total number of bases remains the same. In the second, one or a small number of bases are added to the message or subtracted from it.

There are now extensive data on base-substitution mutants, mainly from studies of three rather convenient proteins: human hemoglobin, the protein of tobacco mosaic virus and the A protein of the enzyme tryptophan synthetase obtained from the colon bacillus. At least 36 abnormal types of human hemoglobin have now been investigated by many different workers. More than 40 mutant forms of the protein of the tobacco mosaic virus have been examined by Hans Wittmann of the Max Planck Institute for Molecular Genetics in Tübingen and by Akita Tsugita and Heinz Fraenkel-Conrat of the University of California at Berkeley [see "The Genetic Code of a Virus," by Heinz Fraenkel-Conrat; SCIENTIFIC AMERICAN Offprint 193]. Charles Yanofsky and his group at Stanford University have characterized about 25 different mutations of the A protein of tryptophan synthetase.

RNA BASE SEQUENCE	READ AS	AMINO ACID SEQUENCE EXPECTED
$(X Y)_n$ . . .	X Y X / Y X Y / X Y X / Y X Y . . .	αβαβ
$(X Y Z)_n$ . . .	X Y Z / X Y Z / X Y Z . . .	ααα
	Y Z X / Y Z X / Y Z X . . .	βββ
	Z X Y / Z X Y / Z X Y . . .	γγγ
$(X X Y Z)_n$ . . .	X X Y Z / X X Y Z / X X Y Z . . .	αβγδαβγδ
$(X Y X Z)_n$ . . .	X Y X Z / X Y X Z / X Y X Z . . .	αβγδαβγδ

VARIETY OF SYNTHETIC RNA's with repeating sequences of bases have been produced by H. Gobind Khorana and his colleagues at the University of Wisconsin. They contain two or three different bases (X, Y, Z) in groups of two, three or four. When introduced into cell-free systems containing the machinery for protein synthesis, the base sequences are read off as triplets (middle) and yield the amino acid sequences indicated at the right.

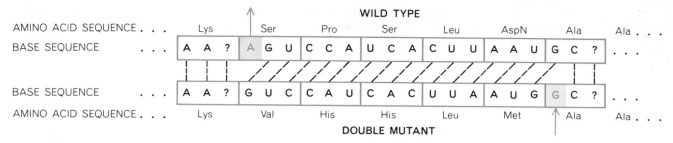

WILD TYPE

| AMINO ACID SEQUENCE . . . | Lys | Ser | Pro | Ser | Leu | AspN | Ala | Ala . . . |

| BASE SEQUENCE . . . | A A ? | A G U | C C A | U C A | C U U | A A U | G C ? | . . . |

| BASE SEQUENCE . . . | A A ? | G U C | C A U | C A C | U U A | A U G | G C ? | . . . |

| AMINO ACID SEQUENCE . . . | Lys | Val | His | His | Leu | Met | Ala | Ala . . . |

DOUBLE MUTANT

"PHASE SHIFT" MUTATIONS help to establish the actual codons used by organisms in the synthesis of protein. The two partial amino acid sequences shown here were determined by George Streisinger and his colleagues at the University of Oregon. The sequences are from a protein, a type of lysozyme, produced by the bacterial virus T4. A pair of phase-shift mutations evidently removed one base, A, and inserted another, G, about 15 bases farther on. The base sequence was deduced theoretically from the genetic code.

The remarkable fact has emerged that in every case but one the genetic code shows that the change of an amino acid in a polypeptide chain could have been caused by the alteration of a single base in the relevant nucleic acid. For example, the first observed change of an amino acid by mutation (in the hemoglobin of a person suffering from sickle-cell anemia) was from glutamic acid to valine. From the genetic code dictionary on page 5 we see that this could have resulted from a mutation that changed either GAA to GUA or GAG to GUG. In either case the change involved a single base in the several hundred needed to code for one of the two kinds of chain in hemoglobin.

The one exception so far to the rule that all amino acid changes could be caused by single base changes has been found by Yanofsky. In this one case glutamic acid was replaced by methionine. It can be seen from the genetic code dictionary that this can be accomplished only by a change of *two* bases, since glutamic acid is encoded by either GAA or GAG and methionine is encoded only by AUG. This mutation has occurred only once, however, and of all the mutations studied by Yanofsky it is the only one not to back-mutate, or revert to "wild type." It is thus almost certainly the rare case of a double change. All the other cases fit the hypothesis that base-substitution mutations are normally caused by a single base change. Examination of the code shows that only about 40 percent of all the possible amino acid interchanges can be brought about by single base substitutions, and it is only these changes that are found in experiments. Therefore the study of actual mutations has provided strong confirmation of many features of the genetic code.

Because in general several codons stand for one amino acid it is not possible, knowing the amino acid sequence, to write down the exact RNA base sequence that encoded it. This is unfortunate. If we know which amino acid is changed into another by mutation, however, we can often, given the code, work out what that base change must have been. As an example, glutamic acid can be encoded by GAA or GAG and valine by GUU, GUC, GUA or GUG. If a mutation substitutes valine for glutamic acid, one can assume that only a single base change was involved. The only such change that could lead to the desired result would be a change from A to U in the middle position, and this would be true whether GAA became GUA or GAG became GUG.

It is thus possible in many cases (not in all) to compare the nature of the base change with the chemical mutagen used to produce the change. If RNA is treated with nitrous acid, C is changed to U and A is effectively changed to G. On the other hand, if double-strand DNA is treated under the right conditions with hydroxylamine, the mutagen acts only on C. As a result some C's are changed to T's (the DNA equivalent of U's), and thus G's, which are normally paired with C's in double-strand DNA, are replaced by A's.

If 2-aminopurine, a "base analogue" mutagen, is added when double-strand DNA is undergoing replication, it produces only "transitions." These are the same changes as those produced by hydroxylamine—plus the reverse changes. In almost all these different cases (the exceptions are unimportant) the changes observed are those expected from our knowledge of the genetic code.

Note the remarkable fact that, although the code was deduced mainly from studies of the colon bacillus, it appears to apply equally to human beings and tobacco plants. This, together with more fragmentary evidence, suggests that the genetic code is either the same or very similar in most organisms.

The second method of checking the code using intact cells depends on phase-shift mutations such as the addi-tion of a single base to the message. Phase-shift mutations probably result from errors produced during genetic recombination or when the DNA molecule is being duplicated. Such errors have the effect of putting out of phase the reading of the message from that point on. This hypothesis leads to the prediction that the phase can be corrected if at some subsequent point a nucleotide is deleted. The pair of alterations would be expected not only to change two amino acids but also to alter all those encoded by bases lying between the two affected sites. The reason is that the intervening bases would be read out of phase and therefore grouped into triplets different from those contained in the normal message.

This expectation has recently been confirmed by George Streisinger and his colleagues at the University of Oregon. They have studied mutations in the protein lysozyme that were produced by the T4 virus, which infects the colon bacillus. One phase-shift mutation involved the amino acid sequence ...Lys —Ser—Pro—Ser—Leu—AspN—Ala—Ala— Lys.... They were then able to construct by genetic methods a double phase-shift mutant in which the corresponding sequence was ...Lys—Val— His—His—Leu—Met—Ala—Ala—Lys....

Given these two sequences, the reader should be able, using the genetic code dictionary on page 165, to decipher uniquely a short length of the nucleic acid message for both the original protein and the double mutant and thus deduce the changes produced by each of the phase-shift mutations. The correct result is presented in the illustration above. The result not only confirms several rather doubtful codons, such as UUA for leucine and AGU for serine, but also shows which codons are actually involved in a genetic message. Since the technique is difficult, however, it may not find wide application.

Streisinger's work also demonstrates what has so far been only tacitly as-

ANTICODON	CODON
U	A G
C	G
A	U
G	U C
I	U C A

"WOBBLE" HYPOTHESIS has been proposed by the author to provide rules for the pairing of codon and anticodon at the *third* position of the codon. There is evidence, for example, that the anticodon base I, which stands for inosine, may pair with as many as three different bases: U, C and A. Inosine closely resembles the base guanine (G) and so would ordinarily be expected to pair with cytosine (C). Structural diagrams for standard base pairings and wobble base pairings are illustrated at the bottom of this page.

sumed: that the two languages, both of which are written down in a certain direction according to convention, are in fact translated by the cell in the same direction and not in opposite directions. This fact had previously been established, with more direct chemical methods, by Severo Ochoa and his colleagues at the New York University School of Medicine. In the convention, which was adopted by chance, proteins are written with the amino (NH$_2$) end on the left. Nucleic acids are written with the end of the molecule containing a "5 prime" carbon atom at the left. (The "5 prime" refers to a particular carbon atom in the 5-carbon ring of ribose sugar or deoxyribose sugar.)

Finding the Anticodons

Still another method of checking the genetic code is to discover the three bases making up the anticodon in some particular variety of transfer RNA. The first tRNA to have its entire sequence worked out was alanine tRNA, a job done by Robert W. Holley and his collaborators at Cornell University [see "The Nucleotide Sequence of a Nucleic Acid," by Robert W. Holley; SCIENTIFIC AMERICAN Offprint 1033]. Alanine tRNA, obtained from yeast, contains 77 bases. A possible anticodon found near the middle of the molecule has the sequence IGC, where I stands for inosine, a base closely resembling guanine. Since then Hans Zachau and his colleagues at the University of Cologne have established the sequences of two closely related serine tRNA's from yeast, and James Madison and his group at the U.S. Plant, Soil and Nutrition Laboratory at Ithaca, N.Y., have worked out the sequence of a tyrosine tRNA, also from yeast.

A detailed comparison of these three sequences makes it almost certain that the anticodons are alanine–IGC, serine–IGA and tyrosine–GΨA. (Ψ stands for pseudo-uridylic acid, which can form the same base pairs as the base uracil.) In addition there is preliminary evidence from other workers that an anticodon for valine is IAC and an anticodon for phenylalanine is GAA.

All these results would fit the rule that the codon and anticodon pair in an antiparallel manner, and that the pairing in the first two positions of the codon is of the standard type, that is, A pairs with U and G pairs with C. The pairing in the third position of the codon is more complicated. There is now good experimental evidence from both Nirenberg and Khorana and their co-workers that one tRNA can recognize several codons, provided that they differ only in the last place in the codon. Thus Holley's alanine tRNA appears to recognize GCU, GCC and GCA. If it recognizes GCG, it does so only very weakly.

The "Wobble" Hypothesis

I have suggested that this is because of a "wobble" in the pairing in the third place and have shown that a reasonable theoretical model will explain many of the observed results. The suggested rules for the pairing in the third position of the anticodon are presented in the table at the top of this page, but this theory is still speculative. The rules for the first two places of the codon seem reasonably secure, however, and can be used as partial confirmation of the genetic code. The likely codon-anticodon pairings for valine, serine, tyrosine, alanine and phenylalanine satisfy the standard base pairings in the first two places and the wobble hypothesis in the third place [see illustration on page 169].

Several points about the genetic code remain to be cleared up. For example, the triplet UGA has still to be allocated.

STANDARD AND WOBBLE BASE PAIRINGS both involve the formation of hydrogen bonds when certain bases are brought into close proximity. In the standard guanine-cytosine pairing (*left*) it is believed three hydrogen bonds are formed. The bases are shown as they exist in the RNA molecule, where they are attached to 5-carbon rings of ribose sugar. In the proposed wobble pairing (*right*) guanine is linked to uracil by only two hydrogen bonds. The base inosine (I) has a single hydrogen atom where guanine has an amino (NH$_2$) group (*broken circle*). In the author's wobble hypothesis inosine can pair with U as well as with C and A (*not shown*).

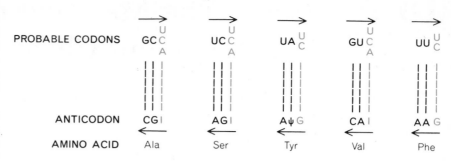

CODON-ANTICODON PAIRINGS take place in an antiparallel direction. Thus the anti-codons are shown here written backward, as opposed to the way they appear in the text. The five anticodons are those tentatively identified in the transfer RNA's for alanine, serine, tyrosine, valine and phenylalanine. Color indicates where wobble pairings may occur.

The punctuation marks—the signals for "begin chain" and "end chain"—are only partly understood. It seems likely that both the triplet UAA (called "ochre") and UAG (called "amber") can terminate the polypeptide chain, but which triplet is normally found at the end of a gene is still uncertain.

The picturesque terms for these two triplets originated when it was discovered in studies of the colon bacillus some years ago that mutations in other genes (mutations that in fact cause errors in chain termination) could "suppress" the action of certain mutant codons, now identified as either UAA or UAG. The terms "ochre" and "amber" are simply invented designations and have no reference to color.

A mechanism for chain initiation was discovered fairly recently. In the colon bacillus it seems certain that formylmethionine, carried by a special tRNA, can initiate chains, although it is not clear if all chains have to start in this way, or what the mechanism is in mammals and other species. The formyl group (CHO) is not normally found on finished proteins, suggesting that it is probably removed by a special enzyme. It seems likely that sometimes the methionine is removed as well.

It is unfortunately possible that a few codons may be ambiguous, that is, may code for more than one amino acid. This is certainly not true of most codons. The present evidence for a small amount of ambiguity is suggestive but not conclusive. It will make the code more difficult to establish correctly if ambiguity can occur.

Problems for the Future

From what has been said it is clear that, although the entire genetic code is not known with complete certainty, it is highly likely that most of it is correct. Further work will surely clear up the doubtful codons, clarify the punctuation marks, delimit ambiguity and extend the code to many other species. Although the code lists the codons that *may* be used, we still have to determine if alternative codons are used equally. Some preliminary work suggests they may not be. There is also still much to be discovered about the machinery of protein synthesis. How many types of tRNA are there? What is the structure of the ribosome? How does it work, and why is it in two parts? In addition there are many questions concerning the control of the rate of protein synthesis that we are still a long way from answering.

When such questions have been answered, the major unsolved problem will be the structure of the genetic code. Is the present code merely the result of a series of evolutionary accidents, so that the allocations of triplets to amino acids is to some extent arbitrary? Or are there profound structural reasons why phenylalanine has to be coded by UUU and UUC and by no other triplets? Such questions will be difficult to decide, since the genetic code originated at least three billion years ago, and it may be impossible to reconstruct the sequence of events that took place at such a remote period. The origin of the code is very close to the origin of life. Unless we are lucky it is likely that much of the evidence we should like to have has long since disappeared.

Nevertheless, the genetic code is a major milestone on the long road of molecular biology. In showing in detail how the four-letter language of nucleic acid controls the 20-letter language of protein it confirms the central theme of molecular biology that genetic information can be stored as a one-dimensional message on nucleic acid and be expressed as the one-dimensional amino acid sequence of a protein. Many problems remain, but this knowledge is now secure.

15

The Mapping of Human Chromosomes

by Victor A. McKusick
April 1971

The goal is to locate a gene in relation to others and to establish which of the 23 chromosome pairs carries it. This is done primarily by applying statistical techniques to data on inheritance of traits

Slowly and laboriously the location of specific genes on the chromosomes of man is being mapped. It is not as simple a matter as looking for landmarks in an uncharted terrain. Identifying the gene responsible for a particular human trait and finding its locus, or site, on one of the 23 pairs of chromosomes of man is a labor a little like hunting in a cluster of mazes for an invisible animal identifiable only by its odor. To track down the quarry one must resort to indirect clues, family pedigrees, linkages of unusual traits and sophisticated probability theory.

In terms of a metaphor more closely related to cartography, we have a general picture of the various countries (the chromosomes) of the genetic world and have identified many of the municipalities (genes) on the basis of the specific traits to which they give rise. We are still largely in the dark, however, about the location of most of the municipalities, even from the standpoint of deciding in what country they belong. The overall size of the genetic domain (the total number of genes in man) is itself obscure, although we know the number must be very large. More than 1,100 separate enzymes are known, and presumably the structure of each enzyme is specified by at least one gene. Moreover, there are a large number of nonenzymic proteins, each of which is also under genetic control. Besides the structural genes there are other classes of genes controlling various aspects of cell development and activity. Judging from the large number of different gene functions and the known content of DNA in cells, a set of chromosomes must contain many thousands of gene loci.

Obviously mapping this domain will be a long and tedious project. Why go to all the trouble? The work actually has a variety of attractions. Detailed mapping of the chromosomes of man would yield incalculable benefits. Among other things it would make possible very early diagnosis, even in the fetus, of some serious hereditary disorders. And for some of us in human genetics it is sufficient motivation that the mapping of the chromosomes, like the ascent of Mount Everest, is there to be accomplished. We find it an exciting enterprise because of its difficulty and its challenge to ingenuity. I shall relate here the strategies being employed and some of the results that have been obtained.

CHROMOSOMES of a human male body cell undergoing division were treated with a salt solution to make them discrete structures and then photomicrographed (*left*); next they were cut out and arranged conventionally, in pairs and groups according to total

The identification of specific genes is made possible by the fact that most genetic characters have alternate forms, called alleles; for example, the gene that specifies A-type blood can have an alternate form that specifies B-type blood. Many genes therefore can be identified, or "marked," by their observable product. By tracing the pedigree of a character and following the distribution of its alternate forms in the offspring of successive generations, the existence of more than 800 human gene loci has been established and another 1,000 loci have been identified tentatively. Pedigree studies have also provided some information on the chromosomal localization of genes.

The identification of genes with a particular chromosome began with the very helpful circumstance that the transmission of some genetic traits is sexlinked; more precisely, X-linked. The pedigrees of color blindness and of hemophilia, for example, show that these hereditary conditions typically affect males and are transmitted by females. What this means is that there is a recessive gene for color blindness or hemophilia on the X chromosome, of which the female has two and the male only one. When such a gene is present on one of the X chromosomes of a female, its effect is masked by a dominant gene on the paired X chromosome; when it is present on the single X chromosome of a male, its effect is expressed.

A considerable number of gene loci (79 at the latest count) have now been definitely assigned to the X chromosome. Having placed loci on a particular chromosome, one is in a position to try to estimate their relative locations on that structure. The strategy in this exploration is to examine the consequences of the exchange of segments between the two members of the pair of X chromosomes in a female, the process called crossing-over. During meiosis, the process that leads to the splitting of a cell into two germ cells, each with 23 chromosomes, the paired chromosomes in the mother cell line up parallel to each other and exchange segments. Under the microscope the points of exchange are visible; they are called chiasmas. Thus during the meiotic process in the ovary segments of the two homologous X chromosomes switch places, the chiasmas appearing essentially at random along the chromosomes [*see illustration on next page*]. As a result the offspring will possess a "recombination" (that is, a changed combination) of the traits borne by the mother if there is an odd number of crossovers.

Now, it is evident that when two traits are involved, the farther apart the loci for these traits are on the chromosome (that is, the less closely linked), the greater is the chance that they will be separated onto opposite X chromosomes by a crossover. This fact therefore gives us a measure of the distance between loci. We can estimate the distance from the relative frequency with which a switched combination of the traits in question

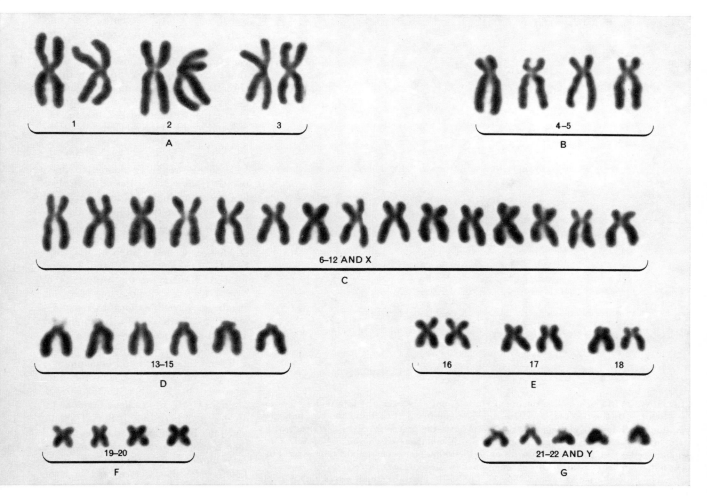

length and relative length of arms, in a karyotype (*right*). At this stage each chromosome has replicated in preparation for cell division and consists of two strands (chromatids) held together by a centromere. There are 23 pairs of chromosomes: 22 autosome pairs (one homologous member from each parent) and two sex chromosomes (two X chromosomes in females, an X and a Y in males).

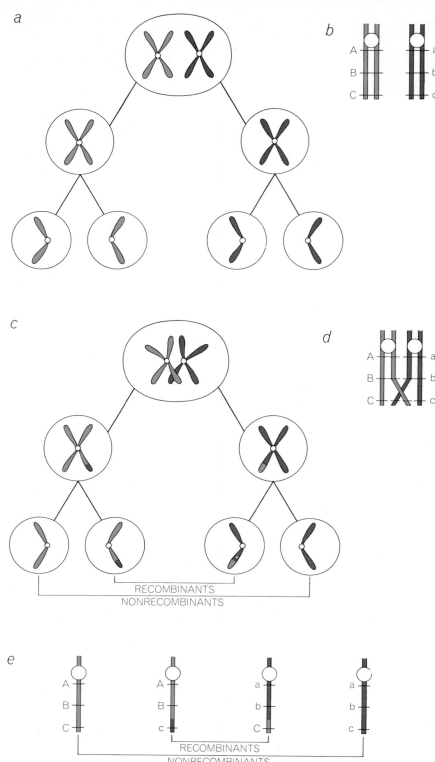

CROSSING-OVER, in which segments of chromosomes are exchanged, provides clues to the distance between two gene loci. Crossing-over and its effect on three loci are shown in simplified form for one chromosome pair. In meiosis, the process whereby germ cells with a single set of chromosomes are produced, two homologous chromosomes separate into daughter cells; then the two chromatids of each chromosome separate into four germ cells (*a*). In diagrammatic form (*b*) the chromosomes are seen to carry three gene loci each: *A*, *B*, *C* on one and alternative forms (alleles) *a*, *b*, *c* on the other. In crossing-over homologous segments become exchanged (*c*), with the alleles they carry (*d*), giving rise to four possible arrangements of genes in the ultimate germ cells (*e*). The closer two loci are linked, the less likely it is that crossing-over will occur between them and produce recombination.

shows up in the mother's sons. Let me illustrate with a study Ian Porter, Jane Schulze and I conducted on certain families in Baltimore.

In this case the pair of traits, linked to the *X* chromosome, was a form of color blindness (controlled by a locus called *dn*) and deficiency of an enzyme in red cells known as glucose-6-phosphate dehydrogenase (whose synthesis is controlled from a locus called *gd*). Our subjects were women who were double heterozygotes, that is, they carried both of these unusual alleles. Both aberrant genes might be on the same *X* chromosome, or they might be separated, one on each of the two *X*'s. We were able to determine which was the case by examining the woman's father. If he showed just one of the traits, for example, she would have received an *X* with this mutant allele from him and the other mutant allele would be on her other *X*. In either case, with this information we could recognize recombinations if they occurred [*see upper illustration on opposite page*]. We examined the sons of these doubly heterozygous mothers and found that about 5 percent of their sons were "recombinants," showing changes in the combination of traits. On this basis we estimated the *dn* and *gd* loci to be about five "map units" apart on the *X* chromosome. At the same time investigators in Israel and in Sardinia arrived at a similar estimate of the distance between the *dn* and the *gd* loci.

Step by step other loci on the *X* chromosome are being related to these two. It turns out that the *gd* locus, two loci for color blindness (*dn* and *pn*) and the locus for one type of hemophilia (hemophilia *A*) are clustered rather close together. S. H. Boyer III of our Division of Medical Genetics at the Johns Hopkins University School of Medicine and John B. Graham of the University of North Carolina School of Medicine found no recombinations by crossing-over between the loci for hemophilia *A* and red-cell glucose-6-phosphate dehydrogenase in families they studied; this indicated that the *gd* and hemophilia *A* loci must be closely linked on the chromosome. On the other hand, C. A. B. Smith of University College London, analyzing pedigrees that J. B. S. Haldane and Julia Bell had studied earlier, noted that hemophilia was closely linked to color blindness in some families but not in other families; this means that the locus for one form of hemophilia (now identified as hemophilia *B*) must be some distance away from the *dn* locus.

In 1962 a new *X*-chromosome marker was described; this locus, responsible for the occurrence of a particular blood group, is called *Xg* because it is *X*-linked and the antibody showing the existence of the blood group was first discovered in a patient in Grand Rapids, Mich., who had had many transfusions. Studies of families in the Mediterranean area have indicated that the *Xg* locus is about 40 map units from the *gd* locus. Several other loci have now been more or less closely linked to this new locus; among these are a locus related to the presence or absence of eye pigment and another

that is responsible for a hereditary condition of skin roughness called ichthyosis. Then there are other identified loci on the *X* chromosome whose positions have been found to be distant from both the *Xg* and the *gd–dn–pn*–hemophilia *A* cluster.

This brings up the question: What is the overall length, in terms of map units, of the *X* chromosome? We can deduce an approximate answer from the number of chiasmas formed between the paired chromosomes during meiosis. The chiasmas can be seen under the micro-

scope most conveniently in cells of the testis, and the counts indicate that on the average there is a total of about 50 chiasmas between the 22 pairs of autosomes, or nonsex chromosomes, in the human male. There are reasons to assume that on the average the number of crossovers is directly proportional to the number of chiasmas.

By the definition of a map unit each potential crossing-over (hence each chiasma) represents 50 map units of length along a chromosome strand. This implies that the male autosomes, with 50 chiasmas, have a total length of about 2,500

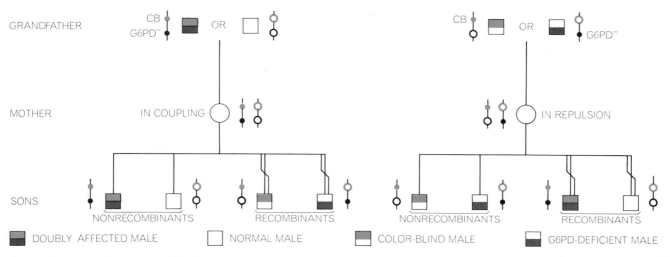

X-CHROMOSOME LOCI are mapped by the "grandfather method," based on phenotypes (physical traits) of sons of women who carry alleles for two unusual traits, in this case color blindness and a deficiency in glucose-6-phosphate dehydrogenase. Whether the "doubly heterozygous" mother carries both unusual alleles on the same *X* chromosome (in coupling) or one on each (in repulsion) is determined by checking her father's phenotype; for example, if he had both traits, his *X* chromosome bore both alleles (*top left*). If the mother's unusual alleles are in coupling, sons with only one trait or the other reflect recombination; if her unusual alleles are in repulsion, sons with both traits or neither are recombinants. The proportion of recombinants is index of distance between loci.

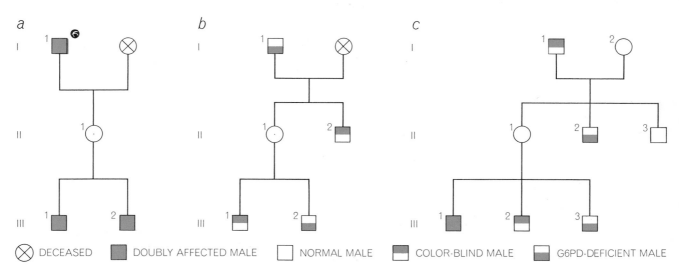

THREE PEDIGREES illustrate the grandfather method. The question is: What males, if any, in the third generation are recombinants? Examination of the generation I (grandfather) phenotypes indicates that the two unusual alleles are in coupling in kindred *a*, in repulsion in kindreds *b* and *c*. Generation III phenotypes indicate that the only recombinant is son No. 1 in kindred *c*.

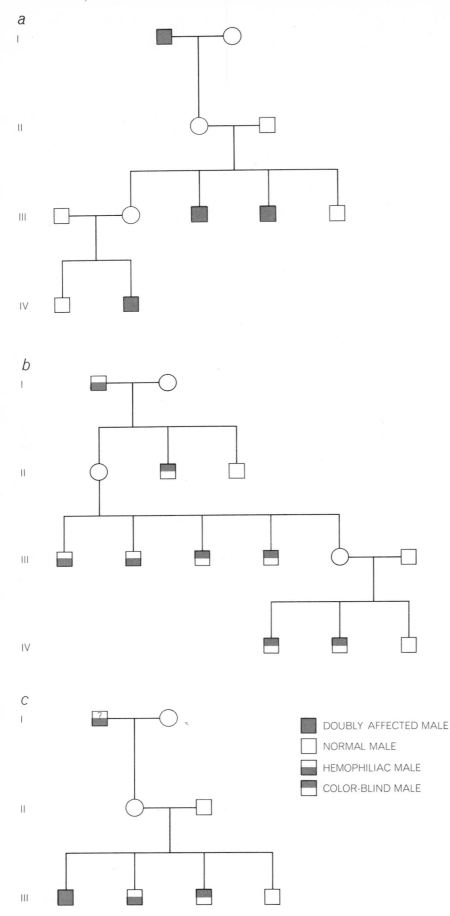

DOUBLY AFFECTED MALE

NORMAL MALE

HEMOPHILIAC MALE

COLOR-BLIND MALE

map units. In women crossovers are about 40 percent more frequent than they are in men; hence in terms of map units their autosomes may be 40 percent longer, or about 3,500 map units.

The physical length of the chromosomes in males and females is of course identical; the map units refer to genetic length. What about the genetic length of the X chromosome? Under the microscope it can be seen that during meiosis the physical length of the X chromosome is about a sixteenth of the total length of the autosomes. Assuming that the length in map units is proportional to the physical length, this means that the X chromosome is more than 200 map units long. That length is sufficient to allow many pairs of loci, not closely linked on the chromosome, to become separated by a crossover and thus produce X chromosomes carrying recombinations of the traits being studied.

When it comes to mapping the autosomes, the nonsex chromosomes, the task is much more difficult than it is for X-linked traits, where to start with we at least know in what country (the X chromosome) the loci are situated. Now, the loci we are hunting are hidden somewhere in a field of 22 pairs of chromosomes. The search must therefore begin with an attempt to find traits or characters that are linked together on the same autosome, even though we do not know what particular chromosome that may be.

As guideposts for establishing such linkages we need first of all to identify readily observable marker traits. The traits should have alternate forms that are inherited in a segregating Mendelian fashion and occur frequently enough to maximize, in the families being studied, the number of heterozygous individuals: individuals carrying genes for both alleles of a pair. About 30 marker traits have proved to be particularly useful; they include more than a dozen types of red-cell antigens identifiable by immu-

LINKAGE between loci for color blindness and two forms of hemophilia is examined in three pedigrees. On the logic developed in the preceding two illustrations, families *a* and *b* are seen to demonstrate no recombination of the two traits, but two of the four sons in family *c* demonstrate recombination. Families *a* and *b* have hemophilia *A*, closely linked to color blindness; family *c* has hemophilia *B*, which is not closely linked to color blindness, as indicated by the frequency of recombination (in about half of the sons in pedigrees such as this).

nologic techniques (ABO, Rh, Duffy, Lutheran, MNSs and others), serum proteins (such as haptoglobin) and red-cell enzymes (such as adenylate kinase) that can be identified by the analytical technique of electrophoresis. These 30 markers themselves provide 435 possible pairs of loci for linkage investigation. Beyond such links one looks for the linkage of individual marker loci with disorders that are attributable to a single gene, such as myotonic dystrophy (a form of muscular dystrophy) or elliptocytosis (abnormal, elliptically shaped red cells).

How can one go about determining that the loci of the genes for two given traits are situated on the same autosome? In the case of the X chromosome, as we have noted, linkages are evidenced by the occurrence of recombinations. The rarer the recombination, the closer the linkage of the loci being studied. In order to decide whether or not a given combination of traits was created by a recombination, however, we need to know whether the doubly heterozygous parent carried these traits on a single chromosome or on the opposite members of a pair. With regard to autosomes we often have no information on this question. The problem has therefore been attacked with probability reasoning, which tests likelihoods in the light of a priori assumptions. In other words, we consider various hypotheses in order to arrive at an estimate of the relative likelihood that the observed traits are or are not linked on the same chromosome pair. For example, we examine the pattern of inheritance of two traits in the children of a double backcross mating (one parent being doubly heterozygous, the other doubly homozygous) and we ask: What is the likelihood that the observed pattern with which traits are distributed in the offspring would have occurred if we assume that the traits are linked on an autosome and recombine in a certain proportion of cases, as compared with the likelihood that the pattern would occur if the traits were not linked? We can also turn the question around and ask: Given the observed and computed data, what are the relative probabilities that recombination will occur with frequency a or b (or with other assumed frequencies)? The answer to this question can give us an estimate of the most likely distance between two loci on an autosome.

Testing the various sets of assumptions is a complex job, and the application of this procedure to the large num-

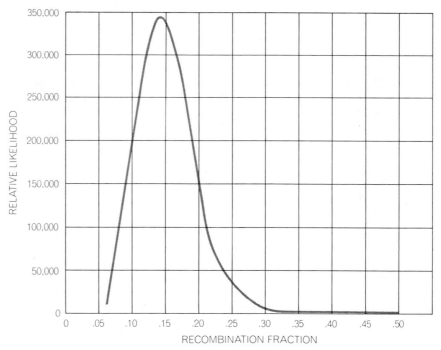

HETEROZYGOUS PARENT LUTHERAN POSITIVE, SECRETOR OR		HOMOZYGOUS PARENT LUTHERAN NEGATIVE, NONSECRETOR	
OFFSPRING: LUTHERAN POSITIVE, SECRETOR	LUTHERAN NEGATIVE, NONSECRETOR	LUTHERAN POSITIVE, NONSECRETOR	LUTHERAN NEGATIVE, SECRETOR
SIBSHIP			
1	0	0	6	2

SIBSHIP	LUTHERAN POSITIVE, SECRETOR	LUTHERAN NEGATIVE, NONSECRETOR	LUTHERAN POSITIVE, NONSECRETOR	LUTHERAN NEGATIVE, SECRETOR
1	0	0	6	2
2	4	1	0	0
3	0	0	4	1
4	1	0	1	5
5	0	1	0	1
6	1	1	0	0
7	1	1	1	1
8	0	0	3	3
9	4	1	0	0
10	0	3	0	1
11	1	3	0	1
12	2	2	0	0
13	0	0	1	1
14	1	2	0	0
15	1	2	0	1
16	1	1	0	2
TOTAL OFFSPRING	17	18	16	19

AUTOSOMES, the nonsex chromosomes, are mapped by applying statistical procedures to the pattern of inheritance of two unusual traits, in this case the Lutheran blood type and the "secretor" trait. One parent has both, the other has neither; their chromosomes must be as shown at the top of the chart. For each sibship (set of offspring) one asks: What is the likelihood that the observed pattern of transmission would occur assuming a particular recombination fraction (probability of recombination), or map distance, compared with the likelihood in the absence of linkage? The pattern in sibship 14, for example, provides data for calculating that complete linkage is four times as likely as no linkage.

LIKELIHOOD is similarly worked out for all the sibships in a series and for multiple recombination-fraction values. The recombination fraction corresponding to the peak of the curve drawn from the summed values is the maximum-likelihood estimate of the recombination fraction and, indirectly, of the distance between two loci. This plot of data derived from the series at the top of the page indicates a recombination fraction of .14, or a map distance of about 14 units between Lutheran and secretor loci on the same chromosome.

ber of possible pairs of marker loci and the great amount of data involved requires the services of a computer. Computer programs have been written for the analysis of linkage data. In the Division of Medical Genetics at Johns Hopkins, James H. Renwick has set up a World Linkage Center where pedigree data can be submitted for analysis.

We and others have studied the pedigrees of a number of families, singly and in groups, and it turns out that linkages of certain loci on the same autosome can be indicated with a high degree of prob-ability, in some cases a probability of 95 percent or better. At least six pairs and three triplets of linked loci have been uncovered. The pairings are:

1. The Duffy blood-type locus and a locus for cataract.

2. The locus for transferrin (a beta globulin of blood) and a locus for a blood cholinesterase.

3. The albumin locus and the locus for another serum protein known as group-specific component (*Gc*).

4. The MNSs blood-group locus and the locus for sclerotylosis (a skin disease).

5. The beta hemoglobin locus and the delta hemoglobin locus.

6. The *IgA* locus and the locus or cluster of loci for *IgG*. Both terms refer to immunoglobulins of the blood.

The triplets of linked loci are:

1. The ABO blood-type locus, the locus for the red-blood-cell enzyme adenylate kinase and the locus for the nail-patella syndrome (abnormalities in the fingernails and kneecaps).

2. The elliptocytosis locus, the Rh blood-group locus and the locus for the enzyme 6-phosphogluconate dehydrogenase.

3. The Lutheran blood-group locus, the locus for secretor trait (the secretion of the ABO blood-type substance into the saliva and other body fluids) and the locus for myotonic dystrophy.

In addition to these pairs and triplets of loci several pairs and at least one triplet appear to be linked but complete proof is not yet at hand.

We come now to the problem of assigning loci to their particular autosomes. The first firm assignment by the method of family study was achieved by one of my graduate students, Roger P. Donahue. Examining samples of his own white blood cells under the microscope, he noticed that one of his autosomes, the one designated No. 1 in the classified array of chromosomes, was unusually long, evidently because part of one arm of the chromosome was relatively uncoiled [*see illustration at left*].

Exhibiting laudable intellectual curiosity, Donahue looked into cells from other members of his family and traced the uncoiled version of chromosome No. 1 through three generations. Wilma B. Bias then obtained data on marker traits, including blood types, in the same pedigree. When this collection of information was subjected to computer analysis, it was found that chromosome No. 1 carried the locus for the Duffy blood type, a finding confirmed in other families.

By similarly searching for linkage with

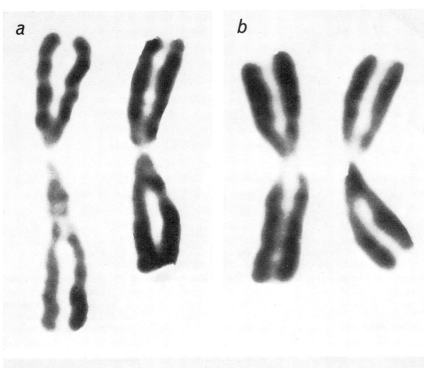

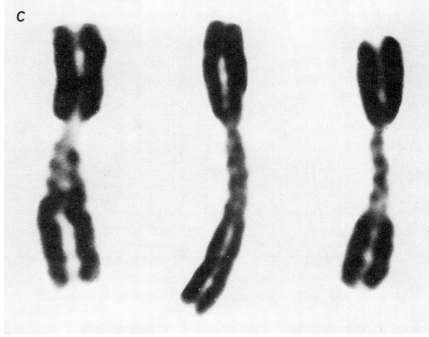

ABNORMAL CHROMOSOME NO. 1 in a member of the Donahue family is longer than its homologous chromosome because one arm is relatively uncoiled (*a*). The No. 1 chromosomes in some members of the family are normal (*b*). In others No. 1 chromosomes from several cells show the anomaly (*c*). Correlation of the transmission of the unusual chromosome with that of the Duffy blood type locates the Duffy locus on the No. 1 chromosome.

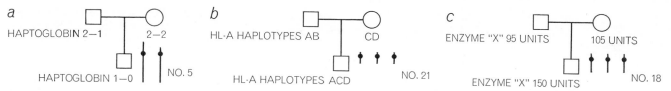

ASSIGNING GENES to chromosomes is theoretically possible on the basis of observations of chromosomes and marker traits in families, as illustrated by these hypothetical examples. Deletion mapping (a) would suggest that the haptoglobin locus is on the segment of chromosome No. 5 missing in the son; actually it is on No. 16. Presence of both alleles from one parent in a son with three No. 21 chromosomes instead of two (b) implies that the HL-A locus is on No. 21, but it appears actually to be on No. 16. Similarly, the 50 percent increase in the level of a red-cell enzyme in a child with three No. 18 chromosomes (c) might suggest that the enzyme is determined by a gene on that chromosome. To date no firm assignments of genes to chromosomes have been made by such methods.

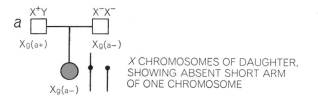

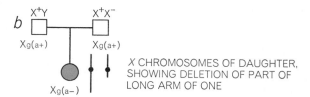

FAILURE OF DELETION MAPPING is shown by pedigrees for blood group Xg. Pedigree a suggests that the daughter's lack of an Xg(a+) allele—indicated because Xg(a+) is dominant—is due to deletion of the short arm of the X chromosome from the father. Pedigree b suggests that the locus is on the long arm of the X chromosome, however; the two findings are mutually invalidating. (The anomalous X chromosome is regularly "inactivated" through a mechanism called lyonization, unique to the X chromosome.)

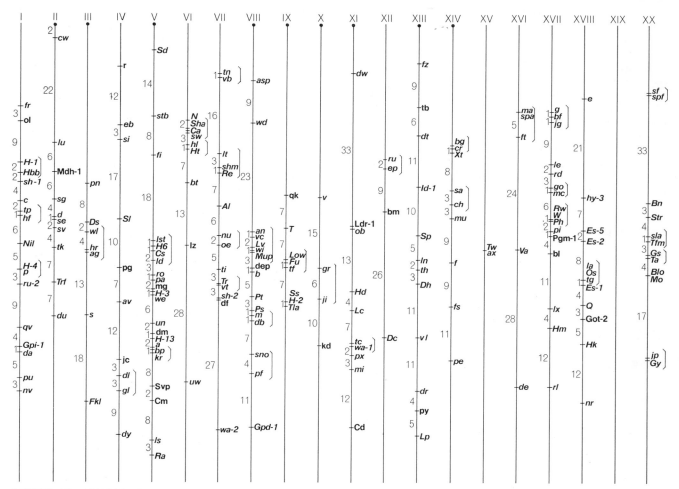

MOUSE CHROMOSOMES have been extensively mapped into linkage groups but, except for the X chromosome, most groups have not been assigned to specific chromosomes because these are not individually very distinctive in the mouse. The map, prepared by Margaret C. Green of the Jackson Laboratory, shows about 200 loci, of which the ones whose location is well established are in italics, and the map distances between loci. The knobs indicate the location of the centromere where it is known. Linkage groups whose order is not established are bracketed. Except for the X chromosome (XX) numbering of the linkage groups is arbitrary.

HYBRID CLONES	1	2	3	4	5	6	7	8	9	10	11	12
PHENOTYPE A	−	−	+	−	−	+	+	+	−	−	+	+
PHENOTYPE B	+	−	−	−	+	−	+	+	+	−	+	+
PHENOTYPE C	−	−	+	−	−	+	+	+	−	−	+	+
CHROMOSOME Z	+	−	−	−	+	−	+	+	+	−	+	+

CELL HYBRIDIZATION offers a technique for linkage analysis and chromosome assignment. In successive generations of mouse-human hybrid cells, human chromosomes tend to disappear gradually. Examining a number of clones, or lines of cells, one notes what human phenotypes are present (+) or absent (−) and what human chromosomes remain. In this example phenotypes A and C appear to be determined by genes on a single chromosome other than chromosome Z; phenotype B's locus appears to be on chromosome Z.

a marker chromosome in family pedigrees it has been established that the locus controlling the synthesis of one part of the haptoglobin molecule lies on the autosome designated No. 16. In general, however, attempts to assign loci to specific chromosomes through linkage with physical anomalies or defects in the chromosome have not been successful. In the case of the X chromosome efforts to determine whether the color-blindness locus, the Xg blood-group locus and other loci are on the short arm of the chromosome or the long arm have been foiled by the circumstance that abnormal X chromosomes are always inactivated. The various types of approach that are used in family studies to assign loci to specific chromosomes are explained in greater detail in the top and middle illustrations on the preceding page.

New methods for seeking out genetic loci are emerging—methods that do not depend on searching through family pedigrees. One of these focuses the search on hybridized cells formed by a union between human cells (usually fibroblasts grown in a tissue culture of a small piece of skin) and cells of another animal species, such as the mouse. Hybrids of this kind can be produced with the aid of a virus, inactivated by ultraviolet treatment, that damages the cell wall so that the cells fuse when the wall heals. (This type of breeding has been called an "alternative for sex.") As the hybrid cells divide, the human chromosomes are selectively and progressively lost until they are reduced to a few whose biochemical products can be identified if the mouse parent cell lacked the capacity to make those products. In this way Howard Green and Mary C. Weiss, who were then working at the New York University School of Medicine, pinned down the genetic responsibility for synthesis of the enzyme thymidine kinase; the locus of the gene is now known to be on the No. 17 autosome of man [see "Hybrid Somatic Cells," by Boris Ephrussi and Mary C. Weiss; SCIENTIFIC AMERICAN Offprint 1137].

Walter F. Bodmer and his co-workers at the Stanford University School of Medicine and Frank H. Ruddle and his colleagues at Yale University have adopted this approach in order to discover linkages of pairs of loci in clones of hybrid cells. They look for pairings of human biochemical traits; if two traits are either both present or both absent in every clone examined, the fact can be taken as evidence that the loci for both traits are on the same autosome [see illustration at left]. This approach has established that the locus for serum LDH-B (one of the lactate dehydrogenase enzymes) and the locus for the serum enzyme known as peptidase-B are on the same chromosome (so far unidentified), that LDH-A and LDH-B are not linked on one chromosome, and that LDH-A is on some chromosome in the C group (No. 6 through No. 12).

Many chromosomes are not individually distinguishable from one another under the microscope (which is one reason for their assignment to groups in the classification); this is particularly true of the C group. A new staining technique that makes the chromosomes fluorescent may help to identify them individually and thus facilitate the assignment of loci to particular chromosomes. It seems that the method of cell hybridization and clone culture may be more productive than the study of family pedigrees for finding linkages between loci. The findings from clones, however, do not indicate the distance between loci on a chromosome, and for this aspect of the exploration we shall have to depend on family studies or more efficient methods that may be developed. Furthermore, medically important gene-determined diseases cannot yet be identified at the cellular level. For them linkage study must be done by the family method.

Extensive mapping of the chromosomes has been done in the mouse and in certain other animals, and some of the information gained there may provide clues for the cartographic work on man. For example, it has been found that in the mouse and in the rat there is a close linkage between the locus for a form of albinism and the locus controlling the formation of the beta chain of the hemoglobin molecule; this suggests that in man the albinism locus may be linked with the one responsible for the sickle-cell trait or other anomalies of the beta chain. There are reasons to believe that the chromosomes, particularly the X chromosome, are evolutionarily conservative and do not change much from spe-

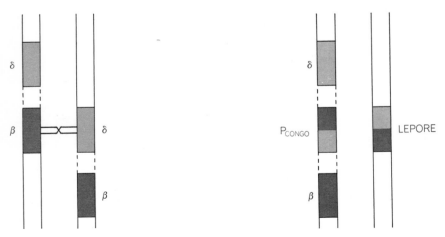

FINE STRUCTURE of chromosomes can be mapped. An anomalous hemoglobin called Lepore includes part of the beta and part of the delta hemoglobin chains. It can be explained by nonhomologous pairing, in which homologous chromosomes are out of alignment, so that crossing-over is unequal (left). The result would be a Lepore recombination and another anomalous one that has now been identified as P_CONGO hemoglobin (right).

cies to species. In the dog as in man the loci for the two forms of hemophilia, *A* and *B,* are on the *X* chromosome, for instance, and in the mouse, the horse and a number of other species the *X* chromosome also carries the *gd* locus.

It appears that even the fine structure of the chromosomes may be mappable by inferences based on the sequences of amino acids in the protein molecules that the genes determine. A mutant hemoglobin called Lepore is interesting in this connection. This hemoglobin contains a polypeptide composed of part of the delta chain and part of the beta chain, which suggests that the loci for the beta and delta chains of hemoglobin are close together on a chromosome, the Lepore hemoglobin gene having arisen from an accident called "nonhomologous pairing and unequal crossing-over."

The hypothesis advanced to explain the origin of the Lepore gene is nicely supported by family studies that show tight linkage of the delta and beta chains and by findings in connection with another mutant hemoglobin called P_{CONGO}. People with this anomalous hemoglobin, which has the amino acid sequence of part of the beta chain and part of the delta chain, also have on the same chromosome a normal beta gene and a normal delta gene. The situation is thus complementary to that of the Lepore gene [*see bottom illustration on opposite page*].

Finally, one can suppose that studies and experiments on the sequence of nucleotides in the DNA molecule itself (and in RNA) might yield the most illuminating information for the mapping of the genes in the chromosomes. After all, these molecules could tell directly the map story that can only be inferred indirectly from studies of linkages of traits.

Meanwhile the investigation of linkages has already progressed far enough to make possible prenatal diagnosis of hereditary conditions such as myotonic dystrophy. The key to the diagnosis of myotonic dystrophy is the secretor trait, whose locus is closely linked to the locus that gives rise to the dystrophy. It has been shown by my associate Peter Harper that the presence or absence of the secretor factor can be determined in the fetus on the basis of a sample of amniotic fluid taken as early as the 14th week of gestation. If one of the parents carries the gene for myotonic dystrophy, and if the two parents' genotypes for the secretor factor are appropriate, one can predict with an accuracy of 90 percent or better whether or not the child will be afflicted with the disorder.

[*A further contribution by Victor A. McKusick is contained in the Addendum beginning on the following page*].

Addendum

Victor A. McKusick delivered the following Joseph C. Wilson Lecture at the University of Rochester in November 1973. It is entitled "Mapping the Chromosomes of Man":

In the first few years of this century, Sutton and Boveri independently concluded that the chromosomes carry the "factors" whose existence Mendel deduced in the 1860s and which Bateson later called genes. Since the work of Thomas Hunt Morgan and his colleagues in 1910 and the immediately following years, it has been known that the genes are arranged linearly along the chromosomes and that the relative distances between gene loci on a chromosome can be inferred from the frequency with which recombination of traits determined by genes at these loci occurs among the offspring of particular parental pairs. In 1910 Morgan's associate E. B. Wilson first assigned a specific gene to a specific human chromosome; this was the assignment of the color blindness gene to the X chromosome on the basis of the characteristic pedigree pattern of sex linkage. The number of human chromosomes (46) has been known since 1956. The fact that the Y chromosome carries male-determining, or specifically, testis-determining factors has been known since 1959. In the last four years new methods of staining the chromosomes—the so-called "banding" techniques—have revealed hills, valleys, and other regional landmarks in the individual chromosomes.

Thus, in our exploration of the genetic planet which is the cell nucleus of man we now have the broad outline of the continents and some of the gross details of their topography. In this survey we are concerned with the location of the political jurisdictions, or functional units—that is, the genes on the human chromosomes.

At the distance from which we view them the individual genes are not distinguishable by any landmarks. Genes are far beyond the resolution of the light microscope; and even when more powerful devices are used to investigate the chromosome, one gene looks like another. The very existence of the genes as specific and individual entities must be inferred from the messages which they transmit and which we pick up from afar—that is, the traits which the genes determine.

How many genes does man have? Estimates based on the total amount of DNA, plus approximations of the total number of protein gene products, plus guesses at the amount of DNA needed for control functions (that is, the turning on and off of other genes), plus estimates of the amount of DNA which is in multiple identical copies, and so on, place the number at a minimum of about 10,000 genes in man and a maximum of something over 50,000.

What specific genes are there? Until the era of molecular genetics, the presence of a gene was inferred from the existence of alternative forms of a given trait and their distribution in families according to Mendelian rules. Over 1000 gene loci have been confidently identified by the investigations of alternative forms of a given trait. Some of the loci have, of course, more than merely two alternative forms of the gene at the given locus. Examples of known gene loci include those for different blood types: ABO, Rh, and all the others. About 850 of the gene loci are known because of the occurrence of disorders, most of them rare, resulting from mutation in the genes. A list of genetic diseases determined by genes on the X chromosome is like a photographic negative from which a positive picture of the genetic constitution of the X chromosome can be deduced.

The era of molecular genetics has brought us other ways to infer the existence of specific genes. The trinitarian dogma of DNA-RNA-protein and the related principle of one gene-one polypeptide chain means that once a polypeptide chain is fully amino-acid sequenced or even clearly defined as a specific entity, existence of a gene which determines its structure can be reasonably inferred even though no variant form of the polypeptide is known. Indeed, the principle of the colinearity of nucleotide bases in DNA on the one hand and of amino acids in the protein on the other hand permits, within limits, deductions about the chemical structure of the gene.

A first step in the mapping of genes on chromosomes is determination of which genes are on the X chromosome and which are on one of the other 22 pairs of chromosomes, called the autosomes. The characteristic pedigree pattern allows us to identify genes carried on the X chromosome. Furthermore, pedigree patterns supported by biochemical and statistical approaches often permit us to say whether a given trait is determined by a gene on an autosome.

For several years we have been maintaining catalogs of known Mendelian traits. These are essentially human gene catalogs. Table I shows the numbers of genes that have been assigned to the X chromosome and to the autosomes.

Table I
Assignment of Genes to X Chromosome and Autosomes

	Verschuer 1958	McKusick's *Mendelian Inheritance in Man* 1966	1968	1971	Oct. 31, 1973
On the X chromosome	38	68	68	86	92
On the autosomes	374	506	624	780	953
Total	412	574	692	866	1045

Table II lists the methods used for mapping genes on chromosomes. Until as recently as 1967 family studies were the only productive method. If one can show that two traits determined by different genes tend to travel together in their transmission through successive generations of a family, then this is evidence that the genes responsible are located on the same chromosome reasonably close together. Indeed, the frequency with which the traits disassociate in transmission from one generation to another is a measure of the distance separating the two loci. If two traits assort quite independently, one concludes that the two gene loci are either on separate chromosomes or are so far apart on the same chromosome that abundant crossing-over occurs between them. This is the family method of study.

Table II
Methods of Chromosome Mapping

Family studies°
1. Are two given loci on the same chromosome within genetically measurable distance of each other and if so, how far apart are they?
2. Is a particular locus on a particular chromosome?

Somatic cell hybridization°
1. Are two particular loci on the same chromosome (that is, syntenic)?
2. Is a particular locus on a particular chromosome?
3. More precisely, where on the particular chromosome is the given locus?

In situ RNA-DNA hybridization°

Study of gene product°
1. Indirect identification of fusion gene resulting from unequal crossing-over involving neighboring genes.
2. Dosage effects, for example, deletion mapping.°

°These terms are explained in the text.

By the family method it was first shown in the early 1950s that the loci for the Lutheran blood group, and for that "honorary" blood group called secretor

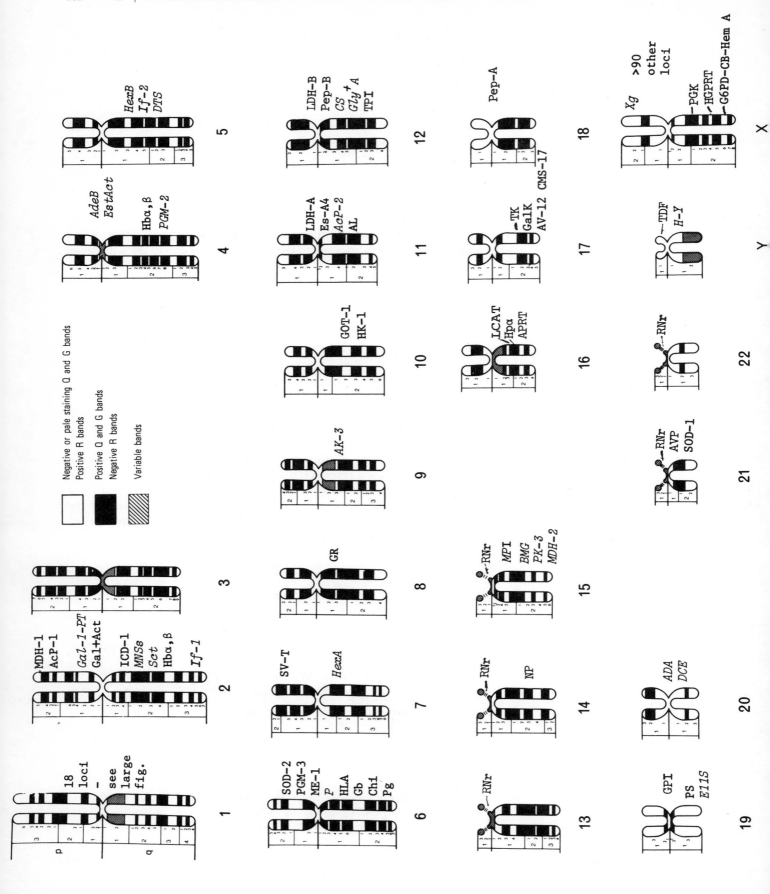

Figure 1 A human gene map (1 September 1974). The banding pattern of the human chromosomes as indicated by special staining techniques is diagrammed. To the left of each chromosome the symbols of genes which have been assigned to the given chromosome are given. When the assignment is inconclusive, the symbol is indicated in italics. [Courtesy of Victor A. McKusick.]

THE X CHROMOSOME

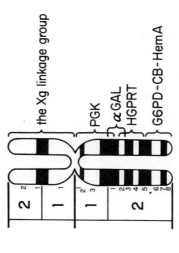

Figure 3 A gene map of the human chromosome X (1 September 1974). [Courtesy of Victor A. McKusick.]

CHROMOSOME NO. 1

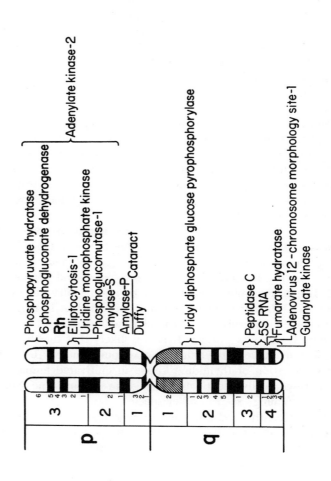

Figure 2 A gene map of the human chromosome No. 1 (1 September 1974). [Courtesy of Victor A. McKusick.]

factor, are on the same autosome; soon thereafter it was found that the Rh gene locus and the locus for elliptocytosis, and the ABO gene locus and that for the nail-patella syndrome, were similarly linked. It was, of course, not then known which specific chromosome carried these three pairs of loci. (We now know that the Rh blood group, and by inference elliptocytosis, are on the short arm of chromosome No. 1.)

Some families have chromosome peculiarities, normal variations. For example, a long chromosome No. 1 is a normal trait in some families, like a long nose in other families. If one can show that the peculiar chromosome, called a marker chromosome, and a given trait are passed down in the family together, this constitutes proof that the gene locus is on this specific chromosome. The first such assignment was achieved in my department in 1968 when Roger Donahue, then a graduate student, showed by studying his own family that the gene locus determining for Duffy blood type is carried on chromosome No. 1.

The family method of study has serious limitations. Alternative forms of the trait determined by the genes at the locus under study must be present in the family. Human families, especially these days, are small in size and geographically dispersed. Study of more than two generations may be difficult because generation time is long. Because matings cannot, of course, be made by design as in linkage studies in the mouse, for example, the raw data must be taken as found. Consequently complex or at least arduous computer-aided computations are often necessary to extract maximal information from available raw family data. Because of these limitations, when the methodology was limited to the family approach progress in chromosome mapping was slow.

The method of somatic cell hybridization has great advantages for gene mapping. It is, as one geneticist has put it, a "substitute for sex." If cells of man and mouse are mixed and a virus which causes damage to cell membranes is added, fusion will occur between the nuclei of cells of the different species. One ends up with a hybrid cell containing at the outset the 46 chromosomes of the human cell and the 40 chromosomes of the mouse. In subsequent cell divisions the human chromosomes are preferentially lost. In due course one may end up with a derivative cell line that has only a single human chromosome persisting along with the full complement of mouse chromosomes. A correlation between persistence of a single human chromosome and a given human biochemical cell trait is an indication that the gene for that trait is on the retained chromosome. Furthermore, if cells derived from the hybrid show persistence of human traits A and B together or loss of traits A and B together, this is an indication of so-called synteny (that is, genes for A and B are on the same human chromosome). The cell hybridization method is especially sensitive if there are selective methods which guarantee the persistence of one particular human chromosome because it carries a gene without which the hybrid cell cannot survive. In 1967 Weiss and Green found—and subsequently Migeon at Johns Hopkins corroborated—that the thymidine kinase locus is on chromosome No. 17. When the mouse cell was one deficient in thymidine kinase the hybrid cell could survive in a particular medium only if the human gene for thymidine kinase was present. It is now likely that the thymidine kinase gene is near the middle of the long arm of chromosome No. 17; a virus which stimulates formation of thymidine kinase in cultivated human cells also causes a microscopically identifiable change in chromosome No. 17, probably similar to "puffing" seen in other species.

A third and most recently used approach to gene mapping is a different type of hybridization. As every high school student and most well-read laymen now know, the gene DNA does its work through the intermediacy of a messenger RNA, which passes out of the nucleus into the cytoplasm where it serves as a blueprint for the linear assemblage of amino acids into a protein.

There are other genes whose function it is to determine another type of RNA—ribosomal RNA, the RNA which is the backbone structure in the cytoplasm on which proteins are assembled. Ribosomal RNA and specific messenger RNA for proteins such as hemoglobin can be radioactively labelled and isolated in relatively pure and abundant form. If cells are treated in a particular way the DNA of the chromosome will unravel to some extent. When RNA is applied to these cells and the conditions of the medium are so changed as to favor reconstitution of the chromosome, RNA tends to anneal to the DNA which is complementary to it in nucleotide sequence. Thus, ribosomal RNA attaches to the gene for it and theoretically hemoglobin messenger RNA attaches to the gene for it. If the RNA is radioactively labelled, one can by autoradiography identify the location of the specific genes on specific chromosomes.

By this method the genes for one class of ribosomal RNA have been localized to the centromeric ends of chromosomes Nos. 13, 14, 15, 21, and 22, and a special type of ribosomal RNA to the long arm of chromosome No. 1. Also by this method it has been proposed that the gene for the beta chain of hemoglobin may be on chromosome No. 2, but this conclusion can be considered only tentative because technical considerations make it unlikely, in the view of some, that the method is sufficiently sensitive. Only when many copies of the gene in question are present is the radioactivity expected to be adequate to show up the location of the gene. Work with other species suggests that the genes for histones, proteins present in chromosomes, and genes for immunoglobulins, being present in multiple forms, can be mapped in man by the presently available technique.

A fourth method of deducing close linkage of gene loci might be called the Lepore method. One polypeptide chain of an anomalous hemoglobin called Hb Lepore is a curious hybrid as to its amino acid sequence. One part has the sequence of the normal delta polypeptide chain that occurs in hemoglobin A_2; the rest has the sequence of the normal beta polypeptide chain that occurs in hemoglobin A. It is entirely probable that the genes for delta and beta hemoglobin chains are close together and that the gene for the anomalous Lepore chain originated by nonhomologous pairing and unequal crossing-over. This interpretation has been strengthened by finding patients in Japan and in Africa with an anomalous protein which is the reciprocal product of the accident postulated to cause the Lepore gene. Hemoglobin Kenya is a similar fusion hemoglobin chain that tells us that the gamma and beta loci are closely linked. Among the immunoglobulins, the fact that variant proteins have been found tells us that the genes for different types of gamma globulin are closely linked.

Deletion mapping is another way to make deductions about gene localization. The approach has given dubious results in the past, but recently assignment of the Rh locus to the short arm of chromosome No. 1 and of the LDH-B locus to the short arm of chromosome No. 12 has been achieved by the method of deletion mapping.

Rapid advances in assignment of specific genes to specific chromosomes have been possible particularly with the cell hybridization approach. Last June an International Workshop on Human Gene Mapping held at Yale University gave workers an opportunity to collate their findings, many of them not yet published. With the approaches outlined above, now at least one gene has been assigned with some confidence to each of 19 of the 22 pairs of autosomes, and the largest chromosome, No. 1, is becoming rather densely populated with 16 loci known to be situated thereon. Only chromosomes Nos. 3, 8, and 9 remain no man's land. The family and the cell methods have complemented each other well. The family method can give information on the distance separating two loci assigned to a given chromosome. Cell hybridization studies using human cells with broken and rearranged chromosomes can give information on what specific part of a chromosome carries a particular gene locus. For a total of over 60 loci there is now some information on the autosome which carries them. Unassigned linkage groups involve over 20 other loci, so that all told some mapping information is available on about 85 gene loci. Fortunately, information is accumulating at an accelerating pace, so that the numbers given today, November 1, 1973, will not hold a month or two from now.

Figure 1 gives a résumé of the present status of our knowledge of the human chromosome map. The relatively dense mapping of chromosome No. 1 is noteworthy (Parts 1 and 2). I find great intellectual satisfaction in the fact that the Rh blood group can be assigned to the distal half of the short arm of chromosome No. 1. The locus of the gene for galactosemia may be on chromosome No. 2; the locus of HL-A tissue type, important in kidney transplantation, is on chromosome No. 6; and the locus of the mutation causing Tay-Sachs disease may be on chromosome No. 7.

Self-potentiation is evident in the mapping of chromosome No. 1 (Figure 2). From its length one would estimate that about 9% of the autosomal genetic material is on chromosome No. 1, but about 20% of the assigned loci are on that chromosome. The first locus assigned was Duffy—in 1968. Now five years later the assigned loci total 16.

Studies of aberrant chromosomes No. 1 in families and in somatic cell culture lead to the conclusion that the Rh locus and PGM_1 locus are on the short arm.

The mapping of the X chromosome has proceeded through several steps. Mainly by means of pedigree patterns, 92 loci have, as mentioned earlier, been assigned to the X chromosome.

Two groups of genes closely linked on the X chromosome have been discovered: Haldane and colleagues showed that the color blindness loci and hemophilia A are closely situated, and my colleagues and I as well as others showed that color blindness and G6PD are closely linked and G6PD and hemophilia A are closely linked. Thus, there is a tight cluster of these 3 loci which are not within mappable distance with the Xg blood group locus. On the other hand, the Xg blood group locus is linked with those for ocular albinism, a form of hereditary retinal detachment, X-linked mental retardation and an X-linked skin disorder.

Studies of various aberrant X chromosomes in somatic cell hybrids indicate that the G6PD locus is situated toward the distal end of the long arm of the X and that the HGPRT locus and PGK locus are situated toward the centromere in the approximate position indicated. There is suggestive evidence that the Xg locus is situated toward the distal end of the short arm of the X. Thus one can arrive at the tentative map of the X chromosome presented in Figure 3. Again, I find it a great intellectual satisfaction to know that the color blindness genes and the gene for classic hemophilia are on the distal third of the long arm of the X chromosome.

Since this symposium is entitled "The impact of genetics on medicine," some indication of the connection of gene mapping to applied medicine should be indicated. Even in this day of shrinking funding for basic research, I have limited patience with people who ask, "Why do you want to know the human gene map?" It is *terra incognita* which is a challenge to the human intellect just as is any uncharted terrain on this planet. The practical value of the information will certainly be great, although I must confess that at this point this statement is largely an article of faith. The *in utero* diagnosis of genetic disorders which are not per se biochemically identifiable at that stage or perhaps at any stage can theoretically be achieved if closely linked loci which are identifiable in amniotic cells are known. Confirmation of theory has been achieved in the case of at least one autosomal and one X-linked disease. The autosomal disorder is myotonic muscular dystrophy, which we now know is linked to the locus for the so-called secretor trait. The X-linked disorder is classic hemophilia, which as we saw is determined by a gene situated close to the locus for the enzyme glucose-6-phosphate dehydrogenase. Both secretor status and G6PD can be determined in the fluid around the fetus or cells in the fluid. Thus, if the genetic make-up of the parents is sufficiently clear, one can determine whether the unborn baby has hemophilia or has myotonic dystrophy by testing for G6PD or secretor, respectively, in the amniotic cells or fluid.

November 1973   *Victor A. McKusick*

16 . Ionizing Radiation and Evolution

by James F. Crow
September 1959

Living things evolve as a result of random mutations in hereditary characteristics that survive when they make the organism more fit. What role does ionizing radiation play in the evolutionary process?

The mutant gene—a fundamental unit in the mechanism of heredity that has been altered by some cause, thereby changing some characteristic of its bearers—is the raw material of evolution. Ionizing radiation produces mutation. Ergo, ionizing radiation is an important cause of evolution.

At first this seems like a compelling argument. But is it really? To what extent is the natural rate at which mutations occur dependent upon radiation? Would evolution have been much the same without radiation? Is it possible that increased exposure to radiation, rising from human activities, has a significant effect upon the future course of human evolution?

Radiation has been of tremendous value for genetic research, and therefore for research in evolution. To clarify the issue at the outset, however, it is likely that ionizing radiation has played only a minor role in the recent evolutionary history of most organisms. As for the earliest stages of evolution, starting with the origin of life, it is problematical whether ionizing radiation played a significant role even then. Laboratory experiments show that organic compounds, including the amino acid units of the protein molecule, may be formed from simple nitrogen and carbon compounds upon exposure to ionizing radiation or an electric discharge. But ultraviolet radiation serves as well in these demonstrations, and was probably present in large amounts at the earliest ages of life. In the subsequent history of life the development of photosynthesis in plants and of vision in animals indicates the much greater importance of nonionizing radiation in the terrestrial environment.

Nonetheless, as will be seen, man presents an important special case in any discussion of the mutation-inducing effects of ionizing radiation. The mutation rate affects not only the evolution of the human species but also the life of the individual. Almost every mutation is harmful, and it is the individual who pays the price. Any human activity that tends to increase the mutation rate must therefore raise serious health and moral problems for man.

H. J. Muller's great discovery that radiation induces mutations in the fruit fly *Drosophila*, and its independent confirmation in plants by L. J. Stadler, was made more than 30 years ago. One of the first things to be noticed by the Drosophila workers was that most of the radiation-induced changes in the characteristics of their flies were familiar, the same changes having occurred repeatedly as a result of natural mutation. Not only were the external appearances of the mutant flies recognizable (white eyes, yellow body, forked bristles, missing wing-veins); it could also be shown that the mutant genes were located at the same sites on the chromosomes as their naturally occurring predecessors. Thus it seems that radiation-induced mutants are not unique; they are the same types that occur anyhow at a lower rate and that we call spontaneous because we do not know their causes.

The prevailing hypothesis is that the hereditary information is encoded in various permutations in the arrangement of subunits of the molecule of deoxyribonucleic acid (DNA) in the chromosomes. A mutation occurs when this molecule fails, for some reason, to replicate itself exactly. The mutated gene is thereafter reproduced until its bearer dies without reproducing, or until, by chance, the altered gene mutates again.

A variety of treatments other than radiation will induce mutation. Most agents, including radiation, seem to affect the genes indiscriminately, increasing the mutation rate for all genes in the same proportion. But some chemical mutagens are fairly selective in the genes they affect. It is even conceivable that investigators may find a chemical that will regularly mutate a particular gene and no other. This will probably be very difficult to achieve: A mutagen capable of affecting a specific gene would probably have to have the same order of informational complexity as the gene itself in order to recognize the gene and influence it.

Moreover, different mutant genes known to be at different locations on the chromosome frequently produce effects that mimic each other. Geneticists who work with fruit flies are familiar with several different genes that result in indistinguishable eye colors. This is not surprising when we consider the complexity of the relationship between the genes and the characteristics that they produce. There are many different paths by which any particular end-point may be reached; it is to be expected that many different gene changes can lead to the same result, though the chemical pathways by which this is accomplished may be greatly different.

To consider another kind of example, many insects have come to survive insecticides. They do so by such diverse means as behavior patterns that enable them to avoid the insecticide, mechanisms that interfere with the entrance of the insecticide into the body, enzymes that detoxify the insecticide, and by somehow becoming able to tolerate more of the insecticide. All these modes of survival develop by selection of mutant genes that are already present in low frequency in the population. This is one of the characteristic features of evolution: its opportunism. It makes use of the raw materials—that is, the mutant genes—that happen to be available.

As a first conclusion it appears that radiation-induced mutations do not play any unique role in evolution. The same gene mutations would probably occur anyhow. Even if they did not, the same end result could be achieved with other mutants.

One might still suspect that spontaneous mutations are caused by natural radiations. This was quickly ruled out as a possibility in Drosophila. For one thing, the spontaneous-mutation rate is strongly dependent upon temperature, which would be surprising if mutation were a simple and direct consequence of

radiation. But much more decisive evidence comes from the fact that the amount of natural radiation is entirely inadequate to account for the rate of spontaneous mutation. The natural-mutation rate in Drosophila, if it were caused solely by radiation, would require 50 or more r. Yet the amount of radiation received by a fly in the 12-day interval between egg and mature adult is about .004 r. Natural radiation would have to be increased more than 10,000 times to account for the natural Drosophila mutation rate! Thus, in Drosophila at least, radiation accounts for only a trivial part of the spontaneous rate. The same is true for mice. Although the fraction of spontaneous mutations that owe their origin to radiation is higher than that in Drosophila, it is still less than .1 per cent.

It is clear that natural-mutation rates, if they are measured in absolute time-units, cannot be the same in all organisms. One example will demonstrate this decisively. The spontaneous-mutation rate in Drosophila is such that about one embryo in 50 carries a lethal mutation (a mutation harmful enough to cause death) that occurred during the preceding generation. Most such mutations are recessive, that is, they have a lethal effect only when they are in a double dose, but this does not prevent the death; it only postpones it. The reproductive life-cycle in man is approximately 1,000 times as long as that of a fly: some 30 years as compared with 12 days. If the absolute mutation-rate in man were the same as that in Drosophila, each human embryo would bear an average of 20

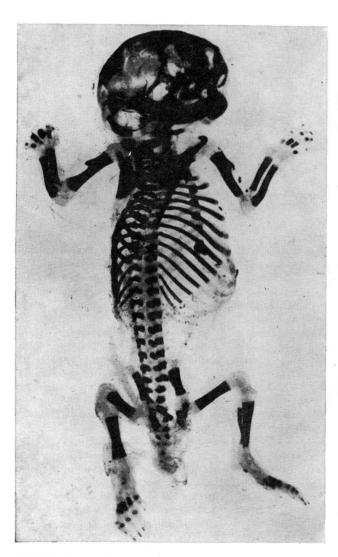
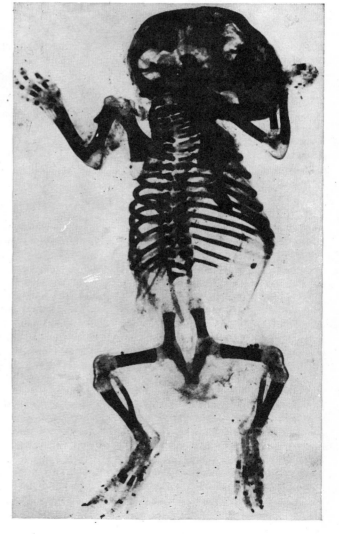

MUTATION of a single gene in a mouse results in offspring that have an unusually short tail (*skeleton at left*). A mouse that receives such a mutant gene from both of its parents has more serious defects, including the absence of the lower part of its spine (*skele-* *ton at right*); it dies soon after birth. These specimens were prepared in the laboratory of L. C. Dunn of Columbia University. The soft tissues were treated with strong alkali and glycerin to make them transparent; the bones were stained with a red dye.

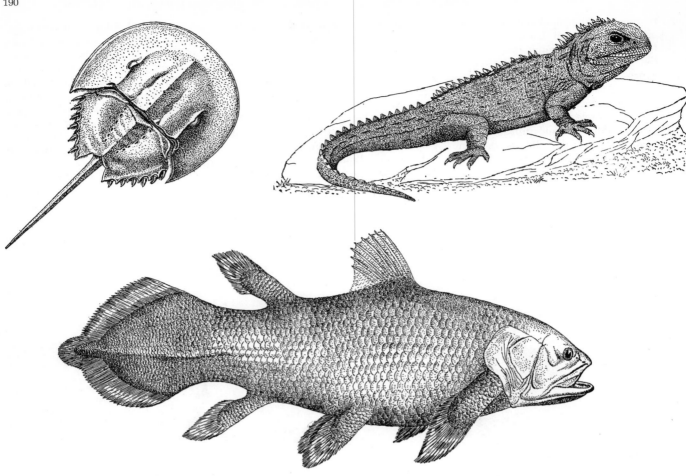

RATE OF EVOLUTION in certain organisms is extremely slow. Depicted in these drawings are four animals that have not changed appreciably over a period of millions or even hundreds of millions of years. At top left is the horseshoe crab; at top center, the tuatara;

new lethal mutations; man would quickly become extinct.

Actually, if the rate is measured in mutations per generation, the spontaneous-mutation rate of those few human genes whose mutation rates can be effectively measured is roughly the same as that of Drosophila genes. The rule seems to be that the absolute mutation-rate divided by the generation period is much more nearly constant from one species to another than the rate itself. The implication of this is exciting. It can only mean that the mutation rate itself is capable of modification; that it, too, is changed by natural selection. By being brought into adjustment with the life cycle, the underlying mechanism of evolution itself is undergoing evolution!

It appears, however, that the rates of radiation-induced mutations are not as readily modified. If these rates were being adjusted along with the rates of mutations from other causes, we would expect that mice would show a lesser response to radiation than do fruit flies be-

cause their life cycle is longer. The facts are otherwise; mouse genes average some 15 times as many mutations per unit of radiation as Drosophila genes.

This strongly suggests that the process whereby mutations are produced by radiation is less capable of evolutionary adjustment than other mutation-producing processes. The implication is that organisms with a long life-cycle— Sequoia trees, elephants, men—have a larger fraction of mutations due to natural radiations. It may be that the majority of mutations in a very long-lived organism are due to radiations. Possibly this sets an upper limit on the length of the life cycle.

Unfortunately the rate of radiation-induced mutations is not known for any organism with a long life-cycle. If we assume that the susceptibility of human genes to mutation by radiation is the same as that of mouse genes, we would conclude that less than 10 per cent of human mutations are due to natural radiations. But the exact fraction is quite

uncertain, because of inaccurate knowledge of the rate of spontaneous human mutations. So it cannot be ruled out that even a majority of human mutations owe their origin to radiation.

Thus the over-all mutation rate is not determined by radiation to any significant extent, except possibly in some very long-lived organisms. In general, radiation does not seem to play an important role in evolution, either by supplying qualitatively unique types of mutations or by supplying quantitatively significant numbers of mutations.

There is another question: To what extent is the rate of evolution dependent on the mutation rate? Will an organism with a high mutation-rate have a correspondingly higher rate of evolution? In general, the answer is probably no.

The measurement of evolutionary rates is fraught with difficulty and doubt. There is always some uncertainty about the time-scale, despite steady improvements in paleontology and new techniques of dating by means of the decay

at bottom center, the recently discovered coelacanth; at the far right, the opossum.

rate of evolution of tooth size in the ancestors of the horse was about 40 millidarwins.)

More difficult to quantify, but more significant, are changes in structure. Some animals have changed very little in enormous lengths of time. There are several examples of "living fossils," some of which are depicted on the preceding two pages. During the time the coelacanth remained practically unchanged whole new classes appeared: the birds and mammals, with such innovations as feathers, hair, hoofs, beaks, mammary glands, internal temperature-regulation and the ability to think conceptually. What accounts for such differences in rate?

The general picture of how evolution works is now clear. The basic raw material is the mutant gene. Among these mutants most will be deleterious, but a minority will be beneficial. These few will be retained by what Muller has called the sieve of natural selection. As the British statistician R. A. Fisher has said, natural selection is a "mechanism for generating an exceedingly high level of improbability." It is Maxwell's famous demon superimposed on the random process of mutation.

Despite the clarity and simplicity of the general idea, the details are difficult and obscure. Selection operates at many levels—between cells, between individual organisms, between families, between species. What is advantageous in the short run may be ruinous in the long run. What may be good in one environment may be bad in another. What is good this year may be bad next year. What is good for an individual may be bad for the species.

A certain amount of variability is necessary for evolution to occur. But the comparison of fossils reveals no consistent correlation between the measured variability at any one time and the rate of evolutionary change. George Gaylord Simpson, now at Harvard University, has measured contemporary representatives of low-rate groups (crocodiles, tapirs, armadillos, opossums) and high-rate ones (lizards, horses, kangaroos) and has found no tendency for the latter to be more variable. Additional evidence comes from domesticated animals and plants. G. Ledyard Stebbins, Jr., of the University of California has noted that domesticated representatives of slowly evolving plant groups produce new horticultural varieties just as readily as those from more rapidly evolving groups. Finally, the rates of "evolutionary" change in domestic animals and

plants under artificial selection by man are tremendous compared with even the more rapidly evolving natural forms—perhaps thousands of times as fast. This can only mean that the genetic variability available for selection to work on is available in much greater abundance than the variability actually utilized in nature. The reasons why evolution is so slow in some groups must lie elsewhere than in insufficient genetic variability.

Instances of rapid evolution are probably the result of the opening-up of a new, unfilled ecological niche or environmental opportunity. This may be because of a change in the organism itself, as when the birds developed the power of flight with all the new possibilities this offered. It may also be due to opening-up of a new area, as when a few fortunate colonists land on a new continent.

One of the best-known examples of rapid change is to be found in the finches of the Galápagos Islands that Charles Darwin noted during his voyage on the *Beagle*. Darwin's finches are all descendants of what must have been a small number of chance migrants. They are a particularly striking group, especially in their adaptations to different feeding habits. Some have sparrow-like beaks for seed feeding; others have slender beaks and eat insects; some resemble the woodpeckers and feed on insect larvae in wood; still others feed with parrot-like beaks on fruits. The woodpecker type is of special interest. Lacking the woodpecker's long tongue it has evolved the habit of using a cactus spine or a twig as a substitute—it is the only example of a tool-using bird. In the rest of the world the finches are a relatively homogeneous group. Their tremendous diversity on these islands must be due to their isolation and the availability of new, unexploited ecological opportunities. A similar example of multiple adaptations is found in the honey creepers of the Hawaiian Islands [*see illustration on page 193*].

When paleontologists look into the ancestry of present-day animals, they find that only a minute fraction of the species present 100 million years ago is represented by descendants now. It is estimated that 98 per cent of the living vertebrate families trace their ancestry to eight of the species present in the Mesozoic Era, and that only two dozen of the tens of thousands of vertebrate species that were then present have left any descendants at all. The overwhelmingly probable future of any species is extinction. The history of

of radioactive isotopes. In addition there is the difficulty of determining what a comparable rate of advance in different species is. Is the difference between a leopard and a tiger more or less than that between a field mouse and a house mouse? Or has man changed more in developing his brain than the elephant has by growing a trunk? How is it possible for one to devise a suitable scale by which such different things can be compared?

Despite these difficulties, the differences in rates of evolution in various lines of descent are so enormous as to be clear by any standard. One criterion is size. Some animals have changed greatly. The horse has grown from a fox-sized ancestor to its present size while many other animals have not changed appreciably. (The British biologist J. B. S. Haldane has suggested that the word "darwin" be used as a unit for rate of size change. One darwin is taken to be an increase by a factor *e* per million years. By this criterion the

RAPID RATE OF EVOLUTION is illustrated by the horse. Comparisons of the skulls, hindfeet and forefeet of animals of successive periods indicate the changes which led from a fox-sized ancestor in the Eocene period, 60 million years ago, to the modern horse (top).

evolution is a succession of extinctions along with a tremendous expansion of a few fortunate types.

The causes of extinctions must be many. A change of environment—due to a flood, a volcanic eruption or a succession of less dramatic instances—may alter the ecological niche into which the species formerly fitted. Other animals and plants are probably the most important environmental variables: one species is part of the environment of another. There may be a more efficient predator, or a species that competes for shelter or food supply, or a new disease vector or parasite. As Theodosius Dobzhansky of Columbia University has said, "Extinction occurs either because the ecological niche disappears, or because it is wrested away by competitors."

Extinction may also arise from natural selection itself. Natural selection is a short-sighted, opportunistic process. All that matters is Darwinian fitness, that is, survival ability and reproductive capacity. A population is always in danger of becoming extinct through "criminal" genes—genes that perpetuate themselves at the expense of the rest of the population. An interesting example is the so-called SD gene, found in a wild Drosophila population near the University of Wisconsin by Yuichiro Hiraizumi. Ordinarily the segregation ratio—the ratio of two alternative genes in the progeny of any individual that carries these genes —is 1:1. In this strain the segregation is grossly distorted to something like 10:1 in favor of the SD gene; hence its name, SD, for segregation distorter. The SD gene somehow causes the chromosome opposite its own chromosome to break just prior to the formation of sperm cells. As a result the cells containing the broken chromosome usually fail to develop into functional sperm. The SD-bearing chromosome thus tends to increase itself rapidly in the population by effectively killing off its normal counterpart. Such a gene is obviously harmful to the population. But it cannot be eliminated except by the extinction of the population, or by the occurrence of a gene that is immune to the SD effect.

A similar gene exists in many mouse populations. Causing tail abnormalities, it is transmitted to much more than the usual fraction of the offspring, though in this case the detailed mechanism is not known. L. C. Dunn of Columbia University has found this gene in many wild-mouse populations. Most of these genes are highly deleterious to the mouse (a mouse needs a tail!), and some are lethal when they are borne in a double dose, so that the gene never completely takes over despite its segregational advantage. The result is an equilibrium frequency determined by the magnitude of the two opposing selective forces: the harmfulness of the gene and its segregational advantage. The population as a whole suffers, a striking illustration of the fact that natural selection does not necessarily improve the fitness of the species.

A gene causing extremely selfish, antisocial behavior—for example genes for cannibalism or social parasitism—could have similar effects in the human population. Any species must be in constant danger from the short-sightedness of the process of natural selection. Those that are still here are presumably the descendants of those that were able to avoid such pitfalls.

Aside from mutation itself, the most important evolutionary invention is sexual reproduction, which makes possible Mendelian heredity. The fact that such an elaborate mechanism exists throughout the whole living world—in viruses and bacteria, and in every major group of plants and animals—attests to its significance.

In a nonsexual population, if two potentially beneficial mutations arise in separate individuals, these individuals and their descendants can only compete with each other until one or the other type is eliminated, or until a second mutation occurs in one or the other

HONEY CREEPERS of Hawaii are a striking example of rapid evolution. Dozens of varieties, adapted to different diets, arose from a common ancestor. The long bills of *Hemignathus lucidus affinis* (1), *Hemignathus wilsoni* (4) and *Hemignathus o. obscurus* (7) are used to seek insects as woodpeckers do or to suck nectar. The beaks of *Psittirostra kona* (2), *Psittirostra cantans* (3), and *Psittirostra psittacea* (6) are adapted to a diet of berries and seeds. *Loxops v. virens* (5) sucks nectar and probes for insects with its sharp bill. *Pseudonestor xanthrophrys* (8) wrenches at hard wood to get at burrowing insects. Some of these species are presently extinct.

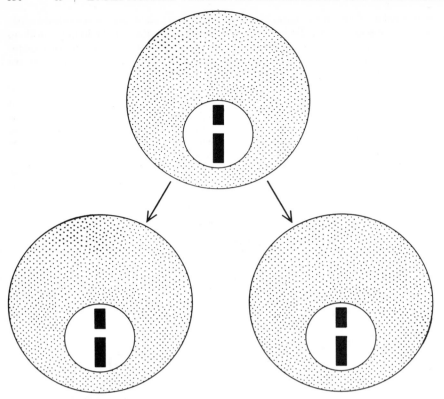

ASEXUAL REPRODUCTION permits little variability in a population; the evolution of asexual organisms depends entirely on mutation. At top is a schematic diagram of an asexual cell. Within its nucleus (*open circle*) are chromosomes (*rectangles*). When the cell divides (*bottom*), its two daughter cells have replicas of the original chromosomes and are exactly like the parent. To simplify the diagram only two of the chromosomes of a cell are shown.

group. A Mendelian species, with its biparental reproduction and consequent gene-scrambling, permits both mutants to be combined in the same individual. An asexual species must depend upon newly occurring mutations to provide it with variability. Sexual reproduction permits the combination and recombination of a whole series of mutants from the common pool of the species. Before they enter the pool the mutants have been to some extent pretested and the most harmful ones have already been eliminated.

Suppose that a population has 50 pairs of genes: Aa, Bb, Cc, etc. Suppose that each large-letter gene adds one unit of size. The difference between the smallest possible individual in this population (aa bb cc . . .) and the largest possible (AA BB CC . . .) is 100 units. Yet if all the genes are equally frequent, the size of 99.7 per cent of the population will be between 35 and 65 units. Only one individual in 2^{100} (roughly 1 followed by 30 zeros) would have 100 size units. Yet if the population is sexual, this type can be produced by selection utilizing only the genes already in the population.

This example illustrates the evolution-ary power of a system that permits Mendelian gene-assortment. In an asexual system the organism would have to wait for new mutations. Most of the size-increasing mutations would probably have deleterious side effects. If the asexual organism had a mutation rate sufficient to give it the potential variability of a sexual population, it would probably become extinct from harmful mutations.

The very existence of sexual reproduction throughout the animal and plant kingdoms argues strongly for the necessity of an optimum genetic variability. This is plain, even though there is no consistent correlation between evolution rates as observed in the fossil record and the variability of the animals observed. It must be that a certain level of genetic variability is a necessary, but by no means sufficient, condition for progressive evolution.

Evolution is an exceedingly complex process, and it is obviously impossible, even in particular cases, to assign relative magnitudes to the various causal factors. Perhaps species have become extinct through mutation rates that are too high or too low, though there is no direct observational evidence for this. Probably many asexual forms have become extinct because they were unable to adapt to changes. Other forms have become overspecialized, developing structures that fit them for only a particular habitat; when the habitat disappears, they are lost. The population size and structure are also important. To be successful in evolution, by the criterion of having left descendants many generations later, a species has the best chance if it has an optimum genetic system. But among a number of potentially successful candidates, only a few will succeed, and probably the main reason is simply the good luck of having been at the right place at the right time.

Of all the natural selection that occurs, only a small fraction leads to any progressive or directional change. Most selection is devoted to maintaining the status quo, to eliminating recurrent harmful mutations, or to adjusting to transitory changes in the environment. Thus much of the theory of natural selection must be a theory of statics rather than dynamics.

The processes that are necessary for evolution demand a certain price from the population in the form of reduced fitness. This might be said to be the price that a species pays for the privilege of evolving. The process of sexual reproduction, with its Mendelian gene-shuffling in each generation, produces a number of ill-adapted gene combinations, and therefore a reduction in average fitness. This can be avoided by a nonsexual system, but at the expense of genetic variability for evolutionary change in a changing environment.

The plant breeder knows that it is easy to maintain high-yielding varieties of the potato or sugar cane because they can be propagated asexually. But then his potential improvement is limited to the varieties that he has on hand. Only by combining various germ plasms sexually can he obtain varieties better than the existing best. But the potato and cane breeder can have his cake and eat it. He gets his new variants by sexual crosses; when he gets a superior combination of genes, he carries this strain on by an asexual process so that the combination is not broken up by Mendelian assortment.

Many species appear to have sacrificed long-term survival for immediate fitness. Some are highly successful. A familiar example is the dandelion; any lawn-keeper can testify to its survival value. In dandelion reproduction, although seeds are produced by what looks superficially like the usual method, the chromosome-assorting features of the sexual process are bypassed and the seed contains exactly the same combination of genes as the plant that produced it. In the long run the dandelion will probably become extinct, but in the present environment it is highly successful.

The process of mutation also produces ill-adapted types. The result is a lowering of the average fitness of the population, the price that asexual, as well as sexual, species pay for the privilege of evolution. Intuition tells us that the effect of mutation on fitness should be proportional to the mutation rate; Haldane has shown that the reduction in fitness is, in fact, exactly equal to the mutation rate.

The environment is never constant, so any species must find itself continually having to adjust to transitory or permanent changes in the environment. The most rapid environmental changes are usually brought about by the continuing evolution of other species. A simple example was given by Darwin himself. He noted that a certain number of rabbits in every generation are killed by wolves, and that in general these will be the rabbits that run the slowest. Thus by gradual selection the running speed of rabbits would increase. At the same time the slower wolves would starve, so that this species too has a selective premium on speed. As a result both improve, but the position of one with respect to the other does not change. It is like the treadmill situation in Lewis Carroll's famous story: "It takes all the running *you* can do, to keep in the same place."

A change in the environment will cause some genes that were previously favored to become harmful, and some that were harmful to become beneficial. At first it might seem that this does not make any net difference to the species. However, when the change occurs, the previously favored genes will be common as a result of natural selection in the past. The ones that were previously deleterious will be rare. The population will not return to its original fitness until the gene numbers are adjusted by natural selection, and this has its costs.

Just how much does it cost to exchange genes in this way? Let us ask the question for a single gene-pair. If we start with a rare dominant gene present in .01 per cent of the population, it requires the equivalent of about 10 selective "genetic deaths" (*i.e.*, failure to survive or reproduce) per surviving individual in the population to substitute this gene for its predecessor. This means

that if the population is to share an average of one gene substitution per generation, it must have a sufficient reproductive capacity to survive even though nine out of 10 individuals can die without offspring in each generation. The cost is considerably greater if the gene is recessive. The surprising part of this result is that the number does not depend on the selective value of the gene. As long as the difference between two alternative genes is small, the cost of replacing one by the other depends only on the initial frequency and dominance of the gene and not at all on its fitness.

If the gene is less rare, the cost is lowered. Thus the species can lower the price of keeping up with the environment by having a higher frequency of deleterious genes that are potentially favorable. One way to accomplish this is to have a higher mutation rate, but this, too, has its price. Once again there is the conflict between the short-term objective of high fitness and the longer-term objective of ability to change with

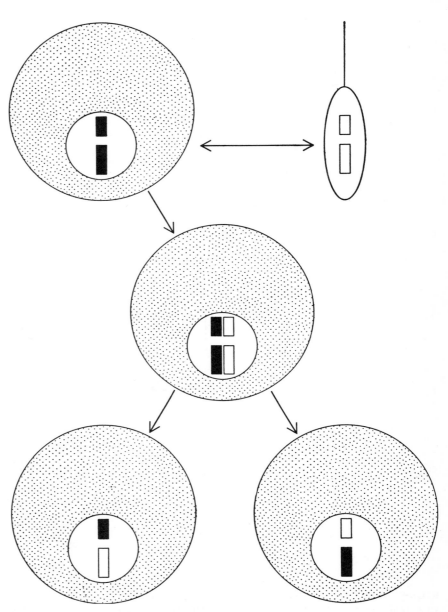

SEXUAL REPRODUCTION, also depicted in highly schematic form, depends on the union of two cells that may be from different lines of descent. At top left is an egg cell; at top right, a sperm cell. Each contains one set of chromosomes (*rectangles*). They join to form a new individual with two sets of chromosomes in its body cells (*center*). When this organism produces its own sperm or egg cells (*bottom*), each receives a full set of chromosomes. Some, however, may be from the father and some from the mother. Evolution in sexual organisms thus does not depend entirely on new mutations, because the genes already present in the population may be combined in different ways leading to improvements in the species.

the environment.

There are known to be genes that affect the mutation rate. Some of them are quite specific and affect only the mutation rate of a particular gene; others seem to enhance or depress the over-all rate. A gene whose effect is to lower the mutation rate certainly has selective advantage: it will cause an increase in fit-ness. This means that in most populations there should be a steady decrease in the mutation rate, possibly so far as to reduce the evolutionary adaptability of the organism. This is offset by selection for ability to cope with fluctuating environments.

How does man fare in this respect? From the standpoint of his biological evolution, is his mutation rate too high, is it too low or is it just right? It is not possible to say.

In general one would expect the evolutionary processes to work so that the mutation rate would usually be below the optimum from the standpoint of long-term evolutionary progress, because selection to reduce the mutation load has an immediate beneficial effect. Yet selection for a mutation-rate-adjusting gene is secondary to selection for whatever direct effects this gene has on the organism, such as an effect on size or metabolic rate. So we do not have much idea about how rapidly such selection would work.

Our early simian ancestors matured much more rapidly than we do now. This means that the mutation rate would have to be lowered in order to be brought into adjustment with the lengthening of our life cycle. To whatever extent the adjustment is behind the times, the mutation rate is too high. Furthermore, if it is true (as it appears to be) that radiation-induced mutation rates are less susceptible to evolutionary adjustment than those due to other causes, then an animal with a life cycle so long that it receives considerable radiation per generation may have too many from this cause.

I think it is impossible, however, to say whether man has a mutation rate that is too high or too low from the viewpoint of evolutionary advantage. It is worth noting that man, like any sexually reproducing organism, already has a tremendous store of genetic variability available for recombination. If all mutation were to stop, the possibilities for evolution would not be appreciably altered for a tremendous length of time —perhaps thousands of generations. Consider the immense range of human variability now found, for example the difference between Mozart, Newton, da Vinci and some of our best athletes, in contrast to a moron or the genetically impaired. Haldane once said: "A selector of sufficient knowledge and power might perhaps obtain from the genes at present available in the human species a race combining an average intellect equal to that of Shakespeare with the stature of Carnera." He goes on to say: "He could not produce a race of angels. For the moral character or for the wings he would have to await or produce suitable mutations." Surely the most hopefully naive eugenist would settle for considerably less!

I would argue that from any practical standpoint the question of whether

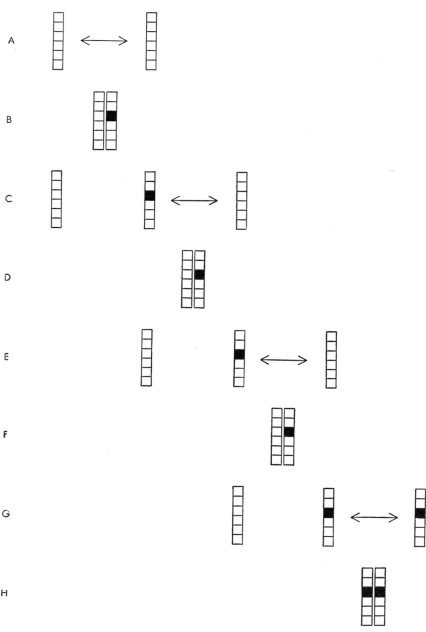

RECESSIVE MUTATION cannot be expressed in a sexual organism unless the corresponding gene of the paired chromosome has the same defect. Thus a harmful mutation can remain latent for generations. In this diagram the bars representing chromosomes are divided into squares, each symbolizing the gene for a different character. In row A the chromosomes of normal parents are paired (*arrows*). In row B a gene of their offspring mutates (*black*). In row C the mutant gene has been transmitted to the next generation but is still latent because the other parent has supplied a normal gene. This continues (*rows E and F*) until two individuals harboring the mutant gene mate (*row G*). The full effect of the mutation, harmful or otherwise, is expressed in offspring receiving a pair of mutant genes (*row H*).

man's mutation-rate is too high or too low for long-term evolution is irrelevant. From any other standpoint the present mutation rate is certainly too high. I suspect that man's expectations for future progress depend much more on what he does to his environment than on how he changes his genes. His practice has been to change the environment to suit his genes rather than vice versa. If he should someday decide on a program of conscious selection for genetic improvement, the store of genes already in the population will probably be adequate. If by some remote chance it is not, there will be plenty of ways to increase the number of mutations at that time.

There can be little doubt that man would be better off if he had a lower mutation-rate. I would argue, in our present ignorance, that the ideal rate for the foreseeable future would be zero. The effects produced by mutations are of all sorts, and are mostly harmful. Some cause embryonic death, some severe disease, some physical abnormalities, and probably many more cause minor impairments of body function that bring an increased susceptibility to the various vicissitudes of life. Some have an immediate effect; others lie hidden to cause their harm many generations later. All in all, mutations must be responsible for a substantial fraction of human premature death, illness and misery in general.

At the present time there is not much that can be done to lower the spontaneous-mutation rate. But at least we can do everything possible to keep the rate from getting any higher as the result of human activities. This is especially true for radiation-induced mutations; if anything they are probably more deleterious and less likely to be potentially useful than those from other causes. It is also important to remember that there are very possibly things in the environment other than radiation that increase the mutation rate. Among all the new compounds to which man is exposed as a result of our complex chemical technology there may well be a number of mutagenic substances. It is important that these be discovered and treated with caution.

The general conclusion, then, is that ionizing radiation is probably not an important factor in animal and plant evolution. If it is important anywhere it is probably in those species, such as man, that have a long life span, and at least for man it is a harmful rather than a potentially beneficial factor.

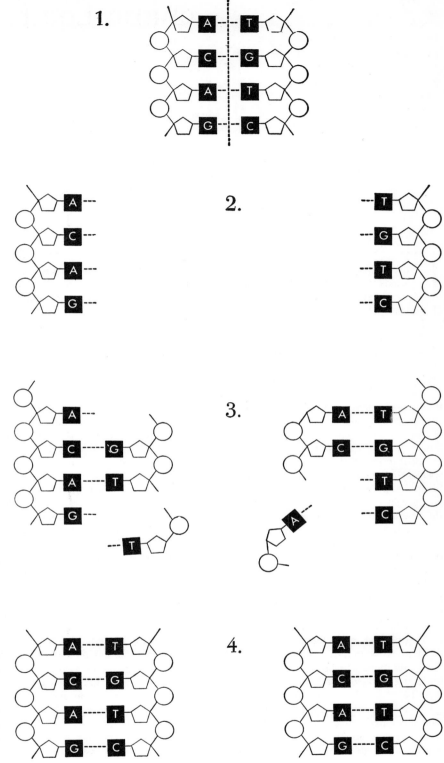

THE GENETIC MATERIAL, deoxyribonucleic acid (DNA), consists of a chain of sugar units (*pentagons*) and phosphate groups (*circles*) with side chains of bases: adenine (A), cytosine (C), thymine (T) and guanine (G). One possible mechanism for replication postulates that DNA normally contains two complementary strands, linked A—T and C—G (1). The chains then separate (2), and separate precursor units assemble along each chain (3). When they are completed, the double strands are identical to the original (4).

17 Genetic Load

by Christopher Wills
March 1970

The term refers to the accumulated mutations in the gene pool of an entire species. Part of the load reduces the viability of the species; the rest may be a priceless genetic resource

Every human being has tens of thousands (possibly hundreds of thousands) of genes, each a small part of the long chains of deoxyribonucleic acid in his cells. When this DNA is duplicated and passed on to the next generation through the reproductive cells, there is a certain probability that one or more genes have mutated. That is, they have changed in such a way that the enzyme or other protein they specify is also changed. Over a period of time, as each generation gives rise to the next, such mutations accumulate in the pool of genes of all members of the species living at a particular moment. Since the process of evolution consists of changes in the quality and quantity of the genetic variability stored in the gene pool, it is a matter of some importance to consider the role of mutations, which provide this variability.

Some mutations are "beneficial," that is, the individual in whom they are expressed is better able to adapt to a given set of environmental circumstances. The large majority of mutations, however, are harmful or even lethal to the individual in whom they are expressed. Such mutations can be regarded as introducing a "load," or genetic burden, into the pool. The term "genetic load" was first used by the late H. J. Muller, who recognized that the rate of mutations is increased by numerous agents man has introduced into his environment, notably ionizing radiation and mutagenic chemicals. We now know that this mutational load is not the only kind of genetic load. We must ask the question: What is the overall load on the gene pool, and how does it affect living populations? The answer is currently being sought in genetic studies of many different organisms from man to yeasts.

One might suppose that harmful or lethal genes could not survive for very long in the gene pool because the individuals who carry them are less likely to reproduce than other individuals. The fact is, however, that such genes can survive in spite of the strong negative pressures of natural selection. The reason is that the genetic material of man, like that of all other sexually reproducing organisms, is diploid: human body cells (as distinct from human reproductive cells) have a double set of genes. As is well known, each individual receives a complete set of chromosomes from each parent. Hence every individual has two genes for every genetic function, one from his mother and one from his father. (The sex chromosomes, two of the 46 chromosomes in man, are a complication that need not concern us here.)

For each maternal chromosome, then, there is a corresponding chromosome in the paternal set. If each of these chromosomes has the same gene at exactly the same locus, the individual is said to be homozygous for that gene. If the gene happens to be a lethal mutant, the individual will of course die, by definition without being able to reproduce. If the gene is "subvital" (harmful without being lethal), the homozygous individual will often survive to transmit it to the next generation.

An individual who has two different genes at the same locus is said to be heterozygous. He might be heterozygous for (1) a mutant gene and a "normal" one, (2) two different "normal" genes or (3) two different mutant genes. The effect of the mutant genes in the heterozygote can vary from complete recessiveness (their effect is completely masked by a normal gene) to complete dominance (the normal gene is masked). Partial dominance is not uncommon; what it means is that the effect of the mutant

gene is not completely masked but leaks through to a greater or lesser degree. Because of the masking effect a heterozygote can carry either lethal or subvital genes and transmit them to the next generation. All that is required is that the individual have a normally functioning gene that compensates for the mutant one.

Considering the complexity of the genetic material, mutations are remarkably rare. Nonetheless, they do arise con-

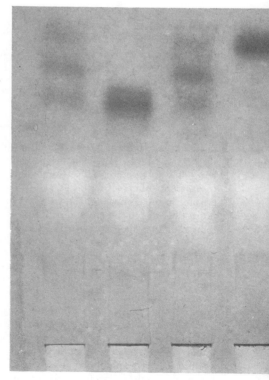

HIDDEN DIFFERENCES in the genetic material of fruit flies are revealed by this electrophoretic pattern on a slab of polyacrylamide gel. Such genetic variation, originally caused by mutation, can form a part of the genetic load. Each slot at the bottom of the slab was filled with juice from an instantly; indeed, they are occurring in the reader as he reads this article. Fortunately most of them take place in cells that are not involved in reproduction, and hence they are not conveyed to the next generation. Any influence that increases the rate of mutation of those genes that are passed on to the next generation will also increase the chance of homozygosity for recessive genes. If the mutation rate remains constant for some time, there will be an equilibrium in the population between the rate at which new recessive lethals appear at a particular locus, and the rate at which they are removed by premature death as two of them turn up by chance in the same individual. If a harmful gene is dominant or partially dominant, its effects will appear right away in the heterozygote, and it will not be as common in a population at equilibrium as a completely recessive lethal with the same mutation rate would be.

From studies of marriages between close relatives Muller, Newton E. Morton and James F. Crow estimated that between 6 and 15 percent of human egg and sperm cells carry new recessive lethal mutations or mutations that are so harmful that they are "lethal equiva-

lents." These workers calculated that the average individual is heterozygous for three to five lethals or lethal equivalents. Will such a gene leak through a masking gene? In order to find out Terumi Mukai and his co-workers at the National Institute of Genetics in Japan and later at North Carolina State University conducted a Herculean set of experiments with the fruit fly Drosophila. Mukai patterned his experiments on a technique developed by Muller that has become standard in modern genetics.

The consequences of a given level of genetic load can be examined experimentally by causing mutations in the gene pool of the experimental population through exposure to X rays or a chemical mutagen. There is, however, a difficulty in this simple strategy. The effects of such agents may not be easy to detect because the mutations they cause are mostly recessive. In fact, Muller worked for a decade before he was able to show in 1927 that X rays actually do produce mutations in Drosophila. Muller and later workers solved the problem by taking advantage of certain genetic peculiarities of Drosophila that allowed an entire chromosome to be passed from one generation to the next as a unit. This

made it possible to produce flies that were, for example, completely homozygous for one or more chromosomes, so that new mutations would be revealed. Once the effects of a chromosome have been demonstrated in this way, new crosses can be made to pair it with other chromosomes of known effects in order to form heterozygous combinations. The results of these crosses reveal what consequences the genes have when they are heterozygous [see illustration on pages 202 and 203].

Mukai and his colleagues examined millions of flies that had been made either homozygous or heterozygous for chromosomes that had a known effect on the flies' survival. They discovered (among other interesting facts) that recessive lethals were hardly expressed at all in the heterozygote but that subvital genes leaked through the masking gene to a startling extent: about 40 percent of the homozygous effect.

Why should a subvital gene be expressed while a lethal one is almost completely concealed? There may be a good biochemical reason. If the product of a recessive lethal gene is so changed that it no longer functions, then in the hetero-

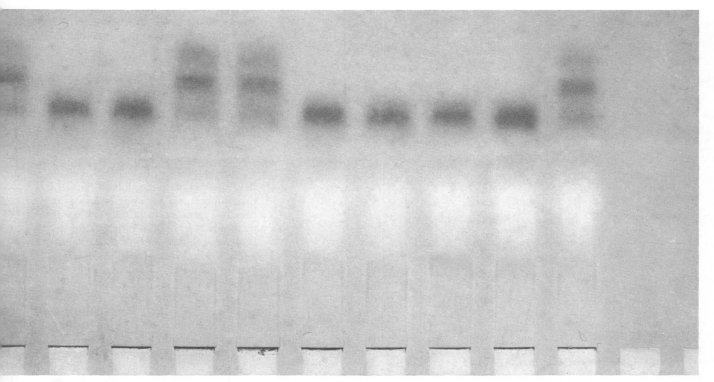

dividual fly containing the enzyme octanol dehydrogenase (among many others). When an electric current was passed through the gel, each enzyme was carried toward the top at a characteristic speed determined by minute charge differences among enzyme molecules. After current was stopped, staining of the product of the octanol dehydrogenase revealed three types (visible as purple bands). Fly second from left has two genes, each of which produces a slow-moving form of the enzyme. Fly fourth from left carries two genes for a fast-moving form of the enzyme. Some flies, such as the one at left and the one third from left, have genes for "fast" and "slow" enzymes and therefore also produce an intermediate form (middle band) made up of fast and slow subunits. Subunits produced by genes are polypeptide chains that are not yet functional. Such subunits must combine to form a normal enzyme or other protein.

zygote the normal gene for that function could take over completely without too much harm to the organism. The product of a subvital gene may be partially functional (as is suggested by the fact that some of the homozygotes survive), and it may interfere in some way with the "good" product from the other gene in the heterozygote so that its effect is felt. For example, many genes give rise to protein subunits rather than complete gene products, and these subunits are put together in the cell. Subunits from normal and subvital genes could combine to yield an abnormal product [see bottom illustration on opposite page].

In order to test this assumption my colleagues and I at Wesleyan University turned to the common one-celled brewer's yeast Saccharomyces, which has the advantage over Drosophila that millions of cells can quickly be screened for mutants. Yeast also has the interesting property that during its life cycle it exists in both a diploid phase and a haploid phase. In the haploid phase the yeast cells have only one set of chromosomes instead of two. Both of these phases can be maintained and studied at leisure. The effect of mutations can be observed in the haploid phase, when they are fully expressed, and then in the heterozygous diploid phase, when they are masked. The system thus resembles the Drosophila one, but the experiments are much easier to do. It is impractical to follow individual yeast cells to see if they die or exhibit defects, and so we used as a measure of genetic effect the rate of increase in the size of a small yeast colony viewed under the microscope.

The yeast cells were exposed to two types of chemical mutagen. One kind of agent apparently inserts or deletes bits of genetic code, so that the sense of that particular gene is usually destroyed. Agents of this type produced large numbers of recessive genes that were completely masked in the heterozygote, and these colonies grew at normal rates. The other kind of agent produces small mistakes in the genes that do not destroy sense completely; these genes did show through in the heterozygote by diminishing the growth of the experimental colonies. In outline, then, the theory seems to be correct, but we are now working on individual genes in an effort to determine the actual mechanisms involved in this partial dominance.

A start has thus been made on classifying the genes that constitute the mutational load. There is, however, a different kind of burden that is also a part of the genetic load. This burden primarily consists not of harmful mutations that are masked in the heterozygote but strangely enough of apparently normal homozygotes. In order for the load to appear the gene pool must contain two or more functioning genes at a locus, and circumstances must be such that organisms heterozygous for these genes have an apparent selective advantage, that is, they can leave more offspring than the homozygotes can. There is thus a load associated with being homozygous, even for normal genes. Such circumstances might include environmental conditions that favor a heterozygote over a homozygote or conditions that select against the homozygote but do not affect the heterozygote. This kind of load is called a balanced load because, as we shall see, a balance in the population is struck between the heterozygotes and the homozygotes.

The term "balanced load" encompasses many phenomena, but the most important is hybrid vigor, a remarkable effect observable in many organisms that was first put to work by geneticists when they crossed different inbred lines of corn to produce vigorous strains with greatly increased yield. A number of mechanisms have been proposed for hybrid vigor, but regardless of the mechanism the end result is the same: an organism heterozygous at a large number of loci is "fitter" in some sense than one that is heterozygous at fewer loci. There must accordingly be a load attached to being homozygous, because the homozygous organism often leaves fewer and less vigorous offspring than the heterozygous one.

The balanced load is different from the mutational load in another respect. The frequency of a recessive gene in the mutational load depends directly on the mutation rate. An altered gene that gives an advantage to the heterozygote, however, might appear only once and then

MASKING of a harmful or a lethal gene by a normal gene is demonstrated in a hypothetical population. Nine out of every 10 of the sperm and the eggs that produced this population carried gene A; the rest carried gene a. When sperm fertilized the eggs at random, 100 individuals were produced. Eighty-one are homozygous, that is, they carry two identical genes, A and A, for the same function. Eighteen individuals are heterozygous (shading); they carry two different genes for the same function, A and a. The a gene is lethal, but because each heterozygote carries a normal A gene that masks the a gene, none displays a defect. One individual, however, carries two lethal genes (solid color). It dies because it has no normal gene to compensate for the lethal one. Two individuals within diagram are mutants (color); they carry an A gene that was changed into an a gene. An average of two mutations must arise in each generation in order to maintain the ratio of A to a as aa homozygotes die.

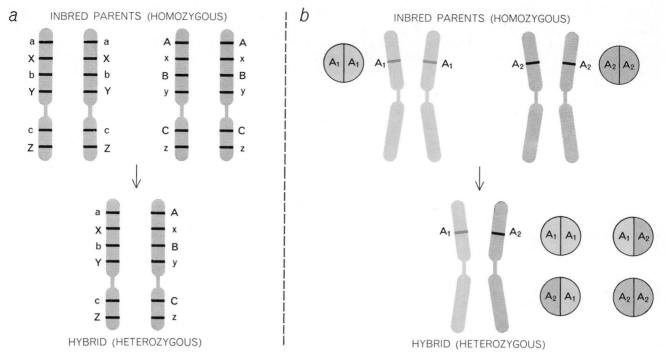

a INBRED PARENTS (HOMOZYGOUS)

b INBRED PARENTS (HOMOZYGOUS)

HYBRID (HETEROZYGOUS)

HYBRID VIGOR may be explained as a masking of harmful genes by normal genes in the heterozygote. In *a* one homozygous parent plant is crossed with another. Both parents carry homozygous harmful genes and homozygous normal genes. The offspring produced is heterozygous (*bottom*). In this hybrid the genes on each parental chromosome are paired so that the harmful genes (*small letters*) are masked by normal genes (*capital letters*). Another ex-

planation of hybrid vigor that does not exclude the first is shown in *b*. Here the *A* genes of homozygous parents at top are each capable of producing only one kind of subunit of the functioning gene product, A_1 or A_2, and one product, A_1A_1 or A_2A_2. The hybrid offspring, however, can produce both kinds of subunit (a nonfunctioning polypeptide chain) and three kinds of gene product (an enzyme or functioning protein) because it has both kinds of *A* gene.

automatically build up to a high level in the population as the number of heterozygotes increases. It is important to realize that no matter how strong the heterozygote appears to be, the homozygotes never disappear; they continue to occur in each generation by the normal mechanisms of the production and the subse-

quent fusion of haploid reproductive cells. In other words, when two heterozygotes mate and reproduce, a certain number of their offspring will inevitably be homozygotes. Eventually, therefore, a balance is struck between the heterozygotes and the homozygotes at that locus [*see illustration on page 204*].

The dependence of the balanced load on environmental conditions has been conclusively demonstrated by Theodosius Dobzhansky and his colleagues at Columbia University and at Rockefeller University. The demonstration has been achieved by experiments with inversions in the chromosomes of *Drosophila*. Such

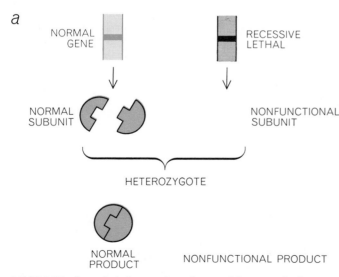

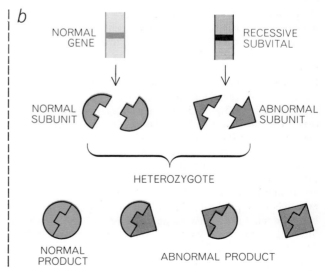

LEAKAGE of a subvital gene through a masking gene is shown schematically. In heterozygote at left (*a*) normal gene (*color*) is paired with a recessive lethal that produces nonfunctional subunits. Because the normal gene produces a normal subunit and normal product, however, the individual carrying the genes appears

normal. In heterozygote at right (*b*) the same normal gene is paired with a subvital gene. The subunit of the subvital is partly functional and therefore can combine randomly with a normal subunit to form an abnormal but functioning product. Only a quarter of the product of this heterozygote is normal and a defect is obvious.

inversions are reversed segments of chromosomes, and they are themselves under genetic control; they have been found in wild populations of many *Drosophila* species. The normal mechanism of crossing-over, which exchanges individual genes between maternal and paternal chromosomes in each generation, is disrupted in flies that are heterozygous for these inversions. Specifically the genes within the inversion are "locked in" and pass from one generation to the next in a group that Kenneth Mather has called a supergene, with inheritance just like that for a single gene. These supergenes are visible in the giant chromosomes of *Drosophila* larvae. In a heterozygous larva one can see corresponding maternal and paternal chromosomes paired so that the normal and the inverted segments form a loop [*see illustration on page 205*]. Because inversions are so easily recognizable their frequencies can be followed in either laboratory populations or wild ones.

One of Dobzhansky's experimental populations consisted of flies carrying a normal chromosome and an inverted chromosome from a particular wild population, maintained in the laboratory at 25 degrees Celsius. The population included three kinds of flies: flies homozygous for the normal chromosome, flies homozygous for the inverted chromosome and heterozygous flies, that is, flies that carried both the inverted chromosome and the normal one. If the conditions of the experiment are such as to give a selective advantage to the heterozygotes, one would predict that, whatever the initial ratios in the population, the proportions of the three types of flies would reach some specific equilibrium value.

Such was the case. Regardless of the number of each type of fly present in the original population, the population reached an equilibrium after a certain number of generations. In this equilibrium state 49 percent of the flies were homozygous for the normal chromosome, 9 percent were homozygous for the inverted chromosome and the remainder (42 percent) were heterozygous. The unequal numbers of the two types of homozygote in the equilibrium population can be explained if the normal homozygote is fitter than the homozygote for the inverted chromosome. Subsequent experiments showed that this was true, and also showed that the heterozygotes clearly had an advantage over the two kinds of homozygote in many factors that together make up genetic fitness: ability to survive to adulthood, number of eggs

laid and so on. This explained the stability of the frequencies, which were governed not by mutation rate but by the relative genetic fitness of the two kinds of homozygote and the heterozygotes. The two kinds of homozygote carried a balanced load, since they were at a disadvantage compared with the heterozygotes.

When the temperature was lowered to 16.5 degrees C., however, the advantage of the heterozygotes—and the balanced load—disappeared. The frequencies of normal and inverted chromosomes now stayed at about the frequencies in the starting populations. In other words, the homozygote disadvantage was conditional on temperature. One explanation (there are others) might be that certain mutant genes on both the normal and the inverted chromosomes worked well at 16.5 degrees but poorly at 25 degrees. These genes were matched with normal ones in the heterozygote, which would therefore be fitter than the homozygotes at 25 degrees. At the lower temperature, however, the balanced load had disappeared, and all three kinds of flies were equally fit.

Flies homozygous for either of these chromosomes do perfectly well by themselves in the laboratory, producing large, healthy populations that look perfectly normal. Dobzhansky's experiments, and those of many other workers, have repeatedly demonstrated the now-you-see-it, now-you-don't quality of the balanced load, with its extreme dependence on the environment. The heterozygote is often fitter, but not under all conditions.

Could the heterozygous advantage that Dobzhansky observed arise at any locus, or were the supergenes unique in some way? Much indirect evidence had accumulated that they were not, but an elegant experiment performed by Edwin Vann at Cornell University provided a direct answer. If such heterozygosity were common, Vann reasoned, it might be observed at many loci on the chromosomes. The problem was finding a way of detecting the heterozygous loci. Vann solved this problem by creating inversions of varying lengths in the chromosomes of a population of highly homozygous *Drosophila*. Next he mated carriers of the newly created supergenes with members of the same population without the inversion, or with members of other populations. The gene pools of these populations were also homozygous; some were related to the original population and some were not. The offspring of these last matings, because of the diverse genetic background of the parents,

could be expected to be heterozygous at a great many of the loci covered by an inversion. Equally important, the fate of this group of loci could be followed by using the inversion as a marker.

If heterozygous advantage had actually been produced by such matings, the inversions would probably remain in the population and increase in frequency, since heterozygotes for the inversion would also always be heterozygous for the genes within the inversion. After several generations had passed Vann observed that in fact the longer inversions (containing more genes and therefore preserving more heterozygosity) were much less likely to be lost than the shorter ones. He also found that the longer inversions often tended to achieve high frequencies. Finally, because Vann's supergenes covered varying lengths of all the chromosomes, it could be concluded that heterozygote advantage existed up and down the chromosomes and needed only to be revealed by a suitable genetic marker.

One proposition remained to be disproved. It seemed possible that an inversion at any point on a chromosome might have some selective advantage per se that had nothing to do with heterozygosity at all. The reader will recall that Vann also introduced his inversions back into the populations from which the inversions had been derived in the first place. In these crosses the genes on the inverted and the uninverted chromosomes were the same, and little if any heterozygosity was present in these flies. After several generations had passed Vann found that the inversions had completely disappeared. It seemed, then, that the mere production of an inversion, rather than providing an advantage, actually constituted a genetic liability that caused the individuals carrying them to

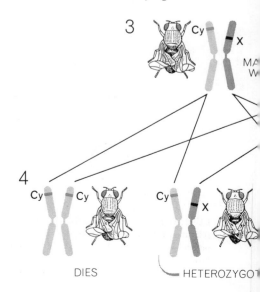

3

4

DIES   HETEROZYGO

be eliminated from the population after a few generations.

Wann had proved that heterozygous advantage could exist at many places on a chromosome, but there was no way of directly determining what functions, if any, these genes performed. Clearly they could not be lethals or subvitals. A fly heterozygous for more than a few severe subvitals would be very sick indeed, and if it were heterozygous for too many lethals, there would be a good chance it would be homozygous for at least one. In order to prove that these genes were normal it was necessary to develop a method for identifying the function of an individual gene.

Until recently population geneticists investigating such problems were in the position of early oceanographers, who tried to reconstruct the bottom of the ocean from a few soundings and samples of sand and mud taken at random over thousands of square miles. If one made a *Drosophila* chromosome homozygous and discovered a lethal gene on it, for example, one had to ignore the thousands of other genes on the same chromosome. There were no markers with which to detect these genes, which were lumped together under the term "wild type." Most mutant genes are nonfunctional or do something very different from wild-type genes, so that they can be

easily distinguished. How can one distinguish one wild-type gene from another when all appear to be perfectly functional? In actuality different wild-type genes with similar functions at the same locus could be detected in a few instances. In man there are three genes at the same locus controlling the ABO blood-type system, and a person may be homozygous or heterozygous for any combination of these genes. He is not distinguishable from his fellows, however, except by immunological tests of himself and in some cases of his parents or children.

Some population geneticists felt that this was only the tip of the iceberg. A few years ago Bruce Wallace at Cornell suggested that a fruit fly from a wild population might be heterozygous at 50 percent of its paired genes, a suggestion that was met with consternation and disbelief. Wallace may have overestimated

the proportion, but it turns out that he was not too far off. The technique of electrophoresis, long used by chemists and adapted to biological systems by Oliver Smithies of the University of Wisconsin, has provided population geneticists with a method for examining the gene pool that is as useful as sonar has been to the mapping of the ocean bottom. Harry Harris of the University of London and Richard C. Lewontin and John L. Hubby of the University of Chicago have used it to examine the wild-type genes of man and *Drosophila*.

The technique is a simple one. A tiny sample of serum from a man or the juice from the body of a single fly is inserted into a strip of a supporting medium such as a slab of starch soaked with an electrolyte, or conducting liquid. When a direct current is passed through the medium, molecules that are very much alike but that differ slightly in size or electric

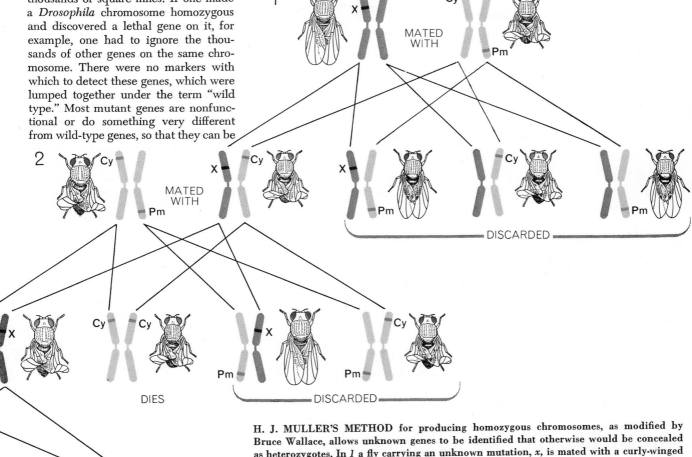

H. J. MULLER'S METHOD for producing homozygous chromosomes, as modified by Bruce Wallace, allows unknown genes to be identified that otherwise would be concealed as heterozygotes. In *1* a fly carrying an unknown mutation, *x*, is mated with a curly-winged (*Cy*), plum-eyed (*Pm*) fly whose chromosomes (*color*) carry dominant genes specifying these marks, which allow gene types to be followed through many generations. *Cy* and *Pm* chromosomes are modified so that they are inherited as single units. In a homozygote these genes are lethal. In *2* one *Cy* fly is mated with a *Cy-Pm* fly. If it is a *Cy-x* fly (*fourth from right*), all *Cy* flies in the next generation carry the *x* gene on their chromosomes. An *x* chromosome cannot recombine with a *Cy* chromosome, so that it must also be inherited as a single unit. In *3 Cy-x* flies are mated with one another. In *4* a quarter are *Cy-Cy* homozygotes, half are heterozygotes and a quarter are *xx* homozygotes. If the *x* gene is lethal, all *xx* flies die. If it is subvital (harmful but not lethal), some may die or be unable to reproduce.

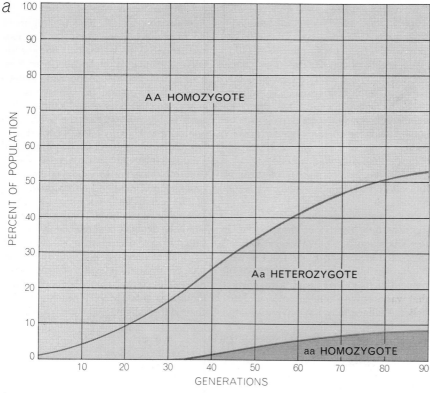

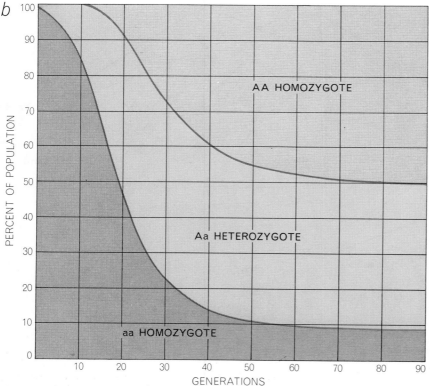

BALANCED LOAD appears in a population when heterozygotes seem to have a selective advantage over homozygotes, so that a load is borne by the normal genes. In this idealized case (*a*) *Aa* heterozygotes have a fitness of 100 percent, *AA* homozygotes are 92 percent as fit as the heterozygotes, and *aa* homozygotes are 80 percent as fit. In first generation 98 percent of the population consist of *AA* homozygotes and about 2 percent are *Aa* heterozygotes. By the 90th generation 42 percent are the favored *Aa* heterozygotes, whereas 9 percent are *aa* homozygotes that have merged through recombination. In the reverse situation (*b*), where *aa* homozygotes form 98 percent of the first generation and 2 percent are *Aa* heterozygotes, the latter still increase to 42 percent. The percentage of *Aa* heterozygotes cannot increase further in this case because the three kinds of gene type balance one another.

charge migrate at different rates in the electric field. When the current is turned off, the protein products of different genes will have migrated to different places in the gel, where each forms a band. The products of two wild-type genes differing by as little as one amino acid can be separated in this way. They can then be made visible in the starch by staining them [*see illustration on pages 198 and 199*].

Not all gene products can be examined by electrophoresis, but from those that can it is possible to make an estimate of the hidden differences between paired wild-type genes. Lewontin and Hubby calculated that their flies were heterozygous at 10 to 14 percent of their gene pairs. They emphasized that, since not all the differences can be detected by electrophoresis, this was a minimum estimate. Harris' results for man, although they were obtained from smaller numbers of genes, agreed. Other workers have found similar differences between the paired genes of organisms as diverse as butterflies and mice.

These slightly different forms of the same gene that perform the same function are called isoalleles. They are, of course, produced by mutation from other forms of the same gene, but mutations to functionally useful isoalleles must occur very rarely. One can take two extreme positions with regard to isoallelic differences. The first is that they are entirely accidental, and that the homozygosity or heterozygosity of the isoalleles makes no difference whatsoever to the fitness of the organism. The second is that the differences (or most of them) are held in the population by heterozygous advantage, and that the homozygotes for the isoalleles contribute to the balanced load. Ingenious mathematical arguments have been advanced in favor of the first view, but strong experimental evidence has now appeared against it.

Satya Prakash, working with Lewontin and Hubby, used electrophoresis to examine populations of *Drosophila* separated from one another by hundreds or thousands of miles. Many of the isoalleles the investigators detected had the same frequencies in these far-flung populations, and those that did not varied in a regular way depending on the geographic location of the sample. Other evidence of strong selection of isoalleles in wild populations of mice has been provided by Robert K. Selander and his co-workers at the University of Texas. Selection must be holding most of these genes in the population, because if they were selectively neutral, their frequency from place to place would vary greatly. It is almost certainly these functional isoalleles, rather than the harmful genes of the mutational load, that provide the variability on which natural selection acts. Isoalleles in the gene pool make a species far more responsive to natural selection than it would be if there were simply one kind of gene at each locus and every organism in the species were homozygous for that gene.

If we can extrapolate from the few genes sampled to the entire gene pool, there would appear to be thousands of isoalleles held in the population by some form of heterozygous advantage, and homozygotes for these isoalleles must be contributing to the balanced load. Therefore either there is a very large load or the selection against any particular gene must be very slight. The former possibility can be ruled out; the balanced load is simply not very large. If it were, most of the offspring of an organism would die from its effects. If we accept the latter possibility, however, we are faced with a difficulty. In any sexually reproducing population (small ones in particular) there is a random effect, known as genetic drift, that causes isoalleles at a locus to be lost simply by chance. Selection pressures have to be large enough to overcome such random forces if these genes are to be retained. The difficulty can be overcome if one assumes that genes, even on chromosomes free of inversions, have a tendency to hold together in groups. Within these groups selection pressures that are individually very small might be large enough in the aggregate to overcome the random drift forces.

Recently John W. Crenshaw of the University of Rhode Island, Joseph N. Vitale of the Yale Computer Center and I collaborated in an attempt to test this assumption by following a population of sexually reproducing organisms simulated by means of a computer program. We gave this "population" a balanced load but left out the mutational one, since it is relatively well understood. In addition we tried to make the balanced load as realistic as possible. It may be recalled that the flies homozygous for chromosomal inversions in Dobzhansky's experiment could fend perfectly well for themselves. In competition and under certain environmental conditions, however, the heterozygotes had a slight advantage. Similarly, the isoalleles discovered by electrophoresis are apparently perfectly functional and do no detectable harm to an organism homozygous for them, but such an or-

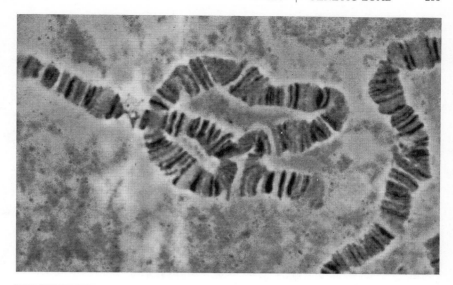

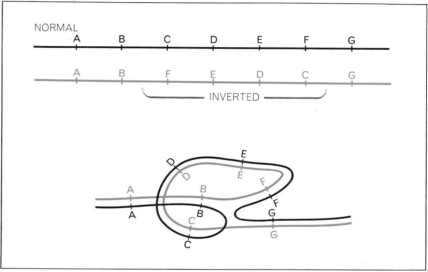

INVERSION in salivary-gland chromosome of a fruit fly (*top*) was produced with X rays by Edwin Vann. The inversion, similar to those found in wild populations, upsets the order of genes (*bottom*). One chromosome must therefore form loop so that genes at the same locus can be paired. A locus is a place on a chromosome for a gene with a specific function.

ganism might not do quite so well in competition as a heterozygote would. This conditional kind of selection has been considered theoretically by a number of workers, notably Wallace, who has called selection against the mutational type of load "hard" selection (since it occurs under almost all conditions) and selection against the balanced type of load "soft" selection.

Our computer organisms consisted of strings of digits. Each organism was a pair of such strings, one representing a maternal chromosome and one a paternal. These "chromosomes" could be manipulated to mimic sexual reproduction and recombination. Genes along the string were represented by a 1 or a 0, so that if an organism had a 1 or a 0 at a particular locus on both of its chromo-

somes, it was homozygous at that locus. If it had a 1 on one chromosome and a 0 on the other, it was heterozygous. At the beginning of each computer run the population contained a mixture of 1's and 0's, so that each organism was heterozygous at many loci. During many generations of simulated sexual reproduction we monitored the population to see how much of this variability would be retained.

Some of our populations were subjected to soft selection, by surveying them each generation and removing a few of the organisms homozygous at the largest number of loci, regardless of which loci. The places of these organisms in the population were then filled with duplicates of those organisms that were heterozygous at the largest number of loci. We found that by doing this we could maintain a surprising amount of variability in the population, even by removing as few as 5 percent of the organisms each generation. As time went on the genes actually did become organized into blocks along the chromosomes, and the patterns that appeared helped to preserve the variability [see upper illustration below]. It will be most interesting to see if such patterns are eventually detected in nature as well as in the computer.

We are learning more about the gene pool and genetic load, but many questions remain unanswered. We know very little about the biochemical reasons for heterozygote advantage, or about the relative proportions of balanced and mutational load produced by the common mutagenic agents. In our laboratory we are able to classify the genetic variability of yeast as "rigid" (expressed in a similar way in many different environments) or "flexible" (expressed in different ways in different environments). Most of the variability we have produced with our mutagenic agents is rigid, and we suspect that this is mutational load. The flexible variability is therefore presumably the same as the balanced load, but this relation has not been proved.

We must seek a better understanding of the size and nature of the human mutational load. Certain genetic diseases are clear-cut members of the mutational load, and until such time as genetic repair work can be done on the chromosomes themselves carriers of these diseases should be informed about the probability of their having defective

LOCUS

```
            1              10            20             30             40
A    1   0 0 1 0 1 1 1 1 1 0 1 1 1 1 1 1 0 1 1 1 1 0 1 0 0 0 1 0 0 0 1 1 0 0 0 1 0 0 0 1 1 1
     2   0 0 1 1 0 1 0 0 1 0 0 0 1 1 1 1 0 1 1 0 1 0 0 0 0 1 0 0 0 1 0 1 0 1 0 1 0 0 0 1 0 1
     3   0 0 0 1 1 1 1 1 1 0 1 1 1 1 0 1 1 1 1 1 0 0 0 1 0 0 0 0 0 1 0 0 0 1 1 1 0 0 1 0 0
     4   0 0 1 0 1 1 1 1 1 0 1 0 0 1 0 1 1 1 1 1 0 1 0 0 0 0 1 0 1 0 1 0 0 1 1 0 0 0 1 0 0
     5   1 0 0 0 1 1 1 0 0 1 0 1 1 0 0 0 0 0 1 0 0 0 0 0 1 0 0 0 0 0 1 1 1 1 0 1 1 0 0
     6   0 1 1 1 0 0 1 1 0 1 1 1 1 1 0 1 0 1 1 0 1 1 1 1 1 0 0 0 0 0 0 0 1 0 0 1 0 0 1 1
     7   1 0 0 1 1 0 1 0 1 0 1 0 1 0 1 0 1 1 0 0 1 0 0 1 0 0 1 0 1 0 1 0 0 0 0 0 0 0 1
     8   0 0 0 1 0 0 1 0 1 1 1 1 1 1 0 1 0 1 0 0 1 0 0 0 0 0 1 1 0 1 0 1 0 1 0 1 1 0
     9   0 0 0 0 0 0 0 1 0 1 0 0 1 1 1 1 1 1 1 0 0 0 0 0 0 0 0 0 1 1 0 0 0 0 1 0 0 0 0 0
    10   0 0 1 1 1 1 1 0 0 1 0 1 1 0 1 1 0 0 1 0 1 0 1 0 1 0 0 0 0 1 0 0 1 1 1 0 0 1 0 0
```

```
            1              10            20             30             40
B    1   0 0 0 1 1 0 0 0 1 1 0 0 1 1 0 1 0 0 1 0 0 0 0 0 0 0 0 0 0 1 0 0 1 0 0 0 0 1 0 1
     2   0 0 0 1 1 1 1 1 0 1 0 1 0 1 1 0 1 1 0 0 1 0 1 0 1 0 0 0 0 0 0 1 0 0 1 1 0 0 0 1 0 0
     3   0 0 0 1 1 0 0 0 1 1 0 0 1 0 1 1 0 0 1 0 1 0 1 0 1 0 0 0 0 0 0 1 0 0 1 1 0 0 0 1 0 1
     4   0 0 0 1 1 1 1 0 1 1 0 0 1 1 0 1 1 0 1 0 0 0 0 0 0 0 1 0 0 1 1 0 0 0 0 1 1 1
     5   0 0 0 1 1 1 1 1 0 1 0 0 1 1 0 1 1 0 1 0 0 0 0 0 0 0 0 1 1 0 1 0 0 0 0 1 0 1
     6   0 0 0 1 1 1 1 0 0 1 1 0 0 1 1 0 1 0 0 1 0 0 0 0 0 0 0 0 0 1 0 0 1 1 0 0 0 1 1 1
     7   0 0 0 1 1 0 0 0 1 1 0 0 1 1 0 1 0 1 0 0 0 0 0 0 0 0 1 0 0 1 1 1 0 0 0 1 0 0
     8   0 0 0 1 1 0 0 0 1 1 0 0 1 1 0 1 0 0 0 0 1 0 1 1 0 0 0 0 0 1 0 1 1 0 0 0 0 1 1 1
     9   0 0 0 1 1 1 1 1 0 1 0 1 1 0 1 1 0 1 1 0 0 0 0 1 0 1 1 0 0 0 0 1 0 1 1 0 0 0 0 1 0 1
    10   0 0 0 1 1 0 0 0 1 1 0 0 1 0 1 1 0 0 0 0 0 0 0 0 1 0 1 1 0 1 0 0 0 0 1 0 0
```

COMPUTERIZED GENE POOL consists of chromosomes made up of genes (represented by 1 or 0) that are simulated in a program and subjected to "natural selection." (Only short sections of a few chromosomes are shown.) The experiment, conducted by the author, John W. Crenshaw and Joseph N. Vitale, consisted of following chromosomes through many generations. Without selective pressure the pronounced variability (*colored digits*) in *A* would have been eradicated by random forces. Column of black digits represents a locus occupied by a "fixed" gene, one for which every "organism" (that is, pair of chromosomes) is homozygous. In *B*, generations later, selection has helped to retain variability (*color*), although homozygosity (*black digits*) has advanced markedly.

LOCUS

```
                1              10            20             30             40
B₁    1   0 0 0 1 1 0 0 0 1 1 0 0 1 1 0 1 0 0 1 0 0 0 0 0 0 0 0 0 1 0 0 1 0 0 0 0 1 0 1
      3   0 0 0 1 1 0 0 0 1 1 0 0 1 0 1 1 0 0 1 0 1 0 1 0 0 0 0 0 0 1 0 0 1 1 0 0 0 1 0 1
      6   0 0 0 1 1 0 0 0 1 1 0 0 1 0 1 1 0 0 1 0 1 0 0 0 0 0 0 0 0 1 0 0 1 1 0 0 0 1 1 1
      7   0 0 0 1 1 0 0 0 1 1 0 0 1 0 1 1 0 1 0 0 0 0 0 0 0 0 1 0 0 1 1 1 0 0 0 1 0 0
      8   0 0 0 1 1 0 0 0 1 1 0 0 1 0 1 1 0 1 0 0 0 0 1 0 1 1 0 0 0 0 1 0 1 1 0 0 0 1 1
     10   0 0 0 1 1 0 0 0 1 1 0 0 1 0 1 1 0 0 0 0 0 0 0 0 1 0 1 1 0 1 0 0 0 0 1 0 0
```

```
B₂    2   0 0 0 1 1 1 1 1 0 1 0 1 1 0 1 1 0 1 1 0 0 1 0 1 0 1 0 0 0 0 0 1 0 0 1 1 0 0 0 1 0 0
      5   0 0 0 1 1 1 1 1 0 1 0 0 1 1 0 1 1 0 1 1 0 1 0 0 0 0 0 0 1 1 0 1 0 0 0 0 1 0 1
      9   0 0 0 1 1 1 1 1 0 1 0 1 1 0 1 1 0 1 1 0 0 0 0 0 1 0 1 1 0 0 0 0 1 0 1 1 0 0 0 0 1 0 1
```

```
B₃    4   0 0 0 1 1 1 1 0 1 1 0 0 1 1 0 1 1 0 1 0 1 0 0 0 0 0 0 0 0 1 0 0 1 1 1 0 0 0 1 1 1
```

HOW HETEROZYGOSITY IS MAXIMIZED by selection is demonstrated with chromosomes of *B* in upper illustration. Chromosomes with genes 0001 at loci 6 through 9 are in B_1; those with genes 1110 at those loci are in B_2. Any organism in the next generation getting one chromosome from B_2 and the other from B_1 will therefore be heterozygous at these loci. Recombination breaks up these groups so that new ones form such as loci 6 through 9 in B_3, a pairing of loci 6 and 7 from B_2 and loci 8 and 9 from B_1. Such chromosomes are selected against because they cannot pair with other chromosomes to give maximum heterozygosity.

children. A small start has been made on this reasonable form of negative eugenics. Genetic counseling services associated with many of our larger hospitals and universities are providing such information, and they are being aided by the fact that an increasing number of genetic diseases can be detected when they are heterozygous. The most important actions that need to be taken, however, are in the area of minimizing the addition of new mutagens to those already present in the environment. Any increase in the mutational load is harmful, if not immediately, then certainly to future generations.

What of positive eugenics? The human gene pool is made up of a complex array of isoalleles, the product of a long and largely unknown genetic history. In most cases there is no way of telling which isoalleles of particular genes are outmoded relics of our past that no longer have a function. We have some examples of such genetic relics, which are detectable because of their striking effects. Populations inhabiting certain malarial regions carry a gene for sickle-cell anemia that kills homozygotes but helps to protect heterozygotes against malaria. In these regions this gene is part (in fact a large part) of the balanced load. It changes to mutational load, however, when malaria is eradicated and the heterozygote advantage disappears. How many less drastic genes of this kind do we still carry that once gave us protection against the plague or smallpox but now serve no useful function? Even if we were to discover many such genes, we dare not select against them. Whatever the optimum gene pool is for technological man, it should enable him to survive if circumstances suddenly change.

Conceivably a changed social climate and increased knowledge will make it possible for positive eugenics to be practiced on man. I suspect that the only rational course would be to select for genetic diversity. Such selection would have to favor isoalleles that pair to produce balanced heterozygosity but are not detectably harmful as homozygotes. This approach would have at least two advantages: actually or potentially valuable isoalleles would not be lost, and the balanced load would not increase directly with added heterozygosity as the mutational load does. No one knows if a more heterozygous human population would in fact be "better" in some sense, but any other kind of selection would literally paint us into an evolutionary corner. Our mutational load is a true burden, but it appears that our balanced load may be a priceless resource.

18

"Genetic Drift" in an Italian Population

by Luigi Luca Cavalli-Sforza
August 1969

Studies of blood-group frequencies and consanguineous marriages among the people of the Parma Valley indicate that this random change in hereditary type distinctly influences human evolution

The variety of hereditary types in a human population originates with mutations in the genetic material. The survival and preferential multiplication of types better adapted to the environment (natural selection) is the basis of evolution. Into this process, however, enters another kind of variation that is so completely independent of natural selection that it can even promote the predominance of genes that oppose adaptation rather than favoring it. Called genetic drift, this type of variation is a random, statistical fluctuation in the frequency of a gene as it appears in a population from one generation to the next. Sometimes genetic drift seems to exert only a moderate influence, causing the frequency of a gene to fluctuate by 5 or 10 percent. At other times it may result in one gene overwhelming other genes responsible for the same characteristic.

How strong is the influence of genetic drift in evolution, and what factors control it? Together with my colleagues Franco Conterio and Antonio Moroni of the University of Parma, Italo Barrai and Gianna Zei of the University of Pavia and our collaborators at other institutions, I have for the past 15 years been investigating genetic drift in the populations of the cities and villages in the Parma Valley in Italy. We have examined parish books, studied marriage records in the Vatican archives, made surveys of blood types, developed mathematical theories and finally simulated some of the region's populations on a computer. We have found that genetic drift can affect evolution significantly, and we have been successful in identifying factors that control it.

Hypothetically genetic drift can happen in the following way. Suppose a small group of Europeans, perhaps 10 people, colonized an island (as the mu-

tinous sailors of the *Bounty* and their Tahitian women did). Among 10 such randomly chosen people there might well be no one with blood of Type B or Type AB, because the genes for these blood types are respectively carried by only 15 percent and 5 percent of Europeans. Forty percent of Europeans have blood of Type O, and the same percentage have blood of Type A. In this small group, then, the frequency of the Type B gene might be zero rather than 15 percent because, in the nature of statistical processes, it is absent and cannot reappear unless a rare mutation takes place. The gene may also be extinguished if only one or a few members of the group

carry the Type B gene and they produce no descendants. Conversely, the frequency of a rare gene may sometimes increase until it becomes "fixed," or predominant. In remote valleys of the Alps, for instance, there is a relatively high frequency of such traits as albinism, mental deficiency and deaf-mutism, which are normally subject to negative selection.

This view of genetic drift suggests that two factors determine its strength: population size and migration. In the population of an alpine village, or among our hypothetical island colonists, a gene might vanish or become fixed in relatively few generations because the popula-

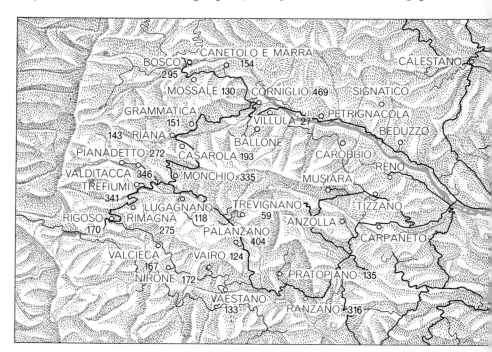

THE PARMA VALLEY stretches from the ridges behind the village of Rigoso at left to the plains of the Po River, 90 kilometers to the north. Because the settlement patterns of the Parma Valley include isolated villages in its steep-sided upper reaches, hill towns at lower

tion is so small that even a slight change in the actual number of people carrying a gene causes a large change in the percentage of the population endowed with that trait. In a larger population a change in gene frequency would affect a smaller percentage of the people, and thus drift would be less pronounced. Migration can offset the movement of a gene toward predominance or extinction by increasing the frequency of rival genes. Like migration, natural selection may also restore equilibrium, by promoting adaptive combinations of genes, even after the situation has been profoundly disturbed by genetic drift.

Isolated observations, however, offer only glimpses of the significance of genetic drift, and speculating on such observations cannot provide us with a basis for measuring the phenomenon or identifying the factors that control it. Accordingly my colleagues and I began to search for an experimental group in which we could conduct tests that would clarify these issues. We decided that the Parma Valley, which stretches for 90 kilometers to the south of the city of Parma, would provide an ideal population.

The Parma Valley, located in north-central Italy, is named after a stream that flows through it into the Po from the Apennines. The river has carved out what in its upper reaches is a steep-sided, inhospitable valley that gradually opens out into gentle hills and finally into a broad plain on which lies the city of Parma. The very geology of the valley creates an almost complete spectrum of the patterns of human habitation. In the highlands the steep countryside encourages people to gather in small villages of about 200 to 300 inhabitants. Farther downstream the rural villages become bigger as the hills give way to the plain, and where the stream flows into the Po stands the city of Parma [*see illustration below*].

People have lived in the Parma Valley since prehistoric times. Because there have been no major immigrations since the seventh century B.C. a certain demographic and genetic equilibrium has been reached. The effect of natural factors such as migration, natural selection and genetic drift can therefore be studied under the simplest conditions: when they are, or can be reasonably believed to be, in equilibrium. On the plain and in the hills, however, immigration and migratory exchanges are more frequent than in the mountains. Important demographic information is supplied by the parish books of marriages, births and deaths in the area since the end of the 16th century. Accordingly the valley offers excellent opportunities for measuring the effects of population size and migration on drift.

One of the first hypotheses we decided to test was the one that drift should be more pronounced in a small, isolated population than in a large one, since a large population has a wide variety of gene types and is more susceptible to migration. If this proposition were true, we could expect to detect the strongest drift in small, isolated mountain villages in the uplands of the Parma Valley, less drift in the hill communities farther down the valley and the least drift on the plain.

The most convenient way to measure drift is suggested by the nature of the phenomenon itself. Under the influence of drift village populations will tend to become more and more different, even if at the beginning they were homogeneous in their composition of hereditary types. Taking a particular hereditary characteristic, say blood of Type A, individuals with blood of this type may become more frequent in one village and rare in other villages. What is needed is a measure of this kind of variation among villages. If we had only two villages, we could take the percentage of individuals with blood of Type A in one village and the percentage in the other village and compute the difference between the two percentages as a measure of the variation between the two villages. In examining many villages we might consider the differences between all possible pairs of villages and average them out. In actuality we use a somewhat different way

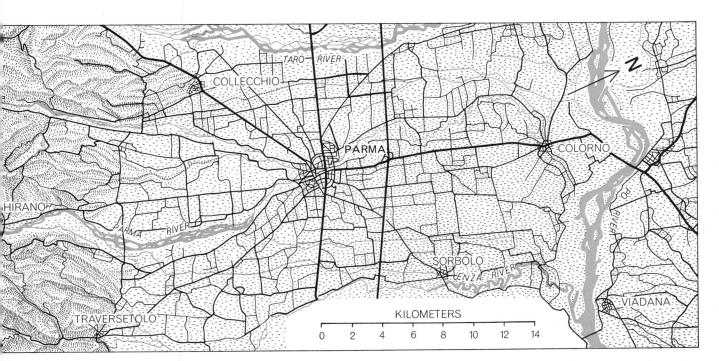

altitudes and the city of Parma on the plain south of the Po, the valley constitutes an excellent natural laboratory for studying how genetic drift affects human evolution. In order to study genetic drift, blood samples were taken throughout the cities and towns of the valley, and those upland villages whose population sizes are indicated by numbers were simulated in a computer experiment.

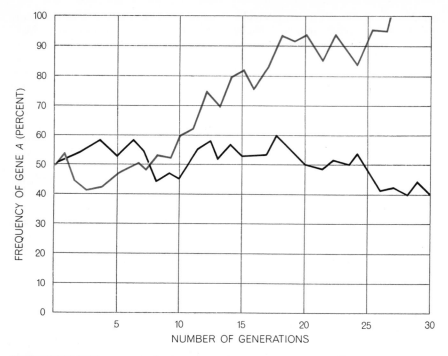

GENETIC DRIFT can cause the frequency of a gene to vary markedly from one population to another. In this calculation performed with random numbers Gene *A* appears in 50 percent of the members of two populations. Only 27 generations later Gene *A* has become "fixed" in one (*color*) and in the other its frequency fluctuates from 40 to 60 percent.

of measuring the variation, but the principle is much the same. Here let us simply call the result "measure of genetic variation between villages." Estimates of the variation were obtained after we had grouped villages in somewhat larger local areas, from the highlands down through the hill towns to the city of Parma. The measure we used excludes the effects due to sampling because we used a fraction of the total population.

As predicted, the variation between villages declined as population size increased, from .03 in the high valley, where the population density was well under 50 people per square kilometer, to less than .01 in the hill country, where there are about 100 people per square kilometer, to almost nothing on the plain, where the density reaches 200 people per square kilometer [*see bottom illustration on page 212*].

It is possible that the variation between villages could be caused by adaptation to different environments rather than by genetic drift. As unlikely as it may seem, it is possible that the environmental conditions differ from village to village so that different genes are favored in each place. It may also be that people of diverse origins and therefore of diverse blood groups have settled in the more populous regions, and that because of these historical accidents there

has not yet been time to reach an equilibrium.

If natural selection or historical accidents were responsible, the percentage of individuals possessing a certain gene would vary from village to village. The percentage would not necessarily vary in the same way for all genes, since there is no reason why the selective factors or historical accidents should operate with equal force on all genes. It would, in fact, be a strange coincidence if they did. If the variations in genes were caused by genetic drift, however, they would be the same, on the average, for any gene. The reason is that genetic drift, being a property of the population rather than of the gene, should affect all genes in the same way. Our evidence shows that the variations between villages are indeed the same for any gene.

This first test of our ideas about genetic drift was convincing, but in order to test our analysis more severely we wanted to make exact forecasts of the amount of genetic variation caused by drift. Such an exercise would require a precise quantitative prediction rather than a simple qualitative statement. Unfortunately the classical mathematical theories of population genetics (put forward by Sewall Wright, Motoo Kimura and Gustave Malécot) require that vil-

lages be of equal size, and that migrations between them follow a highly homogeneous pattern, simplifications that are rather far from reality.

To avoid this difficulty we developed other methods of predicting variations in the frequency of a gene on the basis of population size and migration. With the help of Walter Bodmer of Stanford University it was possible to devise a new theory that takes account of the actual observed migration pattern from village to village, however complex it may be. The model removes many of the oversimplifications of the classical theories but not all of them. We have therefore also developed a more general method that makes it possible on the basis of simple demographic information to predict the expected amount of drift with unlimited adherence to reality. This method consists in the use of artificial populations generated in a computer. Before I describe it, however, I should mention an apparently independent but in fact closely related approach, using a substantially different body of data, that we have followed in parallel with the study of genes.

This alternative approach we have followed is the study of relationships between individuals, which can be obtained from pedigrees or similar sources. One intuitively understands that the relationship between people must be associated with the similarities (or the differences) between the genes they carry. Both depend on common ancestry. Greater isolation between villages implies a lesser degree of common ancestry between the people of the villages, and therefore both a lesser degree of relationship between them and more differences between their genes. Thus the study of pedigrees, making it possible to estimate common ancestry, or degrees of relationship, should yield almost the same information as an analysis of the frequency of genes in the various villages. It has been shown that even data as simple as the identity of surnames can, in indicating common ancestry, supply information similar to what can be obtained from the direct study of genes.

It is the availability of parish books in the Parma Valley that makes it possible to carry on this investigation in parallel with the study of genes. Unfortunately the reconstruction of pedigrees from parish books is a laborious task, and it has not yet been completed. We do, however, have data on relationships from another source: records of consanguineous marriages. We found it particularly interesting to test the validity of this method as an alternative to the direct study of the effects of drift on genes. In the Parma Valley we could compare all these approaches. We could see, for instance, if we could predict drift from consanguinity or vice versa, or better still, predict both from a common source: simple demographic data.

Consanguineous marriages and genetic drift are similarly affected by common factors: population size and migration. A small population encourages consanguineous marriage because after a few generations most marriage partners would also be relatives. Migration, on the other hand, tends to decrease the frequency of consanguineous marriage by introducing new partners who are not relatives, or, if the flow is outward, by removing relatives who would otherwise be available.

The mathematical model with which the frequency of consanguineous marriage can be predicted is relatively simple. It is based on the idea that the population whose size critically affects the frequency of consanguineous marriage and genetic drift is somewhat diffuse, ge-

ographically speaking. As the Swedish geneticist Gunnar Dahlberg pointed out in 1938, this population basically consists of a group of people who are potential marriage partners for one another. This population is therefore not identical with the marriageable population because there are social barriers that reduce marriage choice. A village or a town might also be so large that not all the available partners would know one another. Such factors tend to make the population of eligible partners smaller than it is in a smaller village. The group can, however, extend across political boundaries, so that marriages are made between people living in different villages.

Since a simple census will not yield the size of the population of marriageable individuals, the population must be determined mathematically. By definition the population consists of a circle of N people available to one another for marriage. Assume now that an individual is not prohibited from marrying a blood relative (provided they are not so closely related that the marriage is forbidden by law). In this case the probability that he

(or she) will marry a relative will be equal to the ratio between the number of eligible blood relatives, c, and the number of candidates who are not relatives. The probability of consanguineous marriage, m, will therefore equal c/N. This probability is also identical with the overall frequency of consanguineous marriage; all other factors being excluded, the frequency of consanguineous marriage would depend only on the number of available partners who are also kinsmen. Thus if there were 40 available partners and 20 of them were blood relatives, the frequency of consanguineous marriage would be one in two, or 50 percent. Knowing the number of blood relatives from simple calculations, and the frequency m of consanguineous marriages from ecclesiastical records, we can determine the size N of the population of eligible mates because it is a function of m and c. In other words, if $m = c/N$, then $N = c/m$.

Having determined the population size, it would be convenient at this point if we could simply complete our

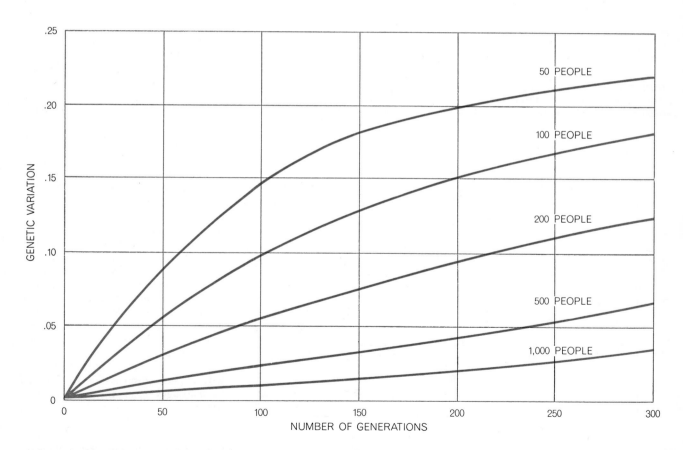

POPULATION AND DRIFT are closely related. The frequency of a particular gene in each population begins in the first generation at 50 percent, equivalent to zero on the vertical scale marked according to a measure of genetic drift called variance. After 300 generations the variation of the gene in the smallest population has increased to .22, almost as far as it can go, whereas in the largest population it has reached only .03. Genetic drift, then, is strongest in smaller populations and weakens as the population size increases.

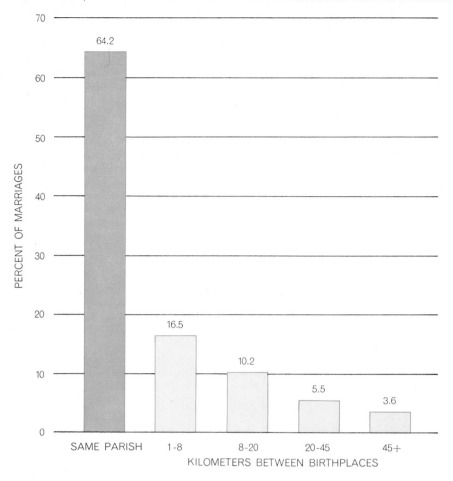

MIGRATION in upper Parma Valley has been infrequent, a conclusion drawn from the fact that most marriages recorded from 1650 to 1950 in parish books unite men and women who are from the same village. The number falls as the distance separating birthplaces increases.

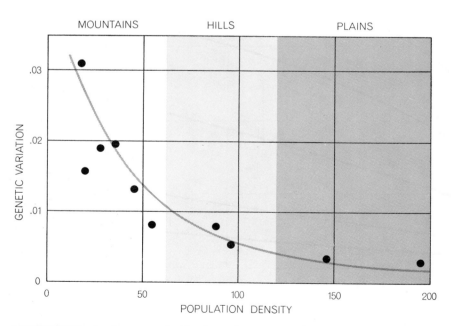

VARIATION in the frequency of a blood type between one village and another was greatest, as predicted, in the isolated upland hamlets, and declined as population density increased farther down the valley in the hill towns, on the plain and in the city of Parma.

model by taking into account the effect of migration on the available supply of marriage partners. We could then predict the frequency of consanguineous marriage and therefore estimate the amount of genetic drift. Reality, however, forces us to make a circuitous detour. It appears that there are certain factors (such as the tendency of people to marry people of a similar age, biases for or against certain kinds of consanguineous marriage and the fact that degrees of kinship too remote are recorded incompletely or not at all) that would distort the prediction of genetic drift because they affect only the frequency of consanguineous marriage without influencing the rate of variation for a gene. In order to calculate genetic drift on the basis of consanguineous marriage we must identify and compensate for such factors.

These factors can be inferred from the study of consanguineous marriages. The Vatican archives contain records of 590,-000 dispensations for consanguineous marriages granted from 1911 to 1964, the year in which our gathering of data temporarily ended. Only the dispensations for the more distantly consanguineous marriages that were granted directly by the bishops in certain areas such as Sicily and Sardinia and a few other remote dioceses are excluded. This material provided our investigators (led by Moroni, who had been a student of mine at the University of Parma) with a mass of valuable information. The records provide, among other data, the given name and the family name of the parents of the couple and the degree to which the marriage is consanguineous.

These records exist because the Roman custom and religious belief that prohibited marriage between blood relatives was inherited and diffused by the Catholic church. During the Middle Ages only the Pope could grant dispensations from the prohibition, and the dispensations (at least those known to us) were not numerous. The degree of consanguinity eligible for dispensation, however, has varied through the centuries, and a progressively more liberal trend can be detected. In the 16th century the Council of Trent recommended that a special dispensation be required for marriages up to "the fourth degree" (third cousins). Since 1917 dispensation has been required only for marriages between second cousins. The Vatican Council has recently pushed the liberalization one degree further, so that today only a marriage between first cousins, or between uncle and niece, require dispen-

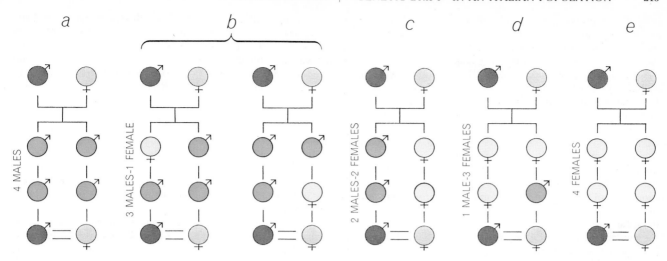

FAMILY TREES affect the frequency of consanguineous marriage. Different family trees associated with second-cousin marriages show that when spouses share only male ancestors (a), the number of consanguineous marriages reaches 774. As the number of female ancestors rises the number of marriages falls. Trees such as b (two varieties are shown) have produced 652 marriages, c 325 marriages, d 262 marriages and e 252 marriages, according to diocesan records from 1850 to 1950. Since land passes from father to son, men do not usually emigrate and marriages among relatives are therefore much more likely. There are 10 other trees for second-cousin marriages.

sation. Marriages between closer relatives are not and never have been eligible for dispensation.

The dispensation must be requested by the parish priest from the Curia before the marriage can be celebrated. In some cases the bishop can grant dispensations, but customarily he must forward a copy of the request to Rome (or, in other countries, to the representative of the Pope in that country). The Vatican will then reply to the bishop, and he will reply to the priest. The Vatican practically always grants dispensations in allowed cases, and therefore the dispensation request has constituted, or at least constitutes today, only a formal obstacle.

Of the factors that seem to alter the frequency of consanguineous marriage, one is the very closeness of the blood relationship. Apart from legal and religious restrictions, there is the widespread knowledge that consanguineous marriages may result in hereditary handicaps for the offspring.

Age can also have an important effect. As the archives show, marriages in which the consanguineous mates are a generation apart, such as those between uncle and niece and between first cousins once removed, are rarer than those between first cousins and between second cousins. We can explain this fact if we assume that in both consanguineous marriages and nonconsanguineous marriages age affects the choice of mates in the same way. In Italy, for instance, there is a mean age difference between husband and wife of about five years; the differ-

ence is smaller for young spouses and larger and more variable for older spouses. Therefore by considering the age differences among children of the same family, between parents and children and between normal spouses we can predict that marriages between uncle and niece will be only 3 percent of what would be expected on the basis of the frequency of this relationship, and marriages between aunt and nephew will be still rarer. By the same token one could expect a higher frequency of marriage between first cousins, because they tend to be of a similar age.

Migration also tends to reduce the frequency of consanguineous marriage. In places where the population is small and migration is low, blood relatives remain in contact. Hence we are not surprised to find most of the consanguineous marriages in rural areas whose populations have been rooted in the same soil for many generations. In industrial areas migration tends to disperse blood relatives so that they may not even meet, much less marry. Therefore consanguineous marriage tends to be diluted in frequency, or even to vanish, just as genetic drift does.

The effects of migration become more complex when we study specific types of genealogical trees. From data gathered in northern Emilia, a broad region including the Parma Valley, it appears that in the past century the number of consanguineous marriages diminishes when among the immediate ancestors of husband and wife there are more females

than males. The reason is that men and women migrate in different patterns. In a largely rural area such as the one we were examining, where land is inherited by the male child, fewer sons emigrate than daughters. Moreover, a woman who marries someone from another village will emigrate in the process, and the distance between the villages will make her descendants a little less available for marriage with descendants remaining in the original place. The more women there are in the genealogical tree, the more significant this pattern is [see illustration above].

We have also isolated a factor of a sociological nature. It is scarcely important enough on the statistical level to merit consideration, but I shall cite it as a curiosity. It is the tendency of children of consanguineous mothers to intermarry. Probably this is because the mothers, when related, have a greater tendency to conserve bonds that favor marriage among the children.

With the help of Kimura (who is with the National Institute of Genetics in Japan) and Barrai, we incorporated these inhibiting factors and the effects of migration into a mathematical model that predicts the incidence of consanguineous marriage with some accuracy.

Even this carefully derived mathematical theory suffers, as all applications of mathematics in biology do, from the necessity of simplifying reality in order to make results calculable. The difficulty lies not only in solving complicated mathematical problems but also in successfully simplifying the terms of the problem to allow the use of appropriate mathematical instruments without losing essential features of the problem. Computers, however, make possible another technique for attacking these problems. If we have enough data available on the population under examination, we can reconstruct it in the computer and see what happens in experiments. The repetition of these experiments a sufficient number of times gives us a view of what we can expect in reality. In this way we can, without the use of higher mathematics and with the employment of real data, forecast the complicated effects of the genetic structure of a population on phenomena such as the frequency of consanguineous marriages or genetic drift.

Naturally we simplify the artificial population that we reconstruct in a computer as much as we can. Our computer "men" and "women" do not have hands and brains, only a number (0 or 1) that indicates sex, a number of several digits representing a name, and other numbers

that identify the father and the mother of each individual, his distant ancestors and his descendants. If we study the effects of age, we must give our artificial subjects an age, and by the same token we can characterize their geographic location and social class [see illustration below].

An artificial population so constructed marries, reproduces and dies according to certain probability tables drawn from reality. For reasons of economy we make the time advance crudely, in steps of 10 years. Thus if we have a 30-year-old person, we ask the probability of his dying before 40, and on the basis of tables of the real population we make him die according to a random procedure that has a probability equal to the real one. To determine whether a 30-year-old man dies before 40, for example, we calculate from the program a random number between 00 and 99. Such a number has equal probability of being one of the 100 numbers from 00 to 99. Since the probability of a man of this age dying is 12 percent, the individual dies if the chosen

number lies between 00 and 11 and survives if it falls between 12 and 99. In the same way, using a random-number table that gives real probabilities, we decide if he marries and whom he marries by making the choice based on age, social class and geographical location. Finally, computer-generated marriages can be analyzed to determine the degree of consanguinity.

The results obtained by simulating the population of the Parma Valley confirm the impressions we had gained from our mathematical analysis of the actual population. That is, taking into account age, migration and the number of blood relatives of a given degree, the frequency of consanguineous marriages is about the same as what one would expect it to be if such marriages happened randomly. This is particularly true for the more remote degrees of consanguinity. Among first cousins, however, it seems that the frequency of consanguineous marriages is only half what it would have been if such marriages had been random.

Our final experiment consisted in sim-

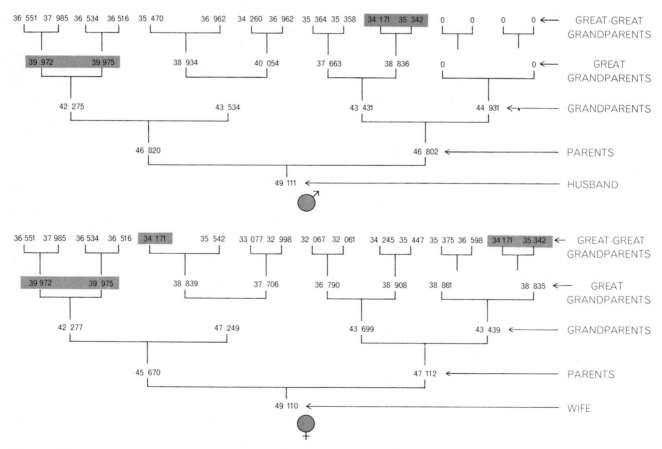

MAN AND WIFE are programmed for a computer run that simulates populations in order to determine the rate of genetic drift through the frequency of consanguineous marriage. The male's name is encoded in the digits 49 111. Other numbers (not shown) can be programmed that indicate the person's sex, age, social class and genetic endowment. Shading indicates ancestors shared by man and wife.

ulating the populations of 22 villages in order to test our hypotheses of genetic drift. The 5,000 individuals in the test population were given genes of the three blood-group systems: ABO (governed by the gene types A_1, A_2, B and O), Rh (seven gene types) and MN (two gene types). At the beginning of the simulation the frequencies of these genes in each simulated village were the same as the average of the frequencies in the actual villages. With the passage of each simulated generation, however, the frequencies began to change by a factor that was approximately the same for each blood-group system. They finally leveled off when the number of people belonging to a blood group was two or three times the original value. This equilibrium was reached fairly soon (after about 15 generations) as a consequence of the establishment of a balance between drift, which tends to make villages different, and migration, which tends to make them more nearly the same.

We found that the variations among the simulated villages quite closely matched the variations predicted by Bodmer's theory, thus confirming its capacity to represent real data. We also found that the variations among the simulated villages matched, although less closely, the variations observed among the real villages. In both the simulated and the real villages no single gene type either vanished or became predominant; the drift was not strong enough to achieve this result. Fairly divergent proportions of genes could be found in the different villages. Which gene increased in which particular village was of course a matter of chance. We did not expect a real village to show the same proportion of a given gene as its artificial counterpart [see illustration on this page].

It is clear that since the observed variation corresponds—within limits that we are now investigating—to the expected one it is not necessary to invoke explanations other than the action of genetic drift. The methods we have used in our study of the Parma Valley have now been applied to other populations as diverse as African pygmies, New Guinea tribesmen and the descendants of the Maya Indians. The results so far have confirmed the concept that genetic drift is the principal agent responsible for the variations among villages, tribes or clans. In fact, at the microgeographical and microevolutionary levels on which we worked the differences attributable to natural selection were not large (apart

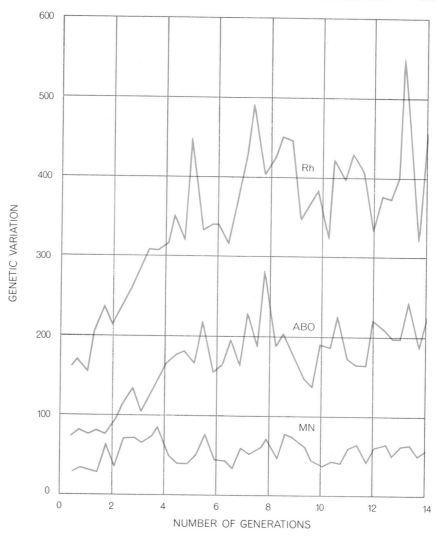

GENE FREQUENCIES for the ABO, Rh and MN blood-group systems in the populations of the villages from the upper part of the Parma Valley vary with the passing of each generation. Differences in gene frequency between villages simulated in a computer program and measured by "chi square" were similar to the differences in the real villages. Therefore migration, population size and other demographic influences that control the simulated genetic drift are probably equivalent to the forces at work in the real villages.

from some minor ones we intend to reexamine). Furthermore, there is evidence that drift can operate on a macroevolutionary scale extending over millions of years. Recent comparisons of the sequences of amino acids in the proteins of separate species show differences that are at least in part caused by drift, although the evidence is still controversial.

In seeking to extend these conclusions one could study populations distributed over large areas. In that case, however, it would be easier to encounter disturbing factors. For example, in a large enough region one might encounter selective pressures whose diversifying effects would be added to the effects of

drift on certain genes, whereas in another area or in the case of another gene natural selection might oppose drift and reduce the variations.

In any case, the discovery that genetic drift can affect evolution on a small scale over a short period of time gives the phenomenon a more important role in evolution than was once thought. It would be an error to assume, however, that evolution is almost entirely random. Only natural selection can bring about adaptation to the environment, and its importance must not be underestimated. The relative importance of drift and natural selection in determining the course of evolution remains to be assessed.

RACE AND INDIVIDUALITY

III RACE AND INDIVIDUALITY

INTRODUCTION

Linnaeus first characterized all the living peoples of the world as members of one genus and species, *Homo sapiens*. Biological anthropologists, in addition to studying the origins of the genus and species, have also traditionally dealt with questions concerning subspeciation, or race, especially along the lines of the evolutionary framework developed in the previous section. Central to this research into the nature of race lies one of the most significant transitions in physical anthropology, and biology in general. The shift is from Linnaean typological thinking to the use of the neo-Darwinian population concept. Basically, typological thinking is a taxonomic remnant of the past when species were thought to be immutable. In man, the concept was applied to classifying the obvious subspeciation which had evolved and led to the formation of approximately six major races or, according to Garn (1970) as many as thirty-two, depending upon the definition used. Under this taxonomic concept, the subspecies or racial "type," was represented by a composite of the averages of various morphological features, such as skin color, hair texture, nose shape, eye shape, body weight, height, and limb and head proportions. While at the time this was a perfectly reasonable approach to describing the variations of living humans, it had very significant limitations. For instance, it is practically impossible for an individual of a particular race to have a set of morphological features each of which is the average for his race; to say that an individual is typical for this or that race is simply fallacious. An individual may have some features in common with other individuals of the same race, but there is considerable variation among the individuals in any population. Nevertheless, many people, through sheer misinterpretation or for racist reasons, continue to use typological concepts such as "pure race" to label the features of an individual.

While the typological concept has been replaced by the population concept in studies of the variation of living humans, it has been very difficult, however desirable, for paleontologists to apply the population concept to the taxonomic questions underlying the interpretation of the fossil record, due to the very limited number of finds. Those who have attempted it have been severely criticized, not because their approach was invalid, but because it required too many assumptions and led to improbable extrapolations. (A provocative article on this topic is Eckhardt's "Population Genetics and Human Origins," *Scientific American* Offprint 676.)

When the population concept is applied to living humans, it represents a statistical approach for describing the variability of a whole population, not of each individual within it. Most of the morphological features in any individual are polygenic in origin. This means that they are undoubtedly the product of many genes whose phenotypic expression is conditioned by their interaction with the particular environment in which they developed. Thus the highly plastic and comparatively long period of child growth and development is particularly important in understanding the genetic and environmental components of adult variation in any human population. It is quite possible that even twins with identical genotypes (genetic constitutions) could show different phenotypes (observable characteristics) if they were riased in significantly different environments. It has been domonstrated that the variation of polygenic traits, such as I.Q., is usually greater among the *individuals* of a given population or race than between *populations* or races.

The study of blood groups and other serological and biochemical traits with simple or monogenic modes of inheritance at first produced exciting new taxonomic criteria for racial analysis. However, the problems with this approach quickly became apparent when, as Garn mentions (1970), the initial use of the ABO blood group system led to the grouping of Asia, India, and Africa in one population and the Amerindians and Australians in another! Although this kind of problem has been resolved to a considerable extent, it nevertheless points out the incongruencies that can develop if classification is based on serological determinations alone and without reference to the other characteristics of the natural populations under study.

With regard to the individual and the population, the same argument generally applies to serological data as applies to morphological data. Most human populations have all of the common blood groups within their boundaries, and therefore even if the average is very high for a particular group, such as the high frequency of blood group O in Amerindian populations, this does not rule out the occurrence of another blood group in an individual within this population. Nor, if an individual from some other area of the world happened to have the same pattern of alleles as the average distribution in a population of a different area of the world, would we characterize that individual as a member of the faraway population unless there were direct evidence linking his or her lineage to it. Jean Hiernaux (1968) was able to demonstrate, from a study of several hundred sub-Saharan African populations, that some populations had a few distinct and characteristic biochemical traits, but that when a larger number of biochemical traits were considered together none of these distinct traits appeared to be consistent with either the morphological characteristics or natural history of the particular population. The most consistent finding was that the degree of variation tended to be different for each trait in any given population and that each trait was continuously distributed in most cases throughout the populations.

The numerous difficulties encountered in describing subspeciation have led to a reanalysis of its meaning and of the usefulness of biochemical and morphological techniques in determining subspeciation. This reanalysis has produced important changes in the thinking of biological anthropologists about populations. Diversity has increasingly been seen as a real asset to the species, especially in the light of studies of the relations between human variation and human adaptability in the widely differing ecosystems of the world. Differences between populations have been analyzed, with the aid of new methods from population genetics, as the products of the process of evolutionary change. (See the introduction to Section IV.) Finally, the analysis of major race per se has become somewhat outmoded because few useful generalizations can be made about such large population units.

Nevertheless, race remains a very controversial subject. In order to present a more complete picture of the concept of race, I have included the statement on race enamating from the 1964 UNESCO-sponsored conference in Moscow.° Although the 1964 statement was not voted upon by UNESCO as a

---

°The UNESCO statement issued in 1950 was voted on by UNESCO as a body. The statement was, however, widely criticized by scientists and underwent revision in 1951 (UNESCO, 1969).

body, it represents one of the best statements on the complexity of the problem and should provide a useful focus for further consideration and discussion of this important topic.

PROPOSALS ON THE BIOLOGICAL ASPECTS OF RACE

The undersigned, assembled by Unesco in order to give their views on the biological aspects of the race question and in particular to formulate the biological part for a statement foreseen for 1966 and intended to bring up to date and to complete the declaration on the nature of race and racial differences signed in 1951, have unanimously agreed on the following:

1. All men living today belong to a single species, *Homo sapiens*, and are derived from a common stock. There are differences of opinion regarding how and when different human groups diverged from this common stock.

2. Biological differences between human beings are due to differences in hereditary constitution and to the influence of the environment on this genetic potential. In most cases, those differences are due to the interaction of these two sets of factors.

3. There is great genetic diversity within all human populations. Pure races—in the sense of genetically homogeneous populations—do not exist in the human species.

4. There are obvious physical differences between populations living in different geographic areas of the world, in their average appearance. Many of these differences have a genetic component.

    Most often the latter consist in differences in the frequency of the same hereditary characters.

5. Different classifications of mankind into major stocks, and of those into more restricted categories (races, which are groups of populations, or single populations) have been proposed on the basis of hereditary physical traits. Nearly all classifications recognize at least three major stocks.

    Since the pattern of geographic variation of the characteristics used in racial classification is a complex one, and since this pattern does not present any major discontinuity, these classifications, whatever they are, cannot claim to classify mankind into clear-cut categories; moreover, on account of the complexities of human history, it is difficult to determine the place of certain groups within these racial classifications, in particular that of certain intermediate populations.

    Many anthropologists, while stressing the importance of human variation, believe that the scientific interest of these classifications is limited, and even that they carry the risk of inviting abusive generalizations.

    Differences between individuals within a race or within a population are often greater than the average differences between races or populations.

    Some of the variable distinctive traits which are generally chosen as criteria to characterize a race are either independently inherited or show only varying degrees of association between them within each population. Therefore, the combination of these traits in most individuals does not correspond to the typological racial characterization.

6. In man as well as in animals, the genetic composition of each population is subject to the modifying influence of diverse factors: natural selection, tending towards adaptation to the environment, fortuitous mutations which lead to modifications of the molecules of desoxyribonucleic acid which determine heredity, or random modifications in the frequency of qualitative hereditary characters, to an extent dependent on the patterns of mating and the size of populations.

    Certain physical characters have a universal biological value for the survival of the human species, irrespective of the environment. The differences on which racial classifications are based do not affect these characters and, therefore, it is not possible from the biological point of view to speak in any way whatsoever of a general inferiority or superiority of this or that race.

7. Human evolution presents attributes of capital importance which are specific to the species.

    The human species, which is now spread over the whole world, has a past rich in migrations, in territorial expansions and contractions.

As a consequence, general adaptability to the most diverse environments is in man more pronounced than his adaptations to specific environments.

For long millennia, progress made by man, in any field, seems to have been increasingly, if not exclusively, based on culture and the transmission of cultural achievements and not on the transmission of genetic endowment. This implies a modification in the role of natural selection in man today.

On account of the mobility of human populations and of social factors, mating between members of different human groups, which tend to mitigate the differentiations acquired, has played a much more important role in human history than in that of animals. The history of any human population, or of any human race, is rich in instances of hybridization and those tend to become more and more numerous.

For man, the obstacles to interbreeding are geographical as well as social and cultural.

8. At all times, the hereditary characteristics of the human populations are in dynamic equilibrium as a result of this interbreeding and of the differentiation mechanisms which were mentioned before. As entities defined by sets of distinctive traits, human races are at any time in a process of emergence and dissolution.

Human races in general present a far less clear-cut characterization than many animal races and they cannot be compared at all to races of domestic animals, these being the result of heightened selection for special purposes.

9. It has never been proved that interbreeding has biological disadvantages for mankind as a whole.

On the contrary, it contributes to the maintenance of biological ties between human groups and thus to the unity of the species in its diversity.

The biological consequences of a marriage depend only on the individual genetic make-up of the couple and not on their race.

Therefore, no biological justification exists for prohibiting intermarriage between persons of different races, or for advising against it on racial grounds.

10. Man since his origin has at his disposal ever more efficient cultural means of nongenetic adaptation.

11. Those cultural factors which break social and geographic barriers enlarge the size of the breeding populations and so act upon their genetic structure by diminishing the random fluctuations (genetic drift).

12. As a rule, the major stocks extend over vast territories encompassing many diverse populations which differ in language, economy, culture, etc.

There is no national, religious, geographic, linguistic or cultural group which constitutes a race *ipso facto*; the concept of race is purely biological.

However, human beings who speak the same language and share the same culture have a tendency to intermarry, and often there is as a result a certain degree of coincidence between physical traits on the one hand, and linguistic and cultural traits on the other. But there is no known causal nexus between these and therefore it is not justifiable to attribute cultural characteristics to the influence of the genetic inheritance.

13. Most racial classifications of mankind do not include mental traits or attributes as a taxonomic criterion.

Heredity may have an influence in the variability shown by individuals within a given population in their responses to the psychological tests currently applied.

However, no difference has ever been detected convincingly in the hereditary endowments of human groups in regard to what is measured by these tests. On the other hand, ample evidence attests to the influence of physical, cultural and social environment on differences in response to these tests.

The study of this question is hampered by the very great difficulty of determining what part heredity plays in the average differences observed in so-called tests of over-all intelligence between populations of different cultures.

The genetic capacity for intellectual development, like certain major anatomical traits peculiar to the species, is one of the biological traits essential for its survival in any natural or social environment.

The peoples of the world today appear to possess equal biological potentialities for attaining any civilizational level. Differences in the achievements of different peoples must be attributed solely to their cultural history.

Certain psychological traits are at time attributed to particular peoples. Whether or not such assertions are valid, we do not find any basis for ascribing such traits to hereditary factors, until proof to the contrary is given.

Neither in the field of hereditary potentialities concerning the over-all intelligence and the capacity for cultural development, nor in that of physical traits, is there any justification for the concept of 'inferior' and 'superior' races.

The biological data given above stand in open contradiction to the tenets of racism. Racist theories can in no way pretend to have any scientific foundation and the anthropologists should endeavour to prevent the results of their researches from being used in such a biased way that they would serve non-scientific ends.

Moscow, 18 August 1964.

Professor Nigel Barnicot, Department of Anthropology, University College, London (United Kingdom).

Professeur Jean Benoist, Directeur du Départment d'Anthropologie, Université de Montréal, Montréal (Canada).

Professor Tadeusz Bielicki, Institute of Anthropology, Polish Academy of Sciences, Wroclaw (Poland).

Dr. A. E. Boyo, Head, Federal Malaria Research Institute, Department of Pathology and Haematology, Lagos University Medical School, Lagos (Nigeria).

Professor V. V. Bunak, Institute of Ethnography, Moscow (U.S.S.R.).

Professor Carleton S. Coon, Curator, The University Museum, University of Pennsylvania, Philadelphia, Pennsylvania (U.S.A.).

Professor G. F. Debetz, Institute of Ethnography, Moscow (U.S.S.R.).

Mrs. Adelaide G. de Diaz Ungría, Curator, Museo de Ciencias Naturales, Caracas (Venezuela).

Professeur Robert Gessain, Directeur du Centre de Recherches Anthropologiques, Musée de l'Homme, Paris (France).

Professor Santiago Genovés, Instituto de Investigaciones Históricas, Faculty of Science, University of Mexico, Mexico 20 D.F. (Mexico).

Professor Jean Hiernaux, Laboratoire d'Anthropologie, Faculté des Sciences, Université de Paris, Paris (France); Institut de Sociologie, Université Libre de Bruxelles, Bruxelles (Belgique). (Scientific Director of the meeting.)

Dr. Yaya Kane, Directeur du Centre National de Transfusion Sanguine du Sénégal, Dakar (Senegal).

Professor Ramakhrishna Mukherjee, Head, Sociological Research Unit, Indian Statistical Institute, Calcutta (India).

Professor Bernard Rensch, Zoological Institute, Westfälische Wilhelms-Universität, Münster (Federal Republic of Germany).

Professor Y. Y. Roguinski, Institute of Ethnography, Moscow (U.S.S.R.).

Professor Francisco M. Salzano, Instituto de Ciencias Naturais, Pôrto Alegre, Rio Grande do Sul (Brazil).

Professor Alf Sommerfelt, Rector, Oslo University, Oslo (Norway).

Professor James N. Spuhler, Department of Anthropology, University of Michigan, Ann Arbor, Michigan (U.S.A.).

Professor Hisashi Suzuki, Department of Anthropology, Faculty of Science, University of Tokyo, Tokyo (Japan).

Professor J. A. Valsík, Department of Anthropology and Genetics, J. A. Komensky University, Bratislava (Czechoslovakia).

Dr. Joseph S. Weiner, London School of Hygiene and Tropical Medicine, University of London, London (United Kingdom).

Professor V. P. Yakimov, Moscow State University, Institute of Anthropology, Moscow (U.S.S.R.).

Science and the Citizen
June 1972

The Male Presence

The age at menarche, or first menstrual period, for girls in the U.S. and in Europe has declined at the rate of three to four months per decade for the past 100 years. Although the trend toward earlier sexual maturity is amply documented, little is known about the causal factors. Investigators have tried to relate the onset of menstruation to climate, altitude, season, nutrition, hygiene, disease, race and social and psychological factors. Because many of the factors are interrelated, however, it has not been possible to determine their individual effects. Now J. G. Vandenbergh and his associates at the North Carolina Department of Mental Health report an interesting animal model of accelerated sexual maturation that may help to identify some of the dominant factors.

In earlier studies Vandenbergh had found that when young female mice that had not yet attained puberty were housed with an adult male mouse, they first ovulated 20 days earlier than young female mice housed without a male present. The apparent cause was stimulation by a pheromone: a substance secreted by one member of a species that affects the behavior of other members of the same species. When soiled bedding from cages housing males was added to cages housing isolated young females, the sexual maturation of the females was accelerated. On the other hand, some investigators have found that sexual maturation in mice was dependent on the amount of protein in the diet or on reaching a critical body weight. Vandenbergh and his colleagues decided to conduct an experiment to determine the relative importance of these factors.

Female mice were weaned at 21 days of age and placed in individual cages. They were exposed to three levels of male stimulation: (1) an adult male mouse lived with a young female, (2) soiled bedding from adult-male cages was added daily to the cage of a young female and (3) young females were maintained with no male contact. Three levels of dietary protein were also tested: 8 percent, 16 percent and 24 percent. Each diet contained equal amounts of fats, vitamins and minerals.

The findings, presented in *Journal of Reproductive Fertility,* show a relation between the level of dietary protein and the age of sexual maturation. Female mice fed a diet with 8 percent protein matured later than female mice reared on higher levels of protein. Moreover, of the females housed with males only 69 percent of the mice reared on 8 percent protein produced litters, whereas 81 percent of those on 16 percent protein and 100 percent of those on 24 percent protein bore young.

The presence of a male, however, advanced the age of first ovulation on the average to about eight days after weaning. Females exposed only to male bedding began to ovulate about 13 days after weaning; isolated females began about 15 days after weaning. Analysis of variance indicated that although both dietary protein and the presence of males (or their odor) were significant factors in regulating sexual maturation, the male presence contributed 47.3 percent of the total variance and·diet accounted for only 4.8 percent. Body weight appeared to have no influence on the onset of ovulation.

Vandenbergh and his colleagues also found that female mice housed in groups with a male ovulated later than female mice housed singly with males. Although the effect of male stimulation is strong under both conditions, the presence of other females appears to inhibit sexual maturation. Moreover, female mice housed singly and not exposed to a male matured sexually at an earlier age than females in a group exposed to a male did. Vandenbergh and his associates observe: "[The fact that] social stimulation was more effective than protein intake may have relevance to the phenomenon of accelerated sexual maturation in human females."

Science and the Citizen
March 1969

Slow Aging

Experiments with substances that scavenge free radicals in the body have significantly increased the normal lifespan of mice, according to Denham Harman of the University of Nebraska. Writing in the *Journal of Gerontology,* Harman describes work designed to test the hypothesis that free radicals, which are highly reactive molecular fragments, play a role in aging by randomly causing the deterioration of cells. The radicals, which are highly reactive because they have at least one unpaired electron, can be produced by normal metabolic processes or by exposure to ionizing radiation. Whatever the mechanism, a molecule such as water (H_2O) can give rise to a free radical such as OH. The radical reacts readily with other substances, thereby disrupting them or changing their character.

On Harman's hypothesis reactions with free radicals might, for example, change the properties of cell membranes or cause the release of lysosomal enzymes that damage DNA. He believes that if such changes do play a role in aging, the process might be slowed by the addition of nontoxic antioxidants to food. In that way one would raise the concentration in the body of compounds capable of reacting rapidly with free radicals so that fewer of them would be available for harmful reactions. In his experiments with mice Harman has added small amounts of such free-radical inhibitors as butylated hydroxytoluene (BHT) and 2-mercaptoethylamine to the food given the mice. The results of his most recent experiments, he reports, indicate an increase of 30 to 40 percent in the mean longevity of mice receiving .5 percent BHT in their diet.

Science and the Citizen
February 1967

Death in America

After reaching an all-time low in 1954, the U.S. death rate climbed by 4.7 percent in the next decade, from 919 deaths per 100,000 population to 961.9 in 1963. Although much of this increase can be attributed to the changing age composition of the population, there were also significant changes in the death rate from different causes. Among diseases showing the sharpest 10-year increase were two closely associated with cigarette smoking: arteriosclerotic heart disease and respiratory cancer (chiefly lung cancer). The former increased by 23 percent and the latter by 46 percent in the decade 1954–1963.

The 13 leading causes of death and the 10-year change for each are shown in the following table. (The first number is the 1963 death rate per 100,000 population; the second number is the percent change since 1954; a blank indicates that the change is less than 7 percent.)

Arteriosclerotic heart disease	290.0	+23%
Stroke	106.7	
Cancer of the digestive organs	49.3	−7%
Pneumonia and influenza	37.5	+48%
Diseases of infancy	33.3	−15%
Hypertensive heart disease	32.4	−30%
Accidents (except motor vehicle)	30.3	−10%
Nonrheumatic endocarditis	29.7	−28%
Respiratory cancer	24.9	+46%
Motor vehicle accidents	23.1	
Genital cancer	21.2	−7%
General arteriosclerosis	19.9	
Diabetes mellitus	17.2	+10%

As in the past, there continue to be striking differences between white death rates and nonwhite rates in certain categories. Among whites, for example, the death rate from arteriosclerotic heart disease is more than 70 percent higher than it is among nonwhites. Whites also experience higher death rates than nonwhites for cancer of the stomach and lung. On the other hand, nonwhites have a death rate from hypertensive heart disease that is nearly 130 percent higher than the white death rate. Nonwhites also have a higher death rate than whites for diabetes, pneumonia and accidents other than those caused by motor vehicles.

In the 10-year period 1954–1963 there was a slight decline of about 5 percent in the infant mortality rate. This is another category, however, in which the nonwhite death rate is significantly higher than the white death rate: 41.5 deaths per 1,000 live births for nonwhite infants compared with 22.2 deaths per 1,000 for white infants. In the category of infant mortality even the white U.S. rate is higher than that in countries such as Australia (19.5 deaths per 1,000), Finland (18.2), the Netherlands (15.8) and Sweden (15.4).

The data are from recent booklets in the series "Vital and Health Statistics," published by the U.S. Department of Health, Education, and Welfare.

Science and the Citizen
May 1971

The American Way of Death (Cont.)

American men under 65 are twice as likely to die of heart attack as men living in Norway, Sweden or the Netherlands. Although American women of the same age are only about a third as prone to fatal heart attack as American men, even their rate is more than double that of Norwegian, Swedish and Dutch women. Each year about 175,000 Americans in the age group 35 to 64 die prematurely of coronary heart disease. A 14-year study in Framingham, Mass., has shown that a coronary attack often strikes without prior medical warning and that the majority of victims die within an hour of the event, two-thirds of them without ever reaching a hospital. A report on the Framingham experience by Tavia Gordon and William B. Kannel in *The Journal of the American Medical Association* concludes that improved medical care *after* a heart attack has occurred offers little hope for combating what the World Health Organization has described as potentially "the greatest epidemic mankind has faced."

In the Framingham study 102 men and 18 women died of coronary heart disease before their 65th year. For 58 percent of the men death was "sudden," defined as occurring within an hour of the attack; among women somewhat fewer deaths (39 percent) were sudden.

For both men and women sudden death was more likely if they were less than 55 years old at the time of the attack. "If we define an unexpected [coronary-heart-disease] death," the authors write, "as the death of a person without previous clinical evidence of *any* form of definite heart disease—a conservative definition, indeed—one half of all sudden CHD deaths were unexpected.... The progression from nil or inapparent disease to death appears to be very swift."

The authors acknowledge that although programs and techniques for preventing coronary heart disease are controversial, "a great deal is known about what kind of people die prematurely [of coronary heart disease]." The Framingham study and many others have shown that the risk of a heart attack is increased by such factors as hypertension, excessive body weight, elevated cholesterol in the blood and cigarette smoking. Commenting on the Framingham victims who had exhibited no previous sign of heart disease, the authors report that except for one person whose smoking habits were unknown all were cigarette smokers. They conclude: "Epidemiological studies have marshaled impressive evidence that the development of [coronary heart disease] is controlled by the local habits and conditions of life. It seems highly plausible... that modifications of our present way of life could be specified today that would ...dramatically reduce the premature toll of this disease and lower overall mortality in persons before age 65."

Since individual variation is central to the study of variation in a population, the course of individual development from conception to death—a course determined by the interaction of genes and environment—can provide the most useful framework within which to understand the phenotypic variability of most polygenic characteristics in humans. Within this framework, the period of child growth and development before sexual maturation represents the most plastic phase of the extrauterine life cycle. During this period, environmental (including social) differences produce behavioral, morphological, physiological, and biochemical adaptations that can become permanent if the influence is of significant intensity and duration.

Hence we can look at physiological, morphological, and behavioral growth and development as a dynamic process of adaptation at the phenotypic level to varying environmental conditions. For example, height can be dramatically increased if inadequate nutrition is improved or if a chronic illness is cured before sexual maturation occurs. Just how this increase is mediated through the neuroendocrine system is only now becoming better understood: it appears that a complex series of psychoendocrine factors act more or less in consort with nutrition, exercise, health, emotion, and possibly other more obscure environmental factors, such as light, temperature, and even odors. (See "The Male Presence" in Science and the Citizen, page 223) More specifically, the onset of pubescence is controlled by a change in the sensitivity of the hypothalamic centers controlling gonadotrophin-releasing factors to the circulating prepubertal levels of sex hormones (testosterone, estrogen, progesterone). The evidence suggests that as soon as these centers in the hypothalamus lose their inhibition to the feedback effects of these steroid sex hormones, the hypothalamic neurons begin to secrete sufficient releasing factors to trigger larger release of pituitary gonadotrophins, which, in turn, stimulate gonadal maturation. It is currently believed that a detailed knowledge of the environmentally sensitive endocrine mechanisms controlling child growth and development will contribute greatly to the understanding of human variation, especially when we are able to combine what we know of these endocrine factors with related genetic factors in a particular population.

How these endocrine processes relate to the adaptability of individuals over the various phases of their life cycles is another question with very broad ramifications, which merit serious investigation by biological anthropologists. Nathan Shock, in his article "The Physiology of Aging," (Scientific American, January, 1962), supplies us with a unique diagram showing the different sites of aging and the problems associated with senescence. That we have much to learn about how aging takes place in the body is evident from the Science and the Citizen excerpt on aging (page 225). We are under increasing pressure, however, to understand the processes of aging, now that increases in fertility and decreases in infant and adult mortality have brought about worldwide demographic changes. The immediate effect of these changes throughout most of the world has been a pyramidal age structure in which the percentage of children is much greater than the percentage of adults in many populations; however, the combination of measures to decrease fertility and measures to increase longevity will ultimately result in a stable population structure in which the number of individuals of every age will be approximately equal. The result of this change will be the rapid relative increase in the percentage of elderly people in the population. Hence, problems associated with aging are certain to increase as more stable population structures are attained.

Within this context, biological anthropology has begun to expand its already established focus on child growth and development to include the entire life cycle. There are several practical and theoretical reasons for this broadened view. First, we can learn as much about human adaptability to various environmental factors by studying the aged as we can by focusing upon patterns of child growth and development. The method is of course different since in the elderly the principal variable is disease, while in children it is the continued rate of growth. Secondly, disorders such as lung and cardiac diseases, which are best studied among the aged, are present to some extent during the reproductive years and hence can influence differential fertility. Finally, among primates, only in the human species do females live well beyond their reproductive years. This suggests some kind of evolutionary significance for grandmothers! The possible selective advantage may in part be due to certain responsibilities for child care and socialization frequently given them by their daughters. However, these evolutionary and adaptive considerations are only a part of what will be a growing area of investigation by biological anthropologists.

Science and the Citizen
February 1971

Intelligence and Race (Cont.)

Some light on the factors influencing intelligence is provided by a study of the I.Q. scores of 88 children each of whom had one white parent and one black parent. Sixty-one of the children had a white mother (and a black father); the remaining 27 had a black mother (and a white father). When tested at four years of age, the children of white mothers achieved a mean I.Q. score significantly higher than the children of black mothers did. The mean scores were respectively 100.9 and 93.7. In the absence of evidence that intelligence is genetically linked to the sex of the parent, the provisional interpretation is that environmental factors rather than inherited capacity are primarily responsible for the difference in the two scores.

Reporting these findings in *Science*, Lee Willerman, Alfred F. Naylor and Ntinos C. Myrianthopoulos of the National Institute of Neurological Diseases and Stroke review the pitfalls that beset efforts to compare the I.Q.'s of U.S. whites and U.S. Negroes. They point out, for example, that U.S. Negroes and U.S. whites have about 21 percent of their genes in common, and that in surveys 70 percent of U.S. Negroes report having at least one white ancestor. The authors accept the designations "white" and "Negro" as useful, however, "in providing insights concerning the occurrence of many biological and social phenomena." They undertook their study on the assumption that intelligence is "determined by additive genetic factors which are not sex-linked." Any test differences that emerged could then be regarded as environmental in origin because the mother "is the primary socializing agent during preschool years."

The subjects of the investigation were provided by a study sponsored by the National Institutes of Health involving the children born to some 42,000 women who were registered during pregnancy in 12 institutions throughout the U.S. The children are given neurological and psychological examinations at intervals during the first eight years of life. The first 88 children of racially mixed parentage to reach four years of age were given an abbreviated form of the Stanford-Binet test to measure I.Q. A study of the children's weight and length at birth and their gestation period showed that there were no significant differences between children born to white mothers and those born to Negro mothers. The number of years of education of all the parents, white and Negro, male and female, also was remarkably similar: the means ranged from 10.9 to 11.5 years. The I.Q. scores of the parents, however, were not known.

In addition to the overall difference of 7.2 points in the mean I.Q. scores favoring the children of white mothers, there were some other results of interest. For example, when the sex of the child is ignored, it is the children of the unmarried Negro mothers that have the lowest I.Q. On the other hand, if marital status is ignored, it is only the males born to Negro mothers who have a significantly low I.Q. The authors suggest that the first of these findings may be attributable to the disorganization assumed to exist in one-parent families. The second finding is consistent with other studies showing that males in general score lower than females on certain I.Q. tests. The authors conclude: "Interpretation of the race effect should be tentative since the number of interracial subjects is small. The evidence presented here suggests that environmental factors may play an important role in the lower intellectual performance of Negro preschool children."

Science and the Citizen
December 1967

Poverty and Mental Retardation

A Duke University psychologist suggests that physically and mentally normal children can be transformed into retarded ones during the interval between their first and third birthdays. Since only one out of four mentally retarded individuals is handicapped as a consequence of known hereditary defects or other physical causes, 75 percent of retardation may thus be environmental in origin.

Analyzing the reports of several experimental preschool programs, Donald J. Stedman, research director of Duke University's Education Improvement Program in Durham, N.C., found that among children from deprived backgrounds nearly 80 percent scored as "borderline retardates" when tested at school-entrance age, compared with only 15 percent of children from all income levels. Stedman obtained the same low scores when he tested deprived Durham children between the ages of four and six. He next tested infants with similarly deprived backgrounds at the ages of one, three, six, nine, 12 and 15 months; their scores proved to be better than the national average.

Seeking out the specific environmental factors that may be responsible for retardation, Stedman points to studies in Mexico and elsewhere that show a correlation between malnutrition and intellectual underdevelopment. He believes that an effect of equal or greater importance is produced by an impoverished external environment on children from 12 to 36 months old. During these critical months, Stedman points out, the child's use of language accelerates, as does the associated intellectual experience of classifying in logical fashion the increasing number of things the child encounters in the surrounding world. Because the ability to classify depends on memory processes, tests of memory efficiency provide a sensitive measure of the child's intellectual growth. The children from deprived backgrounds enrolled in Duke's Education Improvement Program, Stedman reports, show a "horrendous" deficiency in this respect.

Science and the Citizen
December 1969

Blood of the Pharaohs

A problem in Egyptian history of the 14th century B.C. is whether two of the successors to the pharaoh Ikhnaton were brothers. Using a new microserological technique, investigators in England and Egypt have cast additional light on the question. R. G. Harrison and R. C. Connolly of the University of Liverpool and A. Abdalla of the University of Cairo report in *Nature* that their blood-type analysis strengthens the case for those who believe the two were brothers (although it does not fatally weaken the case for those who believe they were not).

Ikhnaton is famous as a religious reformer whose campaign to substitute a kind of monotheism for the bizarre polytheism of his time collapsed after his death. Neither of his immediate successors would be remembered by nonspe-

cialists today except that the tomb of one —Tutankhamen—astonished the world by its riches when it was opened in 1922. The mummy of "King Tut" is in the custody of the United Arab Republic's Department of Antiquities; another of the department's treasures, until recently believed to be the mummy of the great Ikhnaton himself, has now been shown to be more probably that of his immediate successor, one Smenkhkare.

Tutankhamen and Smenkhkare had one bond in common: each was married to a daughter of Ikhnaton. The three investigators thought that knowledge of the two successors' blood type might settle the question of whether they were also brothers. Because the usual serological analysis requires quantities of tissue that were not available from either mummy, they developed a refined method that needed only a few milligrams of tissue dust. Both mummies proved to belong to the A_2 blood group and also to harbor the serum antigen MN.

It does not follow that because the pharaohs had two blood fractions in common they were brothers. If A_2 and MN were the only fractions existing within the Egyptian population of the second millennium B.C., for example, the two pharaohs need not even have been relatives. Other investigators, however, have established the existence of other blood fractions among Egyptians of that period. Harrison, Connolly and Abdalla therefore conclude that, because their findings are not negative, the probability that the two pharaohs were close relatives is correspondingly increased.

Science and the Citizen
July 1960

Primitive Coexistence

An early variety of modern man apparently lived almost side by side with Neanderthal man about 50,000 years ago in the Near East. So concludes T. Dale Stewart of the Smithsonian Institution after studying human remains from the cave of Shanidar in Iraq and the caves of Mount Carmel in Palestine. It has generally been thought that Neanderthal man preceded modern man by tens of thousands of years.

The Shanidar cave contained Neanderthal bones, while the caves at Mount Carmel contained both Neanderthal and modern skeletons. Carbon-14 dating indicates that all the cave dwellers lived in the same general period, although the Mount Carmel skeletons appear to be somewhat older.

Fragments of a female pelvis from one of the Mount Carmel caves, and a male pelvis from Shanidar have proved to be almost indistinguishable from the classic Neanderthal skeletons of central Europe, Stewart reported in *Science*. But the bones found in the other Mount Carmel cave were remarkably similar to those of modern man. Stewart suggests that the two human varieties occupied the caves at slightly different times, and did not interbreed.

As William W. Howells notes in his article "The Distribution of Man," the question of racial origins has inspired a variety of theories about human adaptation and evolution, upon which have been based the definitions of the great geographic races of man in various parts of the world. Several lines of evidence have been used to develop these theories. First, differences in cranial and other skeletal remains found in various parts of the world roughly correspond to the current distribution of the human species. Use of this evidence assumes, among other things, that contemporary geography and differences in distribution of races conform to prehistoric geography and distributions, and that the skeletal or fossil remains discovered are representative of the population from which they came. These assumptions are representative of the kinds of assumptions that must be made routinely by specialists in the study of human skeletal populations. An important advantage for the biological anthropologist studying the skeletal remains of the more recent past is the possibility of studying larger populations than the human paleontologist, who frequently deals with more fragmentary fossil finds. A larger sample allows broader inferences to be made about the period in question, including the variation in fossil remains. Examples of inferences made about the more recent past on the basis of skeletal and dental evidence are genetic traits; diseases and their primitive medical treatment, which influenced skeletal and dental development and structure; demographic implications of the approximate age at death; behavioral adaptations and the structure and function of limbs; environmental information based on structural—functional considerations of such regions as the face, long bone, and chest cavity; and dietary information based on the effects of nutritional stress on bone, cartilage, and dental development and the presence of various major and trace minerals.

Howells, in a recent letter, outlines new evidence for the dating of *Homo Sapiens* and comments on his current view of race.

> If I had made yearly records from 1960 of my private feelings as to a best estimate for the time of appearance of strictly modern humans (*Homo sapiens* of the article), I think a graph of these would have shown a swing toward more recent dates and then back again (the article itself was fortunately rather vague on this point). Since 1960, we have had new evidence of early modern man in East Africa from at least 60,000 to 70,000 years ago, in Indonesia, from 40,000 years ago (with the occupation of Australia at before 32,000), and in North America, from nearly 50,000 years ago, hitherto almost unthinkable (although the same issue of the *Scientific American* carried a notice of cultural evidence from Valsequillo, Mexico, suggesting a date of 30,000). Only Europe, with North Africa and an unknown fraction of western and central Asia, seems to have definitely continued as a bastion of Neanderthal and Neanderthal-like populations for any length of time after 40,000. At the moment, however, among such early evidences only Indonesia (with the Niah Cave skull) and South Africa with the Fish Hoek skull from probably 35,000) give rather clear signs of foreshadowing living peoples of their regions.

I have had certain general changes of mind, which would affect the distribution maps more than anything else. I have concluded from various kinds of evidence that Melanesians are not connected with Africans but owe their resemblances more to convergent evolution and are actually closer to Australian aboriginals, probably deriving from a general population occupying southeasternmost Asia and then-connected Indonesia in the later Pleistocene. Similarly, I would look on other major races more as what could better be called population complexes, having a certain general community of features but marked by much local individualization in physical details. Thus I would not view Ainus of northern Japan as displaced Caucasoids (see maps) but rather as a remnant of a very broad proto-Mongoloid complex parental to American Indians, to other prehistoric aboriginals of Japan and Formosa, and to Micronesians and Polynesians, as well as, of course, to Mongols, Chinese, and Japanese. Coon (1962) published a major study suggesting some conclusions of this sort but mainly intended to buttress Weidenreich's hypothesis of derivation. Otherwise, however, my views remain as stated in the article, which portrays a general pattern of gradual variation from a fundamentally unitary branch of mankind.

William W. Howells, January 1974

Another approach has been the age-old attempt to explain the environmentally adaptive significance of the major anthroposcopic, or readily observable, variations in living humans. Facial features and skin color, for example, are two characteristics that have attracted a wide degree of research interest. In the case of facial variation, there have been a considerable number of investigations concerning the fact that the human face is so exposed to the environment that structural modifications in the bony sinuses and soft tissue parts about the eyes and cheeks of the Mongoloid populations may be adaptations to the cold (Steegman, 1970). Taking these considerations a step further, it is possible, for example, that the nasal air passages may also be modified in dry climates to help humidify the air properly before it reaches the delicate tissues of the lungs. Just as facial features have been related to climactic differences of temperature and humidity, so have skin pigmentation and keratin content been related to differential effects of ultraviolet sunlight. There are two theories which are not mutually exclusive. One theory holds that increased melanin, the pigment found in one of the skin's layers and which, in large amounts, produces the dark skin color of black people, also absorbs ultraviolet light at the wavelength necessary to prevent the overproduction of Vitamin D. Another theory holds that melanin possibly protects the skin from the mutagenic effects of excessive ultraviolet light which may lead to skin cancer.

Finally, biochemical features have been used to describe racial and subracial differences. Examples are differences in the frequencies of blood groups of plasma and red blood cell enzymes, and of hemoglobin variants and the various serum proteins.

Apart from the methodological issues, the study of human race, whether it focuses on racial origins or morphological variation, is a complicated mixture of science, prejudice, and public policy. The whole issue of human racial differences and similarities was quietly dropped by biological anthropologists in the early 1960s following the publication of Carleton Coon's (1962) scholarly but highly controversial *The Origin of Races*. Coon's work implied to some scientists that evolutionary development was more advanced in some races than others, although it is not clear that Coon meant to imply this. Theodosius Dobzhansky's review of Coon's book argues that such a theory of differential advancement is scientifically untenable. However, the reader should also study Coon's interesting exchange of letters with Dobzhansky (See Letters to the Editor, p. 247). Rather than using the so-called major geographic races of man as the basis for studies of human variation, anthropologists have been doing more studies of differentiation on a small population level. This change reflects the scientific conclusion that we do not know enough about the interaction of local environmental factors, particularly physical and sociocultural factors, with the genomes of individuals in isolated populations to understand the larger geographic population differences. It also reflects the increasing concern that any study involving race somehow supports racist factions within our society.

The article "Intelligence and Race" by Walter F. Bodmer and Luigi Luca Cavalli-Sforza summarizes a number of issues underlying the study of the inheritance of I.Q. and the difficulty of making meaningful comparisons between American black and white populations. Noting that there are inherent dangers in limiting scientific research, they nevertheless conclude on the basis of current evidence that few justifications exist for carrying out research in this area. This conclusion, particularly if it is generalized to the whole field remains controversial, especially as new evidence in studies of behavioral genetics raises the possibility of new questions relevant to human behavior (See Seymour Benzer's "Genetic Dissection of Behavior," *Scientific American* Offprint 1285). Moreover, stopping research at a low level of development because it might lend support to racists would be like advocating in the nineteenth century that all research that might alter in any way the early Darwinian concepts of evolution should be stopped because any alteration would give the antievolutionists new evidence with which to criticize the theory. The whole history of human adaptation has been built on knowledge and it would be ridiculous to stop research on any issue for fear it would give the racists new fodder for their cannons. Social bigotry has never been based on carefully investigated facts, only on carefully twisted facts.

The letters by Heinz and Shockley and the authors' answers to their letters, as well as the very recent comments by Bodmer following the article indicate other dimensions of this issue. Undoubtedly, the issue is far from settled. It will take careful studies to separate scientific fact from the myths surrounding the issue of the significance of racial differences of all kinds.

In a very recent article entitled "The Genetics of Human Populations," L. L. Cavalli-Sforza expounds further on the concepts underlying the application of population genetic principles to the history of human races. Within an important and potentially controversial discussion on the use and possible misuse of genetic and other anthropological data to determine the relations among human populations, he provides us with some of his latest insights on a number of topics pertaining to the interaction of genes and environment at population levels. For example, he discusses the importance of the sickle cell gene not only for its classic contribution to evolutionary theory but also for its limitations in helping bioanthropologists to resolve questions about the relations between and among human populations. In this context he goes on to broader questions concerning subspeciation and reveals some striking results about the genetic distances among populations representative of major racial subdivisions. In this regard, he suggests that all races could have branched out from a core population approximately 50,000 years ago. Continuing on with this analysis, he goes on to demonstrate how models built on archaeological evidence of early agriculture could be integrated with genetic evidence to develop the working hypothesis that Caucasians are mostly descendant from a Near Eastern population which was intermediate between Africans and Asians.

Crucial to the whole issue of genetically based differences in human populations is the variable effect of enriched and deprived environment during child growth and development. James Tanner, in his article "Growing Up," has carefully documented that over the past 100 years in many of the economically developed nations of the world the children have been reaching sexual maturation earlier and actually growing taller. If sexual maturation in humans is associated with final adult behavior, as it is in other animal species, then this very recent trend may be producing an earlier emotional and cognitive maturation, which is yet to be investigated by biological anthropologists for its significance to the behavioral adaptability of modern man. The evolutionary trend called *neoteny* suggests that human evolution has favored quite a different situation; its supposed selective advantage lies in the prolongation of parent-child interrelations, which allows the child to learn all of the factors necessary to become a productive culture-bearing adult.

Another link between environment and physical development is provided by Lytt I. Gardner's article "Deprivation Dwarfism," which establishes a clear relationship between emotional factors and endocrine function. It demonstrates that behavioral adaptation involves the endocrine mechanisms and that growth and development can be significantly altered by various emotional disorders. Hence sociocultural factors that influence the development of child behavior can play an important role in the endocrine mediated long-term growth processes as well as the moment-to-moment metabolic adjustments of body physiology. This theory, that emotional disorders have profound physiological effects, agrees with information on the effects of early deprivation such as resulted from the Harlows' experimental studies of primates (see H. F. Harlow and M. K. Harlow, "Social Deprivation in Monkeys," *Scientific American* Offprint 473) and various researchers' findings on orphaned children. Gardner's demonstration of the complexity and sensitivity of the growth processes to various environmental factors should, therefore, enable us to appreciate more fully the plasticity of growth processes in the production of human variation.

How these behavioral, endocrinological, and genetic factors influence the populations Alexander Leaf describes in "Getting Old" is a question that at this time is open for investigation. The Science and the Citizen articles on death in this nation (p. 291) suggest that these factors are important but are not the only ones operating. Nevertheless, through the careful analysis of the populations Leaf describes, we should be able to make some headway in understanding the processes of human aging and the incredible longevity experienced by some human populations.

Science and the Citizen
March 1968

Sirs:

The facts on early maturation presented in J. M. Tanner's lucid article ["Earlier Maturation in Man"; SCIENTIFIC AMERICAN, January] have important implications for education to which I should like to draw attention.

While the age of physical maturity has fallen steadily, the age of university education has remained almost unchanged. As a result the campuses are now peopled by grown men and women yet are governed by traditions of organization and discipline which were made for adolescents. No wonder that those who remember themselves as striplings at college are outraged by the beards and the bosoms they see there now—and by the intransigence that is natural in the bearded and the bosomed, especially when they have to be treated as children. The university system as it is, historically, is two years out of step with the attitudes and emotions of contemporary students, and is only suited to the young who are now in high school.

A part of this difficulty will no doubt be repaired by giving university education more of the character of adult education. But the one change which is radical and inevitable is that students will go to college at least a year earlier, and in time two years earlier. This will require children to get through the present school curriculum one to two years faster than they do now, and the signs are that this is possible. Tanner's article of course is concerned only with body functions, and does not deal directly with brain and with intelligence. But even in the evidence for earlier physical maturation, these are grounds for seeing an implication that the brain is also maturing earlier. And there is at least a presumption from this (which has some support in tests) that intelligence quotient in its turn is rising in children.

At the least, Tanner's article should put an end to a classical fallacy about intelligence. This is the argument (popularized by Sir Ronald Fisher and copied by pundits ever since) which goes: *There is a positive correlation between the I.Q. of parents and the average I.Q. of their children. The average I.Q. of the children in large families is lower than in small families. Large families contribute more members to the next generation than do small families. Therefore the average I.Q. of the population must be falling.* There are several logical flaws in the statistical reasoning here. But what is more practical, Tanner's article proves in the most concrete way that the argument *must* be fallacious. For the argument can be repeated word for word about weight and about height, simply by putting the word "weight" or "height" in place of "I.Q." Yet as we see, the conclusion for weight and for height is demonstrably wrong.

J. BRONOWSKI

Salk Institute for Biological Studies
La Jolla, Calif.

234

COLOR OF HUMAN SKIN is sometimes measured by physical anthropologists on the von Luschan scale. Reproduced here somewhat larger than natural size, the scale consists of numbered ceramic tiles which are compared visually to color of the underside of subject's forearm. Both sides of the scale are shown; colors range from almost pure white (*top right*) to black (*bottom left*).

The Distribution of Man

by William W. Howells
September 1960

Homo sapiens arose in the Old World, but has since become the most widely distributed of all animal species. In the process he has differentiated into three principal strains

Men with chins, relatively small brow ridges and small facial skeletons, and with high, flat-sided skulls, probably appeared on earth in the period between the last two great continental glaciers, say from 150,000 to 50,000 years ago. If the time of their origin is blurred, the place is no less so. The new species doubtless emerged from a number of related populations distributed over a considerable part of the Old World. Thus *Homo sapiens* evolved as a species and began to differentiate into races at the same time.

In any case, our direct ancestor, like his older relatives, was at once product and master of the crude pebble tools that primitive human forms had learned to use hundreds of thousands of years earlier. His inheritance also included a social organization and some level of verbal communication.

Between these hazy beginnings and the agricultural revolution of about 10,-000 years ago *Homo sapiens* radiated over most of the earth, and differentiated into clearly distinguishable races. The processes were intimately related. Like the forces that had created man, they reflected both the workings of man's environment and of his own invention. So much can be said with reasonable confidence. The details are another matter. The when, where and how of the origin of races puzzle us not much less than they puzzled Charles Darwin.

A little over a century ago a pleasingly simple explanation of races enjoyed some popularity. The races were separate species, created by God as they are today. The Biblical account of Adam and Eve was meant to apply only to Caucasians. Heretical as the idea might be, it was argued that the Negroes appearing in Egyptian monuments, and the skulls of the ancient Indian mound-builders of Ohio, differed in no way from their living descendants, and so there could have been no important change in the only slightly longer time since the Creation itself, set by Archbishop Ussher at 4004 B.C.

With his *Origin of Species*, Darwin undid all this careful "science" at a stroke. Natural selection and the immense stretch of time provided by the geological time-scale made gradual evolution seem the obvious explanation of racial or species differences. But in his later book, *The Descent of Man*, Darwin turned his back on his own central notion of natural selection as the cause of races. He there preferred sexual selection, or the accentuation of racial features through long-established ideals of beauty in different segments of mankind. This proposition failed to impress anthropologists, and so Darwin's demolishing of the old views left something of a void that has never been satisfactorily filled.

Not for want of trying. Some students continued, until recent years, to insist that races are indeed separate species, or even separate genera, with Whites descended from chimpanzees, Negroes from gorillas and Mongoloids from orangutans. Darwin himself had already argued against such a possibility when a contemporary proposed that these same apes had in turn descended from three different monkey species. Darwin pointed out that so great a degree of convergence in evolution, producing thoroughgoing identities in detail (as opposed to, say, the superficial resemblance of whales and fishes) simply could not be expected. The same objection applies to a milder hypothesis, formulated by the late Franz Weidenreich during the 1940's. Races, he held, descended separately, not from such extremely divergent parents as the several great apes, but from the less-separated lines of fossil men. For example, Peking man led to the Mongoloids, and Rhodesian man to the "Africans." But again there are more marked distinctions between those fossil men than between living races.

Actually the most reasonable—I should say the only reasonable—pattern suggested by animal evolution in general is that of racial divergence within a stock already possessing distinctive features of *Homo sapiens*. As I have indicated, such a stock had appeared at the latest by the beginning of the last glacial advance and almost certainly much earlier, perhaps by the end of the preceding glaciation, which is dated at some 150,000 years ago.

Even if fossil remains were more plentiful than they are, they might not in themselves decide the questions of time and place much more accurately. By the time *Homo sapiens* was common enough to provide a chance of our finding some of his fossil remains, he was probably already sufficiently widespread as to give only a general idea of his "place of origin." Moreover, bones and artifacts may concentrate in misleading places. (Consider the parallel case of the australopithecine "man-apes" known so well from the Lower Pleistocene of South Africa. This area is thought of as their home. In fact the region actually was a geographical *cul-de-sac*, and merely a good fossil trap at that time. It is now clear that such prehumans were widespread not only in Africa but also in Asia. We have no real idea of their first center of dispersion, and we should assume that our earliest knowledge of them is not from the actual dawn of their existence.)

In attempting to fix the emergence

of modern races of man somewhat more precisely we can apply something like the chronological reasoning of the pre-Darwinians. The Upper Paleolithic invaders of Europe (*e.g.*, the Cro-Magnons) mark the definite entrance of *Homo sapiens*, and these men were already stamped with a "White" racial nature at about 35,000 B.C. But a recently discovered skull from Liukiang in China, probably of the same order of age, is definitely not Caucasian, whatever else it may be. And the earliest American fossil men, perhaps 20,000 years old, are recognizable as Indians. No other remains are certainly so old; we cannot now say anything about the first Negroes. Thus racial differences are definitely older than 35,000 years. And yet—this is sheer guess—the more successful *Homo sapiens* would probably have overcome the other human types, such as Neanderthal and Rhodesian men, much earlier if he had reached his full development long before. But these types survived well into the last 50,000 years. So we might assume that *Homo sapiens*, and his earliest racial distinctions, is a product of the period between the last two glaciations, coming into his own early during the last glaciation.

When we try to envisage the causes of racial development, we think today of four factors: natural selection, genetic drift, mutation and mixture (interbreeding). With regard to basic divergence at the level of races, the first two are undoubtedly the chief determinants. If forces of any kind favor individuals of one genetic complexion over others, in the sense that they live and reproduce more successfully, the favored individuals will necessarily increase their bequest of genes to the next generation relative to the rest of the population. That is selection; a force with direction.

Genetic drift is a force without direction, an accidental change in the gene proportions of a population. Other things being equal, some parents just have more offspring than others. If such variations can build up, an originally homogeneous population may split into two different ones by chance. It is somewhat as though there were a sack containing 50 red and 50 white billiard balls, each periodically reproducing itself, say by doubling. Suppose you start a new population, drawing out 50 balls without looking. The most likely single result would be 25 of each color, but it is more likely that you would end up with some other combination, perhaps as extreme as 20 reds and 30 whites. After this population divides, you make a new drawing, and so on. Of course at each

subsequent step the departure from the then-prevailing proportion is as likely to favor red as white. Nevertheless, once the first drawing has been made with the above result, red has the better chance of vanishing. So it is with genes for hereditary traits.

Both drift and selection should have stronger effects the smaller and more isolated the population. It is easy to imagine them in action among bands of ancient men, living close to nature. (It would be a great mistake, however, to imagine that selection is not also effective in modern populations.) Hence we can look upon racial beginnings as part accident, part design, design meaning any pattern of minor change obedient to natural selection.

Darwin was probably right the first time, then, and natural selection is more important in racial adaptation than he himself later came to think. Curiously, however, it is extremely difficult to find demonstrable, or even logically appealing, adaptive advantages in racial features. The two leading examples of adaptation in human physique are not usually considered racial at all. One is the tendency among warm-blooded animals of the same species to be larger in colder parts of their territory. As an animal of a given shape gets larger, its inner bulk increases faster than its outer surface,

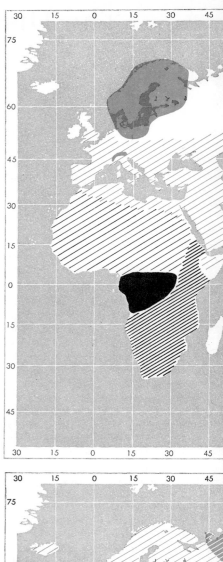

DISTRIBUTION OF MAN and his races in three epochs is depicted in the maps on these and the following two pages. Key to the races appears in legend below. Solid blue areas in map at top represent glaciers. According to available evidence, it is believed that by 8000 B.C. (*map at top*) early Mongoloids had already spread from the Old World to the New World, while late Mongoloids inhabited a large part of northern Asia. Distribution in A.D. 1000 (*map at bottom*) has late Mongoloids dominating Asia, northern Canada and southern Greenland, and early Mongoloids dominating the Americas. The Pygmies and Bushmen of Africa began a decline that has continued up to the present (*see map on next two pages*).

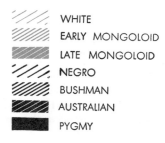

WHITE
EARLY MONGOLOID
LATE MONGOLOID
NEGRO
BUSHMAN
AUSTRALIAN
PYGMY

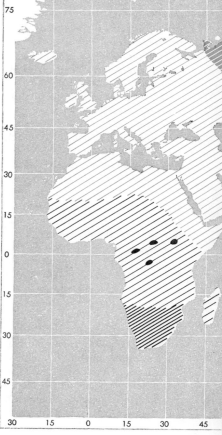

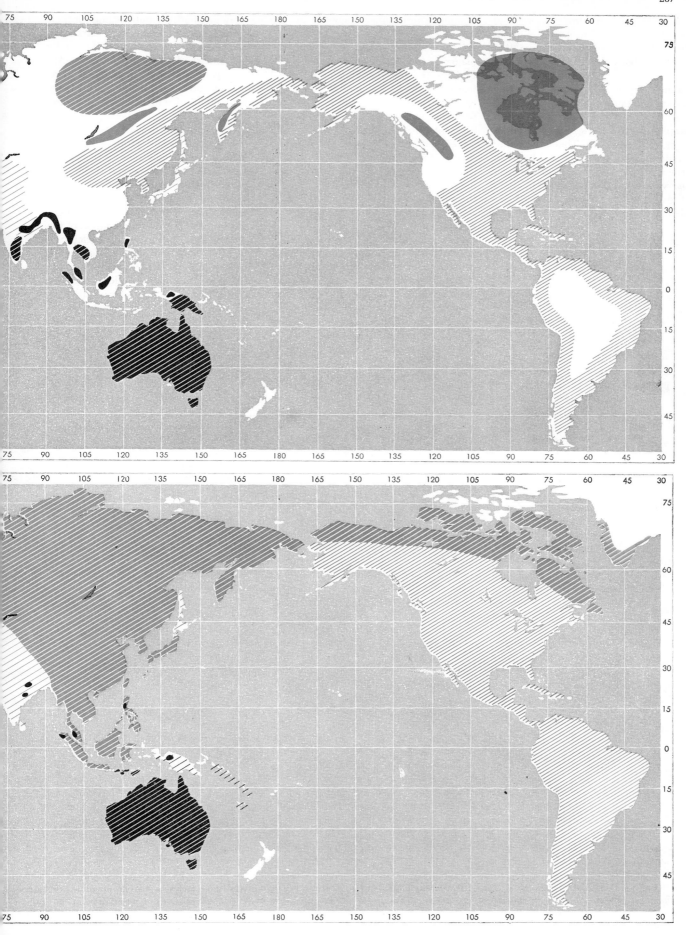

so the ratio of heat produced to heat dissipated is higher in larger individuals. It has, indeed, been shown that the average body weight of man goes up as annual mean temperature goes down, speaking very broadly, and considering those populations that have remained where they are a long time. The second example concerns the size of extremities (limbs, ears, muzzles). They are smaller in colder parts of the range and larger in warmer, for the same basic reason—heat conservation and dissipation. Man obeys this rule also, producing lanky, long-limbed populations in hot deserts and dumpy, short-limbed peoples in the Arctic.

This does not carry us far with the major, historic races as we know them. Perhaps the most striking of all racial features is the dark skin of Negroes. The color of Negro skin is due to a concentration of melanin, the universal human pigment that diffuses sunlight and screens out its damaging ultraviolet component. Does it not seem obvious that in the long course of time the Negroes, living astride the Equator in Africa and in the western Pacific, developed their dark skins as a direct response to a strong sun? It makes sense. It would be folly to deny that such an adaptation is present. But a great deal of the present Negro habitat is shade forest and not bright sun, which is in fact strongest in the deserts some distance north of the Equator. The Pygmies are decidedly forest dwellers, not only in Africa but in their several habitats in southeastern Asia as well.

At any rate there is enough doubt to have called forth other suggestions. One is that forest hunters needed protective coloration, both for stalking and for their protection from predators; dark skin would have lowest visibility in the patchy light and shade beneath the trees. Another is that densely pigmented skins may have other qualities—e.g., resistance to infection—of which we are unaware.

A more straightforward way out of the dilemma is to suppose that the Negroes are actually new to the Congo forest, and that they served their racial apprenticeship hunting and fishing in the sunny grasslands of the southern Sahara. If so, their Pygmy relatives might represent the first accommodation of the race to the forest, before agriculture but after dark skin had been acquired. Smaller size certainly makes a chase after game through the undergrowth less exhausting and faster. As for woolly hair, it is easy to see it (still without proof) as an excellent, nonmatting insulation against solar heat. Thick Negro lips? Every suggestion yet made has a zany sound. They may only be a side effect of some properties of heavily pigmented

- WHITE
- EARLY MONGOLOID
- LATE MONGOLOID
- NEGRO
- BUSHMAN
- AUSTRALIAN
- PYGMY

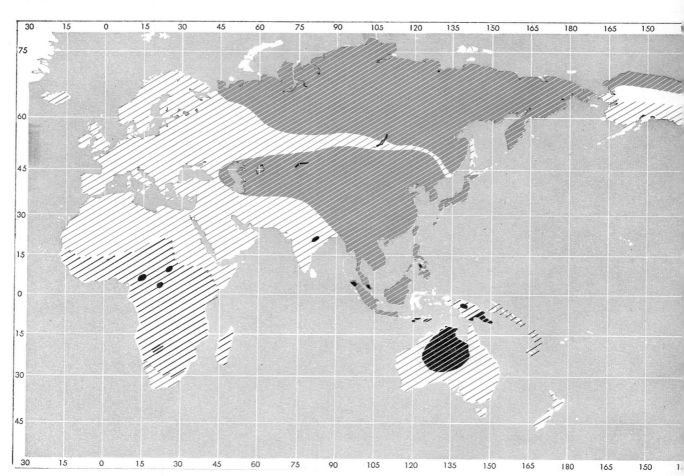

PRESENT DISTRIBUTION OF RACES OF MAN reflects dominance of White, late Mongoloid and Negro races. Diffusion of Whites has been attended by decline of early Mongoloids in America, Bushmen in Africa and indigenous population in Australia.

skin (ability to produce thick scar tissue, for example), even as blond hair is doubtless a side effect of the general depigmentation of men that has occurred in northern Europe.

At some remove racially from Negroes and Pygmies are the Bushmen and Hottentots of southern Africa. They are small, or at least lightly built, with distinctive wide, small, flat faces; they are rather infantile looking, and have a five-cornered skull outline that seems to be an ancient inheritance. Their skin is yellowish-brown, not dark. None of this has been clearly interpreted, although the small size is thought to be an accommodation to water and food economy in the arid environment. The light skin, in an open sunny country, contradicts the sun-pigment theory, and has in fact been used in favor of the protective-coloration hypothesis. Bushmen and background blend beautifully for color, at least as human beings see color.

Bushmen, and especially Hottentots, have another dramatic characteristic:

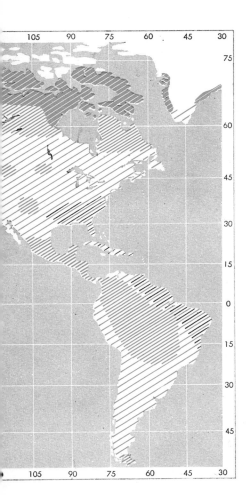

Narrow band of Whites in Asia represents Russian colonization of southern Siberia.

steatopygia. If they are well nourished, the adult women accumulate a surprising quantity of fat on their buttocks. This seems to be a simple storehouse mechanism reminiscent of the camel's hump; a storehouse that is not distributed like a blanket over the torso generally, where it would be disadvantageous in a hot climate. The characteristic nicely demonstrates adaptive selection working in a human racial population.

The Caucasians make the best argument for skin color as an ultraviolet screen. They extend from cloudy northern Europe, where the ultraviolet in the little available sunlight is not only acceptable but desirable, down to the fiercely sun-baked Sahara and peninsular India. All the way, the correspondence with skin color is good: blond around the Baltic, swarthy on the Mediterranean, brunet in Africa and Arabia, dark brown in India. Thus, given a long enough time of occupation, and doubtless some mixture to provide dark-skinned genes in the south, natural selection could well be held responsible.

On the other hand, the Caucasians' straight faces and often prominent noses lack any evident adaptive significance. It is the reverse with the Mongoloids, whose countenances form a coherent pattern that seems consistent with their racial history. From the standpoint of evolution it is Western man, not the Oriental, who is inscrutable. The "almond" eyes of the Mongoloid are deeply set in protective fat-lined lids, the nose and forehead are flattish and the cheeks are broad and fat-padded. In every way, it has been pointed out, this is an ideal mask to protect eyes, nose and sinuses against bitterly cold weather. Such a face is the pole toward which the peoples of eastern Asia point, and it reaches its most marked and uniform expression in the cold northeastern part of the continent, from Korea north.

Theoretically the Mongoloid face developed under intense natural selection some time during the last glacial advance among peoples trapped north of a ring of mountain glaciers and subjected to fierce cold, which would have weeded out the less adapted, in the most classic Darwinian fashion, through pneumonia and sinus infections. If the picture is accurate, this face type is the latest major human adaptation. It could not be very old. For one thing, the population would have had to reach a stage of advanced skill in hunting and living to survive at all in such cold, a stage probably not attained before the Upper Paleolithic (beginning about 35,000 B.C.). For an-

other, the adaptation must have occurred after the American Indians, who are Mongoloid but without the transformed face, migrated across the Bering Strait. (Only the Eskimos reflect the extension of full-fledged, recent Mongoloids into America.) All this suggests a process taking a relatively small number of generations (about 600) between 25,000 and 10,000 B. C.

The discussion so far has treated human beings as though they were any mammal under the influence of natural selection and the other forces of evolution. It says very little about why man invaded the various environments that have shaped him and how he got himself distributed in the way we find him now. For an understanding of these processes we must take into account man's own peculiar abilities. He has created culture, a milieu for action and development that must be added to the simplicities of sun, snow, forest or plain.

Let us go back to the beginning. Man started as an apelike creature, certainly vegetarian, certainly connected with wooded zones, limited like all other primates to tropical or near-tropical regions. In becoming a walker he had begun to extend his range. Tools, social rules and intelligence all progressed together; he learned to form efficient groups, armed with weapons not provided by nature. He started to eat meat, and later to cook it; the more concentrated diet widened his possibilities for using his time; the hunting of animals beckoned him still farther in various directions.

All this was probably accomplished during the small-brained australopithecine stage. It put man on a new plane, with the potential to reach all parts of the earth, and not only those in which he could find food ready to his hand, or be comfortable in his bare skin. He did not actually reach his limits until the end of the last glaciation, and in fact left large tracts empty for most of the period. By then he had become *Homo sapiens*, with a large brain. He had tools keen enough to give him clothes of animal skin. He had invented projectiles to widen the perimeter of his striking power: bolas, javelins with spear throwers, arrows with bows. He was using dogs to widen the perimeter of his senses in tracking. He had found what could be eaten from the sea and its shores. He could move only slowly, and was probably by no means adventurous. But hunting territory was precious, and the surplus of an expanding population had

240

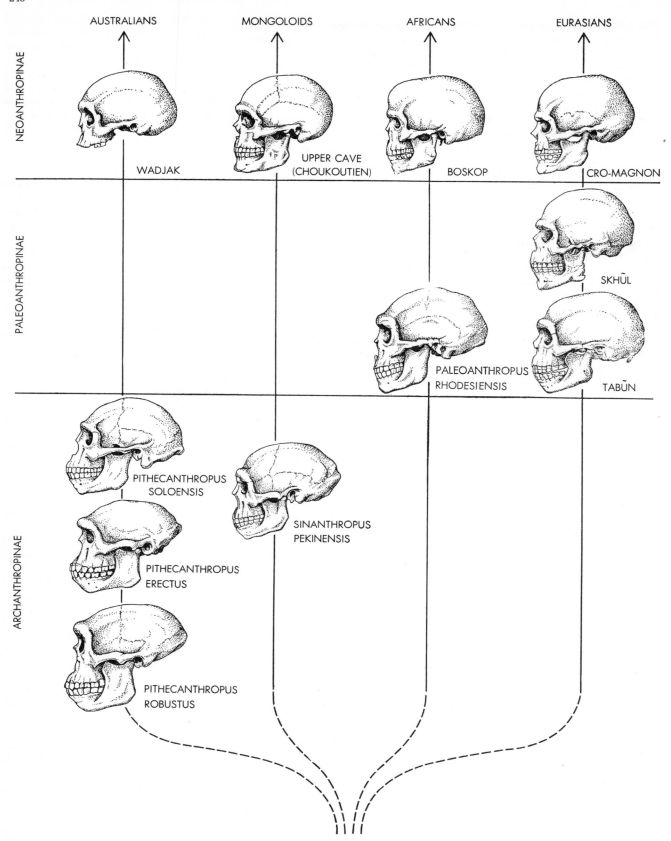

NEOANTHROPINAE

AUSTRALIANS MONGOLOIDS AFRICANS EURASIANS

WADJAK UPPER CAVE (CHOUKOUTIEN) BOSKOP CRO-MAGNON

PALEOANTHROPINAE

SKHŪL

PALEOANTHROPUS RHODESIENSIS TABŪN

ARCHANTHROPINAE

PITHECANTHROPUS SOLOENSIS

PITHECANTHROPUS ERECTUS

SINANTHROPUS PEKINENSIS

PITHECANTHROPUS ROBUSTUS

POLYPHYLETIC SCHOOL of anthropology, chiefly identified with Franz Weidenreich, conceives modern races of man descending from four ancestral lines. According to this school, ancestors of Australians (*left*) include *Pithecanthropus soloensis* (Solo man) and *Pithecanthropus erectus* (Java man). Original ancestor of Mongoloids is *Sinanthropus pekinensis* (Peking man); of Africans, *Paleoanthropus rhodesiensis* (Rhodesian man). Four skulls at top are early *Homo sapiens*. Alternative theory is shown on next page.

to stake out new preserves wherever there was freedom ahead. So this pressure, and man's command of nature, primitive though it still was, sent the hunters of the end of the Ice Age throughout the Old World, out into Australia, up into the far north, over the Bering Strait and down the whole length of the Americas to Tierra del Fuego. At the beginning of this dispersion we have brutes barely able to shape a stone tool; at the end, the wily, self-reliant Eskimo, with his complicated traps, weapons and sledges and his clever hunting tricks.

The great racial radiation carried out by migratory hunters culminated in the world as it was about 10,000 years ago. The Whites occupied Europe, northern and eastern Africa and the Near East, and extended far to the east in Central Asia toward the Pacific shore. Negroes occupied the Sahara, better watered then, and Pygmies the African equatorial forest; south, in the open country, were Bushmen only. Other Pygmies, the Negritos, lived in the forests of much of India and southeastern Asia; while in the open country of these areas and in Australia were men like the present Australian aborigines: brown, beetle-browed and wavy-haired. Most of the Pacific was empty. People such as the American Indians stretched from China and Mongolia over Alaska to the Straits of Magellan; the more strongly Mongoloid peoples had not yet attained their domination of the Far East.

During the whole period the human population had depended on the supply of wild game for food, and the accent had been on relative isolation of peoples and groups. Still close to nature (as we think of nature), man was in a good position for rapid small-scale evolution, both through natural selection and through the operation of chance in causing differences among widely separated tribes even if selection was not strong.

Then opened the Neolithic period, the beginning of a great change. Agriculture was invented, at first inefficient and feeble, but in our day able to feed phenomenally large populations while freeing them from looking for food. The limit on local numbers of people was gradually removed, and with it the necessity for the isolation and spacing of groups and the careful observation of boundaries. Now, as there began to be surpluses available for trading, connections between communities became more useful. Later came a spreading of bonds from higher centers of trade and of authority. Isolation gave way to contact,

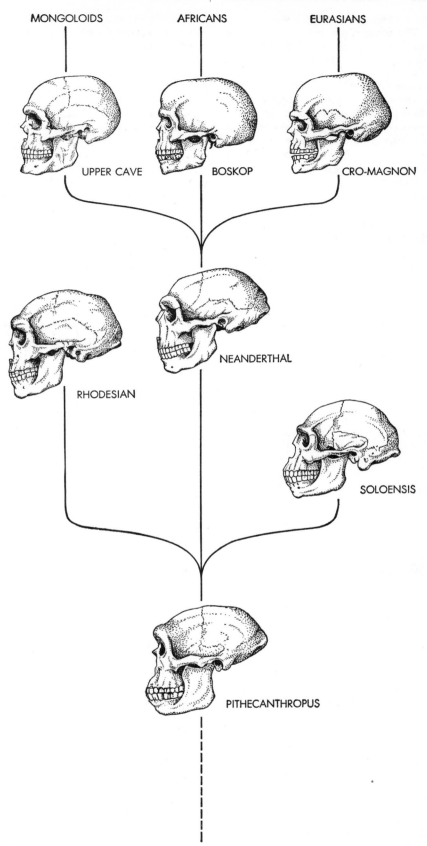

UNILINEAR OR "HAT-RACK" SCHOOL predicates three races descending from single ancestral line, as opposed to polyphyletic theory depicted at left. Rhodesian, Neanderthal and Solo man all descend from *Pithecanthropus*. Neanderthal is ancestor of early *Homo sapiens* (Upper Cave, Boskop and Cro-Magnon) from which modern races descended.

even when contact meant war.

The change was not speedy by our standards, though in comparison with the pace of the Stone Age it seems like a headlong rush. The new economy planted people much more solidly, of course. Farmers have been uprooting and displacing hunters from the time of the first planters to our own day, when Bushman survivors are still losing reservation land to agriculturalists in southwestern Africa. These Bushmen, a scattering of Australian aborigines, the Eskimos and a few other groups are the only representatives of their age still in place. On the other hand, primitive representatives of the Neolithic level of farming still live in many places after the thousands of years since they first became established there.

Nevertheless mobility increased and has increased ever since. Early woodland farmers were partly nomadic, moving every generation following exhaustion of the soil, however solidly fixed they may have been during each sojourn. The Danubians of 6,000 years ago can be traced archeologically as they made the same kind of periodic removes as central Africans, Iroquois Indians and pioneer Yankee farmers. Another side of farming—animal husbandry—gave rise to pastoral nomadism. Herders were much lighter of foot, and historically have tended to be warlike and domineering. With irrigation, villages could settle forever and evolve into the urban centers of high civilizations. Far from immobilizing man, however, these centers served

as fixed bases from which contact (and conflict) worked outward.

The rest of the story is written more clearly. New crops or new agricultural methods opened new territories, such as equatorial Africa, and the great plains of the U. S., never successfully farmed by the Indians. New materials such as copper and tin made places once hopeless for habitation desirable as sources of raw material or as way stations for trade. Thus an island like Crete rose from nothing to dominate the eastern Mediterranean for centuries. Well before the earliest historians had made records, big population shifts were taking place. Our mental picture of the aboriginal world is actually a recent one. The Bantu Negroes moved into central and

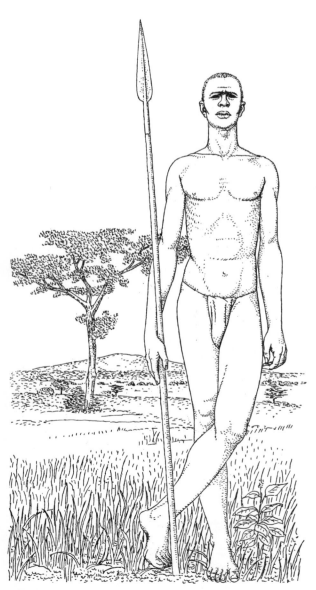

HUMAN ADAPTATION TO CLIMATE is typified by Nilotic Negro of the Sudan (*left*) and arctic Eskimo (*right*). Greater body surface of Negro facilitates dissipation of unneeded body heat; proportionately greater bulk of the Eskimo conserves body heat.

southern Africa, peoples of Mongoloid type went south through China and into Japan, and ancient folk of Negrito and Australoid racial nature were submerged by Caucasians in India. Various interesting but inconsequential trickles also ran hither and yon; for example, the migration of the Polynesians into the far Pacific.

The greatest movement came with the advent of ocean sailing in Europe. (The Polynesians had sailed the high seas earlier, of course, but they had no high culture, nor did Providence interpose a continent across their route at a feasible distance, as it did for Columbus.) The Europeans poured out on the world. From the 15th to the 19th centuries they compelled other civilized peoples to accept contact, and subjected or erased the uncivilized. So today, once again, we have a quite different distribution of mankind from that of 1492.

It seems obvious that we stand at the beginning of still another phase. Contact is immediate, borders are slamming shut and competition is fierce. Biological fitness in races is now hard to trace, and even reproduction is heavily controlled by medicine and by social values. The racial picture of the future will be determined less by natural selection and disease resistances than by success in government and in the adjustment of numbers. The end of direct European dominance in Africa and Asia seems to mean the end of any possibility of the infiltration and expansion of the European variety of man there, on the New World model. History as we know it has been largely the expansion of the European horizon and of European peoples. But the end in China of mere absorption of Occidental invention, and the passionate self-assertion of the African tribes, make it likely that racial lines and territories will again be more sharply drawn than they have been for centuries. What man will make of himself next is a question that lies in the province of prophets, not anthropologists.

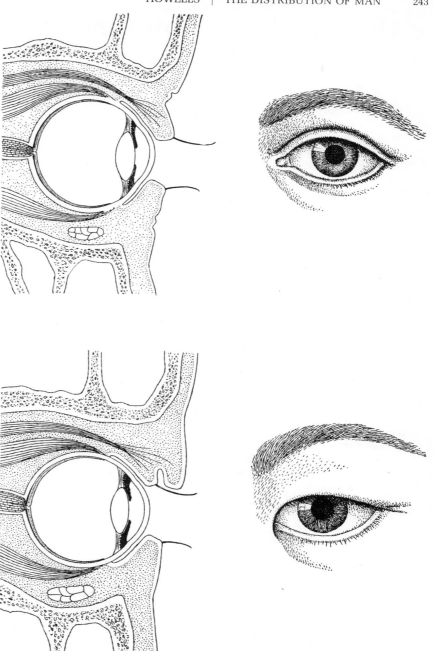

"ALMOND" EYE OF MONGOLOID RACES is among latest major human adaptations to environment. The Mongoloid fold, shown in lower drawings, protects the eye against the severe Asian winter. Drawings at top show the Caucasian eye with its single, fatty lid.

20

The Origin of Races

by Carleton S. Coon

Reviewed by Theodosius Dobzhansky
February 1963

A debatable account of the origin of races

The Origin of Races is an important book. It is also a controversial one. It is important because it provides a detailed and critical review of what is known about fossil man, and in such a way as to create order and a system in a field of study that has traditionally suffered from an accumulation of disconnected and undigested observations. It is the subject of controversy because Professor Coon states some of his conclusions in a way that makes his work susceptible to misuse by racists, white supremacists and other special pleaders. This misuse began even before the book was published, and it is continuing. Some of the points that cause the trouble are rather subtle, and they merit careful consideration and analysis.

Human evolution and human origins are naturally more interesting to most humans than the evolution of other organisms. It is hardly surprising, therefore, that a considerable effort has been made to find the fossil remains of men and their ancestors. Every scrap of bone that is found is studied and described in the minutest detail. Although human fossils are relatively rare, they have been unearthed at dozens of sites distributed over every continent except Antarctica. The remains of several hundred individuals are represented, often, of course, by different parts of the skeleton. The rate of discovery has been so high in recent years that it is not unreasonable to hope that future finds will throw new light on critical chapters in the story of human evolution. Of the 724 pages in Professor Coon's book, 438 (chapters 7 through 12) are devoted to a painstaking description of the available hominid fossils. This is unquestionably the most valuable part of the book; no other work in English, nor as far as I know any in another language, gives as complete and up-to-date an account of the matter. The introductory chapters (1 through 6)

outline the principles of the theory of evolution, particularly as it applies to man, and review briefly the living and fossil primates and man's relation to them. A short 13th chapter summarizes the conclusions. Professor Coon is an experienced and clear writer; the bones he describes may be as dry as dust, but his account of them is so engrossing that the interest of the reader will not flag.

The interest of humans in human evolution is not, however, an unadulterated blessing. Investigators working in this field are often tempted to draw from the bones they study conclusions that these scraps of evidence cannot really support. One difficulty, which at first might seem unimportant, is that the discoverers of hominid fossils like to give to their finds generic and specific names in Latin. The name *Pithecanthropus erectus* is assigned to fossils found in Java; *Sinanthropus pekinensis,* to those found in the vicinity of Peking. Did the Java and Peking men belong to different zoological genera and species? Not at all; judging from their bones they differed only about as much as do some of the races of men now living. Neanderthal man has been assigned to the separate species *Homo neanderthalensis,* and on occasion even to a separate genus, *Protanthropus neanderthalensis.* On the basis of Latin names it appears that there existed some two dozen hominid species and genera during the geologically rather short Pleistocene epoch.

Does it really matter what Latin name one bestows on a fossil? Unfortunately it does. It flatters the discoverer's ego to have found a new hominid genus, or at least a new species, rather than a mere new race. But generic and specific names are not just arbitrary labels; they imply a biological status. Living men constitute a single species: *Homo sapiens.* Now, *Homo sapiens* can be descended from only one ancestral species living at any

given time in the past. To be sure, some plant species arise from the hybridization of two ancestral species, followed by a doubling of the complement of chromosomes, but it is most unlikely that mankind could have arisen by such a process. It follows, then, that if two or several hominid species lived at a given time in the past, only one of them can possibly be our ancestor. All other species must be assumed to have died out without leaving descendants.

This creates an issue that for years was quite troublesome to students of human origins. Consider, for example, the fact that in Europe some 30,000 years ago Neanderthal man was replaced by men whose bones so closely resemble our own that almost all authorities consider them a race of *Homo sapiens.* If the Neanderthalers belonged to a really different species, they were probably wiped out by *Homo sapiens.* If, however, this was an early episode of genocide, where did the invading *Homo sapiens* come from? The rest of the world was at that time, and in earlier times, inhabited by hominids with other specific or generic names. There are similar puzzles to be found in other parts of the world; to give just one more example, what happened to Peking man, and where did the ancestors of the present inhabitants of eastern Asia come from?

A solution to these puzzles was suggested about two decades ago by the eminent human anatomist and paleontologist Franz Weidenreich. He realized that, in spite of the riot of Latin names given to the fossils, the world was inhabited, at least since the middle Pleistocene, by only one human or prehuman species at any one time. Our middle Pleistocene ancestors all belonged to a species that we may call *Homo erectus.* In time this species was gradually transformed into *Homo sapiens.* Weidenreich's solution seemed rather too radical to some authorities, but it was accepted by Professor Coon and others, including this reviewer. Coon has acknowledged Weidenreich's contribution by dedicating his book to Weidenreich's memory.

As so often happens in science, the solving of one problem opens up several new ones. Living men are a single species, but men in different parts of the world are not alike. Most biological species are composed of races, and *Homo sapiens* is no exception. Even though *Homo erectus* inhabited a much smaller territory than *Homo sapiens* (for example, it did not colonize the New World), there were also races of *Homo erectus*. Two of these races have been mentioned above: *Homo erectus erectus* of Java and *Homo erectus pekinensis* of China. In comparing the races of *erectus* with those of *sapiens* Weidenreich noted that the bones of Java man have some features in common with those of modern Australoids, and that Peking man shares some skeletal traits with Mongoloids. Weidenreich's idea has been developed much further by Coon. It is, in fact, pivotal to his interpretation of human evolution as presented in his book. This interpretation may well be right, although it is certainly not proved, and specialists will dispute him on many of its points. What is important is how he states it.

Coon divides living *Homo sapiens* into five races, or "subspecies": Australoids, Mongoloids, Caucasoids, Congoids (African Negroes) and Capoids (Bushmen and Hottentots). He thinks that these races have existed for a very long time; indeed, he believes that some of their skeletal traits were present in the races of the ancestral species *Homo erectus*. Following Weidenreich, Coon connects the Australoid race of *sapiens* with the Java race of *erectus* and the Mongoloid race with the race *erectus pekinensis;* similarly, the Caucasoid race of *sapiens* is linked to a European form of *erectus* and to the early Neanderthalers, and the Congoid race to the Rhodesian man, who becomes *Homo erectus rhodesiensis.*

So far so good. Now, however, Coon says: "*Homo erectus* then evolved into *Homo sapiens* not once but five times, as each subspecies, living in its own territory, passed a critical threshold from a more brutal to a more *sapient* state." Moreover, they passed this "threshold" at different times, the Caucasoid race becoming *sapiens* first, during the second interglacial period, whereas the Congoids arrived in the *sapiens* fold some 200,000 years later, or only 40,000 to 50,000 years ago. At this point Coon leaps straight from bones to culture. To him it is "a fair inference that fossil men now extinct were less gifted than their descendants who have larger brains, that the subspecies which crossed the evolutionary threshold into the category of *Homo sapiens* the earliest have evolved the most, and that the obvious correlation between the length of time a subspecies has been in the *sapiens* state and the levels of civilization attained by some of its populations may be related phenomena." He relents somewhat on the last page of the book and points out that until recently all five "subspecies" of *Homo sapiens* included some populations living as hunters and gatherers, and that some of the most backward populations belonged to the putatively advanced Mongoloid and Caucasoid subspecies.

Can these sweeping conclusions be sustained? The arguments in favor of the view that there were exactly five races of *Homo erectus* and that there are exactly five living races of *Homo sapiens* are not convincing, let alone conclusive. A race is an entity that is not clearly defined biologically. The number of races of living men has been set by different anthropologists anywhere from two to more than 200. In a book published by Coon jointly with Stanley M. Garn and Joseph B. Birdsell in 1950 the number of "racial stocks" is given as 30. In a more recent book Garn recognizes nine "geographical races" and 32 "local races." As noted above, Coon calls his five races "subspecies." This is a term used in zoological systematics but not in anthropological; however, a subspecies is merely a race given a name in Latin in accordance with the rules of zoological nomenclature. It is biologically no more and no less clearly defined. The fivefold division encounters just as many difficulties as all the others; for example, Coon places the Polynesians in his Mongoloid subspecies and the Melanesians in his Australoid, a far from convincing arrangement. When it comes to *Homo erectus,* the basis for assuming five subspecies is flimsy in the extreme.

Let us suppose, for the sake of argument, that *Homo sapiens* consists of exactly five subspecies, and that there were just five subspecies of *Homo erectus.* What, then, is the meaning of the claim that *erectus* evolved into *sapiens* not once but five times? Coon's interpretation is, as he acknowledges, an extension of that of Weidenreich. But this is not a matter of priority; it is something more important. Weidenreich was an adherent of the theory of orthogenesis, according to which evolutionary changes are directed from within the organism by a sort of inner urge. To Weidenreich the name *Homo erectus* stood for a stage in the evolutionary progression of the hominid stock; a race of *erectus*, if it survived at all, was predestined to evolve into *sapiens*. Today most evolutionists consider the theory of orthogenesis obsolete. Coon, in the second and third chapters of his book, interprets the evolutionary development of the human stock in terms of the modern biological theory of evolution. Evolution is not orthogenesis; the directing agency of evolution is natural selection, which makes a living species respond to the challenges of its environment by genetic modifications. The independent but parallel development of five separate lines into a single species is no less puzzling than the old "*sapiens* problem," which arose, as we have seen, because the discoverers of human fossils were overgenerous in assigning generic and specific names.

It *is* a fair inference that *Homo sapiens* is genetically better adapted to human ways of life than *Homo erectus* was. We can agree with Coon that natural selection has favored, in human races everywhere in the world, a *sapiens*-like genotype over the *erectus*-like one. This can be stated most clearly as follows. The transformation of prehuman populations into human populations involved a feedback process between the genotype and the environment; *sapiens* genes favored the development of capacities for symbolic thinking, language and eventually for civilization. These human adaptations in turn made human genes essential for survival and opened the way for further adaptations.

The possibility that the genetic system of living men, *Homo sapiens,* could have independently arisen five times, or even twice, is vanishingly small. A biological species can be likened to a cable consisting of many strands; the strands—populations, tribes and races—may in the course of time subdivide, branch or fuse; some of them may fade away and others may become more vigorous and multiply. It is, however, the whole species that is eventually transformed into a new species. Adaptively valuable gene patterns arise in different populations of the species. The populations, or races, in which these evolutionary inventions have occurred then increase in number, spread, come in contact with other populations, hybridize with them, form superior new gene patterns that spread from new centers and thus continue the process of change. Coon is too competent an anthropologist not to know that man is, and apparently always was, a wanderer and a colonizer, and that as people come in contact gene exchange takes place. But if this is true, the assumed separate evolution of the five subspecies becomes a practical impossibility. Coon believes that the ancestors of his Capoid race lived in Africa somewhere to the north of the ancestors of the Congoid race. At present the Capoids live to the south of the Congoids. Are we to assume that these peoples practiced racial segregation during their wanderings?

Organizations engaged in propaganda against the desegregation decision of the Supreme Court have seized on the supposed demonstration that Negroes are some 200,000 years behind the whites in their evolutionary development. What Coon himself says is that some of his subspecies, particularly the Caucasoid and the Mongoloid, ceased to be *Homo erectus* and became *Homo sapiens* much earlier than the other subspecies. He does not, however, contend that the transition from *erectus* to *sapiens* was sudden or instantaneous. Assigning a date to this transition is therefore a ticklish task. Since the transition was gradual, cutting a continuous process into two or more sections called "species" is arbitrary. Coon so chooses his criteria for the application of the names *erectus* and *sapiens* that the latter appears to be much more ancient in Europe than it is in Africa. Other anthropologists will dispute his choices. For example, the fossils of Solo man in Java and of Broken Hill man in Africa are classified by Coon as *erectus*, whereas others classify them as *sapiens*. These remains are geologically rather recent, which in Coon's view indicates that the transition from *erectus* to *sapiens* occurred much later in Java

and in Africa than it did in Europe. Coon seems not to notice that this leads him into a major inconsistency. His classification makes *Homo erectus* contemporaneous with *Homo sapiens* for some 200,000 years, although the two lived in different parts of the world. The division of an evolutionary line into species succeeding each other in time is arbitrary, but the division of contemporaneous forms into species is not. If *erectus* lived at the same time as *sapiens*, it must have been genetically isolated from *sapiens*. Yet its modern descendants are not genetically isolated; they belong to the same species. For a single species to have arisen from two species that could not interbreed would indeed be extraordinary.

Attempts to assign dates to *Homo erectus'* becoming *Homo sapiens* in Europe, in Africa or elsewhere are misleading in another respect. The transmutation of *erectus* into *sapiens* is not like receiving an academic degree or being admitted to an exclusive club. One basic consideration that should always be kept in mind is that evolution is a continuous process. Suppose the skeletal characteristics that are chosen as being characteristic of *erectus* make us label the bones of an individual who lived in Africa 40,000 years ago as belonging to that species. It surely does not follow that this *erectus* resembled in every respect, including its mental capacities, all other members of the species that lived in Europe and elsewhere at much earlier times. If it were true that the Caucasoids 200,000 years ago attained the state that the Congoids achieved only 40,000 years ago, would it not follow that the rate of the evolutionary development of the Congoids was since then

about five times faster than that of the Caucasoids? This is surely not a conclusion that white supremacists would embrace with pleasure.

Professor Coon's book will stand as a milestone in the study of fossil man. Specialists will dispute many of his interpretations of particular fossils, and new discoveries will almost certainly change many parts of the picture. But after Coon the hodgepodge of species and genera of fossil hominids will give way to a biologically more meaningful system. Mankind is and was, at least from the middle Pleistocene to the present time, a single polytypic species consisting of varying numbers of races of varying degrees of distinctness. It is most unfortunate that some semantic mischief in Coon's work has made it usable as grist for racist mills. A scientist should not and cannot eschew studies on the racial differentiation of mankind, or examine all possible hypotheses about it, for fear that his work will be misused. But neither can he disclaim all responsibility for such misuses. Scientists living in ivory towers are quaint relics of a bygone age. The work and writing of scientists is used, and anthropology—the science of man—is particularly vulnerable to misuse. Race prejudice is a psychological and social disease and is not based on reason, yet those who suffer from it have repeatedly sought the support of bogus "science." There are absolutely no findings in Coon's book that even suggest that some human races are superior or inferior to others in their capacity for culture or civilization. There are, however, some unfortunate misstatements that are susceptible to such misinterpretation.

LETTERS TO THE EDITOR
April 1963

Sirs:

In commenting on Dobzhansky's review of my book, *The Origin of Races,* in the February *Scientific American,* space does not allow me to answer him point by point. I shall ignore his dislike of my style and his godlike strictures—unbecoming to a scientist—about the immorality of telling the truth and shall concentrate my remarks on a few key points.

Had he read my first chapter carefully he would have seen that I discussed the problem of peripheral gene flow as being a mechanism of transforming, from one population to another, the critical genetic innovation that gradually transferred *Homo erectus* into *Homo sapiens.* I consider it very likely that this is exactly what happened, and said so. However, not being a professional geneticist, I am not so sure of it as he is, nor am I sure that all similar phenotypical effects can be attributed to the same gene locus, or that we really know the mutation rates of all racially important changes.

But I am, as he is not, a physical anthropologist of 40 years' experience, and I consider his rejection, without detail, of my criteria of grades and lines as being professionally incompetent.

Dobzhansky challenges the idea that a population bearing genes for the *sapiens* condition could interbreed with one lacking them, but he admits that anagenesis is a continuous process. Paleontology provides no evidence to support his view. Dobzhansky seems to be thinking of cladogenetically differentiated, contemporaneous species, which

is all that a laboratory geneticist has to work with. That is an entirely different kettle of fish from a genetic sequence in time. Furthermore, he seems not to have realized that nearly all, if not all, the differences between *Homo erectus* and *Homo sapiens* could have been produced by minor changes in endocrine balance and in the growth sequence, changes that would have required relatively little chromosomal innovation.

As for the lag in time between the races in crossing the *erectus-sapiens* threshold, Dobzhansky should note that, unlike his fruit flies, human beings do not mate at random but are kept apart to a large extent and quite effectively by cultural barriers such as language and religion, and by such other customs as feelings about integration and segregation. These cultural roadblocks help geography to prolong periods of separation and impede, but do not prevent, gene flow.

CARLETON S. COON

West Gloucester, Mass.

Sirs:

Far from disliking Dr. Coon's style of writing, I find it admirable. The fact I have felt compelled to point out is that Dr. Coon uses his writing ability in such a way that his book is being utilized by racists in support of their propaganda. Dr. Coon has not seen fit to disavow these misuses of his book. If, on the other hand, his book is being used with his consent, he should have the courage to

say so openly. A scientist cannot assume a pose of disdain and unconcern when what he believes to be truth is being misrepresented. There is no need for me to criticize in detail his criteria for delimiting what he calls *Homo sapiens* and *Homo erectus* because, first, this is too technical a matter for a review such as mine and, second, because this has been done by anthropologists who are Coon's peers in professional competence. His belief that *sapiens* evolved from *erectus* five times independently involves, however, a serious misconception of the mechanisms of evolution. And, contrary to Coon, this misconception happens to be particularly serious exactly because human evolution involved a combination of anagenesis and cladogenesis, with a predominance of the former. Neither humans nor, I can assure Dr. Coon, fruit flies mate at random. Human culture and human mobility may not only impede but also promote the gene flow. If, as Dr. Coon seems to suggest, *erectus* differed from *sapiens* in only one or a few genes, then they were not different species at all; it is far more likely that the transition from *erectus* to *sapiens* involved rebuilding of the whole genetic system, and if so, this transition could not have happened five times independently. It is chiefly this misconception that opens Dr. Coon's work to misuse for racist propaganda.

THEODOSIUS DOBZHANSKY

The Rockefeller Institute
New York, N.Y.

Intelligence and Race

21

October 1970

Do the differences in I.Q. scores between blacks and whites have a genetic basis? Two geneticists, reviewing the evidence, suggest that the question cannot be answered in present circumstances

To what extent might behavioral differences between social classes and between races be genetically determined? This question is often discussed, although generally not at a scientific level. Recently attention has been focused on the average differences in intelligence, as measured by I.Q., between black and white Americans by the educational psychologist Arthur R. Jensen and the physicist William Shockley. We are geneticists who are interested in the study of the interaction between heredity and environment. Our aim in this article is to review, mainly for the nongeneticist, the meaning of race and I.Q. and the approaches to determining the extent to which I.Q. is inherited. Such a review can act as a basis for the objective assessment of the evidence for a genetic component in race and class I.Q. differences.

We should first define what we mean by terms such as "heredity," "intelligence" and "race." Heredity refers to those characteristics of an individual that are inherited from past generations. The primary functional unit of heredity is the gene. The human genome—the complete set of genes in an individual—consists of perhaps as many as 10 million genes. Some of these genes and their expression can now be analyzed at the biochemical level. Complex behavioral traits such as intelligence, however, are most probably influenced by the combined action of many genes. The inheritance of differences known to be deter-

mined by one gene or a few genes can be reliably predicted, but the tools for dealing with the inheritance of more complex characteristics are still relatively ineffective.

What is intelligence? A rigorous, objective definition of such a complicated characteristic is not easy to give, but for the purposes of this discussion one can focus on qualities that can actually be observed and measured. One instrument of measurement for intelligence is a test such as the Stanford-Binet procedure. Such a test is devised to measure a capacity to learn or, more generally, the capacity to benefit from experience.

Intelligence tests are based on the solution of brief problems of various kinds and on the response to simple questions. The total score is standardized for a given age by comparing it with the values of a large sample of a given reference population (such as native-born American whites). The final standardized score, which is called the intelligence quotient, is usually computed so that it is given on a scale for which the average of the reference population is 100, and for which the spread is such that about 70 percent of the individuals have I.Q.'s in the range of 85 to 115 and 5 percent have I.Q.'s either below 70 or above 130 (corresponding to a standard deviation of about 15 points).

The Stanford-Binet test and other procedures yield results that correspond

reasonably well to one another. More ambitious attempts have been made to measure the "general intelligence factor." There is a tendency among the more optimistic psychologists to consider such tests as measuring an "innate" or potential ability. Any given test, however, depends on the ability acquired at a given age, which is inevitably the result of the combination of innate ability and the experience of the subject. Intelligence tests are therefore at most tests of achieved ability.

This limitation is confirmed by the dependence of all intelligence tests on the particular culture of the people they are designed to test. The transfer of tests to cultures different from the one for which they were designed is usually difficult, and sometimes it is impossible. Attempts to design tests that are genuinely "culture-free" have so far failed.

A check on the usefulness of I.Q. measurements is provided by examining their reliability (equivalent to short-term consistency), their stability (equivalent to long-term consistency) and their validity. For the Stanford-Binet test the average difference between repeat tests after a short time interval ranges from 5.9 points at an I.Q. of 130 to 2.5 for I.Q.'s below 70, indicating a fairly high reproducibility. The long-term consistency of the test is less impressive, particularly if the age at the first test is lower than five or six. Repetitions of testing after a period of years may show large discrepancies (up to 20 to 30 I.Q. points), and these differences increase with the number of years between tests.

There is at present no definition of intelligence that is precise enough to answer questions of validity in general terms. The validity of a particular test must therefore be related to its predictive aims. If the aim is to predict future school performance, then the validity is measured by how well I.Q. predicts that performance. The prediction will be on a probability basis, meaning that a higher I.Q. will usually but not always be associated with better school performance. There is, in fact, fairly general agreement that there is a high correlation between intelligence tests and success in school. The same is true for success in jobs and, in general, in society. I.Q. tests do have some predictive value on a probability basis, although this is limited to performance in contemporary American and European society. In this sense I.Q. tests do have some validity.

Races are subgroups that emerge within the same species. Like other species, the human species is made up of individuals whose genetic composition is so similar that in principle any male can mate with any female and give rise to fertile progeny. In the course of evolution this highly mobile species has spread over the entire surface of the earth. Even today, however, most individuals live out their lives within a small area. This pattern, together with geographic and other barriers, leads to considerable reproductive isolation of groups living in different regions.

Ecological factors, such as geology, climate and flora and fauna, may differ widely in the different habitats of a species. Natural selection, that is, the preferential survival and reproduction of individuals better fitted to their local environment, inevitably creates differences among these somewhat localized groups. In addition the isolation of one group from another allows differences to arise by the random sampling to which genes are subject from generation to generation; this process results in what is called random genetic drift.

Isolated subgroups of the same species therefore tend to differentiate. The process is a slow one: hundreds—more probably thousands—of generations may be necessary for biological differences to become easily noticeable. When sufficient time has elapsed for the differences to become obvious, we call the subgroups races.

In man biological differentiation is usually accompanied or preceded by cultural differentiation, which is a much faster process than biological evolution. The two kinds of differentiation inevitably interact. Cultural differences may contribute to perpetuation of the geographic barriers that lead to reproductive isolation. For example, religious differences may promote reproductive isolation. In the U.S. differences in skin color, which reflect biological differentiation, usually reduce the chances of marriage between groups. This effect, however, is probably a direct psychological consequence not of the difference in skin color but of the parallel cultural divergence.

The relative contributions of biological and cultural factors to complex characteristics such as behavioral differences, including those that distinguish one race from another, are exceedingly difficult to identify. In this connection it is instructive to consider characteristics in which differences can easily be attributed to biological factors. It is clear, for example, that differences in skin color are mostly biological. There is a predominantly nongenetic factor—tanning—that operates during the life of an individual; it is a short-term physiological adaptation and is generally reversible. Apart from this adaptation, most of the differences in skin color both within and among races are genetic.

There are many differences among individuals that are totally under genetic control, that is, they are not subject to even the small physiological adaptation mentioned for skin color. These genetic differences are called genetic polymorphisms when the alternative versions of the genes determining them each occur within a population with a substantial frequency. Such genetic traits are generally detected by chemical or immunological tests, as in the case of the "blood groups." (There are three genes, A, B and O, that determine the ABO blood type.)

The frequencies of polymorphic genes vary widely among races. For example, in Oriental populations the frequencies of the A, B and O genes are respectively 49 percent, 18 percent and 65 percent; in Caucasian populations they are 29 percent, 4 percent and 68 percent. Such polymorphisms are a valuable aid in understanding the nature and magnitude of the biological similarities and differences among races, since they show what kinds of factor can be due solely to heredity. The inheritance of the more conspicuous face and body traits, however, is complex and not well understood, which decreases their value for the biological study of races.

The analysis of genetic polymorphisms demonstrates three very important features of the nature and extent of genetic variation within and among races. First, the extent of variation with-

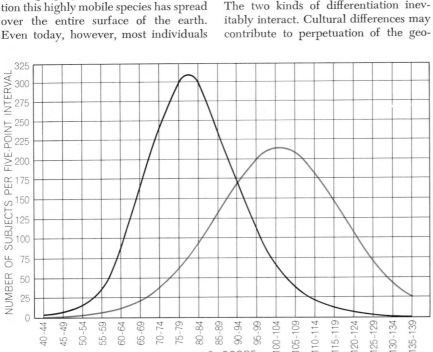

I.Q. DIFFERENCE BETWEEN U.S. BLACKS AND WHITES emerges from a comparison of the I.Q. distribution in a representative sample of whites (*colored curve*) with the I.Q. distribution among 1,800 black children in the schools of Alabama, Florida, Georgia, Tennessee and South Carolina (*black curve*). Wallace A. Kennedy of Florida State University, who surveyed the students' I.Q., found that the mean I.Q. of this group was 80.7. The mean I.Q. of the white sample is 101.8, a difference of 21.1 points. The two samples overlap distinctly, but there is also a sizable difference between the two means. Other studies show a difference of 10 to 20 points, making Kennedy's result one of the most extreme reported.

in any population generally far exceeds the average differences between populations. Second, the differences between populations and races are mostly measured by differences in the relative frequencies of a given set of genes rather than by qualitative differences as to which gene is present in any particular population. Thus any given genetic combination may be found in almost any race, but the frequency with which it is found will vary from one race to another. Third, the variation from race to race is mostly not sharp but may be almost continuous at the boundaries between races. This is the consequence of hybridization's occurring continuously at these boundaries in spite of isolation, or of the formation of hybrid groups by recent migration followed by the more complete mixing of formerly isolated groups.

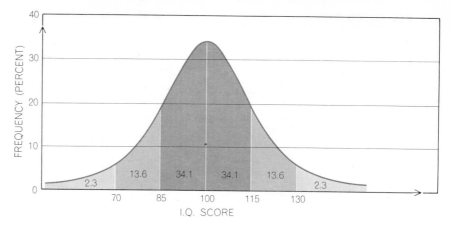

NORMAL DISTRIBUTION OF I.Q. for a population whose mean is 100 is shown by curve. The standard deviation, that is, the usual measure of variation, is about 15 points and the distance in either direction from this mean is measured in multiples of the standard deviation. Thus about 34 percent have an I.Q. with a value that lies between 85 and 100, another 34 percent of the population have an I.Q. score of 100 to 115 points (*dark color*). Those with very high or low scores are a smaller part of population: about 2 percent have an I.Q. below 70, whereas another 2 percent have an I.Q. above 130 (*light color*).

As we have noted, intelligence must be a complex characteristic under the control of many genes. Extreme deviations from normal levels, as in cases of severe mental retardation, can, however, be attributed to single gene differences. Such deviations can serve to illustrate important ways in which genetic factors can affect behavior. Consider the disease phenylketonuria. Individuals with this disease receive from both of their parents a mutated version of the gene controlling the enzyme that converts one amino acid, phenylalanine, into another, tyrosine. That gene allows phenylalanine to accumulate in the blood and in the brain, causing mental retardation. The accumulation can be checked early in life by a diet deficient in phenylalanine.

The difference between the amounts of phenylalanine in the blood of people with phenylketonuria and that in the blood of normal people, which is closely related to the primary activity of the gene causing phenylketonuria, clearly creates two genetic classes of individuals [*see bottom illustration on next page*]. When such differences are compared with differences in I.Q., there is a slight overlap, but individuals afflicted with phenylketonuria can be distinguished clearly from normal individuals. This simply reflects the fact that the phenylketonuric genotype, that is, the genetic constitution that leads to phenylketonuria, is associated with extreme mental retardation. If differences in head size and hair color in phenylketonuric individuals and normal individuals are compared, however, they show a considerable overlap. Although it can be said that the phenylketonuric genotype has

on the average a significant effect on both head size and hair color, measurements of these characteristics cannot be used to distinguish the phenylketonuric genotype from the normal one. The reason is that the variation of head size and hair color is large compared with the average difference. Thus the genetic difference between phenylketonuric and normal individuals contributes in a major way to the variation in blood phenylalanine levels but has only a minor, although significant, effect on head size and hair color.

The phenylketonuric genotype is very rare, occurring with a frequency of only about one individual in 10,000. It therefore has little effect on the overall distribution of I.Q. in the population. It is now known, however, that a large fraction of all genes are polymorphic. Among the polymorphic genes must be included many whose effect on I.Q. is comparable to the effect of the phenylketonuric genotype on head size or hair color. These genotype differences cannot be individually identified, but their total effect on the variation of I.Q. may be considerable.

The nature of phenylketonuria demonstrates another important point: The expression of a gene is profoundly influenced by environment. Phenylketonuric individuals show appreciable variation. This indicates that the genetic difference involved in phenylketonuria is by no means the only factor, or even the major factor, affecting the level of phenylalanine in the blood. It is obvious that dietary differences have a large effect, since a phenylalanine-deficient diet

brings the level of this amino acid in the blood of a phenylketonuric individual almost down to normal. If an individual receives the phenylketonuric gene from only one parent, his mental development is not likely to be clinically affected. Nevertheless, he will tend to have higher than normal levels of phenylalanine in his blood. The overall variation in phenylalanine level is therefore the result of a combination of genetic factors and environmental factors. Measuring the relative contribution of genetic factors to the overall variation is thus equivalent to measuring the relative importance of genetic differences in determining this type of quantitative variation.

When we turn to the analysis of a complex characteristic such as I.Q., which is influenced by many genes each contributing on the average a small effect, we can expect the characteristic to be even more strongly affected by the previous history of the individual and by a host of other external, nongenetic or in any case unrelated factors, which can together be called the "environment." It is necessary to resort to statistical analysis in order to separate the effects of these various factors. Consider an experiment of nature that allows the separation, at least roughly, of environmental factors from genetic factors. This is the occurrence of two types of twins: twins that are "identical," or monozygous (derived from only a single zygote, or fertilized egg, and therefore genetically identical), and twins that are "fraternal," or dizygous (derived from two separate zygotes and therefore genetically different).

Clearly the difference between the

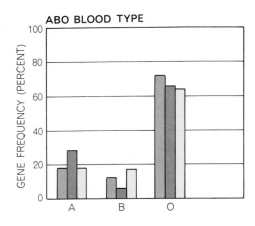
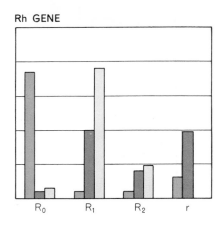
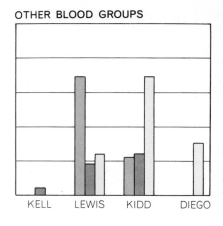

FREQUENCIES OF POLYMORPHIC GENES among Africans, Caucasians and Orientals provide a means of differentiating these three races. (A polymorphic gene is one of a group that accounts for variability in a particular characteristic.) About half of the

two members of a monozygous pair is determined only by environmental factors. It would seem that the distribution of such differences among a number of pairs might tell us how much two individuals can differ because of environmental factors alone. The members of monozygous pairs do not generally have identical I.Q.'s. The members of a given twin pair can differ by as much as 20 I.Q. points, although in the majority of cases they differ by less than 10. Hence environmental differences can have an effect on I.Q. whose average magnitude is comparable to, or slightly larger than, the difference between the I.Q. scores of the same individual who has been tested more than once over a period of time.

To see whether or not, and if so to what extent, genetic differences are found, we turn to dizygous twins. Here we know that in addition to the environment genetic factors also play a role in differentiating the members of a pair. The differences in I.Q. among dizygous pairs show a greater spread than those among monozygous pairs, indicating

that the addition of genetic diversity to the purely environmental factors increases, on the average, the overall difference between members of a pair. Hence genetic factors that can contribute to the differentiation of I.Q.'s also exist among normal individuals.

It might seem that the twin data could easily provide a measure of the relative importance of genetic variation and environmental variation. A comparison of the average difference between the members of a monozygous pair and the average difference between the members of a dizygous pair should be a good index of the comparative importance of genetic factors and environmental ones. (A minor technical point should be mentioned here. As is customary in all modern statistical analysis, it is better to consider not the mean of the differences but the mean of their squares. This is comparable to, and can easily be transformed into, a "variance," which is a well-known measure of variation.)

There are two major contrasting reasons why such a simple measure is not entirely satisfactory. First, the difference

between members of a dizygous pair represents only a fraction of the genetic differences that can exist between two individuals. Dizygous twins are related to each other as two siblings are; therefore they are more closely related than two individuals taken at random from a population. This implies a substantial reduction (roughly by a factor of two) in the average genetic difference between dizygous twins compared with that between two randomly chosen individuals. Second, the environmental difference between members of a pair of twins encompasses only a fraction of the total environmental difference that can exist between two individuals, namely the difference between individuals belonging to the same family. This does not take into account differences among families, which are likely to be large. Within the family the environmental differences between twins are limited. For instance, the effect of birth order is not taken into account. Differences between ordinary siblings might therefore tend to be slightly greater than those between dizygous twins. It also seems possible

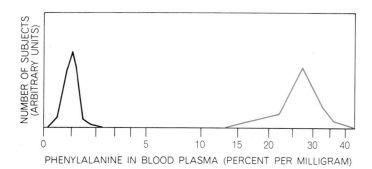
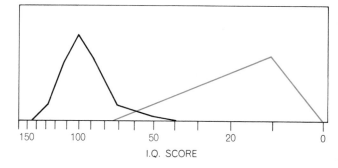

PHENYLALANINE LEVELS in blood plasma shown in first set of curves at left distinguish those who carry a double dose of the defective gene that causes high phenylalanine levels (*colored curve*), a condition called phenylketonuria, from those with normal phenylalanine levels (*dark curve*). Second set of curves shows

that this genotype has a direct effect on intelligence: phenylketonurics (*colored curve*) have low I.Q.'s because accumulation of phenylalanine and its by-products in blood and nerve tissue damages the brain. Individuals with functioning gene (*dark curve*) have normal I.Q.'s. In the third set phenylalanine levels are related

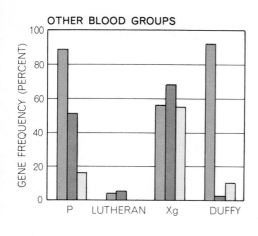

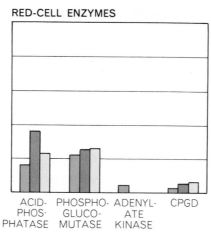

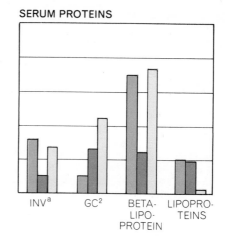

OTHER BLOOD GROUPS   RED-CELL ENZYMES   SERUM PROTEINS

polymorphic systems in man are shown. Average differences in frequencies between Africans (*color*) and Caucasians (*dark color*) are 22 percent, those between Africans and Orientals (*light color*) are 30 percent, those between Caucasians and Orientals are 22 percent.

that the environmental differences between monozygous twins, who tend to establish special relations with each other, are not exactly comparable to those between dizygous twins. In short, whereas the contrast between monozygous and dizygous twin pairs minimizes genetic differences, it also tends to maximize environmental differences.

In order to take account of such difficulties one must try to use all available comparisons between relatives of various types and degrees, of which twin data are only a selected case. For technical reasons one often measures similarities rather than differences between two sets of values such as parent I.Q.'s and offspring I.Q.'s. Such a measure of similarity is called the correlation coefficient. It is equal to 1 when the pairs of values in the two sets are identical or, more generally, when one value is expressible as a linear function of the other. The correlation coefficient is 0 when the pairs of measurements are completely independent, and it is intermediate if there is a relation between the two sets such

that one tends to increase when the other does.

The mean observed values of the correlation coefficient between parent and child I.Q.'s, and between the I.Q.'s of pairs of siblings, are very nearly .5. This is the value one would expect on the basis of the simplest genetic model, in which the effects of any number of genes determine I.Q. and there are no environmental influences or complications of any kind. It seems probable, however, that the observed correlation of .5 is coincidental. Complicating factors such as different modes of gene action, tendencies for like to mate with like and environmental correlations among members of the same family must just happen to balance one another almost exactly to give a result that agrees with the simplest theoretical expectation. If we ignored these complications, we might conclude naïvely (and in contradiction to other evidence, such as the observation of twins) that biological inheritance of the simplest kind entirely determines I.Q.

Instead it is necessary to seek a means

of determining the relative importance of environmental factors and genetic factors even taking account of several of the complications. In theory this measurement can be made by computing the quotients known as heritability estimates. To understand what such quotients are intended to measure, consider a simplified situation. Imagine that the genotype of each individual with respect to genes affecting I.Q. can be identified. Individuals with the same genotype can then be grouped together. The differences among them would be the result of environmental factors, and the spread of the distribution of such differences could then be measured. Assume for the sake of simplicity that the spread of I.Q. due to environmental differences is the same for each genotype. If we take the I.Q.'s of all the individuals in the population, we obtain a distribution that yields the total variation of I.Q. The variation within each genotype is the environmental component. The difference between the total variation and the environmental component of variation leaves a component of the total variation

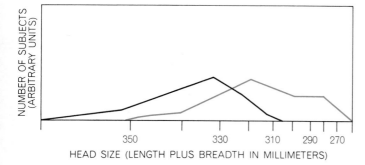

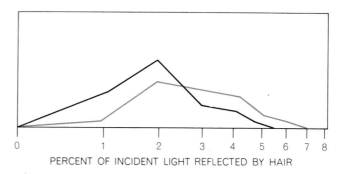

to head size (displayed as the sum of head length and breadth), and in the fourth set phenylalanine levels are related to hair color (displayed as the percentage of light with a wavelength of 700 millimicrons reflected by the hair). In both cases it is obvious that the phenylketonuric genotype has a significant effect on each of these

characteristics: the reflectance is greater and the head size is smaller (*colored curves*) among phenylketonurics than they are among normal individuals (*dark curves*). Yet the distribution of these characteristics is such that they cannot be used to distinguish those afflicted with phenylketonuria from those who are not.

that may be accounted for by genetic differences. This component, when expressed as a fraction of the total variance, is one possible measure of heritability.

In practice, however, the estimation of the component of the total variation that can be accounted for by genetic differences (from data on correlations between relatives) always depends on the construction of specific genetic models, and is therefore subject to the limitations of the models. One problem lies in the fact that there are a number of alternative definitions of heritability depending on the genetic model chosen, because the genetic variation may have many components that can have quite different meanings. A definition that includes only those parts of the genetic variation generally considered to be most relevant in animal and plant breeding is often used. This is called heritability in the narrow sense. If all genetic sources of variation are included, then the heritability estimate increases and is referred to as heritability in the broad ense.

The differences between these esti-

mates of heritability can be defined quite precisely in terms of specific genetic models. The resulting estimates of heritability, however, can vary considerably. Typical heritability estimates for I.Q. (derived from the London population in the early 1950's, with data obtained by Sir Cyril Burt) give values of 45 to 60 percent for heritability in the narrow sense and 80 to 85 percent for heritability in the broad sense.

A further major complication for such heritability estimates has the technical name "genotype-environment interaction." The difficulty is that the realized I.Q. of given genotypes in different environments cannot be predicted in a simple way. A given genotype may develop better in one environment than in another, but this is not necessarily true for any other genotype. Even if it is true, the extent of the difference may not be the same. Ideally one would like to know the reaction of every genotype in every environment. Given the practically infinite variety of both environments and genotypes, this is clearly impossible. Moreover, in man there is no way of con-

trolling the environment. Even if all environmental influences relevant to behavioral development were known, their statistical control by appropriate measurements and subsequent statistical analysis of the data would still be extremely difficult. It should therefore be emphasized that because estimates of heritability depend on the extent of environmental and genetic variation that prevails in the population examined at the time of analysis, they are not valid for other populations or for the same population at a different time.

In animals and plants the experimental control of the environment is easier, and it is possible to explore "genotype-environment" interactions. An interesting experiment was conducted by R. Cooper and John P. Zubek of the University of Manitoba with two lines of rats in which genetic differences in the rats' capacity to find their way through a maze had been accumulated by artificial selection. The two lines of rats had been selected to be either "bright" or "dull" at finding their way through the maze. When rats from these lines were raised for one generation in a "restricted" environment that differed from the "normal" laboratory conditions, no difference between the lines could be found. Both bright and dull animals performed at the same low level. When they were raised in a stimulating environment, both did almost equally well [*see illustration on page 259*]. Since the difference between the lines is genetic, the effect of environmental conditions should be reversible in future generations. This experiment is particularly relevant to differences in I.Q. because of the structure of human societies. If "ghetto" children tend to have I.Q. scores lower, and the children of parents of high social and economic status to have scores higher, than the level one would expect if both groups of children were reared in the same environment, then heritability estimates may be biased upward.

The only potential safeguard against such bias is provided by the investigation of the same genotype or similar genotypes in different environments. In man this can be done only through the study of adopted children. A particularly interesting type of "adoption" is that in which monozygous twins are separated and reared in different families from birth or soon afterward. The outcome is in general a relatively minor average decrease in similarity. Following the same line of reasoning, the similarity between foster parents and adopted children can be measured and contrasted with that between biological parents and their

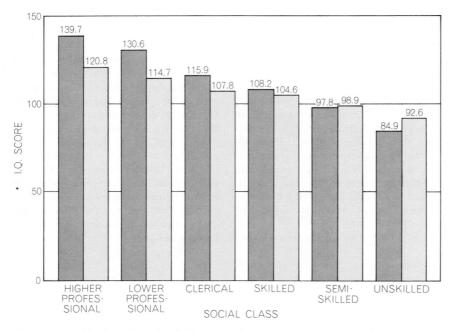

SOCIAL CLASS AND INTELLIGENCE are closely related, a study by Sir Cyril Burt of the University of London indicates. Set of bars at left shows the mean I.Q. for higher professionals (*dark bar*) is 139.7, children of higher professionals have a mean I.Q. of 120.8 (*light bar*). Second set of bars shows that lower professionals have a mean I.Q. of 130.6, children of lower professionals have a mean I.Q. of 114.7. Third set shows that clerical workers have a mean I.Q. of 115.9, their children have a mean I.Q. of 107.8. Fourth set shows that skilled workers have a mean I.Q. of 108.2, their children have a mean I.Q. of 104.6. Fifth set shows that semiskilled workers have a mean I.Q. of 97.8, their children have a mean I.Q. of 98.9. Sixth set shows that unskilled workers have a mean I.Q. of 84.9, their children have a mean I.Q. of 92.6. Mean I.Q.'s of wives (*not shown*) correlate well with husbands'. Above the mean children's I.Q. tends to be lower than that of parents. Below it children's I.Q. tends to be higher. Social mobility maintains distribution because those individuals with high I.Q.'s tend to rise whereas those with low I.Q.'s tend to fall.

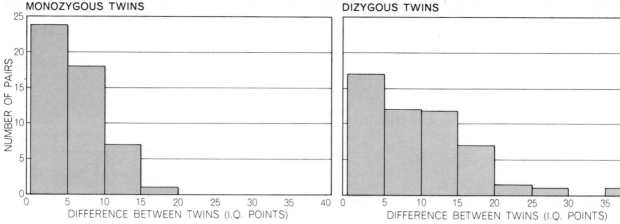

MONOZYGOUS TWINS

DIZYGOUS TWINS

NUMBER OF PAIRS

DIFFERENCE BETWEEN TWINS (I.Q. POINTS)

DIFFERENCE BETWEEN TWINS (I.Q. POINTS)

EXPERIMENT OF NATURE based on I.Q. data collected by Horatio H. Newman of the University of Chicago gives a rough measurement of the relative influence of heredity and environment on intelligence. Chart at left shows I.Q. differences between the members of 50 pairs of monozygous twins, that is, twins who developed from the same egg and have identical genotypes. I.Q. differences between members of these pairs tend to be low: 24 pairs (or almost half of the sample) show a difference of from zero to five points. Only one pair shows a difference of between 15 and 20 points. The mean difference between the members of each pair is 5.9 points. Since the genotypes in each pair are identical it appears that the environmental effect tends to be small. Second chart shows I.Q. differences between 45 pairs of dizygous twins, that is, twins with different genotypes who developed from separate eggs. In this case the mean difference in I.Q. between the members of these pairs is about 10 points. Thus a fairly large difference appears to be attributable to heredity. Such a comparison does not separate the effects of heredity and environment precisely. Members of monozygous pairs have very similar environments, whereas genotypes of dizygous twins are less different on the average by a factor of two than those of unrelated individuals. Comparison thus underestimates effect of heredity but also minimizes environmental influence.

children. A few such studies have been conducted. They show that the change of family environment does indeed have an effect, although it is not as great as that of biological inheritance. The correlation between foster parents and their adopted children is greater than 0, but it is undoubtedly less than that between biological parents and their offspring.

A complete analysis of such data is almost impossible because environmental variation among families and genotype-environment interactions of various kinds must be responsible for the observed effects in ways that make it difficult to disentangle their relative importance. Adoption and rearing apart take place in conditions far from those of ideal experiments, and so any conclusions are bound to be only semiquantitative. On the basis of all the available data, with allowance for these limitations, the heritability of intelligence, as measured by I.Q., is still fairly high. It must be kept in mind, however, that the environmental effects in such studies are generally limited to the differences among and within families of a fairly homogeneous section of the British or American population. They cannot be extrapolated to prediction of the effects of greater differences in environment, or of other types of difference.

There are significant differences in mean I.Q. among the various social classes. One of the most comprehensive and widely quoted studies of such differences and the reasons for their apparent stability over the years was published by Burt in 1961 [see illustration on opposite page]. His data come from schoolchildren and their parents in a typical London borough. Socioeconomic level was classified, on the basis of type of occupation, into six classes. These range from Class 1, including "university teachers, those of similar standing in law, medicine, education or the church and the top people in commerce, industry or civil service," to Class 6, including "unskilled laborers, casual laborers and those employed in coarse manual work." There are four main features of these data:

1. Parental mean I.Q. and occupational class are closely related. The mean difference between the highest and the lowest class is over 50. Although occupational class is determined mostly by the father, the relatively high correlation between the I.Q.'s of husband and wife (about .4) contributes to the differentiation among the classes with respect to I.Q.

2. In spite of the significant variation between the parental mean I.Q.'s, the residual variation in I.Q. among parents within each class is still remarkably large. The mean standard deviation of the parental I.Q.'s for the different classes is 8.6, almost three-fifths of the standard deviation for the entire group. That standard deviation is about 15, and it is usual for the spread of I.Q.'s in any group.

3. The mean I.Q. of the offspring for each class lies almost exactly between the parental mean I.Q.'s and the overall population mean I.Q. of 100. This is expected because it is only another way of looking at the correlation for I.Q. between parent and child, which as we have already seen tends to be about .5 in any given population.

4. The last important feature of the data is that the standard deviations of the I.Q. of the offspring, which average 13.2, are almost the same as the standard deviation of the general population, namely 15. This is another indication of the existence of considerable variability of I.Q. within social classes. Such variability is almost as much as that in the entire population.

The most straightforward interpretation of these data is that I.Q. is itself a major determinant of occupational class and that it is to an appreciable extent inherited (although the data cannot be used to distinguish cultural inheritance from biological). Burt pointed out that, because of the wide distribution of I.Q. within each class among the offspring and the regression of the offspring to the population mean, appreciable mobility among classes is needed in each generation to maintain the class differences with respect to I.Q. He estimated that to maintain a stable distribution of I.Q. differences among classes, at least 22 percent of the offspring would have to change class, mainly as a function of I.Q., in each generation. This figure is

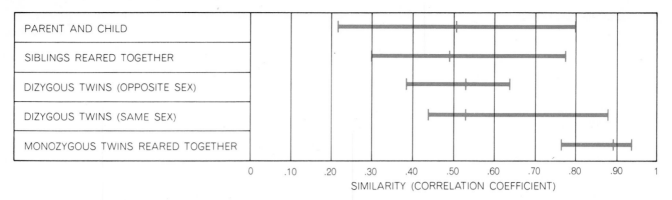

CORRELATION COEFFICIENTS are calculations of similarity, for example, between the I.Q.'s of two sets of relatives such as parents and children. A coefficient of 1 indicates identity, 0 indicates independence of one value from the other. These data were collected from published literature by L. Erlenmeyer-Kimling and Lissy F. Jarvik of the New York State Psychiatric Institute to derive measurements of comparative effects of heredity and environment, taking into account all possible effects of relatedness between individuals. The horizontal line at top indicates that the coefficients of samples of parents and children from different studies range from about .20 to .80. Second horizontal line indicates that coefficients for siblings reared together range from .30 to about .78. Range for dizygous (fraternal) twins of opposite sex is .38 to .65; for dizygous twins of same sex it is .43 to .88. The mean (*vertical line intersecting each horizontal line*) for each of these four sets of relatives is about .50. Monozygous (identical) twins, however, have a range of .77 to .92 with a mean of .89. Mean coefficient of .50 is that which would be expected if there were no environmental effects in I.Q. Since other evidence indicates that environment exerts a significant effect, these calculations must be further refined.

well below the observed intergenerational social mobility in Britain, which is about 30 percent.

Fears that there may be a gradual decline in I.Q. because of an apparent negative correlation between I.Q. and fertility have been expressed ever since Francis Galton pointed out this correlation for the British ruling class in the second half of the 19th century. If there were such a persistent association, if I.Q. were at least in part genetically determined and if there were no counteracting environmental effects, such a decline in I.Q. could be expected. The fact is that no significant decline has been detected so far. The existing data, although they are admittedly limited, do not support the idea of a persistent negative correlation between I.Q. and overall reproductivity.

The existence of culturally, and often racially, reproductively isolated subgroups within a human population almost inevitably leads to social tensions, which are the seeds of racism. This has been true throughout the history of mankind, and is by no means unique to the present tensions among different racial groups such as those between blacks and whites in the U.S. Conflicts between religious groups, such as Protestants and Catholics in Northern Ireland, are examples of the same type of social tension. Cultural divergence is often accompanied by relative economic deprivation in one group or the other, which aggravates the tensions between them.

The striking outward differences between blacks and whites, mainly of course the color of their skin, must be a major extra factor contributing to the racial tensions between them. If the cultural differences between the Protestants and Catholics of Ireland disappeared, there would be no way of telling the two groups apart. The same is not true for black and white Americans. Many generations of completely random mating would be needed to even out their difference in skin color.

Such mating has not taken place in the U.S. The average frequency of marriages between blacks and whites throughout the U.S. is still only about 2 percent of the frequency that would be expected if marriages occurred at random with respect to race. This reflects the persistent high level of reproductive isolation between the races, in spite of the movement in recent years toward a strong legal stand in favor of desegregation. Hawaii is a notable exception to this separation of the races, although even there the observed frequency of mixed marriages is still only 45 to 50 percent of what would be expected if matings occurred at random.

The socioeconomic deprivation of one racial group with respect to another inevitably raises the question of whether or not the difference has a significant genetic component. In the case of U.S. blacks and whites the question has recently been focused on the average difference in I.Q. Many studies have shown the existence of substantial differences in the distribution of I.Q. in U.S. blacks and whites. Such data were obtained in an extensive study published by Wallace A. Kennedy of Florida State University and his co-workers in 1963, based on I.Q. tests given to 1,800 black children in elementary school in five Southeastern states (Florida, Georgia, Alabama, Tennessee and South Carolina). When the distribution these workers found is compared with a 1960 sample of the U.S. white population, striking differences emerge. The mean difference in I.Q. between blacks and whites is 21.1, whereas the standard deviation of the distribution among blacks is some 25 percent less than that of the distribution among whites (12.4 v. 16.4). As one would expect, there is considerable overlap between the two distributions, because the variability for I.Q., like the variability for most characteristics, within any population is substantially greater than the variability between any two populations. Nevertheless, 95.5 percent of the blacks have an I.Q. below the white mean of 101.8 and 18.4 percent have an I.Q. of less than 70. Only 2 percent of the whites have I.Q.'s in the latter range.

Reported differences between the mean I.Q.'s of blacks and whites generally lie between 10 and 20, so that the value found by Kennedy and his colleagues is one of the most extreme reported. The difference is usually less for blacks from the Northern states than it is for those from the Southern states, and clearly it depends heavily on the particular populations tested. One well-known study of Army "Alpha" intelligence-test results, for example, showed that blacks from some Northern states achieved higher average scores than whites from some Southern states, although whites always scored higher than blacks from the same state. There are many uncertainties and variables that influence the outcome of I.Q. tests, but the observed mean differences between U.S. blacks and whites are undoubtedly more or less reproducible and are quite striking.

There are two main features that clearly distinguish I.Q. differences among social classes described above from those between blacks and whites. First, the I.Q. differences among social classes relate to the environmental variation within the relatively homogeneous British population. It cannot be assumed that this range of environmental variation is comparable with the average environmental difference between black and white Americans. Second, and more important, these differences are maintained by the mobility among occupational classes that is based to a significant extent on selection for higher I.Q. in the higher occupational classes. There is clearly no counterpart of this mobility with respect to the differences between U.S. blacks and whites; skin color effectively bars mobility between the races.

The arguments for a substantial genetic component in the I.Q. difference between the races assume that existing heritability estimates for I.Q. can reasonably be applied to the racial difference. These estimates, however, are based on observations within the white population. We have emphasized that heritability estimates apply only to the population studied and to its particular environment. Thus the extrapolation of existing heritability estimates to the racial differences assumes that the environmental differences between the races are comparable to the environmental variation within them. Since there is no basis for making this assumption, it follows that there is no logical connection between heritabilities determined within either race and the genetic difference between them. Whether or not the variation in I.Q. within either race is entirely genetic or entirely environmental has no bearing on the question of the relative contribution of genetic factors and environmental factors to the differences between the races.

A major argument given by Jensen in favor of a substantial genetic component in the I.Q. difference is that it persists even when comparisons are made between U.S. blacks and whites of the same socioeconomic status. This status is defined in terms of schooling, occupation and income, and so it is necessarily a measure of at least a part of the environmental variation, comparable to the class differences we have discussed here.

Taken at face value—that is, on the assumption that status is truly a measure of the total environment—these data would indicate that the I.Q. difference is genetically determined. It is difficult to see, however, how the status of blacks and whites can be compared. The very existence of a racial stratification correlated with a relative socioeconomic deprivation makes this comparison suspect. Black schools are well known to be generally less adequate than white schools, so that equal numbers of years of schooling certainly do not mean equal educational attainment. Wide variation in the level of occupation must exist within each occupational class. Thus one would certainly expect, even for equivalent occupational classes, that the black level is on the average lower than the white. No amount of money can buy a black person's way into a privileged upper-class white community, or buy off more than 200 years of accumulated racial prejudice on the part of the whites, or reconstitute the disrupted black family, in part culturally inherited from the days of slavery. It is impossible to accept the idea that matching for status provides an adequate, or even a substantial, control over the most important environmental differences between blacks and whites.

Jensen has suggested other arguments in defense of his thesis that the average I.Q. difference between blacks and whites is entirely genetic or mostly so,

and he has challenged readers of his paper in the *Harvard Educational Review* to consider them. One is a set of data on blacks that is quite similar to those we have cited for whites; it shows the filial regression of I.Q. or related measurements as a function of the social class of the parents. The only conclusion one can draw is that among blacks the inheritance of I.Q. must also be fairly high. No conclusion can be drawn from these data concerning environmental differences between blacks and whites that affect I.Q., and it is this that is the real issue.

Jensen also discusses differences between the races in rates of early motor development, and in other developmental rates, which are believed to be correlated with I.Q. The argument must, by implication, be that developmental rates are determined mostly by genetic factors. Environmental influences on such rates are widely recognized, so that this information does not help to clarify the situation concerning I.Q. Moreover, Jensen makes the statement, based on the well-known "Coleman report," that American Indians, in spite of poor schooling, do not show the same I.Q. gap as blacks. According to the Coleman report, however, American Indians typically go to schools where whites are in the majority, which is not the case for most of the schools attended by black children. (The actual difference between whites and Indians may be greater, be-

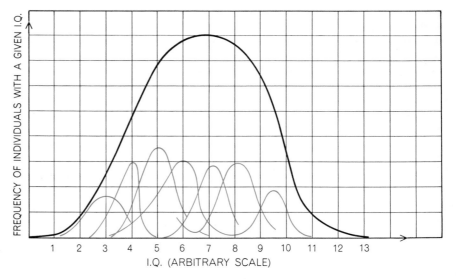

HERITABILITY is a measure of the relative effects of heredity and environment on characteristics such as I.Q. The heritability estimate is based on the assumption that a population consists of several groups each distinguished by a different genotype and I.Q. distribution (*colored curves*). The total of these I.Q. distributions equals the I.Q. spread for the population (*black curve*). By definition those in each group have the same genotype, thus any variation in a group is environmental. Heredity's effect on the total I.Q. distribution can be calculated by averaging together the I.Q. spread of each group and subtracting the result from the total I.Q. spread. The remainder is the total variation due to genetic factors.

cause the sample may not have adequately represented the 70 to 80 percent of American Indians who live on reservations.) The differences between Indians and blacks or whites are clearly no easier to assess than those between blacks and whites.

Jensen states that because the gene pools of whites and blacks are known to differ and "these genetic differences are manifested in virtually every anatomical, physiological and biochemical comparison one can make between representative samples of identifiable racial groups . . . there is no reason to suppose that the brain should be exempt from this generalization." As geneticists we can state with certainty that there is no a priori reason why genes affecting I.Q., which differ in the gene pools of blacks and whites, should be such that on the average whites have significantly more genes increasing I.Q. than blacks do. On the contrary, one should expect, assuming no tendency for high-I.Q. genes to accumulate by selection in one race or the other, that the more polymorphic genes there are that affect I.Q. and that differ in frequency in blacks and whites, the less likely it is that there is an average genetic difference in I.Q. between the races. The same argument applies to the differences between any two racial groups.

Since natural selection is the principal agent of genetic change, is it possible that this force has produced a significant I.Q. difference between American blacks and whites? Using the simple theory with which plant and animal breeders predict responses to artificial selection, one can make a rough guess at the amount of selection that would have been needed to result in a difference of about 15 I.Q. points, such as exists between blacks and whites. The calculation is based on three assumptions: that there was no initial difference in I.Q. between Africans and Caucasians, that the heritability of I.Q. in the narrow sense is about 50 percent and that the divergence of black Americans from Africans started with slavery about 200 years, or seven generations, ago. This implies a mean change in I.Q. of about two points per generation. The predictions of the theory are that this rate of change could be achieved by the complete elimination from reproduction of about 15 percent of the most intelligent individuals in each generation. There is certainly no good basis for assuming such a level of selection against I.Q. during the period of slavery.

It seems to us that none of the above arguments gives any support to Jensen's conclusion. The only observation that could prove his thesis would be to compare an adequate sample of black and white children brought up in strictly comparable environments. This seems practically impossible to achieve today.

What can be said concerning environmental differences that are known or suspected to affect I.Q.? First it should be mentioned that, in spite of high I.Q. heritability estimates, the mean intrapair I.Q. difference found by Horatio H. Newman and his co-workers at the University of Chicago between monozygotic twins reared apart was 8 and the range was from 1 to 24. Therefore even within the white population there is substantial environmental variation in I.Q.

The following known environmental effects are also worth mentioning:

1. There is a systematic difference of as much as five I.Q. points between twins and nontwins, irrespective of socioeconomic and other variables. This reduction in the I.Q. of twins could be due either to the effects of the maternal environment *in utero* or to the reduced attention parents are able to give each of two very young children born at the same time.

2. It has been reported that the I.Q. of blacks tested by blacks was two to three points higher than when they were tested by whites.

3. Studies of the effects of protein-deficient diets administered to female rats before and during pregnancy (conducted by Stephen Zamenhof and his co-workers at the University of California School of Medicine in Los Angeles) have shown a substantial reduction in total brain DNA content of the offspring and hence presumably a reduction in the number of brain cells. The reductions were correlated with behavioral deficiencies and in man could be the basis for substantial I.Q. differences. There can be no doubt that in many areas the poor socioeconomic conditions of blacks are correlated with dietary deficiency. Dietary deficiencies in early childhood are likely to have similar consequences.

4. The very early home environment has long been thought to be of substantial importance for intellectual development. There are clear-cut data that demonstrate the detrimental effects of severe early sensory deprivation. There can be little doubt that both the lower socio-

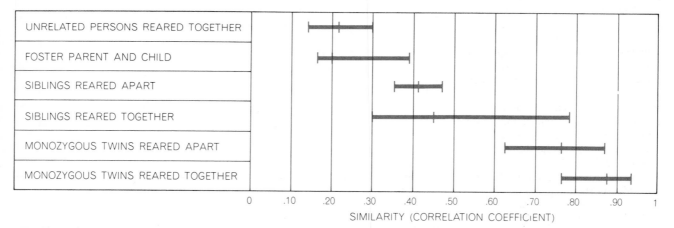

EFFECTS OF ENVIRONMENT can be measured by comparing correlation coefficients of individuals with similar genetic backgrounds reared in different environments and those with different backgrounds reared in the same environment. Published data collected by Erlenmeyer-Kimling and Jarvik show that unrelated persons reared together have coefficients that range from about .15 to slightly over .30. Coefficients for foster-parents and children range from .16 to almost .40. Siblings reared apart have coefficients that range from more than .30 to more than .40. Siblings reared together have coefficients that range from .30 to almost .80. Monozygous twins reared apart have coefficients that range from more than .60 to above .80, and monozygous twins reared together have coefficients of more than .70 to more than .90. It appears that environment affects intelligence but not as strongly as heredity does.

economic status of U.S. blacks and a cultural inheritance dating back to slavery must on the average result in a less satisfactory home environment; this may be particularly important during the preschool years. Here again animal experiments support the importance of early experience on brain development.

5. Expectancy of failure usually leads to failure.

In his *Harvard Educational Review* article Jensen chooses to minimize environmental effects such as these. We believe, however, that there is no evidence against the notion that such influences, among other environmental factors, many of which doubtless remain to be discovered, could explain essentially all the differences in I.Q. between blacks and whites.

We do not by any means exclude the possibility that there could be a genetic component in the mean difference in I.Q. between races. We simply maintain that currently available data are inadequate to resolve this question in either direction. The only approach applicable to the study of the I.Q. difference between the races is that of working with black children adopted into white homes and vice versa. The adoptions would, of course, have to be at an early age to be sure of taking into account any possible effects of the early home environment. The I.Q.'s of black children adopted into white homes would also have to be compared with those of white children adopted into comparable white homes. To our knowledge no scientifically adequate studies of this nature have ever been undertaken. It is questionable whether or not such studies could be done in a reasonably controlled way at the present time. Even if they could, they would not remove the effects of prejudice directed against black people in most white communities. We therefore suggest that the question of a possible genetic basis for the race I.Q. difference will be almost impossible to answer satisfactorily before the environmental differences between U.S. blacks and whites have been substantially reduced.

Apart from the intrinsic difficulties in answering this question, it seems to us that there is no good case for encouraging the support of studies of this kind on either theoretical or practical grounds. From a theoretical point of view it seems unlikely that such studies would throw much light on the general problem of the genetic control of I.Q., because any racial difference would be a small fraction of the total variation in I.Q. The mere fact that even the rela-

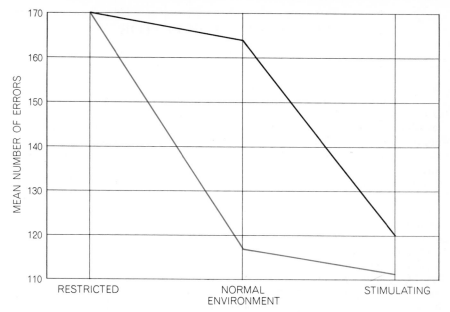

GENOTYPE-ENVIRONMENT INTERACTION is measured in these results from an experiment carried out by R. Cooper and John P. Zubek of the University of Manitoba. The experiment involved two strains of rats: those that were bred to be "bright," that is, clever at finding their way through a maze, and those that were "dull." In a normal environment bright rats (*colored curve*) made only 120 errors, whereas dull rats made about 168 errors. When both strains were raised in a restricted environment, however, both made about 170 errors. When raised in a stimulating environment, both kinds of rats did equally well.

tively crude studies on the inheritance of I.Q. conducted so far have not taken advantage of racial differences suggests that these are not the most convenient differences to investigate. Much basic work on the biology and biochemistry of mental development under controlled conditions, making use of known genetic differences, is needed before a fuller understanding of the inheritance of I.Q. can be achieved.

Perhaps the only practical argument in favor of research on the race I.Q. difference is that, since the question that the difference is genetic has been raised, an attempt should be made to answer it. Otherwise those who now believe—we think on quite inadequate evidence—that the difference is genetic will be left to continue their campaigns for an adjustment of our educational and economic systems to take account of "innate" racial differences.

A demonstration that the difference is not primarily genetic could counter such campaigns. On the other hand, an answer in the opposite direction should not, in a genuinely democratic society free of race prejudice, make any difference. Our society professes to believe there should be no discrimination against an individual on the basis of race, religion or other a priori categorizations, including sex. Our accepted ethic holds that each individual should be given equal and maximum opportunity, ac-

cording to his or her needs, to develop to his or her fullest potential. Surely innate differences in ability and other individual variations should be taken into account by our educational system. These differences must, however, be judged on the basis of the individual and not on the basis of race. To maintain otherwise indicates an inability to distinguish differences among individuals from differences among populations.

We are not unaware of the dangers of either overt or implicit control of scientific inquiry. The suppression of Galileo and the success of T. D. Lysenko are two notorious examples of the evils of such control. Most investigators, however, do accept certain limitations on research on human beings, for example in the right of an individual not to be experimented on and in the confidentiality of the information collected by organizations such as the Bureau of the Census. In the present racial climate of the U.S. studies on racial differences in I.Q., however well intentioned, could easily be misinterpreted as a form of racism and lead to an unnecessary accentuation of racial tensions. Since we believe that, for the present at least, no good case can be made for such studies on either scientific or practical grounds, we do not see any point in particularly encouraging the use of public funds for their support. There are many more useful biological problems for the scientist to attack.

LETTERS TO THE EDITOR
January 1971

Sirs:

"Intelligence and Race," by Walter F. Bodmer and Luigi Luca Cavalli-Sforza [SCIENTIFIC AMERICAN, October, 1970], neglects the possibility that I have stressed since 1966 of using gene frequencies, for example T. Edward Reed's Caucasian gene (*Science*, August 22, 1969), to analyze the effect of race mixture on intelligence within uniform slum environments. My own preliminary research suggests that an increase of 1 percent in Caucasian ancestry raises Negro I.Q. about one point on the average for low-I.Q. populations. The authors' neglect of these research possibilities is in keeping with their irresponsibility toward the essential moral point.

If what I fear is true, our society is being profoundly irresponsible. Our nobly intended welfare programs may be encouraging dysgenics—retrogressive evolution through disproportionate reproduction of the genetically disadvantaged. This national illness probably occurs for whites as well as blacks. But it may be much easier to diagnose for the blacks because of the research possibilities offered by the Caucasian-gene effect.

To fail to use this method of diagnosis for fear of being called a racist is irresponsible. It may also be a great injustice to black Americans themselves. If those Negroes with the fewest Caucasian genes are in fact the most prolific and also the least intelligent, then genetic enslavement will be the destiny of their next generation. The consequences may be extremes of racism and agony for both blacks and whites.

I believe that a nation that achieved its 10-year objective of putting a man on the moon can wisely and humanely solve its human-quality problems once the objective is stated and relevant facts are courageously sought. I urge your readers to write to their legislators to demand high-priority research on what I maintain is our nation's most agonizing problem.

W. SHOCKLEY

Stanford, Calif.

Sirs:

Although I agree with the statement of Bodmer and Cavalli-Sforza that in a genuinely democratic society the demonstration that there are genetically determined racial differences in I.Q. should not "make any difference," I must disagree with their conclusion that the only approach to the question of the existence of such differences is through the study of transracially adopted children.

Another approach is available owing to the peculiarity that American society treats as black anyone who derived even a relatively small portion of his genes from the African gene pool. Consequently it should be possible to obtain a series of I.Q. measurements from persons living under essentially identical social conditions but who have different portions of their genotype derived from the African gene pool.

If the hypothesis of a genetically controlled inferiority of I.Q. in the black as compared with the Caucasian race is correct, then there should be a strong positive correlation between I.Q. and the fraction of the genotype derived from the Caucasian gene pool. I personally do not expect such a correlation to exist.

WERNER G. HEIM

Professor of Biology
Colorado College
Colorado Springs, Colo.

Sirs:

I sincerely hope that the article "Intelligence and Race" in the October *Scientific American* is published as a result of a momentary lapse of consciousness on the part of your editorial board and is not indicative of a new policy regarding the quality of material acceptable to your magazine. Quite aside from the outrageous conclusion regarding acceptable areas of research, the article is a mine of unwarranted assumptions, logical inconsistencies, unfounded conclusions and biased emotional rhetoric.

Publication of such material, more properly in the realm of the radical press, detracts severely from the status of *Scientific American* and, by implication, the work of other scientists who are published in your journal. In the now slightly passé phrase, your credibility is diminished by articles such as this. In an era in which intellectual rigor is increasingly scorned and pride of place given to emotional "relevance," a journal such as *Scientific American* has an even greater responsibility to maintain standards in the material it accepts for publication. Let us have no more of this kind of thing.

ALFRED E. BIGOT

Minneapolis, Minn.

Sirs:

Both Dr. Shockley and Dr. Heim suggest another method for attempting to demonstrate the existence of a genetic component in the racial differences in I.Q. The method is based on the estimation of the degree of racial admixture, mainly using polymorphic genes but also perhaps using skin color and other phenotypic differences. An assessment is then made of the correlation between the degree of racial admixture and the average I.Q. We omitted this possibility not, as Dr. Shockley suggests, because of lack of responsibility but because we believe the method does not allow the necessary separation of genetic and environmental components of the variation between races. With the use of a single marker, as Shockley is apparently suggesting, the method has to be applied to entire groups and not to single individuals, and even then there are appreciable problems in establishing, even approximately, the extent of racial admixture; this has been shown by the work of Glass and Li, of Workman and his colleagues and of Reed, in which several markers were actually employed. Groups with different degrees of admixture of white and black genes would have to be studied for their average I.Q. It is known, however, that the degree of white admixture in different U.S. black communities varies from less than 10 percent to 30 percent or more, with a South-North gradient and possibly other important sources of geographical variation. For this knowledge to be useful in solving the problem at issue, the assumption has to be made that the environment is the same for all these populations and that there is no correlation between differences in the environment and the extent of black-white admixture. It is difficult to believe such an assumption could be correct.

It is of interest that the preliminary report by Dr. Shockley that "an increase of 1 percent in Caucasian ancestry raises Negro I.Q. about one point on the average" in itself throws considerable doubt on the validity of the approach, although it is not clear what Shockley really means by "low-I.Q. populations." If there were a clear-cut genetic difference between blacks and whites for I.Q. based on a mean race I.Q. difference of 15 to 20 points, an increase of 1 percent in Caucasian ancestry should lead to an increase in I.Q. of at most .1 to .2 point, which is at least five times smaller than what is claimed by Shockley. The discrepancy is such that the increase he claims would make a black with 50 percent white genes much more intelligent on the average than an average white, and a black with 100 percent white genes (who would be an average white) an absolute genius. This absurd result must derive from there being in the material examined genetic components that are far from additive or, more probably, from complex genotype-environment interactions. To put it simply, "uniform slum environments" surely do not exist, and sociocultural effects are too complex to be straightened out by some simple statistical analysis.

The letter from Mr. Bigot reflects the kind of emotional and irrational response that any attempt to discuss such delicate social issues as the race-I.Q. difference can engender. We leave it to the reader to judge how seriously such a response should be taken—or whether in fact Mr. Bigot himself is serious.

Dr. Shockley and Dr. Heim obviously disagree on the social conclusions to be drawn from the research they suggest. Dr. Shockley does not in his letter, and to our knowledge has not in the past, clearly stated what social measures (other than the differential restriction of reproduction) would follow if his fears concerning dysgenic effects turned out to be true. As we have stated, we believe that neither the existence nor the nonexistence of a genetic component in race-I.Q. differences should have an effect on educational and social practices. Our suggestion that appropriation of public funds for the support of studies on the genetic component of the race-I.Q. difference should not be particularly encouraged was not meant as a proposal to bar well-founded research on this question but was especially directed against the "putting a man on the moon" approach apparently being advocated in the last paragraph of Dr. Shockley's letter. In our view it would be more responsible to devote that kind of effort in the U.S. to solving social and economic problems, racial or otherwise, in terms of the environment.

WALTER F. BODMER

Oxford, England

LUIGI LUCA CAVALLI-SFORZA

Pavia, Italy

*Commentary by Bodmer**

Thank you for your letter about the inclusion of the article of intelligence and race in your *Scientific American* collection. . . . Firstly, I should like to ask that an error which crept into the original article and which has not been corrected in its reprinted form be put right. On page 7 of the Offprint the first full sentence on the page should read, "In short, whereas the contrast between monozygous and dizygous twin pairs minimizes genetic differences, it also tends to *minimize* environmental differences."

Since our article was written calculations have been done which back up specifically our statement that the extent of variation within a population generally far exceeds the average differences between populations. Specifically one can say that the contribution of racial differences to genetic variation is, at the very most, of the order of 30% of the total genetic variation in the human species as a whole. To the discussion of environmental effects on I.Q. I think we would now have added more detail on the question of differences between twins and non-twins, and an analysis of Skodac and Skeel's data showing the difference between the I.Q. of adopted children and their biological parents. . . .

Otherwise, there really is not much I feel that we would have wanted to change had we been writing the article now. In fact in a recent review of A. Jensen's books I stated that I could see no basis for changing the viewpoint that Cavalli-Sforza and I expressed in our article, though I noted an apparent change in Jensen's attitude since in his Harvard Educational Review article in 1969 he wrote "All we are left with are various lines of evidence no one of which is definitive alone but which viewed all together make it a not unreasonable hypothesis that genetic factors are strongly implicated in the average negro-white intelligence difference. The preponderance of the evidence is, in my opinion, less consistent with a strictly environmental hypothesis than with a genetic hypothesis, which of course does not exclude the influence of environment or its interaction with genetic factors." The first paragraph of his summary of the final chapter of *Educability and Group Differences* ends, however, with the following statement: "All the major facts would seem to be comprehended quite well by the hypothesis that something between one half and three fourths of the average I.Q. difference between American negroes and whites is attributable to genetic factors, and the

*Professor Bodmer also suggests examining the critical editorial in *Nature*, Vol. 223, 12 December 1970 and then his and Professor Cavalli-Sforza's reply in *Nature*, Vol. 229, 1 January 1971 (p. 71) for an analysis of questions concerning "the more political aspects of the race IQ difference.

remainder to environmental factors and their interaction with genetic differences." It seems that in the intervening years Jensen became sufficiently convinced of the hypothesis of a genetic contribution to the race I.Q. difference to give quite specific numbers, something he was clearly not prepared to do in 1969. I myself can see no evidence in his or anyone else's writings that should have made him so change his mind. I note that recently new books have been published by Eysenck and by Hernstein on these same issues and find it a little depressing that the arguments drag on and on with nothing new to be said. One can only suspect that the motive for writing the books is to capitalise on the commerical potential of writing repeatedly on such controversial issues.

Walter F. Bodmer, November 1973

Jheronimus bosch

The Genetics of Human Populations

by L. L. Cavalli-Sforza
September 1974

Since the species Homo sapiens emerged less than 100,000 years ago it has by definition shared a common pool of genes. The differences within a human population are greater than those between populations

In *The Comedy of Errors* Shakespeare makes use of a device that was dear to the hearts of Greek and Roman playwrights. He brings onto the stage identical twins; as he puts it, "the one so like the other, as could not be distinguish'd but by names." To add to the confusion he gives each twin the same name. Moreover, each twin has a servant, and they too are identical twins with the same name. It is no wonder that errors arise. Nature, however, seldom imitates art so closely. Twins are relatively rare, particularly identical ones; they represent only some .3 percent of all births. Therefore not everyone has had the benefit of observing identical twins closely. Those who have done so are usually struck by their remarkable similarity. For all we know, identical twins have identical sets of genes, represented by identical sequences of the paired nucleotides of DNA. They thus provide a tangible and simple proof of the power of inheritance. When in contrast we look at two people selected at random, enough differences are apparent so that the likelihood of confusion between them is remote. Individuality is a familiar property of man; it marks not only facial features

and bodily traits but even such details as fingerprints and voice. Indeed, not even identical twins are wholly identical in every respect; it is only that the differences between them are almost always smaller than those between unrelated individuals.

Until recently there existed no precise measure of the full extent of the differences between unrelated individuals. Now, however, the systematic use of electrophoresis as a means of analyzing proteins enables us to make some estimates of this kind. Proteins are simply long chains of amino acids in various sequences. Each type of protein performs a highly specific function in the body. For example, some serve as enzymes that catalyze specific chemical reactions, transforming one compound into another. Other proteins serve for transport; an example is the hemoglobin that carries oxygen from the lungs to the rest of the body. Still others serve other purposes. All the functions of an organism are performed with the assistance of one or another specific protein, and so proteins exist in enormous variety.

Electrophoresis was first used as a technique of genetic analysis by Linus

Pauling, Harvey A. Itano, S. J. Singer and I. C. Wells at the California Institute of Technology in 1949. The method basically consists in applying an electric field to a solution of proteins. If two or more proteins present in the solution have different electric charges, they will migrate in the electric field at different rates and thus will separate. The first application of the technique by Pauling and his colleagues clarified the molecular basis of sickle-cell anemia. Electrophoresis showed that the hemoglobin contained in the red blood cells of individuals with the disease is different from normal hemoglobin. It had been known from work done by J. V. Neel of the University of Michigan that the disease, which is particularly frequent among African blacks, is inherited in a precise way. The difference between the hemoglobin found in sickle-cell anemia (called Hb-S) and normal hemoglobin (Hb-A) is due to a single amino acid difference at position 6 on one of the two amino acid chains that make up the hemoglobin molecule [*see top illustration on next page.*]

Since the time of this first study several other workers have used the electrophoresis technique to examine genetic differences among other proteins. For example, many enzymes in human blood have been separated by means of electrophoresis and then stained for purposes of identification. The importance of these methods of genetic analysis cannot be overemphasized. In the great majority of cases differences in the electrophoretic mobility of different enzymes is likely to be a consequence of the substitution of one amino acid for another in the long chain of amino acids that comprises the enzyme molecule. The substitution of one amino acid for another in a protein

"ADORATION OF THE MAGI," painted in 1510 by Hieronymus Bosch (*opposite page*), is an example of postmedieval conceptions of the races of man. By the Middle Ages legends that were based on the mention in the New Testament of "three wise men from the east" who had brought gifts to the newborn King of the Jews had promoted the Magi into kings who ruled the three divisions of mankind: the Asians, the Africans and the Europeans. Long before Bosch artists had begun to portray the supposed King of the Moors, Gaspar, as being dark-skinned and even, as Bosch has done (*left*), with plainly Negroid features. White-haired Balthasar (*kneeling in foreground*) is the king who is usually held to be the ruler of the Europeans. Melchior, with his offering of Arabian frankincense, is supposedly the ruler of the Asians. Some artists have portrayed Melchior with Oriental features rather than as a Middle Easterner. The half-naked man standing in the doorway is an allegorical figure who is evidently intended to represent the Antichrist. Bosch further symbolized the world's burden of evil in the attitude of the shepherds on the roof: they exhibit not reverence but only rustic curiosity. The painting, the central panel of a triptych, is in the Prado.

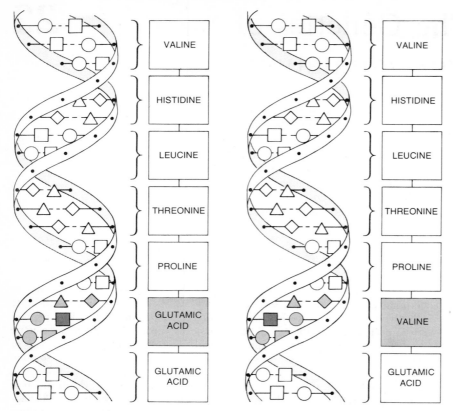

ONE-GENE MUTATION is responsible for the difference between the beta chain of a normal hemoglobin molecule (*left*) and that of hemoglobin S, the variant form responsible for sickle-cell anemia (*right*). Because the middle pair of nucleotides in the sixth nucleotide triplet of the DNA that encodes the beta chain fall in the order thymine-adenine rather than the reverse, the sixth amino acid in the chain is valine (*color*) instead of glutamic acid. The other triplets are shown with arbitrary components; the sequence of amino acids in both beta chains is known, but the sequence of nucleotides in the DNA has not been established.

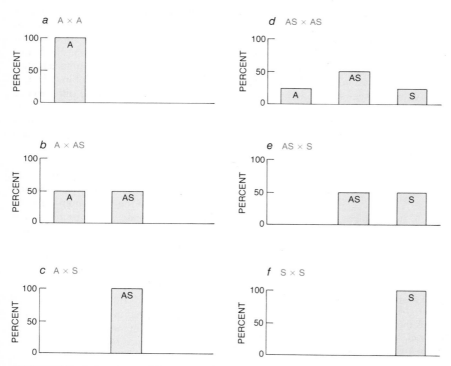

OFFSPRING of the six possible matings between parents with normal hemoglobin (*A*), those with the sickling trait (*AS*) and those with sickle-cell anemia (*S*) are affected as is shown here. The matings (*color*) are $A \times A$, $A \times AS$, $A \times S$, $AS \times AS$, $AS \times S$ and $S \times S$.

molecule is due to the substitution of one nucleotide pair for another in the segment of DNA that is responsible for the synthesis of the protein or of that part of the protein. There are almost no exceptions to the rule that when different individuals show differences in the electrophoretic band or bands that a given enzyme produces, the differences have a simple genetic origin.

The systematic analysis of a large number of enzymes and other proteins has brought a remarkable discovery: a given gene (the DNA segment responsible for the synthesis of a given protein) is by no means identical among the individuals in a population. This observation was made in quantitative terms almost simultaneously by Harry Harris at University College London with respect to man and by Richard C. Lewontin at the University of Chicago with respect to the fruit fly *Drosophila*. When one examines a small sample, say 100 individuals, roughly one in three of the enzymes taken from one of the 100 individuals will show electrophoretic bands that are different from the enzyme bands of some of the remaining 99 individuals. Geneticists customarily call such an enzyme (more precisely, the gene responsible for it) polymorphic. It would be wrong, however, to think that the other two of the three enzymes are invariant from one individual to another. If one analyzes a sample that includes many more than 100 individuals, one finds electrophoretically different forms of nearly every protein studied.

Exactly what these differences mean is far from clear. In many cases there is little evidence that an individual finds it an advantage or a disadvantage to possess a protein in form *A* rather than in form *B* or *C*. There are usually subtle differences in the activity of each form, but all of them are well tolerated by their carriers. As far as we can tell, it often does not seem to matter which form of a polymorphic enzyme we carry, except perhaps in special circumstances. Of course, the differences may seem trivial to us only because we do not know enough about them. For example, we know what function a particular enzyme performs because we identify an enzyme on the basis of which compounds it transforms into which other compounds. The precise importance to the economy of the organism of a specific enzyme, or of small differences in the activities of two slightly different forms of an enzyme, may nonetheless escape us.

In summary, then, electrophoresis analyses have shown that there is an extraordinary diversity among individuals at the biochemical level, that the diversity is genetic in origin and that it must therefore be due to differences in the DNA. We can also estimate what the extent of the differences can be. We get roughly half of our DNA from our father and half from our mother. Let us limit our estimate of differences to the DNA obtained from one parent only. (Apart from the DNA of the sex chromosomes, which accounts for about 5 percent of the total, the DNA received from the father is quite similar to that received from the mother.) If we can count the differences between the father's DNA and the mother's, we shall have some basis for calculating the differences that exist within populations. On the assumption that the differences counted for enzyme-producing genes can be extrapolated to the rest of the genes, the DNA of paternal origin in an average individual differs from the DNA of maternal origin by some 200,000 nucleotide pairs. Compared with the total DNA contribution from each parent, which is about five billion nucleotide pairs, a mere 200,000 differences may seem few. In absolute value, however, they are many: they are some 1 percent of the nucleotide-pair differences that separate man from his closest zoological relatives, the chimpanzee and the gorilla.

The original source of all the differences between two individuals is the phenomenon we call mutation. When new DNA is formed by the replication of existing DNA, errors can occur. Usually such errors involve the substitution of one nucleotide pair for another, but sometimes more drastic changes, involving a cluster of nucleotide pairs or even entire chromosomes with their millions of nucleotide pairs, take place. Mutations are rare events; this is fortunate because a mutation that changes the functioning of even a single gene in a complex organism can jeopardize the life of the organism just as a clogged carburetor or an interrupted electric circuit is enough to stop an automobile. The rate at which mutations take place is of such a low order of magnitude that any individual carries only perhaps 10 to 100 nucleotide pairs, different from those present in his parents, that can be attributed to the mutation process. How, then, have we accumulated hundreds of thousands of changes?

Let us trace the history of a human mutation that has just arisen. There are three immediate possibilities: the change will affect the individual carrying it in a negative way, in a positive way or not at all. If the influence is negative, the carri-

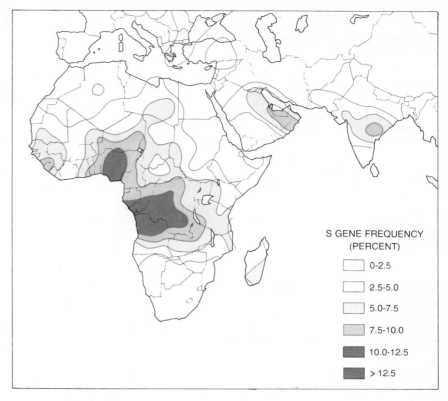

SICKLE-CELL GENE is commonest in populations of tropical Africa; in Zaire, for example, the S gene frequency is about 18 percent, which means that some 30 percent of the population carry the AS trait. The sickle-cell gene is also found in the Mediterranean, particularly in Greece and Turkey, in northwestern Africa, southern Arabia, Pakistan, India and Bangladesh. Individuals who carry the AS trait are more resistant to malaria than others.

S GENE FREQUENCY (PERCENT)

- 0-2.5
- 2.5-5.0
- 5.0-7.5
- 7.5-10.0
- 10.0-12.5
- > 12.5

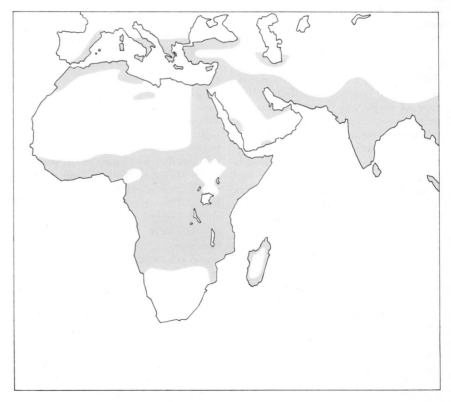

MALIGNANT MALARIAS caused by the parasite *Plasmodium falciparum* were common in the 1920's in the parts of Old World indicated on this map; data are from M. F. Boyd. Overlap with sickle-cell gene distribution is extensive, as seen in illustration at top of page.

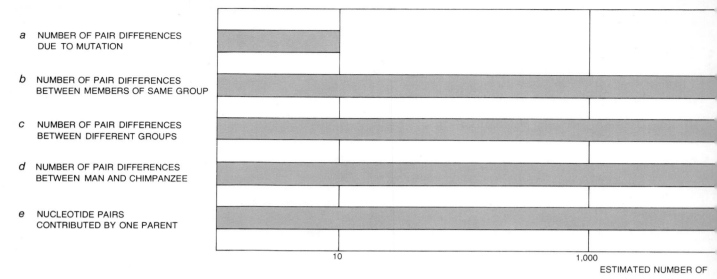

a NUMBER OF PAIR DIFFERENCES DUE TO MUTATION

b NUMBER OF PAIR DIFFERENCES BETWEEN MEMBERS OF SAME GROUP

c NUMBER OF PAIR DIFFERENCES BETWEEN DIFFERENT GROUPS

d NUMBER OF PAIR DIFFERENCES BETWEEN MAN AND CHIMPANZEE

e NUCLEOTIDE PAIRS CONTRIBUTED BY ONE PARENT

10   1,000

ESTIMATED NUMBER OF

NUMBERS OF GENETIC DIFFERENCES that are estimated to exist between individuals who are more and more distantly related are plotted on a logarithmic scale in this graph. The data used are the number of differences in the nucleotide pairs of the DNA that encodes proteins; these differences are observable as amino acid substitutions in the proteins. The observed number is then extrapolated to estimate the total number of nucleotide-pair differences. For comparison purposes the size of the haploid genome, that is, the number of nucleotide pairs contributed to an offspring by one parent only, is shown at the bottom of the graph.

er of the mutation may even die before having a chance to reproduce; then the mutation is lost. It will not be found in later generations unless it reoccurs spontaneously. If the mutation has no discernible effect on the carrier, then its reappearance in future generations is entirely a matter of chance. That is because the carrier may die before reproducing or may have no children or, even if he or she has children, may not pass the mutation to any of them. The probability that the mutation will be passed to any one child is only 50:50, so that it is possible, even if there are several children, that none of them will carry the mutated gene.

The outcome in both cases is the loss of the new mutation; that is what happens in about a third of all mutations. For another third or so there will be one descendant of the original carrier who will carry the new gene, which can then be passed on to further progeny. For the remaining third there will be more than one carrier among the progeny: two, three, four or more. Then the gene, entirely by chance, will have increased in relative frequency. Although the mutation started as a single copy, there are now several copies of it in the population.

This increase by chance can repeat itself until, after a large number of generations, the original mutant gene will be found in a great many individuals of a population. It can even happen, again always by chance, that all the individuals in a population will eventually carry the mutant gene that arose many genera-

tions earlier in a single individual. The chances of this happening are small, but they are greater than zero. Since mutations occur continuously in every new individual, this chance mechanism, known technically as random genetic drift, can contribute to the differences that we observe among individuals of a population or between populations [*see bottom illustration on page 270*].

What about the remaining possibility, a mutation that is advantageous to the carrier? This is the most interesting of the three possibilities because it allows an advance in what may be called a genetic adaptation to the environment. When a mutation confers some advantage on its carrier, the carrier may have a better chance than others to have progeny and thereby to pass on the advantageous mutation. This, of course, is the well-known phenomenon of natural selection. Chance will still play a role: even an advantageous mutation may disappear from a population as a result of random processes. On the average, however, an advantageous mutated gene will become more prevalent in a population and will eventually supplant the original gene.

Perhaps the most intensively studied example of this process is the mutation that gives rise to the sickle-cell trait. The mutation responsible for the sickle-cell trait results in three different genetic types of individuals. They are labeled *AA*, *AS* and *SS*. The *AA* type is normal. The *AS* type has the sickle-cell trait, which can be distinguished by laboratory tests, but enjoys essentially normal

health. The *SS* type has the hereditary disease called sickle-cell anemia.

It happens that in an environment where malaria is prevalent the genetic type *AS* has a distinct advantage over the type *AA*, because *AS* individuals have a 10 to 15 percent better chance of surviving invasion by the most dangerous of the malarial parasites: *Plasmodium falciparum*. The total number of *AS* types will therefore tend to increase in proportion to the other genetic types in the population by the process of natural selection. We can follow the entire process mathematically starting from one *AS* individual who arose by mutation in a population consisting only of type *AA*. At the start, and for many generations thereafter, only *AS* and *AA* individuals will be found in the population. The *AS* individuals will increase with respect to the *AA* ones because of their greater resistance to malaria. Later on, however, *SS* individuals will also appear. Unlike *AS* and *AA* individuals they are subject to sickle-cell anemia whether malaria is present or not. The *SS* individuals have only a poor chance (between 20 and 40 percent) of surviving long enough to have children.

With respect to the gene that gives rise to the sickle-cell trait, then, natural selection cannot accomplish what would seem to be (and usually is) the natural outcome of the process: the replacement of gene *A* by gene *S*. The reason is the poor viability of *SS* individuals. Their high mortality acts as a brake, and the more *AS* individuals there are, the

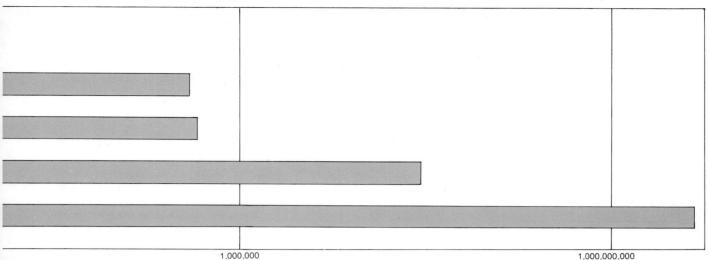

DNA NUCLEOTIDE-PAIR DIFFERENCES

It is about five billion (*e*). The smallest number of differences, perhaps as few as 10 (*a*), is the number that arises in the haploid genome because of random mutation in one generation. A much larger number of differences, half a million or more (*b*), exists between the haploid genomes of two randomly chosen members of a single ethnic group. The number is not greatly increased when the randomly chosen individuals belong to different major divisions of the human population, such as Caucasian and Oriental (*c*). Differences between man and his near relative the chimpanzee number in the millions (*d*). The figures are approximations only.

more SS individuals will be born and the more effective the brake is. Eventually an equilibrium is reached that is affected by the environmental incidence of malaria. When malaria is prevalent, as many as 30 percent of all individuals in the population can be of the AS type; at this level the frequency of SS individuals is just above 2 percent. The process comes close to equilibrium within 2,000 years or so. In biological terms that is a rapid process; the human species rarely experiences natural selection at this level of intensity.

Other kinds of genetic adaptation to malaria, involving other genes, have also occurred. Thalassemia and the disease resulting from a defect in the enzyme glucose-6 phosphate dehydrogenase are well-known examples that involve similar selection intensities. Still other genetic adaptations, although they are less well known, are believed to involve lower selection intensities. Many of them, however, are not barred from proceeding to completion by the mischance, encountered with sickle-cell anemia, that makes the SS individual the victim of a generally fatal disease. If this were not so, the population that harbors the S gene would in the end consist entirely of SS individuals.

The sickle-cell trait thus provides an example of how swiftly genetic changes can occur in a population. In almost all other cases the process is much slower. The differences we find between individuals is evidence that the process whereby one gene is substituted for another is an ongoing one. Many of these processes are clearly under way simultaneously; that is why we are able to count so many differences between two individuals. Some of the processes—an unknown number—may have reached the level of equilibrium we have noted with respect to sickle-cell anemia in the presence of malaria, namely that both gene A and gene S coexist in the population in a ratio that does not change any further, once equilibrium is reached, unless the environment also changes. This change in the environment has in fact begun to materialize. The incidence of sickle-cell anemia among blacks who have now lived for 200 or 300 years in the relatively malaria-free environments of the U.S. is only 25 percent of the incidence among equivalent populations in malarial Africa.

Many other mutant genes are similarly not at equilibrium, and their prevalence will change substantially with time. If we could visit the earth 10,000 years from now, we might find substantial changes in the comparative frequencies of all gene types. Some of these gene frequencies may change with the passage of time because one form of a gene has an advantage over another, and its frequency will tend to increase. With other genes the changes can proceed randomly. As mutations keep pouring in at every generation there is a constant state of flux.

How do such processes bear on the genetics of race? When we look at the main divisions of mankind, we find many differences that are visible to the unaided eye. It is not hard to assess the origin of an individual with respect to the major racial subdivisions: the straight-haired, tan Orientals, the wiry-haired, dark Africans and the lank-haired, pale Caucasians. If we analyze our impressions in detail, we find that they come down to a few highly visible characteristics: the color of the skin, the color and form of the hair and the gross morphology of the face, the eye folds, the nose and the lips. It is highly likely that all these differences are determined genetically, but they are not determined in any simple way. For example, where skin color is concerned there are at least four gene differences that contribute to variations in pigmentation.

If we return to the mechanisms by which differences in genes give rise to differences in proteins, we find that differences in proteins parallel the superficial differences of race only to a limited extent. The differences between individuals that have been assessed by the random sampling of enzymes total some 200,000 for any two Caucasians. Protein differences of the same order of magnitude also exist between two Orientals and between two African blacks. If, in choosing individuals for comparison, we take two Caucasians from the same village, the nucleotide-pair differences will be slightly less; if we take two Caucasians from the geographical extremes of Europe, they will be slightly more. If we compare a Caucasian with a black African, the differences increase somewhat, but not by a great deal. Much the same is true if we compare a Caucasian with an Oriental. (A black African and an Ori-

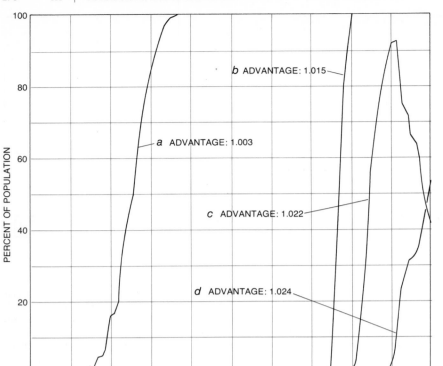

FOUR ADVANTAGEOUS MUTATIONS are traced over 10,000 generations in a computer simulation. The first to appear (*a*), with a fitness advantage only .003 greater than unity (1.0), was present in all the population some 2,300 generations later. The most advantageous mutation (*d*) swamped the next most advantageous one in only 1,000 generations.

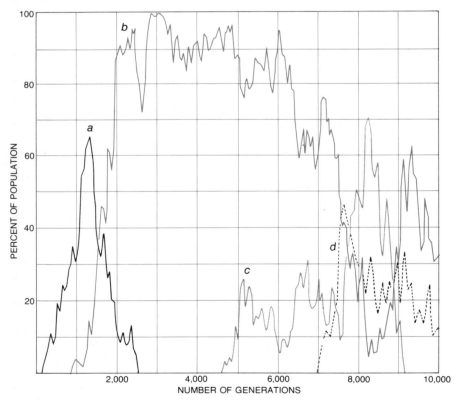

NEUTRAL MUTATIONS are traced over the same 10,000 generations in a second computer simulation. Although the gene-frequency fluctuations are random, the second mutation (*color*) succeeds in supplanting the first and even regains a majority position after a temporary swamping. Fluctuations of this kind are classified as random genetic drift.

ental may show slightly greater differences.) Race as a factor thus adds remarkably little to the differences we can detect between any two individuals. Why, then, are there such differences in some traits, differences profound enough to enable us to diagnose the origin of a Caucasian, an Oriental or an African at a glance? Which is a better measure of difference, the genes that give rise to proteins or what we perceive when we simply look at a person?

As we have seen, the genes for enzymes are similar in different populations. The same seems to be true of all the other genes we can analyze, for example the substances that account for the various blood groups: *A, B, AB, O* and so on. In contrast to this relative uniformity it seems likely that the genes that determine the color of the skin, the color and form of the hair and the morphology of facial characteristics are atypical in being much more diversified. How did such differences arise? Our best answer to the question is embarrassingly vague. For example, we are prepared on a commonsense basis to accept the notion that a darker skin is advantageous in the Tropics: it is less subject to sunburn. Why, however, do Caucasians have a light-colored skin? An answer has been suggested by W. F. Loomis of Brandeis University, and it is somewhat unexpected. His hypothesis is that at latitudes where solar radiation is not particularly intense the skin must be light in color if ultraviolet radiation is to penetrate it and produce enough vitamin D. An adequate supply of vitamin D is critical for growth; if it is not obtained directly through the diet (and it rarely is), it must be formed from precursors in the diet. Ultraviolet radiation is necessary to effect the transformation.

Several details of the Loomis hypothesis are open to criticism, but its general conclusion has not been refuted. Archaeology may provide substantiation; if there was a shortage of vitamin D among early Europeans, one should be able to see the effects in the form of rickets in skeletons. I have calculated that several hundred skeletons from suitable populations would need to be observed in order to test the Loomis hypothesis; so far only a small number of skeletons have been examined. The diet of the Neolithic Europeans who may have been the direct ancestors of today's Caucasians fits well, however, with the vitamin D hypothesis of skin-color selection pressure. These people were cereal-eaters and, unlike the earlier inhabitants of Europe, did not consume much animal protein. Cereals contain the precursors of vitamin D but not the vitamin itself, so that a need for ultraviolet radiation would have existed. At the time of the Industrial Revolution in England, when farming folk moved to the cities and lived in dark slums, rickets became a very common disease. Even the English were not sufficiently light-skinned when the usual quota of ultraviolet radiation was reduced. Hygienists of the period soon learned that exposure to the sun was all that was needed to prevent rickets.

Whatever role the vitamin-D need may have played in Caucasian skin color, it is likely that variations in skin color generally express genetic adaptation to climate. Hair form and such ranges of facial traits as a large nose as opposed to a small one or a narrow eye opening as opposed to a wide one may also represent adaptations to different climatic conditions. Body size too seems to be related to climate. It is always possible, of course, that sexual selection—the "tastes" of our ancestors—also played a part in shaping us one way or another. Climatic adaptation nonetheless makes sense, even if its role in selection pressure is far from being rigorously proved.

If this assumption is correct, we have a good explanation of why some differences among races are so large and others are so small. The differences we see when we look at people are genuinely superficial; the interface between the body and the environment, particularly the climatic dimension of the environment, is the body surface. It is therefore no wonder that the interface has been changed by natural selection to fit the environment to a far greater extent than the rest of our genes have.

The key prerequisite for the differentiation of any animal population into races is some kind of separation of groups that prevents interbreeding. In man's development separation must have been achieved mainly by geography. Today geographic separation has largely broken down, but even in prehistoric times there was considerable movement. An outstanding example is the migration from Asia to the Western Hemisphere across the Bering Strait land bridge roughly between 50,000 and 12,000 years ago.

Geographic distance favors local differentiation even where there are no major barriers to movement. Unless there are strict barriers of some kind, however, the differences are not sharp but gradual, continuous rather than discontinuous. This kind of gradation is characteristic of most human racial differentiation. When on occasion geological

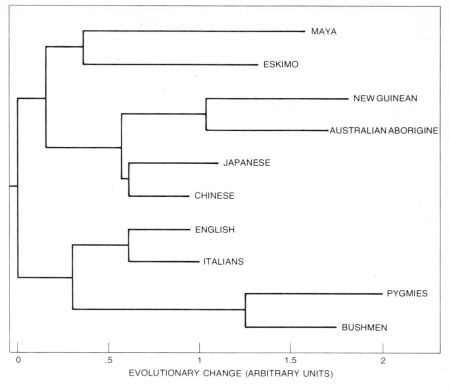

EVOLUTIONARY TREE groups 10 populations, measuring their separation from a common beginning on a scale proportional to the number of substitutions evident in 58 genes. Three main groups emerge: Africans, Europeans and one including Orientals, Oceanians and native Americans. Europeans trail in evolutionary change, possibly owing to intermixture.

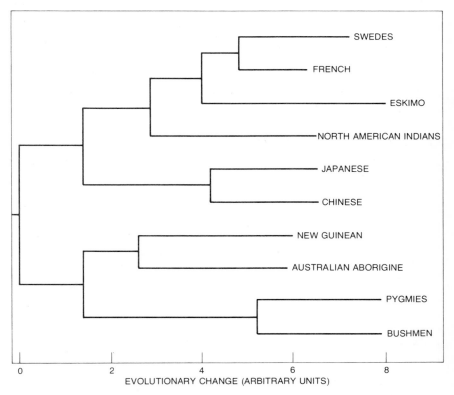

ANTHROPOMETRIC TREE, based on 26 external measurements and observations, shows 10 comparable populations; the array differs from the evolutionary tree's. Europeans now join Orientals and native Americans, whereas Oceanians are with Africans. This suggests that anthropometric characteristics are more affected by climate than genes are, so that the relations shown here are due more to similar environments than to similar descents.

events created insuperable barriers, human genetic differentiation was intensified. This is what happened, for example, when communication between southeastern Asia and Australia and between northeastern Asia and the New World was reduced or totally inhibited by an increase in sea level some 12,000 years ago.

It is possible to reconstruct in the form of a tree some of the history of the genetic differences generated in this way. The reconstruction assumes a fairly sharp separation between an original group and a group that moved away, a separation distinct enough to prevent any (or almost any) contact between the descendants of the two groups. The fact that the migrations may have taken

place over long periods presents no major difficulty. Later migrations and exchanges may blur the picture, but they do not necessarily erase it.

Can one use the genetic data obtained from present human racial groups to reconstruct the history of these past separations? More than 10 years ago I undertook such an effort in collaboration with Anthony Edwards. We made use of the available genetic data on a sample of populations representing the aboriginal inhabitants of five continents. The data covered 15 different genes. With the accumulation of information on more genes, it became possible to repeat the reconstruction with a larger data base. Recently, in collaboration with A. Piazza, L. Sgaramella-Zonta and P. Gluck-

man, I have analyzed the data for 58 genes. The result is in remarkable agreement with the earlier one [see top illustration on preceding page].

The analysis has also made it possible to better understand the origins of many populations, such as the Lapps and the Ainu of Japan. The position of both groups has been a matter of controversy. We find, however, that the Ainu cannot be genetically distinguished from other Orientals and that the Lapps are essentially main-stem Caucasians.

It would be desirable to add time estimates to the tree to indicate the approximate dates when the separations took place. In some instances, for example the occupation of Australia or of the Americas, approximate dates are

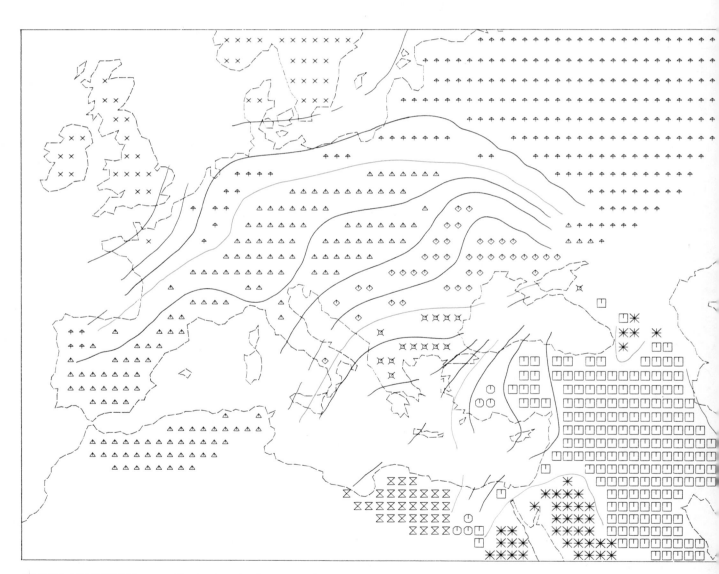

SPREAD OF FARMING across Europe from nuclear areas where agriculture was known more than 9,000 years ago is traced on this computer-generated map. Data are carbon-14 age determinations from some 90 early Neolithic sites, collated by the author and Albert J. Ammerman. The map was produced at the IBM Research Laboratory in San Jose, Calif., with Donald E. Schreiber's program for analysis and display of such data. The rate of spread proves to be about one kilometer per year. If, as is probable, not only

known. In other instances the estimates depend on the constancy of evolutionary rates, and as the tree shows such constancy has not been the case. Caucasians and some Orientals apparently have evolved rather slowly; both groups exhibit shorter branches than Africans. Even though about the same amount of time has elapsed since these groups separated, the amounts of genetic change in them are vastly different. One possible reason for these differences will be examined below.

Perhaps the most interesting estimate to be obtained in this way is the one referring to the time of the original split, the oldest separation in the tree. Allowing for the sources of uncertainty I have mentioned, the time can be given, with

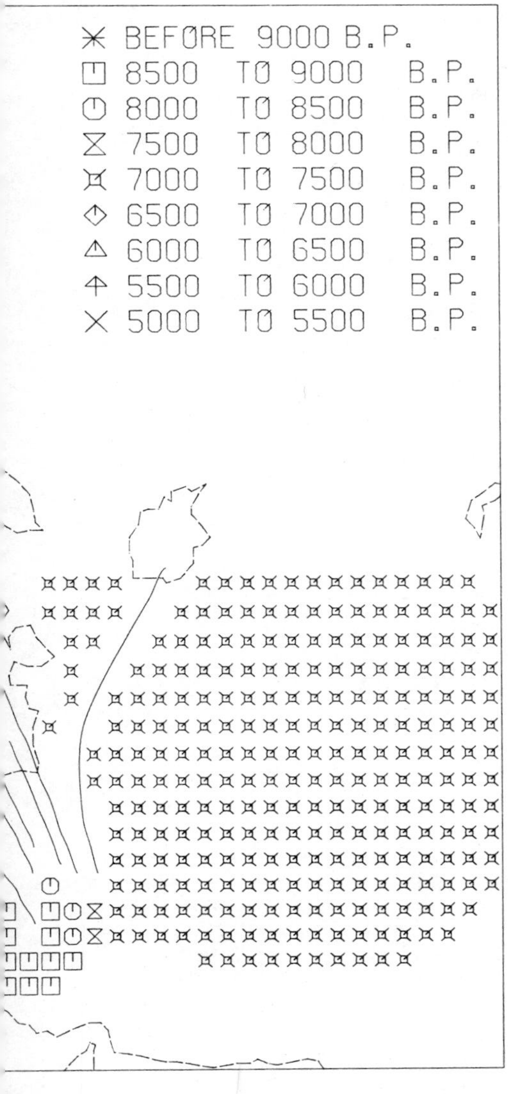
BEFORE 9000 B.P.
8500 TO 9000 B.P.
8000 TO 8500 B.P.
7500 TO 8000 B.P.
7000 TO 7500 B.P.
6500 TO 7000 B.P.
6000 TO 6500 B.P.
5500 TO 6000 B.P.
5000 TO 5500 B.P.

Near Eastern farming but also Near Eastern farmers entered Europe, it could explain why modern Europeans are genetically intermediate between Africans and Orientals.

reservations, as being approximately 35,000 to 40,000 years ago. It is encouraging to note that the oldest-known fossil remains that are classified as *Homo sapiens sapiens,* that is, modern man in the strict sense, are between 40,000 and 60,000 years old. Thus two independent estimates are compatible and indicate that the differentiation among races began not long after the appearance of modern man.

The simplest interpretation of these conclusions today would envision a relatively small group starting to spread not long after modern man appeared. With the spreading, groups became separated and isolated. Racial differentiation followed. Fifty thousand years or so is a short time in evolutionary terms, and this may help to explain why, genetically speaking, human races show relatively small differences. Future discoveries may of course alter these conclusions. It should also be noted that there are fossils of manlike primates that are a great deal more than 60,000 years old. Indeed, some of these fossils may be three million years old. All of them, however, are quite distinct from the fossils of modern man.

It is interesting to pursue the genetic details of one of these differentiations, even though it is a comparatively recent one. One of modern man's most important technological innovations, the domestication of plants and animals, was achieved in various relatively restricted areas of the earth; the domestications were probably independent of one another. Of no less than three such nuclear areas, the best-known is the Near East, where the domestication of wheat, barley and other cereals and of cattle, sheep, goats and pigs began some 10,000 years ago.

With my colleague Albert J. Ammerman, an archaeologist now working at Stanford University, I have plotted the carbon-14 dates for the oldest remains of domesticated plants in Europe; this is an area where carbon-14 determinations are not only abundant but also reliable. The spread is rather regular and relatively slow [*see illustration at left*]. The average rate of spread is about one kilometer per year. We have asked the question: Did the new technology spread, or was it the people of the nuclear areas who spread, bringing their technology with them? One consequence of the introduction of agriculture, of course, is an increase in the number of people who can live in a given area. Such an increase in population is often accompanied by a wave of expansion.

Early farming was in itself a shifting type of agriculture that required frequent movement from old fields to new ones. Furthermore, the transition from a hunting and gathering economy to an agricultural economy is a radical one. Little is known about how many people inhabited Europe just before the arrival of farming, but what data there are suggest a low population density. Therefore it is not very likely that the new technology alone spread across Europe.

There is no clear evidence, either archaeological or genetic, opposing the hypothesis that it was the farmers of the nuclear area themselves who spread to Europe, not to mention in other directions. Further analysis is needed, but the hypothesis seems a useful one. On this basis the Caucasians could be mostly the descendants of farmers from the Near East, although it is clear that they would also have mixed with the indigenous inhabitants of Europe. This could account for the fact that Caucasians are genetically somewhat intermediate between Africans and Orientals; if the Near East was their center of origin, they began as a group geographically intermediate between Africans and Asians. Their admixture with local elements during their subsequent spread (together with other factors, some of them linked to the increase in numbers following the adoption of agriculture) can also help to explain the apparent lower rate of genetic change among Caucasians.

It is worth noting that the study of single genes is probably more useful for reconstructing a common ancestry than the study of superficial traits or of bone shape and size, which are probably the effects of many genes and are subject to short-term environmental effects. This limitation is not widely realized and has been the source of some misunderstanding. Moreover, even some single genes are less useful than others for reconstructing the history of the human population. For example, genes that are rapidly selected under specific environmental conditions, such as the sickle-cell gene, may be providing us with misleading information. The fact is that we do not know enough about how natural selection affects most of the genes we study. If we knew more, we would choose those genes that show fewer (or less systematic) effects from natural selection and have differentiated in a more random fashion. Strange as it may seem, chance-determined effects are the ones most useful for reconstructing the genetic history of the human population.

Growing Up

by J. M. Tanner
September 1973

Events in the interaction between the environment and the genetic potential during the growth of the child are critical to the health of the adult. At the same time "normal" growth is highly variable

Over the past 100 years there has been a deep change in attitudes toward the years of childhood, following the realization of how crucial the process of growing up is to the entire subsequent life of the individual. Instead of child labor we have universal education; instead of birch rods we have psychotherapists. The study of child growth and development is central to modern educational theory and practice. It also bears heavily on social policy concerning the distribution of food, the condition of housing and the control of population. The study of growth in this context has made us appreciate more than ever before the intricate way in which genetic endowment and cultural forces continuously interact to mold the life of the individual child. For example, what are we to make of the fact that in most industrial countries the age of menarche (first menstruation) has shown a steady downward trend of three to four months per decade for the past century? Identical twins growing up in the same environment attain menarche within a month or two of each other, so that the genes are clearly involved. Yet the trend suggests that the environmental factors can exert a powerful influence.

There are two ways of plotting a child's growth. One is to simply show the child's height at successive ages. Another is to show the increments of height gained from one age to the next, expressed as the rate of growth per year. If we think of growth as a form of motion, the first curve shows the distance traveled and the second shows the velocity of growth. The velocity curve reflects the child's state at any particular time better than the distance curve, because the distance curve depends largely on how much the child has grown in the preceding years. Children of the same age show a wide variation in their height. In fact, this variation is so great that if a child who was of exactly average height at his seventh birthday grew not at all for two years, he would still be just within the normal limits of height attained at age nine.

In general the velocity of growth decreases from the fourth month of fetal life until the early teen-age years. At that time there is a marked acceleration of growth called the adolescent growth spurt. The adolescent spurt is a constant feature in all human growth curves. On the average it comes two years earlier in girls than in boys. It is less pronounced in girls because it is caused partly by testosterone, the male sex hormone.

Human growth itself is a rather regular process. Contrary to opinions still heard occasionally, growth in height does not proceed by fits and starts, nor does growth in upward dimensions alternate with growth in transverse dimensions. The more carefully the measurements are made, the more regular the succession of points in the graph of a child's growth becomes. A good technique of positioning the child for measurement is as important as the proper apparatus for accurately measuring his height. Careful positioning minimizes the decrease in height that occurs during the day for postural reasons. The decrease is significant: it can be as much as three centimeters with a bad positioning technique but is less than half a centimeter with good technique.

Mathematical curves have been fitted with great success to measurements of individuals followed during the adolescent spurt. Not only the height of the children has been fitted in this way but also the length of the arms, legs and trunk and the width of the shoulders and hips. Such serial studies of individuals are called longitudinal, as opposed to the studies of populations called cross-sectional, in which each child is measured only once.

The average boy is slightly taller than the average girl until the girl's adolescent spurt begins. Between the ages of about 11 and 13 the average girl is taller. Moreover, she is also heavier, in most

"LAS MENINAS" ("THE MAIDS OF HONOR"), painted by Diego Velazquez in 1656, shows among other things three conditions of human growth. At left center in the portion of the painting reproduced on the opposite page is the Infanta Margarita Maria, the daughter of Philip IV of Spain and his second wife, Marianna of Austria. The Infanta is a normal child of five. (She is dressed as a miniature adult, which reflects a difference in attitudes toward children between then and now.) The two figures at the far right are dwarfs. The woman suffers from achondroplasia, in which the growth of the trunk is normal but the limbs are stunted and the face is characteristically altered. The man, who appears to be a child with his foot playfully on the back of the dog, suffers from the principal form of dwarfism: isolated growth-hormone deficiency. In this form of dwarfism growth is severely limited but the proportions of the body are normal. The Infanta later married Leopold I, the Holy Roman Emperor. Her mother and father appear in the picture as reflections in the mirror to the left of the man in the illuminated doorway. Velazquez, who painted the scene as though he were making a portrait of the king and queen while the Infanta looked on, put himself in the picture at the far left. The painting has a room to itself at the Prado in Madrid.

respects as strong and sexually much more mature. Only when the boy's spurt begins does he pass the girls, to take up his adult status of being the larger and more physically powerful sex. This changeover in size and maturity in the sexes is just one example of how the biology of growth presents problems in the organization of activities in schools.

Nearly all the bones and muscles take part in the adolescent growth spurt. The increase in the size of the muscles is much more marked in boys than in girls. This growth, perhaps combined with changes in the muscles themselves toward more power per unit of cross-sectional area of muscle, results in a large increase in the strength of adolescent boys. Boys also develop a larger heart and lungs in relation to their size than girls. In addition they develop a higher systolic blood pressure, a lower rate of heartbeat while they are resting, a greater capacity for oxygen in the blood and a greater power for neutralizing the chemical products of muscular exercise (such as lactic acid), resulting in a faster rate of recovery from physical exhaustion.

At the same time the male's shoulders show a proportionally greater spurt in width than the female's, while the female's hips widen more than the male's. In short, at adolescence the male becomes more adapted for the tasks of hunting, fighting and manipulating heavy objects, as is necessary in some forms of food gathering. It is as a direct result of these anatomical and physiological changes that athletic ability increases to such a marked degree in boys at adolescence. The notion of a boy outgrowing his strength at this stage has little observational support. Strength, athletic skill and physical endurance all progress rapidly throughout adolescence; if the adolescent feels weak and becomes easily exhausted, it is for psychological and social reasons.

Important sex differences develop in the individual long before puberty. During prenatal life the Y chromosome of the male induces the growth of the testes. These organs manufacture testosterone, the hormone that causes the development of the external male genitalia. In addition fetal testosterone has a specific action on the hypothalamic portion of the brain, transforming it into a male hypothalamus. The action is irrevocable, at least in experimental animals, and has to happen during a short period when the hypothalamus is particularly sensitive. If no testosterone is received during that period, the hypothalamus differen-

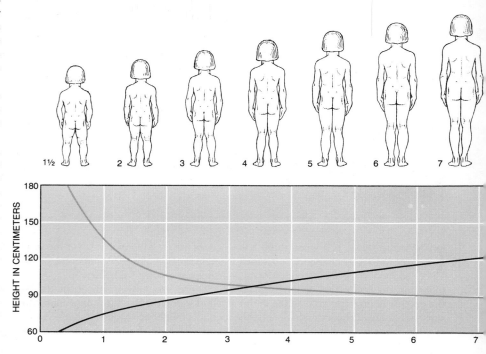

GIRL GROWING UP is shown at regular intervals from infancy to maturity (*top*). The figures show the change in the form of her body as well as her increase in height. The

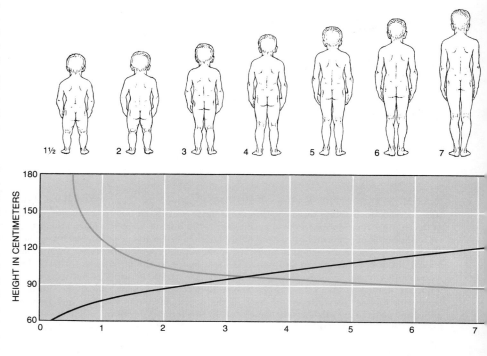

BOY GROWING UP is shown at the same age intervals as the girl. Again the height curve and velocity curve of his growth are below the figures that show the development of his

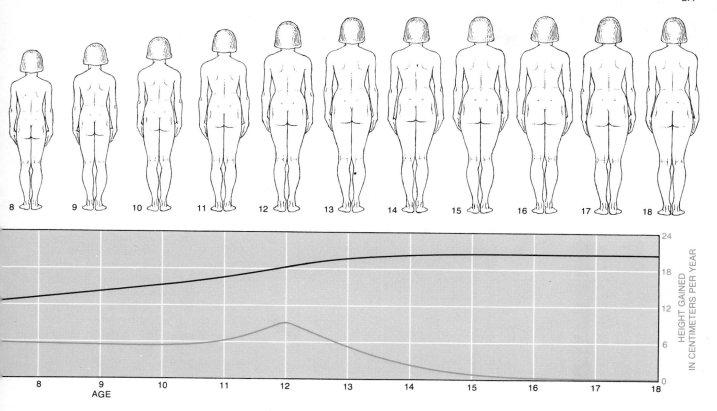

height curve (*black*) is an average for girls in North America and western Europe. Superposed on it is a curve for velocity of growth (*color*), which displays the increments of height gained from one age to the next. The sharp peak is the adolescent growth spurt.

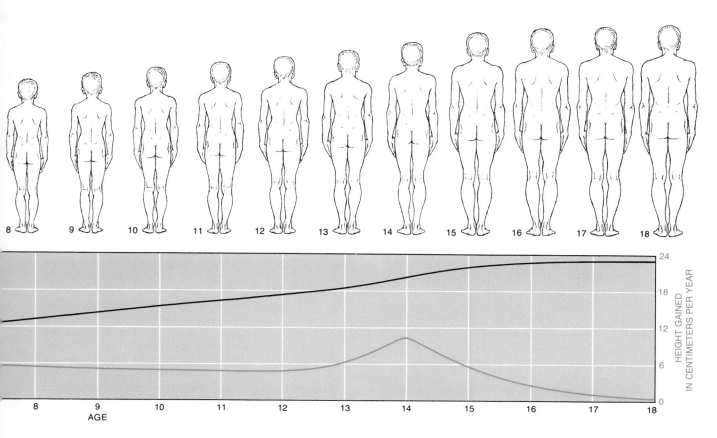

body. His adolescent growth spurt comes some two years later than the girl's. The human figures in both of these illustrations are based on photographs in the longitudinal-growth studies of Nancy Bayley and Leona Bayer of the University of California at Berkeley.

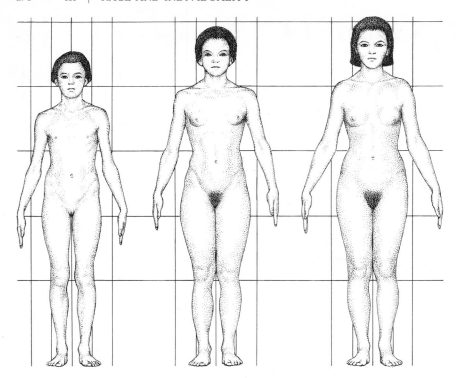

THREE GIRLS, all with the chronological age of 12.75 years, differed dramatically in development according to whether the particular girl had not yet reached puberty (*left*), was part of the way through it (*middle*) or had finished her development (*right*). This range of variation is completely normal. This drawing and the one below are based on photographs made by author and his colleagues at Institute of Child Health of University of London.

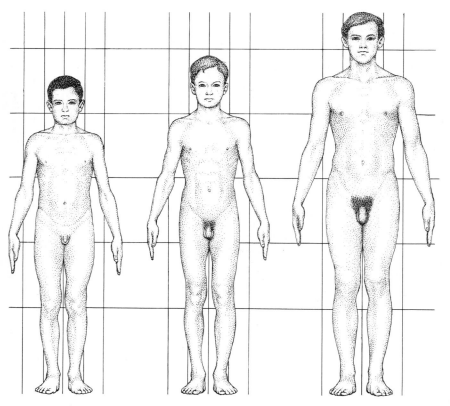

THREE BOYS, all of the chronological age of 14.75 years, showed a similar variation in the range of their development. As is indicated in the charts on page 22, evidently some boys have entirely finished their growth and sexual maturation before others even begin theirs.

tiates as female, that is, as an organ that will mediate the endocrinological functions of the female's sexual cycle. The same is probably true in man, with the sensitive period coming in the fourth month of fetal life.

Other sex differences develop gradually during the entire course of childhood growth. From birth onward males have larger forearms than females with respect to the length of their upper arms or to total body height. The velocity of growth in the length of the male's forearm is always slightly greater than the velocity of growth in the female's.

At puberty some of the more distinct sex differences appear, and the majority of them result in immediate differences in behavior. At about the same time that the adolescent growth spurt is under way, the reproductive system of both the male and the female begins to mature. In boys the growth of the penis and the testes accelerates. In girls the breasts begin to develop. In both sexes the pubic hair first appears. Even though girls experience their adolescent growth spurt two years earlier than boys, the sexes are separated only by six months in the first changes of puberty. Menarche is a late event in female puberty and invariably comes after the peak of the growth spurt is over.

Just as there are large variations in the normal range of childhood heights at any particular age, there are wide individual differences in the rates at which children develop—in what has been called the tempo of growth. These differences are present at all ages but their effects are seen most dramatically at adolescence. For example, the range of ages for the beginning of penis growth in males is from 10.5 to 14.5 years, and the range of ages for the completion of that development is from 12.5 to 16.5 years. Evidently some boys have finished their growth before others have even begun.

The importance of this variation in individuals for educational practice is obvious enough, although how to deal with it is less so. Body-contact sports between boys who are early maturers with boys of the same age who are late maturers are scarcely to be recommended. The situation is complicated by the fact that ability in school work and formal examinations is significantly, although not closely, linked to body size and the degree of development. Thus examinations administered to a group of children purely on the basis of their chronological age, such as the 11-plus examination in Britain, tend to pick out more than the fair share of earlier maturers for future advancement without any evidence that

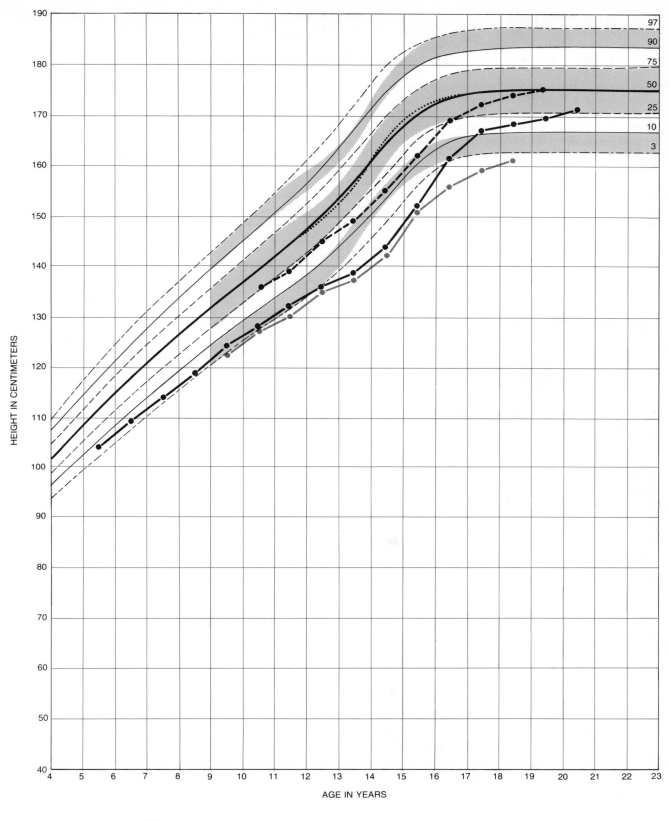

SECULAR TREND IN HEIGHT is shown by surveys of the height of English boys in the years 1833, 1874, 1878 and 1965. Data are reproduced on a standard growth chart. "Single-time standard (cross-sectional)" refers to the average result from cross-sectional surveys. "Repeated-visit standard (longitudinal)" refers to average result from longitudinal surveys. The numbers 97, 90, 75 and so on indicate percent of the male population shorter than a given height.

these would ultimately prove to be the brightest individuals in the group.

There is little doubt that being an early or a late maturer can have considerable and perhaps lasting effects on the individual's behavior. Perhaps boys are at more risk than girls, since the changes in their size and strength are greater. In one case two boys who were of equal height at age 11 differed three years later in height by 12 centimeters (five inches), by many kilograms of weight-lifting performance and by an entire dimension of sexual development. Part of the duty of teachers is to understand this aspect of biological variability, to recognize the late maturers and to reassure them that their ultimate status is not a jot different from that of the early maturers.

In the light of the variation in the tempo of growth, we need some measure of developmental age or physiological maturity that would be applicable throughout the entire period of growth. Numerous possible measurements have been tried, ranging from the number of teeth that have erupted to the amount of water in muscle cells. The various scales do not necessarily coincide; the most commonly used is bone age, or skeletal maturity. This measurement rests on the fact that the bones (in practice those of the hand and wrist) pass through the same developmental stages, independently of size, in all children. Therefore a scale can be constructed corresponding to how close the bone is to the adult appearance at any given time.

Bone age can be used to help in certain problems of educational guidance. The Royal School of Ballet in the United Kingdom insists that the height of dancers in its corps de ballet be within rather narrow limits. Its associated school takes in prospective dancers mostly at ages nine to 11. A considerable number of the children were found to end up as adults who were unacceptably tall or short. Their training had been wasted, their hopes dashed and their life disoriented. At the Institute of Child Health of the University of London, R. H. Whitehouse, W. A. Marshall and I developed a method for predicting adult height, derived originally from the work of Nancy Bayley of the University of California at Berkeley. Adult height is predicted by an equation involving present height, chronological age and bone age. The coefficients of the equations differ at age nine, 10 and so on; in puberty the importance of the bone-age coefficient increases and that of the chronological-age coefficient decreases. Thus for a 12-year-old girl one has a measure of whether she is advanced and nearing the end of her growth period or whether she is delayed and has much more growth to come.

The predictions are moderately successful. The great majority of the children are within five centimeters (two inches) of the actual height attained. We thus give the prediction in the form of a 10-centimeter band of adult height. If part of this band overlaps the required band for dancers, well and good; if it does not, the child is told of her limited chances for a dancing career. We are seeking ways of making the prediction better. Allowance for parental height improves it slightly, but the chief errors seem to come from our being unable to predict how large the adolescent spurt will be. The amount of height added in the spurt is largely independent of pre-adolescent growth. Very likely it has a separate genetic control.

The rate of growth at any age is clearly the outcome of the interaction of genetic and environmental factors. The child inherits possible patterns of growth from his parents. The environment, however, dictates which (if any) of the patterns will become actual. In an environ-

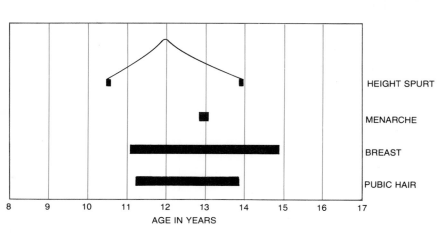

SEQUENCE OF EVENTS OF PUBERTY IN GIRLS at various ages is diagrammed for the average child. The hump in the bar labeled "Height spurt" represents the peak velocity of the spurt. The bars represent the beginning and completion of the events of puberty. Although the adolescent growth spurt for girls typically begins at age 10.5 and ends at age 14, it can start as early as age 9.5 and end as late as age 15. Similarly, menarche (the onset of menstruation) can come at any time between the ages of 10 and 16.5 and tends to be a late event of puberty. Some girls begin to show breast development as early as age eight and have completed it by age 13; others may not begin it until age 13 and complete it at age 18. First pubic hair appears after the beginning of breast development in two-thirds of all girls.

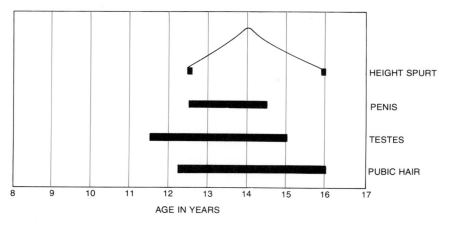

SEQUENCE OF EVENTS OF PUBERTY IN BOYS is also shown at various ages for the average child. The adolescent growth spurt of boys can begin as early as age 10.5 or as late as age 16 and can end anywhere from age 13.5 to age 17.5. Elongation of the penis can begin from age 10.5 to 14.5 and can end from age 12.5 to age 16.5. Growth of the testes can begin as early as age 9.5 or as late as age 13.5 and end at any time between the ages of 13.5 and 17.

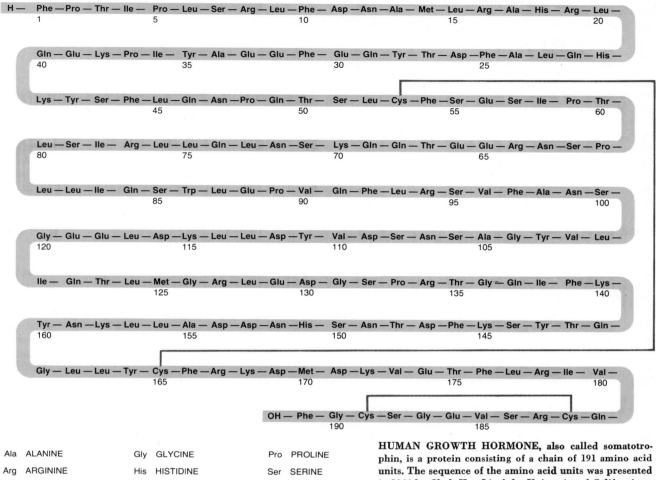

Ala	ALANINE	Gly	GLYCINE	Pro	PROLINE
Arg	ARGININE	His	HISTIDINE	Ser	SERINE
Asn	ASPARAGINE	Ile	ISOLEUCINE	Thr	THREONINE
Asp	ASPARTIC ACID	Leu	LEUCINE	Trp	TRYPTOPHAN
Cys	CYSTINE	Lys	LYSINE	Tyr	TYROSINE
Gln	GLUTAMINE	Met	METHIONINE	Val	VALINE
Glu	GLUTAMIC ACID	Phe	PHENYLALANINE		

HUMAN GROWTH HORMONE, also called somatotrophin, is a protein consisting of a chain of 191 amino acid units. The sequence of the amino acid units was presented in 1966 by Choh Hao Li of the University of California at Berkeley and was later modified by Hugh Niall of the Massachusetts General Hospital. Somatotrophin, acting with other hormones, regulates the normal growth of children. Lines joining two pairs of cystine (*Cys*) units represent disulfide bonds. Growth-hormone molecule is folded in such a way that paired cystine units are adjacent to each other.

ment where nutrition is always adequate, where the parents are caring and where social factors are adequate it is the genes that largely determine differences between members of the population in growth and in adult physique. In an environment that is suboptimal and perhaps changes from time to time, as in the periodic famines characteristic of much of the world, differences between members of the population reflect the social history of the individuals as much as their genetic endowment.

The genetic-environment interaction need not be additive. A child whose genes enable him to grow very well in an optimal environment may be less able to do so under poor circumstances than a child who in the good environment was smaller than he. Such differences in the degree to which growth can be regulated probably themselves depend largely on genetic factors. Girls are on the average better able to cope with environmental changes than boys, and their growth is less affected by such adverse factors as atomic radiation or poor nutrition. The same holds true in at least some other mammalian species.

The shape of the body is under closer genetic control than size. Identical twins may be so nearly the same in shape that they cannot be distinguished, yet one may be larger in absolute dimensions, usually from the time of birth. Japanese reared in California grew to be larger than Japanese in the then poorer nutritional circumstances of Japan, but their characteristic facial and trunk-limb proportions did not change. It seems that between blacks and whites in the U.S. and Jamaica there is very little difference in height when the circumstances of the two groups can be matched, but differences in the two groups' body proportions remain, American blacks having longer legs and arms and slenderer hips than American whites. Similar genetically controlled differences in proportion are observed between, for example, the Tutsi and Hutu, two African populations living side by side in Rwanda.

Since growth is so sensitive to malnutrition and other environmental upsets, surveys of the growth of children are an essential part of any country's monitoring of its social and nutritional status. When such surveys are carried out with the proper attention to sampling, the proper training of the measurers and the proper recording of the relevant social data, they can clearly indicate the factors causing childhood disadvantage. These factors usually include the number of siblings in the family, the occupation and income of the parents and the physical geography of the region: whether it is mountainous or low-lying, hot or cold.

Complications arise in countries where the population is not genetically homogeneous, or where social class and ethnic origin are related. Even in these cases, however, standards can be set for each ethnic group. In my opinion standards for developing countries should not be constructed from a random sample of the entire population, as standards in well-nourished countries are. In countries that are subject to general malnutrition, standards should be based on a sample of the population that is environmentally faring the best, since these individuals represent the currently attainable range of desired norms for the population as a whole.

As the environmental and social conditions of a country improve, the children grow up faster and reach a greater final size. The variation between individuals of different social classes becomes less. This process is termed the secular trend of growth. In Europe and North America the process has been going on continuously for about 100 years. The first survey of a population in the United Kingdom was the measurement of the height of boys working in factories in 1833. The results of this early survey can be compared with the results of a survey of boys of the working classes and of the upper middle classes carried out from 1874 through 1878 and with the results of a modern survey of London boys in 1965.

The effect of the environment on the boys' rate of maturation is considerably greater than its effect on the boys' final size. In the 19th century working-class boys went on growing far into their middle twenties and thus eventually made up for some of their earlier deficit. Victor Oppers of the Amsterdam department of health has estimated that the secular trend of final adult size in the Netherlands was zero between 1820 and 1860. Between 1860 and 1960, however, it was one centimeter per decade. In other words, the average adult in 1960 was 10 centimeters (four inches) taller than his counterpart of a century ago.

There has also been a downward secular trend in the age of menarche. In some countries where the statistics are adequate there was a trend of three to four months per decade from 1840 to 1960. There are indications that the trend has ceased in some populations, such as in Oslo, in London and in the

upper social classes in the U.S. In others, however, it is still active. The trend of increasing height has also nearly ceased in American and British populations that are economically well off.

Although the reasons for secular trends are not fully understood, it seems likely that better nutrition, particularly in infancy, is chiefly responsible. In many countries today, however, there is a danger that children are being overfed. Childhood obesity is becoming common, particularly where children are fed from bottles and are given solid food very early instead of (or in addition to) breast-feeding. In these circumstances surveys of growth are still highly important, but measurements of skin folds, which are an indication of the amount of subcutaneous fat, have to be added to measurements of height and weight.

The mechanisms through which growth is genetically controlled are obscure. Indeed, the reason one child grows faster and to a greater adult height than another is quite unknown. All we can say at present is that certain hormones are essential for normal growth. Among them are the pituitary growth hormone, the thyroid hormone, insulin and the gonadotropic and sex hormones.

Lack of growth hormone causes a particular form of dwarfism. (The term is never used in the clinic, since it tends to conjure up associations with elves and demons. We refer to these children as suffering from short stature.) Such children are normal at birth but fail to grow adequately in length thereafter (although they may at first apparently gain weight normally, due to the accumulation of excessive fat). Human growth hormone, extracted from the pituitary gland of cadavers, is now available for the treatment of short stature due to growth-hormone deficiency. Such treatment results in a period of supernormal growth, which has been called "catch up" growth. Catch-up growth is characteristic of all children whose normal development has been retarded (for example by malnutrition) and then resumes when the retarding factor is removed. Growth-hormone-deficient children require growth hormone continuously throughout childhood and adolescence in order to attain normal adult stature.

The condition seems to be due to a malfunction of the hypothalamus rather than of the pituitary gland itself. Like all pituitary hormones, growth hormone is controlled by a specific releasing hormone secreted by the cells of the hypothalamus. The deficiency may be simply

in the amount of growth hormone, or it may extend to the release of other pituitary hormones as well. The deficiency occurs in families. Some 15 percent of the siblings of these patients and 1 to 2 percent of the parents also lack growth hormone.

Growth hormone seems to completely restore the capacity of these children to grow. If it is given early enough, the child catches up totally and ends up at, or very near, his genetically programmed curve. Interestingly enough, giving excess growth hormone produces no excess growth. By the same token giving growth hormone to normal children, who have their own supply, fails to increase their size.

Growth hormone does not act directly on growing cartilage. It causes the liver to secrete another hormone: somatomedin. The somatomedin molecule is much smaller than the growth hormone molecule, but its structure is not yet known. Whether or not somatomedin could be administered to cause normal small children to grow to be normal large children is not known. The possibility, however, seems unlikely. The ultimate control of the size of a child probably lies in the number of cartilage cells he has and their responsiveness to the various hormones.

In certain forms of dwarfism it is these cartilage cells that are at fault. The best-known of these growth disorders is called achondroplasia. Here the defect is localized chiefly in the bones of the upper arm and the thigh. Achondroplasia is an inherited disorder; a single dominant gene is responsible.

In some children the secretion of the growth-hormone releaser may be switched off as a result of psychosocial upset. Such children resemble others who have a deficiency of growth hormone, except that they usually also have a history of psychiatric disturbance and abnormal behavior. Furthermore, when these children are removed from their stressful surroundings, their growth hormone switches on again and they show typical catch-up growth. This phenomenon was first described under the name of deprivation dwarfism by Lytt I. Gardner of the Upstate Medical Center of the State University of New York and by Robert M. Blizzard and his colleagues at the Johns Hopkins Hospital [see the article "Deprivation Dwarfism," by Lytt I. Gardner, beginning on page 284]. It is now more usually called psychosocial short stature, since "deprivation" does not always adequately describe the social process that gives rise to it.

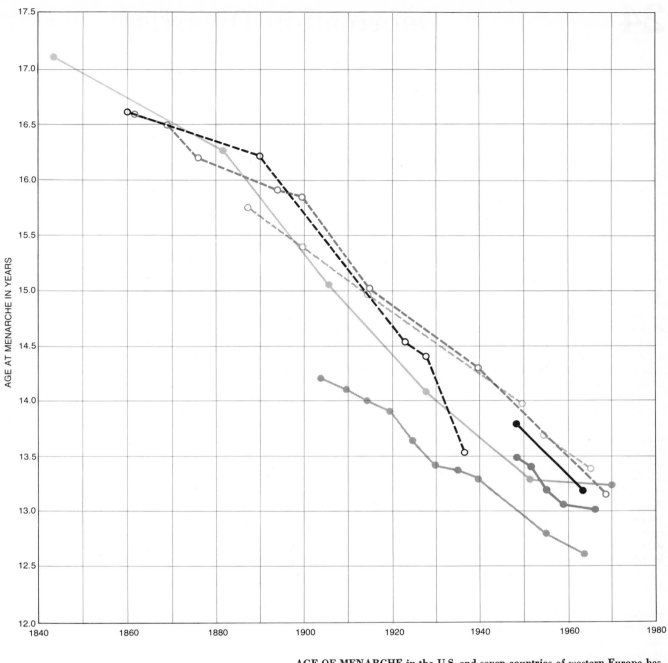

AGE OF MENARCHE in the U.S. and seven countries of western Europe has declined greatly from what it was 120 years ago. For example, in the mid-1840's an average Norwegian girl began menstruating at 17; today she is just over 13. The downward trend appears to be leveling off in the case of some countries. Trend is probably chiefly due to advances in nutrition over the past century.

In addition to growth hormone the sex hormones are required for normal growth in prenatal life and at puberty, and perhaps also in the years before puberty. They are present in small quantities in the blood throughout growth, but the quantities increase greatly at puberty. Testosterone is responsible for much of the adolescent spurt in boys, although growth hormone is still necessary; the growth rate of boys deficient in growth hormone is greater when they

are given growth hormone plus testosterone than when they are given either hormone alone. The adolescent growth spurt in girls, however, seems to be caused by growth hormone plus androgenic hormones from the adrenal gland. The female sex hormone (estrogen) does not give rise to growth, except growth of the breasts and of the reproductive tract.

Much about the mechanism of growth and maturation still remains obscure.

Our lack of specific information does not prevent the use of growth rates as a guide for improving the health of populations, nor does it impair the importance of a knowledge of variation in growth rates, both between and within the sexes. Nevertheless, human biologists would dearly like to know the movement of each of the particular hormonal shuttles that weave the complex and unique patterns that constitute an individual's growing up.

24

Deprivation Dwarfism

by Lytt I. Gardner
July 1972

*Children raised in an emotionally deprived
environment can become stunted. The reason
may be that abnormal patterns of sleep inhibit
the secretion of pituitary hormones, including
the growth hormone*

It has long been known that infants will not thrive if their mothers are hostile to them or even merely indifferent. This knowledge is the grain of truth in a tale, which otherwise is surely apocryphal, told about Frederick II, the 13th-century ruler of Sicily. It is said that Frederick, himself the master of six languages, believed that all men were born with an innate language, and he wondered what particular ancient tongue—perhaps Hebrew—the language was. He sought the answer through an experiment. A group of foster-mothers was gathered and given charge of certain newborn infants. Frederick ordered the children raised in silence, so that they would not hear one spoken word. He reasoned that their first words, owing nothing to their upbringing, would reveal the natural language of man. "But he labored in vain," the chronicler declares, "because the children all died. For they could not live without the petting and the joyful faces and loving words of their foster mothers."

Similar emotional deprivation in infancy is probably the underlying cause of the spectacularly high mortality rates in 18th- and 19th-century foundling homes [see "Checks on Population Growth: 1750–1850," by William L. Langer; SCIENTIFIC AMERICAN Offprint 674]. This, at least, was the verdict of one Spanish churchman, who wrote in 1760: "In the foundling home the child becomes sad, and many of them die of sorrow." Disease and undernourishment certainly contributed to the foundlings' poor rate of survival, but as recently as 1915 James H. M. Knox Jr., of the Johns Hopkins Hospital noted that, in spite of adequate physical care, 90 percent of the infants in Baltimore orphanages and foundling homes died within a year of admission.

Only in the past 30 years or so have the consequences of emotional deprivation in childhood been investigated in ways that give some hope of understanding the causative mechanisms. One pioneer in the field, Harry Bakwin of New York University, began in 1942 to record the physiological changes apparent in infants removed from the home environment for hospital care. These children, he noted, soon became listless, apathetic and depressed. Their bowel movements were more frequent, and even though their nutritional intake was adequate, they failed to gain weight at the normal rate. Respiratory infections and fevers of unknown origin persisted. All such abnormalities, however, quickly disappeared when the infants were returned to their home and mother.

Another early worker, Margaret A. Ribble, studied infants at three New York maternity hospitals over a period of eight years; in several instances she was able to follow the same child from birth to preadolescence. When normal contact between mother and infant was disrupted, she noted, diarrhea was more prevalent and muscle tone decreased. The infants would frequently spit up their food and then swallow it again. This action is called "rumination" by pediatricians. Largely as the result of studies by Renata and Eugenio Gaddini of the University of Rome, it is recognized today as a symptom of psychic disturbance. Ribble concluded that alarm over a lack of adequate "mothering" was not mere sentimentality. The absence of normal mother-infant interaction was "an actual privation which may result in biological, as well as psychological, damage to the infant."

Two other psychiatrically oriented investigators of this period, René Spitz of the New York Psychoanalytic Institute and his colleague Katherine Wolf, took histories of 91 foundling-home infants in the eastern U.S. and Canada. They found that the infants consistently showed evidence of anxiety and sadness. Their physical development was retarded and they failed to gain weight normally or even lost weight. Periods of protracted insomnia alternated with periods of stupor. Of the 91, Spitz and Wolf reported, 34 died "in spite of good food and meticulous medical care." The period between the seventh and the 12th month of life was the time of the highest fatalities. Infants who managed to survive their first year uniformly showed severe physical retardation.

The comparative irrelevance of good diet, as contrasted with a hostile environment, was documented with startling clarity in Germany after World War II. In 1948 the British nutritionist Elsie M. Widdowson was stationed with an army medical unit in a town in the British Zone of Occupation where two small municipal orphanages were located. Each housed 50-odd boys and girls between four and 14 years of age; the children's average age was 8½. They had nothing except official rations to eat and were below normal in height and weight. The medical unit instituted a program of physical examinations of the orphans every two weeks and continued these observations for 12 months. During the first six months the orphanages continued to receive only the official rations. During the last six months the children in what I shall call Orphanage A received in addition unlimited amounts of bread, an extra ration of jam and a supply of concentrated orange juice.

The matron in charge of Orphanage A at the start of this study was a cheerful young woman who was fond of the children in her care. The woman in charge of Orphanage B was older, stern and a strict disciplinarian toward all the children in her care except a small group of favorites. It so happened that at the end of the first six months the cheerful matron left Orphanage A for other employment and the disciplinarian was transferred from Orphanage B to Orphanage A, bringing her eight favorites.

The examinations revealed that during the first six months the weight gained by the children in the "cheerful" orphanage was substantially more than the weight gained by the children in the "strict" orphanage. The strict matron's favorites of course did much better than the rest of her charges. The shift in matrons then occurred, coinciding with the provision of extra food for Orphanage A.

During the next six months the children of Orphanage B, whose food supply was not increased but who no longer had the stern matron, showed a rapid rise in weight. In spite of orange juice, jam and unlimited bread the disciplinarian's new charges in Orphanage A only gained weight at about the same rate as before; indeed, the figures showed that their average weight gain was slightly

less. The matron's favorites were an exception; their weight gain exceeded all the other children's [see illustration on page 290]. An identical trend was recorded with respect to increases in height.

It seems clear that the reaction of the orphans to an adverse emotional environment was a reduction in the normal growth rate. Although the operative mechanism is not easily identified from observations such as these, a unique opportunity arose recently in the U.S. to study in detail the effect of emotional deprivation on an infant's digestive apparatus. In 1965 a mother in upper New York state gave birth to a daughter with an underdeveloped esophagus. A surgical opening was made into the infant's stomach, a feeding tube was inserted and the mother was instructed in its use.

The mother and daughter soon left the hospital for home, where over the next 15 months the mother meticulously fed her child a standard daily dosage of nutrient formula, using a syringe to push the food through the feeding tube. The

mother was fearful, however, of dislodging the feeding tube, and she did not play with the child or cuddle her for the entire period. At the end of 15 months the child had become extremely depressed. She showed evidence of motor retardation, and her physical development was that of an eight-month-old. The child was brought to the University of Rochester Medical Center, where George L. Engel, Franz K. Reichsman and Harry L. Segal conducted extensive observations.

Engel and his associates described the child at the time of admission as exhibiting a "depression withdrawal" reaction. Her facial expression was sad and her muscles flaccid. She was inactive and withdrawn; the withdrawal frequently led to abnormally long periods of sleep. Her stomach secretions were deficient in pepsin and hydrochloric acid. Doses of histamine, which ordinarily stimulate a profuse outpouring of acid by the stomach lining, failed to elicit the normal response.

The investigators began to monitor

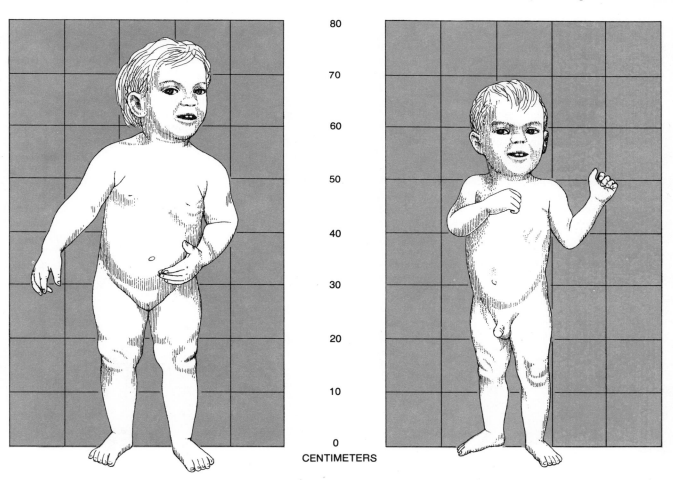

80

70

60

50

40

30

20

10

0

CENTIMETERS

TWINS, NORMAL AND DWARFED, offer evidence of the effect of emotional deprivation on infants. This drawing is based on photographs made when the children were almost 13 months old. The girl was near normal in weight and stature but her twin brother was the size of a seven-month-old. Some four months after the twins were born a period of stress began between the parents; the father then lost his job and left home. It appears that the mother's hostility toward her husband included the son but not the daughter.

the child's activities and keep a record of her emotional state as reflected in facial expressions, at the same time analyzing her gastric secretions. They found that the condition of the stomach was intimately linked with her behavior and emotions. When she was depressed and withdrawn, her production of hydrochloric acid was markedly reduced. When she was angry, talking or eating or otherwise actively relating to external objects, acid production increased.

The child quickly responded to the attention she received from the hospital staff. She gained weight and made up for lost growth; her emotional state improved strikingly. Moreover, these changes were demonstrably unrelated to any change in food intake. During her stay in the hospital she received the same standard nutrient dosage she had received at home. It appears to have been the enrichment of her environment, not of her diet, that was responsible for the normalization of her growth.

A relation between such a physiological deficiency and deprivation dwarfism had been observed in Boston nearly 20 years earlier. On that occasion the abnormality documented was endocrine imbalance. In 1947 Nathan B. Talbot, Edna H. Sobel and their co-workers at the Massachusetts General Hospital were reviewing the clinical findings with respect to some 100 children who were abnormally short for their age. In about half of the cases they found that physiological causes, including lesions of the pituitary gland, were responsible for the stunted growth. In 51 other cases, however, they could find no organic abnormalities. Within this group were 21 children who were not only dwarfed in stature but also abnormally thin. All 21 proved to have a history of emotional disturbance and disordered family environment; the most common finding was

rejection of the child by one parent or both. The investigators concluded that the children's poor condition was the result of an emotionally induced pituitary deficiency.

Some years after this initial observation of psychologically induced endocrine imbalance, Robert Gray Patton and I, working at the State University of New York's Upstate Medical Center in Syracuse, undertook the study of six such "thin dwarfs." We were able to continue observations of two of the children from infancy to late childhood. As we expected, all six were not only short but also far underweight for their age. They were also retarded in skeletal maturation: their "bone age" was substantially less than their actual age in years. In this connection the findings of Austin H. Riesen and Henry W. Nissen are of interest. Working at the Yerkes Laboratory of Primate Biology in the late 1940's, they subjected young chimpanzees to environmental deprivation by keeping them in the dark for long periods. The chimpanzees' "bone age" was considerably retarded as a result.

Our six patients all came from disordered family environments. For example, one of them, a girl 15 months old, was kept in a dark room, isolated and unattended; she was removed from this setting only at feeding times. The child was lethargic and slept as much as 16 or 18 hours a day. Following the children's hospital admission and the provision of a normal emotional environment, all six of them showed a rapid gain in weight, improvement in motor abilities and increased social responsiveness. Indeed, the changes were so consistently dramatic that we believe their presence or absence can serve as a diagnostic test for deprivation dwarfism.

In spite of these short-term gains few

of the children recovered entirely from their experience of deprivation dwarfism. They tended to remain below average in height, weight and skeletal maturation. Furthermore, the two we were able to follow until late childhood gave evidence of residual damage to personality structure and to intellect.

A remarkably vivid example of deprivation dwarfism, affecting one of a pair of twins, came to the attention of Joseph G. Hollowell and myself in 1964. The mother had given birth to a boy and a girl. Some four months later she found herself unwelcomely pregnant. A few weeks later her husband lost his job and after a few more weeks he left home.

Almost up to the time of the mother's new pregnancy the twins had been growing at the normal rate. Indeed, the boy, although he had begun to ruminate early in infancy, was progressing somewhat more rapidly than the girl. The mother's hostility toward the father, however, evidently became directed, consciously or unconsciously, toward her son as well. From the 15th week onward the boy's growth rate fell progressively behind his sister's. By the time he was a little over a year of age his height was only that of a seven-month-old.

The boy was then hospitalized. He began to recover lost ground and his rumination gradually subsided. Before the child was released from the hospital the father had returned to the mother. The boy's progress continued in the improved home environment; by his second birthday he had caught up to his sister.

Patton and I have postulated a physiological pathway whereby environmental deprivation and emotional disturbance might affect the endocrine apparatus and thereby have an impact on a child's growth. Impulses from the higher brain centers, in our view, travel along neu-

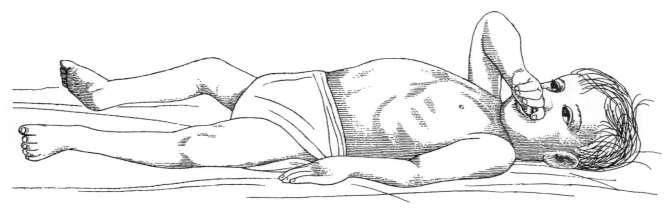

THREE-YEAR-OLD, treated for deprivation dwarfism 18 months earlier, actually lost weight on return to the care of a mother who appeared detached and unemotional in her relationship with the boy. His skeletal maturity on return to the hospital was at the level of a 15-month-old's; he was listless and lay on his back most of the time, his legs spraddled in a characteristic "frog" position.

ral pathways to the hypothalamus and thence, by neurohumoral mechanisms, exert influence on the pituitary gland. Research on "releasing factors" secreted by the hypothalamus, which in turn are responsible for the secretion of various trophic hormones by the anterior pituitary, has shown that hypothalamic centers exercise a major influence over this neighboring gland. Moreover, it is now known that virtually all the blood reaching the pituitary has first bathed the hypothalamic median eminence. Apparently the releasing factors are transported to the pituitary in the blood flowing from the median eminence through the pituitary portal veins.

Evidence of pituitary involvement in deprivation dwarfism is now becoming increasingly abundant. For example, one of the six children that Patton and I had studied came to the attention of my colleague Mary Voorhess in 1963. Following the child's earlier discharge from the hospital, he had spent two years in his disordered home environment and once again exhibited deprivation dwarfism. He was depressed and in an advanced state of malnutrition. An X-ray examination showed that in terms of maturation his bone age was three years less than his chronological age.

A determination was made of the boy's reserve of one important hormone secreted by the anterior pituitary: the adrenocorticotrophic hormone (ACTH). This hormone stimulates the secretion of the steroid hydrocortisone by the adrenal cortex. The steroid is an important regulator of carbohydrate metabolism; it promotes the conversion of protein into sugar, thereby raising the level of blood sugar. The examination showed that the child's reserve of ACTH was abnormally low.

The child entered the hospital, and following his recovery he was placed in a foster home with a favorable emotional environment. Eighteen months after the first measurement of his ACTH reserve the examination was repeated. The child's pituitary function was normal with respect to ACTH reserve. Furthermore, his formerly lagging bone age had almost caught up with his age in years. Both observations provide support for the working hypothesis that the chain of events leading to the clinical manifestations of deprivation dwarfism involves disturbances in pituitary trophic hormone secretion.

Another important pituitary hormone is somatotrophin, the growth hormone. Like most chemical messengers, the growth hormone is present in the blood-

BALD SPOT had developed on the head of child shown on opposite page. This occurs frequently among emotionally deprived children, who will lie in one position for long periods.

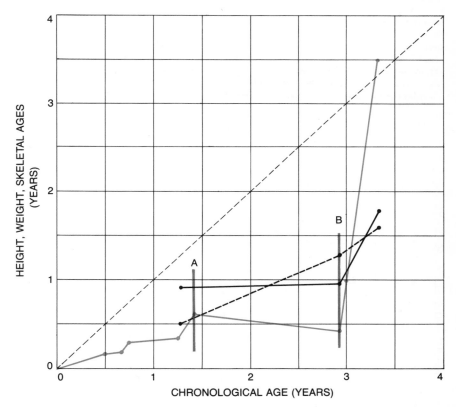

GROWTH RECORD of the boy shown on the opposite page traces his slow decline in weight (*color*) following his release from the hospital at about 18 months of age (*A*). By the age of three he weighed no more than the average six-month-old and was also severely retarded in height (*black curve*) and in bone maturation (*broken curve*). Reentering the hospital (*B*), the child gained weight at a dramatic rate. Placed in a foster home thereafter, he reached a weight above average for his age. Height, weight and skeletal ages of the vertical scale refer to the height, weight or skeletal development of an average child of that age.

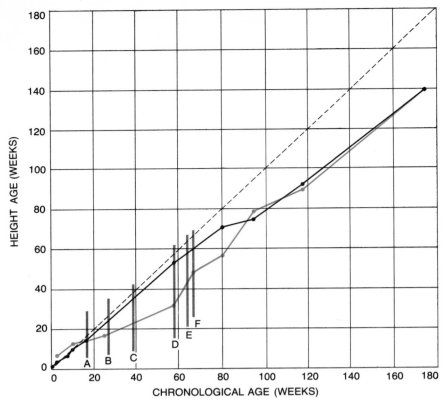

TWINS' INCREASE IN HEIGHT over a 3½-year period is plotted on this graph in terms of normal children's average growth. (The diagonal line marks the 50th percentile.) The boy who developed deprivation dwarfism also exhibited "rumination," that is, he spat up his food and swallowed it again. Nevertheless, his increase in height (color) was equal to or better than his sister's until his mother became pregnant (A). From that time on he fell steadily behind his sister as his father first lost his job (B) and then left home (C). Recovery of lost growth, begun when the boy was admitted to the hospital (D), continued on his return home (F), an event that followed his father's return (E). Before his second birthday the boy once more equaled his sister in height; both, however, were below normal.

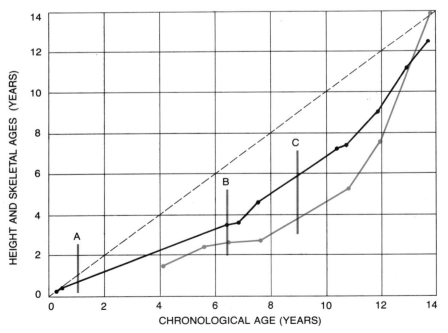

THIRTEEN YEARS of subnormal growth are shown in a child with a disordered home environment. Deserted by her husband (A), the mother worked full time. Six years later (B) the parents were divorced; then (C) the mother remarried and resumed keeping house. The child's bone development (color) but not his stature (black) finally became average.

stream in very small quantities; the normal adult on waking will have less than three micrograms of growth hormone in each liter of blood plasma. Even with refined assay techniques measurements at this low level of concentration are difficult. As a result ways have been sought to briefly stimulate the production of growth hormone. Such stimulation not only makes measurement easier but also, if there is little or no response to the stimulus, provides direct evidence for a pituitary deficiency.

Bernardo A. Houssay of Argentina was the first investigator to point to the metabolic antagonism between insulin and the growth hormone. Subsequent research showed that an injection of insulin lowers the recipient's blood-sugar level, and the reaction is normally followed by an increased output of growth hormone. Jesse Roth and his colleagues at the Veterans Administration Hospital in the Bronx perfected an insulin-stimulation test for growth-hormone concentration in the blood in 1963.

Several quantitative assessments of the relation between emotional deprivation and abnormalities in growth-hormone concentration have been made in recent years. For example, in 1967 George Powell and his colleagues at the Johns Hopkins Hospital worked with a group of children over three years old suffering from deprivation dwarfism. They found that the children's growth-hormone response to insulin stimulation was subnormal. After the children had been transferred to an adequate emotional environment insulin stimulation was followed by the normal increase in growth-hormone concentration. At the Children's Hospital of Michigan patients over the age of three with deprivation dwarfism showed a similar picture. Working there in 1971, Ingeborg Krieger and Raymond Mellinger found that the response to insulin stimulation in these children was subnormal. When they repeated the test with deprived children below the age of three, however, they were surprised to find that the concentration of growth hormone under fasting conditions was abnormally high, and that after insulin stimulation the concentration was normal. It is likely that the difference in the responses of the two age groups is related to maturation, perhaps the maturation of the cerebral cortex. In any event both the Johns Hopkins and the Michigan studies are further evidence of the connection between deprivation dwarfism and impaired pituitary function.

Loss of appetite is a well-known com-

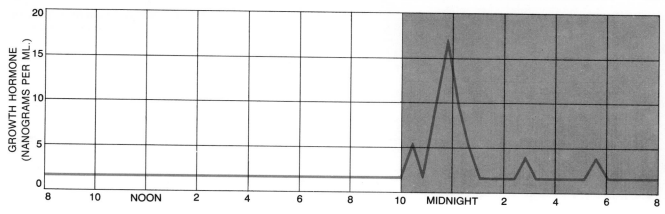

RELEASE OF GROWTH HORMONE increases during early hours of sleep (*shaded area*). This record of the growth hormone in the blood of a preadolescent child was collected by Jordan W. Finkelstein and his associates at Montefiore Hospital in the Bronx.

plaint in adolescents; in a few cases it is so extreme that it is termed anorexia nervosa. The disorder is usually attributable to adverse interpersonal relations between parent and child, particularly between mother and daughter. The clinical similarities between adolescent anorexia nervosa and infant and child deprivation dwarfism have long interested investigators. For example, adolescent girls with anorexia nervosa may stop menstruating; the adverse emotional climate evidently halts secretion of the pituitary hormones that mediate ovarian function. It now appears that some patients with anorexia nervosa also respond to insulin stimulation with a subnormal release of growth hormone.

Because it can be difficult to distinguish between anorexia nervosa and organic disorders of the pituitary, John Landon and his associates at St. Mary's Hospital in London recently tested the pituitary function of five patients with anorexia nervosa. All five showed the reaction typical of individuals with impaired pituitary function: after injections of insulin their level of blood sugar was excessively low. Two of the five also showed the reaction that typifies many instances of deprivation dwarfism: the concentration of growth hormone in the blood did not increase. The investigators also noted that before the injection of insulin the concentration of growth hormone in their patients' blood was significantly higher than normal. This paradoxical finding is not unlike the reaction observed among the younger deprivation-dwarfism patients in Michigan.

The significance of the St. Mary's findings is not yet clear, but they could prove to be important clues in unraveling the relations among the higher brain centers, the hypothalamus and the pituitary. We may be observing here a series of differing, age-mediated physiological

responses to what are essentially identical psychosocial stimuli.

An important new direction for future investigation is suggested by the recent discovery of a connection between the release of growth hormone and individual modes of sleep. This connection was uncovered in 1965 by W. M. Hunter and W. M. Rigal of the University of Edinburgh, who observed that the total amount of growth hormone secreted during the night by older children was many times greater than the amount secreted during the day. Soon thereafter Hans-Jürgen Quabbe and his colleagues at the Free University of Berlin measured the amount of growth hormone secreted by adult volunteers during a 24-hour fast and detected a sharp rise that coincided with the volunteers' period of sleep. Pursuing this coincidence, Yasuro Takahashi and his co-workers at Washington University and Yutaka Honda and his colleagues at the University of Tokyo found that the rise in growth-hormone concentration occurs in adults during the first two hours of sleep, and that it equals the increase produced by insulin stimulation. If the subject remains awake, the growth hormone is not secreted. Honda and his associates propose that activation of the cerebral cortex somehow inhibits the secretion of growth hormone, whereas sleep—particularly the sleep that is accompanied by a high-voltage slow-wave pattern in encephalograph readings—induces the secretion of a growth-hormone-releasing factor in the hypothalamus.

Collecting such data calls for the frequent drawing of blood samples from sleeping subjects through an indwelling catheter, with the result that studies of growth-hormone concentration in infants and young children have been relatively

few. What findings there are, however, fall into a pattern. For example, there appears to be no correlation between the concentration of growth hormone in the blood of normal newborn infants and the infants' cycle of alternate sleep and wakefulness. Such a correlation does not appear until after the third month of life. In normal children between the ages of five and 15 the maximum growth-hormone concentration is found about an hour after sleep begins. Maturation therefore appears to be a factor in establishing the correlation. Whether there is any link between these maturation-dependent responses and similar responses in instances of deprivation dwarfism is not clear.

The existence of a cause-and-effect relation between deprivation dwarfism and abnormal patterns of sleep had been suggested by Joseph Schutt-Aine and his associates at the Children's Hospital in Pittsburgh. They and others found that in children with deprivation dwarfism there were spontaneous and transient decreases in reserves of ACTH, the hormone that stimulates the secretion of the adrenal-cortex steroid that raises the level of blood sugar in the bloodstream. They also found that the decrease in ACTH reserve was accompanied by a temporary lowering of the child's blood-sugar level. Taking a position much like Honda's with respect to the growth hormone, Schutt-Aine and his colleagues suggest that any preponderance of inhibitory cerebral-cortex influences on the hypothalamus would tend to interfere with the normal release of ACTH and other pituitary hormones. An abnormal sleep pattern, they conclude, could lead to such a preponderance.

Is it in fact possible to attribute the retarded growth of psychosocially deprived children to sleep patterns that in-

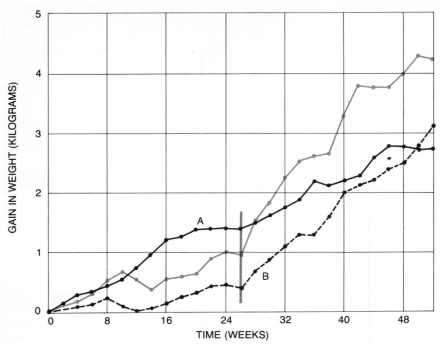

QUALITY OF CARE proved more important than quality of food in two postwar German orphanages studied by Elsie M. Widdowson. For six months during 1948 the 50-odd war orphans in each home received nothing but basic rations, yet the children in Orphanage *A*, supervised by a kindly matron, gained more weight than most of those in Orphanage *B*, whose matron was a stern disciplinarian. An exception was a group of favorites of the stern matron at *B* (*color*); they did better than their companions. After six months the matron at *B* was transferred to *A* and brought her favorites with her. Simultaneously the children at *A* were given extra rations, whereas the children at *B* remained on the same basic diet. (The transition is indicated by the vertical gray line.) Relieved of the stern matron's discipline, the children at *B* began to show a sharp increase in weight; those at *A* showed a weight gain that averaged somewhat less than it had during the preceding six months in spite of the larger ration. Again matron's favorites were an exception: their gain was greatest of any.

hibit the secretion of growth hormone? Certainly there is evidence that deprivation dwarfism and sleep abnormalities, both of commission and omission, often go together. The infants observed by Spitz and Wolf alternated between insomnia and stupor. One of the six thin dwarfs that Patton and I studied slept as much as 18 hours a day; another spent the hours while his family slept roaming the dark house. The tube-fed 15-month-old in Rochester, when admitted to the hospital, appeared to use sleep as a means of withdrawing from the world.

Georg Wolff and John W. Money of the Johns Hopkins Hospital have attempted a quantitative assessment of this question by studying the sleep patterns of a group of children with deprivation dwarfism. Analysis of their data suggests that the sleep pattern of children with deprivation dwarfism is disturbed in periods of subnormal growth and undisturbed in periods of normal growth. Thus far, however, the data are insufficient to establish whether or not there is an abnormal pattern in the secretion of growth hormone by sleeping children with deprivation dwarfism.

It has been proposed that the human infant is born with an innate, species-specific repertory of responses that includes clinging, sucking, "following" with the eyes, crying and smiling. These are the responses that John Bowlby of the Tavistock Institute of Human Relations in London identifies as having survival value for the infant; he believes their existence is a product of natural selection. In Bowlby's view the primary function of the mother is to integrate these responses into "attachment behavior," a more mature and more complicated pattern. In addition there evidently are "sensitive" periods in the course of human development, such as those familiar from animal experimentation. Exactly when these periods occur in human infancy, however, and just what conditions and experiences are necessary if the child is to develop normally remain uncertain. One conclusion nevertheless seems clear. Deprivation dwarfism is a concrete example—an "experiment of nature," so to speak—that demonstrates the delicacy, complexity and crucial importance of infant-parent interaction.

Getting Old

by Alexander Leaf
September 1973

*Everyone ages, but some seem to age less quickly
than others. In search of clues to the phenomenon
the author visits three communities where vigorous
oldsters are remarkably numerous*

"The patient, Mr. *X*, is 81 years old. A resident of the Dunhill Nursing Home, he has had two strokes, the first three years ago and the second a year ago. Since the last stroke he has been bedridden, incontinent and senile. He no longer recognizes members of his own family. For the past two months he has been eating poorly and failing generally. He was brought in last night by ambulance to our Emergency Service, where we found pulmonary congestion from a failing arteriosclerotic heart and pneumonia. Treatment was started with diuretics and digitalis for his congestive heart failure and high doses of penicillin for his pneumonia. This morning his fever is gone and he is breathing quietly."

I listen to this familiar story related by my intern at the Massachusetts General Hospital and mentally fill in the remainder of the picture. Sometimes the patient is 65, sometimes 70 or 90. Sometimes there is an underlying cancer. Usually, however, cardiovascular or respiratory problems dominate the clinical situation but are superimposed on a substrate of debility, wasting and senility. In the past pneumonia usually terminated such stories with some degree of dignity. Today modern medicine, with its antibiotics, intravenous infusions, cardiac pacemakers, respirators, diuretics and the like can often resolve the immediate problem (pneumonia and congestive heart failure in this instance) and return the patient to his nursing home again.

In a large metropolitan teaching hospital some 40 percent of the medical (as opposed to surgical) beds are occupied by patients over 65, many of them in a condition similar to Mr. *X*'s. More than 20 million citizens are 65 or older in the U.S. today. They are the major reservoir of illness and medical needs. When I chose a career in medicine 35 years ago,

I did so with the conviction that regardless of my eventual specialization my work would promote health and relieve human suffering. Today I contemplate Mr. *X* and wonder if my initial conviction was right. Of course, medicine does more than treat the Mr. *X*'s, but are we doing the best we can for contemporary society? The proportion of the population over 65 is between 10 and 11 percent now and will come close to 15 percent in the next few decades. What is medicine doing about it? Are we applying our resources wisely? Should we devote proportionately more of our efforts to trying to learn how we can prevent the infirmities of old age?

In the U.S. in 1969 the life expectancy at birth for white males was 67.8 years and for white females 75.1 years. That is some 23 years longer than life expectancy was in 1900. However, an adult who had reached 65 at the turn of the century could expect to live another 13 years and an adult who reaches 65 today can expect to live another 15 years, or only two years longer than in 1900. The seemingly large increase in life expectancy at birth actually reflects the great reduction in infant mortality. Little progress has been made in controlling the major causes of death in adults: heart disease, cancer and stroke. Accidents, of which nearly half are caused by motor vehicles, are a fourth major cause of adult deaths.

At the Ninth International Congress of Gerontology in July, 1972, M. Vacek of Czechoslovakia discussed the increase in mean age and the rising proportion of old people in the population. He pointed out the fact that the rise in the number of people over 65 toward 15 percent in the populations of stable, industrial countries could be attributed to a falling birthrate. When at the conclusion of his

remarks someone in the audience timidly asked if the achievements of the medical sciences had played a role in the rise in mean age, he responded that indeed they had, but that the simultaneous deterioration of the environment had canceled out any positive effect from medicine.

Mere length of life, however, may be a poor concern on which to focus. Most would agree that the quality of life, rather than its duration, should be the prime issue. The active life, so warmly espoused by Theodore Roosevelt, has been the American model. If one can extend the period of productive activity as did Verdi and Churchill, so much the better.

Most students of the field would agree with the statement of Frederic Verzár, the Swiss dean of gerontologists. "Old age is not an illness," says Verzár. "It is a continuation of life with decreasing capacities for adaptation." The main crippler and killer, arteriosclerosis, is not a necessary accompaniment of aging but a disease state that increases in incidence with age; the same is true of cancer. If we could prevent arteriosclerosis, hypertension and cancer, the life-span could be pushed back closer to the biological limit, if such a limit in fact exists.

In order to observe aged individuals who are free of debilitating illness I recently visited three remote parts of the world where the existence of such individuals was rumored. These were the village of Vilcabamba in Ecuador, the small principality of Hunza in West Pakistan and the highlands of Georgia in the Soviet Caucasus.

A census of Vilcabamba taken in 1971 by Ecuador's National Institute of Statistics recorded a total population of 819 in this remote Andean village. Nine of the 819 were over 100 years old. The

NINE REMBRANDT SELF-PORTRAITS, painted between the ages of 27 or 28 and 63, document the progress of aging in the case of a generally prosperous Dutch burgher of the mid-17th century. The painter was born in July, 1606, and died in October, 1669. His self-portrait of 1633 or 1634 (*top left on opposite page*) is now in the Uffizi Gallery in Florence. Next (*top center*) is his self-portrait of 1652, when he was 46 years old. This is one of three portraits reproduced here that are in the Kunsthistorisches Museum in Vienna. Next (*top right*) is a portrait at age 49, also in Vienna. The second row begins (*left*) with a portrait in the National Gallery of Scotland in Edinburgh, painted at the age of 51. Next is the third of the Vienna paintings, which may show Rembrandt one year older (*center*). At the right is his portrait at age 54, now in the Louvre. The bottom row begins (*left*) with a portrait at age 55, now in the Rijksmuseum in Amsterdam. The next portrait (*center*) may have been painted in 1664 when Rembrandt was 58; it is also in the Uffizi. The last portrait (*right*) Rembrandt painted in the year of his death; it is at the Mauritshuis in The Hague.

proportion of the population in this small village over 60 is 16.4 percent, as contrasted with a figure of 6.4 percent for rural Ecuador in general. The valley that shelters Vilcabamba is at an altitude of some 4,500 feet. Its vegetation appears quite lush. The people live by farming, but the methods are so primitive that only a bare subsistence is extracted from the land.

A team of physicians and scientists from Quito under the direction of Miguel Salvador has been studying this unique population. Guillermo Vela of the University of Quito, the nutritionist in the group, finds that the average daily caloric intake of an elderly Vilcabamba adult is 1,200 calories. Protein provided 35 to 38 grams and fat only 12 to 19 grams; 200 to 250 grams of carbohydrate completed the diet. The contribution of animal protein and animal fat to the diet is very low.

The villagers of Vilcabamba, like most inhabitants of underdeveloped countries, live without benefit of modern sanitation, cleanliness and medical care. Cleanliness is evidently not a prerequisite for longevity. A small river skirts the village and provides water for drinking, washing and bathing. When we asked various villagers how long it had been since they had last bathed, the responses showed that many had not done so for two years. (The record was 10 years.) The villagers live in mud huts with dirt floors; chickens and pigs share their quarters. As one might expect in such surroundings, infant mortality is high, but so is the proportion of aged individuals. By extrapolation it stands at 1,100 per 100,000, compared with three per 100,000 in the U.S. Statistically, of course, such an extrapolation from so small a number is unwarranted; nonetheless, it shows how unusual the age distribution is in this little village.

The old people of Vilcabamba all appeared to be of European rather than Indian descent. We were able to validate the reported ages of almost all the elderly individuals from baptismal records kept in the local Catholic church. Miguel Carpio, aged 121, was the oldest person in the village when we were there. José Toledo's picture has appeared in newspapers around the world with captions that have proclaimed his extreme old age; actually he is only 109. All the old people were born locally, so that what is sometimes called the Miami Beach phenomenon, that is, an ingathering of the elderly, cannot account for the age distribution.

Both tobacco and sugarcane are grown in the valley, and a local rum drink, *zuhmir,* is produced. We did not, however, witness any drunkenness, and although most villagers smoke, there is disagreement among visiting physicians about how many of them inhale. The villagers work hard to scratch a livelihood from the soil, and the mountainous terrain demands continuous and vigorous physical activity. These circumstances are hardly unique to Vilcabamba, and one leaves this Andean valley with the strong suspicion that genetic factors must be playing an important role in the longevity of this small enclave of elderly people of European stock.

The impression that genetic factors are important in longevity was reinforced by what we saw in Hunza. This small independent state is ruled over by a hereditary line of leaders known as Mirs. In 1891 the Mir of that day surrendered control over defense, communications and foreign affairs to the British when they conquered his country. In 1948, after the partition of Pakistan and India,

IN SOVIET GEORGIA, one of three widely separated parts of the world visited by the author, a 105-year-old man has the place of honor (*at head of table, left*) at a party held near the village of Gurjanni. The centenarian was the oldest guest but the man and the two women on his left are all over 80. The average diet of those over 80 in the Caucasus is relatively rich in proteins (70 to 80 grams a day) and fats (40 to 60 grams), but the daily caloric intake, 1,700 to 1,900 calories, is barely half the U.S. average.

ON THE PAKISTAN FRONTIER old men of the principality of Hunza, another area visited by the author, winnow threshed wheat in a mountain village. Ibriham Shah (*right*) professes to be 80 years old but Mohd Ghraib (*left*) says he is only 75. Both vigorous work and a low-calorie diet are factors in the fitness of Hunza elders. An adult male's daily diet includes 50 grams of proteins, 36 grams of fats and 354 grams of carbohydrate. This combination provides a somewhat higher daily total than in the Caucasus: 1,923 calories.

the present Mir yielded the same right to Pakistan. Hunza is hidden among the towering peaks of the Karakorum Range on Pakistan's border with China and Afghanistan and is one of the most inaccessible places on the earth. After a day's travel from Gilgit, first by jeep and then on foot from the point where a rockslide had cut the mountain road, we found ourselves in a valley surrounded on all sides by peaks more than 20,000 feet high, blocked at the far end by Mount Rokaposhi, which rises to 25,500 feet in snow-clad splendor.

The valley is arid, but a system of irrigation canals built over the past 800 years carries water from the high surrounding glaciers, converting the valley into a terraced garden. The inhabitants work their fields by primitive agricultural methods, and the harvests are not quite sufficient to prevent a period of real privation each winter. According to S. Maqsood Ali, a Pakistani nutritionist who has surveyed the diet of 55 adult males in Hunza, the daily diet averages 1,923 calories: 50 grams are protein, 36 grams fat and 354 grams carbohydrate. Meat and dairy products accounted for only 1 percent of the total. Land is too precious to be used to support dairy herds; the few animals that are kept by the people are killed for meat only dur-

ing the winter or on festive occasions.

As in Vilcabamba, everyone in Hunza works hard to wrest a living from the rocky hills. One sees an unusual number of vigorous people who, although elderly in appearance, agilely climb up and down the steep slopes of the valley. Their language is an unwritten one, so that no documentary records of birth dates are available. In religion the Hunzakuts are Ismaili Moslems, followers of the Agha Khan. Their education is quite limited. Thus, although a number of nonscientific accounts have attributed remarkable longevity and robust health to these people, no documentation substantiates the reports.

Unfortunately there is no known means of distinguishing chronological age from physiological age in humans. When we asked elderly Hunzakuts how old they were and what they remembered of the British invasion of their country in 1891, their answers did little to validate their supposed age. If, however, they are as old as both they and their Mir, a well-educated and worldly man, maintain, then there are a remarkable number of aged but lean and fit-looking Hunzakuts who can climb the steep slopes of their valley with far greater ease than we could. Putatively the oldest citizen was one Tulah Beg,

who said he was 110; the next oldest, also a male, said he was 105.

In addition to their low-calorie diet, which is also low in animal fats, and their intense physical activity, the Hunzakuts have a record of genetic isolation that must be nearly unique. Now, there do not seem to be "good" genes that favor longevity but only "bad" genes that increase the probability of acquiring a fatal illness. One may therefore speculate that a small number of individuals, singularly lacking such "bad" genes, settled this mountain valley centuries ago and that their isolation has prevented a subsequent admixture with "bad" genes. This, of course, is mere speculation.

The possible role of genetic factors in longevity seemed of less importance in the Caucasus. In Abkhasia on the shores of the Black Sea and in the adjoining Caucasus one encounters many people over 100 who are not only Georgian but also Russian, Jewish, Armenian and Turkish. The Caucasus is a land bridge that has been traveled for centuries by conquerors from both the east and the west, and its population can scarcely have maintained any significant degree of genetic isolation. At the same time, when one speaks to the numerous centenarians in the area, one invariably discovers that each of them has parents or siblings who have similarly attained great age. The genetic aspect of longevity therefore cannot be entirely dismissed.

In contrast to the isolated valleys of Vilcabamba and Hunza, the Caucasus is an extensive area that includes three Soviet republics: Georgia, Azerbaijan and Armenia. The climate varies from the humid and subtropical (as at Sukhumi on the Black Sea, with an annual rainfall of 1,100 to 1,400 millimeters) to drier continental conditions, marked by extremes of summer heat and winter cold. The population extends from sea-level settlements along the Black and Caspian seas to mountain villages at altitudes of 1,000 to 1,500 meters. More old people are found in the mountainous regions than at sea level, and the incidence of atherosclerosis among those who live in the mountains is only half that in the sea-level villages. G. Z. Pitzkhelauri, head of the Gerontological Center in the Republic of Georgia, told me that the 1970 census placed the number of centenarians for the entire Caucasus at between 4,500 and 5,000. Of these, 1,844, or an average of 39 per 100,000, live in Georgia. In Azerbaijan there are 2,500 more, or 63 per 100,000. Perhaps of more pertinence to my study was the record of activity among the elderly of the Caucasus. Of 15,000 individuals over 80 whose records were kept by Pitzkhelauri, more than 70 percent continue to lead very active lives. Sixty percent of them were still working on state or collective farms.

I returned from my three surveys convinced that a vigorous, active life involving physical activity (sexual activity included) was possible for at least 100 years and in some instances for even longer.

Longevity is clearly a multifactorial matter. First are the genetic factors; all who have studied longevity are convinced of their importance. It is generally accepted that the offspring of long-lived parents live longer than others. Yet a long life extends beyond the period of fertility, at least in women, so that length of life can have no direct evolutionary advantage. It has been suggested that living organisms are like clocks: their life-span ends when the initial endowment of energy is expended, just as the clock stops when its spring becomes unwound. L. V. Heilbrunn estimated in the 1900's that the heart of a mouse, which beats 520 to 780 times per minute, would contract 1.11 billion times

IN THE ANDES OF ECUADOR an 85-year-old woman of the village of Vilcabamba works in a cornfield, continuing to contribute to the economic welfare of the community at an age when many women no longer work. Of the areas visited by the author, Vilcabamba afforded the elderly the most sparse diet. The daily intake was less than 40 grams of proteins, 20 grams of fats and 250 grams of carbohydrate for a total intake of 1,200 calories.

BLACK SEA VILLAGER from the coast near Sukhumi is over 100 years old. To live to be 100 or older in the Caucasus gains one a kind of elder statesman's place in local society.

during the 3.5 years of the mouse's normal life-span. The heart of an elephant, which beats 25 to 28 times per minute, would have beaten 1.021 billion times during the elephant's normal life-span of 70 years. The similarity between these two figures seems to suggest some initial equal potential that is gradually dissipated over the animal's life-span. Such calculations, however, are probably more entertaining than explanatory of longevity.

As I have mentioned, genes evidently influence longevity only in a negative way by predisposing the organism to specific fatal diseases. Alex Comfort of University College London has pointed out the possible role of heterosis, or "hybrid vigor." The crossbreeding of two inbred strains—each with limited growth, size, resistance to disease and longevity—can improve these characteristics in the progeny. This vigor has been manifested in a wide variety of species, both plant and animal, but its significance in human longevity is not known.

Next are the factors associated with nutrition. Since we are composed of what we eat and drink, it is not surprising that students of longevity have emphasized the importance of dietary factors. Indeed, the only demonstrable means of extending the life-span of an experimental animal has been the manipulation of diet. The classic studies of Clive M. McCay of Cornell University in the 1930's showed that the life-span of albino rats could be increased as much as 40 percent by the restriction of caloric intake early in life. Rats fed a diet otherwise balanced but deficient in calories showed delayed growth and maturation until the caloric intake was increased. At the same time their life-span was extended. The significance of these experiments with respect to human longevity is not known, but they raise questions about the current tendency to overfeed children.

The role of specific dietary factors in promoting longevity remains unsettled. When the old people we visited were asked to what they attributed their long life, credit was usually given to the local alcoholic beverage, but this response generally came from the more vocal and chauvinistic males. Much publicity is given today to the possible role of animal fats in the development of arteriosclerosis. Saturated fatty acids and cholesterol have also been suggested as the causal agents of coronary atherosclerosis. Since the atheromas themselves—the deposits that narrow and occlude the blood vessels of the heart, the brain and other organs—contain cholesterol, the suspicion

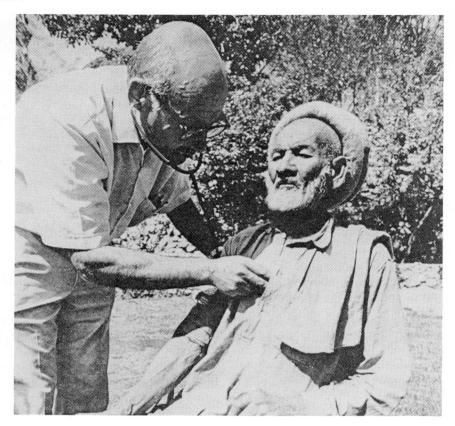

ELDER OF HUNZA is examined by the author. A resident of the village of Mominabad, the man professed to be 110 years old. Birth records are not kept in Hunza, however, and evidence supporting his claim and other Hunza elders' claims of extreme age did not exist.

of complicity comes easily. It is also well documented that the level of cholesterol in the blood serum has a positive prognostic relation to the likelihood of heart attacks.

Since the diet of affluent societies has a high content of animal fats, which are rich in cholesterol and saturated fatty acids, the suspicion further arises that these dietary constituents are contributing to the increase in the number of heart attacks affecting young adult males. The marked individual variability in tolerance to the quantity of fat and cholesterol in the diet, however, makes it difficult to ascribe prime importance to this single factor. We have seen that in both Vilcabamba and Hunza the diet was not only low in calories but also low in animal fats. In the Caucasus an active dairy economy allows cheese and milk products to be served with every meal. Perhaps it is significant that in this area the cheese is low in fat content and the total fat intake is only some 40 to 60 grams per day. This level is in sharp contrast to figures from a recent U.S. Department of Agriculture report stating that the average daily fat intake for Americans of all ages is 157 grams. The best-informed medical opinion today

generally agrees that the Americans' average daily intake of 3,300 calories, including substantial quantities of fat, is excessive and conducive neither to optimal health nor to longevity.

Let us now consider physical activity. There is increasing awareness that early heart disease is a price we are paying for our largely sedentary existence. In the three areas I visited physical fitness was an inevitable consequence of the active life led by the inhabitants. My initial speculation that their isolated lives protects them from the ravages of infectious diseases and from acquiring "bad" genes is probably incorrect. A simpler explanation for their fitness is that their mountainous terrain demands a high level of physical activity simply to get through the day.

A number of studies have examined the effects of physical activity on the incidence and severity of heart attacks among various sample populations. For example, among British postal workers it was found that those who delivered the mail had a lower incidence of heart attacks and, when attacks did occur, a lower mortality rate than their colleagues who worked at sedentary jobs. This same study also compared the relative incidence of heart attacks among London bus drivers and conductors. The conductors, who spent their working hours climbing up and down the double-deck buses collecting fares, had less heart trouble than the sedentary drivers. It has been reported recently that the weekend athlete who engages in vigorous physical activity is only one-third as prone to heart disease as his age-matched sedentary neighbor. It is well known that exercise increases the oxygenation of the blood and improves the circulation. Exercise will also improve the collateral circulation of blood to the heart muscle. When the exercises are carefully graded and performed under appropriate supervision, they are undoubtedly the best means of rehabilitating the heart muscle after a heart attack.

Exercise improves circulation to nearly all parts of the body. Circulation is increased to the brain as well as to the heart and skeletal muscles. Recently it has been asserted that improvement in the oxygen supply to the brain will actually improve thinking. In a resting sedentary individual, however, the blood supplied to the brain contains more oxygen than the brain is able to extract. It is difficult to explain how an added overabundance of a constituent that is normally not a rate-limiting factor in

cerebral function would enhance that function. It may nonetheless be that the sense of well-being that the exercising individual enjoys is likely to increase self-confidence and as a result improve both social and intellectual effectiveness.

Finally, physical activity helps to burn off excess calories and dispose of ingested fats. Exercise may thus counteract the deleterious effects of a diet that includes too many calories and too much fat. Indeed, it may well be one factor that helps to account for the great individual differences in tolerance for dietary factors.

Psychological factors must also be considered. It is characteristic of each of the areas I visited that the old people continue to be contributing, productive members of their society. The economy in all three areas is agrarian, there is no fixed retirement age and the elderly make themselves useful doing many necessary tasks around the farm or the home. Moreover, increased age is accompanied by increased social status. The old people, with their accumulated experience of life, are expected to be wise, and they respond accordingly. In Hunza the Mir rules his small state with the advice of a council of elders, who sit on the ground in a circle at his feet and help him with his decisions and pro-

nouncements. When we met Temur Tarba in the Caucasus just three weeks after his 100th birthday, it was clear from his manner that he was delighted to have at last "arrived." He proudly displayed his Hero of Labor medal, the highest civilian award of the U.S.S.R. He had won it only seven years earlier for his work in hybridizing corn. The cheerful centenarian still picked tea leaves, rode his horse and worked on a collective farm.

People who no longer have a necessary role to play in the social and economic life of their society generally deteriorate rapidly. The pattern of increasingly early retirement in our own society takes a heavy toll of our older citizens. They also find that their offspring generally have neither any room nor any use for them in their urban apartment. These are economic determinants that cannot be reversed in our culture today. Their devastating effect on the happiness and life-span of the elderly could be countered at least in part by educational programs to awaken other interests or avocations to which these people could turn with zest when their contribution to the industrial economy is no longer needed. The trend toward shorter working hours and earlier retirement makes the need for such education urgent. It seems a corruption of the very purpose of an economy that instead of freeing us from drudgery and need and allowing us to enjoy a better life, it holds us slaves to its dictates even though affluence is at hand.

In their remote farms and villages the old people I visited live oblivious to the pressures and strains of modern life. Such American controversies as the fighting in Southeast Asia, conflict in the Middle East, environmental pollution, the energy crisis and the like that fill our news media were unknown to them. Of course, most of the stresses and tensions to which mankind is subject arise from more personal social interactions, such as a quarrel with a spouse or misbehavior by an offspring. As a result it is impossible for any social group to entirely escape mental stress and tensions. Nonetheless, in societies that are less competitive and less aggressive even these personal stresses can be less exhausting than they are in our own. The old people I met abroad showed equanimity and optimism. In the Caucasus I asked Gabriel Chapnian, aged 117, what he thought of young people, of his government and of the state of the world in general. When he repeatedly responded "Fine, fine," I asked with some annoy-

FEW LIVE TO GROW OLD in underdeveloped nations, whereas the opposite is true in the developed nations. For example, half of the women who died in India (*color*) from 1921 to 1930 were 24 or younger; only 5 percent of the women who died in New Zealand from 1934 to 1938 were that young. Half of the New Zealand women who died in the same period were 74 or older. In India only 5 percent of women's deaths were in this age group.

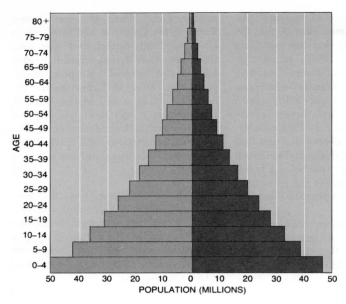

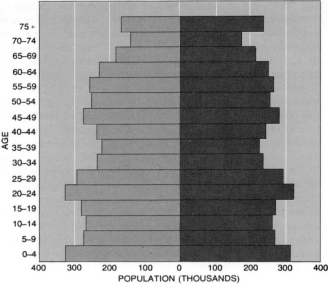

EXAGGERATED PYRAMID appears when the males (*left*) and females (*right*) of a population with a high growth rate are counted in ascending five-year steps. The graph shows the 1970 population of India; many more Indians are below the age of 20 than are above that age. In such an expanding population the elderly, although numerous, comprise a small percentage of the total.

UNEVEN COLUMN, rather than a pyramid, appears when the number of males (*left*) and females (*right*) in a slow-growing population are similarly displayed. The graph shows the population of Sweden in 1970; about as many Swedes are above the age of 35 as are below that age. In this population, noted for its low birthrate, the elderly comprise an increasingly large percentage of the total.

ance, "Isn't there anything today that disturbs you?" He replied cheerfully, "Oh yes, there are a number of things that are not the way I would want them to be, but since I can't change them I don't worry about them."

One cannot discuss the quality of life at advanced age without considering sexual activity. In most societies the combination of male boasting about sexual prowess and taboos against discussing the subject makes it difficult to collect reliable information about sexual activity in the elderly. Women's ovaries stop functioning at menopause, usually in the late 40's or early 50's, but this has little influence on the libido. Similarly, aging is associated with a gradual decrease in the number of cells in certain organs, including the male testes. The cells that produce sperm are the first to be affected, but later the cells that produce the male hormone testosterone may also diminish in number and activity. Sexual potency in the male and libido in the female may nonetheless persist in advanced old age. Herman Brotman of the Department of Health, Education, and Welfare reports that each year there are some 3,500 marriages among the 20 million Americans over the age of 65, and that sexual activity is cited along with companionship as one reason for these late unions.

Research on aging is proceeding in two general directions. One aims at a better understanding of those disease states that, although they are not an integral part of the aging process, nevertheless increase in incidence with age and constitute the major cripplers of the aged. Here both arteriosclerosis and cancer are prominent. Knowledge of the causes and prevention of these diseases is still very limited, and much more work is necessary before there can be sufficient understanding to allow prevention of either. If both arteriosclerosis and cancer could be prevented, it should be possible to extend man's life-span close to its as yet undetermined biological limit.

There is reason to believe that a limit does exist. Even if one could erase the cumulative wear and tear that affects the aging organism, it seems probable that the cells themselves are not programmed for perpetual activity. The differences in the life-spans of various animals suggest some such natural limit. The changes that are observed in the tissues of animals that undergo metamorphosis—for example insects—are indicative of the programmed extinction of certain tissues. So is the failure of the human ovaries at menopause, long before other vital organs give out. Leonard Hayflick of the Stanford University School of Medicine has reported that the cells in cultures of human embryonic connective tissue will divide some 50 times and then die. If growth is interrupted by plunging the culture into liquid nitrogen, the cells will resume growth on thawing, continue through the remainder of their 50 di-

visions and then die. Although one may question whether the cells are not affected by adverse environmental influences, Hayflick's studies support the notion of programmed death. Only cancer cells seem capable of eternal life in culture. One familiar line of cancer cells, the "HeLa" strain, has often been the subject of cell-culture studies; it originated as a cervical cancer 21 years ago and has been maintained in culture ever since.

As investigations and speculations seek an answer to the question of the natural limits of life, other workers have noted that the giant molecules of living matter themselves age. Collagen, the main protein of connective tissue, constitutes approximately 30 percent of all the protein in the human body. With advancing age collagen molecules show a spontaneous increase in the cross-linking of their subunits, a process that increases their rigidity and reduces their solubility. Such a stiffening of this important structural component of our bodies might underlie such classic features of aging as rigidity of blood vessels, resistance to blood flow, reduced delivery of blood through hardened arteries and, as a final consequence, the loss of cells and of function. Other giant molecules, including the DNA molecule that stores the genetic information and the RNA molecule that reads out the stored message, may also be subject to spontaneous cross-linking that would eventually prevent the normal self-renewal of tissues.

A new area in aging research appears to be opening up in studies on the immune system of the body. In addition to providing antibodies against bacteria or foreign substances introduced into the body, the immune system recognizes and destroys abnormal or foreign cells. When these functions of the immune system diminish, as happens with advancing age, there may be errors in the system that result in antibodies that attack and destroy normal body cells or impair their function. The net result of this disturbed activity of the immune system, like the cross-linking of collagen, would be what is recognized as the aging process.

Takashi Makinodan of the Baltimore City Hospitals thinks that methods of rejuvenating the immune system are possible. The hope that some medicine will be discovered that can block the fundamental process of aging, however, seems to me very remote until the nature of the aging process is far better understood.

Much research is needed before such an understanding can be attained. It is nonetheless encouraging that aging research is finding increased interest and support in several countries. It is also encouraging to perceive a parallel interest in the aged among scientists, physicians, economists, politicians and others. To consider any extension of the human life-span without a serious effort to anticipate and plan for the impact of increased longevity on society would be entirely irresponsible.

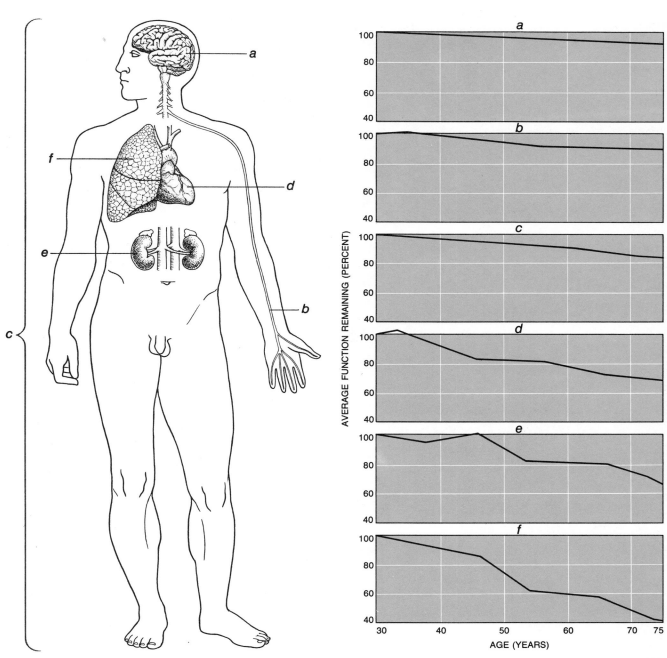

LOSS OF FUNCTION with increasing age does not occur at the same rate in all organs and systems. Graphs (*right*) show loss as a percentage, with the level of function at age 30 representing 100 percent. Thus brain weight (*a*) has diminished to 92 percent of its age-30 value by age 75 and nerve-conduction velocity (*b*) to about 90 percent. The basal metabolic rate (*c*) has diminished to 84 percent, cardiac output at rest (*d*) to 70 percent, filtration rate of the kidneys (*e*) to 69 percent and maximum breathing capacity (*f*) to 43 percent. Diseases, however, rather than gradual diminution of function, are at present the chief barrier to extended longevity.

IV

ADAPTATION AND ADAPTABILITY

IV ADAPTATION AND ADAPTABILITY

INTRODUCTION

Associated with the shift over the last several decades from typological approaches to population approaches in biological anthropology, there has been a significant shift of emphasis away from concern with the *products* of evolution and adaptation toward understanding the *processes* of human adaptation in evolution. This reorientation of the paradigm was critical to the developments that subsequently occurred in this field of study. Biological anthropologists were no longer concerned simply with human differences or variations but went a step further in using these variations as a data base from which to study microevolutionary and adaptive processes. The products of human evolution and adaptation, then, provided insights into the very processes which produced them.

In order to use this processual approach, the biological anthropologist first considers some combination of the genetic, biochemical, physiological, morphological, and behavioral features of naturally occurring populations of individuals and then considers the microevolutionary processes through which these variations could have occurred. In order to use this approach a variety of ecological factors must be considered. Studying the effects of specific environmental stresses on a human population is one highly productive approach to the question of adaptation and microevolution. Paul Baker (1969) used this approach in his studies of high altitude adaptations of acclimatized native populations and other unacclimatized populations in the Peruvian Andes. His team was able to demonstrate both the biological and cultural adaptations that take place in response to this environmental stress. It was noted, for instance, by Robert Frisancho, a member of Baker's team, that there are particularly important changes in the morphology of children growing and developing at high altitudes.

In a closely related study Joel Hanna (1970) was able to demonstrate the biocultural adaptability of the use of *coca* and alcohol in the same population. Elsewhere, studies of temperature adaptation under arctic or desert conditions were carried out to determine the effects of these environmental extremes. Still other studies have dealt with the effects of nutritional stresses —either deprivation, as in the case of studies of kwashiorkor, or plenty, as in the case of obesity. Finally, the whole issue of infectious disease in human populations has been regarded as a highly significant problem amenable to research using the same approach.

These studies all indicate the overwhelming need for the development of integrated and holistic approaches to evaluating the adaptive processes of human populations. We must understand as much about the sociocultural basis for adaptation as we do about the environmental stresses and the biogical mechanisms capable of adjusting to them. In studying adaptability to cold temperatures it is not sufficient, for example, to know only of the micro-circulation of the fingers or of the operation of the hypothalamic mechanism for regulating temperature, without understanding the entire context in which temperature adaptation occurs. Thus, knowing that in the Arctic, tradition and necessity dictated that an Eskimo man select a wife on the basis of how well she could sew a fur parka or make *muck-luks* (boots) is as important in understanding Eskimo adaptability to cold temperatures as knowing the biological mechanism that this cultural practice supplemented. Other molecularly based variations have also been shown to depend on complex ecological relationships as in the case of the interrelations of Glucose-6-PD deficiency, malaria, and consumption of fava beans. Hence, we must try to analyze the entire ecosystem of a human population with its multiple inter-actions of biological, sociocultural (including technological), demographic, and environmental variables. The ecosystem becomes the framework within which a particular biochemical or physiological adaptation is traced through the levels of complexity from the elementary biological level to the inter-actions with human behavior within a particular sociocultural system.

Another strategy for tracing the significant interrelations within a human ecosystem has developed out of cultural ecology. Rather than focusing on the biological variables, the cultural ecologists have tended to emphasize the interaction of environmental and sociocultural variables. Hence social institutions and economics are studied, for example, within the context of the evaluation of energy and food resources. However, increasingly, both biological anthropologists and cultural ecologists are developing comprehensive models to take into account all of the variables in a human ecosystem.

Although it is obvious that research in human adaptability and microevolution is continuing to proceed in these more holistic directions, up to now it has been more productive for biological anthropologists, for example, to investigate the effects of a particular environmental stress on the adaptability of a particular genetic polymorphism rather than to investigate broader problems. However, in an attempt to expand these lines of inquiry, George Masnick and I at the University of Pennsylvania, recently carried out an ecosystems analysis of the changing patterns of fertility in North Alaskan Eskimo communities in relation to the other interacting demographic, bio-medical, environmental, sociocultural, and economic variables. Since differential fertility is a key consideration in microevolutionary studies, and since it is also related to many other facets of adaptability in the human ecosystem, we used an ecological framework for this particular problem to generate a more comprehensive analysis of the significant problems of the population. Already the ecosystems framework has proven to be highly successful in the analysis of health-related problems in this population. It holds the promise of demonstrating complex interrelations among the biological and socio-cultural variables involved in human adaptability and evolution.

Science and the Citizen
October 1963

Stress and the Zulu

A study of high blood pressure among Zulus in the Union of South Africa strongly suggests that stress is a major factor in the condition, and it also sheds some light on the nature of stress itself. Writing in the *American Journal of Public Health,* Norman A. Scotch of the Harvard University School of Public Health reports on a survey conducted in two Zulu communities, one a rural "reserve" and the other an urban "location" near the city of Durban. Hypertension, or high blood pressure, was significantly more prevalent among the urban Zulus. Scotch first attributed this to the greater severity and variety of stress in the location, where the predictable strains of city life and detribalization are complicated by the stressful effects of apartheid, the South African policy of strict separation of the races.

In an effort to define "stress" more specifically, Scotch examined the effect of a number of social variables on the incidence of hypertension in both communities. He found that only four variables were clearly associated with hypertension in both communities: age, sex, obesity and marital status (widowed women and women separated from their husbands were more likely to be hypertensive). But a number of other factors that were correlated with high blood pressure in one community were correlated with normal pressures in the other. For example, in the city women with many children were more hypertensive than those with few children; in the rural area there was no such correlation. Country women who had passed the menopause were more likely to be hypertensive than those who were premenopausal, whereas in the city the menopause had no such clear relation to hypertension. Scotch points out that a large number of children is stressful in the city but not in the country. Menopause, on the other hand, is stressful for the rural Zulu woman because it marks the end of her high-status period of childbearing; in the city, however, it frees her for greater productivity as a wage earner and is nonstressful. Scotch concludes that whether or not a variable is stressful depends on the social context in which it arises.

In general, Scotch believes, urbanization may not be stressful in itself. "It is not simply a case of change but rather of success or failure in change." The individuals most likely to be hypertensive were "those who maintained traditional cultural practices and who were thus unable to adapt successfully to the demands of urban living."

Science and the Citizen
May 1974

Cancer on the Caspian

Among the least common but most fatal forms of cancer is one that be-

gins as a tumor of the cells lining the esophagus, the section of the alimentary tract between the pharynx and the stomach. In two sizable districts bordering on the Caspian Sea, however, cancer of the esophagus is so common that the chance of a person's developing this kind of tumor before the age of 65 is about one in six. One of the areas, in Iran, is the Caspian coastal province of Mazenderan; the other, in Soviet Kazakhstan, is centered on a Caspian port city, Ghuryev. Why are the inhabitants of these areas, nomadic Turkomans in Iran and Kazakh tribesmen in the U.S.S.R., so prone to esophageal cancer?

Since 1966 a team of epidemiologists headed by J. Kmet and E. Mahboubi has been searching for an answer to this question among the Turkomans of Mazenderan. A recent review of their interim findings in *The Lancet* notes that the investigators have been able to rule out genetic factors. Because the Turkomans are strict Moslems, the ingestion of alcohol, which is believed to contribute to the considerable incidence of esophageal cancer in Brittany and Normandy, for example, can also be disregarded. Nor are the Turkomans exposed to any known natural or man-made environmental carcinogens. Kmet, Mahboubi and their colleagues are now focusing on the role that may be played by the mineral deficiencies of the region's soil and the shortcomings of the traditional Turkoman diet. Not only are trace metals absent from the soil in some parts of Mazenderan but also the staple foodstuff, unleavened bread, is rich in a chelating agent that binds metal ions. The Turkoman diet, moreover, is deficient in animal protein and vitamins A, B_2 and C. Iron and B-complex-vitamin deficiencies are believed to make surface cells more sensitive to stimulation by carcinogens, and the Turkomans both smoke and chew tobacco.

Perhaps the best single example of human microevolution is the natural selection of mutant genes for abnormal hemoglobins that increase resistance to malaria. The article by L. L. Cavalli-Sforza entitled "The Genetics of Human Populations," (also see Anthony C. Allison's "Sickle Cells and Evolution," *Scientific American* Offprint 1065) relates the history, population genetics, and significance of this important genetic polymorphism. The fact that millions of black Americans now live in an environment where the sickle cell gene no longer has a selective advantage poses a critical challenge to modern medicine. The problem involves medically alleviating the debilitating and often deadly effects of the gene in its homozygous condition, and simultaneously promoting eugenic counseling programs to reduce the overall frequency of diseased homozygotes in future generations. Thus when we speak of human evolution in the twentieth century we must begin to consider not only the effects of naturally occurring selective factors such as infectious disease, but also the effects of our ability to alter reproductive behavior, environments, and even genomes in specific ways. The full implications of these processes may mean a new kind of human evolution.

Lactose intolerance is one of the interesting recent discoveries in the interaction of nutrition and disease in human populations and illustrates the unique fit between human biology and cultural subsistence practices. In his article "Lactose and Lactase" Norman Kretchmer points out that adults in most populations historically dependent on fresh milk have lactase, an enzyme that digests the lactose sugar in milk, while most non-dairying populations lack this enzyme. It is likely that the presence of this enzyme is associated with a genetic characteristic. Hence the strong selective pressures produced by nutritional practices may have been involved in the apparent evolutionary persistence of this enzyme in the adult population.

> Since this article was written, many data have accumulated which support the contention that the ability for some peoples to digest lactose in adult life is genetically controlled. This characteristic is genetically dominant. Consequently, when an individual who can digest lactose has children with an individual who cannot digest the carbohydrate, the progeny will invariably be completely or partially composed of individuals who are lactose digestors. Union between two lactose non-digestors results in offspring who are lactose non-digestors. Based on knowledge of the cultural mores and history of people in regard to milk-drinking, it is possible to make reasonable predictions of where, geographically, one would expect to find lactose-digestors and lactose non-digestors.
>
> Linguistic data can be used to distinguish peoples and their origins. In contrast to the statements in the article, the Fulani cannot be classified as Hamites; they probably originated in Northwest Africa. The Ibo and Yoruba probably derive from the area in which they now live.
>
> The exciting aspect of these studies is the possibility that an amalgamation of biochemistry, genetics, and anthropology will produce more knowledge of human development.
>
> *Norman Kretchmer, February 1974*

Studies of this nature may have important implications for food supplementation programs where powdered milk is added, since it contains lactose that may be indigestible to the individuals who receive the food. Still at another level it is thought that there are biocultural adaptations involved in preparing yogurts or cheeses which are digestible to lactose intolerant individuals. Still another highly significant ramification of this finding is its theoretical implications for other examples of the interaction of nutritional practices and pathological conditions in human adaptability and evolution. This concept prompts us to ask new questions about the effects of cooking some foods and leaving others raw or about special recipes in cooking which result in significant enhancement of nutrition. For example a group of co-workers and I recently investigated a group of recipes for the preparation of maize which is traditionally the principal agricultural crop in the Western Hemisphere and is a highly important source of nutrition to much of the remaining world. We were able to demonstrate a highly significant relationship between alkali treatment of maize with limestone or ashes (a technique which sharply enhances the nutritional quality of maize) and the high production and consumption of this crop (Katz, Hediger, and Valleroy, 1974). Similarly, there is the finding that the consumption of fava beans by populations with a red blood cell deficiency of Glucose-6–phosphate dehydrogenase (G6PD) a condition prevalent in some regions with endemic malaria, leads to a serious hemolytic anemia.

As the means of storing and distributing foods becomes more developed, the incidence of maladaptive nutritional interaction will probably increase. We can only hope that our growing knowledge of the diversity of genetic incapacities and cultural practices of modern populations will be sufficient to allow us to prevent some of these problems in the future.

Within the human ecosystem one of the most important components of natural selection is infectious disease. Frequently infectious disease interacts with the genome of the individual to produce an illness. As the biomedical sciences become more sophisticated, an ever-increasing number of debilitating diseases are associated either directly or indirectly with the effects of some infectious agent. In certain forms of cancer, infectious hepatitis, yaws, and a variety of other infectious diseases, important genetic components are thought to be related to susceptibility to infection. In the case of sickle cell anemia, for example, (See Allison's "Sickle Cells and Evolution") there is strong evidence to suggest that the gene for Hemoglobin S is associated with resistance to certain forms of malaria. Blumberg (1970) has also suggested that there are simple autosomal traits associated with the incidence of acute infectious hepatitis.

The article by Geoffrey Dean on the "Multiple Sclerosis Problem," however, emphasizes that careful geographic analysis indicates heavy dependence on an environmental component for development of this disease. More specifically, Dean suggests that multiple sclerosis follows a pattern of infection much like the virus producing poliomyelitis. The infection rate of poliomyelitis is highest among those individuals who are not continuously exposed to an oral-fecal infection route. In populations lacking modern sewage systems the continuous contamination of the environment by human feces provides a continuous exposure to polio; this exposure allows the infant to develop antibodies against the virus, probably while it is still protected by maternal antibodies passed along to the infant in maternal breast milk. Where there are more modern sanitation systems the contamination of the environment by human feces is so low that the child is not exposed to polio until later in life when he has lost the protective effects of the maternal breast milk antibodies; never having developed his own antibodies, he has no immunity to the disease, and may even have gained an increased sensitivity to the paralytic effects of the disease.

When we consider the problems of infectious disease in a human population, it is important to take into account the behavioral and sociocultural responses to disease in order to understand more fully the levels at which adaptations to this basically biological phenomenon occur. With good historical records, it is possible to analyze the debilitating effects of a very serious infection such as bubonic plague upon a wide range of biosocial and economic adjustments in a population. William L. Langer's article "The Black Death" demonstrates from analyses of historical records the profound effects that this single disease had upon everything from the arts and philosophy to the rapid emergence of cities and the important interruption in the exponential growth of population in Europe in the middle ages. This article certainly serves to document the phenomenal impact of infectious disease upon biosocial evolution. In a supplementary note, Langer commented on the more recent studies of the plague and its effects. Following are excerpts from that note.

The threat of nuclear cataclysm has stimulated interest in the great plague epidemic of 1348–1350, which is generally acknowledged to have been the greatest disaster thus far to have befallen the human race.

No one doubts that such an enormous mortality in so short a time must have disrupted the social and economic conditions. But whether these effects were relatively transitory or whether they provoked the deepening economic depression of the later Middle Ages continues to be a subject hotly debated among economists. So much is certain: the Black Death should be viewed as the first and most destructive of a long series of plague epidemics which afflicted Europe every few years for several centuries and which admittedly must have had a baneful effect on all human activity. . . .

Recent studies have left no doubt that plague occurs in the pneumonic as well as the bubonic form. The former type is communicable by fleas from man to man and is more deadly than the bubonic, which is carried by fleas from plague-infected rats. The evidence suggests that the great plague of 1348–1350 and probably some later plagues were largely if not exclusively of the pneumonic type, which attacks the lungs and leads to almost certain death within twenty-four hours. It has been called "probably the deadliest bacterial disease of man." . . .

One of the great mysteries has been and still is the quite sudden disappearance of plague from Europe in the second half of the seventeenth century. The theory that an invasion of Europe by the brown field rat led to the expulsion or extermination of the black house rat, which was the prime vector of the plague bacillus, has been generally discarded. It has since been proved that the plague disappeared before the arrival of the brown rat, in the eighteenth century, and that in any case the black rat continued to exist in close contact to humans in several places. It may be that the replacement of mud huts and thatched roofs by stone structure with slate roofs deprived the house rat of its most congenial habitat, but this explanation seems at least inadequate. It is more likely that there was an "attenuated virulence" on the part of the plague bacillus or possibly a growing immunity on the part of mankind. The terrible plague epidemic that struck Marseilles and southeastern France as late as 1720, however, casts some doubt on the notion that either the fleas or the men had undergone any significant alteration. The question therefore remains open.

William L. Langer, November 1973

When biological anthropologists deal with the past interaction of diseases and human populations, frequently there is little more to go on than the skeletal remains of the people. Hence analyses of what diseases occurred are limited usually to the diseases that influence the skeleton, such as osteoarthritis, syphilis, and other diseases of bone. Paleopathology takes on added interest, however, when we consider the very careful job of body preservation developed in ancient Egypt; in Egyptian mummies, actual tissues from body organs can be identified. Using careful rehydration techniques a tissue section can be reconstituted and microscopically investigated for evidence of disease —sometimes with remarkable results (see the Science and the Citizen excerpt "Blood of the Pharaohs," page 228). By studying the history of infectious disease with these methods, we should be able to gain new insights into the adaptation and evolution of both the organisms producing a particular disease and the human populations contracting the disease.

Although infectious disease is very important in the understanding of human adaptation and evolution, other environmental stresses are equally important. In studies of adaptation to specific environmental stresses, a major question is the relative significance of acclimatization and genetic adaptation. Raymond J. Hock, in an article entitled "The Physiology of High Altitude," uses an experimental animal model to investigate adaptation to hypoxia (oxygen deficiency) at high altitudes. He concludes that the acclimatization that occurs during growth and development accounts for the vast majority of adaptations. However, these findings do not necessarily rule out the operation of one or more important genetic factors. The recent work, for example, with the product 2,3-diphosphoglycerate (2,3-DPG) suggests that this compound greatly facilitates rapid shifts in the effective carriage and transfer of oxygen by hemoglobin in the red blood cells. The enzyme responsible for producing this compound (2,3-DPG mutase) may thus provide an important source of genetic adaptation to hypoxic stress. Should these findings lead to the discovery of genetic variants that are important in adaptations to altitude, they could reshape our thinking about the whole mechanism of adaptation at the tissue level since it would help resolve a long-standing controversy regarding whether or not genetic factors underly these adaptive responses.

Studying organs of adaptation, William Montagna in his article "The Skin" introduces us to another approach in the study of human adaptability. This approach is largely physiological, centering on the adaptive functions of the skin which is considered a body organ. In discussing all of the physiological functions of the skin, he develops a highly inclusive perspective of the known adaptations served by this organ. The advantage of the physiological approach is that the knowledge can be integrated into a variety of questions about human adaptation, such as the adaptive significance of this organ within the variation found in a particular population within its ecosystem, the analysis of any particular physiological trait across various populations in related ecosystems, and analysis of the function that skin serves with respect to its integration with other body organs and behavior in general.

Laurence Irving's article "Adaptations to Cold" attempts to delineate some of the adaptive mechanisms various animals use in cold climates. Irving suggests that the most significant cold adaptation for humans in the Arctic is clothing; although biological mechanisms are called into play, they seem to be outweighed in significance by the effective insulation that arctic clothing provides. As Irving's article shows, the Arctic provides one of the most extreme environments in which to study the ways man satisfies his energy needs.

William B. Kemp's article "The Flow of Energy in a Hunting Society," which deals with the energy exchanges in an Eskimo community in the Canadian Arctic, nicely complements Irving's biologically based study of cold adaptation with an analysis of the relationships between biological constraints and sociocultural patterns. The flow of food and fuel energy for the people in this community is highly adapted to their mode of subsistence, which in turn is limited by the arctic environment. The interaction of environmental limitations and energy sources inevitably influences population size and age-sex composition. However, outside energy and technological resources mitigate this impact, and even differentially support one Eskimo family more than another of the same village. The contrast between such families demonstrates in microcosm the shifts in the sources and uses of technology and energy that have occurred in the Arctic over the last several decades. Once again we see the complexity of the dynamic interactions of environment, rapidly changing technology, and sociocultural responses. How these changes will influence the biosociocultural evolution and adaptations of this population remains an unanswered and exciting question for future investigators.

Moving to the agricultural society of the Tsembaga of New Guinea, described by Roy A. Rappaport in his article "The Flow of Energy in an Agricultural Society," we can observe the intricate way in which this population has teased a highly productive subsistence out of its tropical ecology by preserving the ecological balance. As Rappaport analyzes the energy transfers within this ecosystem, he expands his discussion to the broader considerations of basic ecological principles—particularly the importance of ecosystemic diversity and stability—and suggests that the complex industrialized agricultural societies could learn an important lesson from the Tsembaga about the limits and potentials of the human ecosystem.

Science and the Citizen
December 1972

Rubella and Autism

The outbreak of rubella ("German measles") in 1964 was one of the most costly epidemics in American history. An estimated 30,000 infants carried by mothers who had contracted the disease during pregnancy were born with congenital abnormalities such as deafness and cataracts. It now seems likely that the abnormalities include the childhood psychic disorder known as autism. This grave syndrome, which is characterized by almost total withdrawal from interaction with other people, has been ascribed to various psychogenic and organic causes. Until recently, however, the neurological damage done by rubella did not rank very high among the possibilities.

According to surveys in Britain and the U.S., the rate of autism in the general population is less than five cases per 10,000 live births. For a group of 243 "rubella children" being investigated at the New York University Medical Center the rate is a thousandfold higher, equivalent to 412 cases per 10,000. A smaller group being studied at the Baylor University College of Medicine shows a rate twice that of the New York University group.

One of the participants in the New York University studies, Stella Chess, professor of child psychiatry at the Medical Center, has found that 20 percent of the 243 rubella children escaped organic damage of any kind and that nearly 50 percent show no evidence of psychiatric disorder. Nine of the 243, who also exhibit various degrees of mental retardation, are autistic, and one unretarded child is autistic. Partial autism is evident in one unretarded child, in six who are retarded and in one with combined cerebral dysfunction and mental retardation. Noting that 65 others in the group are more or less severely retarded but that none of these children is autistic, Chess judges that the overlap between retardation and autism is coincidental. The fact remains that 10 of the 243 are autistic and eight are partially so.

Chess notes that the New York University studies clearly imply the existence of a link between rubella and autism, even though the exact mechanism whereby the organic damage manifests itself behaviorally remains to be determined. She speculates that the link was largely overlooked by most medical workers in the U.S. until after the 1964 epidemic and suggests that mothers of autistic children be routinely questioned about a possible history of rubella during pregnancy.

the bones of older people and may also affect the course of atherosclerosis, or degeneration of the arteries. Investigators from the Harvard School of Public Health have found that people who regularly drink water with a high fluoride content have less osteoporosis, a disease characterized by a reduction in bone mass, and less calcification of the aorta, which is evidence of severe atherosclerosis in the major artery of the body.

These conclusions were drawn on the basis of X-ray studies of two population groups in North Dakota: 300 men and women, ranging in age from 45 to over 65, from a region in the southwestern part of the state where the water supply is rich in fluorides (from 4 to 5.8 parts per million) and 1,015 people in the same age group from an area in the northeastern part of the state where the water has a low fluoride content (.15 to .3 part per million). About twice as many women had decreased bone density and two to six times as many had collapsed vertebrae in the low-fluoride area as in the high-fluoride area. A similar but less marked tendency was noted in the men. Calcification of the aorta was less prevalent in the high-fluoride area, with the difference in this case appreciably more significant in men. Differences in the amounts of cheese and milk (good sources of calcium) consumed in the two areas did not appear to affect the incidence of either disease.

The Harvard group included Daniel S. Bernstein, Norman Sadowsky, D. Mark Hegsted, Charles D. Guri and Fredrick J. Stare. They point out that fluoride is known to enhance the growth and architectural integrity of crystalline material in the enamel of teeth and in bone. "The enlarged and more nearly perfect bone crystal may be less susceptible to resorption, accounting for our observations." An editorial in the issue of the *Journal of the American Medical Association* in which their report is published comments: "It appears as though the fluoride ion helps to keep calcium deposited in the hard tissues of the body."

Science and the Citizen
January 1967

Bones, Arteries and Fluorides

The consumption of fluorides has an important effect on the fragility of

LACTOSE IS DIGESTED BY LACTASE in the intestine, a single epithelial cell of which is enlarged 37,500 diameters in this scanning electron micrograph made by Jeanne M. Riddle of the Wayne State University School of Medicine. The cell, on the surface of one of the finger-like villi that stud the lining of the intestine, is in turn covered by innumerable fine processes called microvilli.

Lactose and Lactase

by Norman Kretchmer
October 1972

*Lactose is milk sugar; the enzyme lactase breaks it
down. For want of lactase most adults cannot digest
milk. In populations that drink milk the adults have
more lactase, perhaps through natural selection*

Milk is the universal food of newborn mammals, but some human infants cannot digest it because they lack sufficient quantities of lactase, the enzyme that breaks down lactose, or milk sugar. Adults of all animal species other than man also lack the enzyme—and so, it is now clear, do most human beings after between two and four years of age. That this general adult deficiency in lactase has come as a surprise to physiologists and nutritionists can perhaps be attributed to a kind of ethnic chauvinism, since the few human populations in which tolerance of lactose has been found to exceed intolerance include most northern European and white American ethnic groups.

Milk is a nearly complete human food, and in powdered form it can be conveniently stored and shipped long distances. Hence it is a popular source of protein and other nutrients in many programs of aid to nutritionally impoverished children, including American blacks. The discovery that many of these children are physiologically intolerant to lactose is therefore a matter of concern and its implications are currently being examined by such agencies as the U.S. Office of Child Development and the Protein Advisory Group of the United Nations System.

Lactose is one of the three major solid components of milk and its only carbohydrate; the other components are fats and proteins. Lactose is a disaccharide composed of the monosaccharides glucose and galactose. It is synthesized only by the cells of the lactating mammary gland, through the reaction of glucose with the compound uridine diphosphate galactose [see *illustrations on next page*]. One of the proteins found in milk, alpha-lactalbumin, is required for the synthesis of lactose. This protein apparently does not actually enter into the reaction; what it does is "specify" the action of the enzyme galactosyl transferase, modifying the enzyme so that in the presence of alpha-lactalbumin and glucose it catalyzes the synthesis of lactose.

In the nonlactating mammary gland, where alpha-lactalbumin is not present, the enzyme synthesizes instead of lactose a more complicated carbohydrate, N-acetyl lactosamine. Test-tube studies have shown that alpha-lactalbumin is manufactured only in the presence of certain hormones: insulin, cortisone, estrogen and prolactin; its synthesis is inhibited by the hormone progesterone. It is when progesterone levels decrease late in pregnancy that the manufacture of alpha-lactalbumin, and thus of lactose, is initiated [see "Milk," by Stuart Patton; SCIENTIFIC AMERICAN Offprint 1147].

The concentration of lactose in milk from different sources varies considerably. Human milk is the sweetest, with 7.5 grams of lactose per 100 milliliters of milk. Cow's milk has 4.5 grams per 100 milliliters. The only mammals that do not have any lactose—or any other carbohydrate—in their milk are certain of the Pinnipedia: the seals, sea lions and walruses of the Pacific basin. If these animals are given lactose in any form, they become sick. (In 1933 there was a report of a baby walrus that was fed cow's milk while being shipped from Alaska to California. The animal suffered from severe diarrhea throughout the voyage and was very sick by the time it arrived in San Diego.) Of these pinnipeds the California sea lion has been the most intensively studied. No alpha-lactalbumin is synthesized by its mammary gland. When alpha-lactalbumin from either rat's milk or cow's milk is added to a preparation of sea lion mammary gland in a test tube, however, the glandular tissue does manufacture lactose.

In general, low concentrations of lactose are associated with high concentrations of milk fat (which is particularly useful to marine mammals). The Pacific pinnipeds have more than 35 grams of fat per 100 milliliters of milk, compared with less than four grams in the cow. In the whale and the bear (an ancient ancestor of which may also be an ancestor of the Pacific pinnipeds) the lactose in milk is low and the fat content is high.

Lactase, the enzyme that breaks down lactose ingested in milk or a milk product, is a specific intestinal beta-galactosidase that acts only on lactose, primarily in the jejunum, the second of the small intestine's three main segments. The functional units of the wall of the small intestine are the villus (composed of metabolically active, differentiated, nondividing cells) and the crypt (a set of dividing cells from which those of the villus are derived). Lactase is not present in the dividing cells. It appears in the differentiated cells, specifically within the brush border of the cells at the surface of the villus [see *illustrations on page 314*]. Lactase splits the disaccharide lactose into its two component monosaccharides, glucose and galactose. Some of the released glucose can be utilized directly by the cells of the villus; the remainder, along with the galactose, enters the bloodstream, and both sugars are metabolized by the liver. Neither Gary Gray of the Stanford University School of Medicine nor other investigators have been able to distinguish any qualitative biochemical or physical difference among the lactases isolated from the intestine of infants, tolerant adults and intolerant adults. The difference appears to be

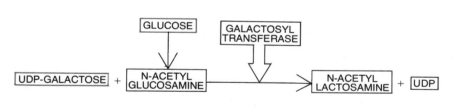

LACTOSE, a disaccharide composed of the monosaccharides glucose and galactose, is the carbohydrate of milk, the other major components of which are fats, proteins and water.

merely quantitative; there is simply very little lactase in the intestine of a lactose-intolerant person. In the intestine of Pacific pinnipeds, Philip Sunshine of the Stanford School of Medicine found, there is no lactase at all, even in infancy.

Lactase is not present in the intestine of the embryo or the fetus until the middle of the last stage of gestation. Its

activity attains a maximum immediately after birth. Thereafter it decreases, reaching a low level, for example, immediately after weaning in the rat and after one and a half to three years in most children. The exact mechanism involved in the appearance and disappearance of the lactase is not known, but such a pattern of waxing and waning

activity is common in the course of development; in general terms, one can say that it results from differential action of the gene or genes concerned.

Soon after the turn of the century the distinguished American pediatrician Abraham Jacobi pointed out that diarrhea in babies could be associated with the ingestion of carbohydrates. In 1921 another pediatrician, John Howland, said that "there is with many patients an abnormal response on the part of the intestinal tract to carbohydrates, which expresses itself in the form of diarrhea and excessive fermentation." He suggested as the cause a deficiency in the hydrolysis, or enzymatic breakdown, of lactose.

The physiology is now well established. If the amount of lactose presented to the intestinal cells exceeds the hydrolytic capacity of the available lactase (whether because the lactase level is low or because an unusually large amount of lactose is ingested), a portion of the lactose remains undigested. Some of it passes into the blood and is eventually excreted in the urine. The remainder moves on into the large intestine, where two processes ensue. One is physical: the lactose molecules increase the particle content of the intestinal fluid compared with the fluid in cells outside the intestine and therefore by osmotic action draw water out of the tissues into the intestine. The other is biochemical: the glucose is fermented by the bacteria in the colon. Organic acids and carbon dioxide are generated and the symptoms can be those of any fermentative diarrhea, including a bloated feeling, flatulence, belching, cramps and a watery, explosive diarrhea.

At the end of the 1950's Paolo Durand of the University of Genoa and Aaron Holzel and his colleagues at the University of Manchester reported detailed studies of infants who were unable to digest lactose and who reacted to milk sugar with severe diarrhea, malnutrition and even death. This work stimulated a revival of interest in lactose and lactase, and there followed a period of active investigation of lactose intolerance. Many cases were reported, including some in which lactase inactivity could be demonstrated in tissue taken from the patient's intestine by biopsy. It became clear that intolerance in infants could be a congenital condition (as in Holzel's two patients, who were siblings) or, more frequently, could be secondary to various diseases and other stresses: cystic fibrosis, celiac disease, malnutrition, the ingestion of certain drugs, surgery and even non-

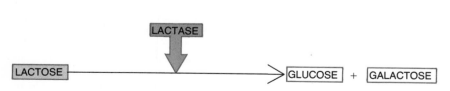

SYNTHESIS OF LACTOSE in the mammary gland begins late in pregnancy when specific hormones and the protein alpha-lactalbumin are present. The latter modifies the enzyme galactosyl transferase, "specifying" it so that it catalyzes the synthesis of lactose from glucose and galactose (top). In the nonlactating gland the glucose takes part in a different reaction (middle). In intestine lactase breaks down lactose to glucose and galactose (bottom).

specific diarrhea. During this period of investigation, it should be noted, intolerance to lactose was generally assumed to be the unusual condition and the condition worthy of study.

In 1965 Pedro Cuatrecasas and his colleagues and Theodore M. Bayless and Norton S. Rosensweig, all of whom were then at the Johns Hopkins School of Medicine, administered lactose to American blacks and whites, none of whom had had gastrointestinal complaints, and reported some startling findings. Whereas only from 6 to 15 percent of the whites showed clinical symptoms of intolerance, about 70 percent of the blacks were intolerant. This immediately suggested that many human adults might be unable to digest lactose and, more specifically, that there might be significant differences among ethnic groups. The possibility was soon confirmed: G. C. Cook and S. Kajubi of Makerere University College examined two different tribes in Uganda. They found that only 20 percent of the adults of the cattle-herding Tussi tribe were intolerant to lactose but that 80 percent of the nonpastoral Ganda were intolerant. Soon one paper after another reported a general intolerance to lactose among many ethnic groups, including Japanese, other Orientals, Jews in Israel, Eskimos and South American Indians.

In these studies various measures of intolerance were applied. One was the appearance of clinical symptoms—flatulence and diarrhea—after the ingestion of a dose of lactose, which was generally standardized at two grams of lactose per kilogram (2.2 pounds) of body weight, up to a maximum of either 50 or 100 grams. Another measure was a finding of low lactase activity (less than two units per gram of wet weight of tissue) determined through an intestinal biopsy after ingestion of the same dose of lactose. A third was an elevation of blood glucose of less than 20 milligrams per 100 milliliters of blood after ingestion of the lactose. Since clinical symptoms are variable and the biopsy method is inconvenient for the subject being tested, the blood glucose method is preferable. It is a direct measure of lactose breakdown, and false-negative results are rare if the glucose is measured 15 minutes after lactose is administered.

By 1970 enough data had been accumulated to indicate that many more groups all over the world are intolerant to lactose than are tolerant. As a matter of fact, real adult tolerance to lactose has so far been observed only in northern Europeans, approximately 90 percent of whom tolerate lactose, and in the

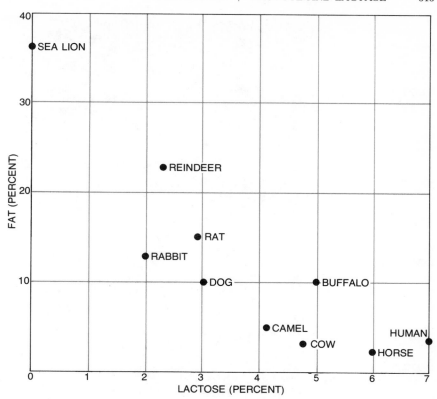

CONCENTRATION OF LACTOSE varies with the source of the milk. In general the less lactose, the more fat, which can also be utilized by the newborn animal as an energy source.

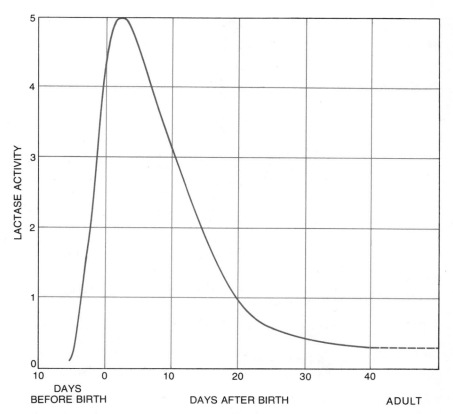

LACTASE is present in mammals other than man, and in most humans, in the fetus before birth and in infancy. The general shape of the curve of enzyme activity, shown here for the rat, is about the same in all species. Enzyme activity, given here in relative units, is determined by measuring glucose release from intestinal tissue in the presence of lactose.

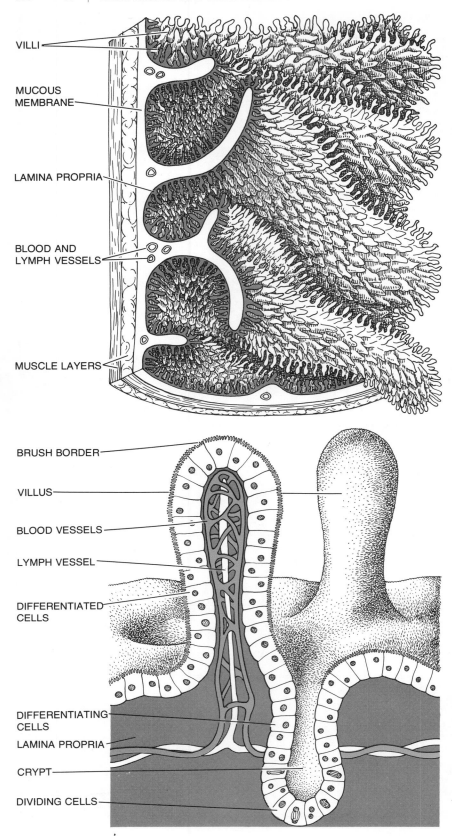

VILLI

MUCOUS
MEMBRANE

LAMINA PROPRIA

BLOOD AND
LYMPH VESSELS

MUSCLE LAYERS

BRUSH BORDER

VILLUS

BLOOD VESSELS

LYMPH VESSEL

DIFFERENTIATED
CELLS

DIFFERENTIATING
CELLS

LAMINA PROPRIA

CRYPT

DIVIDING CELLS

WALL OF SMALL INTESTINE, seen in longitudinal section (*top*), has outer muscle lay-ers, a submucosa layer and an inner mucous membrane. The mucous membrane (*bottom*) has a connective-tissue layer (lamina propria), which contains blood and lymph capillaries, and an inner surface of epithelial cells. The cells multiply and differentiate in the crypts and migrate to the villi. At what stage the lactase is manufactured is not known; it is found primarily in the microvilli, which constitute the brush border of the differentiated cells.

members of two nomadic pastoral tribes in Africa, of whom about 80 percent are tolerant. Although many other gen-erally tolerant groups will be found, they will always belong to a minority of the human species. In this situation it is clearly more interesting and potentially more fruitful to focus the investigation on tolerant people in an effort to explain adult tolerance, a characteristic in which man differs from all other mammals.

There are two kinds of explanation of adult tolerance to lactose. The first, and perhaps the most immediately apparent, originates with the fact that most people who tolerate lactose have a history of drinking milk. Maybe the mere pres-ence of milk in the diet suffices to stimu-late lactase activity in the individual, perhaps by "turning on" genes that en-code the synthesis of the enzyme. In-dividual enzymatic adaptation to an en-vironmental stimulus is well known, but it is not transferable genetically. The other explanation of tolerance is based on the concept of evolution through natural selection. If in particular popu-lations it became biologically advan-tageous to be able to digest milk, then the survival of individuals with a genetic mutation that led to higher intestinal lactase activity in adulthood would have been favored. An individual who de-rived his ability to digest lactose from this classical form of Darwinian adapta-tion would be expected to be able to transfer the trait genetically.

These two points of view have become the subject of considerable contro-versy. I suspect that each of the expla-nations is valid for some of the adult tolerance being observed, and I should like to examine both of them.

The possibility of individual adapta-tion to lactose has been considered since the beginning of the century, usually through attempts to relate lactase ac-tivity to the concentration of milk in the diet of animals. Almost without excep-tion the studies showed that although there was a slight increase in lactase activity when a constant diet of milk or milk products was consumed, there was no significant change in the characteris-tic curve reflecting the developmental rise and fall of enzymatic activity. Re-cently there have been reports pointing toward adaptation, however. Some stud-ies, with human subjects as well as rats, indicated that continued intensive feed-ing of milk or lactose not only made it possible for the individual to tolerate the sugar but also resulted in a measurable increase in lactase activity. The discrep-ancy among the findings could be partly attributable to improvement in methods for assaying the enzyme activity.

On balance it would appear that individual adaptation may be able to explain at least some cases of adult tolerance. I shall cite two recent studies. John Godell, working in Lagos, selected six Nigerian medical students who were absolutely intolerant to lactose and who showed no physiological evidence of lactose hydrolysis. He fed them increasing amounts of the sugar for six months. Godell found that although the students did develop tolerance for the lactose, there was nevertheless no evidence of an increase of glucose in the blood—and thus of enzymatic adaptation—following test doses of the sugar. The conjecture is that the diet brought about a change in the bacterial flora in the intestine, and that the ingested lactose was being metabolized by the new bacteria.

In our laboratory at the Stanford School of Medicine Emanuel Lebenthal and Sunshine found that in rats given lactose the usual pattern of a developmental decrease in lactase activity is maintained but the activity level is somewhat higher at the end of the experiment. The rise in activity does not appear to be the result of an actual increase in lactase synthesis, however. We treated the rats with actinomycin, which prevents the synthesis of new protein from newly activated genes. The actinomycin had no effect on the slight increase in lactase activity, indicating that the mechanism leading to the increase was not gene activation. It appears, rather, that the presence of additional amounts of the enzyme's substrate, lactose, somehow "protects" the lactase from degradation. Such a process has been noted in many other enzyme-substrate systems. The additional lactase activity that results from this protection is sufficient to improve the rat's tolerance of lactose, but that additional activity is dependent on the continued presence of the lactose.

Testing the second hypothesis—that adult lactose tolerance is primarily the result of a long-term process of genetic selection—is more complicated. It involves data and reasoning from such disparate areas as history, anthropology, nutrition, genetics and sociology as well as biochemistry.

As I have noted, the work of Cuatrecasas, of Bayless and Rosensweig and of Cook and Kajubi in the mid-1960's pointed to the likelihood of significant differences in adult lactose tolerance among ethnic groups. It also suggested that one ought to study in particular black Americans and their ancestral populations in Africa. The west coast of Africa was the primary source of slaves for the New World. With the objective of studying lactose tolerance in Nigeria, we developed a joint project with a group from the University of Lagos Teaching Hospital headed by Olikoye Ransome-Kuti.

The four largest ethnic groups in Nigeria are the Yoruba in western Nigeria, the Ibo in the east and the Fulani and Hausa in the north. These groups have different origins and primary occupations. The Yoruba and the Ibo differ somewhat anthropometrically, but both are Negro ethnic groups that probably came originally from the Congo Basin; they were hunters and gatherers who became farmers. They eventually settled south of the Niger and Benue rivers in an area infested with the tsetse fly, so that they never acquired cattle (or any other beast of burden). Hence it was not until recent times that milk appeared in their diet beyond the age of weaning. After the colonization of their part of Nigeria by the British late in the 19th century, a number of Yoruba and Ibo, motivated by their intense desire for education, migrated to England and northern Europe; they acquired Western dietary habits and in some cases Western spouses, and many eventually returned to Nigeria.

The Fulani are Hamites who have been pastoral people for thousands of years, originally perhaps in western Asia and more recently in northwestern Africa. Wherever they went, they took their cattle with them, and many of the Fulani are still nomads who herd their cattle from one grazing ground to another. About 300 years ago the Fulani appeared in what is now Nigeria and waged war on the Hausa. (The Fulani also tried to invade Yorubaland but were defeated by the tsetse fly.) After the invasion of the Hausa region some of the Fulani moved into villages and towns.

As a result of intermarriage between the Fulani and the Hausa there appeared a new group known as the town-Fulani or the Hausa-Fulani, whose members no longer raise cattle and whose ingestion of lactose is quite different from that of the pastoral Fulani. The pastoral Fulani do their milking in the early morning and drink some fresh milk. The milk reaches the market in the villages and towns only in a fermented form, however, as a kind of yogurt called *nono*. As the *nono* stands in the morning sun it becomes a completely fermented, watery preparation, which is then thickened with millet or some other cereal. The final product is almost completely

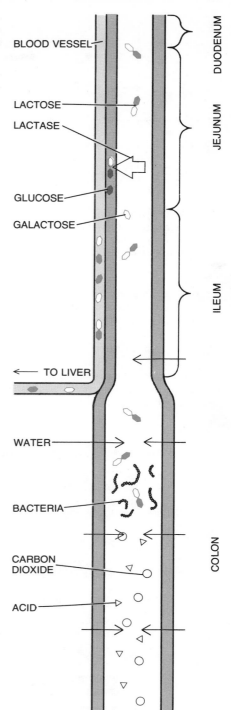

DIGESTION OF LACTOSE is accomplished primarily in the jejunum, where lactase splits it into glucose and galactose. Some glucose is utilized locally; the rest enters the bloodstream with the galactose and both are utilized in the liver. In the absence of enough lactase some undigested lactose enters the bloodstream; most goes on into the ileum and the colon, where it draws water from the tissues into the intestine by osmotic action. The undigested lactose is also fermented by bacteria in the colon, giving rise to various acids and carbon dioxide gas.

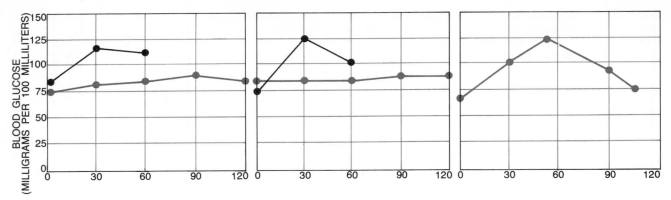

LACTOSE INTOLERANCE is determined by measuring blood glucose after ingestion of lactose. The absence of a significant rise in blood glucose after lactose ingestion (color) as contrasted with a rise in blood glucose after ingestion of sucrose, another sugar (black), indicates that a Yoruba male (left) and an American Jewish male (middle) are lactose-intolerant. On the other hand, the definite rise in blood glucose after ingestion of lactose in a Fulani male (right) shows that the Fulani is tolerant to lactose.

free of lactose and can be ingested without trouble even by a person who cannot digest lactose.

We tested members of each of these Nigerian populations. Of all the Yorubas above the age of four who were tested, we found only one person in whom the blood glucose rose to more than 20 milligrams per 100 milliliters following administration of the test dose of lactose. She was a nurse who had spent six years in the United Kingdom and had grown accustomed to a British diet that included milk. At first, she said, the milk disagreed with her, but later she could tolerate it with no adverse side effects. None of the Ibos who were studied showed an elevation of glucose in blood greater than 20 milligrams per 100 milliliters. (The major problem in all these studies is determining ethnic purity. All the Yorubas and Ibos who participated in this portion of the study indicated that there had been no intermarriages in their families.) Most of the Hausa and Hausa-Fulani

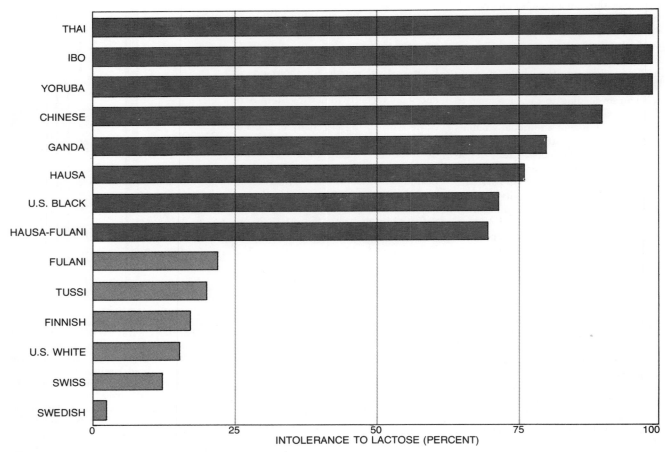

INTOLERANCE VARIES WIDELY among populations. The bars are based on tests conducted by a number of investigators by different methods; they may not be strictly comparable or accurately reflect the situation in entire populations. Among the groups studied to date lactose intolerance is prevalent except among northern Europeans (and their descendants) and herders in Africa.

(70 to 80 percent) were intolerant to lactose. In contrast most of the nomadic Fulani (78 percent) were tolerant to it. In their ability to hydrolyze lactose they resembled the pastoral Tussi of Uganda and northern Europeans more than they resembled their nearest neighbors.

Once the distribution of lactose intolerance and tolerance was determined in the major Nigerian populations, we went on to study the genetics of the situation by determining the results of mixed marriages. One of the common marriages in western Nigeria is between a Yoruba male and a British or other northern European female; the reverse situation is less common. Our tests showed that when a tolerant northern European marries a lactose-intolerant Yoruba, the offspring are most likely to be lactose-tolerant. If a tolerant child resulting from such a marriage marries a pure Yoruba, then the children are also predominantly tolerant. There is no sex linkage of the genes involved: in the few cases in which a Yoruba female had married a northern European male, the children were predominantly tolerant.

On the basis of these findings one can say that lactose tolerance is transmitted genetically and is dominant, that is, genes for tolerance from one of the parents are sufficient to make the child tolerant. On the other hand, the children of two pure Yorubas are always intolerant to lactose, as are the children of a lactose-intolerant European female and a Yoruba male. In other words, intolerance is also transmitted genetically and is probably a recessive trait, that is, both parents must be lactose-intolerant to produce an intolerant child. When the town-dwelling royal line of the Fulani was investigated, its members were all found to be unable to digest lactose—except for the children of one wife, a pastoral Fulani, who were tolerant.

Among the children of Yoruba-European marriages the genetic cross occurred one generation ago or at the most two generations. Among the Hausa-Fulani it may have been as much as 15 generations ago. This should explain the general intolerance of the Hausa-Fulani. Presumably the initial offspring of the lactose-tolerant Fulani and the lactose-intolerant Hausa were predominantly tolerant. As the generations passed, however, intolerance again became more prevalent. The genes for lactase can therefore be considered incompletely dominant.

The blacks brought to America were primarily Yoruba or Ibo or similar West African peoples who were originally

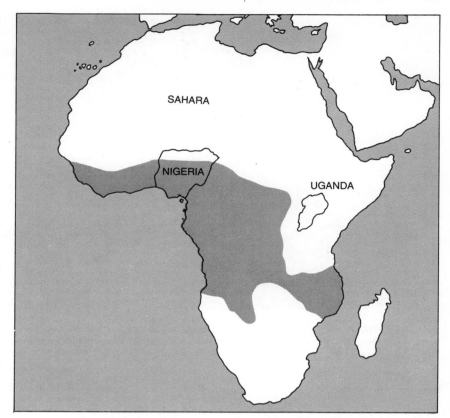

GEOGRAPHICAL EXTENT of dairying coincides roughly with areas of general lactose tolerance. According to Frederick J. Simoons of the University of California at Davis, there is a broad belt (color) across Africa in which dairying is not traditional. Migrations affect the tolerance pattern, however. For example, the Ganda, a lactose-intolerant group living in Uganda, came to that milk-drinking region from the nonmilking central Congo.

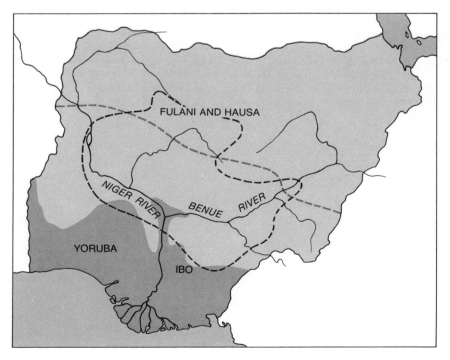

LARGEST ETHNIC GROUPS in Nigeria are the Ibo in the east, the Yoruba in the west and the Hausa and Fulani in the north. Map shows regions of mangrove swamp or forest (dark color) and grassland or desert (light color). Southern livestock limit (broken colored line) is set by climate, vegetation and tsetse fly infestation (broken black line).

FULANI WOMAN offers *nono,* a yogurt-like milk drink, for sale in the marketplace of a town in northern Nigeria. The pastoral Fulani drink fresh milk. The partially fermented *nono,* with reduced lactose content, is tolerated by villagers who could not digest milk.

intolerant to lactose. American blacks have been in this country for between 10 and 15 generations, in the course of which a certain complement of white northern European genes has entered the black population. Presumably as a result lactose intolerance among American blacks has been reduced to approximately 70 percent. One can speculate that if this gene flow eventually stopped, lactose intolerance would approach 100 percent among American blacks.

What events in human cultural history might have influenced the development of tolerance to lactose in the adults of some groups? Frederick J. Simoons of the University of California at Davis has proposed a hypothesis based on the development of dairying. It would appear that the milking of cattle, sheep, goats or reindeer did not begin until about 10,000 years ago, some 100 million years after the origin of mammals and therefore long after the mammalian developmental pattern of lactase activity had been well established. Man presumably shared that pattern, and so adults were intolerant to lactose. When some small groups of humans began to milk animals, a selective advantage was conferred on individuals who, because of a chance mutation, had high enough lactase activity to digest lactose. A person who could not digest lactose might have difficulty in a society that ingested nonfermented milk or milk products, but the lactose-tolerant individual was more adaptable: he could survive perfectly well in either a milk-drinking or a non-milk-drinking society.

The genetic mutation resulting in the capability to digest lactose probably occurred at least 10,000 years ago. People with the mutation for adult lactase activity could be members of a dairying culture, utilize their own product for food (as the Fulani do today) and then sell it in the form of a yogurt (as the Fulani do) or cheese to the general, lactose-intolerant population. These statements are presumptions, not facts, but they are based soundly on the idea that tolerance to lactose is a mutation that endowed the individual with a nutritional genetic advantage and on the basic assumption, which is supported by fact, that lactose intolerance is the normal genetic state of adult man and that lactose tolerance is in a sense abnormal.

What are the implications of all of this for nutrition policy? It should be pointed out that many people who are intolerant to lactose are nevertheless able to drink some milk or eat some milk products; the relation of clinical symptoms to lactose ingestion is quantitative. For most people, even after the age of four, drinking moderate amounts of milk has no adverse effects and is actually nutritionally beneficial. It may well be, however, that programs of indiscriminate, large-scale distribution of milk powder to intolerant populations should be modified, or that current moves toward supplying lactose-free milk powder should be encouraged.

The Black Death

by William L. Langer
February 1964

The plague that killed a quarter of the people of Europe in the years 1348–1350 is still studied to shed light on human behavior under conditions of universal catastrophe

In the three years from 1348 through 1350 the pandemic of plague known as the Black Death, or, as the Germans called it, the Great Dying, killed at least a fourth of the population of Europe. It was undoubtedly the worst disaster that has ever befallen mankind. Today we can have no real conception of the terror under which people lived in the shadow of the plague. For more than two centuries plague has not been a serious threat to mankind in the large, although it is still a grisly presence in parts of the Far East and Africa. Scholars continue to study the Great Dying, however, as a historic example of human behavior under the stress of universal catastrophe. In these days when the threat of plague has been replaced by the threat of mass human extermination by even more rapid means, there has been a sharp renewal of interest in the history of the 14th-century calamity. With new perspective, students are investigating its manifold effects: demographic, economic, psychological, moral and religious.

Plague is now recognized as a well-marked disease caused by a specific organism (*Bacillus pestis*). It is known in three forms, all highly fatal: pneumonic (attacking primarily the lungs), bubonic (producing buboes, or swellings, of the lymph glands) and septicemic (killing the victim rapidly by poisoning of the blood). The disease is transmitted to man by fleas, mainly from black rats and certain other rodents, including ground squirrels. It produces high fever, agonizing pain and prostration, and it is usually fatal within five or six days. The Black Death got its name from dark blotches produced by hemorrhages in the skin.

There had been outbreaks of plague in the Roman Empire in the sixth century and in North Africa earlier, but for some reason epidemics of the disease in Europe were comparatively rare after that until the 14th century. Some historians have suggested that the black rat was first brought to western Europe during the Crusades by expeditions returning from the Middle East. This seems unlikely: remains of the rat have been found in prehistoric sites in Switzerland, and in all probability the houses of Europe were infested with rats throughout the Middle Ages.

In any event, the 14th-century pandemic clearly began in 1348 in the ports of Italy, apparently brought in by merchant ships from Black Sea ports. It gradually spread through Italy and in the next two years swept across Spain, France, England, central Europe and Scandinavia. It advanced slowly but pitilessly, striking with deadliest effect in the crowded, unsanitary towns. Each year the epidemic rose to a peak in the late summer, when the fleas were most abundant, and subsided during the winter, only to break out anew in the spring.

The pandemic of 1348–1350 was followed by a long series of recurrent outbreaks all over Europe, coming at intervals of 10 years or less. In London there were at least 20 attacks of plague in the 15th century, and in Venice the Black Death struck 23 times between 1348 and 1576. The plague epidemics were frequently accompanied by severe outbreaks of typhus, syphilis and "English sweat"—apparently a deadly form of influenza that repeatedly afflicted not only England but also continental Europe in the first half of the 16th century.

From the 13th to the late 17th century Europe was disease-ridden as never before or since. In England the long affliction came to a climax with an epidemic of bubonic plague in 1665 that killed nearly a tenth of London's estimated population of 460,000, two-thirds of whom fled the city during the outbreak. Thereafter in western and central Europe the plague rapidly died away as mysteriously as it had come. The theories advanced to explain its subsidence are as unconvincing as those given for its rise. It was long supposed, for instance, that an invasion of Europe early in the 18th century by brown rats, which killed off the smaller black rats, was responsible for the decline of the disease. This can hardly be the reason; the plague had begun to subside decades before, and the brown rat did not by any means exterminate the black rat. More probably the answer must be sought in something that happened to the flea, the bacillus or the living conditions of the human host.

This article, however, is concerned not with the medical but with the social aspects of the Black Death. Let us begin by examining the dimensions of the catastrophe in terms of the death toll.

As reported by chroniclers of the time, the mortality figures were so incredibly high that modern scholars long regarded them with skepticism. Recent detailed and rigorously conducted analyses indicate, however, that many of the reports were substantially correct. It is now generally accepted that at least a quarter of the European population was wiped out in the first epidemic of 1348 through 1350, and that in the next 50 years the total mortality rose to more than a third of the population. The incidence of the disease and the mortality rate varied, of course, from place to place. Florence was reduced in population from 90,000 to 45,000, Siena from 42,000 to 15,000; Hamburg apparently lost almost two-thirds of its inhabitants. These estimates are borne out by accurate records that were kept in later epidemics. In Venice, for example, the Magistrato della Sanità (board of health) kept a meticulous count of the victims of a severe plague attack in 1576 and 1577; the deaths totaled 46,721 in a total estimated population of about 160,000. In 1720 Marseilles lost 40,000 of a population of 90,000, and in Messina about half of the inhabitants died in 1743.

It is now estimated that the total population of England fell from about 3.8 million to 2.1 million in the period from 1348 to 1374. In France, where the loss of life was increased by the Hundred Years' War, the fall in population was even more precipitate. In western and central Europe as a whole the mortality was so great that it took nearly two centuries for the population level of 1348 to be regained.

The Black Death was a scourge such as man had never known. Eighty per cent or more of those who came down with the plague died within two or three days, usually in agonizing pain. No one knew the cause of or any preventive or cure for the disease. The medical profession was all but helpless, and the desperate measures taken by town authorities proved largely futile. It is difficult to imagine the growing terror with which the people must have watched the inexorable advance of the disease on their community.

They responded in various ways. Almost everyone, in that medieval time, interpreted the plague as a punishment by God for human sins, but there were arguments whether the Deity was sending retribution through the poisoned arrows of evil angels, "venomous moleculae" or earthquake-induced or comet-borne miasmas. Many blamed the Jews,

accusing them of poisoning the wells or otherwise acting as agents of Satan. People crowded into the churches, appealing for protection to the Virgin, to St. Sebastian, to St. Roch or to any of 60 other saints believed to have special influence against the disease. In the streets half-naked flagellants, members of the century-old cult of flagellantism, marched in processions whipping each other and warning the people to purge themselves of their sins before the coming day of atonement.

Flight in the face of approaching danger has always been a fundamental human reaction, in modern as well as ancient times. As recently as 1830, 60,-000 people fled from Moscow during an epidemic of cholera, and two years later, when the first cases of this disease turned up in New York City, fully a fourth of the population of 220,000 took flight in

RAPHAEL'S "LA PÈSTE" ("The Plague") reflects the preoccupation of European art with plague and its consequences during the plague-ridden three centuries following the Black Death. This picture, now worn with time, is divided into two parts: night at right and day at left. Among other plague themes of artists were the dance of death and the terrors of the Last Judgment.

steamboats, stagecoaches, carts and even wheelbarrows. The plague epidemics of the 14th to 16th century of course produced even more frightened mass migrations from the towns. Emperors, kings, princes, the clergy, merchants, lawyers, professors, students, judges and even physicians rushed away, leaving the common people to shift for themselves. All who could get away shut themselves up in houses in the country.

At the same time drastic efforts were made to segregate those who were forced to remain in the towns. In an epidemic in 1563 Queen Elizabeth took refuge in Windsor Castle and had a gallows erected on which to hang anyone who had the temerity to come out to Windsor from plague-ridden London. Often when a town was hit by the plague a cordon of troops would be thrown around the town to isolate it, allowing no one to leave or enter. In the afflicted cities entire streets were closed off by chains, the sick were quarantined in their houses and gallows were installed in the public squares as a warning against the violation of regulations. The French surgeon Ambroise Paré, writing of a plague epidemic in 1568,

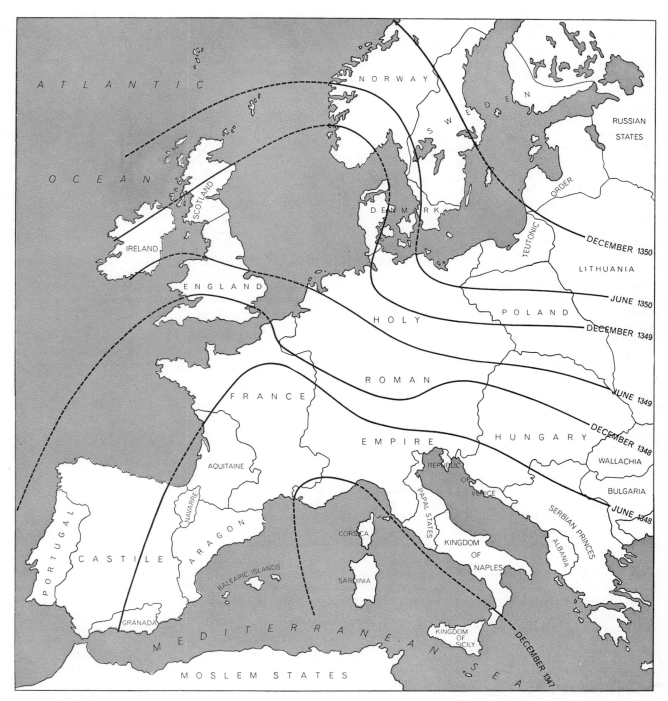

APPROXIMATE CHRONOLOGY of the Black Death's rapid sweep through Europe in the middle of the 14th century is indicated on this map, which shows the political divisions as they existed at the time. The plague, which was apparently brought from Asia by ships, obtained a European foothold in the Mediterranean in 1347; during the succeeding three years only a few small areas escaped.

reported that husbands and wives deserted each other, that parents sometimes even abandoned their children and that people went mad with terror and committed suicide.

Victims of the disease often died in the streets, as is shown in Raphael's "La Pèste," now in the Uffizi Gallery in Florence. Gravediggers were understandably scarce. For the most part those hired for the job, at fantastic wages, were criminals and tramps—men who could not be expected to draw fine distinctions between the dying and the dead. The corpses and the near corpses were thrown into carts and dumped indiscriminately into huge pits outside the town walls.

The sufferings and reactions of humanity when the plague came have been depicted vividly by writers such as Boccaccio, Daniel Defoe, Alessandro Manzoni and the late Albert Camus (in his novel *The Plague*) and by artists from Raphael and Holbein to Delacroix. Boccaccio's *Decameron*, an account of a group of well-to-do cavaliers and maidens who shut themselves up in a country house during the Black Death in Florence and sought to distract themselves with revelry and spicy stories, illustrates one of the characteristic responses of mankind to fear and impending disaster. It was most simply described by Thucydides in his report of the "Plague of Athens" in 430 B.C.:

"Men resolved to get out of life the pleasures which could be had speedily and would satisfy their lusts, regarding their bodies and their wealth alike as transitory.... No fear of gods or law of men restrained them; for, on the one hand, seeing that all men were perishing alike, they judged that piety or impiety came to the same thing, and, on the other hand, no one expected that he would live to be called to account and pay the penalty for his misdeeds. On the contrary, they believed that the penalty already decreed against them and now hanging over their heads was a far heavier one, and that before it fell it was only reasonable to get some enjoyment out of life."

From this philosophy one might also develop the rationalization that hilarity and the liberal use of liquor could ward off the plague. In any event, many people of all classes gave themselves up to carousing and ribaldry. The Reformation theologian John Wycliffe, who survived the Black Death of the 14th century, wrote with dismay of the lawlessness and depravity of the time. Everywhere, wrote chroniclers of the

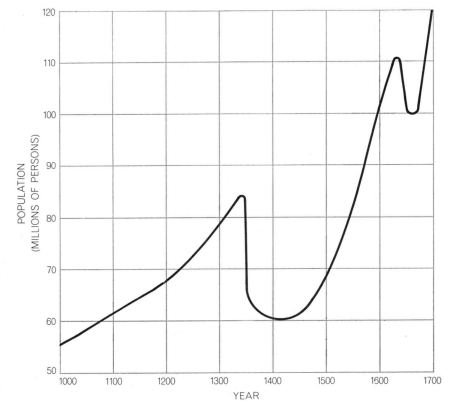

IMPACT ON POPULATION from recurrent plagues in Europe is indicated. For more than 300 years after 1347 the plagues checked the normal rise in population; sometimes, as in the 14th and 17th centuries, they resulted in sharp reductions. The figures shown on this chart derive from estimates by students of population; actual data for the period are scarce.

epidemics in London then and later, there was "drinking, roaring and surfeiting.... In one house you might hear them roaring under the pangs of death, in the next tippling, whoring and belching out blasphemies against God." Even the sober Samuel Pepys admitted to his diary that he had made merry in the shadow of death, indulging himself and his wife in a "great store of dancings." The university town of Oxford, like London, also was the scene of much "lewd and dissolute behavior."

The outbreak of an epidemic of plague was almost invariably the signal for a wave of crime and violence. As Boccaccio wrote, "the reverend authority of the laws, both human and divine, was all in a manner dissolved and fallen into decay, for lack of the ministers and executors thereof." In the midst of death, looting and robbery flourished. Burial gangs looted the houses of the dead and stripped the corpses of anything of value before throwing them into the pits. On occasion they even murdered the sick.

Just as desperation drove some to a complete abandonment of morality, it drove others, perhaps the majority, to

pathetic extravagances of religiosity or superstition. The poet George Wither noted this contrast in the London epidemic of 1625:

*Some streets had Churches full
   of people, weeping;
Some others, Tavernes had, rude-revell
   keeping;
Within some houses Psalmes
   and Hymnes were sung;
With raylings and loud scouldings
   others rung.*

Many people threw themselves on God's mercy, showered the church with gifts and made extravagant vows for the future. Others hunted down Jews and witches as the originators of the plague. The Black Death generated a startling spread of belief in witchcraft. Even as learned a scholar and theologian as John Calvin was convinced that a group of male and female witches, acting as agents of Satan, had brought the plague to Geneva. In the cult of Satanism, as in that of flagellantism, there was a strong strain of sexuality. It was believed that the women accused of being witches had intercourse with the

Devil and could strike men with sexual impotence. From the psychoanalytic point of view this belief may have stemmed from an unconscious reaction to the tremendous shrinkage of the population.

Jews and witches were not the only victims of the general panic. The wrath of the people also fell on physicians. They were accused of encouraging or helping the spread of the plague instead of checking it. Paré tells us that some of them were stoned in the streets in France. (In the 19th century physicians were similarly made scapegoats during epidemics of cholera. Some people accused them of poisoning public water supplies, at the behest of the rich, in order to kill off the excessive numbers of the poor.)

Although we have fairly accurate knowledge of the immediate effects of the great plagues in Europe—they were fully and circumstantially chronicled by many contemporary writers—it is not so easy to specify the long-term effects of the plagues. Many other factors entered into the shaping of Europe's history during and after the period of the plague epidemics. Nevertheless, there can be no doubt that the Great Dying had a profound and lasting influence on that history.

In its economic life Europe suffered a sudden and drastic change. Before the Black Death of 1348–1350 the Continent had enjoyed a period of rather rapid population growth, territorial expansion and general prosperity. After the pandemic Europe sank into a long depression: a century or more of economic stagnation and decline. The most serious disruption took place in agriculture.

For a short time the towns and cities experienced a flush of apparent prosperity. Many survivors of the epidemic had suddenly inherited substantial amounts of property and money from the wholesale departure of their relatives. They built elegant houses and went on a buying spree that made work (and high prices) for the manufacturing artisans. The churches and other public institutions, sharing in the wealth of the new rich, also built imposing and expensive structures.

The rural areas, on the other hand, virtually collapsed. With fewer people to feed in the towns and cities, the farmers lost a large part of the market for their crops. Grain prices fell precipitately. So did the farm population. Already sadly depleted by the ravages of the plague, it was now further reduced by a movement to the towns, which offered the impoverished farmers work as artisans. In spite of strenuous efforts by landlords and lords of the manor to keep the peasants on the land by law and sometimes by force, the rural population fled to the cities en masse. Thousands of farms and villages were deserted. In central Germany some 70

DESERTED ENGLISH VILLAGE, typical of many medieval communities made ghost towns by the Black Death and succeeding plagues, occupied the site shown in this aerial photograph. This site is Tusmore in Oxfordshire; most of the lines are earthworks that bounded farm enclosures behind cottages. Aerial photography has been used to locate many abandoned medieval villages.

per cent of all the farm settlements were abandoned in the period following the Black Death. (Many of these "lost" farms and villages, long overgrown, have recently been located by aerial photography.)

Farms became wilderness or pasture. Rents and land values disappeared. The minor land-owning gentry sank into poverty. In the words of the 14th-century poet Petrarch, "a vast and dreadful solitude" settled over the land. And of course in the long run the depression of agriculture engulfed the cities in depression as well.

Some authorities believe that Europe had begun to fall into a period of economic decay before the Black Death and that the epidemics only accentuated this trend. The question is certainly a complicated one. Wars and other economic forces no doubt played their part in Europe's long recession. It seems probable, however, that the decisive factor was the repeated onslaught of epidemics that depleted and weakened the population. The present consensus on the subject is that population change is a main cause of economic change rather than vice versa. Surely it must be considered significant that Europe's economic revival in the 17th and 18th centuries coincided with the disappearance of the plague and a burst of rapid population growth [see "Population," by Kingsley Davis; SCIENTIFIC AMERICAN Offprint 645].

The psychological effects of the ordeal of the plague are at least as impressive as the economic ones. For a long time it held all of Europe in an apocalyptic mood, which the Dutch historian Johan Huizinga analyzed brilliantly a generation ago in his study *The Waning of the Middle Ages*. As Arturo Castiglioni, the eminent Yale University historian of medicine, has written: "Fear was the sovereign ruler of this epoch." Men lived and worked in constant dread of disease and imminent death. "No thought is born in me that has not 'Death' engraved upon it," wrote Michelangelo.

Much of the art of the time reflected a macabre interest in graves and an almost pathological predilection for the manifestations of disease and putrefaction. Countless painters treated with almost loving detail the sufferings of Christ, the terrors of the Last Judgment and the tortures of Hell. Woodcuts and paintings depicting the dance of death, inspired directly by the Black Death, enjoyed a morbid popularity. With pitiless realism these paintings portrayed Death as a horridly grinning skeleton that seized, without warning, the prince and the peasant, the young and the old, the lovely maiden and the hardened villain, the innocent babe and the decrepit dotard.

Along with the mood of despair there was a marked tendency toward wild defiance—loose living and immoralities that were no doubt a desperate kind of reassertion of life in the presence of death. Yet the dominant feature of the time was not its licentiousness but its overpowering feelings of guilt, which arose from the conviction that God had visited the plague on man as retribution for his sins. Boccaccio, a few years after writing his *Decameron*, was overcome by repentance and a sense of guilt verging on panic. Martin Luther suffered acutely from guilt and fear of death, and Calvin, terror-stricken by the plague, fled from each epidemic. Indeed, entire communities were afflicted with what Freud called the primordial sense of guilt, and they engaged in penitential processions, pilgrimages and passionate mass preaching.

Some 70 years ago the English Catholic prelate and historian (later cardinal) Francis Gasquet, in a study entitled *The Great Pestilence,* tried to demonstrate that the Black Death set the stage for the Protestant Reformation by killing off the clergy and upsetting the entire religious life of Europe. This no doubt is too simple a theory. On the other hand, it is hard to deny that the catastrophic epidemics at the close of the Middle Ages must have been a powerful force for religious revolution. The failure of the Church and of prayer to ward off the pandemic, the flight of priests who deserted their parishes in the face of danger and the shortage of religious leaders after the Great Dying left the people eager for new kinds of leadership. And it is worth noting that most if not all of the Reformation leaders—Wycliffe, Zwingli, Luther, Calvin and others—were men who sought a more intimate relation of man to God because they were deeply affected by mankind's unprecedented ordeal by disease.

This is not to say that the epidemics of the late Middle Ages suffice to explain the Reformation but simply that the profound disturbance of men's minds by the universal, chronic grief and by the immediacy of death brought fundamental and long-lasting changes in religious outlook. In the moral and religious life of Europe, as well as in the economic sphere, the forces that make for change were undoubtedly strengthened and given added impetus by the Black Death.

Adaptations to Cold

by Laurence Irving
January 1966

*One mechanism is increased generation of heat by a
rise in the rate of metabolism, but this process has
its limits. The alternatives are insulation and changes
in the circulation of heat by the blood*

All living organisms abhor cold. For many susceptible forms of life a temperature difference of a few degrees means the difference between life and death. Everyone knows how critical temperature is for the growth of plants. Insects and fishes are similarly sensitive; a drop of two degrees in temperature when the sun goes behind a cloud, for instance, can convert a fly from a swift flier to a slow walker. In view of the general hostility of cold to life and activity, the ability of mammals and birds to survive and flourish in all climates is altogether remarkable.

It is not that these animals are basically more tolerant of cold. We know from our own reactions how sensitive the human body is to chilling. A naked, inactive human being soon becomes miserable in air colder than 28 degrees centigrade (about 82 degrees Fahrenheit), only 10 degrees C. below his body temperature. Even in the Tropics the coolness of night can make a person uncomfortable. The discomfort of cold is one of the most vivid of experiences; it stands out as a persistent memory in a soldier's recollections of the unpleasantness of his episodes in the field. The coming of winter in temperate climates has a profound effect on human well-being and activity. Cold weather, or cold living quarters, compounds the misery of illness or poverty. Over the entire planet a large proportion of man's efforts, culture and economy is devoted to the simple necessity of protection against cold.

Yet strangely enough neither man nor other mammals have consistently avoided cold climates. Indeed, the venturesome human species often goes out of its way to seek a cold environment, for sport or for the adventure of living in a challenging situation. One of the marvels of man's history is the endurance and stability of the human settlements that have been established in arctic latitudes.

The Norse colonists who settled in Greenland 1,000 years ago found Eskimos already living there. Archaeologists today are finding many sites and relics of earlier ancestors of the Eskimos who occupied arctic North America as long as 6,000 years ago. In the middens left by these ancient inhabitants are bones and hunting implements that indicate man was accompanied in the cold north by many other warm-blooded animals: caribou, moose, bison, bears, hares, seals, walruses and whales. All the species, including man, seem to have been well adapted to arctic life for thousands of years.

It is therefore a matter of more than idle interest to look closely into how mammals adapt to cold. In all climates and everywhere on the earth mammals maintain a body temperature of about 38 degrees C. It looks as if evolution has settled on this temperature as an optimum for the mammalian class. (In birds the standard body temperature is a few degrees higher.) To keep their internal temperature at a viable level the mammals must be capable of adjusting to a wide range of environmental temperatures. In tropical air at 30 degrees C. (86 degrees F.), for example, the environment is only eight degrees cooler than the body temperature; in arctic air at −50 degrees C. it is 88 degrees colder. A man or other mammal in the Arctic must adjust to both extremes as seasons change.

The mechanisms available for making the adjustments are (1) the generation of body heat by the metabolic burning of food as fuel and (2) the use of insulation and other devices to retain body heat. The requirements can be expressed quantitatively in a Newtonian formula concerning the cooling of warm bodies. A calculation based on the formula shows that to maintain the necessary warmth of its body a mammal must generate 10 times more heat in the Arctic than in the Tropics or clothe itself in 10 times more effective insulation or employ some intermediate combination of the two mechanisms.

We need not dwell on the metabolic requirement; it is rarely a major factor. An animal can increase its food intake and generation of heat to only a very modest degree. Moreover, even if metabolic capacity and the food supply were unlimited, no animal could spend all its time eating. Like man, nearly all other mammals spend a great deal of time in curious exploration of their surroundings, in play and in family and social activities. In the arctic winter a herd of caribou often rests and ruminates while the young engage in aimless play. I have seen caribou resting calmly with wolves lying asleep in the snow in plain view only a few hundred yards away. There is a common impression that life in the cold climates is more active than in the Tropics, but the fact is that for the natural populations of mammals, including man, life goes on at the same leisurely pace in the Arctic as it does in warmer regions; in all climates there is the same requirement of rest and social activities.

The decisive difference in resisting cold, then, lies in the mechanisms for conserving body heat. In the Institute of Arctic Biology at the University of Alaska we are continuing studies that have been in progress there and elsewhere for 18 years to compare the

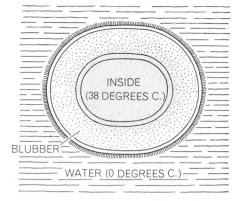

TEMPERATURE GRADIENTS in the outer parts of the body of a pig (*left*) and of a seal (*right*) result from two effects: the insulation provided by fat and the exchange of heat between arterial and venous blood, which produces lower temperatures near the surface.

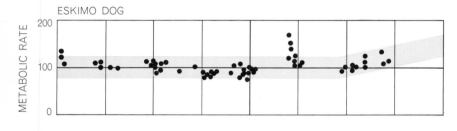

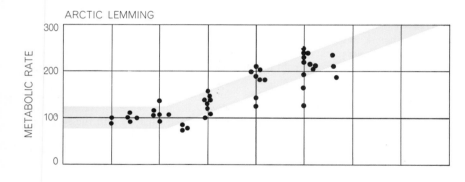

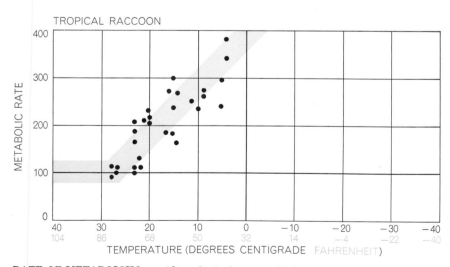

RATE OF METABOLISM provides a limited means of adaptation to cold. The effect of declining temperatures on the metabolic rate is shown for an Eskimo dog (*top*), an arctic lemming (*middle*) and a tropical raccoon (*bottom*). Animals in warmer climates tend to increase metabolism more rapidly than arctic animals do when the temperature declines.

mechanisms for conservation of heat in arctic and tropical animals. The investigations have covered a wide variety of mammals and birds and have yielded conclusions of general physiological interest.

The studies began with an examination of body insulation. The fur of arctic animals is considerably thicker, of course, than that of tropical animals. Actual measurements showed that its insulating power is many times greater. An arctic fox clothed in its winter fur can rest comfortably at a temperature of −50 degrees C. without increasing its resting rate of metabolism. On the other hand, a tropical animal of the same size (a coati, related to the raccoon) must increase its metabolic effort when the temperature drops to 20 degrees C. That is to say, the fox's insulation is so far superior that the animal can withstand air 88 degrees C. colder than its body at resting metabolism, whereas the coati can withstand a difference of only 18 degrees C. Naked man is less well protected by natural insulation than the coati; if unclothed, he begins shivering and raising his metabolic rate when the air temperature falls to 28 degrees C.

Obviously as animals decrease in size they become less able to carry a thick fur. The arctic hare is about the smallest mammal with enough fur to enable it to endure continual exposure to winter cold. The smaller animals take shelter under the snow in winter. Weasels, for example, venture out of their burrows only for short periods; mice spend the winter in nests and sheltered runways under the snow and rarely come to the surface.

No animal, large or small, can cover all of its body with insulating fur. Organs such as the feet, legs and nose must be left unencumbered if they are to be functional. Yet if these extremities allowed the escape of body heat, neither mammals nor birds could survive in cold climates. A gull or duck swimming in icy water would lose heat through its webbed feet faster than the bird could generate it. Warm feet standing on snow or ice would melt it and soon be frozen solidly to the place where they stood. For the unprotected extremities, therefore, nature has evolved a simple but effective mechanism to reduce the loss of heat: the warm outgoing blood in the arteries heats the cool blood returning in the veins from the extremities. This exchange occurs in the *rete mirabile* (wonderful net), a network of small arteries and veins near the junction between the trunk of the animal and the extremity [see "'The Wonderful Net,'" by P. F. Scholander; SCIENTIFIC AMERICAN Offprint 1117]. Hence the extremities can become much colder than the body without either draining off body heat or losing their ability to function.

This mechanism serves a dual purpose. When necessary, the thickly furred animals can use their bare extremities to release excess heat from the body. A heavily insulated animal would soon be overheated by running or other active exercise were it not for these outlets. The generation of heat by exercise turns on the flow of blood to the extremities so that they radiate heat. The large, bare flippers of a resting fur seal are normally cold, but we have found that when these animals on the Pribilof Islands are driven overland at their laborious gait, the flippers become warm. In contrast to the warm flippers, the rest of the fur seal's body surface feels cold, because very little heat escapes through the animal's dense fur. Heat can also be dissipated by evaporation from the mouth and tongue. Thus a dog or a caribou begins to pant, as a means of evaporative cooling, as soon as it starts to run.

In the pig the adaptation to cold by means of a variable circulation of heat in the blood achieves a high degree of refinement. The pig, with its skin only thinly covered with bristles, is as naked as a man. Yet it does well in the Alaskan winter without clothing. We can read the animal's response to cold by its expressions of comfort or discomfort, and we have measured its physiological reactions. In cold air the circulation of heat in the blood of swine is shunted away from the entire body surface, so that the surface becomes an effective insulator against loss of body heat. The pig can withstand considerable cooling of its body surface. Although a man is highly uncomfortable when his skin is cooled to 7 degrees C. below the internal temperature, a pig can be comfortable with its skin 30 degrees C. colder than the interior, that is, at a temperature of 8 degrees C. (about 46 degrees F.). Not until the air temperature drops below the freezing point (0 degrees C.) does the pig increase its rate of metabolism; in contrast a man, as I have mentioned, must do so at an air temperature of 28 degrees C.

With thermocouples in the form of needles we have probed the tissues of pigs below the skin surface. (Some pigs, like some people, will accept a little

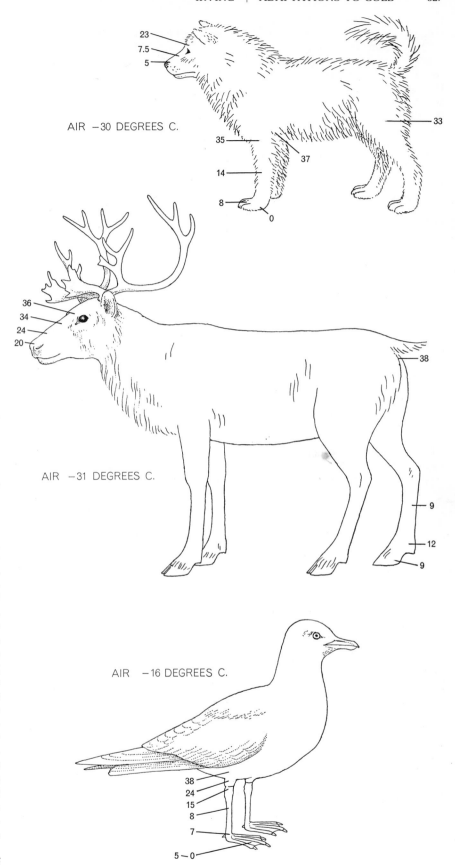

TEMPERATURES AT EXTREMITIES of arctic animals are far lower than the internal body temperature of about 38 degrees centigrade, as shown by measurements made on Eskimo dogs, caribou and sea gulls. Some extremities approach the outside temperature.

pain to win a reward.) We found that with the air temperature at −12 degrees C. the cooling of the pig's tissues extended as deep as 100 millimeters (about four inches) into its body. In warmer air the thermal gradient through the tissues was shorter and less steep. In short, the insulating mechanism of the hog involves a considerable depth of the animal's fatty mantle.

Even more striking examples of this kind of mechanism are to be found in whales, walruses and hair seals that dwell in the icy arctic seas. The whale and the walrus are completely bare; the hair seal is covered only with thin, short hair that provides almost no insulation when it is sleeked down in the water. Yet these animals remain comfortable in water around the freezing point although water, with a much greater heat capacity than air, can extract a great deal more heat from a warm body.

Examining hair seals from cold waters of the North Atlantic, we found that even in ice water these animals did not raise their rate of metabolism. Their skin was only one degree or so warmer than the water, and the cooling effect extended deep into the tissues—as much as a quarter of the distance through the thick part of the body. Hour after hour the animal's flippers all the way through would remain only a few degrees above freezing without the seals' showing any sign of discomfort. When the seals were moved into warmer water, their outer tissues rapidly warmed up. They would accept a transfer from warm water to ice water with equanimity and with no diminution of their characteristic liveliness.

How are the chilled tissues of all these animals able to function normally at temperatures close to freezing? There is first of all the puzzle of the response of fatty tissue. Animal fat usually becomes hard and brittle when it is cooled to low temperatures. This is true even of the land mammals of the Arctic, as far as their internal fats are concerned. If it were also true of extremities such as their feet, however, in cold weather their feet would become too inflexible to be useful. Actually it turns out that the fats in these organs behave differently from those in the warm internal tissues. Farmers have known for a long time that neat's-foot oil, extracted from the feet of cattle, can be used to keep leather boots and harness flexible in cold weather. By laboratory examination we have found that the fats in the bones of the lower leg and foot of the caribou remain soft even at 0 degrees C. The melting point of the fats in the leg steadily goes up in the higher portions of the leg. Eskimos have long been aware that fat from a caribou's foot will serve as a fluid lubricant in the cold, whereas the marrow fat from the upper leg is a solid food even at room temperature.

About the nonfatty substances in tissues we have little information; I have seen no reports by biochemists on the effects of temperature on their properties. It is known, however, that many of the organic substances of animal tissues are highly sensitive to temperature. We must therefore wonder how the tissues can maintain their serviceability over the very wide range of temperatures that the body surface experiences in the arctic climate.

We have approached this question by studies of the behavior of tissues at various temperatures. Nature offers many illustrations of the slowing of tissue functions by cold. Fishes, frogs and water insects are noticeably slowed down by cool water. Cooling by 10 degrees

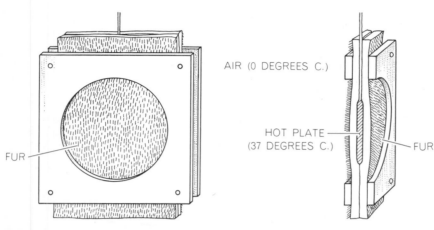

INSULATION BY FUR was tested in this apparatus, shown in a front view at left and a side view at right. The battery-operated heating unit provided the equivalent of body temperature on one side of the fur; outdoor temperatures were approximated on the other side.

INSULATING CAPACITY of fur is compared for various animals. A "clo unit" equals the amount of insulation provided by the clothing a man usually wears at room temperature.

ARCTIC ZONE (20 TO −60 DEGREES C.)

TEMPERATE ZONE (20 TO −20 DEGREES C.)

TROPICAL ZONE (35 TO 25 DEGREES C.)

RANGE OF TEMPERATURES to which warm-blooded animals must adapt is indicated. All the animals shown have a body temperature close to 100 degrees Fahrenheit, yet they survive at outside temperatures that, for the arctic animals, can be more than 100 degrees cooler. Insulation by fur is a major means of adaptation to cold. Man is insulated by clothing; some other relatively hairless animals, by fat. Some animals have a mechanism for conserving heat internally so that it is not dissipated at the extremities.

C. will immobilize most insects. A grasshopper in the warm noonday sun can be caught only by a swift bird, but in the chill of early morning it is so sluggish that anyone can seize it. I had a vivid demonstration of the temperature effect one summer day when I went hunting on the arctic tundra near Point Barrow for flies to use in experiments. When the sun was behind clouds, I had no trouble picking up the flies as they crawled about in the sparse vegetation, but as soon as the sun came out the flies took off and were uncatchable. Measuring the temperature of flies on the ground, I ascertained that the difference between the flying and the slow-crawling state was a matter of only 2 degrees C.

Sea gulls walking barefoot on the ice in the Arctic are just as nimble as gulls on the warm beaches of California. We know from our own sensations that our fingers and hands are numbed by cold. I have used a simple test to measure the amount of this desensitization. After cooling the skin on my fingertips to about 20 degrees C. (68 degrees F.) by keeping them on ice-filled bags, I tested their sensitivity by dropping a light ball (weighing about one milligram) on them from a measured height. The weight multiplied by the distance of fall gave me a measure of the impact on the skin. I found that the skin at a temperature of 20 degrees C. was only a sixth as sensitive as at 35 degrees C. (95 degrees F.); that is, the impact had to be six times greater to be felt.

We know that even the human body surface has some adaptability to cold. Men who make their living by fishing can handle their nets and fish with wet hands in cold that other people cannot endure. The hands of fishermen, Eskimos and Indians have been found to be capable of maintaining an exceptionally vigorous blood circulation in the cold. This is possible, however, only at the cost of a higher metabolic production of body heat, and the production in any case has a limit. What must arouse our wonder is the extraordinary adaptability of an animal such as the hair seal. It swims in icy waters with its flippers and the skin over its body at close to the freezing temperature, and yet under the ice in the dark arctic sea it remains sensitive enough to capture moving prey and find its way to breathing holes.

Here lies an inviting challenge for all biologists. By what devices is an animal able to preserve nervous sensitivity in tissues cooled to low temperatures? Beyond this is a more universal and more

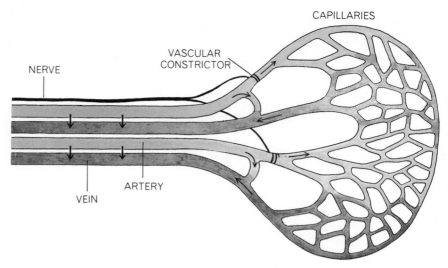

ROLE OF BLOOD in adaptation to cold is depicted schematically. One mechanism, indicated by the vertical arrows, is an exchange of heat between arterial and venous blood. The cold venous blood returning from an extremity acquires heat from an arterial network. The outgoing arterial blood is thus cooled. Hence the exchange helps to keep heat in the body and away from the extremities when the extremities are exposed to low temperatures. The effect is enhanced by the fact that blood vessels near the surface constrict in cold.

interesting question: How do the warm-blooded animals preserve their overall stability in the varying environments to which they are exposed? Adjustment to changes in temperature requires them to make a variety of adaptations in the various tissues of the body. Yet these changes must be harmonized to maintain the integration of the organism as a whole. I predict that further studies of the mechanisms involved in adaptation to cold will yield exciting new insights into the processes that sustain the integrity of warm-blooded animals.

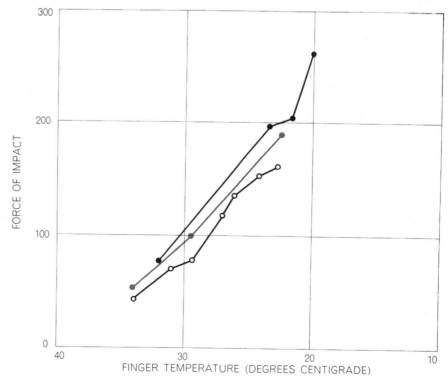

FINGER EXPERIMENT performed by the author showed that the more a finger was chilled, the farther a one-milligram ball had to be dropped for its impact to be felt on the finger. The vertical scale is arbitrary but reflects the relative increase in the force of impact.

29

The Physiology of High Altitude

by Raymond J. Hock
February 1970

To meet the stress of life at high altitude, notably lack of oxygen, a number of changes in body processes are required. What are these adaptations, and are they inborn or the result of acclimatization?

At altitudes above 6,000 feet the human organism leaves its accustomed environment and begins to feel the stresses imposed by an insufficiency of oxygen. Yet 25 million people manage to live and work in the high Andes of South America and the Himalayan ranges of Asia. More than 10 million of them live at altitudes above 12,000 feet, and there are mountain dwellers in Peru who daily go to work in a mine at an elevation of 19,000 feet. How does the human physiology contrive to acclimatize itself to such conditions? Over the past half-century, ever since the British physiologist Joseph Barcroft led an expedition to study the physiology of the mountain natives of Peru in the early 1920's, a small host of fascinated investigators has been exploring this puzzle. We now know many of the details of the body's remarkable ability to accommodate itself to life in an oxygen-poor environment.

The study has an intrinsic lure, akin to the challenge of an Everest for a mountain climber, and in these days of man's travels beyond the earth's atmosphere the subject of oxygen's relation to life has taken on added interest. The problem also has its practical aspects on our own planet. Already more and more people each year have recourse to mountain heights for recreations such as camping and skiing; for example, in 1968 there were five million visitor-days in the Inyo National Forest of California, nearly all at elevations of 7,000 feet or higher. From studies of the physiology of adjustment to oxygen deprivation we can expect some beneficial dividends, not only for the problems of living or vacationing in the high mountains but also for medical problems in diseases involving hypoxia.

The native mountain dwellers of Peru and the Sherpa people of Tibet in the Himalayas have served as very helpful subjects for the investigation of acclimatization to high-altitude life. British expeditions led by L. G. C. E. Pugh have conducted several important studies of the Sherpas. In the Andes the research has been centered principally in the Institute of Andean Biology, a permanent station founded in 1928 as a division of the University of San Marcos by Carlos Monge with Alberto Hurtado as director of research [see "Life at High Altitudes," by George W. Gray; SCIENTIFIC AMERICAN, December, 1955]. Recently Pennsylvania State University established another station in Peru at Nuñoa under the supervision of Paul T. Baker and Elsworth R. Buskirk. In the U.S. the University of California has a major center for high-altitude research on White Mountain, with Nello Pace as director. I was associated with the White Mountain Research Station for several years as resident physiologist, working primarily with experimental animals. There are four laboratories in the complex: the Barcroft Laboratory at 12,500 feet and others at 14,250 feet, 10,150 and 4,000 feet. Investigators from the U.S. Army Laboratory of the Fitzsimons Hospital have also been active in human high-altitude research in the Rockies, principally on Pikes Peak.

The High-Altitude Environment

One may wonder why people choose to live in the hostile environment of mountain heights, as the Quechua Indians of Peru, for example, have done for centuries. Life on the mountains is made rigorous not only by hypoxia but also by cold. Even in the equatorial Andes the air temperature decreases by one degree Celsius with each 640 feet of altitude. The winters are long, snowy and windy; summers are short and cool. At the 12,500-foot station on White Mountain in California temperature records over a period of 10 years showed that the mean temperature is below freezing during eight months of the year, and even in some of the summer months the nighttime minimum averages below freezing. Plant life at high altitudes has an extremely short growing season, and few animals can breed successfully at these altitudes. The relatively strong ultraviolet radiation, ionization of the air and other harsh factors no doubt affect life there. There are a few compensating factors. The intense sunlight in the thin atmosphere heats the rocks and provides warm niches for life. The heavy winter snowfall lays down a greater store of moisture than may be available in the surrounding lowlands. For a few months the highlands offer grazing for herdsmen's flocks (which are brought down to lower altitudes when the summer season ends).

Most of the people in the highlands live on herding or agriculture, raising short-season crops such as potatoes or some grains. In the Andes mining also is an important factor in the economy. The highest inhabited settlement in the world is a mining camp at 17,500 feet in Peru. The residents there work in the mine at 19,000 feet that I have already mentioned. The miners daily climb the 1,500 feet from their camp to the mine. Significantly, they rebelled against living in a camp that was built for them at 18,500 feet, complaining that they had no appetite, lost weight and could not sleep. It seems, therefore, that 17,500 feet is the highest altitude at which even acclimatized man can live permanently.

Notwithstanding the rigors of life on the heights, the Peruvian Indians of the "altiplano" have thrived in their environment. It is said that the Incas had

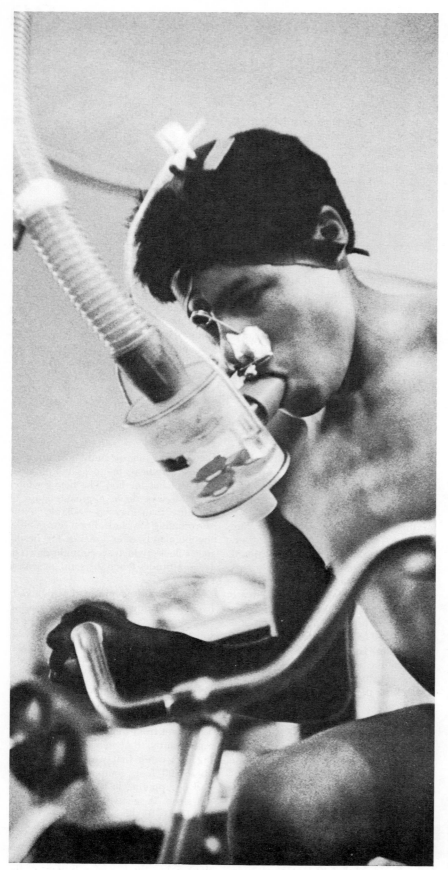

QUECHUA INDIAN breathes from a device that records oxygen intake and carbon dioxide output while he exercises on a bicycle ergometer, which measures the work performed.

two separate armies, one for the lowlands and one for high-mountain duty. Monge and Hurtado believe the high-altitude natives have become a distinctive breed ("Andean man") superbly fitted for life on the heights but probably incapable of surviving long in the lowlands. This is open to doubt. It may be that at sea level the highlanders would succumb to diseases to which they have not been exposed in the mountains, but it has not yet been demonstrated that they would be unable to adjust physiologically to the conditions at low altitudes.

Nevertheless, it is incontestable that high-altitude man, in the Andes and the Himalayas, does indeed possess unusual physiological capabilities. They are evidenced in his responses to hypoxia (defined here as a deficient supply of oxygen in the air). To see his special attributes in perspective, let us first examine the usual reactions of an unacclimatized person to hypoxia.

The Physiological Responses

The proportion of oxygen in the air is not reduced at high altitudes (it is constant at 21 percent throughout the atmosphere), but as the barometric pressure of the air as a whole declines with increasing altitude the partial pressure of the oxygen also declines correspondingly. Thus at 12,500 feet the barometric pressure drops to 480 millimeters of mercury (from 760 millimeters at sea level) and the partial pressure of oxygen is only 100 millimeters, as against 159 millimeters at sea level. That is to say, the number of oxygen and other molecules per cubic foot of air is reduced.

This decrease in oxygen tension, reducing the transfer of oxygen from inspired air to the blood in the lungs, calls forth several immediate reactions by the body. The breathing rate increases, in order to bring more air into the lungs. The heart rate and cardiac output increase, in order to enhance the flow of blood through the lung capillaries and the delivery of arterial blood to the body tissues. The body steps up its production of red blood cells and of hemoglobin to improve the blood's oxygen-carrying capacity. The hemoglobin molecule itself has a physicochemical property that enables it to take in and unload oxygen more readily when necessary at high altitudes. In a person who remains at high altitude these acclimatizing changes take place over a period of time. Investigators who measured them during a Himalayan expedition found that the hemoglobin content of the blood continued to in-

NUÑOA, at an altitude of 13,000 feet in the Andes Mountains of Peru, is the site of an experimental station operated by Pennsylvania State University for the study of human adaptation to high altitude. The native Indians herd llamas and alpacas, as shown here.

BARCROFT LABORATORY of the University of California is at an altitude of 12,500 feet in the White Mountains, a range just east of the Sierra Nevada in California. The environment appears uninhabitable but is the home of a number of small animal species.

crease for two or three months and then leveled off. As the climbers moved up from 13,000 feet to 19,000 feet and beyond, the number of red cells in the blood increased continuously for as long as 38 weeks.

The adjustments I have just recounted are not sufficient to enable a newcomer to high altitude to expend normal physical effort. Because of the interest stimulated by the holding of the 1968 Olympic Games in Mexico City (at an altitude of 7,500 feet) much study has recently been given to the effects of high altitude

on the capacity for exercise. It has been found that at 18,000 feet, for instance, a man's capacity for performing exercise without incurring an oxygen debt is only about 50 percent of that at sea level. The tolerance of such a debt, and of the accumulation of lactic acid in the muscles, also is reduced. This accounts for the fact that mountain climbers at extreme altitudes can take only a few tortured steps at a time and must rest for a considerable period before going on. The limits on the capacity for work are set, of course, by the limits of the body's pos-

sible physiological adjustments to the high-altitude conditions. These limits affect the rate of ventilation of the lungs, the heart rate, the cardiac output and the blood flow to the exercising muscles. The limit for hyperventilation, for example, is a flow of 120 liters of air per minute through the lungs. This maximum, invoked at an altitude of about 16,400 feet, supplies two liters of oxygen per minute to the blood. At extreme altitudes the heart can speed up its beat during moderate exercise, but under the stress of maximum exercise the limit for both the

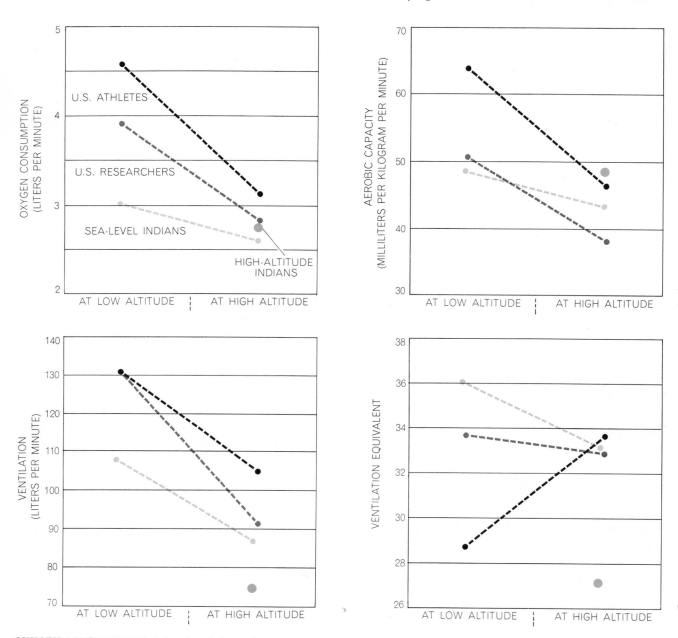

OXYGEN CONSUMPTION of Quechua Indians who were natives of Nuñoa, at 13,000 feet in the Andes (*solid color*), was compared with that of sea-level Quechua (*light color*), U.S. athletes (*black*) and U.S. research workers (*gray*) in a study made by Paul T. Baker of Pennsylvania State University. The data were collected during a bicycle exercise test. (The low-altitude subjects had been at Nuñoa at least four weeks before their high-altitude tests.) Aerobic capacity relates oxygen consumption to an individual's weight and therefore measures the success of his oxygen-transport system. Ventilation is the total volume of air breathed by the individual. Ventilation equivalent is ventilation divided by oxygen consumption; the lower the value, the greater the oxygen-extracting efficiency.

heart rate and the cardiac output is lower than at sea level.

Mountain Natives' Physiology

Let us now turn to the mountain natives' extraordinary adjustments for living at high altitudes. To begin with, the Quechua Indians of the Andes and the Sherpas of the Himalayas have developed an exceptionally large chest and lung volume, enabling them to take in a greater volume of air with each breath. Their breathing rate also is higher than that of dwellers at sea level, but they do not need to hyperventilate as much as lowlanders do when the latter go to high altitudes. The mountain natives also have a high concentration of red cells and hemoglobin in their blood, and their hemoglobin is geared to unload oxygen readily to the tissues.

In the high-altitude native the lung capillaries are dilated, so that the pulmonary circulation carries an unusually large percentage of the body's total blood volume. Moreover, the blood pressure in the lungs is higher than in the rest of the circulatory system. The heart is unusually large, apparently because of the heightened pressure in the pulmonary arteries. The heartbeat is slower than in sea-level dwellers. The mountain dwellers' metabolism also appears to be affected by the hypoxic conditions. Their basal metabolic rate is slightly higher than it is in lowlanders, and when this is considered in terms of body mass, it turns out that the rate of oxygen consumption per unit of metabolizable tissue is unusually high. That is, the hypoxic conditions exact a cost in lowered efficiency in the use of oxygen.

The mountain natives show their superior acclimatization most markedly in their capacity for exercise at high altitude. Sherpas show a smaller increase in ventilation, similar oxygen consumption and a greater heart-rate increase when performing the same exercise as low-altitude subjects who have become thoroughly acclimatized to a high altitude. The ability of mountain natives to perform physical labor daily at altitudes where even acclimatized visitors are quickly exhausted by exercise is itself obvious evidence of the mountaineers' extraordinary physiology.

In general, the physiological adjustments of the permanent mountain dwellers are similar in kind to those developed by sojourners in the mountains after a year of residence there. Furthermore, even mountain natives sometimes lose their acclimatization to high altitude and incur *soroche* (chronic mountain sickness), which is characterized by extreme elevation of the relative number and mass of red cells in the blood, pulmonary hypertension, low peripheral blood pressure, enlargement of the right lobe of the heart and ultimately congestive heart failure if the victim remains at high altitude. In general, the differences between mountain natives and sea-level natives are most apparent in the mountaineers' superior capacity for exercise at high altitude and their ability to produce children in that habitat; newcomers to the mountains, even after extended acclimatization, are much less successful in reproduction. The Spanish conquistadors who settled in the high Andes, for example, found themselves afflicted with relative infertility and a high rate of infant mortality.

Does the special physiology of the mountain people arise from genetic adaptation or is it acquired during their lifelong exposure (from the womb onward) to high altitude? One approach to answering that question has been through investigations with experimental animals. The laboratory studies of animals have also explored the physiological aspects of acclimatization much more exhaustively than is possible in man. Much of this animal work has been done at the White Mountain Research Station.

Hypoxia and Rats

Pace and an associate, Paola S. Timiras, carried out a series of investigations on rats at the White Mountain Research Station. Rats that had been bred at sea level were brought to the Barcroft Laboratory (at 12,500 feet), and the investigators examined the responses to hypoxia in these animals and in the second generation of offspring produced at the high altitude. The development of the animals exposed to the high altitude was compared with that of a control group of rats kept at sea level.

The rats at the Barcroft Laboratory exhibited acclimatizing reactions like those of human newcomers to high altitude. There was a marked increase, for example, in their red cells and hemoglobin: in the imported animals the red-cell concentration rose to 54.6 percent of the blood volume, and in their second-generation offspring it was 66.7 percent, as against 47.5 percent in the control rats of the same age at sea level. The rats also developed an enlargement of the heart like that of human mountain natives. After 10 months at the high altitude they had a 20 percent higher ratio of heart weight to body weight than the sea-level controls did, and in the second-generation rats born at the Barcroft station the increase in heart-weight ratio was 90 percent. An increase in the relative weight of the adrenal glands was also observed in the rats exposed to the high altitude.

The exposure to hypoxia stunted the rats' growth. Up to the age of about 120 days the rats brought to Barcroft (at age 30 days) gained weight at the same rate as the rats left at sea level, but thereafter their growth slowed, and their maximum weight (at about 300 days) was significantly lower than that of the sea-level controls. The growth rate of the second-generation rats at high altitude was lower still: at 130 days they weighed only 250 grams, whereas their parents and the sea-level controls attained this weight in 84 days.

Fenton Kelley at the Barcroft Laboratory investigated the rats' reproduction and high-altitude effects on their young. The hypoxic conditions did not impair the ability to conceive in young, healthy rats: more than 85 percent of the females that were mated after 30 days of acclimatization became pregnant. Their fetuses, however, suffered considerable attrition: by the 15th day of pregnancy 25 percent of the females had abnormally stunted fetuses. Whether this is due to inadequacy of the oxygen supply to the fetus, disturbance of hormone production, neurological anomalies or metabolic disturbances has not yet been determined. At all events, the females bred at high altitude bore substantially smaller litters of live young than those bred at sea level.

The offspring were generally normal in weight at birth, but by the age of 10 days their weight was 30 percent less than the sea-level norm. Their mortality rate in the first 10 days was about 20 percent, 10 times higher than in the sea-level control group. This was not attributable to lack of nursing ability in their mothers; in fact, the high-altitude infant rats had more milk in their stomachs than the sea-level young of the same age did. There were indications that the high-altitude young had metabolic defects that may account for their high mortality and for the slow rate of growth in those offspring that survived the postpartum period. The high-altitude young had a subnormal content of glycogen in the liver, apparently reflecting a defect in carbohydrate metabolism, and there is reason to believe the metabolism of fats and proteins also is affected by hypoxia. The dry atmosphere of high altitude may be another hazard for the newborn, affecting the

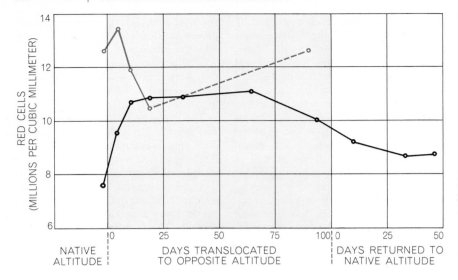

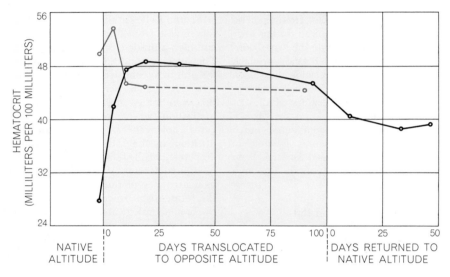

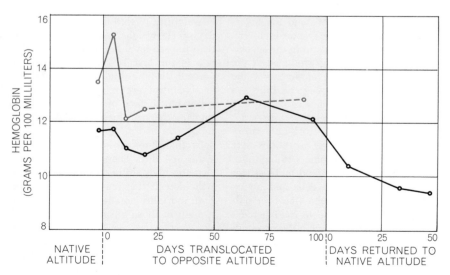

DEER MICE trapped at 12,500 feet (*color*) have more red blood cells, a higher hematocrit (red cells as a proportion of total blood volume) and more hemoglobin than mice trapped at sea level (*black*). As the curves indicate, these values increase in sea-level mice that are transported to the high altitude and decline again with their return to sea level. There is less long-term change, however, in high-altitude mice that are brought down to sea level.

body's water balance, temperature regulation, respiration and vulnerability to infection.

The Deer Mouse

My own investigations focused on the deer mouse (*Peromyscus maniculatus*), a small, white-footed species that is noted for its ubiquitous presence throughout North America and its ability to live in all climatic zones except extreme desert. Deer mice of various species are found inhabiting all altitudes from below sea level to about 15,000 feet. This one species is ideal for our studies not only because of its great variety of physiological responses to different conditions but also because a mouse spends its entire life in the same locality. A tiny deer mouse on White Mountain probably does not range more than a quarter of a mile from its birthplace during its lifetime; consequently we could be sure that a mouse trapped at 12,500 feet on White Mountain had been born at about that altitude (within 500 feet) and had been exposed to it throughout its life.

I trapped deer mice at seven different altitudes, ranging from below sea level to the 14,250-foot White Mountain summit, and for comparison of their native differences each population was examined at the altitude at which it was caught. It was apparent at once that the mice followed only in part the well-known rule that body size increases with exposure to cold: their body weight increased with increasing altitude up to a point. The heaviest weight was found at 10,150 feet; beyond that the oxygen scarcity apparently limits growth in deer mice as it was found to do in the experiments on rats.

There was also a clear progression, with increasing altitude, in the ratio of the heart size to the body weight. In the deer mice caught at 14,250 feet the relative heart weight was one and a half times greater than it was in mice living at an altitude of 4,000 feet. The relative number and mass of red cells and the amount of hemoglobin in the blood also increased with altitude in the deer mice as it does in rats and men. Contrary to what had been observed in rats, however, the mice's adrenal glands shrank with increasing altitude, both in absolute weight and in relation to body weight. Presumably this phenomenon in the mice reflects a different physiological response to the stresses of high altitude from that shown by the rats.

In an effort to determine whether the differences among the natives of various altitudes were genetic or simply the

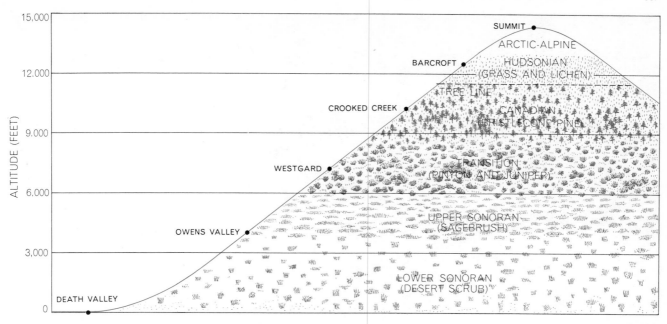

ALTITUDE RANGE of the deer mouse *Peromyscus maniculatus,* the animal the author studied, is remarkably large, extending from sea level to the summit of White Mountain in California. It en-compasses six of the seven "life zones" described some years ago by the American naturalist C. Hart Merriam, which are indicated, with their characteristic vegetation, on this schematic diagram.

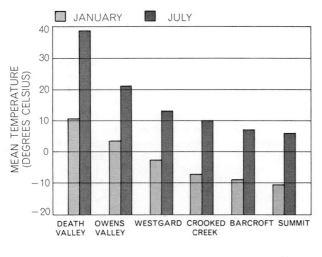

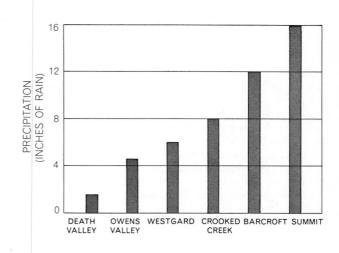

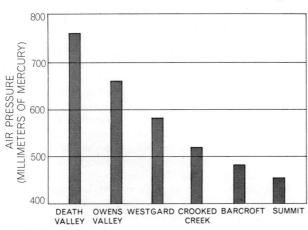

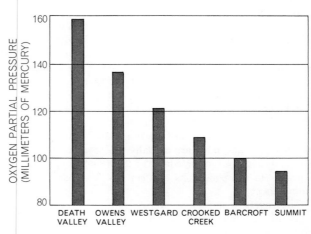

ENVIRONMENTAL DATA are given for the four laboratories of the White Mountain Research Station and two other places where the author worked, Death Valley and Westgard. Altitudes are in-dicated at the top of the page. (Summit precipitation is estimated.)

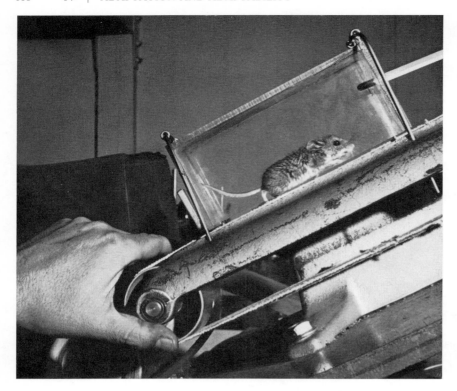

MINIATURE TREADMILL for testing the capacity of deer mice for strenuous exercise was improvised by mounting a linen belt on an old belt sander. The belt was moved at a speed of a mile and a half an hour. The mouse ran on it, restrained by the plastic barriers, until it was exhausted, and the length of time it ran was the measure of its endurance.

result of acclimatization from birth, I then began to transfer mice from one altitude to another for study of their responses to the change. When mice from the sea-level colony were transferred to our 12,500-foot laboratory, their relative heart weight did not increase. They showed definite signs of acclimatization, however, in other responses. The adrenal glands diminished in size. The weight of the spleen decreased and the lung weight increased, indicating that circulatory and respiratory adjustments were taking place. The red-cell mass and the hemoglobin content of the cells increased to about the same values as in native high-altitude mice. When the surviving mice were later returned to sea level, they soon reverted to their original sea-level condition: the adrenal glands gained in weight and the red-cell mass and hemoglobin fell back to sea-level norms. It appears, therefore, that most of the adaptive mechanisms found in native high-altitude mice are actually adjustments acquired in the course of their exposure to the conditions of their environment.

The reverse experiment—transferring high-altitude mice to sea level—produced a mixed picture. In these mice the relative heart weight decreased and the spleen weight increased, but the adre-nals and the lungs showed no change in relative weight. After 90 days of acclimatization to the low altitude the number of red cells in the mice's blood remained unchanged from what it had been at high altitude. This seems to suggest that the high red-cell count in high-altitude mice may represent a genetic adaptation, but it might be explainable on the basis that the translocated animals simply retained their original high red-cell count because there was nothing in the change to low-altitude conditions that would foster destruction of the cells. The total mass of the red cells in proportion to the blood volume did decrease to sea-level values; this may have been due to an increase in the amount of plasma. The concentration of hemoglobin, however, changed only slightly if at all.

The high-altitude natives showed no inferiority to low-altitude mice in fertility; in fact, the average litter size at 10,000 feet or above was six, as against five for females living at 4,000 feet. The high-altitude young, however, had a poor survival rate: mortality among them by the 30th day after birth was 23 percent, whereas all the low-altitude young survived beyond that age. I found that the rate of growth for the young was about the same at all levels during the first 45 days of life, but thereafter it decreased with altitude. By the age of maturity (120 days) the average weight of mice born at 4,000 feet was 22.5 grams; of those born at 14,250 feet, 18.8 grams.

Exercise and Metabolism

In order to test the capacity of the mice for strenuous exercise I developed a miniature treadmill that could be run at various speeds. As was to be expected, the natives at low altitudes showed more endurance than those at higher levels. The mean time before exhaustion on the treadmill in one series of tests, for example, was 16.7 minutes for natives at 4,000 feet and only 11.2 minutes for natives at 12,500 feet. Was the difference in performance due to the handicap of hypoxia at the higher altitude or to some innate physical or physiological difference in the mice themselves? I examined this question by switching the environment for the mice, testing the low-altitude natives at the high station and the high-altitude natives at the lower station.

The 4,000-foot natives, when taken to the 12,500-foot level, at first showed a drop in endurance on the treadmill. Their performance slowly improved, however, as they became acclimatized over a period of 90 days. The transfer of 12,500-foot natives to tests at the 4,000-foot level, on the other hand, yielded a major surprise. Although they were now performing in an atmosphere richer in oxygen, their endurance on the treadmill declined instead of improving. At the end of 90 days of "acclimatization" they were able to run on the treadmill only half as long, before exhaustion, as they had done in their oxygen-poor native environment! The explanation may lie in abnormalities of the heart and certain other functions in the high-altitude mice and in the change to a new climate at the lower altitude.

In one study I compared low-altitude and high-altitude mice with regard to their consumption of oxygen during exercise. When sea-level natives were transferred to high altitude, they did not increase their oxygen consumption more while exercising than they had at sea level. High-altitude natives, on the other hand, showed a considerably greater increase in oxygen consumption during exercise than the low-altitude mice did, both at high and at low altitudes. In short, under both conditions the high-altitude mice paid a higher cost (that is, were less efficient) in the use of oxygen during exercise.

I measured the basal metabolic rate

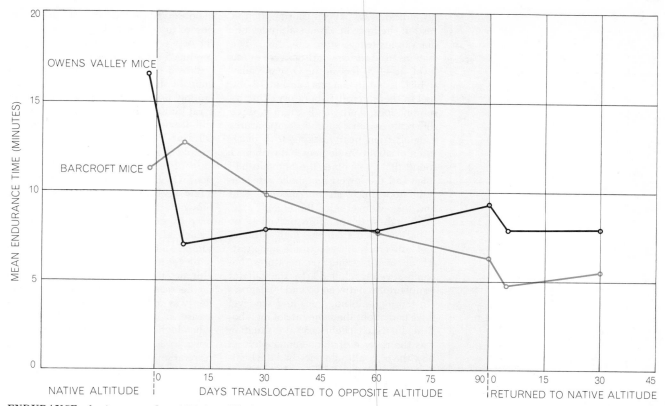

ENDURANCE of mice trapped at 4,000 feet (*black*) was greater than that of mice trapped at 12,500 feet (*color*) when both groups were in their home environments (*left*). The low-altitude mice showed a decided decrease in endurance when they were first taken to 12,500 feet but then improved somewhat. Surprisingly, the high-altitude natives did less well at 4,000 feet than at 12,500.

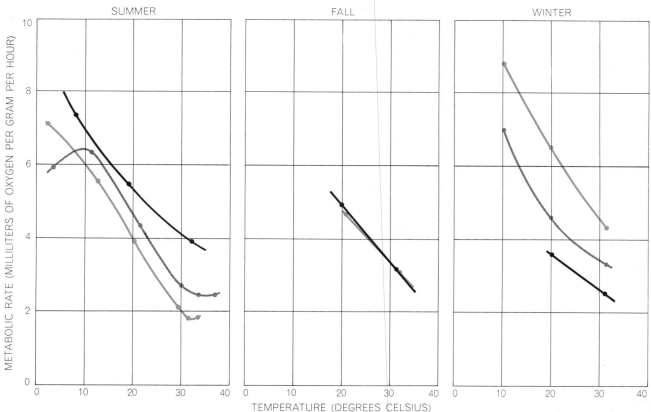

BASAL METABOLIC RATE (oxygen consumption at rest) of mice native to sea level (*black*), 4,000 feet (*gray*) and 12,500 feet (*color*) was measured at their native altitudes in the summer and winter over a wide range of ambient temperatures; two of the three groups were tested in the fall over a narrower temperature range. In the summer the sea-level mice had the highest rates and the 12,500-foot animals had the lowest rates; in the fall they were about equal, and in the winter the summertime findings were reversed (*see text*).

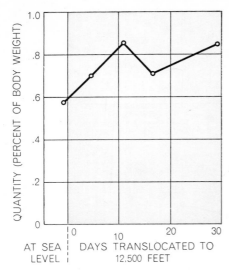

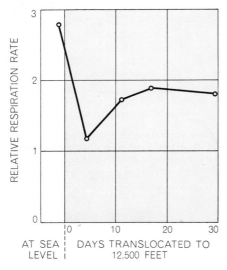

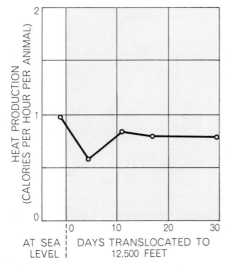

BROWN FAT, a tissue that generates heat, increased in quantity in sea-level deer mice transported to 12,500 feet (*top*). The rate of respiration of the tissue decreased, however, because of the relative lack of oxygen (*middle*). As a result the animal's total heat production was somewhat reduced (*bottom*).

(as indicated by oxygen consumption at rest) of the mice at various altitudes under various temperature conditions. The stations used for comparison were at sea level, at 4,000 feet in the Owens Valley (which is hot in summer) and at 12,500 feet in the Barcroft Laboratory. The determinations were made during three different seasons and at temperatures ranging from near freezing to a maximum of about 99 degrees Fahrenheit. I found that in summer the high-altitude mice had the lowest metabolic rate, the 4,000-foot mice an intermediate rate and the sea-level mice the highest rate. (The highest temperature proved to be lethal for mice from the high altitude, and conversely lower-altitude mice tested at near-freezing temperatures became severely chilled.) In the fall (at temperatures between 68 and 90 degrees F.) the high-altitude mice and sea-level mice had about the same rate of metabolism. In winter (February) the situation was the reverse of the summer picture: now the high-altitude mice had the highest rate at all temperatures, the sea-level mice the lowest.

These observations could be interpreted as follows. At the high altitude the comparatively mild temperatures of summer enable the native mouse to adjust to the hypoxic environment by reducing oxygen consumption to the minimum required for nourishing the body tissues. Because of the mouse's small size it cannot grow a thick enough hair covering to insulate it effectively against the winter cold. Consequently the high-altitude mouse is forced to increase its metabolism in winter to maintain its body temperature. The sea-level mouse, on the other hand, is not subjected to extreme cold in winter. Hence it is adequately protected from the drop in the ambient temperature by a small increase in its furry insulation and by an adjustment in the form of "physiological insulation," that is, reduction of its body temperature, which cuts down heat loss by reducing the temperature difference between the body and the ambient air. (I found that the deep-body temperature of the sea-level mouse does indeed decrease in winter.) Moreover, the sea-level mouse in winter can afford to reduce its metabolic rate from the high rate associated with summer activities without stinting its tissues' needs for oxygen.

With two associates, Robert E. Smith and Jane C. Roberts, I looked into the metabolic response of mice at the cell and tissue levels. We found several marked differences in cell activities at low altitudes and at high altitudes. In most cases it was difficult to tell whether

the observed differences were due to exposure to cold or to hypoxia. Studies of the brown fat in these animals, however, produced some significant findings.

Brown fat, found mainly between an animal's shoulder blades, is a heat-generating tissue [see "The Production of Heat by Fat," by Michael J. R. Dawkins and David Hull; SCIENTIFIC AMERICAN Offprint 1018]. In response to exposure to cold there is an increase in both the mass of brown fat and its heat production, which may multiply severalfold in a few weeks. We found that the mass of brown fat could be increased in deer mice by exposure to cold or to hypoxia (which also lowers the body temperature). It turned out, however, that when sea-level mice were transferred to high altitude, the respiration of their brown fat decreased, so that its heat production was reduced in spite of a clear increase in its mass. On the other hand, when high-altitude natives were brought down to sea level, both the mass and the respiration of their brown fat increased, and its heat production apparently equaled that of sea-level mice that had been acclimated to cold. Evidently the transfer to the oxygen abundance at sea level had improved the tissue's respiration so that it increased its production of heat. From these findings we concluded that hypoxia, although it gives rise to the growth of brown fat, may suppress heat production by limiting the tissue's respiration.

Heredity or Environment?

The extensive investigations leave unsettled the question of whether men native to high altitude are a race apart or merely human beings with a normal heredity who have adjusted to the conditions over a lifetime of habituation beginning in the uterus. In some respects the mountain natives, both animals and men, do seem to show innate physiological differences from their kindred species at sea level. There is a serious objection to considering them a separate strain, however, namely the lack of genetic isolation. There has been no barrier in this case to the pooling of genes, either for the deer mouse or for man. We know that Andean man has intermarried freely with lowlanders. Indeed, many of the mountain miners came from the lowlands and many highlanders have come down to live in the lowlands. It seems likely that the highlanders have derived their special qualities from acclimatization—in short, that their response to their environment is phenotypic rather than genotypic.

The Skin

30

by William Montagna
February 1965

*The human body's largest organ, this protective
envelope not only stabilizes temperature and blood
pressure but also gives rise to the hair patches, odors
and shades of color characteristic of man*

As a naked animal who is apparently becoming progressively more hairless as his evolution advances, man is extraordinarily dependent on the properties of his skin. Skin is a remarkable organ—the largest and by far the most versatile of the body. It is an effective shield against many forms of physical and chemical attack. It holds in the body's fluids and maintains its integrity by keeping out foreign substances and microorganisms. It acts to ward off the harsh ultraviolet rays of the sun. It incorporates mechanisms that cool the body when it is warm and retard the loss of heat when it is cold. It plays a major role in regulating blood pressure and directing the flow of blood. It embodies the sense of touch. It is the principal organ of sexual attraction. It identifies each individual, by shaping the facial and bodily contours as well as by distinctive markings such as fingerprints. The skin crowns all these properties with the ability to regenerate itself and thereby heal wounds. As A. E. Needham of the University of Oxford has remarked, scratches and other minor wounds are so common (probably, at a conservative estimate, averaging one a week per person) that few human beings would survive very long if it were not for the skin's property of self-repair.

We shall survey in this article the highlights of what has been learned about man's skin: its anatomical properties, functions and evolution. The subject has many aspects, because skin is a complex tissue that forms a great variety of structures. In mammals the same tissue that produces the epidermis also differentiates into hair, spines, nails, claws, hooves, scales and horns; in birds it produces feathers, the beak, scales and claws; in reptiles it gives rise to scales, spines and claws. In

man the glands of the skin deserve particular attention, because they perform several vital roles.

The skin is composed of two principal layers: (1) the underlying dermis, a thick, fibrous tissue that forms its main bulk, and (2) the epidermis, the thin surface coat, which consists of four or five sheets of cells veneered on one another. The top layer of the epidermis is made up of flattened, dead cells—necessarily dead, because living cells cannot survive exposure to air or water. It is this mantle of dead tissue, called the horny layer, that serves as the principal shield of the body. Thin, flexible and transparent, it is nevertheless a sturdy structure, with its cells held together by "attachment plaques." In protected areas of the body this layer is smooth and very supple; on surfaces that get a good deal of wear, such as the palms of the hands, it is thicker and more rugged.

If you scratch your skin with your fingernails, you will scrape off tiny flakes of the dead surface tissue. The skin of the whole body is continually exfoliated by the wear and tear of rubbing and exposure to the environment. The deeper layers of the epidermis steadily replenish the horny layer, however, by moving up more cells. As the cells ascend toward the surface, they die by degrees as they produce keratin, the fibrous protein that constitutes the bulk of the dead surface structures, not only of the skin proper but also of the hair, nails and other skin growths. Death is the goal of every epidermal cell, and it is achieved in an orderly manner. Like the leaves of autumn, the epidermal cells, having lived for their season, eventually dry out and peel off.

The horny layer they form is a relatively effective barrier against the entry of most foreign substances, but its

effectiveness is not complete. Among some of the noxious substances it fails to keep out are metallic nickel and the oleoresins of poison ivy. The skin is so sensitive to nickel that even the comparatively few molecules that are rubbed off on contact may produce a violent reaction with the living tissues if the nickel penetrates the epidermis. The skin's sensitivity to an encounter with the leaves of poison ivy, or even the smoke from its burning leaves, is well known. A thicker horny layer might have made man impervious to all invasions, as it has the elephant, but man would then have had to pay the price of a loss of suppleness and agility. The human skin, all things considered, has achieved a remarkably effective compromise.

To continue with our examination of the skin's surface, we observe that, like a very detailed map, it is heavily marked with topographical features: furrows, ridges, pores, hair follicles, pebbled areas and so on. Each area of the body has its own characteristic topography. Some of the markings have obvious general usefulness. The hands and feet need rough surfaces; if they were perfectly smooth, they could not get a good grip. Some features are clearly the result of long habit in the exercise of certain muscles that pull on the skin; among these are the wrinkles formed by smiling and by knitting the brow. By and large, however, most of the patterns in the skin are strictly genetic. Largely determined by the orientation of the fibers in the dermis and by other anatomical factors, they are peculiar to each individual and therefore serve as a means of personal identification.

Look at the skin of your palm or a finger under a magnifying lens. Its ridges, forming whorls, loops and arch-

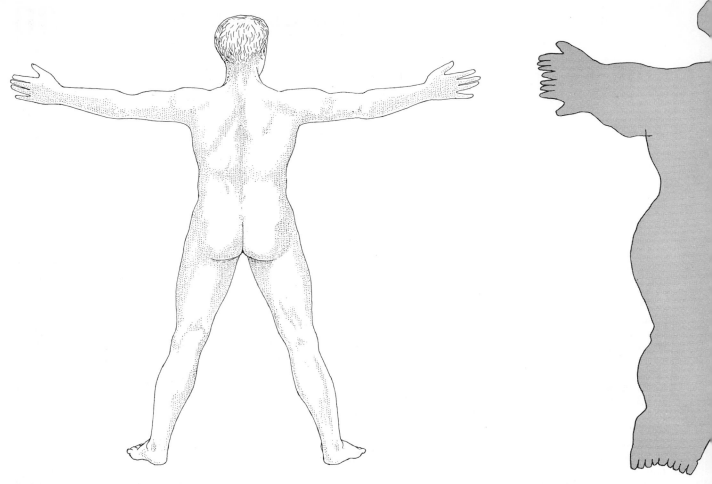

TOTAL SURFACE AREA of the skin, which seems surprisingly large in contrast to the outline of a human figure (*left*), is calcu- lated by adding the areas of a series of cylinders constructed from an average of leg, arm and torso circumferences. A man six feet

es, make up specific pattern designs, called dermatoglyphics. No two individuals, not even identical twins, have exactly the same dermatoglyphics. The patterns are formed before birth; they are laid down in the fetus during the third and fourth months of development. Their congenital origin shows itself in certain graphic ways. For example, women's fingerprints are distinctly different from men's: women have fewer whorls and more arches. In an individual the dermatoglyphics of the right hand show major differences from those of the left, which suggests that handedness may be established during the third or fourth month of fetal life. There are even indications that unusual skin markings may be associated with congenital brain abnormalities, such as mental deficiency and epilepsy [*see bottom illustration on page 346*]. Dermatoglyphic peculiarities have shown up consistently in such individuals; this implies that the factors responsible for the brain abnormalities may have operated during the third and

fourth fetal months, when the skin patterns were being formed.

The development of skin begins very early in the human embryo. The epidermal cells soon differentiate further into the skin's suborgans: hair follicles, nails, sebaceous glands and sweat glands. At about three months, for example, hair follicles start to form on the head, the part of the body that develops first, and as the fetus grows the trunk and limbs also acquire hair follicles. By the time the infant is born it has as many hairs or rudiments of hairs on its body as it will ever have. The common notion that hair does not begin to form on some parts of the body until one matures (for instance, that a boy's cheeks are hairless until he approaches the age of shaving) is incorrect. The hairs are there all the time, although they may not grow noticeably before puberty. Moreover, there is no substantial difference between men and women with respect to the number of hair follicles: a woman has about as many hairs on her body as a man, but

many of them are so small and colorless that they escape notice. Indeed, the same observation holds for the comparison between man and his furrier relatives—the gorilla, the orangutan and the chimpanzee. Man has about the same number of hair follicles as these animals; the difference is simply that most of his are obsolescent and fail to grow much.

Man's skin follows a charactertistic life cycle. In infancy and early childhood it is dry, soft, velvety, clear and apparently almost hairless. Because it is so free of blemishes and presumably because it suggests the clear, soft skin of a sexually attractive young woman, baby skin has come to be regarded as the epitome of skin beauty. With adolescence comes an enlargement of the hair follicles and a more active growth of the hair. The sweat glands and sebaceous glands (which produce a fatty secretion) go from a nearly dormant state to full activity. Physiologically speaking, the skin arrives at full bloom with puberty. Its ensuing history, however, is not completely happy, partly

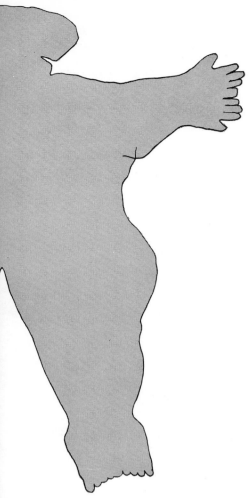

tall and of average weight and body build has about 3,000 square inches of skin area.

because its owner proceeds to subject it to daily abuses.

In the effort to enhance its attractiveness, men and women submit their skin to systematic stretching, scraping, gouging, soaking and burning. In our fastidious society the skin is treated with daily baths, which remove its natural emollients and essential substances. It is doused with powders, poultices, oils and other chemical and physical treatments that may cause varying degrees of irritation. To give it a "healthy" tan, the skin is ritualistically exposed to excessive and injurious doses of sunlight and wind.

That the skin survives these daily torments is a remarkable tribute to its toughness. But age and decades of indignities do, of course, take their toll. Man's most obvious sign of age is the dry, wrinkled, flaccid skin that marks his late years. It is then a tired organ—a relic of what it was in its youth.

From place to place on the body the skin is a study in contrasts. On the eyebrows it is thick, coarse and hairy;

on the eyelids, thin and hairless. On the red border of the lips it is completely hairless; on the upper lip, chin and jowl of a man, so hairy that bristles are visible within a few hours after shaving. On the nose, the cheeks and the forehead the skin is oily; on the jowls, dry and greaseless. The rest of the body shows contrasts as striking as those on the face. The skin areas of the chest, the pubic region, the scalp, the abdomen and the soles of the feet are as different from one another, structurally and functionally, as if they belonged to different animals.

A brief examination of a few specific properties of the skin will serve to illustrate how exquisitely it is adapted to its functions. As a wrapping that must accommodate itself to changes in the shape and size of the body, the skin is highly elastic. Pull the skin and it will snap back. Cut out a piece and the detached piece will contract, whereas the skin around the wound will widen the cut by elastically pulling away from it. During pregnancy the skin of the lower trunk of a woman is highly stretched. Afterward, when her body returns to its normal size, the skin makes heroic efforts to regain its former area, but the stretching may leave permanent scars—the light streaks in the skin that commonly appear on the abdomen of a woman who has borne children. Similar streaks appear on the body of a person who has gone through repeated bouts of gaining weight and reducing. Such bouts sometimes leave the fatigued skin sagging in pendulous folds that refuse to shrink back.

Another conspicuous property of the skin is its pigmentation. Evenly scattered deep in the epidermis are the melanocytes, cells that produce the dark pigment melanin. Spider-shaped, with long tentacle-like processes, these cells inject granules of melanin into the surrounding epidermal cells, where the pigment forms a protective awning over each cell nucleus on the side toward the skin surface. The prime function of the pigment is to shield the cells by absorbing the ultraviolet rays of the sun. All human beings, regardless of race, have about the same number of melanocytes; the darker races are distinguished from the lighter ones only by the fact that their melanocytes manufacture more pigment. This protective capacity has evolved in the tropical peoples of the world as an asset with high survival value.

Dense webs of blood vessels course through the skin all over the body.

They transport through the skin a great deal more blood than is needed to nourish the skin itself; this immense circulation performs two important functions for the entire body. First, it acts as a cooling system. The skin's sweat glands pour water onto the skin's surface, and the evaporation of the water cools the blood circulating through the skin. When the outside environment is warm or the body is engaged in strenuous exercise, the blood vessels assist the cooling process by relaxing and allowing a maximum flow of blood through the skin, which accounts for the flushed appearance of the skin at such times. On the other hand, when the environment is cold, the vessels contract rapidly and greatly reduce the blood flow in the skin, thus conserving the internal body heat.

Second, the skin's circulation serves to help regulate the blood pressure. The blood vessels in the skin have sphincter-like passages that can shut off the flow through the capillaries and thereby cause the blood to bypass them so that it flows directly from the small arteries into the veins. This mechanism for speeding the flow acts like a safety valve when the blood pressure rises to a dangerous level.

The skin's extraordinary network of blood vessels is matched by an equally massive network of nerves. Much of this nervous system is concerned with controlling the glands, blood vessels and other organs in the skin. There is also a vast complex of sensory nerve endings. These are particularly prominent in the most naked surfaces of the body: the fingers, palms, soles, lips and even the cornea of the eye, which has no blood vessels. These specialized nerves are sensitive to tactile and thermal stimuli. Without them the human body would be almost as out of touch with the outside world as it would be if it lacked the major sense organs.

The Hair

Hairs are products of the skin that man shares with all the rest of the mammalian order. In many ways hair is a paradoxical growth. For other mammals it serves a wide variety of useful functions, but man is able to dispense with most of them. In fact, in man hair has become largely an ornamental appendage; it seems to survive mainly as a means of sexual attraction.

The most obvious function of a heavy coat of hair for mammals in the natural state is protective insulation against the

344 ADAPTATION AND ADAPTABILITY

weather and other hazards of the environment. This is as true in a warm climate as in a cold one: the fur-covered animals of the Tropics are insulated by their hair against the strong sun and heat. Hair, however, is only one of the devices that have evolved among mammals for this purpose. The whale, a completely naked mammal, is adapted to living in polar waters by a thick layer of insulating blubber, capped by a heavy skin with a thick, horny layer. Man's nakedness and his thin skin plain-

ly indicate that he originated in a tropical or temperate environment. His spread into the colder regions of the earth was made possible only by his development of artificial clothing and shelter.

A few special protective functions of hair remain important to the human body. The hairs inside the nostrils slow incoming air currents, trap dust particles, keep out insects and prevent the nasal mucus from pouring down over the lips. The hairs in the outer ear and

around the anogenital orifices act as barriers against the entry of foreign matter and small invaders such as insects. The bushy eyebrows and the eyelashes help to shield the vulnerable eyeballs.

Man also retains some use of the sensory function of hair. Most hair follicles in a mammal's skin have a collar of sensory nerves around them, and the animal therefore senses any slight movement of the hair due to contact with an object. The nerve supply is par-

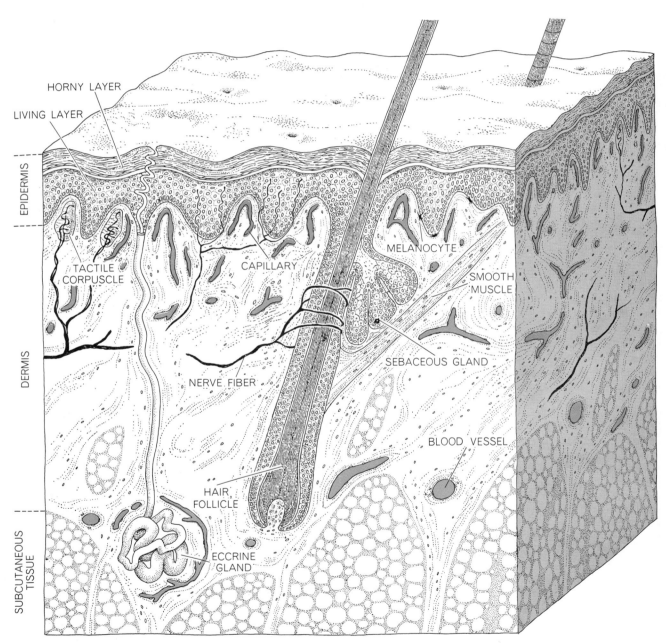

ZONES OF THE SKIN are displayed in an idealized section. The underlying dermis, the thickest part of the organ, is supported by a fat-rich subcutaneous stratum. Intermingled with the cells of the dermis are fine blood vessels (color), tactile and other nerves, the smooth muscles that raise the hair when contracted, and a variety of specialized glands. Above the dermis are the twin levels of the epidermis: a lower zone of living cells capped by a horny layer of dead cells filled with the fibrous protein keratin. Melanocytes, the pigment organs that produce the granules responsible for varying skin colors, lie at the base of the epidermis.

ticularly rich around hair follicles in certain sensitive regions of the body, among them the face, the anogenital areas and certain special areas that are important to a given animal's activities. A squirrel, for instance, is sensitized in this way on the surface of the abdomen, so that it feels its way with its abdominal hairs as it runs along the bark of a tree. Lemurs, which use their hands to move about in trees, have patches of sensory hairs on the inner surface of their wrists. Nearly all mammals have long, sensitive vibrissae, or whiskers, around the muzzle; these hairs communicate their motion directly to nerves and indirectly through pressure on blood-filled sacs around the follicles. The whiskers are particularly well developed in nocturnal animals, and they attain large size in seals and walruses. Man, although he lacks the blood-filled sacs around the follicles, possesses nerve endings around many of his hair follicles, particularly those that surround the mouth.

Obviously, aside from a few special functions such as the screening of external passages, hair is not really essential to man. It is not so easy to see, however, what positive advantages may have been responsible for his evolution toward nakedness, as compared with other primates. It has been suggested that lack of a heavy fur may have had some adaptive value for running and hunting in the open savannas, but this is conjectural. At all events, there is no doubt that, although man still has as many hair follicles as his primate cousins, his hair growth is gradually declining, and one of the most obvious indications of this is the increasing prevalence of baldness.

Hair Growth

The follicle that produces a hair is a tube that extends all the way through the skin and widens into a bulb—the hair root—at its deep end. When the hair has attained its characteristic length, it stops growing (except on the scalp, where the hair may grow very long if it is not cut). Having reached its limit, the hair forms a clublike base and puts out rootlets that anchor it to the surrounding follicle. The follicle shrinks and goes into a resting period. After a time it forms the germ of a new hair, which then works its way toward the surface, loosening the old hair and causing it to be shed. Thus hair growth is a matter of alternate growing and resting periods, with new hairs arising period-

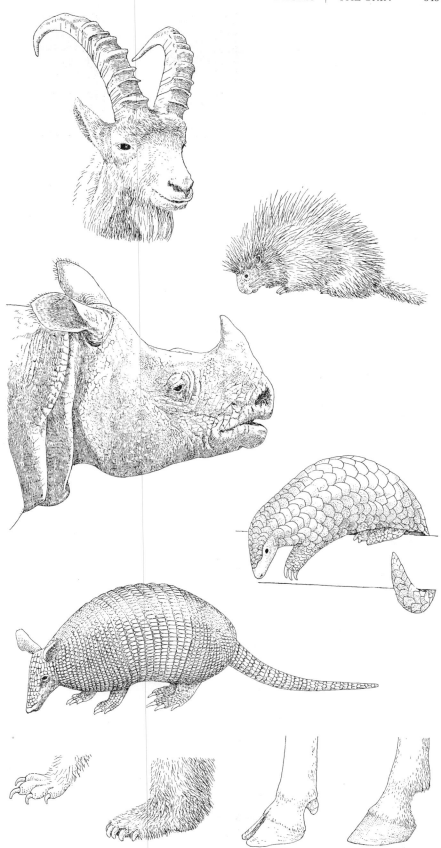

THE VERSATILE SKIN gives rise to a wide variety of superficial structures; among the mammals these include, from top to bottom, the bold horns of the ibex, the quills of the porcupine, the hairy "horn" of the rhinoceros, the scales of the pangolin and the armadillo, and various claws and hooves. Like all of these, man's hair and nails are special skin structures.

INDIVIDUALITY OF FINGERPRINTS is one of the best-known characteristics of the skin. These thumbprints can be readily told apart, although they are those of identical twins. The same individual quality exists on any skin surface, but the strong pattern of ridges and grooves found on the ventral surfaces of hands and feet are the most easily identified.

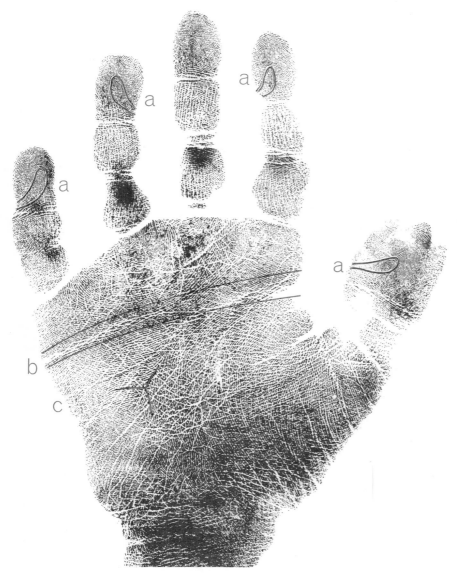

GENETIC BASIS of skin patterns is shown by the existence of similar patterns among unrelated individuals with similar chromosomal abnormalities. None of the patterns outlined (*color*) on this palm print of a mongoloid imbecile is abnormal, yet the simultaneous presence of these configurations is a very rare event among normal people. These patterns are ulnar loops on the digits (*a*), the simian crease (*b*) and an off-center axial triradius (*c*). The palm print was made by Irene A. Uchida of the Children's Hospital in Winnipeg, Canada.

ically to displace the old. In many animals this is a seasonal process; the animal sheds nearly all its hair at one time, starting a completely new crop.

The pelt of such an animal makes a good fur piece only if it is taken during the resting period, when the clubbed hairs are firmly attached to the follicles and will remain so after the skin is tanned. In man and some other mammals the pattern of growth and shedding is different: in any given area there are always some follicles growing and some resting, so that normally there is no wholesale shedding and the total hair growth remains constant in all seasons of the year.

Human hair grows at the rate of about a third of a millimeter per day. The follicle is at an angle to the skin surface, hence the emerging hair lies over on the skin except when certain muscle fibers attached to the follicle pull on it and cause the hair to stand erect. The same muscle action also forms the mounds known as goose pimples. Thus proverbial references to goose pimples and hair standing on end in moments of fright have a real basis; it will happen when the hormones released by the emotion activate the muscles of the hair follicles.

The individual hairs of man may be round (which causes the hair to be straight), alternately round and oval (which makes the hair wavy) or ribbon-shaped (which makes it kinky). The color of the hair depends on the amount and distribution of melanin in it and on the hair's surface structure, which affects the reflection of light. A study of how hair grows helps to explain some of the superstitions about it. One of these is the notion that a traumatic experience may turn the hair gray or white overnight. The idea is incorrect, but it has this much basis: a shock may cause some shedding of fine, normally pigmented hairs, thereby exposing to greater prominence the coarser graying hairs, which were already present and are more resistant to stress.

Another common misconception is the one that shaving causes the hair to grow increasingly coarse. It is true that the stubble after shaving feels rough, but the reason is simply that the soft, tapered ends of the hairs have been cut off; the new hairs that will succeed them later will still have soft, tapered ends. Then there are the startling stories about corpses that have been observed to grow a beard in the days after death. This phenomenon too has a simple explanation: after the skin of a dead person dries and shrinks it may expose a millimeter or two of hair that was below the surface before death.

From the evolutionary point of view the most interesting aspect of man's hair is the baldness that develops on the top of his head. This baldness is actually an extension of a natural process that occurs in all human beings and begins before birth. In the young fetus the entire head is covered with hairs—the forehead as well as the scalp. After the fifth month the hair follicles on the forehead gradually become involuted and diminish in size. At birth the infant often still has some visible hair on its brow, but the forehead continues to become increasingly naked, and by late childhood it establishes a high, well-defined hairline. (There are, however, freakish cases in which an individual retains a bushy growth of hair on his forehead like that on his scalp.) The same balding process that occurs on the forehead also takes place elsewhere on the body; babies are often visibly hairier at birth than they are later. Thus man's nakedness is the result of a progressive involution of his hair follicles. Although he has as many follicles as other primates, most of them are so small that the hairs they produce are not visible on the surface.

Exactly the same process of involution of follicles is responsible for balding of the scalp, which may begin in young men as early as the twenties. It is curious that this dramatic loss of hair should take place on the scalp, which, unlike other parts of the body, will normally grow hair to almost unlimited length (as much as 12 feet) if the hair is not cut. The explanation lies in the action of androgenic (male) hormones, which paradoxically are responsible not only for the growth of all hair but also, under certain circumstances, for the reduction of the scalp hair. Eunuchs, having a deficiency of androgenic hormones, rarely become bald on top—a fact that was noted by Aristotle, who himself was bald. I should emphasize at this point that once involution of the scalp follicles has taken place no agency will avail to grow a new crop of hair.

Significantly, man is not the only primate that develops baldness. The stump-tailed macaque and the orangutan become virtually bald on the forehead when they mature. The ouakari monkey of South America, starting with a full head of hair in its youth, loses all the hair on its scalp and forehead by the time it reaches adulthood. We hope to learn a great deal about baldness by studying these animals. Whether

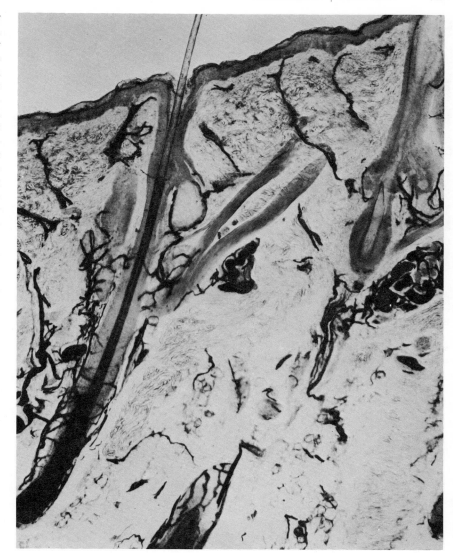

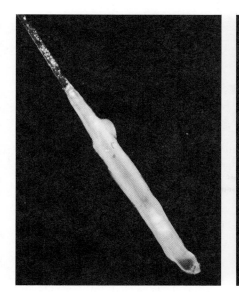

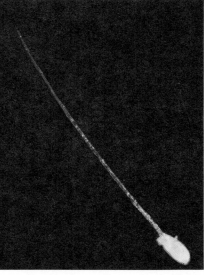

HAIR GROWTH alternates between active and dormant phases. The human hair at the left in the upper photograph is growing; the follicle that produces it is surrounded by many blood vessels. In contrast, the hair at the right is not growing; its follicle is quiescent and shriveled and the base of the hair is clubbed. The lower pair of photographs contrasts an active hair (*left*) with a dormant one (*right*). Each hair has been plucked from its follicle.

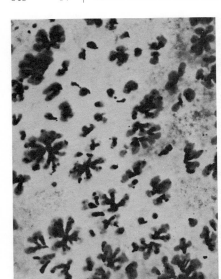
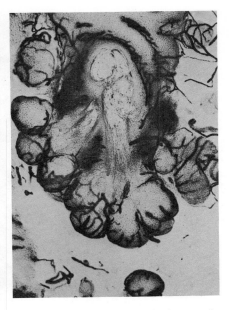

SEBACEOUS GLANDS are not always associated with hair follicles; these photographs show the numerous nests of these glands situated on the inside of the human cheek (*left*) and the abundance of fine blood vessels surrounding one such cheek gland (*right*). Wherever located, the cells of these glands synthesize and accumulate globules of fat (*see below*).

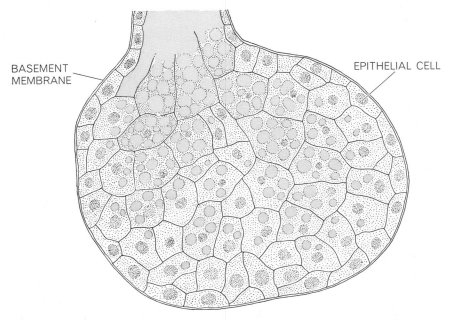

BASEMENT
MEMBRANE

EPITHELIAL CELL

PRODUCTION OF SEBUM, a mixture of fatty acids, triglycerides, waxes and cholesterol, occurs as the sebaceous gland cells become choked with accumulated fat globules (*color*), die and disintegrate. As the sebum accumulates in the gland's duct, capillary traction and the pressure from skin movements bring the semiliquid material to the surface of the skin.

some odorless and some extraordinarily malodorous, some fatty and some watery, some colorless and some strikingly pigmented, perform a wide range of functions, prominent among which is sexual attraction. The skin of man has two main kinds of secretory gland: the sebaceous glands and the sweat glands.

The former produce an odd material called sebum, which is a semiliquid mixture of fatty acids, triglycerides, waxes, cholesterol and cellular debris. The production of sebum is somewhat like the production of the horny layer by the epidermis. The cells of the sebaceous glands synthesize globules of fat, gradually become bloated with the accumulation of these globules and eventually break up. This mélange of dead and decaying cell fragments is the sebum.

Investigators who have studied sebum are at a loss to imagine what useful purpose it may serve. The secretion does not emulsify readily, it is toxic to living tissues, produces skin blemishes and in general seems to do more harm than good. The sebaceous glands themselves offer no clear clues, only a confusion of inconsistencies. Most of them are attached to hair follicles and deposit their sebum on the hairs inside the follicles, but in some areas of the skin the glands are not connected with follicles; there the sebum oozes out on the skin through ducts. The glands are particularly prominent around the nose and mouth, on the inside of the cheeks, on the hairless border of the upper lip, on the forehead, over the cheekbones, on the inside edge of the eyelids (where they are so large that one can easily see them with the naked eye by turning up a lid before a mirror), on parts of the neck and upper torso and on the genital organs. All this suggests that the sebum may play useful roles, although it is hard to see what they are. It does not seem likely that sebum is only a lubricant.

The human body often appears to contain senseless appendages and even to make outright mistakes, but the sebaceous glands are too numerous and active to be dismissed as trivial. Nor do they seem to be mere survivals from earlier stages of evolution in which they were more important to the body; man has a greater number of and more active sebaceous glands than most other mammals and has them in places where they do not appear in other animals.

In spite of a considerable amount of research, very little has been learned about the cause or treatment of acne,

we like it or not, it seems clear that in the long run we shall have to accept the fact that man is becoming increasingly bald and must reconcile himself to the ornamental value of nakedness.

Most of the members of the animal kingdom possess skin glands of one sort or another, which produce a remarkable variety of secretions. Fishes and amphibians secrete slime; toads produce

poisons that make them unpalatable to most predators; the duckbill platypus secretes toxic substances from rosettes of glands on its hind legs; most birds have a pair of preen glands over the tail (in chickens and turkeys vulgarly known as "the pope's nose") that secretes a preening ointment that contains precursors of vitamin D. The many varieties of mammalian skin secretions,

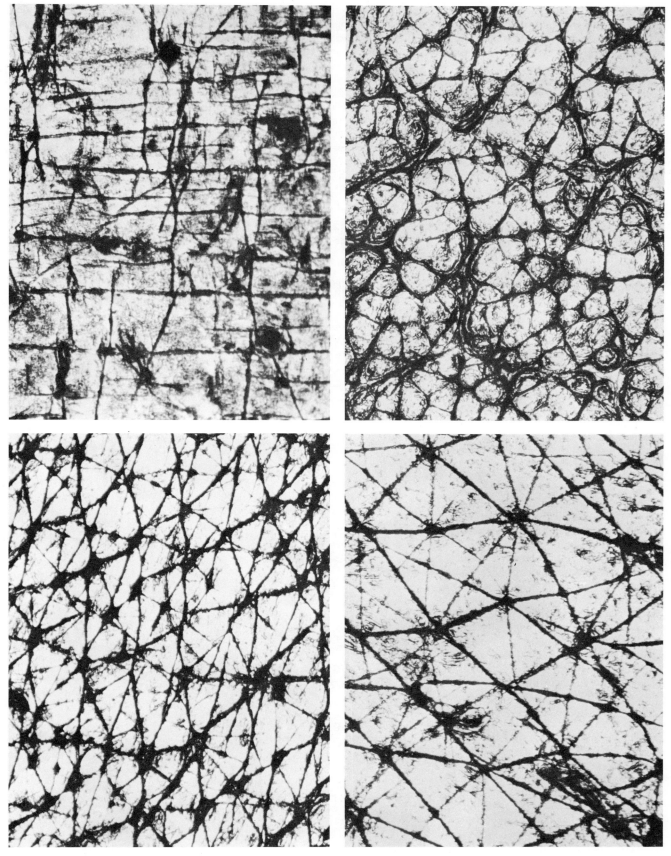

SKIN TEXTURE varies from place to place on the human body, as is evidenced by varying patterns of lines and pores. From left to right, the four illustrations show impressions in plastic of forehead and elbow skin (*top*) and of chest and back skin (*bottom*). The work of H. D. Chim and R. L. Dobson at the University of Oregon Medical School, the impressions are here enlarged 75 diameters.

for which the sebaceous glands are in some way responsible. Why do these lesions occur particularly in young adolescents? Why do they break out on the face, neck and upper torso but not on the scalp or the anogenital areas, where the sebaceous glands are also large and numerous? The only facts about acne that seem definitely established are that there is a hereditary disposition to it and that it is connected in some way with diet and with the activity of the androgenic hormones. These hormones have a great deal to do with the development and functioning of the sebaceous glands. The glands are large in a newborn infant, become dormant during childhood, begin to enlarge again in early puberty and grow to full bloom in adults. They show a definite relation to the level of androgenic hormones in the individual. The glands are larger and more active in men than in women; they are only poorly developed in eunuchs, and they increase in size and number when a eunuch is treated with androgens.

The Two Kinds of Sweat Gland

In the usage of physiologists the term "sweat glands" lumps together many different organs, most of which have nothing to do with sweating. Some produce scent or musk, others mucoid substances, still others colored secretions. What all the so-called sweat glands have in common is that they are tubular in form and are found only among the mammals.

The glands that actually produce sweat are of two general kinds: the apocrine glands, which are usually associated with hair follicles, and the eccrine glands, which are not. The two types have different origins, structures and functions. Because the eccrine glands predominate in the more advanced primates, some evolutionists have supposed that this type evolved more recently and that the apocrine type is more primitive; actually one of the most primitive of all mammals, the duckbill platypus, has well-developed eccrine glands, and man not only is richer in eccrine glands than any other primate but also has more and better-developed apocrine glands in certain parts of his body. It is not possible to say definitely that either type is more ancient or more primitive than the other.

The apocrine glands secrete the odorous component of sweat. They are primarily scent glands, and they produce their secretions in response to stress or sexual stimulation. Before the deodorant and perfume industries usurped their function of creating a person's body odor, the apocrine glands no doubt played an important role in human society. Aside from their odor-generating property, these glands are quite unnecessary to man. There are clear signs that man's apocrine glands, like his hair, are much less luxuriant than they were in his ancestors.

A human fetus in its fifth month produces rudiments of apocrine sweat glands over almost its entire body. Within a few weeks, however, most of these rudiments disappear, and the human body eventually has well-developed apocrine glands only in the armpits, the navel, the anogenital areas, the nipples and the ears. This seems to be a clear case of ontogeny mirroring phylogeny—the fetus recapitulating

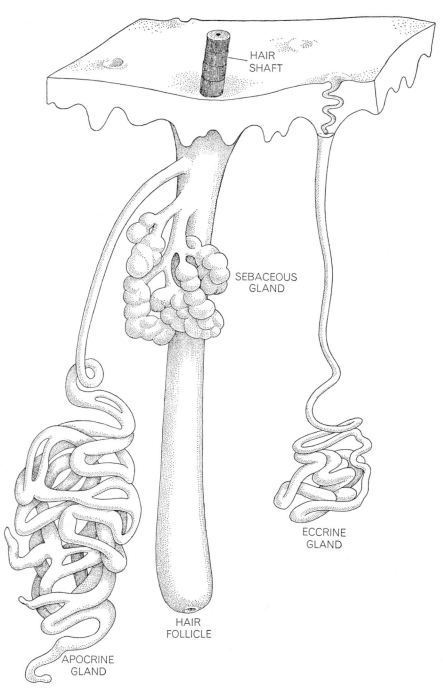

SWEAT GLANDS comprise two major categories: apocrine glands, which secrete a milky, odorous fluid (*left*), and eccrine glands, which secrete water (*right*). The former, together with the sebaceous glands, produce the body's odors; the latter help to regulate body heat.

man's evolutionary history. Oddly, although man no longer has apocrine glands all over his body, in his armpits these glands are larger and more numerous than in all other animals. Man is distinguished from all other mammals by a highly developed axillary organ in his armpits, made up of very large apocrine glands with eccrine glands interspersed among them.

The apocrine secretion is a milky, sticky fluid of varying color—pale gray, whitish, yellow or reddish. Although the glands are large, the amount of their secretion is very small; most of the fluid in the copious sweat of the armpits is supplied by the eccrine glands, which provide the vehicle for the spread of the odorous apocrine substances. The freshly secreted apocrine sweat is actually rather odorless, but it becomes malodorous when its substances are decomposed by the action of bacteria on the skin's surface.

The eccrine glands, the source of most of man's sweat, secrete water, which has two main functions: (1) cooling the body by evaporation and (2) moistening the friction surfaces, such as those of the palms and the soles, which prevents flaking of the horny layer, improves the grip and assists the tactile sensitivity. The glands responsible for the two functions show clear-cut differences, both in their response to stimuli and in their embryonic development. Eccrine glands of the first category produce sweat in response to heat; those in the second category, sweat in response to psychic stimuli. As for development, the eccrine glands on the palms and soles appear in the fetus at the age of three and a half months, whereas those in the rest of the body do not develop until

the fifth month and are the last structures to form. This suggests that the secretions for gripping arrived early in evolution and the cooling secretions may be a recent development.

Cats, dogs and rodents have eccrine glands only in the pads of their paws. Some South American monkeys have a hairless surface on the lower side of the prehensile tail, and this surface is copiously supplied with eccrine glands. So are the knuckles of the gorilla's and the chimpanzee's hands, which they use in walking. In the monkeys and the apes the hairy skin of the body also has a considerable sprinkling of eccrine glands, but it is significant that these are not nearly so active as man's. The skin of a monkey remains dry even on the hottest days. Obviously profuse sweating would be a liability to a furry animal: if its hair were soaked with sweat, the animal would continually be wrapped in a wet and chilling blanket.

For naked man, on the other hand, the array of active sweat glands all over the body skin is a highly useful adaptation. It endows him with an essential cooling system that compensates for his lack of an insulating pelage. Man has millions of eccrine glands on his body, the number varying with individuals and ranging from two million to five million, or an average of about 150 to 340 per square centimeter of skin surface. Some of the individual differences may depend on differences in body size. Some people sweat much more profusely than others, but this is not strictly related to the individual's total number of sweat glands; the difference lies, rather, in the relative activity of the glands.

The human sweating response has

been investigated by means of such experiments as the administration of drugs, spices and other treatments. The results are not very enlightening. Sweating can be evoked by different drugs of apparently opposite chemical properties; individuals often respond differently to a given drug; the drug may produce inconsistent responses even in the same individual. Moreover, sweating is an enigma that amounts to a major biological blunder: it depletes the body not only of water but also of sodium and other essential electrolytes that are carried off with the water.

Perhaps the eccrine glands are still an experiment of nature—demonstrably useful to man but not yet fully refined by the evolutionary process. In view of its indispensability to the human body, sweating is likely to survive, in spite of the determined efforts of antiperspirant technologists.

To sum up, the outstanding features of man's skin are its nakedness and its ability to sweat profusely. His hair is largely ornamental, the only luxuriant growths of his body having no practical value for protecting him from the environment. One of the important mechanisms man has developed as an adaptation to his increasing nakedness is the body-temperature control system regulated by the eccrine sweat glands, which adjust their output of cooling water both to changes in the outside temperature and to the internal heat generated in the body by exercise. All in all, the seemingly delicate skin of man is a remarkably complex and adaptable organ, serving not only as armor against the outside world but also as an important contributor to the body's internal husbandry.

31

The Multiple Sclerosis Problem

by Geoffrey Dean
July 1970

*The cause of this disease of the central nervous system
is unknown. The variations in its incidence around the
world, however, suggest that it results from infection
by a virus with a long latent period*

The written record of multiple sclerosis begins in 1822, when a young English nobleman, Sir Augustus D'Este, noted in his diary unmistakable evidence that he was a victim of some mysterious disease. When he died at the age of 54, D'Este had spent at least 26 years of his life fighting this unseen enemy. In 1838, while D'Este was traveling all over Europe in a vain search for a cure, Sir Robert Carswell, a British medical illustrator, included in his *Pathological Anatomy* a watercolor of a strange-looking spinal cord he had seen during an autopsy. On the otherwise seemingly healthy cord were scattered spots of hardened and discolored tissue. Carswell described the condition as "a peculiar diseased state of the spinal cord accompanied by atrophy of the discoloured portions."

Almost at the same time a French physician, Jean Cruveilhier, observed similar spots on the spinal cord at the autopsy of a woman who had been hospitalized for many years. He called the spots "islands of sclerosis," from the Greek for "hardening," and speculated that they might have actually caused the disease. Thirty more years were to pass before multiple sclerosis was properly identified. It was Jean Martin Charcot, one of France's most famous medical investigators, who in 1868 gave the world a detailed description of the disease. Working at the Salpêtrière hospital in Paris, Charcot found that many of his patients were suffering from varying degrees of tremor and paralysis. Some of these patients suffered from the shaking palsy ("paralysis agitans"), which had been first described by James Parkinson in England in 1817. Charcot realized, however, that another distinct disease was present, evidenced by tremor and varying degrees of spastic paralysis, or

stiff and jerky body and limb movements. At autopsy victims of this disease showed plaques, or hardened flat patches, scattered throughout the central nervous system. He called the disease *sclerose en plaques.*

Charcot found that patients frequently experienced alternating exacerbation and remission of symptoms, that the severity of the symptoms varied greatly from patient to patient and that often the illness appeared to remain stationary for many years. In its advanced stages he found that the disease was characterized by paralysis and by three additional symptoms now known as Charcot's triad. One of these symptoms is "intention tremor": the limbs, particularly the arm and hand, shake violently whenever the patient tries to control his movements. The second symptom is slow and "scanning" speech, characterized by a pause after each syllable. The third is ocular abnormalities, particularly nystagmus: an involuntary flicking of the eye back and forth, up and down or around and around. In England the disease is called disseminated sclerosis; in the U.S. it is called multiple sclerosis (sometimes abbreviated MS).

Today multiple sclerosis is the commonest disease of the nervous system affecting men and women in the prime of life in northern Europe and North America. We have learned that the neurological symptoms of the disease are apparently caused by the patchy destruction of the material known as myelin, a system of membranes wrapped in a spiral around the central component of the nerve fiber, the axon. This fatty substance can be compared to the insulation around a telephone wire. When the myelin sheath surrounding a nerve fiber breaks down, the conduction of impulses along the now exposed fiber is disrupted.

Eventually scar tissue forms in the demyelinated areas, producing the hard plaques for which the disease is named.

Although its clinical history, its symptoms and signs and the characteristic scarring of the brain and spinal cord it produces have long been well known, the cause of multiple sclerosis has remained a mystery. I remember my old professor Henry Cohen (now Lord Cohen of Birkenhead) once asking a student what was the cause of disseminated sclerosis. The student scratched his head, looked up and down and replied: "Oh, sir, if you had only asked me ten minutes ago, I could have told you." Cohen said: "What a catastrophe. Ten minutes ago you knew and now no one knows."

A social phenomenon that has developed in recent decades is the founding of societies to support intensive investigation into the causes of crippling diseases of humanity. Perhaps the best-known of these societies has been the National Foundation for Infantile Paralysis; it is because of the great research work organized and financed by this foundation that the problem of poliomyelitis has been solved. On May 1, 1945, a New York woman named Sylvia Lawry, whose brother had developed multiple sclerosis, inserted a small advertisement in *The New York Times* asking for information from anyone who had recovered from the disease. The response Miss Lawry received came instead from hundreds of multiple sclerosis patients and their families seeking the same information. From this very small beginning grew the National Multiple Sclerosis Society. Today the society has about 200 chapters throughout the U.S. and has helped to found the International Federation of Multiple Sclerosis Societies, which today has 18 member

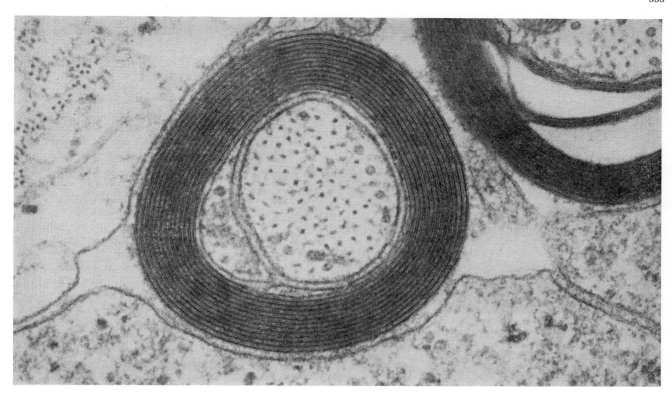

SHEATHS OF MYELIN, single membranes that are wrapped in a tight protective spiral around the central axons of normal nerve fibers, are shown in cross section at a magnification of 105,000 diameters in this electron micrograph. Myelin, a fatty substance, is analogous in function to the insulation on wire; in its absence the conduction of nerve impulses along the axon is disrupted.

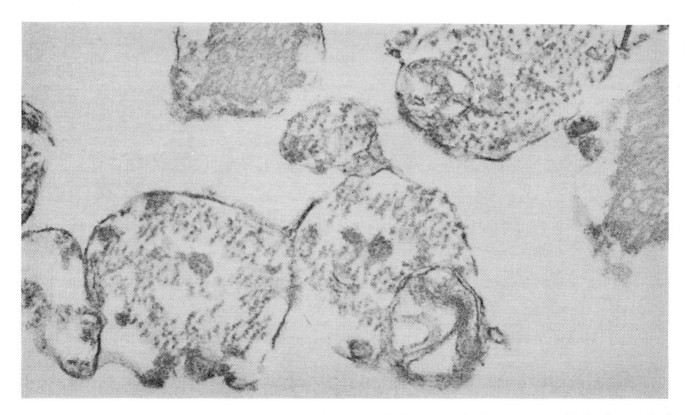

DENUDED NERVE FIBERS, lacking the protection of a myelin sheath, are shown in cross section in this electron micrograph at a magnification of 33,000 diameters. The fibers lie within one of the sclerotic, or hardened, patches whose abundance in the nervous tissue of sufferers from the disease is responsible for the term "multiple sclerosis." Like the micrograph at top of page, this one was made in the Department of Pathology at the Albert Einstein College of Medicine for a study of the neuropathology of the disease.

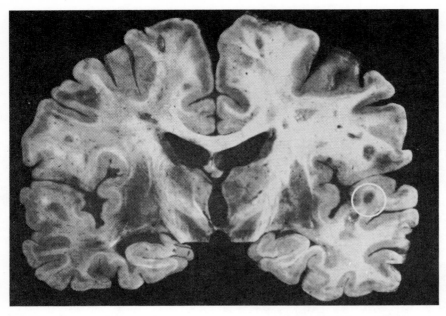

BRAIN CROSS SECTION shows the sclerotic patches, called "islands" and "plaques" by early observers of multiple sclerosis, that lie scattered throughout the subcortical white matter. For purposes of identification one of the plaques (*right*) has been circled in white.

societies in 17 nations around the world. Miss Lawry was also extremely active in convincing Congress to set up (in 1951) the National Institute of Neurological Diseases and Stroke as one of the National Institutes of Health. The society and the institute are today the chief supporters of multiple sclerosis research in the U.S. and elsewhere.

Among the great advances in medical science since World War II has been the growth of a new discipline: geographical medicine. This field of investigation involves intensive study of populations, particularly of populations that have migrated from one environment to another. In this way one may discover what environmental factors are responsible for various diseases. Much of the rather skimpy body of hard fact so far known about multiple sclerosis has been gathered in just this manner.

For example, in 1953 Leonard T. Kurland, who now works at the Mayo Clinic, compared cases of multiple sclerosis in Halifax, Nova Scotia, with cases in New Orleans and found that the disease was three times more prevalent in the northern city than in the southern one. Kurland also found that multiple sclerosis was more prevalent among the whites of each city than among the blacks (most of Nova Scotia's 14,000 blacks live in Halifax). A similar north-south gradient has been found in Europe, where multiple sclerosis appears to be three times commoner in the countries of northern Europe than it is in areas along the Mediterranean [*see illustration on pages 356 and 357*]. For a long time climate was thought to be the factor responsible for such differences. This hypothesis, however, seems to be contradicted by surveys of countries such as Japan; multiple sclerosis is equally uncommon in both the northernmost and the southernmost islands of that nation. Moreover, there are areas in northern Europe, such as the Faeroe Islands and the coast of Norway, where the disease is relatively uncommon.

In 1947 I emigrated from England to South Africa, where I was surprised to find a marked difference in the prevalence of certain diseases among white South Africans compared with my experience in England. Multiple sclerosis, for instance, was reported to be extremely uncommon; many neurologists who had been trained in Europe and knew multiple sclerosis well stated that they had not seen a single South-African-born white with the disease. Shortly after my arrival in the country I therefore undertook to study all the patients who had been diagnosed as having multiple sclerosis at the five main teaching hospitals in South Africa during the preceding 10 years. There were, I found, 27 probable cases of multiple sclerosis. Of these 14 were immigrants from the United Kingdom or northern Europe, although such immigrants comprised less than 10 percent of the total white population. Clearly multiple sclerosis was extremely un-

common among white persons born in South Africa.

Since 1956, with support from the U.S. National Multiple Sclerosis Society, I have undertaken an intensive study of the annual incidence, prevalence and mortality of multiple sclerosis in South Africa. This has involved the cooperation of many physicians, lay organizations, the press and the radio. The South African Multiple Sclerosis Society was formed in the course of this work and helped greatly with the research. I found that among immigrants from the United Kingdom and northern Europe multiple sclerosis is common, with an incidence of about 50 cases per 100,000 of population. This incidence is about the same order of magnitude recorded for northern Europe. Among immigrants from southern Europe only a third as many contract the disease. Among the English-speaking South-African-born whites only a fourth as many contract it, and among Afrikaans-speaking South-African-born whites only an eleventh as many do so. Multiple sclerosis does occur but is extremely uncommon among the Cape Colored and among the Asians of Natal (chiefly of Hindu origin). Not a single patient with multiple sclerosis has been found among South Africa's 12 million Bantu, although in the major cities of South Africa there are good Bantu hospitals with neurologists who are well able to diagnose the disease.

The elevenfold difference in the prevalence of multiple sclerosis between the immigrants from the United Kingdom and northern Europe and the Afrikaans-speaking South-African-born whites, who are also of northern European stock, shows that multiple sclerosis must be a disease of the environment. Its incidence within families is far too low for multiple sclerosis to be an inherited disease. Two members of the same family are occasionally affected; the number is a little more than would be expected by chance alone. The reason may be that the two have been subjected to the same home environment or perhaps that certain families are more predisposed to the disorder than others.

In 1962 Milton Alter of the University of Minnesota Medical School reported that Jews who immigrated to Israel from northern Europe also showed a high incidence of multiple sclerosis. Jews who were born in Israel, however, show only a sixth the incidence of the European immigrants, and Jews who came from the ghettos of North Africa run an even smaller risk of multiple sclerosis than the Jews born in Israel. The situation in

Australia, which is very similar to South Africa in climate, is quite different. The prevalence of multiple sclerosis is much the same among native-born white Australians as among immigrants to Australia from northern Europe; immigrants to Australia from southern Europe show a lower prevalence than either. In Britain and America those who are economically better off appear to run a slightly greater risk of developing multiple sclerosis than the poor. One more curious fact is that recent research by Alter and myself indicates that in both South Africa and Israel immigrants who come to those countries from northern Europe before the age of 15 run a much smaller risk of developing multiple sclerosis than those who arrive after the age of 15.

What hypothesis best fits these facts? The earliest one was that multiple sclerosis could be related to climate, particularly to the amount of sunshine. With growing knowledge of the geographical distribution of the disease this hypothesis becomes increasingly unlikely. John S. Barlow of the Massachusetts General Hospital has suggested that the geographical distribution of multiple sclerosis better fits geomagnetic latitude than geographic latitude; this too does not offer a really satisfactory answer to the problem. Some scholars have long considered the possible multiple sclerosis agent to be diet. R. L. Swank of the University of Oregon Medical School has suggested that the disease may be caused by a diet that is rich in animal fat; this is the kind of diet commonest in northern Europe and North America, both economically advanced regions. The hypothesis cannot be correct, however, because the South-African-born whites, particularly the Afrikaans-speaking ones, have a diet that is extremely high in animal fat. Although they have a high death rate from coronary thrombosis, these South Africans run a very low risk of developing multiple sclerosis.

There is a most interesting parallel between the epidemiology of multiple sclerosis and that of poliomyelitis. This was first pointed out by David C. Poskanzer of the Massachusetts General Hospital in 1963. Like multiple sclerosis, poliomyelitis in its paralytic form was a disease of the more advanced nations rather than of the less advanced ones, and of economically better-off people rather than of the poor. It occurred in northern Europe and North America much more frequently than in southern Europe or the countries of Africa, Asia or South America. Immigrants to South Africa

from northern Europe ran twice the risk of contracting paralytic poliomyelitis that South-African-born whites ran, and the South-African-born whites ran a much greater risk than nonwhites. Among the Bantu of South Africa paralytic poliomyelitis was rarely an adult disease. During World War II in North Africa cases of paralytic poliomyelitis were commoner among officers in the British and American forces than among men in the other ranks. At the time various wild hypotheses for the difference were proposed; it was even suggested that it arose from the fact that the officers drank whisky whereas men in the other ranks drank beer!

We now understand very well the reason for the strange distribution of paralytic poliomyelitis. Until this century poliomyelitis was a universal infection of infancy and infants hardly ever suffered paralysis from it. The fact that they were occasionally so affected is what gave the disease the name "infantile paralysis." With the improvement of hygiene in the advanced countries of the world more and more people missed infection in early childhood and contracted the disease for the first time at a later age, when the risk that the infection will cause paralysis is much greater.

This explains why the first epidemics of poliomyelitis did not occur until this century and then only in the economically advanced countries. In South Africa examination of Bantu blood samples

shows that the population is consistently infected with poliomyelitis virus in infancy. Most of the white people who grow up in South Africa, particularly the Afrikaans-speaking whites who as infants are usually cared for by Bantu or Cape Colored servants, are infected by the poliomyelitis virus early in life and seldom become paralyzed. Among the white immigrants, however, a larger number had missed this early infection and were infected for the first time in South Africa. Today we do what nature once did for all of us and deliberately infect our infants with a variety of living poliomyelitis viruses: the Sabin vaccine.

Let us compare prevaccine poliomyelitis with multiple sclerosis. Multiple sclerosis is a common disease of the nervous system in northern Europe and the northern part of the U.S. and is rather rare in the less economically advanced southern regions. Like paralytic poliomyelitis, multiple sclerosis is extremely uncommon in Japan, where until recently human excrement was used to fertilize crops. It is also uncommon in South America. In South Africa the native-born white children, particularly in Afrikaans-speaking families, are cared for by nonwhite servants whose home hygiene is primitive. The children are therefore likely to develop many infections early in childhood. White immigrants from Europe who come before the age of 15 would likewise be infected early, develop natural resistance and so be protected from a later infection. Conversely, in

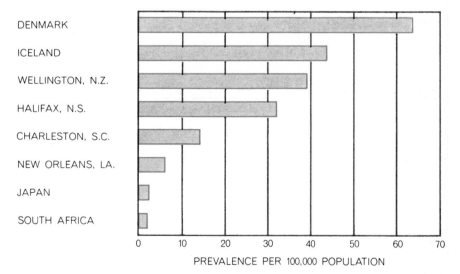

PREVALENCE OF MULTIPLE SCLEROSIS is far from uniform. The graph records the number of victims of the disease per year per 100,000 population, but the data are not all for the same year. In the case of South Africa the figure applies only to native-born white residents and excludes white immigrants. An apparent connection between greater and lesser prevalence of the disease and the coolness or warmness of the climate has been disproved.

Australia the primitive nonwhite population has very limited contact with the white settlers, and the entire white population has a high level of domestic hygiene. In that country there is no great difference in the prevalence of multiple sclerosis between white immigrants from northern Europe and Australian-born whites. Within Australia, multiple sclerosis is commoner in the temperate state of Tasmania, far to the south, than in the more tropical northern states. It is even commoner in New Zealand.

On the basis of the data from Israel and South Africa, John Kurtzke of the Georgetown University Medical School has suggested as an alternative hypothesis that multiple sclerosis is "caught" at about age 15 and that the risk of contracting the disease will depend on where one happens to be on attaining

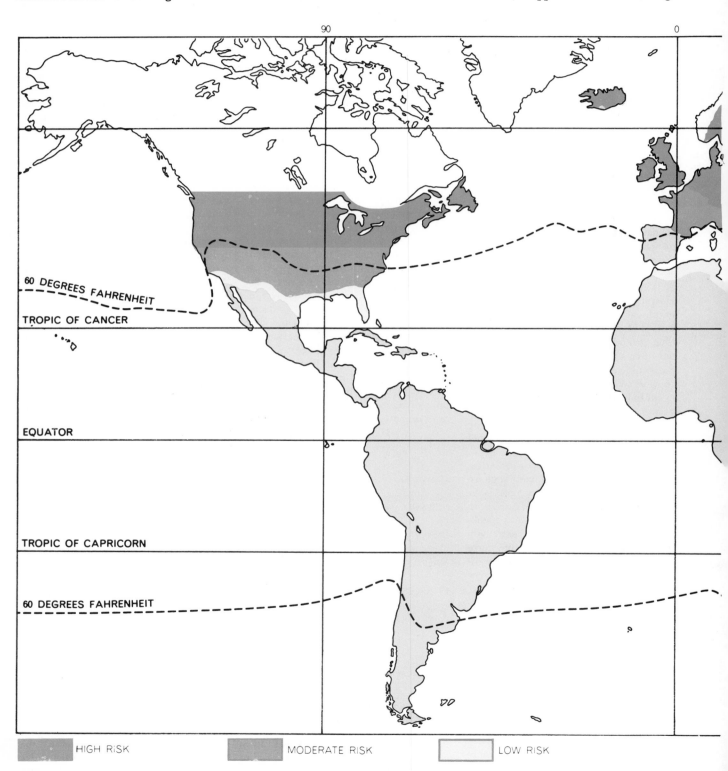

HIGH RISK   MODERATE RISK   LOW RISK

WORLDWIDE DISTRIBUTION of multiple sclerosis is plotted on this map by distinguishing between populations whose risk of contracting the disease is known to be high to moderate (*darker colors*) and those whose risk is known to be low (*lightest color*). For some regions, such as central Asia, Alaska and parts of Canada, the data are too few to allow this distinction. For others the as-that age. If one is in a high-prevalence area at age 15, the risk is high; if one is in a low-prevalence area, the risk is low. Thus immigrants who come to South Africa from Europe after age 15 carry their high risk with them, and those who arrive before that age have the advantage of residence in a low-risk region. Whether my belief (that multiple sclerosis is normally an infection of early childhood) or Kurtzke's hypothesis (that it is caught wherever one happens to be at the age of 15) is correct, we both agree that multiple sclerosis is almost certainly a virus infection of childhood, and that the virus responsible is probably one of the little-understood "slow," or latent, viruses.

It is now known that certain unusual viruses can remain latent in the nervous system for many years without pro-

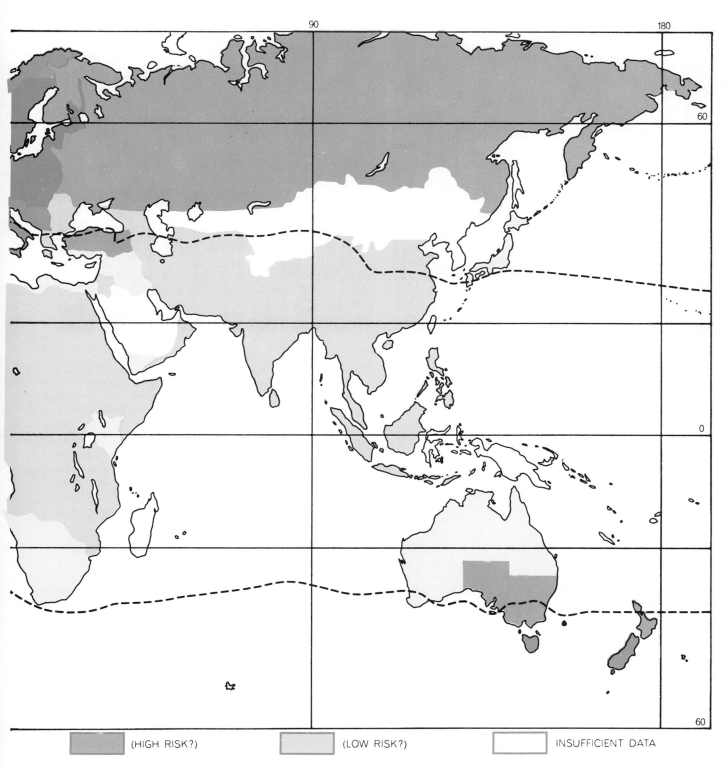

(HIGH RISK?)   (LOW RISK?)   INSUFFICIENT DATA

signment to either extreme is tentative. A comparison of the prevalence of the disease among the native-born and among immigrants to such nations as South Africa, Israel and Australia in the years following World War II suggests strong parallels between multiple sclerosis and infantile paralysis; both diseases are most commonly found among populations with high standards of domestic hygiene.

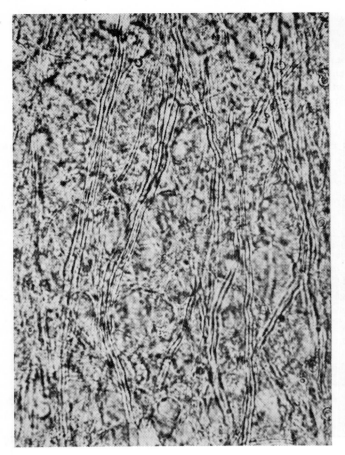
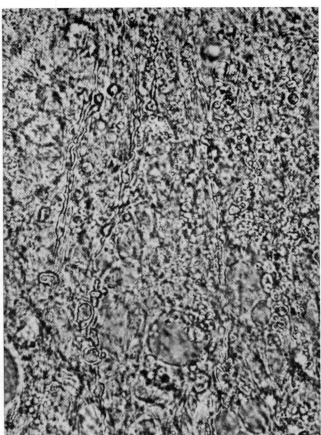

LABORATORY PROOF that a demyelinating factor is present in the blood of multiple sclerosis victims is seen in these two micrographs from an experiment by Murray B. Bornstein of the Albert Einstein College of Medicine. At left is a living culture of rat brain tissue; the numerous strands running generally from top to bottom of the micrograph are normal nerve axons, sheathed in myelin. The culture is seen at right in a micrograph made eight hours after serum from a patient undergoing an acute exacerbation of the disease was added to the nutrient medium. Most of the sheaths have been fragmented and the myelin has been reduced to droplets.

ducing symptoms. A latent virus is suspected as the causative agent of scrapie, a nervous disorder found in sheep. Another example is the agent responsible for "kuru," a disease that once brought death due to generalized paralysis to about 10 percent of the members of the Fore tribe in New Guinea. Originally thought to be the result of genetic factors, kuru has now been transmitted from human patients to chimpanzees and has subsequently been passed on from one chimpanzee to another. The incubation period is initially very long but shortens somewhat with repeated passage, a pattern that is typical of virus infections. It thus appears that kuru is caused by a virus that can remain latent in the nervous system for a long time. In New Guinea the disease was probably spread by the tribal ritual of "cerebrocannibalism," or the eating of human brains, in a situation where the brains were already infected with the kuru virus.

The virus responsible for kuru and other newly discovered latent viruses are strange forms of life indeed. They are difficult to study in our present state of knowledge; we do not yet know how to culture them nor have they been seen even with the electron microscope. They do not cause the biochemical reaction known as complement fixation, which normally assists in the detection of viruses, and what is even more remarkable, their infectivity is affected neither by boiling nor by lengthy immersion in Formalin.

Today, a century after Charcot recognized multiple sclerosis as a distinct medical entity, it remains a disease with an unknown cause, an unpredictable course, an undiscovered cure and not even a simple laboratory test to confirm its diagnosis. So far the best clue to the etiology of the disease has come from the study of multiple sclerosis among populations in different parts of the world. The hypothesis that best fits the few facts is that multiple sclerosis is normally a virus infection of childhood and that it has a long latent period. If the early infection is missed and occurs for the first time in early adult life, there may be a precarious balance between allergy and immunity to the virus that produces the alternating exacerbations and remissions that are characteristic of the disease. To investigate this hypothesis the National Multiple Sclerosis Society has channeled a significant proportion of its resources into improving virus technology and into the search for a multiple sclerosis virus.

The multiple sclerosis problem is going to be solved. All the evidence points to its being a disease of the environment. The most likely environmental factor is infection by one of the latent viruses, infective agents that can remain relatively quiescent in the central nervous system for many years. When the search for the virus eventually succeeds and leads to an effective treatment or preventive for this disease, the key to success will have been provided by geographical medicine.

The Flow of Energy in a Hunting Society

by William B. Kemp
September 1971

Early man obtained food and fuel from the wild plants and animals of his environment. How the energy from such sources is channeled is investigated in a community of modern Eskimos on Baffin Island

The investment of energy in hunting and gathering has provided man's livelihood for more than 99 percent of human history. Over the past 10,000 years the investment of energy in agriculture, with its higher yield per unit of input, has transformed most hunting peoples into farmers. Among the most viable of the remaining hunters are the Eskimos of Alaska, Canada and Greenland. What are the characteristic patterns of energy flow in a hunting group? How is the available energy channeled among the various activities of the group in order for the group to survive? In 1967 and 1968 I undertook to study such energy flows in an isolated Eskimo village in the eastern Canadian Arctic.

I observed two village households in particular. When I lived in the village, one of the two households was characterized by its "modern" ways; the other was more "traditional." I was able to measure the energy inputs and energy yields of both households in considerable detail. (The quantitative data presented here are based on observations made during a 54-week period from February 14, 1967, to March 1, 1968.) The different patterns of energy use exhibited by the two households help to illuminate the process of adaptation to nonhunting systems of livelihood and social behavior that faces all contemporary hunting societies.

For the Eskimos the most significant factor in the realignment of economic and social activity has been the introduction of a cash economy. The maintenance of a hunting way of life within the framework of such an economy calls for a new set of adaptive strategies. Money, or its immediate equivalent, is now an important component in the relation between the Eskimo hunter and the natural environment.

The village where I worked is one of the few remaining all-Eskimo settlements along the southern coast of Baffin Island on the northern side of Hudson Strait [*see illustrations on next page*]. In this village hunting still dominates the general pattern of daily activity. The economic adaptation is supported by the household routine of the women and is reflected in the play of the children. Villages of this type were once the characteristic feature of the settlement pattern of southern Baffin Island. Within recent years, however, many Eskimos have abandoned the solitary life in favor of larger and more acculturated settlements.

The community I studied is in an area of indented coastline that runs in a northwesterly direction extending from about 63 to 65 degrees north latitude. The land rises sharply from the shore to an interior plateau that is deeply incised by valleys, many containing streams and lakes that serve as the only routes for overland travel. At these latitudes summer activities can proceed during some 22 hours of daylight; the longest winter night lasts 18 hours. Perhaps the most noticeable feature of the Hudson Strait environment is tides of as much as 45 feet. Such tides create a large littoral environment; bays become empty valleys, islands appear and disappear and strong ocean currents prevail. In winter the tides build rough barriers of broken sea ice, and at low tide the steeper shorelines are edged with sheer ice walls. In summer coastal navigation and the selection of safe harbors are difficult, and in winter crossing from the sea ice to the land tries the temper of men and the strength of dogs and machines.

The varying length of the day, the seasonal changes of temperature, the tides and to some extent the timing of the annual freeze-up and breakup are predictable events, easily built into the round of economic activity. Superimposed on these events is the variability and irregularity of temperature, moisture and wind, which affect the pattern of energy flow for the community on a day-to-day basis. In winter the temperatures reach −50 degrees Fahrenheit, with a mean around −30. In summer the temperature may climb above 80 degrees, although temperatures in the low 50's are more typical. Throughout the year there may be large temperature changes from one day to the next. Midwinter temperatures have gone from −30 degrees to above freezing in a single night, bringing a thaw and sometimes even rain.

The heaviest precipitation is in the spring and fall, and strong winds can arise any day throughout the year. Winds of more than 40 miles per hour are common; on four occasions I measured steady winds in excess of 70 m.p.h. Speaking generally, the weather is most stable in March and April and least stable from late September into November.

Within this setting the Eskimos harvest at least 20 species of game. All the marine and terrestrial food chains are exploited in the quest for food, and all habitats—from the expanses of sea ice and open water to the microhabitats of

BLEAK TERRAIN of the Canadian Arctic is seen in the aerial photograph shown on page 364. The steep shore and treeless hinterland are part of an islet in Hudson Strait off the coast of southern Baffin Island. By hunting sea mammals the Eskimos of the region can obtain enough food and valuable by-products to keep them well above the level of survival.

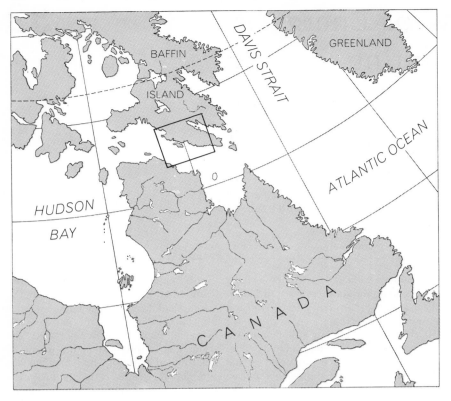

BAFFIN ISLAND extends for nearly 1,000 miles in the area between the mouth of Hudson Bay and the Greenland coast. The villagers' hunting ranges lie within the black rectangle.

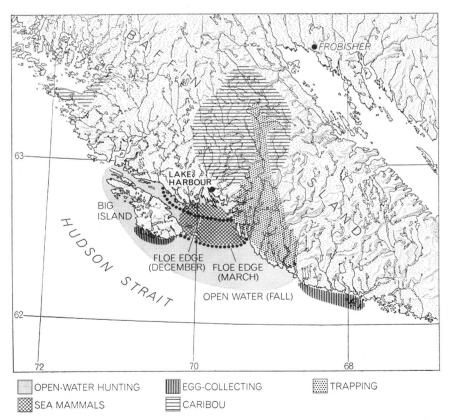

HUNTING RANGES of one Eskimo village in southern Baffin Island change with the season. The most productive months of the year are spent hunting in coastal waters. Trapping and caribou hunting, generally winter activities, carry the hunters into different areas.

tidal flats, leeward waters and protected valleys—are utilized. Traditionally the Eskimos of southern Baffin Island are mainly hunters of sea mammals: the small common (or ring) seal, the much larger bearded seal and on occasion the beluga whale and the walrus.

Survival in such a harsh environment has two primary requirements. The first is an adequate caloric intake in terms of food and the second is maintenance of a suitable microclimate in terms of shelter and clothing. In the village where I worked the Eskimos met these requirements by hunting and trapping and by buying imported foods and materials. They also bought ammunition for their guns and gasoline for two marine engines and two snowmobiles, transportation aids that increased their hunting efficiency. The money for such purchases was obtained by the sale of skins and furs (products of the hunt) and of stone and ivory carvings (products of artistic skill and of the Eskimos' recognition of consumer preferences). Because government "social assistance" and some work for wages were available, certain individuals had an occasional source of additional cash.

The daily maintenance of life in the village called for an initial input of human energy in the pursuit of game, in the mining of soapstone and in the manufacture of handicrafts. The expenditures of human energy for the 54-week period were 12.8 million kilocalories. They were augmented by expenditures of imported energy: 10,900 rounds of ammunition and 885 gallons of gasoline. The result was the acquisition of 12.8 million kilocalories of edible food from the land and seven million kilocalories of viscera that were used as dog food. To this was added 7.5 million kilocalories of purchased food. By eating the game and the purchased food the hunters and their dependents were able to achieve a potential caloric input of 3,000 kilocalories per day, which was enough to sustain a level of activity well above the maintenance level. The general pattern of energy flow into, through and out of the village is shown in the illustration on pages 362 and 363.

During my stay the population of the village varied between 26 and 29. The people lived in four separate dwellings. One, a wood house, had been built from prefabricated materials supplied by the government. The other three were the traditional *quagmaq:* a low wood-frame tent some 20 feet long, 15 feet wide and seven feet high. These structures were covered with canvas, old

BEARDED SEAL (*left*) is a relatively uncommon and welcome kill. It weighs more than 400 pounds, compared with the common seal's 80 pounds, and its skin is a favorite material. Flat-bottomed rowboat (*rear*) is used to retrieve seals killed at the floe-ice edge.

mailbags and animal skins and were insulated with a 10-inch layer of dry shrubs. Inside they were lined with pages from mail-order catalogues and decorated with a fantastic array of trinkets and other objects. The rear eight feet of each *quagmaq* was occupied by a large sleeping platform, leaving some 180 square feet for household activities during waking hours. The wood house (Household II) was occupied by six people comprising a single family unit. One *quagmaq* (Household I) was occupied by nine people: a widower, his son, three daughters, a son-in-law and three grandchildren.

The *quagmaq* was heated in the traditional manner with stone lamps that burned seal oil. The occupants of the wood house heated it with a kerosene stove. In a period when the highest outdoor temperature during the day was −30 degrees, I measured the consumption of fuel and recorded the indoor temperatures of the wood house and the *quagmaq*. The *quagmaq* was heated by three stone lamps, two at each side of the sleeping platform and one near the entrance. In a 24-hour period the three lamps burned some 250 ounces (slightly less than two imperial gallons) of seal oil. The fat from a 100-pound seal shot in midwinter yields approximately 640 ounces of oil, which is about a 60-hour supply at this rate of consumption. The

interior temperature of the *quagmaq* never rose above 68 degrees. The average was around 56 degrees, with troughs in the low 30's because the lamps were not tended through the night.

In the wood house the kerosene stove burned a little less than three imperial gallons every 24 hours. This represented a daily expenditure of about $1 for fuel oil during the winter months. (Since 1969 this cost has been fully subsidized by the government.) The interior temperature of the house sometimes reached 80 degrees, and the nightly lows were seldom below 70. One result of the difference between the indoor and outdoor temperature—frequently more than 100 degrees—was that the members of Household II complained that they were uncomfortably warm, particularly when they were carving or doing some other kind of moderately strenuous work.

Before the Eskimos of southern Baffin Island had acquired outboard motors, snowmobiles and a reliable supply of fuel they shifted their settlements with the seasons. Fall campsites were the most stable element in the settlement pattern and were the location for the *quagmaq* shelters. During the rest of the year the size and location of the camps depended on which of the food resources were being exploited.

The movements of settlements to resources served to minimize the distance

a hunter needed to travel in a day. Thus little energy was wasted traversing unproductive terrain, and good hunting weather could be exploited immediately. This is no longer the practice. Long trips by the hunters are common, but seasonal movements involving an entire household are rare. Therefore the location of the village never shifts. The four dwellings of the village I studied are more or less occupied throughout the year. Tents are still used in summer, but they are set up within sight of the winter houses. There is a major move each August, when the villagers set up camp at the trading post, a day's journey from the village. There they await the coming of the annual medical and supply ships and also take advantage of any wage labor that may be available.

The hunters' ability to get to the right place at the right time is ensured by a large whaleboat with a small inboard engine, a 22-foot freight canoe driven by a 20-horsepower outboard motor, and the two snowmobiles. In addition the villagers have several large sledges and keep 34 sled dogs. The impact of motorized transport (particularly of the marine engines) on the stability of year-round residence and on the increase in hunting productivity is evident in the remark of an older man: "As my son gets motors for the boats, we are always living here. As my son always gets animals we are no longer hungry. Do you know what I mean?"

The threat of hunger is a frequent theme in village conversation, but the oral tradition that serves as history gives little evidence of constant privation for the population of southern Baffin Island. Although older men and women tell stories of hard times, the fear of starvation did not generate the kind of social response known elsewhere. In the more hostile parts of the Arctic female infanticide was common well into the first quarter of this century. The existence of the practice is supported by statistical data compiled by Edward M. Weyer, Jr., in 1932. For example, among the Netsilik Eskimos the ratio of females to males in the population younger than 19 was 48 per 100; in the Barren Grounds area the ratio was 46 per 100.

Census data from Baffin Island in 1912 indicate that female infanticide was not common along the southern coast. In that year a missionary recorded the population for the region; the total was some 400 Eskimos. Among those younger than 19 there were 89 females per 100 males. Among those 19 or older the ratio was 127 females per 100 males; hunters often had short lives. The vital statistics that have been kept since 1927 by the Royal Canadian Mounted Police support the impression that death by starvation was a rare occurrence on southern Baffin Island. On the other hand, hunting accidents were the cause of 15 percent of the deaths. The causes of trouble or death most usually cited by the villagers were peculiarities of the weather, ice conditions and mishaps of the hunt. Starvation was commonplace in the dog population, but for human groups disasters were local. A 75-year-old resident of the southern coast was able to recall only one year when severe hunger affected a large segment of the population.

A major factor in reducing the possibility of hunger is the Eskimos' increasing access to imported goods. Although store foods are obviously of prime importance in this respect, energy in the form of gasoline for fuel is also significant. The snowmobiles in the village are owned by an individual in each household, but all the hunters help to buy the gasoline needed to run these machines and the marine engines. The two snowmobiles consumed about twice as much fuel as the two boat motors. A snowmobile pulling a loaded sled can run for about 35 minutes on a gallon of gasoline. A trip from the village to the

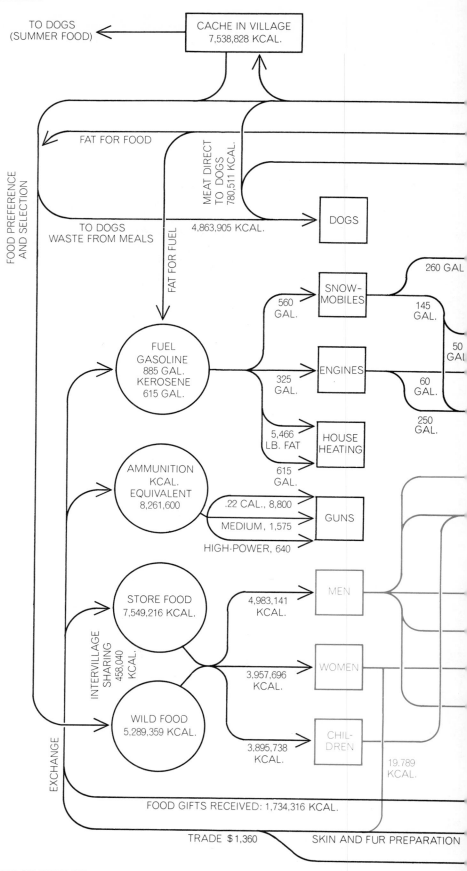

FLOW OF ENERGY within two hunting households is outlined in this diagram. The inputs and yields were recorded by the author in kilocalories and other units during his 13-month residence in an Eskimo hunting village. The input of imported energy in the form of fuel and ammunition, along with the input of native game and imported foodstuffs (*far*

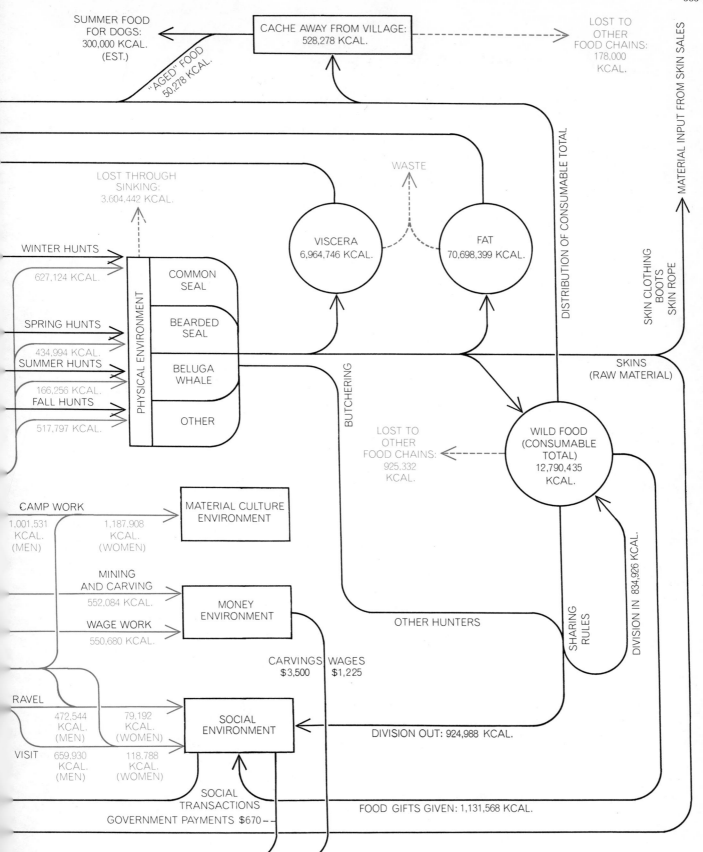

SUMMER FOOD
FOR DOGS:
300,000 KCAL.
(EST.)

CACHE AWAY FROM VILLAGE:
528,278 KCAL.

LOST TO
OTHER
FOOD CHAINS:
178,000
KCAL.

MATERIAL INPUT FROM SKIN SALES

"AGED" FOOD
50,278 KCAL.

LOST THROUGH
SINKING:
3,604,442 KCAL.

WASTE

VISCERA
6,964,746 KCAL.

FAT
70,698,399 KCAL.

DISTRIBUTION OF CONSUMABLE TOTAL

SKIN CLOTHING
BOOTS
SKIN ROPE

WINTER HUNTS

627,124 KCAL.

COMMON
SEAL

SPRING HUNTS

434,994 KCAL.

SUMMER HUNTS

166,256 KCAL.

FALL HUNTS

517,797 KCAL.

PHYSICAL ENVIRONMENT

BEARDED
SEAL

BELUGA
WHALE

OTHER

BUTCHERING

LOST TO
OTHER
FOOD CHAINS:
925,332
KCAL.

SKINS
(RAW MATERIAL)

WILD FOOD
(CONSUMABLE
TOTAL)
12,790,435
KCAL.

CAMP WORK

1,001,531
KCAL.
(MEN)

1,187,908
KCAL.
(WOMEN)

MATERIAL CULTURE
ENVIRONMENT

MINING
AND CARVING

552,084 KCAL.

WAGE WORK

550,680 KCAL.

MONEY
ENVIRONMENT

OTHER HUNTERS

SHARING
RULES

DIVISION IN 834,926 KCAL.

CARVINGS WAGES
$3,500 $1,225

RAVEL

472,544
KCAL.
(MEN)

79,192
KCAL.
(WOMEN)

SOCIAL
ENVIRONMENT

DIVISION OUT: 924,988 KCAL.

VISIT

659,930
KCAL.
(MEN)

118,788
KCAL.
(WOMEN)

SOCIAL
TRANSACTIONS

GOVERNMENT PAYMENTS $670

FOOD GIFTS GIVEN: 1,131,568 KCAL.

left), enabled the four hunters and their kin (*left, color*) to heat their dwellings and power their machines (*left, black*), and also to join in many seasonal activities (*colored arrows*) that utilized various parts of the environment in the manner indicated (*right*).

The end results of these combined inputs of energy are shown as a series of yields and losses from waste and other causes (*far right*). The net yields then feed back through various channels (*lines at borders of diagram*) to reach the starting point again as inputs.

edge of the floe ice 10 miles away took 55 minutes in each direction and cost nearly $3.

Variations in fuel purchases are not necessarily correlated with variations in hunting yield or cash income. Debt can be used to overcome fluctuations in income, and the desire to visit distant relatives may be as important a consideration as the need to hunt. The largest monthly gasoline purchase was made in September, 1967. Wages paid for construction work were used to buy a combined total of 170 gallons of gasoline. This fuel was utilized for the intensive hunting of sea mammals in order to make up for a summer when the Eskimos had been earning wages instead of hunting.

Hunting was a year-long village occupation in spite of considerable seasonal variation in the kind and amount of game available. An analysis of the species represented in the Eskimos' annual kill confirms the predominance of sea mammals. The common seal (with an average weight of 80 pounds) provided nearly two-thirds of the villagers' game calories. When one adds bearded seals (with an average weight of more than 400 pounds) and occasional beluga whales, the sea mammals' contribution was more than 83 percent of the annual total. Caribou accounted for a little more than 4 percent of the total, and all the other land mammals together came to less than 1 percent. Indeed, the contribution of eider ducks and duck eggs to the villagers' diet (some 7 percent) was larger than that of all land mammals

combined. The harvest of birds, fish, clams and small land mammals may not contribute significantly to the total number of calories, but it does provide diversity in hunting activities and in diet.

The common seal is hunted throughout the year and is the basic source of food for both the Eskimos and their dogs. From January through March sea mammals are hunted first at breathing holes in the sea ice and then at the boundary between open water and the landfast ice. The intensity of sea-mammal hunting during the winter months varies according to the amount of food left over from the fall hunt and the alternative prospects for trapping foxes and hunting caribou.

In winter some variety in the food supply is provided by the hunting of sea birds and small land mammals, but for the most part seal meat remains the basic item in the diet. In April hunting along the edge of the floe ice is intensified, and the canoe is hauled to the open water beyond the floe ice for hunting the bearded seals. In May and June hunting along the edge of the floe ice (on foot or by canoe) continues; the quarry is the seal and the beluga whale. In late spring seals are also stalked as they bask on top of the ice. By the middle of July open-water hunting is the most common activity, although much of the potential harvest is lost because the animals sink when they are shot. In 1967 and 1968 the villagers lost five whales, five bearded seals and 47 common seals.

The sinking of marine mammals serves to illustrate the interplay of physi-

cal, biological and technological factors the hunter must contend with. In late spring the seal begins to fast and therefore loses fat. At the same time the melting of snow and sea ice reduces the salinity of the surface waters. These interacting factors reduce the buoyancy of the seal, and a killed seal is likely to sink unless it is immediately secured with a hand-thrown harpoon. The high-powered rifle separates the hunter from his prey; it may increase the frequency of kill but it does not increase the frequency of harvest. In 30 hours of continuous hunting on July 20 and 21 only five out of the 13 seals killed were actually harvested.

From May through July the hunts are usually successful, even with sinkage losses as high as 60 percent. It is at this time of the year that a large amount of meat goes into dog food for the summer and early fall. Meat is also cached in areas the Eskimos expect to visit when they are trapping the following winter. The caches are deliberately only partly secured with rocks; their purpose is to bait areas of potential trapping. In May the variety of foods begins to increase. Seabirds, ptarmigans, geese, fish, clams and duck eggs are taken in large numbers and become the most important component of the food input. Only an occasional seal or the edible skin of a beluga whale is carried home to eat. The great variety of small game is consumed within a few days. With the exception of duck eggs, about half of which are cached until after Christmas, none of these foods is stored.

In September the sea mammals again become the primary objective. Open-water hunting continues until early November, when the sea begins to freeze. Just before freeze-up the beluga whales pass close to the village and are hunted from the shore with the aid of rifles and harpoons. The success of the fall whale-hunting is the key to the villagers' evaluation of the adequacy of their winter provisions.

As the sea ice thickens and extends, hunting seals at their breathing holes in the bays becomes the most common activity. The unfavorable interaction of physical, biological and technological factors that affects open-water seal-hunting in spring and summer is reversed where breathing-hole hunting is concerned. As the sea begins to freeze, some seals migrate away from the land in order to stay in open water. Others remain closer to the shore, using their claws and teeth to maintain a cone-shaped hole through the ice. The seal's breathing is

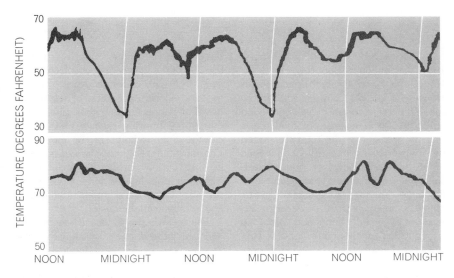

CONTRASTING METHODS of heating maintained different house microclimates with the consumption of different amounts of fuel. In Household I (*top*), the more traditional one, the use of three lamps that burned seal oil produced an average temperature of 58 degrees F. A kerosene stove (*bottom*) in the more modern Household II kept the average closer to 75 degrees. As a result Household II used three gallons a day to the other's two.

now confined to specific points the hunter can easily find on the surface of the ice. The hunting technique calls for locating the breathing holes and distributing the available men to maximize the chance of a kill. The hunting skill calls for the patience to wait motionless for periods of as much as two hours and to depend on hearing rather than sight. By mid-December the new ice is covered by a deep layer of drifting snow, and the breathing holes become harder to locate. The Eskimos then move out to the edge of the floe ice and the seasonal cycle begins anew.

The analysis of hunting success on a month-to-month basis shows great variability in the total caloric input and in each member's contribution to the total [*see illustration on next page*]. The peak hunting months for the two households were June (some 2.5 million kilocalories), October (more than three million) and November (2.9 million). Stockpiling provides the motivation for the big October and November kills. Game taken in these months will remain frozen and unspoiled through the winter and will help to feed the hunters and their dependents in February, March and April.

In the fall days grow short and winds often restrict the choice of hunting areas. Daylight hours are utilized to the full, and the evening darkness is filled with the sound of the hunters struggling to get their catch across the difficult terrain of the tidal flats. In this period almost all the food is brought back to the village; it is stored in a small meat house, on elevated platforms, under the hulls of old boats and on top of the wood house. A few of the seals shot in early fall are cached on the land in order for the meat to "age." These carcasses are retrieved in the spring, and the meat is considered one of the more flavorsome food inputs.

The large kill in June results from the fact that the daylight hours are at a maximum and that there is a much greater choice of resources. If weather conditions hamper open-water hunting, basking seals can be pursued. Under conditions of severe wind or poor ice, spearfishing for arctic char is possible and duck eggs can be collected. Summer hunts last for three or four days; the hunters sleep during the few hours of least light or during brief pauses in the hunt. Game killed in June will thaw in the summer months, so that almost all the two million kilocalories of sea mammals harvested that month is destined for the dogs.

Compared with the high caloric inputs of the spring and fall, winter hunting is much less productive in terms of

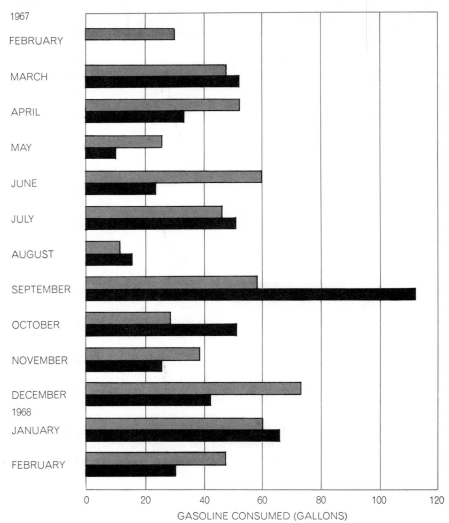

GASOLINE CONSUMPTION by two Eskimo households is shown over a 12-month period. The fuel was used to power the two snowmobiles and the marine engines that greatly increased the villagers' hunting efficiency. Purchases by the three hunters of Household I are shown in black and those by the single hunter of Household II are in gray. Gasoline is second only to imported food among the exotic energy inputs to the Eskimo hunting society.

total harvest. For example, February, 1967, was only a fair hunting month for Household I and a very bad month for Household II. The combined kill (more than 70 percent common seals) provided only 166,500 kilocalories of food; more than 90 percent of the total was taken by Household I. A month of low food input does not, however, mean hardship. Such a February is an example of the important role storage plays in the villagers' management of energy resources. The fall hunt had provided enough food for the winter, and as a result in February the villagers did more visiting than hunting. Visiting is therefore one mechanism that takes hunters out of the productive sector of the economy and creates a better balance between energy availability and energy need. The same pattern holds true

throughout the winter months, so that the 500,000 calories that was harvested from February through April was as much a caloric expression of leisure as it was of poorer hunting conditions. The differential hunting success of individuals or of households in the month of February did not greatly influence energy distribution within the social unit. Although one hunter may have more skins to trade, food is stored in bulk and is generally available to all.

The records show that although caribou are hunted only occasionally, the animals are then present in substantial numbers. In the lean February of 1967 caribou made up some 7 percent of the kill, providing about 11,000 kilocalories of food. The following month caribou comprised more than 37 percent of the kill, amounting to a total of 90,000 kilo-

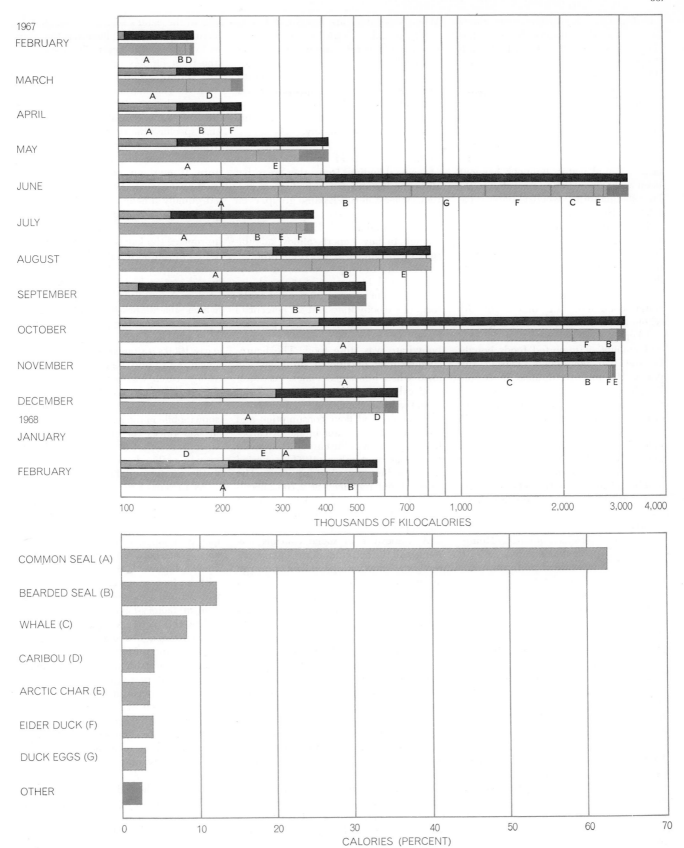

1967
FEBRUARY
MARCH
APRIL
MAY
JUNE
JULY
AUGUST
SEPTEMBER
OCTOBER
NOVEMBER
DECEMBER
1968
JANUARY
FEBRUARY

100   200   300   400   500   600 700   1,000   2,000   3,000 4,000

THOUSANDS OF KILOCALORIES

COMMON SEAL (A)
BEARDED SEAL (B)
WHALE (C)
CARIBOU (D)
ARCTIC CHAR (E)
EIDER DUCK (F)
DUCK EGGS (G)
OTHER

0   10   20   30   40   50   60   70

CALORIES (PERCENT)

HUNTERS' BAG varies considerably from month to month as a result of chance and preference and also because of seasonal fluctuations. The top graph shows the wild foods acquired by Household I (*black*) and Household II (*gray*) in the course of 13 months. A fish known as arctic char, birds such as murres, geese and ducks, duck eggs and even berries add variety to the Eskimo diet from April through October, while caribou contribute to the smaller game bag of winter months. The 13-month totals, however, show that sea mammals (the common seal in particular) provide most of the Eskimo households' consumable kilocalories (*bottom graph*).

calories. After that caribou were almost absent from the villagers' diet until January, 1968, when they furnished nearly 70 percent of the kill for a yield of 245,-000 kilocalories.

Today no Eskimo community depends exclusively on hunting for its food. Each day the adults of the village consumed an average of half a pound of imported wheat flour in the form of a bread called bannock, a pan-baked mixture of flour, lard, salt and water. Bannock has long been an Eskimo staple; it is eaten in the largest quantities where hunting has fallen off the most.

In addition to this basic breadstuff the villagers consumed imported sugar, biscuits, candy and soft drinks, and they fed nonnursing infants and young children a kind of reconstituted milk. A daily ration consisted of 48 ounces of water containing 1.2 ounces of dry whole milk and 1.7 ounces of sugar.

I kept a 13-month record of the kind and amount of imported foods bought by the two households. During this period the more traditional household bought store foods totaling almost 3.3 million kilocalories and the more modern household store foods totaling 3.75 million kilocalories. The purchases provided 531,000 kilocalories of store food per adult in Household I and 477,300 per adult in Household II. The larger number of adults in Household I is reflected in the size of its flour purchase, which made up 53 percent of the total, compared with 40 percent in Household II. The larger purchase of lard by Household II (23 percent compared with 10 percent) is a measure of preference, not consumption. Household I prefers to use the fat from whales for bannock; hence its smaller purchase [*see illustration on next page*]. The consumption of the third imported staple—sugar—was about the same in both households.

The quantities of store food that were bought from month to month showed substantial variations. In March, 1967, the store purchases of the two households rose above one million kilocalories because both households received a social-assistance payment. In February, 1968, social assistance was again given each household, and as before the money was used to buy more than the average amount of food. The rather high caloric input from store food in September, 1967, is attributable to money available from wage labor.

Store foods, unlike food from the land, are not stockpiled and they are not often shared. Except for the staples and tea, tobacco and candy, there is no strong desire for non-Eskimo foods.

When vegetables are bought, it is usually by mistake. Canned meats, although occasionally eaten, are not recognized as "real" food. The villagers like fruit, but it is never bought in large quantity. Jam, peanut butter, honey, molasses, oatmeal and crackers all find their way into the two households. They are consumed almost immediately.

The data on food input support the general findings from other areas that show the Eskimo diet to be high in protein. At least in this Eskimo group, even though imported carbohydrates were readily available and there was money enough to buy imports almost ad libitum, the balance was in favor of protein.

Over the 13-month period the villagers acquired 44 percent of their calories in the form of protein, 33 percent in the form of carbohydrate and 23 percent in fat. Almost all the protein (93 percent) came from game; 96 percent of the carbohydrate was store food. The figures suggest how nutritional problems can arise when hunting declines. As store-food calories take the place of calories from the hunt, the change frequently involves increased flour consumption and consequently a greater intake of carbohydrate. This was the case in Household II during September, 1967, a period when the family worked for wages. The caloric input remained at 2,700 kilocalories per person per day, but 62 percent of the calories were carbohydrate and only 9 percent were protein.

A framework of social controls surrounds all the activities of the village, directing and mediating the flow of energy in the community. For example, even though all the inhabitants are ostensibly related (either by real kinship or by assigned ties), the community is actually divided into two social groups, each operating with a high degree of economic and social independence. Food is constantly shared within each social group, and the boundary between groups is ignored when a large animal is killed.

Village-wide meals serve to divert a successful hunter's caloric acquisitions for the benefit of a group larger than his own household. The meal that follows the arrival of hunters with a freshly killed seal is the most frequent and the most important of these events. It is called *alopaya*, a term that refers to using one's hands to scoop fresh blood from the open seal carcass. The invitation to participate is shouted by one of the children, and all the villagers gather, the men in one group and the women in another, to eat until they are full. The parts of the seal are apportioned according to the eater's sex. The men start by eating a piece of the liver and the women a piece of the heart. The meat from the front flippers and the first third of the vertebrae and the ribs goes to the women. The men eat from the remaining parts of the seal. This meal, like almost all other Eskimo meals, does not come at any specific time of the day. People eat when they are hungry or, in the case of village-wide meals, when the hunters return. If anything remains at the end of an *alopaya* meal, the leftovers are divided equally among all the families and can be eaten by either sex.

Whaleboats and freight canoes began to replace the kayak for water transportation in southern Baffin Island some 30 years ago; by the end of the 1950's outboard motors had been substituted for oars and paddles. The latter change, which made possible more efficient open-water hunting, coincided with a high market price for sealskins. In the early 1960's a single skin might bring as much as $30, and the value of the annual village catch was between $3,000 and $4,000. The good sealskin market enabled the villagers to buy their first snowmobile in the fall of 1963. A decline in skin prices that began in 1964 has since been offset to some extent by the growth of handicraft sales and by the availability of work for wages.

As a result of these new economic inputs a new kind of material flow is now observable. It consists of the movement of secondhand non-Eskimo goods. The flow is channeled through a network of kinship ties between individuals with an income higher than average and those with an income lower than average. By 1971 anyone who wanted a snowmobile or some other item of factory-made equipment could utilize this network and get what he wanted through a combination of salvage, gift and purchase.

For the individual the exploitation of economic alternatives and the pattern of activity vary according to taste and lifestyle. Although life-style is in large degree dictated by age, the effect within the village is integrative rather than disruptive. A son's snowmobile gives the father the advantage of a quick ride to the edge of the floe ice, and the son can rely on the father's dogs to tow a broken machine or to help pull heavy loads over rough terrain. The integration extends to areas beyond the hunt. At home it is not unusual to find the father making sealskin rope or repairing a sledge while the son carves soapstone. Neither considers the other's work either radical or impossibly old-fashioned.

Social controls also affect the expenditure of personal energy within the household. The losers are the teen-age girls. Among the men of the village there is little emphasis on authority structure or leadership; decision-making is left to the individual. Choices for the most part converge, so that joint efforts are a matter of course. Among the women, however, authority structure is emphasized. A girl is subordinate not only to the older women but also to her male relatives. One can make the general statement that those who because of sex, age and kinship ties are most subject to the demands of others expend a disproportionate amount of energy in household and village chores.

One series of social controls has been radically altered by the introduction of non-Eskimo technology, energy and world view. These controls are the beliefs and rituals relating the world of nature to the world of thought. In the traditional Eskimo society the two worlds were closely related. All living organisms, for example, were believed to have a soul. In his ritual the Eskimo recognized the fragility of the Arctic ecosystem and sought to foster friendly relations with the same animals he hunted for food. Obviously the friendship could not be a worldly one, but it did exist in the realm of the spirit. A measure of the strength of this belief was the great care taken by the Eskimo never to invite unnecessary hardship by offending the soul of the animal he killed.

Today ritual control of the forces of nature and of the food supply has almost disappeared; technology is considered the mainspring of well-being. Prayers may still be said for good hunting and good traveling conditions, and the Sunday service may include an analysis of a hunting success and even a request for guidance in the hunts to follow. Hunting decisions may also be affected by dreams. None of these activities, however, has the regulatory powers of the intricate symbols and beliefs of earlier times. The hunters complain of a change in the seals' behavior. Nowadays, they say, only the young animals are curious and can be coaxed to come closer to the boat or the edge of the floe ice. The mutual trust between man and his food supply has evidently been lost in the report of the high-powered rifle and the rumble of the outboard motor.

What conclusions can we draw from the analysis of energy flows in a hunting society? The Eskimos do not differ from other hunters in that the processes surrounding the quest for food involve much more than a simple interplay of

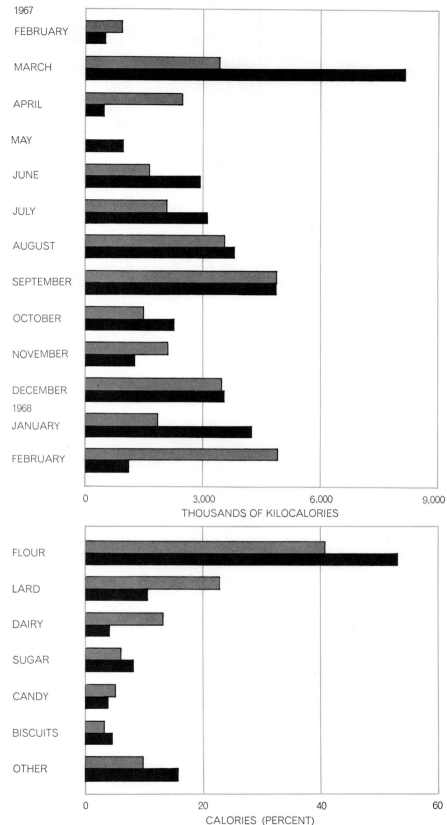

PURCHASES OF IMPORTED FOOD also show large monthly variations. The top graph shows the kilocalorie values of staples such as flour, lard and sugar and of lesser items such as powdered milk, biscuits, soft drinks and candy acquired over 13 months by Household I (*black*) and Household II (*gray*). Most of the flour and lard went to make a kind of bread called bannock. The 13-month totals (*bottom graph*) show how the two households differed in the percentage of all store-food purchases that each allotted to flour and to lard.

COMPOSITION OF DIET is presented for a 13-month period in terms of monthly acquisitions of protein (*top pair of bars*), carbohydrate (*middle pair of bars*) and fat (*bottom pair of bars*), measured in hundreds of grams. The colored bar of each pair indicates the number of grams acquired by hunting and gathering and the black bar indicates the number acquired in the form of store food. Protein outranked the others in total acquisitions: 2.1 million grams, compared with 1.1 million grams of carbohydrate and .7 million grams of fat.

environment and technology. There are many times when a technological advance is fatal to an ecological balance; this was particularly evident in the near-extermination of the caribou herds west of Hudson Bay with the introduction of the rifle and the relaxation of traditional beliefs. In southern Baffin Island, however, there is not yet any evidence of a trend toward "overkill." At the same time that motorized transport has enhanced the ability to kill game, other social and economic factors have acted to reduce the amount of time available for hunting and have kept the kill within bounds. Snowmobiles give quick access to the edge of the floe ice; they also make it easy to visit distant kinsmen. A regular day of rest on Sunday has a religious function; it also contributes to the management of energy resources.

Do hunting societies have a long-term future? In the case of the Eskimo one can reply with a conditional yes. The universal pressure on resources makes continued exploitation of the Arctic a certainty, and Eskimos should be able to profit from these future ventures. Already it is possible to see three distinct groups emerging within Eskimo culture. One of them consists of the wage earners in the larger communities. Another, which is just beginning to make its appearance, is an externally oriented group that seems destined to regulate and control the inputs from the outside world: the non-Eskimo energy flows and material flows that, as we have seen, now play a vital part in the hunters' lives.

Finally, there is a third group, small in numbers but vast in terms of territory, made up of the hunters who will continue the traditional Eskimo participation in the fragile, far-flung Arctic ecosystem. There will be linkages—exchanges of materials and probably of people—between the wage earner and the hunter. Those who choose to live off the land may appear to be the more traditional of the three groups, but their lives will be dynamic enough because the variables that define the hunting way of life are constantly changing. If a snowmobile is perceived to have greater utility than a dog sled, then the ownership of a snowmobile will become one of the criteria defining the traditional Eskimo hunter. With the outward-oriented Eskimos providing stability for the three-group system through their control of exotic inputs, the northern communities should be able to evolve further without developing disastrous strains. But the fundamental linkage—the relation between the hunter and the Arctic ecosystem—will remain the same.

The Flow of Energy in an Agricultural Society

by Roy A. Rappaport
September 1971

*The invention of agriculture gave mankind a more
abundant source of solar energy. The energetics of
a primitive agricultural system are examined in
New Guinea, with a moral for modern agriculturists*

Raising crops and husbanding animals are man's most important means of exploiting the energy that is continuously stored in primary plant production. Man's manipulation through the practice of agriculture of this energy store and of the food chains it supports has enabled him to progress beyond the bare subsistence provided by hunting and gathering, and long ago placed human culture on the road leading to the complex social systems of today. Here we shall examine the flow of energy in an agricultural society that practices a mode of gardening known for millenniums, a mode likely to have been the first to enable pioneer farmers to exploit an almost unpopulated part of the world: the humid Tropics.

An examination of this type of gardening is particularly appropriate to the theme of this issue because the flow of energy within it is easy to trace; its practitioners have no power sources other than fire and their own muscle and have only the simplest tools. At the same time their kind of gardening and swine husbandry makes relatively light demands on the farmers in terms of energy inputs, provides for almost all their dietary needs and, if properly practiced, alters ecosystems less than other modes of agriculture of comparable productivity do. We shall compare this kind of farming with the ecologically more disruptive methods of modern agriculture, and we shall examine how the flow of energy and materials in agricultural systems affects the diversity and stability of ecosystems in general. We shall also consider the relation between social evolution, with its ever increasing demand for expenditures of energy, and ecological degradation.

The system of gardening is called "swiddening," and the place where I observed it is the tropical rain forest of New Guinea. The term comes from the Old Norse word for "singe." The method has often been applied in forest environments outside the Tropics, including the forests of medieval England where it got its name. It has many variants, but basic aspects of the procedure are much the same everywhere in temperate or tropical forests. A clearing is cut in the forest, the cuttings are usually burned (sometimes they are removed by hand or allowed to rot), a garden is planted and harvested and the clearing is then abandoned to the returning forest. On occasion the clearing is planted two or three times before it is abandoned, but a single planting is more typical.

The mature tropical rain forest is probably the most intricate, productive, efficient and stable ecosystem that has ever evolved. Men are able to use directly for food only a tiny fraction of the forest's biomass: its total store of living matter. The unmodified rain forest can support perhaps one human being per square mile. From the human viewpoint such an environment is seriously deficient, and swiddening provides a sophisticated and even elegant means of overcoming its deficiencies. With swiddening population densities comparable to those of industrialized countries are maintained with considerably less degradation of the environment resulting.

The swiddening farmers with whom we are specifically concerned are the Tsembaga, one of several local groups speaking the Maring language that live in the central highlands of the Australian Trust Territory of New Guinea some five degrees south of the Equator [*see top illustration on page 373*]. The Tsembaga occupy a territory on the southern side of the Simbai River valley in the Bismarck Range. From its lowest point along the riverbank, about 2,200 feet above sea level, their land rises in less than three miles to the mountain ridge at an altitude of 7,200 feet. In 1962 and 1963, when I was visiting the Tsembaga, their territory was 3.2 square miles and their population totaled 204.

Not all of the Tsembaga land is arable. The part that lies above 6,000 feet is usually blanketed by clouds and its vegetation consists of a moss forest unaltered by man. The next zone, between 6,000 and 5,000 feet, is cultivable on a marginal basis, but most of it has been left as unaltered mature rain forest. Below this zone, between 5,000 and 2,200 feet, is the main area of agricultural activity, although portions of the land are too rocky or too steep for gardening. Just over 1,000 acres here were occupied either by gardens or by fallow secondary-forest vegetation in 1962.

Forty-six acres—about .2 acre per person—had been newly planted that year. Since some gardens yield a harvest for two years or more, this practice means that as many as 90 to 100 acres of Tsembaga land are often in cultivation simultaneously. Conversely, at any one time at least 90 percent (and sometimes more) is lying fallow. If one adds to these 900-odd acres the 340 acres or so of marginally arable land in the zone between 5,000 and 6,000 feet that have never

GARDEN PLOTS that exemplify a very ancient method of farming lie scattered through the swath of second-growth forest in the aerial photograph shown on page 379. The agricultural area lies on the east bank of the Simbai River in the central highlands of New Guinea. Most gardens are located in the lower third of the area (*see detailed map on next page*). In any year 90 percent of the land lies fallow, slowly returning once again to forest.

been cultivated, the percentage of potentially arable land actually under cultivation becomes even smaller.

In terms of their entire territory the Tsembaga in 1962–1963 were maintaining a population density of 64 per square mile. In terms of all potentially arable land the density was 97 per square mile, and in terms of land that was then or ever had been under cultivation the density was 124 per square mile. Even this figure is below the carrying capacity of the Tsembaga territory; without altering the horticultural regime of keeping 90 percent of the land fallow the Tsembaga's 1,000 best acres might have supported a population of 200 or more per square mile.

Horticulture provides 99 percent of the everyday Tsembaga diet, but the unaltered forest beyond the gardens and the secondary forest that covers the fallow land also play an economic role. For example, the Tsembaga husbandry of pigs depends on feral boars that roam the forests. The Tsembaga castrate their own boars because they believe it makes for larger and more docile animals; the sows (which wander free during the day, returning home at dusk) must thus be impregnated by chance contact with feral boars. Feral pigs are also a source of some protein for the Tsembaga, as are the marsupials, snakes, lizards, birds and woodgrubs also found in the forest. Some forest animals and hundreds of species of forest plants provide the raw materials for tools, house construction, clothing, dyestuffs, cosmetics, medicines, ornaments, wealth objects and the supplies and paraphernalia of ritual. The greatest contribution of the forest, however, is providing a favorable setting for the Tsembaga gardens.

In 1963 I kept detailed records of the activities involved in transforming an 11,000-square-foot area of secondary forest into a garden. (These observations were supplemented by a wide range of measurements of similar activities of the same people and others at different sites.) Situated at an altitude of 4,200 feet, the land had been fallow for 20 to 25 years. On it, in addition to underbrush, were 117 trees with a trunk six inches or more in circumference, including a number that measured at least two feet. The canopy of leaves met some 30 feet overhead and had become dense enough to kill a good deal of the underbrush by its shade. In order to make estimates of energy input during various stages of the clearing work, I conducted time and motion studies in the field. These studies, in conjunction with the findings of E. H. Hipsley and Nancy Kirk of the Commonwealth of Australia Department of Health, provided a basis for my calculations. Hipsley and Miss Kirk, working with other New Guinea highlanders, the Chimbu, measured individual metabolic rates during the performance of everyday tasks. My estimates of crop yields are based on a daily weighing of the harvests from some 25 Tsembaga gardens over a period of almost a year. I have used various standard sources in calculating the energetic values of the produce.

In making a garden the Tsembaga prefer to clear secondary forest rather than primary forest because secondary growth is easier to cut and burn. Even in the secondary forest, clearing the underbrush is hard work, although it was made easier when machetes were introduced to the area in the 1950's. I found that the performance of men and women in clearing the brush was surprisingly uniform. Although in an hour some women clear little more than 200 square feet and some of the more robust men clear nearly 300 square feet, the larger

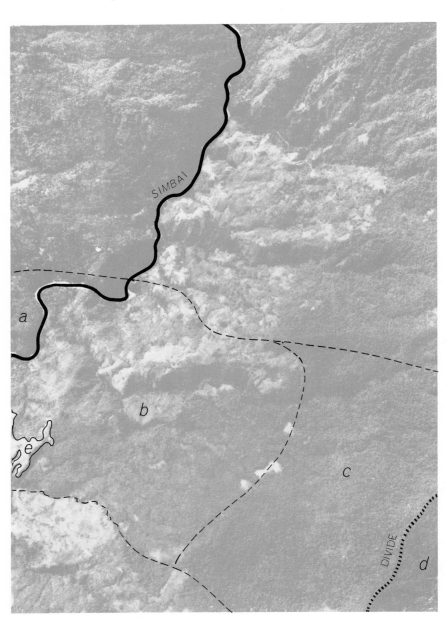

AREA OF STUDY has four major divisions. One forested zone (a) just north of the Simbai River is land as yet little used for gardens. The major agricultural zone is uphill from the river to the south (b); it rises from about 2,300 feet above sea level at the river to about 5,200 feet at its boundary with a zone of largely virgin forest (c) farther uphill. The highest land, which is not farmed, lies in this zone and the adjacent one (d) on both sides of a mountain ridge some 7,200 feet above sea level. The light patch (e) is a stand of kunai grass that has sprung up in a cleared area and is resistant to the process of reforestation.

men expend more energy per minute than the women. The energy input of each sex is approximately equal: some .65 kilocalorie per square foot, or 28,314 kilocalories per acre.

Once the underbrush is cut about two weeks are allowed to pass before the next step: clearing the trees. This is exclusively men's work. On this occasion most of the 117 trees in the garden were felled. Their branches were then lopped off and scattered over the piles of drying underbrush. Trees whose thick trunks would have been hard to burn and a nuisance to drag away were left standing, but most or all of their limbs were removed. The process of tree-clearing is far less strenuous than clearing underbrush: the energy investment is about .26 kilocalorie per square foot, or 11,325 kilocalories per acre.

The next step is to make a fence to keep out pigs, both feral and domestic. The trunks of the felled trees are cut into lengths of from eight to 10 feet and dragged to the edge of the clearing. The thicker logs are split into rails, and the logs and the rails are lashed together with vines to form the fence. Fence-building is heavy work, even without taking into consideration frequent trips to higher altitudes for the gathering of the strong vines needed for lashing. I estimate that the construction effort alone involved an input of something over 46 kilocalories per running foot of fence. Assuming a need for 370 feet of fence per acre of garden and making allowance for the energy expended in gathering vines, I have calculated that the total input for fencing is 17,082 kilocalories per acre. It is little wonder that the Tsembaga tend to cluster their gardens; clustering reduces the length of fence required per unit of area.

After fences are built, and between one month and four months after clearing begins (depending on how steadily the gardener works and on the weather), the felled litter on the site is burned. This is a step of considerable importance in the swiddening regime. Burning not only disposes of the litter but also liberates the mineral nutrients in the cut vegetation and makes them available to the future crop. Since the layer of fertile soil under tropical forests is remarkably thin (seldom more than two inches in Tsembaga territory) and is easily depleted, the nutrients freed from the fallen trees by burning are beneficial, if not crucial, to the growth of garden plants.

Not much energy is expended in the burning process, although one burning is never enough to finish the job. More-

CENTRAL HIGHLANDS of the Australian Trust Territory of New Guinea are drained by the Sepik and Ramu rivers; the Simbai River is a tributary of the Ramu. The colored dot marks the territory of the Tsembaga, the group whose farming practices the author analyzed.

over, since considerable time usually elapses between the clearing of the underbrush and the burning, it is necessary to weed the garden area before the burning. I estimate that two burnings and a weeding involve an energy input of 9,484 kilocalories per acre.

While the women gather the litter into piles for the second burning, the men put aside some of the lighter unburned logs. Some are laid across the grade of the slope to retain the soil. The rest are used to mark individual garden plots. This task is also light work; I estimate

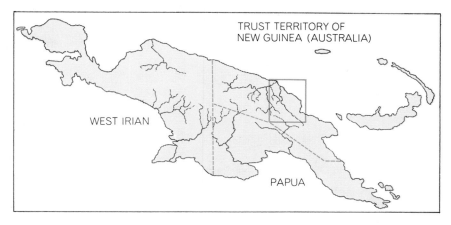

TRUST TERRITORY of New Guinea is one of the island's three political divisions. West Irian (left) is a part of the Republic of Indonesia and Papua is an Australian territory.

LITTER IS BURNED in the clearing where a Tsembaga family is preparing to plant a garden. Tree trunks that are not consumed may be used as soil-retainers or plot-markers. Burning releases nutrients in the cut vegetation that are utilized by the garden plants.

that the total energy input is 7,238 kilocalories per acre.

Burning completed and plot-markers and soil-retainers laid, gardens are ready to be planted. For planting stock the Tsembaga depend primarily on cuttings, although they raise a few crops from seed. The gathering and planting of the cuttings, which are set into holes punched in the untilled soil with a heavy stick, is relatively demanding work. I estimate that the men and women who do the planting expend .38 kilocalorie per square foot, or 16,553 kilocalories per acre.

It is appropriate here to list the plants the Tsembaga grow and also to describe the appearance of a growing garden. The Tsembaga can name at least 264 varieties of edible plants, representing some 36 species. The staples are taro and sweet potato. Other starchy vegetables such as yams, cassavas and bananas are of lesser importance. Sweet potatoes and cassavas are used as pig feed as well as for human consumption. Beans, peas, maize and sugarcane are also grown, along with a number of leafy greens, including hibiscus. Hibiscus leaves are in fact the most important plant source of protein in the Tsembaga diet. An asparagus-like plant, *Setaria palmaefolia*, and a relative of sugarcane

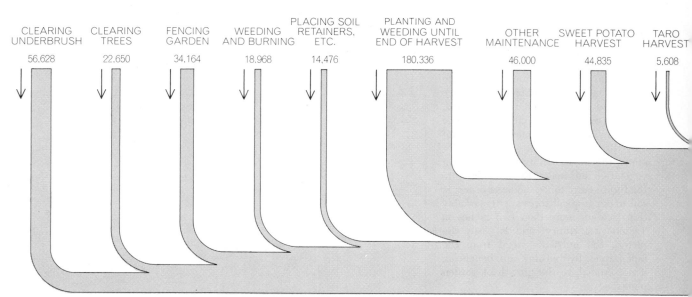

CLEARING UNDERBRUSH	CLEARING TREES	FENCING GARDEN	WEEDING AND BURNING	PLACING SOIL RETAINERS, ETC.	PLANTING AND WEEDING UNTIL END OF HARVEST	OTHER MAINTENANCE	SWEET POTATO HARVEST	TARO HARVEST
56,628	22,650	34,164	18,968	14,476	180,336	46,000	44,835	5,608

TWELVE MAJOR INPUTS of energy are required in gardening. The flow diagram shows the inputs in terms of the kilocalories per acre required to prepare and harvest a pair of gardens (*see illustration on page 376*). Weeding, a continual process after the garden

NEW CLEARING in second-growth forest contains many stumps of trees that have been cut high for use as props for growing plants. Some, although stripped of their leaves, will survive; along with invading tree seedlings they will slowly reforest the garden site.

known as *pitpit* are valued for their edible flowering parts. So is the *Marita* pandanus, one of the screw pines; its fruit is the source of a thick, fat-rich red fluid that the Tsembaga use as a sauce on greens. Minor garden crops include cucumber, pumpkin, watercress and breadfruit.

Most of the principal crops are to be found in most of the gardens and each is often represented by several varieties of the same species. As Clifford Geertz of the University of Chicago has remarked, there is a structural similarity between a swidden garden and a tropical rain forest. In the garden, as in the forest, species are not segregated by rows or sections but are intricately intermingled, so that as they mature the garden becomes stratified and the plants make maximum use of surface area and of variations in vertical dimensions. For example, taro and sweet potato tubers mature just below the surface; the cassava root lies deeper and yams are the deepest of all. A mat of sweet potato leaves covers the soil at ground level. The taro leaves project above this mat; the hibiscus, sugarcane and *pitpit* stand higher still, and the fronds of the banana spread out above the rest. This intermingling does more than make the best use of a fixed volume. It also dis-

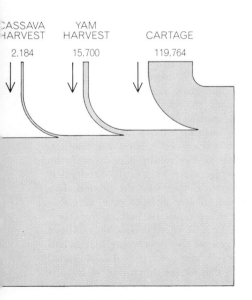

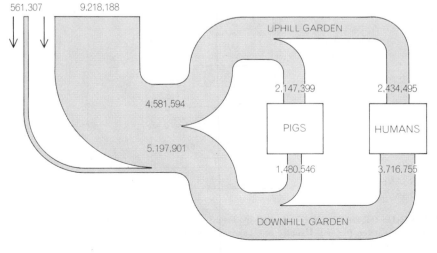

is planted, demands the most energy. Bringing in the garden harvest (*right*) ranks next.

BIOMASS OF CROP YIELD, also measured in kilocalories, gives more than a 16-to-one return on the human energy investment. The Tsembaga use much of the harvest as pig feed.

PLANT   YIELD PER ACRE (KILOCALORIES)

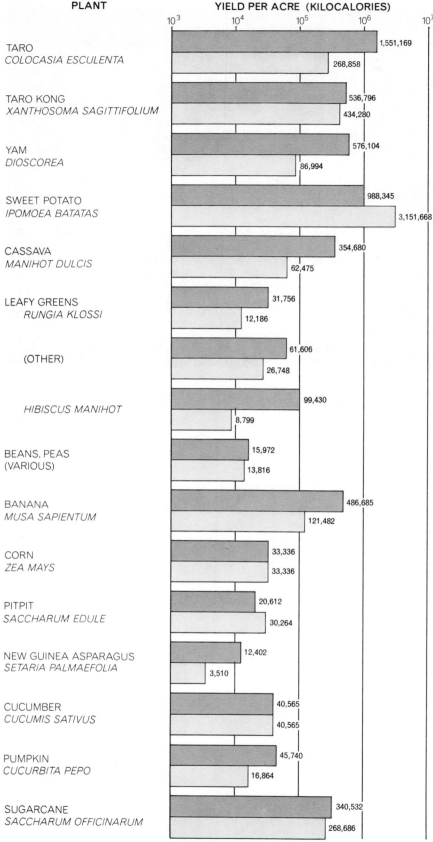

10^3 10^4 10^5 10^6 10^7

TARO
COLOCASIA ESCULENTA — 1,551,169 / 268,858

TARO KONG
XANTHOSOMA SAGITTIFOLIUM — 536,796 / 434,280

YAM
DIOSCOREA — 576,104 / 86,994

SWEET POTATO
IPOMOEA BATATAS — 988,345 / 3,151,668

CASSAVA
MANIHOT DULCIS — 354,680 / 62,475

LEAFY GREENS
RUNGIA KLOSSI — 31,756 / 12,186

(OTHER) — 61,606 / 26,748

HIBISCUS MANIHOT — 99,430 / 8,799

BEANS, PEAS
(VARIOUS) — 15,972 / 13,816

BANANA
MUSA SAPIENTUM — 486,685 / 121,482

CORN
ZEA MAYS — 33,336 / 33,336

PITPIT
SACCHARUM EDULE — 20,612 / 30,264

NEW GUINEA ASPARAGUS
SETARIA PALMAEFOLIA — 12,402 / 3,510

CUCUMBER
CUCUMIS SATIVUS — 40,565 / 40,565

PUMPKIN
CUCURBITA PEPO — 45,740 / 16,864

SUGARCANE
SACCHARUM OFFICINARUM — 340,532 / 268,686

TWO KINDS OF GARDEN are planted by Tsembaga families, whose pigs are too numerous for one garden to feed. Usually one garden is downhill from the other. The downhill garden (*gray*) is planted with more of the family staples: taro and yam. The uphill garden (*color*) is planted with more sweet potato, which is a staple food for pigs. The graph shows the 16 principal Tsembaga garden crops and the comparative yields from two gardens.

courages plant-specific insect pests, it allows advantage to be taken of slight variations in garden habitats, it is protective of the thin tropical soil and it achieves a high photosynthetic efficiency.

If a Tsembaga man and his wife have only one or two pigs, they usually plant one major garden in the middle altitudes, generally between 4,000 and 4,500 feet. But pigs are given a ration from the gardens, and when their numbers increase, their owners are likely to plant two gardens, one above 4,500 feet and the other between 3,000 and 4,000 feet. These gardens differ in the proportions of the major crops with which they are planted. The lower-altitude gardens include more taros and yams and the higher-altitude gardens more sweet potatoes, this last crop forming the largest part of the pigs' ration.

After planting is completed the most laborious of the gardening tasks, weeding, still lies ahead. The Tsembaga recognize and name several successive weedings, but after the first weeding is done (five to seven weeks after planting) the chore becomes virtually continuous. I estimate the total energy input for this task to be about 2.07 kilocalories per square foot, or 90,168 kilocalories per acre. Other miscellaneous tasks performed at the same time (for example tying sugarcane to stumps or other supports) require an additional 14,500 kilocalories per acre. It is noteworthy that weeding aims at uprooting any herbaceous competitors invading the garden but that tree seedlings are spared and even protected. Indeed, a Tsembaga gardener is almost as irritated when a visitor damages a tree seedling as when he heedlessly tramples on a taro plant.

The Tsembaga recognize the importance of the regenerating trees; they call them collectively *duk mi,* or "mother of gardens." Allowing tree seedlings to remain and grow avoids a definite grassy stage in the succession following the abandonment of the garden and for one thing ensures a more rapid redevelopment of the forest canopy. For another, during the cropping period itself the young trees provide a web of roots that penetrate deeper into the ground than the roots of any of the crops and are able to recover nutrients that might otherwise be lost through leaching. Above the ground the developing leaves and branches not only provide additional protection for the thin forest soil against tropical downpours but also immobilize nutrients recovered from the soil for release to future gardens. They also make it increasingly difficult for gardeners to harvest and weed. As a result the people are induced to abandon their gardens before they have seriously depleted the soil, even before the crops are completely harvested. The developing trees, whose growth they themselves have encouraged, make harvesting more laborious at the same time that it is becoming less rewarding. It is interesting to note here that both Ramón Margalef of the University of Barcelona and Howard T. Odum of the University of Florida have argued that in complex ecosystems successful species are not those that merely capture energy more efficiently than their competitors but those that sustain the species supporting them. It is clear that the Tsembaga support not only the garden species that provide them with food but also the species on which they ultimately depend: the species of the forest, which sustain their gardens.

Technological limitations and the nature of crops prevent the Tsembaga from storing most of the food they grow. As a result there is no special harvest period. From the time the crops begin to mature a little harvesting is done every day or two. The strategy is to do as little damage as possible to the plant that yields the crop. For example, hibiscus shrubs are not stripped of all their leaves at one time. Instead every few days a few leaves are plucked from each of several shrubs. This method increases the total yield by allowing the plants to recover in the interval between successive harvestings.

Harvesting continues almost daily from the time crops mature until those in a garden planted in the succeeding year are ready. With the advent of a new garden, harvesting becomes less frequent in the old garden, finally ceasing altogether somewhere between 14 and 28 months after planting. Gardens at lower altitudes are usually shorter-lived than those higher on the mountainside because secondary forest regenerates more quickly on them.

Energy expenditure for harvesting differs slightly between the two types of garden. I estimate that 40,966 kilocalories per acre are expended in harvesting taro-yam gardens and 44,168 kilocalories per acre in sweet potato gardens. Food is consumed at home, homes are at some distance from the gardens and produce therefore must be carried from gardens to houses. An estimated 48,360 kilocalories are expended in transporting produce from sweet potato gardens, which are at approximately the same altitude as the houses. I estimate that 71,404 kilocalories per acre

FENCE-BUILDING is one of the more energy-consuming tasks in preparing a garden. Fences must be pig-proof to keep out both domestic swine and feral swine from the forest.

are needed to bring home produce from the taro-yam gardens, which are usually 1,000 to 2,000 feet lower on the mountainside.

Combining all the inputs and comparing input with yield, I found that the Tsembaga received a reasonable short-term return on their investment. The ratio of yield to input was about 16.5 to one for the taro-yam gardens and about 15.9 to one for the sweet potato gardens. Moreover, in 1963, when these observations were made, the distances between the gardens and the residences of the Tsembaga were greater than usual. It was a festival year and the dwellings, instead of being dispersed among the gardens as is customary, were all clustered around a dance ground. If the normal residential pattern had been in effect, garden-to-house distances might have been reduced by as much as 80 percent, and the yield ratios would have risen respectively to 20.1 to one and 18.4 to one.

I have indicated that swine husbandry is intimately related to gardening among the Tsembaga because they devote a substantial proportion of their principal crops to feeding their pigs. Each adult pig receives a daily ration that equals an adult man's ration in weight, although it differs from the human ration in composition. Around the world most pigs are raised to be eaten. This is the ultimate fate that befalls a Tsembaga pig, but such consumption involves social and political relations and religious beliefs and practices, not simply a desire for meat.

The Tsembaga and other groups that speak the Maring language are prevented by strong religious prohibitions from initiating warfare until they have completed a year-long festival that culminates in large-scale sacrifices of pigs to their ancestors, rewarding them for their presumed support in the last round of warfare. The festival itself is the climax of a prolonged ritual cycle that begins years earlier with the sacrifices terminating warfare, sacrifices in which all adult and many juvenile pigs are killed. The Tsembaga held such a festival during my visit in 1962–1963.

When the festival began, the Tsembaga pigs numbered 169 animals with an average per capita weight of from 120 to 150 pounds. This sizable herd was eating 54 percent of all the sweet potatoes and 82 percent of all the cassavas growing in the Tsembaga gardens: some 36 percent of all the tubers of any kind that the Tsembaga grew. The operation called for the commitment of about a third of all garden land to the production of pig feed (not even taking into account household garbage, which the pigs also consumed). At the end of the festival the Tsembaga herd had been reduced to some 60 juvenile pigs, each weighing an average of from 60 to 70 pounds. Thus in terms of live weight the slaughter had decreased the herd sixfold. In anticipation of this decrease the Tsembaga had earlier in 1963 set the area of new land being put into gardens at what amounted to 36.1 percent below the level of the previous year.

For the Tsembaga swine husbandry is obviously an expensive business. The input in human energy, both in growing pig food and in managing the animals, I estimate to be about 45,000 kilocalories per pig per year. Because 10 years or so are needed to bring the herd up from a minimum following the sacrifices terminating warfare to a size large enough for a festival, the ratio of energy yield to energy input in Tsembaga pig husbandry is certainly no better than two to one and is probably worse than one to one. It is evident that keeping pigs cannot be justified or even interpreted in terms of energetics alone. Other possible benefits must also be considered.

First, Maring pig husbandry is part of the means for regulating relations between autonomous local groups such as the Tsembaga. It has already been indicated that the frequency of warfare is regulated by a ritual cycle, but the timing of the cycle is itself a function of the speed of growth in the pig population. Since it usually takes a decade or more to accumulate enough pigs to hold the festival terminating a cycle, the initiation of warfare is held to once per decade or less.

Second, the animals form a link in the detritus food chain by consuming both garbage and the unassimilated vegetable content of human feces, materials that would otherwise be wasted. Moreover, the pigs are regularly penned in abandoned gardens, where they root up unharvested tubers and where, by eliminating herbaceous growth that competes with tree seedlings, they may hasten the return of the forest.

Third, it must be remembered that a diet must provide more than mere energy to a consumer, and it is as converters of carbohydrates of vegetable origin into high-quality protein that pigs are most important in the Tsembaga diet. The importance of their protein contribution is magnified by the circumstances surrounding their consumption. Except for the once-a-decade festival and for certain rites associated with warfare that are equally infrequent, it is rare for the Tsembaga to kill and eat a pig. The ritual occasions that do call for this unusual behavior are associated with sickness, injury or death. I have argued elsewhere that the sick, the injured, the dying and their kin and associates in Tsembaga society all suffer physiological stress, with an associated net loss of nitrogen (meaning protein) from their body tissues. Now, since the regular protein intake of the Tsembaga is marginal, their antibody production is likely to be low and their rate of recovery from injury or illness slow. In such circumstances nitrogen loss can be a serious matter. The condition of a nitrogen-depleted organism, however, improves rather quickly with the intake of high-quality protein. The nutritional significance of the Tsembaga pigs thus outweighs their high cost in energy input. They provide a source of high-quality protein when it is needed most.

In summary, swiddening and swine husbandry provide the Tsembaga with on the one hand an adequate daily energy ration and on the other an emergency source of protein. The average adult Tsembaga male is four feet 10½ inches tall and weighs 103 pounds; the average adult female is four feet 6½ inches tall and weighs 85 pounds. The garden produce provides the men with some 2,600 kilocalories per day and the women with some 2,200 kilocalories. At the same time the Tsembaga's treatment of the ecosystem in which they live is sufficiently gentle to ensure the continuing regeneration of secondary forest and a continuing supply of fertile garden sites.

We may reflect here on the general strategy of swiddening. It is to establish temporary associations of plants directly useful to man on sites from which forest is removed and to encourage the return of forests to those sites after the useful plants have been harvested. The return of the forest makes it possible, or at least much easier, to establish again an association of cultivated plants sometime in the future. Moreover, the gardens are composed of many varieties of many plant species. If one or another kind of plant succumbs to pests or blight, other plants are available as substitutes. This multiplicity of plants enhances the stability of the Tsembaga subsistence base in exactly the same way that the complexity of the tropical rain forest ensures its stability.

How does such an agricultural pattern compare with farming methods that

LAYERS OF GROWTH characterize the Tsembaga garden. Root crops develop at different depths and their leaves reach different heights. Bananas (*foreground*) are the tallest plants.

remove the natural flora over extensive regions and put in their place varieties of one or a few plant species? Before we take up this question let us consider ecosystems in general and the interactions among the participants in ecosystems in particular. All ecosystems are basically similar. Solar energy is photosynthetically fixed by plants—the primary producers—and then passes along food chains that are chiefly made up of animal populations with various feeding habits: herbivores, one or more levels of carnivores and eventually decomposers (which reduce organic wastes into inorganic constituents that can again be taken up by the plants).

Examined in terms of the flow of matter the ecosystem pattern is roughly circular; the same substances are cycled again and again. The flow of energy in ecosystems is linear. It is not recycled but is eventually lost to the local system.

The energy supply is steadily degraded into heat with each successive step along the food chain. For example, of the organic material synthesized by a plant from 80 to 90 percent is available under ordinary circumstances to the herbivore that consumes the plant. The herbivore expends energy, however, not only in feeding and in other activities but also in metabolic processes. When the amount of energy captured by one organism in a food chain is compared with the amount of energy the organism yields to the organism that preys on it, the figure is usually of the order of 10 to one, which means an energy loss of 90 percent.

Just as there are general similarities among ecosystems, so there are differences in the numbers and the kinds of species that participate in each system and in the relations among them. These differences are the result of evolutionary processes. Associations of species adapt to their habitat, and with the passage of time they pass through more or less distinct stages known as successions. As the work of Margalef and of Eugene P. Odum of the University of Georgia has demonstrated, these successions also show certain general similarities.

One similarity is that in any ecosystem the total biomass increases as time passes. There is a corresponding but not linearly related increase in primary productivity—that is, photosynthesis—whether it is expressed as the total amount of energy fixed or as the total quantity of organic material synthesized. What allows the increase in primary productivity is a parallel increase in the number of plant species that have become specialized and are thus able to

GARDEN MAINTENANCE includes light tasks such as tying up sugarcane. Here the stalks of cane (*left*) have been lashed to a tree stump by a gardener with a length of vine.

conduct photosynthesis under a greater variety of circumstances in a wider range of microhabitats. The increase in plant biomass and plant productivity may allow some increase in animal biomass too. It certainly encourages an increase in the diversity of animal species, since the increase in the diversity of plants favors specialization among herbivores.

Not only are there more species in the maturer stages of a succession but also the species are likely to be of a different kind. Species typical of immature succession stages—"pioneer" species—are characteristically able to disperse themselves over considerable distances, to re-

produce prodigally, to compete strongly for dominance and to survive under unstable and even violently fluctuating conditions. They also tend to be short-lived, that is, their populations are quickly replaced. Therefore in immature ecosystems the ratio of productivity to biomass is high.

In contrast, the species characteristic of more mature stages of succession often cannot disperse themselves easily over long distances, produce few offspring and are relatively long-lived. Their increasing specialization militates against overt competition among them; instead the relations among species are often characterized by an increased mutual reliance. In effect, as the ecosystem becomes maturer it becomes more complex for the number of species, and their interdependence increases. As its complexity increases so does its stability, since there are increasing numbers of alternative paths through which energy and materials can flow. Therefore if one or another species is decimated, the entire system is not necessarily endangered.

The maturing ecosystem also becomes more efficient. In the immature stage productivity per unit of biomass is high and total biomass is likely to be low. As stage follows stage both productivity and biomass increase, but there is a decrease in the ratio of productivity to biomass. For example, it takes less energy to support a pound of biomass in a mature tropical rain forest than it does in the grassy or scrubby forest stages that precede maturity.

It is not really surprising that in-creased stability and increased efficiency should be characteristic of mature ecosystems. Some of the implications of this trend, however, are not altogether obvious. I have alluded to the arguments of Margalef and Howard Odum suggesting that in mature ecosystems selection is not merely a matter of competition between individuals or species occupying the same level in the food chain. Rather, it favors those species that contribute positively to the stability and efficiency of the entire ecosystem. Organisms with positions well up along the food chain can "reward" the organisms they depend on by returning to these lower organisms materials they require or by performing services that are beneficial to them. An exploitive population—one that consumes at a rate greater than the productivity of the species it depends on or does not reward that species—will eventually perish.

Margalef and others have pointed out that human intervention tends to reduce the maturity of ecosystems. Both in terms of the small number of species present and of the lack of ecological complexity a farm or a plantation more closely resembles an immature stage of succession than it does a mature stage. Furthermore, in ecosystems dominated by man the chosen species are usually quick to ripen—that is, they are short-lived—and the productivity per unit of biomass is likely to be high. Yet there is a crucial difference between natural pioneer associations and those dominated by man.

Pioneers in an immature ecosystem are characterized by their ability to survive under unstable conditions. Man's favored cultigens, however, are seldom if ever notable for hardiness and self-sufficiency. Some are ill-adapted to their surroundings, some cannot even propagate themselves without assistance and some are able to survive only if they are constantly protected from the competition of the natural pioneers that promptly invade the simplified ecosystems man has constructed. Indeed, in man's quest for higher plant yields he has devised some of the most delicate and unstable ecosystems ever to have appeared on the face of the earth. The ultimate in human-dominated associations are fields planted in one high-yielding variety of a single species. It is apparent that in the ecosystems dominated by man the trend of what can be called successive anthropocentric stages is exactly the reverse of the trend in natural ecosystems. The anthropocentric trend is in the direction of simplicity rather than complexity, of fragility rather than stability.

We return to our question of how the pattern of Tsembaga agriculture compares with the pattern of agriculture based on one crop. The question really concerns the interaction of man's expanding social, political and economic organization on the one hand and local natural ecosystems on the other. The trend of anthropocentric succession can best be understood as one aspect of the evolution of human society.

We can place the Tsembaga and other "primitive" horticulturists early in such successions. The Tsembaga are politically and economically autonomous. They neither import nor export foodstuffs, and it is necessary for them to maintain as wide a range of crops in their gardens as they wish to enjoy. Economic self-sufficiency obviously encourages a generalized horticulture, but economic self-sufficiency and production for use protect ecological integrity in more

FERAL PIG (foreground) has been roasted and is being dismembered. Feral animals are eaten whenever they are killed, but domestic swine are killed only on ceremonial occasions.

COSTUMED FOR DANCING, a group of Tsembaga men stands ready near the dance ground. During this ceremony in 1963 the Tsembaga butchered and distributed 109 pigs.

important ways. For one thing, the management of cultivation is only slightly concerned, if at all, with events in the outside world. On the contrary, it attends almost exclusively to the needs of the cultivators and the species sustaining them. Moreover, in the absence of exotic energy sources the ability of humans to abuse the species on which they depend is limited by those species, because it is only from them that energy for work can be derived. In such systems, however, abuses seldom need to be repaid by declining yields because they are quickly signaled to those responsible by subtler signs of environmental degradation. Information feedback from the environment is sensitive and rapid in small autonomous ecological systems, and such systems are likely to be rapidly self-correcting.

The fact remains that autonomous local ecological systems such as the Tsembaga system have virtually disappeared. All but a few have been absorbed into an increasingly differentiated and complex social and economic organization of worldwide scope. The increasing size and complexity of human organization is related to man's increasing ability to harness energy. The relationship is not simple; rather it is one of mutual causation. As an example, increases in the available energy allow increases in the size and differentiation of human societies. Increased numbers and increasingly complex organizations require still more energy to sustain them and at the same time facilitate the development of new techniques for capturing more energy, and so on. The system is characterized by positive feedback.

Leslie A. White of the University of Michigan suggested that cultural evolution can be measured in terms of the increasing amount of energy harnessed per capita per annum. This is a yardstick that seems generally to agree with the historical experience of mankind. The development of energy sources that are independent of immediate biological processes has been the factor of greatest importance. Industrialized societies harness many times more energy per capita per annum than nonindustrial ones, and the energy-rich have enjoyed a great advantage in their relations with the energy-poor. In areas where the two have competed the nonindustrial societies have inevitably been displaced, absorbed or destroyed.

Agriculture is not exempt from the increasing specialization that characterizes social evolution generally. Not only individual farms but also regions and even nations have been turned into man-made immature ecosystems such as cotton plantations or cane fields. It is important to note that the transformation would be virtually impossible without sources of energy other than local biological processes. Fossil fuels come into play. When such energy sources are available, the pressures that can be brought to bear on specific ecosystems are no longer limited to the energy that the ecosystem itself can generate, and alterations become feasible that were formerly out of reach. A farmer may even expend more energy in the gasoline consumed by his farm machinery than is returned by the crop he raises. The same nonbiological power sources make it possible to provide the world agricultural community with the large quantities of pesticides, fertilizers and other kinds of assistance that many man-made immature ecosystems require in order to remain productive. Moreover, the entire infrastructure of commercial agriculture—high-speed transportation and communications, large-scale storage facilities and elaborate economic institutions—depends on these same sources of nonbiological energy.

As man forces the ecosystems he dominates to be increasingly simple, however, their already limited autonomy is further diminished. They are subject not only to local environmental stress but also to extraneous economic and political vicissitudes. They come to rely more and more on imported materials; the men who manipulate them become more and more subject to distant events, interests and processes that they may not even grasp and certainly do not control. National and international concerns replace local considerations, and with the regulation of the local ecosystems coming from outside, the system's normal self-corrective capacity is diminished and eventually destroyed.

Margalef has observed that in exchanges among systems differing in complexity of organization the flow of material, information and energy is usually from the less highly organized to the more highly organized. This principle may find expression not only in the relations between predator and prey but also in the relations between "developed" and "underdeveloped" nations. André Gunder Frank has argued that in the course of the development of underdeveloped agrarian societies by industrialized societies the flow of wealth is usually from the former to the latter. Be this as it may, economic development surely accelerates ecological simplification; it inevitably encourages a shift from more diverse subsistence agriculture to the cultivation of a few crops for sale in a world market.

It may not be improper to characterize as ecological imperialism the elaboration of a world organization that is centered in industrial societies and degrades the ecosystems of the agrarian societies it absorbs. Ecological imperialism is in some ways similar to economic imperialism. In both there is a flow of energy and material from the less organized system to the more organized one, and both may simply be different aspects of the same relations. Both may also be masked by the same euphemisms, among which "progress" and "development" are prominent.

The anthropocentric trend I have described may have ethical implications, but the issue is ultimately not a matter of morality or even of *Realpolitik*. It is one of biological viability. The increasing scope of world organization and the increasing industrialization and energy consumption on which it depends have been taken by Western man virtually to define social evolution and progress. It must be remembered that man is an animal, that he survives biologically or not at all, and that his biological survival, like that of all animals, requires the survival of the other species on which he depends. The general ecological perspective outlined here suggests that some aspects of what we have called progress or social evolution may be maladaptive. We may ask if a worldwide human organization can persist and elaborate itself indefinitely at the expense of decreasing the stability of its own ecological foundations. We cannot and would not want to return to a world of autonomous ecosystems such as the Tsembaga's; in such systems all men and women are and must be farmers. We may ask, however, if the chances for human survival might not be enhanced by reversing the modern trend of successions in order to increase the diversity and stability of local, regional and national ecosystems, even, if need be, at the expense of the complexity and interdependence of worldwide economic organization. It seems to me that the trend toward decreasing ecosystemic complexity and stability, rather than threats of pollution, overpopulation or even energy famine, is the ultimate ecological problem immediately confronting man. It also may be the most difficult to solve, since the solution cannot easily be reconciled with the values, goals, interests and political and economic institutions prevailing in industrialized and industrializing nations.

Commentary by Rappaport

I shall take up the matter of maladaptation raised in the last paragraphs of "The Flow of Energy in an Agricultural Society." Before doing so, I must make clear that I take the term "adaptation" to refer to the processes by which living systems maintain homeostasis in the face of both short-term environmental fluctuations and, by transforming their own structures, through long-term non-reversing changes in the composition and structure of their environments as well. Living systems include: (1) organisms, (2) single species assemblages such as populations, troops, tribes, and states, and (3) the multispecies associations of ecosystemic communities. Systemic homeostasis may be given specific meaning if it is conceived as a set of ranges of viability on a corresponding set of variables abstracted from what, for independently established reasons, are taken to be conditions vital to the survival of the system. Any process, physiological, behavioral, cultural or genetic, which tends to keep the states of crucial variables (for example, body temperature, population size, energy flux) within ranges of viability or tends to return them to such ranges should they depart from them, may be taken, other things being equal, to be adaptive. Difficulties in the association of adaptiveness with particular variables will be considered later, but this preliminary formulation does emphasize certain features of adaptive structure.

First, adaptation is basically cybernetic. In response to signals of system-endangering changes in the states of a component or the environment, actions tending to ameliorate those changes are initiated. Corrective actions may eliminate the stressor, make compensatory adjustments, or even effect changes in the system's organization. Adaptation in this view includes both the self-regulatory processes through which living systems maintain themselves in fluctuating environments and the self-organizing processes by which they transform themselves in response to directional environmental changes. These two classes of processes have generally been distinguished in anthropology and have formed the foci of two distinct modes of analysis: "functional" on the one hand, and "evolutionary" on the other. But the distinction has surely been overdrawn: in a changing universe the maintenance of organization demands its continual modification. Self-organizing or evolutionary changes in components of systems are functions of the self-regulatory processes of more inclusive systems and what are called functional changes and evolutionary changes are, in nature, joined together in ordered series of responses to perturbations.

These sequences have certain important properties (Bateson 1963, Slobodkin 1968). The responses most quickly mobilized are likely to be energetically expensive, but they have the advantage of being easily reversible should the stress cease, and they can hold the line, so to speak, until relieved by slower acting, less energetically expensive, less easily reversible changes should it not cease. Such earlier responses may deprive the system of immediate behavioral flexibility while they continue, but while they continue the structure of the system remains unchanged; thus they conserve the long-run flexibility of the system. In contrast, while the later responses do alleviate the strain of the earlier, they are likely to reduce long range flexibility. Put differently, such series ordain a continual and graduated trade-off of adaptive flexibility for adapted efficiency. Since the perturbations to which the system will be subjected in the future are usually unpredictable it is good evolutionary strategy to give up as little long-range flexibility as possible, and evolutionary wisdom seems to be intrinsic to the graduated structure of adaptive response sequences, at least in biological systems. Social systems, on the other hand, can make mistakes of which biological systems may be incapable.

But adaptive structure is not only cybernetic. Special adaptations must be related to each other in structured ways and general adaptations, biological or cultural, must take the form of enormously complex sets of interlocking corrective loops, *hierarchically* arranged and including not only mechanisms regulating material variables, but regulators for the regulators themselves (Kalmus 1966). Regulatory hierarchies, whether or not they are embodied in particular organs or institutions are found in all biological and social systems. To say that regulatory structure is hierarchical is not to say that it is centralized, nor does it imply social stratification; however, two related trends are frequently to be noted in evolving systems. On the one hand there is increased differentiation of special purpose subsystems—organs and specialized institutions. This "progressive segregation" is complimented by "progressive centralization," the increasing concentration of regulatory functions in superordinate controllers.

If adaptive processes are those which tend to maintain homeostasis in the face of perturbations, maladaptations are factors internal to systems interfering with their homeostatic responses. If the maintenance of homeostasis depends upon hierarchically ordered sequences of cybernetic responses, maladaptations may be described in terms of hierarchical and cybernetic structure. Following this, the most simple forms of maladaptation are such cybernetic difficulties as impedence to the detection of deviation of variables from crucial ranges, excessive delay of information transmissions concerning variable states to system regulators, loss or distortion of information in transit and the failure of regulators to understand the signals being received. These and other difficulties are exacerbated by scale. For instance, the more nodes through which it must pass, the more subject is information to distortion or loss. Other things being equal, the higher the administrator the less accurate and adequate his information is likely to be, and the more diverse the subsystems he is regulating the more likely he is to misunderstand the signals upon which he must act. The likelihood of hierarchical anomaly also increases with scale. For instance, the deeper the regulatory hierarchy the more likely are time aberrations. Excessive lag may be a problem, but so may too rapid response by high-order regulators, for such responses may destroy those of lower order if they constantly override them. Moreover, premature responses of the higher order regulators may well be overresponses—resulting in more-or-less irreversible changes when something less drastic would have been sufficient and conservative of long term flexibility.

"Overcentralization" the nonadaptive concentration of regulatory functions in ill-informed controllers remote from the variables for which they are responsible is encouraged by increasing scale, and so is "oversegregation," in which increasingly large units, even whole countries, are turned into special purpose subsystems—such as sugar cane fields—thereby losing their autonomy as well as their ecological stability. Oversegregation and overcentralization, furthermore, encourage "hypercoherence": the components of increasingly encompassing systems become so interdependent that the effects of disruptions occurring anywhere are rapidly felt everywhere.

Oversegregation and overcentralization taken together are complimentary aspects of a more general structural anomaly, which may be called the "hierarchical maldistribution of organization." "Organization" is notoriously difficult to define, but I take it to refer to complexity and the means for maintaining order within it, and have been suggesting that organization at more inclusive levels seems to be increasing at the expense of organization at lower levels. Increasingly complex world organization is based upon decreasingly organized local, regional, and even national social and ecological systems. It seems doubtful that worldwide human organization can persist and elaborate itself indefinitely at the expense of its local infrastructures, and it may be suggested that the ability of the world system to withstand perturbation would be increased by returning to its local subsystems some of the autonomy and diversity that they have lost, as China may be doing.

There is another general class of maladaptations, combining with those discussed so far in complex evolutionary sequences. The basic form has elsewhere been called "usurpation," "escalation," and "overspecification" (Flannery 1972, Rappaport 1969, 1971). I speak here of special purpose subsystems coming to dominate the larger general purpose systems of which they are parts. When particular individuals become identified with special purpose systems they tend to identify the special purposes of those subsystems with their own general purposes, that is, with their own survival, and attempt to promote those purposes to positions of predominance in the larger systems of which they are parts. As they become increasingly powerful they are increasingly able to succeed. The logical end is for a subsystem, or cluster of subsystems, such as a group of industrial firms, to come to dominate a society. No matter how public spirited such subsystems may be this trend is in its nature maladaptive. For the larger system to commit itself to the purposes of one of its subsystems is for it to over-specify or narrow the range of conditions under which it can survive. It is for it to sacrifice evolutionary flexibility.

It has been implied here that where highest order regulation is directed towards economic goals it may impede the maintenance of biological variables—organic, demographic, and ecosystemic—within their ranges of viability. We may ask, even if the cybernetics of the system seem to be in good order, whether this may be properly regarded as adaptive. If the goal of living systems is simply survival, the question of what is ultimately to be maintained in homeostasis is the question of what the term "survival" minimally implies. Here we may be reminded that the term adaptation is basically a biological term and that the systems with which we are concerned have living components. This is to say that "survival," although difficult to specify, has, minimally, a biological meaning and that the adaptiveness of aspects of culture may ultimately be assessed in terms of their effects upon the biological components of the systems in which they occur. This is further to say that "cultural adaptation," the processes through which social structures or institutions maintain themselves in the face of perturbation may contradict or defeat the general or biological adaptation of which culture in its emergence must have been a part. But since survival is nothing if not biological evolutionary changes perpetuating economic or political institutions at the expense of the biological well-being of men, societies and ecosystems may be considered maladaptive. This position is not arbitrary for it reflects the way contingency is structured. There are no particular institutions with which a society could not dispense, but, obviously, if man perished culture would cease to exist.

It is difficult or impossible, however, to assess the long-run effects of any aspect of culture on particular biological variables, nor does it seem possible to identify any particular feature of biological structure or function that will always contribute to survival. Adaptiveness, therefore, is not to be identified with particular biological variables, but with the maintenance of general homeostasis in living systems. The notion of general homeostasis lacks operational precision but it is not mystical. One implication of our argument is that it is intrinsic to orderly adaptive structure, a certain hierarchical ordering of cybernetic processes and the systemic components embodying them with respect to time, reversibility, specificity, and contingency. If such an order is maintained, general homeostasis will prevail. The primacy of biological considerations is implicit in adaptive structure, for the escalation of nonbiological variables to positions of predominance violates adaptive order with respect to both specificity and contingency.

In light of possible contradiction between cultural and biological adaptation it is reasonable to search for the factors impelling maladaptive trends among those that have been taken to be advances in cultural evolution. Causation is, of course, never simple and other suggestions could be made, but increases in energy capture, money, and the division of labor seem to have beem important. High-energy technology itself frees those operating in local ecosystems from the limits imposed upon them by the need to derive energy from the contemporary biological processes of those systems and permits virtually unlimited amounts of energy to be focused upon very small systems. Moreover, the ecological disruption of those systems can be tolerated for a time because of the increased specialization of other systems. In the long run, however, the increasing specialization of larger and larger regions—itself made possible by a technology that provides means for moving even bulky commodities long distances inexpensively and for transmitting information long distances instantaneously—is unstable.

The increasing specialization of increasingly large geographical regions is simply one aspect of increasing internal differentiation of social systems. Progressive segregation and progressive centralization were, of course, encouraged by the emergence of plant and animal cultivation 10,000 or so years ago, for plant and animal cultivation provided significant opportunities for full division of labor. But the emergence of the high-energy technology based upon fossil fuels has accelerated and exaggerated this trend and the maladaptations associated with it. Moreover, it is differentially distributed among the subsystems of societies and it permits or encourages the promotion of the special purposes of powerful subsystems to positions of dominance in higher order systems. All-purpose money has also played a part. In addition to its obvious contribution to overcentralization by facilitating the concentration of real wealth and regulatory prerogative, it flows through virtually all barriers increasing the coherence of the world system enormously.

With increases in monetization, social differentiation, and the amounts of energy harnessed, the disparity between the direction of cultural change and the goal of biological survival has widened. We are led to ask whether civilization, the elaborate stage of culture with which are associated money and banking, high-energy technology, and social stratification and specialization is not maladaptive. It is after all in civilized societies that we observe most clearly oversegregation, overcentralization, oversanctification, hypercoherence, domination of higher by lower order systems, and the destruction of ecosystems. Civilization is, of course, recent, and may yet prove unsuccessful. If civilization is an inevitable outcome of culture it may further be asked if culture is adaptive. To the extent that cultural conventions are arbitrary, men may devise aberrant regulatory structures, and to the extent that their activities are freed from local ecosystemic limitation, they may maintain their aberrant regulatory structures in the face of mounting difficulties. This does not seem possible for other creatures whose activities are dependent upon the ecosystems in which they occur and are, further, much more narrowly specified by their biological characteristics. Nor could others with less powerful intellects develop ideologies that not only mask from themselves the maladaptiveness of their institutions but sanctify those aspects of them that are most maladaptive. If civilization with its maladaptive regulatory hierarchies and misguiding ideologies is an inevitable outcome of culture, and culture of the human level and type of intelligence, and if human intelligence is capable of violating adaptive logic, we may ask, finally, if human intelligence is in the long run adaptive, or merely an evolutionary anomaly bound finally to be destroyed by its own contradictions. Evolutionary "advances" set new problems as well as solve old ones, but to recognize that human intelligence and its products have set as many adaptive problems as they have solved may be the first step toward their solution. That our intelligence causes us difficulties does not mean that it should or could be excluded from the solution of those difficulties. It is, I think the task of anthropologists, among others, to analyze the structures of social systems in terms of adaptation, to develop theories of what the structures of healthy adaptive systems may be like, and also to develop theories of maladaptation and its amelioration. Some crude suggestions have been made here, but the necessary empirical and theoretical work has hardly begun.

Roy A. Rappaport, June 1974

THE CHALLENGE
OF THE PRESENT

V

THE CHALLENGE
OF THE PRESENT

INTRODUCTION

As Dobzhansky leads us into a discussion of the "Present Evolution of Man" it becomes increasingly apparent that any estimate of where we are going as a species must take into account not only our biological potential and our changing environment but also our ability to influence their interaction. For example, research in genetics has introduced the issues of eugenics (the conscious improvement of the gene pool of the population) and euphenics (the alteration of the somatic cell genotype of individuals after conception). The added significance for human evolution of future potentialities such as cloning of ourselves into a population of completely identical individuals or of the selective breeding and artificial insemination which are already being practiced are difficult issues to evaluate. Surely, however, the holistic background attained by being exposed to the kinds of issues subsumed under biological anthropology and covered in many of the articles in this book are enough to suggest that there will be significant evolutionary effects. While it is difficult to predict what the exact effects will be, nevertheless, the moral, legal, and biological questions about various genetically oriented programs with which we will probably have to contend increasingly in the decades to come are certainly with us already as one of the great challenges of the present.

In the environment, dramatic changes have resulted from the agricultural incursion over much of the earth for purposes of feeding our species and from the industrialization of the natural environment for production of goods and energy. In fact, the rates of ecological change are probably as fast or even faster than the ones in Siberia that apparently froze the mastodons in their tracks so long ago. We simply do not know what the long-range effects of these ecological changes will be. What, for example, will be the effects of the rapid decrease in the various animal and plant species over the last 100 years upon the survival of our species over the next 50 years? We can only speculate and look back perhaps at the archeological record, as Paul Martin has done in his interpretation of the rapid disappearance of the Pleistocene mammals in the Americas some 11,000 years ago. (See "Pleistocene Overkill" and "Slaughter in the New World." Science and the Citizen, page 391.)

There are obviously many other major questions that concern the human species. Their complexity requires us to integrate our knowledge of the biological, environmental and sociocultural variables. It has been demonstrated too often that the partial technological social, economic, or biomedical "solutions" to various problems have led to problems equally great or greater than the ones that originally existed. What we clearly need are the *holistic* approaches being developed by anthropologists for the purposes of studying human populations.

Science and the Citizen
December 1966

Pleistocene Overkill

What caused the extinction in North America of large mammals such as the mammoth, the mastodon, the giant sloth and the camel? A change in climate has been the favored hypothesis. Now Paul S. Martin of the University of Arizona has undertaken to show that the cause was another change in the animals' environment: the coming of man.

The remains of 35 mammal genera, Martin writes in *Nature*, have been recovered from California's Rancho La Brea tar pits; they are some 15,000 years old. By 6,000 years ago none of these animals had survived. There is no evidence, however, that there was any catastrophic change in grazing conditions in that period. Moreover, the changes in vegetation that did accompany the last retreat of the Pleistocene ice sheet in the same period had taken place several times before without affecting North America's mammal population. Martin argues that the significant event was not the warming climate but the arrival in the New World of well-armed hunting bands from Asia about 11,000 years ago (see "Elephant-hunting in North America," by C. Vance Haynes, Jr.; SCIENTIFIC AMERICAN, June, 1966).

An argument that has been advanced against the view that man was responsible for the disappearance of North America's largest animals is that Africa, a continent long inhabited by human hunters, still has abundant big game. What this argument overlooks, Martin writes is the fact that at least 25 genera of large mammals (including two genera of primitive elephants and seven or more genera of cattle) became extinct in Africa between 50,000 and 100,000 years ago. The antiquity of this event rules out any possibility that a late Pleistocene change in climate could have been a factor in it.

In recent years the remains of many extinct African mammals have been found in association with large, crude stone hand axes, scrapers, cleavers and other tools. These tools, which are among the earliest specialized human artifacts, belong to a stone-tool industry named the Acheulean (after Saint Acheul, an early Paleolithic site in France). Acheulean industries seem to have disappeared from Africa about 50,-000 years ago—at about the same time by which all but three of the extinct African genera of large mammals had vanished. Proposing that hunters armed with Acheulean weapons did to the fauna of Africa what Paleo-Indian hunters appear to have done in the New World, Martin concludes that in both cases the primary instrument of extinction was "Pleistocene overkill."

Science and the Citizen
May 1973

Slaughter in the New World

When the last continental ice sheet retreated in North America, there were at least 31 kinds of large mammals on the continent, among them mammoths, mastodons, horses, bears, saber-toothed cats, camels, goats, antelopes, tapirs, peccaries, capybaras, four genera of ground sloths and a giant beaver that weighed upward of 400 pounds. All became extinct at about the time man began arriving in the New World from Asia. Could man have been responsible? The question has been difficult to answer on the basis of archaeological evidence. Only seven unmistakable sites where men killed these extinct mammals have been found, and in all seven instances the animals were mammoths.

Paul S. Martin of the University of Arizona, writing in *Science*, has taken another approach to show how a small group of men could have given rise to the great extinction. Martin believes the slaughter began as soon as big-game hunters from Asia invaded the New World. Starting with the assumption that the large mammals of North America were probably as numerous as the large mammals in African game parks are today, he estimates that the ice-free parts of the continent supported some 50,000 pounds of big game per square mile. As the initial event in his hypothetical reconstruction he postulates that an Asiatic hunting band of 100 managed to reach the vicinity of Edmonton, Alberta, 11,500 years ago.

The maximum human population that good hunting ground can support is one person per square mile. Martin visualizes his band strung out in an arc with this average spacing, moving south of Edmonton across the prairie at a net rate of less than a mile per month, preying on the big game as it advanced. Within nine generations the hunters would have reached a point some 400 miles south of Edmonton. At an initial population growth rate of 3.4 percent per year, the number of people in the arc, which would by then have extended from the West Coast to Lake Superior, would have reached 61,000 and the advancing wave, with each person on the average occupying a square mile, would have been 100 miles deep. Within 250 years the arc would have reached the Gulf of Mexico and the total number of people in the hunting bands would have been 300,000.

If during this 250-year advance only one out of every four of these people had on the average killed the equivalent of one 1,000-pound animal per week, the big-game population in the zone of advance would have been reduced by 26 percent per year. Considering the low rate of reproduction among large mammals, an annual loss of this magnitude would have ensured the extinction of the large-mammal population within a decade. A century later the advancing arc would have reached the Isthmus of Panama and most of the big game in North America would have been extinct for more than 100 years.

Thereafter the sweep of the hunters could have been repeated across South America. The nomadic bands would have reached Tierra del Fuego some five centuries later, leaving that continent also stripped of its large mammals. In Martin's view the slaughter went so quickly that "perhaps the only remarkable aspect of New World archaeology is that *any* kill sites have been found."

It seems that the only unique biosocial adaptation we have for dealing with these problems is our ability to store and share useful information about our species and our world (Katz, 1973). We are unlike those species dependent primarily upon their genetic information and the processes of biological evolution for change in their information pools, and even unlike those primate species who, as we learned, for example, from Teleki's article and comments, are fairly imaginative about storing and transferring a good deal of information within their lifetimes. We have evolved an elaborate biosociocultural mechanism that stores the extrasomatic accumulation of information, and this has had the effect of directly augmenting the sum of individuals' learning abilities in the various populations around the world. In other words, through the written word and codes of various kinds we have been able to accumulate the necessary knowledge to continue to adapt to the complex changes in the environment that we, as a species, have produced.

In fact, if we look at the technology developed for purposes of handling this information, it closely mirrors the rate of overall technical changes which have recently occurred. There is undoubtedly a strong relationship, for example, between the complexity and adaptability afforded by a microminiaturized computer and our ability to become extraterrestrial for the first time in the history of the life on our planet. However, all of the "superplexity" of our world is still dependent on individual men and women, with all of the fragility of their personal ontogenies, previous evolution, and behavioral adaptability. Hence, we have an emerging condition where it is becoming just as important to learn about human aggressivity and the potential for waging nuclear war, as it is to learn how to traverse the solar system. As much as we would like to believe that we are free from these human constraints, the reality of our times, the limits of our previous evolution, and the feedback effects of our knowledge about these limits and potentials on our current biosocial adaptability, have to be some of the most awesome sources of burden and inspiration ever experienced by those who come to grips with them.

In a sharply perceptive review of "The Natural History of Aggression," Anatol Rappaport carefully constructs a new kind of framework for critically evaluating the concept of aggression. He rightfully dwells upon the problems of bridging between aggression in individuals and aggression in nation states. Yet from this critical evaluation of aggression at the nation-state level which is one of the most significant problems confronting our survival in the nuclear age, Rappaport touches upon another promising approach for understanding the multi-levelled concept of aggression in a holistic fashion. In this sense it not only closely relates to the kinds of holistic approaches advocated in this book but it also gives us some unusually clear insights into a complex bio-behavioral problem.

The current "population explosion," which in traditional biological terms might be called a successful adaptation, is one of the most important variables ever to influence human evolution. Perhaps if integrated holistic models had been available earlier, and had been used, many of the problems associated with the population explosion could have been averted. Instead, we are probably heading either for some drastic declines in world population or some major changes in the ways in which human populations support themselves.

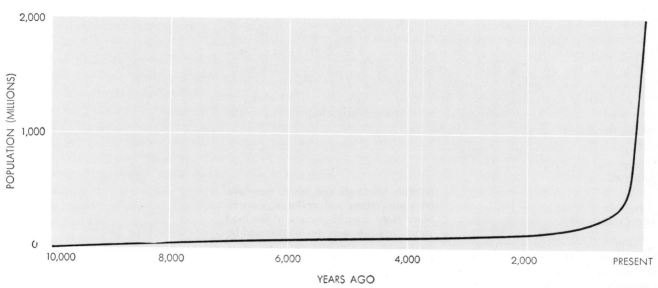

ARITHMETIC POPULATION CURVE (*above*) plots the growth of human population from 10,000 years ago to the present. Such a curve suggests that the population figure remained close to the base line for an indefinite period from the remote past to about 500 years ago, and that is has surged abruptly during the last 500 years as a result of the scientific-industrial revolution.

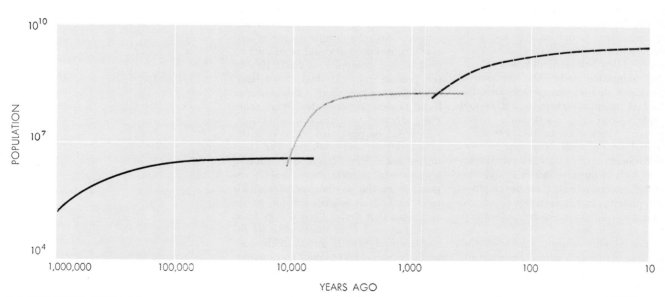

LOGARITHMIC POPULATION CURVE (*below*) makes it possible to plot, in a small space, the growth of population over a longer period of time and over a wider range (from 10^4, or 10,000, to 10^{10}, or 10 billion, persons). The curve, based on assumptions concerning the relationship of technology and population, reveals three population surges reflecting the toolmaking or cultural revolution (*solid line*), the agricultural revolution (*gray line*), and the scientific-industrial revolution (*broken line*).

Several factors over the last few decades probably account for the rapidly increasing rates of world population growth (See Science and the Citizen, articles on population growth, page 402). The development of sophisticated agricultural technologies, interacting with the local resources and populations to raise continually the levels of nutrition, has probably led to increases in fertility. Simultaneously, sophisticated public health technologies have lowered the overall mortality rates of various populations before they have been able to develop socially acceptable mechanisms of limiting fertility. This has led to a phenomenal increase in the number of people being born over the number of people dying each year. Thus, over the last 35 years, the combination of increased food production and its interactive effects with fertility, coupled with the introduction of public health measures which doubled the average life span in some populations without any programs for limiting fertility, quickly produced an uncontrolled expansion of the world-wide human population beyond the demographer's most extreme estimates. The consequences of a world population growth out of control and the possibility that our amazing ability to use our rapidly growing extrasomatic information pool to help us create new technologies to solve the problems of the population explosion, without provoking world-wide conflict and possible nuclear catastrophe, seems to be the most important challenge currently facing the human species.

Science and the Citizen
July 1967

The Protein Gap

Specific measures to cope with the critical protein deficiency in the developing countries of the world have been recommended to the United Nations Economic and Social Council by its Advisory Committee on the Application of Science and Technology to Development. Its report is based on a working paper prepared by Nevin S. Scrimshaw of the Massachusetts Institute of Technology. Many countries are "losing the capacity to feed themselves" as food production lags behind population growth, the committee finds. The problem of quality of diet is even more serious than that of quantity: there is not enough protein available, particularly animal protein, which alone contains certain essential amino acids. The gap between nutritional requirements and protein consumption in these countries is widening and threatens to halt their development completely, and conventional agriculture and animal husbandry cannot cope with the situation.

The committee urges a massive effort to close the protein gap. It recommends, first of all, that production from conventional sources be increased by improving agricultural methods, materials, incentives and credit facilities in the developing countries. The efficiency of fisheries can be improved by new fishing and distribution methods and by an emphasis on conservation and pollution control. Since more than 25 percent of the food supply in some countries is consumed by animal pests, spoilage and processing losses, improved methods of pest control, storage and distribution need to be introduced.

Turning to novel sources of protein, the committee suggests that new plant varieties can be developed through genetic research. Large amounts of protein are available in the form of oilseeds in many developing countries but remain unused; "no other single source of unconventional protein could contribute so greatly and promptly towards closing the protein gap." Methods have been developed for preparing palatable foods from oilseed concentrates. The same thing is true of various fish concentrates, which can be processed to make palatable foods or food additives. The committee notes that "single cell" protein sources can provide more protein regardless of the availability of agricultural land. Such sources include yeasts and algae that derive their energy from petroleum and from photosynthesis respectively. Synthetic amino acids, particularly lysine, tryptophan and methionine, can be added to cereals and other plant products to improve their nutritive value. All these steps require research and training, and the committee proposes new UN-supported programs in these areas.

Science and the Citizen
October 1971

Food and Population

Food production in the Far East rose 5 percent last year, a rate of increase that the Food and Agriculture Organization of the United Nations describes as "comfortably ahead of the population growth." Progress was also made in a number of other developing countries, but a larger number failed to increase their food production fast enough to supply their growing population with more and better food from their own output. Summarizing the situation in a preliminary version of its annual study titled *The State of Food and Agriculture 1971*, the FAO cited "the continued progress of rice and wheat production in the Far East, the world's most concentrated food-deficit zone," but added that "there was little or no increase in the total food production of the developing countries of Africa and the Near East," so that in per capita terms their output declined, and that although food production rose in Latin America, the increase "was just sufficient to keep pace with population growth."

In a foreword to the study Addeke H. Boerma, director-general of the FAO, attributed the gain in rice and wheat output in the Far East to "steadily increasing use... of improved seed varieties" and noted that governments there "are taking measures to spread the new technology over still larger areas and to bring it to farmers who thus far have not been able to profit by it." He advised caution, however, in speaking of "the green revolution as if it were already an accomplished fact." Although the new technology now applied to cultivating rice and wheat in a number of countries has brought many benefits, Boerma said, "this is not yet a green revolution." Even in the most successful countries the increases in rice and wheat production have not been matched by similar increases in the production of other foods, and in many other countries intensive programs to raise yields "are only at a very early stage, if they have been started at all." What is required, he said, is "a widespread introduction of improved agricultural technology... in the developing world as a whole."

Science and the Citizen
January 1974

Supersorghum

Sorghum is the world's fourth most important food grain (after wheat, rice and corn), being the principal subsistence grain for more than 300 million people in underdeveloped countries. It has the advantage of growing on land that is too dry and too infertile for other grains. On the other hand, the most commonly grown strains have the disadvantage of being low in protein and in lysine, one of the amino acids essential in the human diet as a building block for protein. Now investigators at Purdue University have announced a discovery that promises to increase substantially the nutritional value of sorghum.

After analyzing some 9,000 strains of sorghum from many countries the Purdue group, which worked under a $1.7-million contract from the U.S. Agency for International Development (A.I.D.), found two strains from Ethiopia that are much richer than the commonly grown sorghum in protein and in lysine. Presumably the traits can be bred into the strains of sorghum that are grown widely for food. John A. Hannah, administrator of the A.I.D., said when the discovery of the Ethiopian strains was announced that improving the protein quality of sorghum "will amount to a gift of life, especially for children."

Theodosius Dobzhansky's article "The Present Evolution of Man" and Sir Gavin De Beer's review of Dobzhansky's book *Mankind Evolving: The Evolution of the Human Species* epitomizes in many respects the articles presented in earlier sections. The fact, for example, that human genetics and disease resistance of various kinds are closely interwoven is essential for understanding the effects of modern medical technology or, for that matter, the effects of DDT on the malaria-carrying anophales mosquito, or the incidence of plague in the rat-infested cities of the Middle Ages, or even the complex models of modern sanitation involving poliomyelitis or possibly even

multiple sclerosis. All are related to the complex changes that we have introduced into our ecosystem which, in turn, is shaping our evolution. Even our
increasing capability to select certain requisites *in utero* may lead, for
example, to increased selection for intelligence. Along these lines, Dobzhansky points out that human evolution is still going on, and that we are playing
an even greater role both knowingly and unknowingly in the selective processes of our evolution.

The course of human evolution in the next several decades may depend
less on our triumphs over particular diseases or even our ability to manipulate
our genetic composition (though these are very important issues, in the long
run), than it will on an integrated and holistic knowledge of our species. In
this perspective, we must understand the operation of the entire ecosystem of
our species. It may not be enough to understand the genetic evolution of
the species at the individual gene level. We must develop new synthetic
models for the study of human adaptability. We must merge what we know
of biological evolution with what we know of the sociocultural adaptation
and evolution of the species. In short, we need a biosociocultural anthropology. This synthesis would take into consideration not only the biological
dimensions of the species but also the social, cultural, environmental and
demographic variables. In order to "house" this complex set of continuously
interacting variables, we need new kinds of human ecological models. The
remainder of this book is devoted to some of the new building blocks, problems and concepts that must be added to our current theoretical basis of biological anthropology. Although the articles in this section are excellent both
for their individual content and their contribution to this new approach, the
list is incomplete. In one sense, this deficit provides a real challenge to the
reader to explore, analyze, and discover new dimensions necessary for an
understanding of the potentials and limitations of our species as we continue
to evolve in the twentieth century.

As Alfred E. Mirsky suggests in his multidimensional review of *Biology
and the Future of Man*, edited by Philip Handler, we are rapidly acquiring
the ability to alter significantly the genetic basis of our species. He particularly cites the issue of *eugenics*, which traditionally involves genetic counseling to prevent mating of partners whose genotypes would produce a
disadvantageous phenotype. Many genetic screening centers for sickle cell
trait and Tay-Sachs disease trait (see Friedmann, page 424) counsel potential
mates who are heterozygous for the trait against having children, in order
to eliminate the great emotional and economic difficulties stemming from
the birth of a chronically debilitated child who is homozygous for the particular disease.

Theodore Friedmann discusses another eugenic measure in his article
"Prenatal Diagnosis of Genetic Disease." Friedmann notes that there is a
growing list of genetic disorders that can be recognized *in utero* by a technique called *amniocentesis*. Following the discovery of the disorder, the
mother is frequently counseled to undergo an abortion in order to prevent
the birth of a seriously retarded or otherwise maladapted child. In the light
of population policy it might be interesting to ask what the relationships are
between counseling for an abortion of a diseased child and counseling for
an abortion of a so-called "unwanted child." (See Science and the Citizen
for various discussions of abortion.) The answer is important because implicit
in it is the question of a new form of genetic selection based upon the biological and social cost of the child. However, this kind of selection is not new;
for instance, many societies have traditionally performed infanticide on mal-
formed babies. Furthermore, the patterns of infant mortality due to disease
or undernutrition show the results of the interaction of natural biological
selection and socioeconomic factors. The issue of amniocentesis is, however,
more precise. It involves the definition in advance of somewhat arbitrary

grounds of the "cost" of certain phenotypes and the decision to select only against them and not any others. Of course, it is now reasonably easy to make these decisions, but as the list of recognizable problems increase we will need to consider these issues much more seriously.

An alternate proposal, in the realm of genetic engineering, is introduced by Robert Sinsheimer in the Science and the Citizen column "Designed Genetic Change," (page 398). Instead of dealing with prevention of mating, his proposal suggests ways in which the phenotype of an individual could be altered according to his or her needs. This type of genetic engineering has been called *euphenics* (alteration of the somatic cells after the phenotype has been formed). If a genetically based chronic disease were discovered *in utero*, instead of aborting the fetus, it might be possible to change the genetic aberrancy to produce a more adaptive phenotype.

Science and the Citizen
July 1964

Preventing Mental Retardation

Massachusetts and New York are the first states to enact laws specifically designed to prevent mental retardation. The legislation requires a simple blood test of all newborn infants to detect the disease phenylketonuria (PKU), which results from a genetic defect. The PKU patient lacks an enzyme needed to utilize the amino acid phenylalanine, a constituent of all food proteins. Within 30 days after birth waste products that accumulate from the excess of phenylalanine begin to damage the brain irreversibly. Although there is no cure for the condition, a special diet low in phenylalanine can prevent mental retardation.

The testing of nearly 400,000 newborn infants in 28 states and Puerto Rico during the past two years has shown that PKU occurs about once in 10,000 births. As many as 400 children with PKU are born in the U.S. annually. The test, developed by Robert Guthrie of the New York State University School of Medicine in Buffalo, uses the "inhibition assay" principle. A sample of dried blood is placed in an agar culture medium containing a phenylalanine antagonist and spores of *Bacillus subtilis*. The antagonist normally inhibits the multiplication of the bacillus, but in the presence of blood from a baby with PKU a colony of the bacilli develops overnight. Guthrie is now applying the principle to the development of similar tests for several other genetic defects responsible for metabolic diseases.

The New York law requiring tests for PKU [went] into effect [in] 1965. Massachusetts has had its law since 1963.

Science and the Citizen
March 1966

Rh Incompatibility Controlled?

Investigators in several countries are evaluating a technique that may eliminate the hazard arising when a woman with Rh-negative blood bears the children of a man with Rh-positive blood. Some 85 percent of the people in the U.S. are Rh-positive: on the surface of their red blood cells is a substance that is not present on the red cells of the Rh-negative 15 percent. When an Rh-negative woman gives birth to an infant that has inherited its father's Rh-positive blood, Rh-positive red cells leak through the placenta and enter her bloodstream. She may then produce antibodies to remove the cells, a response known as active immunization. When she becomes pregnant with a second Rh-positive child, the response is intensified, that is, she produces antibodies in much larger quantity. These antibodies can destroy Rh-positive red cells in the unborn child and give rise to the serious disorder erythroblastosis fetalis. About one in every 200 infants born in the U.S. suffers from this disorder; three out of four recover completely but one out of four dies.

Several years ago Vincent J. Freda and John G. Gorman of the Columbia University College of Physicians and Surgeons and William Pollack of the Ortho Research Foundation in Raritan, N.J., undertook an attempt to prevent active immunization from arising in pregnant Rh-negative women. Independently R. Finn and his colleagues at the University of Liverpool began a similar effort. Each group injected its subjects with a serum rich in an antibody (sometimes called "anti-D") that is known to destroy Rh-positive red cells. By administering anti-D immediately after delivery the investigators were able to induce a short-lived "passive immunization" that sufficed to destroy the Rh-positive red cells that had entered the woman's blood. This passive immunization can be induced repeatedly without being intensified. Theoretically a woman supplied with anti-D will not produce any antibody of her own, and samples of blood taken from subjects months after delivery contain neither self-produced antibody nor anti-D. The investigators are awaiting the next pregnancies of their subjects.

Science and the Citizen
February 1967

Genetic Passenger

Ever since it became clear that genes are segments of the deoxyribonucleic acid (DNA) molecule some biologists have wondered if it might someday be possible to alter the genetic material of a human being, for example to supply a deleted gene and thereby remedy some metabolic deficiency. How would one introduce the desired genetic information? One possibility that has now received some preliminary experimental support would be to administer a harmless virus that bears the required gene.

The Shope papilloma virus, which causes tumors in rabbits, also induces the synthesis of a distinctive form of the enzyme arginase that lowers the concentration in the rabbits' blood of the amino acid arginine. The question arose whether the same effect might be obtained in human beings, but one may not infect people with animal viruses for experimental purposes. It occurred to Stanfield Rogers of the Oak Ridge National Laboratory that he could get at the question indirectly: he compared the blood of a number of people who had worked with, and therefore been exposed to, the Shope virus with the blood of randomly selected controls.

According to Rogers' report in *Nature*, many of the research workers exposed to the virus were found to be carrying "virus information." They had generally lower arginine levels than controls did and a number of them had lower levels than had ever been reported before. Eight out of 12 serum specimens from people exposed to the Shope virus showed specific antibodies against the distinctive form of arginase but not

against normal rabbit-liver arginase, indicating that the virus DNA had supplied the information for the synthesis. The blood of the research workers did not contain demonstrable neutralizing antibodies against the Shope virus itself, indicating that the infected cells were not synthesizing the protein outer coat of the virus.

The Shope virus, Rogers suggests, is a harmless "passenger" virus in these people. It is possible that there are other such viruses. Perhaps some of them carry genes that would be useful in the treatment of genetic disease. It is conceivable that a harmless virus might even be utilized as a vector for specific information in the form of tailor-made DNA that could be attached to the virus and transferred by the process known as transduction. The evidence for such possibilities is only suggestive at this point; far more experimentation, including more direct tests in animals of the manner in which enzyme production and activity is induced in the host, will be necessary before manipulation of human DNA is considered a serious possibility.

Science and the Citizen
July 1969

Designed Genetic Change

The possibility of human genetic modification is implicit in man's new understanding of the mechanism of the living cell. If an organism's form and function are ordained by its proteins (including its enzymes), if proteins are specified by genes, if genes are segments of nucleic acid molecules whose instructions are written in a genetic code that is now largely deciphered and if means exist whereby bits of DNA can be introduced into living cells—then may it not be possible to design genetic change? The possibility is real, according to Robert L. Sinsheimer of the California Institute of Technology. In an article in the institute's magazine *Engineering and Science* he suggests that the prospect may be analogous to the prospect in the 1930's that the energy of the atomic nucleus might be unlocked: "The principles seem in hand. All that seems really needed is optimism, sustained effort and support commensurate with the importance of the problem."

Sinsheimer defines genetic change as an alteration of any process that appears to be "programmed into us through our inheritance." Such change might be achieved either in a "genetic mode," by changing inheritable characteristics, or in a "somatic (noninheritable) mode," by changing the action of inherited genetic components or supplying components to body cells. Somatic modification is more limited but likely to be achieved sooner. Sinsheimer examines the feasibility of making this kind of change for the "genetic therapy" of diabetes.

In a person with diabetes the beta cells of the pancreas fail to produce enough insulin. In a normal person the genetic instructions for making proinsulin, the precursor of insulin, are probably present in all the body cells but are not activated—are "repressed"—in all but the beta cells. The instructions are presumably present in a diabetic's cells too, but the beta cells have degenerated or the instructions have become repressed even in the pancreas. If that is the case, perhaps one can "turn on" insulin synthesis in the diabetic, if not in the beta cells, then in some other cells. Genes are, in fact, turned on by hormonal and other action in many situations; the beta cells themselves are activated somehow at a stage of embryonic development. The problem is to find an agent that can do this.

An alternative approach would be to supply to some group of cells a new gene or genes that carry the instructions for the synthesis of insulin but that are not subject to repression. The necessary transfer might be accomplished by transduction, in which a virus carries new genetic material into a host cell. Where is one to find a virus carrying the genes of manufacturing insulin? Sinsheimer says: "I propose that we should quite literally, in time, be able to make it to order." In the "not distant future" it should be possible to synthesize the appropriate chain of DNA subunits and wrap it in a proper virus coat.

Beyond such genetic therapy lie the "larger and deeper challenges" of "a new eugenics." One essential in which the new differs from the old eugenics is that the old called for breeding the fit and culling the unfit; the new eugenics can aim to convert all the unfit to the highest genetic level. If that prospect seems frightening, Sinsheimer writes, we should reflect on the alternative; consider "the losers in that chromosomal lottery that so firmly channels our human destinies"—the 200,000 or so children born each year in the U.S. with genetic defects. Faced with this need, he suggests, we should "shoulder the responsibility for intelligent genetic intervention." The

concept of designed genetic change, he writes, "marks a turning point in the whole evolution of life. For the first time in all time a living creature understands its origin and can undertake to design its future."

Science and the Citizen
October 1971

Cause and Effect

In the year since a liberalized abortion law went into effect in New York State (on July 1, 1970), New York City has had a distinct decline in birthrate, in the number of babies born out of wedlock and in the number of maternal deaths related to abortion. The law allows a physician to perform an abortion on any consenting woman who is not more than 24 weeks pregnant; previously an abortion was legal only if it was thought necessary to preserve the life of the mother. The effects of the new law are reported by Jean Pakter and Frieda Nelson of the New York City Department of Health in *Family Planning Perspectives,* a publication of the Planned Parenthood Federation of America. Pakter and Nelson found that the number of births in the first six months of 1971 was 60,695, compared with 64,667 in the first half of 1970; that births out of wedlock, which had been rising since they were first recorded in 1954, were 9,805 in the first four months of 1971 and 10,180 in the same period of 1970, and that the number of maternal deaths related to abortion during the first quarter of 1971 was, at seven deaths per 100,000 live births, only 40 percent of the figure for the first four months of 1970. "If this downturn in maternal deaths continues," they write, "New York City will experience for 1971 its lowest ratio of maternal deaths ever recorded."

Pakter and Nelson take note of predictions at the time the new law was passed that "the state and, more particularly, an unprepared New York City would be subjected to social and medical catastrophe" from an inundation of women seeking abortions. "None of these dire predictions," they find, "has come to pass." About 164,300 legal abortions were performed in the city during the first year under the new law, and most of them were "at costs considerably lower (and, of course, under conditions immeasurably safer) than were prevalent among illegal practitioners."

The authors also report that poor women and black women in particular have benefited from the new law. "New York's experience," they write, "indicates that when abortion is made available and accessible at low cost it will be used to terminate unwanted pregnancies by all ethnic and racial groups."

Another process of selection, *eutelogenesis*, involves the use of preselected sperm donors and artificial insemination. As Muller (1966) has suggested, one male could over his lifetime produce enough sperm to fertilize tens of thousands of eggs. Closely related to this theme is *cloning*, a technique now successfully used with frogs by which a somatic cell nucleus from an individual is transplanted into an ennucleated egg cell and then grown into a genetically identical individual. Another method of so-called "positive eugenics" which has been used by cattle and dog breeders for years, very simply promotes selective breeding for desirable traits. Obviously, before we can undertake further analysis of the evolutionary implications of this theme for the human species, we must take into consideration society's moral and ethical codes. Nevertheless, strong new specific forms of genetic selection and alteration are realities that must be reckoned with in new theories of human evolution.

The rates at which we are changing our ecosystem in the twentieth century probably rank with some of the most extreme changes in the history of life on this planet. Only recently have we begun to notice the effects described by George M. Woodwell in his article "Toxic Substance and Ecological Cycles." The probable truth is that we have only a limited knowledge of what we have already done. In the United States, we have become more wary in recent years of introducing potentially toxic substances into our food and our atmosphere particularly since learning that apparently innocuous substances in fertilizers, pesticides, industrial wastes, and even medicines have proven highly toxic under certain conditions. Just how these substances produce added selective factors, in our environment is not fully understood, but it is known that they are having an effect. For example, the high lead content in the deciduous teeth of Philadelphia children is found not only among those children who eat lead-based paint chips, but also among those in neighborhoods where high lead concentrations are found in the environmental dust.

Of course, various toxic substances have produced partial benefits by improving agricultural production. However, the nutritional success of agriculture has immensely changed the structure and increased the size of human populations throughout the world. These changes have produced a variety of new biological adaptations and precipitated a variety of technological innovations that function in a reciprocal interacting relationship with the greatly increased modern demands of an exponentially increasing population. In this regard, Lester R. Brown's article "Human Food Production as a Process in the Biosphere" demonstrates some of the complex feedback relations among technological innovation, agricultural needs, biomedical problems, and the growth of human population size over the last century.

The phenomenal increase in population growth in the last 500 years may be one of the most important developments in the history of human evolution. We can assume that the demographic variable for most of human evolution was more a constant than a variable. It is unlikely that preagricultural human groups ever varied more than two orders of magnitude (10^1 to 10^3) in population size, and even the upper limits of this range were probably rare. Thus the variations introduced by population size alone throughout most of human evolution were reasonably constant and probably closely reflected the carrying capacity of the local ecosystem to supply their needs. However, with the growth of agricultural products that could be stored and distributed, the population density no longer depended only on the nonagricultural resources of the local ecosystem and new variations in orders of magnitude of supportable population size resulted. This development was hastened by the process of industrialization. Today, a number of cities in the world have more than 10^6 population. (See Science and the Citizen, p. 402.)

The figures on page 393 show the recent upswing in the curve of human population growth. When Edward Deevey prepared these graphs in 1960, he estimated the "present" world population on the upper graph at a little less than two billion people. The incredible fact is that the same graph drawn today would have to be approximately twice as high to show the growth that has occurred since he wrote his article. This has interesting implications for his logarithmic plot of population growth over time. If we accept the idea that at least three sociocultural revolutions led to the population jumps he indicates, then, taking Tomas Frejka's "The Prospects for a Stationary World Population" (*Scientific American* Offprint 683) and projecting population size up to the magnitude of 10^{10} on this kind of graph, we would be forced to conclude that another population revolution is occurring right now! It probably started about 30 years ago, just after World War II, spurred by the technological and communications "explosion" that has allowed almost the entire species to share the total "biosociocultural" information pool. According to all of our current estimates, if the human population should reach 15 billion people over the next 75 to 100 years, then we may be reaching the upper limits of the supportable human biomass and should start various programs to level off population size or reduce it. However, it is more likely that reductions will occur over the next 25 years, before we reach this kind of population problem. In this regard many nations have already expressed their concerns at the first worldwide United Nations sponsored "World Population Year—1974" meetings in Bucharest, Rumania.

The last article, "The History of the Human Population" by Ansley J. Coale, gives us numerous insights on the magnitude of these population changes and, in fact, confirms the concept that another revolution has indeed occurred over the last thirty years. Coale ascribes this principally to the marked reduction in human mortality, particularly among the developing nations of the world. Perhaps more than any other, this article clearly indicates the demographic implications of the unprecedented growth of our species. Along these lines Coale implicitly suggests that it will not be long before we will have a stable world population whose demographic characteristics could vary all the way from one with mothers bearing an average of eight children and living to an average age of fifteen years to one with mothers bearing two children and living to an average age of seventy-five years. Both conditions are possible, and it will soon be common place for decisions about these problems to be made at all levels.

When we consider that for the vast majority of human history people have lived in small groups of several hundred, we can begin to grasp the significance of population growth as an evolutionary force. The growth of mega-populations has no doubt introduced immense changes in the processes of "natural" selection. From the cultural perspective, the sheer numbers of people in highly populated areas have brought about changes in social and economic organization. We know that there have been tremendous changes in expectations of appropriate affective and cognitive behavior (see "Stress and the Zulu," in Science and the Citizen, page 303) as well as in reproductive patterns and health histories. However, if we are going to utilize demographic studies as one of the building blocks in the growing science of current human evolution and adaptation, we must include the interactive inhibitory and self-stabilizing feedback effects of the knowledge of the effects of overpopulation upon human reproductive behavior. Ansley Coale's article gives us a new appreciation of the human ability for self-study and problem-solving even when the problem involves a truly novel set of circumstances.

100 Years Ago
June 1960

JUNE, 1860: "The population of the world is now estimated at 1,279,000,000, viz.: Asia, 755,000,000; Europe, 272,-000,000; Africa, 200,000,000; America, 50,000,000; Australia, 2,000,000."

"The Suez Canal, to unite the Red Sea with the Mediterranean, has been commenced at Port Said, where two large moles, running out nearly a mile into the sea, are being constructed. About 1,700 European workmen and several thousand natives are employed on the works."

"The advent of the Japanese Embassy, and the interest in this but partially known people, has induced us to give some account of their achievements in the agricultural and mechanical departments. Being compelled to make the most of their not very extensive and rather poor soil, they have arrived at a very high state of perfection in the arts of agriculture. Where the land is inaccessible to the plow, it is cultivated by manual labor. Like the Chinese, they pay great attention to manuring and to irrigation. The short time the Embassy has already been with us shows how eager they are to profit by the experience of foreigners, and to imitate their useful arts. The inhabitants of Japan are already supplied with microscopes, telescopes, clocks, watches, knives, spoons, &c., made by themselves from European models. They manufacture Colt revolvers and Sharps rifles, and it is said that they have made improvements upon them. At Nagasaki works have been erected for the manufacture of steam-engines without European assistance."

Science and the Citizen
January 1960

Population Control

Under the pressure of its super-dense population Japan has achieved the most rapid decline of a birth rate in history. A report in *Population Bulletin* states that the rate has dropped from 34.3 births per 1,000 people in 1947 to 18.5 in 1956 and 17.2 in 1957. The annual rate of population growth is now the lowest in Asia: about 1.2 per cent (compared with 1.8 per cent in the

U. S.). The Japanese resorted primarily to abortion and sterilization: In 1957 there were 1,170,000 recorded abortions and probably an equal number of unrecorded ones. More than 42,000 women were reported sterilized in 1955, and the actual total may have been 10 times as high. Recent surveys indicate that contraception is now becoming the principal means of birth control, even in rural areas.

In the U. S. birth control for overpopulated countries has recently been advocated by two governmental advisory groups. The President's Committee to Study the U. S. Military Assistance Program recommended last July that this country furnish assistance in population control to any nation requesting it lest growing populations make other aid expenditures futile. In a study for the Senate Foreign Relations Committee, the Stanford Research Institute pointed out that while population growth in the Western world followed economic development, "in many underdeveloped countries today a very rapid population growth is preceding economic development," thanks to modern medicine and public-health techniques. Its report called for U. S. help in combatting the "world population explosion." It added: "The traditional means have been disease, famine and war. If other means are to be substituted, conscious national and international policies will be required."

Science and the Citizen
May 1961

Three Billion People

The world "population explosion" is even more explosive than has been suspected, a United Nations report indicated in March. Forecasting that the world's population would pass three billion this year, the UN Department of Economic and Social Affairs suggested that current population projections would have to be revised upward on the basis of recent censuses in a number of countries.

India's latest census, conducted in February, illustrates the trend in the populous nations of southeast Asia. The provisional figures for India show a population of 438 million, eight million more than the previous estimate. This represents a 21.5 per cent rise since 1951, when the last census was taken, compared with a 14.5 per cent increase in the 10 years from 1941 to 1951.

An even sharper rise in population was reported from Pakistan, where a new census earlier this year showed a population of 93,812,000. This is an increase of 23.7 per cent in 10 years. Recent census figures from Thailand and the Philippines also show population increases sharper than expected.

World population figures are, of course, estimates, based on data of uneven quality from the various nations. The UN put the world's population at 2,495,000,000 in 1950 and 2,907,000,-000 in mid-1959. The annual rate of increase has been running at about 1.7 per cent but now seems to be approaching 2 per cent; hence the three billion estimate for 1961.

India furnishes statistics to illustrate both the basic cause and the economic effect of the population explosion in the underdeveloped nations. The cause is a lowered death rate. While India's birth rate has held fairly steady at about 40 per 1,000 people per year, the death rate dropped from 25.9 per 1,000 between 1951 and 1956 to 21.6 between 1956 and 1961, and is projected at 18.2 per 1,000 for the period of the new five-year plan of 1961 to 1966. The economic effect is to make it much more difficult to raise the standard of living: a substantial rise of 40 per cent in the national income since 1951 was cut by population growth to an increase of only 19 per cent in per capita income.

Science and the Citizen
June 1964

Fertility and Economic Growth

The way to curb India's rate of population increase is to concentrate on raising the economic level of the country's poorest villagers, argues the Indian demographer P. B. Gupta. In a series of papers published by the Indian Statistical Institute, Gupta points out that the decrease in mortality rates in India and other developing countries today has been brought about by public health measures, not by economic development, and it is therefore unlikely to be followed quickly—as such a decrease was in many Western countries some years ago—by a reduction in the birthrate. Gupta finds, moreover, that India's rural population, which accounts

for 83 per cent of the total population, is not practicing birth control and is not likely to do so until there are changes in education and social structure that require major economic growth.

Gupta studied the relation between the marital fertility rate and the level of living of Indian villagers as revealed in national statistics for 1953 and 1954. He found that fertility is low among people living at a bare subsistence level and tends to rise with some improvement in the level of living. At what he calls a "critical level" of living, fertility reaches a maximum value, and only thereafter does it begin to drop with increasing economic status; the curve of fertility plotted against level of living rises to a peak and then falls. Gupta adapted this curve, a cross section of the rural fertility situation 10 years ago, to construct a curve predicting the relation of fertility to economic growth over the years.

A uniform increase of even as much as 20 per cent in the standard of living of all income groups, without a relative improvement in the condition of the lowest-income group, would cut the birthrate hardly at all, he concluded. He suggests, therefore, that special efforts should be made to improve the status of the poorest villagers in order to transfer as many people as possible from the "rising" portion of the fertility curve to the "falling" portion; that is, "to cause the people at the lower levels of living to cross the critical level." Such a transfer, he says, would not require a very great overall economic advance. Yet it should "automatically" reverse the fertility trend in the poorest segment of the population, paving the way for the greater reduction in fertility that should come with significant economic development.

Science and the Citizen
July 1961

How Many People?

Japan is unique among the major nations in having steadily reduced the rate of growth of its population to a point suggesting that the population will begin to decrease in a generation or so if the present level of reproduction continues. Now concern is rising that the trend will inhibit the rapid economic growth the nation has experienced over the past decade. The situation is described by Minoru Muramatsu, chief of the Section of Public Health Demography of the Institute of Public Health in Tokyo, in "Country Profiles," a publication of the Population Council.

Muramatsu notes that the population of Japan was about 50 million in 1912 and had doubled by 1967. The annual rate of growth of the population during this period therefore averaged 1.3 percent. In the U.S. the population has grown at rates ranging from a high of 21 percent in the first decade of this century to a low of 7.2 percent between 1930 and 1940 (see "The Census of 1970," by Philip M. Hauser, page 17). In recent years the Japanese rate has been about 1.2 percent per year; by 1985, according to the Institute of Population Problems (an agency of the Ministry of Health and Welfare in Japan), it will decline to .7 percent.

The control of population in Japan has been largely voluntary. It is traced by Muramatsu back to the "rice riots" of 1918, when people in many parts of the country demonstrated against the high price of rice; the episode was widely interpreted as being an indication that there was not enough food to go around. "Regardless of official policy decisions or the pros and cons of birth control," he writes, "people proceeded to practice birth control on their own, primarily through induced abortion." Two government policies, however, were "notable influences." The first was the establishment of the Eugenic Protection Law; the second, the establishment of a national program for the promotion of family-planning practice. The chief aim of the law, which was enacted in 1948, was to liberalize induced abortion. The number of reported induced abortions rose sharply to a peak of 1.17 million in 1955; thereafter it declined gradually to 744,451 in 1969. The family-planning policy, inaugurated in 1952, resulted from alarm in the Cabinet about the abortion rate; the policy was that contraception was to be recommended as a far more reasonable method of family limitation.

Then came the economic boom, which has kept Japan's economic growth rate above 10 percent a year since 1963 (except in 1965). During the same period, because of the downward trend in fertility, a shortage of young workers developed. The annual increment of the productive age group (15 to 64) was 960,000 from 1965 to 1970 but will be only 620,000 from 1970 to 1985.

As a result of these effects, according to Muramatsu, "a reaction to the low fertility trend and apprehension of 'diminishing' population are developing. Business magnates and industrial leaders have voiced concern over the shortage of young workers." The Population Problems Council gained wide attention with a report saying that Japan would have to raise its fertility rate slightly in order to bring about a stationary population in the future and recommending that efforts to raise fertility levels should be directed toward the strengthening of social-development problems so that the people encounter fewer economic, social and other deterrents to pregnancy, childbirth and child-rearing. In the present debate over population policy, Muramatsu writes, "some maintain that an increase in the birthrate is imperative, while others wonder why Japan should raise its fertility rates in the face of an inevitable increase of tens of millions in the population expected during the several decades to come." Both groups, however, recognize that "the future fertility trends in this country will be largely determined by the people, not by interventions from outside."

Science and the Citizen
October 1971

Optimism and Population

A comprehensive study of world population growth by a committee of the National Academy of Sciences under the chairmanship of Roger Revelle of Harvard University takes the basically optimistic position that "the natural resources available to present technology are sufficient to allow a vast improvement in the standard of living of all the people who will inhabit the earth 20 to 30 years from now." The committee's report, *Rapid Population Growth: Consequences and Policy Implications*, took three years to prepare. The two-volume work, just published by the Johns Hopkins Press, is concerned with "the most fundamental event of our times—the enormous growth of the world's population during the last 3 decades, and the prospects for continued growth in the future."

The authors observe that "apocalyptic visions of the future are based on simple, mathematical extrapolation of present rates of population growth." They have adopted the modest goal of examining "the population problem as it affects us now—and for the next 5 to 30 years."

They acknowledge that if present fertility rates and mortality trends continue, the world population could reach 7.5 billion in the year 2000. Making "reasonable allowance for reductions in fertility," however, they suggest that seven billion is a more likely figure. They do not believe that "uncontrolled population growth in the earth's poor countries is leading to catastrophe." They write: "It is possible...to take a different view, based on what we know about the history of human populations and on the behavior of many people at the present time—a view that social inventions will lead to a deliberate limitation of fertility by individual couples." As evidence that sharp changes in fertility are possible in a short time, they point to Japan, where birthrates decreased by nearly 50 percent between 1948 and 1960. Decreases nearly as large in Taiwan and South Korea show that a high level of development is not a necessary precondition.

Volume I of the report, subtitled *Summary and Recommendations*, issued in paperback, reviews the history of world population growth, describes the different rates of growth in different regions of the world, presents the economic and social consequences of uncontrolled population growth and outlines a "population policy" with specific recommendations. The authors refer to surveys showing that there is an almost universal desire among parents to have a limited number of children but that in poor countries children are "the poor man's capital." Moreover, this capital is highly perishable. In East Pakistan, for example, the average 45-year-old woman has had 7.6 children, a third of whom have died. "Another important reason for the excess of live births over the number of desired children," the report continues, "is undoubtedly the ineffectiveness, difficulty, and hardship of preventing births with the methods now available to the people of poor countries." The authors state their conviction that "a full range of acceptable, easily used, and effective means of preventing births" are available today and could be provided by governments to everyone "at nominal or no cost."

The report analyzes the arguments sometimes put forward that rapid population growth can be economically beneficial for poor countries under certain circumstances. The authors believe this thesis is almost always misguided if all social costs are considered. Although the report emphasizes that couples must be "given full freedom of choice" on family size, it concludes that a full accounting of "benefits and costs for society as a whole" will "justify social intervention to influence the fertility behavior of the parents.... Many specialists are convinced that governmental population policies to limit fertility must go beyond furnishing contraceptive materials, services, and information.... The freedom of husbands and wives to make reproductive decisions must, therefore, be tempered by concern for the rights and interests of others."

The report recommends a number of policies to help the nations of the world lower fertility rates. It observes that "over a billion births will have to be prevented during the next 30 years to bring down the world's population growth rate from the present 2 percent per year to an annual rate of 1 percent by the year 2000. The task may well be the most difficult mankind has ever faced, for it involves the most fundamental characteristic of all life—the need to reproduce itself."

Science and the Citizen
October 1972

Fertility and Contraception

The modernization of U.S. contraceptive practices, dramatized by a 36 percent decline in the rate of unwanted childbearing between the five-year periods ending in 1965 and 1970, has been a major factor in the remarkable decrease in the U.S. birthrate during the past decade. The birthrate dropped from 23.7 per 1,000 of population in 1960 to 17.3 in 1971 and was below 16 per 1,000 in each of the first five months of this year. The "total fertility rate" (in effect the projected average number of children per completed family based on current age-specific fertility rates) dropped from 3.62 in 1961 to 2.46 in 1968. According to Charles F. Westoff of Princeton University, codirector of the 1970 National Fertility Study, a significant increase in the use by married couples of the most effective means of contraception was "undoubtedly the main explanation" for the decline in unwanted births.

The study, which paralleled one that was made in 1965, was based on extensive interviews with a national sample population of women under 45 who

were married and living with their husbands. Westoff describes the result in
Family Planning Perspectives, a publication of the Planned Parenthood Federation of America. There was little
change, he writes, in the proportion of
couples who were currently using contraception: 63.9 percent in 1965 and 65
percent in 1970. (Most of those who
were not using contraception were either
pregnant, sterile, subfecund or seeking
a pregnancy.) The important change, he
points out, was in the methods used. In
1965 only 37.2 percent of the couples
practicing contraception were using one
of the three most effective methods: the
oral contraceptive pill, sterilization or
the intrauterine device. In 1970, 57.9
percent of such couples were using one
of these most effective methods. Adding
those who were using other effective
methods, Westoff writes, about four out
of five couples practicing contraception
in 1970 were "highly protected from the
risk of unintentional conception." This
high level was being experienced by
blacks and whites and generally by couples of widely varying educational level,
"probably in substantial part due to the
efforts of public and private family planning programs."

Westoff terms the adoption of the oral
contraceptive pill by American women
"an amazing phenomenon." First available to the public in 1960, the pill was
being used in 1965 by 23.9 percent of
the married women currently practicing
contraception; by 1970 the proportion
had increased to 34.2 percent. The pill
was most popular among wives less than
30 years old, almost half of whom were
using the oral contraceptive in 1970.
The intrauterine device (IUD) is still
much less popular than the pill, but its
use grew sixfold, from 1.2 percent of the
wives practicing contraception in 1965
to 7.4 percent in 1970.

Voluntary sterilization (usually a tubal
ligation for women and a vasectomy for
men) was the method selected by 12.1
percent of the couples using contraception in 1965 and by 16.3 percent in
1970. The acceptance of these surgical
procedures by older couples (those in
which the wife is between 30 and 44
years old) was particularly striking: in
1970 a fourth of all older couples who
were currently practicing contraception
had been surgically sterilized, with the
operations about evenly divided between men and women.

Science and the Citizen
October 1972

Rural Earth

Although the fraction of human beings
who live in cities has been increasing at an accelerating rate since about
1850, some 61 percent of the human
population is still in rural areas. "Clearly,
by the standards of a highly industrial
nation, the world is not yet extremely
urbanized," writes Kingsley Davis of the
University of California at Berkeley in
World Urbanization 1950–1970, the second volume of his two-volume study of
the subject. "Yet it is worth noting," he
adds, "that the present degree of world
urbanization is both very recent and
totally unprecedented. Prior to 1850 no
country, no matter how advanced, was
as urbanized as the world is today. It
was not until just after 1850 that the
United Kingdom, the first country to in-
dustrialize, became as urbanized as the
world was in 1970, and not until around
1900 that urbanization reached this level
in the United States. In other words, although the world as a whole is just entering the twentieth century with respect
to urbanization, it is not far behind the
most advanced countries and is certainly
a long way from the Middle Ages. Furthermore ... the global level of urbanization is rising rapidly.... Barring some
great reversal in the process of change,
it will not be long before the world as a
whole is as urbanized as even the most
advanced nations are today."

About 2.2 billion people live in places
classified as rural and about 1.4 billion
in urban places. Since most of the rural
people depend on agriculture for a living, Davis notes, the figures show "the
extent to which the human species, for
all its vaunted science and technology, is
still devoting its labor to meeting the
elementary needs for food and natural
fibers." Even so, he says, the rate of
growth of urbanization has been so rapid
in recent decades that "if [it] continues
in the future, the world will be 100 percent urban in the year 2031." Davis concludes that the recent trend in urbanization "certainly will not endure long in
the future." He also points out that although the rate of growth of urbanization has been rapid, "when the shift in
the world's *level* of urbanization between 1950 and 1970 is compared to

the change during the previous century and a half, it does not seem particularly spectacular or even unprecedented."

Science and the Citizen
February 1973

Leveling Off

The reproductive behavior of Americans appears to have changed significantly, with important implications for the rate of growth and the future structure of the U.S. population and economy. The fertility rate has been falling for some time; so have the crude birthrate and the actual number of births, in spite of an increased number of women of childbearing age. Perhaps most significant, recent statistics show that the total fertility rate—the projected size of completed families—has dropped below 2.1 children per family. That is the level at which the population can eventually attain a steady state, with births just balancing deaths. The present age structure of the population and the likelihood of changes in fertility patterns mean that the U.S. will not soon enter a period of zero population growth, but the Bureau of the Census is apparently convinced that population growth will be slower than had been expected: its latest projections, issued in December, of the population in the year 2000 have been revised sharply downward from the 1971 estimates.

The U.S. birthrate was 23.7 per 1,000 of population in 1960, 17.3 in 1971 and only 15.8 in the 12 months ending last October. The general fertility rate (births per 1,000 women of childbearing age, or 15 through 44) was 82.9 in the first 10 months of 1971 and only 73.6 in the same period last year. As a result it appears that the total increase in the U.S. population last year was only about .7 percent as compared with an average annual increase of 1.1 percent from 1963 to 1970. The total fertility rate is more clearly related to family size. It is derived by summing the age-specific rates for the 30 childbearing years, and thus tells how many children a hypothetical woman would bear if she experienced the current fertility of women at successive ages. (The zero-growth rate is 2.1 rather than 2 per family because some girls die before reaching the age of childbearing.) The total fertility rate was more than 2.2

even during the Depression. It rose to 3.8 in 1957, declined to 2.46 in 1968 and to 2.39 in the first nine months of 1971. In the same period last year it dropped to 2.08.

The reason appears to be primarily that more young women are not marrying, are marrying later or are marrying and nevertheless delaying having children; this could indicate a long-term change in reproductive behavior or it could merely cause a temporary decrease in population growth. Even if the average family size were stabilized at 2.1, the population would grow from its present 209 million to about 320 million in some 70 years before leveling off, because a disproportionately large number of women will be reaching childbearing age in the years ahead.

The fact remains that all current trends point to a period of slower population growth. Notable among these trends are the increase in the proportion of women who work and the expressed intention of women at all economic and educational levels to have smaller families, an objective that will be easier to attain because of the increased efficacy of contraceptive techniques and the increased availability of legal abortion. As a result the Bureau of the Census has modified its population estimates for the year 2000. The bureau makes four projections on the basis of various total fertility rates and it has eliminated its previous "high" projection, based on a rate of 3.1, of 322.3 million. The current high projection, based on a rate of 2.8, is a U.S. population of 300.4 million in 2000. The next two projections, based respectively on rates of 2.5 and 2.1, are 286 million and 264.4 million. A new "low" projection has been introduced based on a rate of only 1.8, which would generate a population of 250.7 million in 2000. As recently as 1967 the highest projection was 361 million and the lowest was 280.7 million.

Science and the Citizen
April 1973

Homo Sapiens

In the middle of 1971, the latest date for which figures are available, the earth was inhabited by 3.7 billion people. They were having children at the rate of 34 per 1,000 per year and dying at the rate of 14 per 1,000. Thus they were increasing their total number by 2 percent per year, which would double the world population by the year 2006 if the rates were maintained (which would be an unlikely occurrence). Population is increasing most rapidly in Latin America (2.9 percent per year), Africa (2.6 percent) and Asia (2.3 percent), and least rapidly in North America (1.2 percent), the U.S.S.R. (1 percent) and Europe (.8 percent). The figures are from the United Nations *Demographic Yearbook* for 1971, which was published in February.

Birth rates are decreasing in much of the world, according to the UN, particularly in Europe. The lowest rates in 1971 were in West Germany (12.8 per 1,000), Luxembourg (13) and Finland (13.1). In 1971 the U.S. rate was 17.3, but last year it dropped to 15.6. Twelve countries in Africa and Asia still had birth rates above 50 per 1,000; the highest rate, 52.3, is shown for Swaziland.

Official figures from China (the first for the *Yearbook*) show that Shanghai is the world's most populous city, with 10,820,000 people. It is thus considerably bigger than Tokyo (8,841,000) and New York (7,895,000). Peking, London and Moscow are the only other cities with more than seven million inhabitants. When it comes to urban agglomerations rather than central cities, the largest are New York (11,572,000), Buenos Aires and Paris.

Urbanization continues to advance throughout the world. Definitions of urban places vary and so it is somewhat misleading to compare different countries, but on the basis of national definitions Belgium is the country with the highest degree of urbanization: 86.8 percent. Australia (which has a broad definition encompassing built-up areas) reports that 85.5 percent of its people live in urban places. Other countries that are more than 80 percent urbanized are Sweden, Israel and Uruguay. The U.S. figure is 73.5. The highest degree of urbanization in Africa is 47.9. Urbanization does not, of course, equal crowding. Australia seems almost empty (two people per square kilometer), whereas (apart from a number of small islands and city-states such as Macau and Monaco) Belgium is one of the most crowded countries (319 inhabitants per square kilometer), along with England and Wales, the Netherlands and South Korea.

The highest life expectancy at birth is found in Sweden and the Netherlands: female infants born in either country can expect to live for 76.5 years. Among males the longest-lived are Swedish (71.9 years), and male life expectancy is more than 70 in only four other countries: Norway, Iceland, the Netherlands and Denmark. Female life expectancy,

on the other hand, is more than 70 in 43 of the 108 countries for which data are available. There are seven countries in which men have a longer life expectancy than women. They are all African or Asian nations with high birth rates and high maternal mortality.

Infant mortality, considered a good indicator of a population's health, is decreasing generally. The Netherlands and Sweden had the lowest rate in 1971: 11.1 per 1,000 live births. Finland (11.8), Japan, Iceland, Norway, Denmark and France (14.4) followed in that order; the U.S. rate was 19.2.

The marriage rate appears to be declining in West Germany, Austria and Sweden; it is going up in Cuba, France, Italy, Ireland, Egypt, Israel and the U.S.S.R. As for divorce, the U.S., with 3.7 divorces per 1,000 of population in 1971, is the undisputed leader, yielding only to its "divorce mill," the Virgin Islands (4.6). Puerto Rico, Cuba and the Spanish Sahara come next, followed by the U.S.S.R. (2.6) and Hungary.

Science and the Citizen
February 1974

Grow, No-Grow

Two extreme positions have been established in the current debate on economic growth, and Ronald G. Ridker of Resources for the Future suggests that both of them "are wrong—indeed, that they border on the irresponsible." The pro-growth school, he writes in *Science*, holds implicitly that material economic growth is the primary social goal, taking precedence over equity and measures to cope with the social and environmental costs of growth. The no-growth school, on the other hand, seems to hold that social problems will disappear if growth ends. "The relevant question," he says, "is not whether to grow or not to grow, but how to channel and redirect economic output . . . in ways that will make it better serve humanity's needs." Ridker grants that the earth is finite, that the law of entropy cannot be violated and that growth must therefore someday cease. But when? It makes a difference if the limitation must come now or in 100, 1,000 or 100,000 years.

Ridker criticizes the well-known study *The Limits to Growth*, which suggests that the limitation must come quickly, on three grounds. Its model, he says, does not include important adjustment mechanisms: prices, which redirect exploration, research and consumption; government, which can do similar things; simple learning from experience, which leads people to change their behavior as they learn its potential consequences. Then too, the model is based on extreme

aggregation, so that it deals with a composite "output," one "resource," one "pollutant" and the world as a whole. This compounds the lack of adjustment mechanisms by eliminating the possibility of substitutions by producers, consumers and society and thereby reducing the choice to one between growth and limitation of growth. Finally, Ridker maintains, *The Limits to Growth* makes pessimistic assumptions about technological progress, reserves, pollution control and population growth. Changing these assumptions makes a significant difference in estimates of when growth must stop even in the absence of the many adjustment mechanisms that would come into play.

For most problems associated with growth, Ridker writes, direct attacks on the problems are probably better than indirect attacks on economic or population growth. He cites a Resources for the Future study's conclusions with regard to various forms of pollution. In each case the amounts of pollutants generated and actually emitted would increase substantially by the year 2000, even assuming low economic and population growth. In the presence of an active abatement policy, however (defined as the application by 2000 of standards that have been recommended by the Environmental Protection Agency for 1976), emissions would be cut well below present levels even in high-growth projections—and at a cost of less than 2 percent of the G.N.P. in the year 2000. In other words, a direct attack through pollution abatement is more effective than a generalized "meat ax" restriction of growth.

There are large areas of ignorance, Ridker concedes, and he asks: "Should we not, in effect, stop the ship, or at least slow it down, until we know more about what lies ahead in the fog?" No, since we are ignorant not only about the negative developments that may accompany growth but also about positive developments, which may improve the well-being of future generations in addition to avoiding disaster. It is therefore "not obvious that the prudent course is to save resources for future generations, at least not obvious to any but the most affluent on this earth."

If society fails to attack such growth-associated problems as pollution directly, then they will indeed build up to the point that they do call for reductions in growth, Ridker writes. Advocates of no-growth may believe that to be the situation; Ridker would hope to prove they are wrong. To do so, however, requires bypassing the conventional debate on limiting growth. "Both schools, it seems to me, are copouts. What we must do is get on with the solution to the problems that obviously and directly face us."

The Present Evolution of Man

by Theodosius Dobzhansky
September 1960

Man still evolves by natural selection for his environment, but it is now an environment largely of his own making. Moreover, he may be changing the environment faster than he can change biologically

In tracing the evolution of man, this issue of SCIENTIFIC AMERICAN deals with a natural process that has transcended itself. Only once before, when life originated out of inorganic matter, has there occurred a comparable event.

After that first momentous step, living forms evolved by adapting to their environments. Adaptation—the maintenance or advancement of conformity between an organism and its surroundings—takes place through natural selection. The raw materials with which natural selection works are supplied by mutation and sexual recombination of hereditary units: the genes.

Mutation, sexual recombination and natural selection led to the emergence of *Homo sapiens*. The creatures that preceded him had already developed the rudiments of tool-using, toolmaking and cultural transmission. But the next evolutionary step was so great as to constitute a difference in kind from those before it. There now appeared an organism whose mastery of technology and of symbolic communication enabled it to create a supraorganic culture. Other organisms adapt to their environments by changing their genes in accordance with the demands of the surroundings. Man and man alone can also adapt by changing his environments to fit his genes. His genes enable him to invent new tools, to alter his opinions, his aims and his conduct, to acquire new knowledge and new wisdom.

The authors of the preceding articles have shown how the possession of these faculties brought the human species to its present biological eminence. Man has spread to every section of the earth, bringing high culture to much of it. He is now the most numerous of the mammals. By these or any other reasonable standards, he is by far the most successful product of biological evolution.

For better or worse, biological evolution did not stop when culture appeared. In this final article we address ourselves to the question of where evolution is now taking man. The literature of this subject has not lacked for prophets who wish to divine man's eventual fate. In our age of anxiety, prediction of final extinction has become the fashionable view, replacing the hopes for emergence of a race of demigods that more optimistic authorities used to foresee. Our purpose is less ambitious. What biological evolutionary processes are now at work is a problem both serious and complex enough to occupy us here.

The impact of human works on the environment is so strong that it has become very hard to make out the forces to which the human species is now adjusting. It has even been argued that *Homo sapiens* has already emancipated himself from the operation of natural selection. At the other extreme are those who still assume that man is nothing but an animal. The second fallacy is the more pernicious, leading as it does to theories of biological racism and the justification of race and class prejudice which are bringing suffering to millions of people from South Africa to Arkansas. Assuming that man's genetic endowment can be ignored is the converse falsehood, perhaps less disastrous in its immediate effects, but more insidious in the long run.

Like all other animals, man remains the product of his biological inheritance. The first, and basic, feature of his present evolution is that his genes continue to mutate, as they have since he first appeared. Every one of the tens of thousands of genes inherited by an individual has a tiny probability of changing in some way during his generation. Among the small, and probably atypical, sample of human genes for which very rough estimates of the mutation frequencies are available, the rates of mutation vary from one in 10,000 to one in about 250,000. For example, it has been calculated that approximately one sex cell in every 50,000 produced by a normal person carries a new mutant gene causing retinoblastoma, a cancer of the eye affecting children.

These figures are "spontaneous" frequencies in people not exposed to any special agents that can induce mutation. As is now widely known, the existence of such agents, including ionizing radiation and certain chemicals, has been demonstrated with organisms other than man. New mutagens are constantly being discovered. It can hardly be doubted that at least some of them affect human genes. As a consequence the members of an industrial civilization have increased genetic variability through rising mutation rates.

There is no question that many mutations produce hereditary diseases, malformations and constitutional weaknesses of various kinds. Some few must also be useful, at least in certain environments; otherwise there would be no evolution. (Useful mutants have actually been observed in experiments on lower organisms.) But what about minor variations that produce a little more or a little less hair, a slightly longer or a slightly shorter nose, blood of type O or type A? These traits seem neither useful nor harmful. Here, however, we must proceed with the greatest caution. Beneficial or damaging effects of ostensibly neutral traits may eventually be discovered. For example, recent evidence indicates that people with blood of type O have a slightly higher rate of duodenal ulcer than does the general population. Does it follow that O blood is bad? Not necessarily; it is the most frequent type in many populations, and it may conceivably confer some advantages yet undiscovered.

Still other mutants that are detrimental when present in double dose (the so-called homozygous condition, where the same type of gene has been inherited from both parents) lead to hybrid vigor in single dose (the heterozygous condition). How frequently this happens is uncertain. The effect surely operates in the breeding of domestic animals and plants, and it has been detected among X-ray-induced mutations in fruit flies. Only one case is thus far known in man. Anthony C. Allison of the University of Oxford has found that the gene causing sickle-cell anemia in the homozygous condition makes its heterozygous carriers relatively resistant to certain forms of malaria. This gene is very frequent in the native population of the central African lowlands, where malaria has long been endemic, and relatively rare in the inhabitants of the more salubrious

highlands. Certainly there are other such adaptively ambivalent genes in human populations, but we do not know how many.

Despite these uncertainties, which cannot be glossed over, it is generally agreed among geneticists that the effects of mutation are on the average detrimental. Any increase of mutation rate, no matter how small, can only augment the mass of human misery due to defective heredity. The matter has rightly attracted wide attention in connection with ionizing radiation from military and industrial operations and medical X-rays. Yet these form only a part of a larger and more portentous issue.

Of the almost countless mutant genes that have arisen since life on earth began, only a minute fraction were preserved. They were preserved because they were useful, or at least not very harmful, to their possessors. A great majority of gene changes were elimi-

nated. The agency that preserved useful mutants and eliminated injurious ones was natural selection. Is natural selection still operating in mankind, and can it be trusted to keep man fit to live in environments created by his civilization?

One must beware of words taken from everyday language to construct scientific terminology. "Natural" in "natural selection" does not mean the state of affairs preceding or excluding man-made changes. Artificially or not, man's environment has altered. Would it now be natural to try to make your living as a Stone Age hunter?

Then there are phrases like "the struggle for life" and "survival of the fittest." Now "struggle" was to Darwin a metaphor. Animals struggle against cold by growing warm fur, and plants against dryness by reducing the evaporating leaf surface. It was the school of so-called social Darwinists (to which Darwin did not belong) who equated "struggle" with violence, warfare and competition

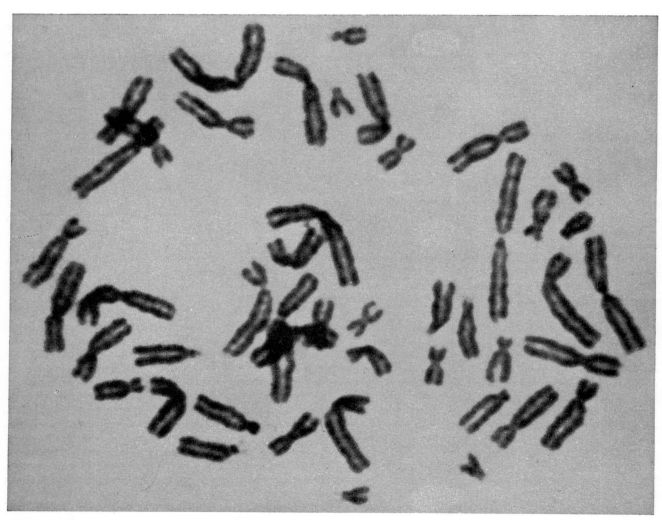

HUMAN CHROMOSOMES are enlarged some 5,000 times in this photomicrograph made by J. H. Tjio and Theodore T. Puck at the University of Colorado Medical Center. The photomicrograph shows all of the 23 pairs of chromosomes in a dividing body cell.

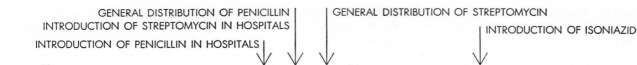

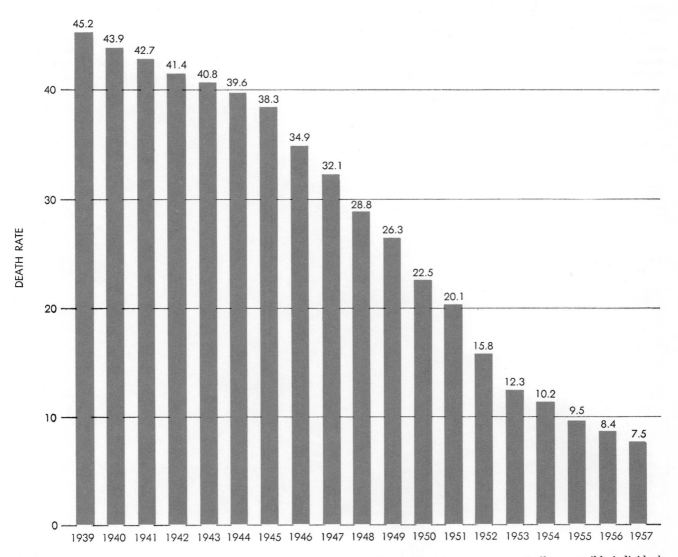

TUBERCULOSIS DEATH RATE per 100,000 people showed a dramatic decline with the introduction of antibiotics and later of the antituberculosis drug isoniazid. As tuberculosis becomes less prevalent, so does its threat to genetically susceptible individuals, who are enabled to survive and reproduce. The chart is based upon information from the U. S. National Office of Vital Statistics.

without quarter. The idea has long been discredited.

We do not deny the reality of competition and combat in nature, but suggest that they do not tell the whole story. Struggle for existence may be won not only by strife but also by mutual help. The surviving fit in human societies may in some circumstances be those with the strongest fists and the greatest readiness to use them. In others they may be those who live in peace with their neighbors and assist them in hour of need. Indeed, co-operation has a long and honorable record. The first human societies, the

hunters of the Old Stone Age, depended on co-operation to kill big game.

Moreover, modern genetics shows that "fitness" has a quite special meaning in connection with evolution. Biologists now speak of Darwinian fitness, or adaptive value, or selective value in a reproductive sense. Consider the condition known as achondroplastic dwarfism, caused by a gene mutation that produces people with normal heads and trunks, but short arms and legs. As adults they may enjoy good health. Nevertheless, E. T. Mørch in Denmark has discovered that achondroplastic dwarfs produce, on

the average, only some 20 surviving children for every 100 children produced by their normal brothers and sisters. In technical terms we say that the Darwinian fitness of achondroplasts is .2 or, alternatively that achondroplastic dwarfism is opposed by a selection-coefficient of .8.

This is a very strong selection, and the reasons for it are only partly understood. What matters from an evolutionary point of view is that achondroplasts are much less efficient in transmitting their genes to the following generations than are nondwarfs. Darwinian fitness is reproductive fitness. Genetically the surviving fittest is neither superman nor conquering hero; he is merely the parent of the largest surviving progeny.

With these definitions in mind, we can answer the question whether natural selection is still active in mankind by considering how such selection might be set aside. If all adults married, and each couple produced exactly the same number of children, all of whom survived to get married in turn and so on,

there would be no selection at all. Alternatively, the number of children, if any, that each person produced might be determined by himself or some outside authority on the basis of the desirability of his hereditary endowment. This would be replacing natural selection by artificial selection. Some day it may come to pass. Meantime natural selection is going on.

It goes on, however, always within the context of environment. As that changes,

the Darwinian fitness of various traits changes with it. Thus by his own efforts man is continually altering the selective pressure for or against certain genes.

The most obvious example, and one with disturbing overtones, is to be found in the advance of medicine and public health. Retinoblastoma, the eye cancer of children, is almost always fatal if it is not treated. Here is "natural" selection at its most rigorous, weeding out virtually all of the harmful mutant genes

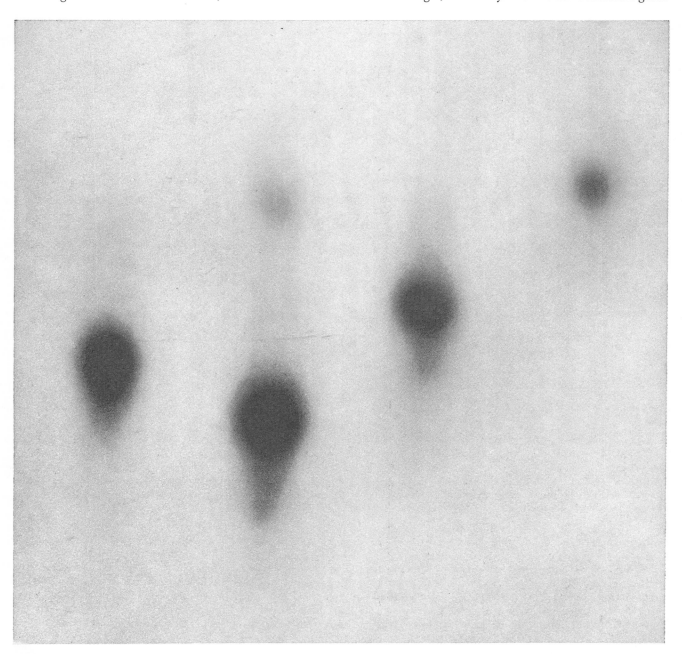

CHEMICAL STRUCTURE OF HEMOGLOBIN in an individual's blood is determined by his genes. Normal and abnormal hemoglobins move at different speeds in an electric field. This photograph, made by Henry G. Kunkel of the Rockefeller Institute, shows surface of a slab of moist starch on which samples of four kinds of human hemoglobin were lined up at top, between a negative electrode at top and a positive electrode at bottom (electrodes are not shown). When current was turned on, the samples migrated toward positive electrode. At right hemoglobin C, the cause of a rare hereditary anemia, has moved down only a short way. Second from right is hemoglobin S, the cause of sickle-cell anemia, which has moved farther in same length of time. Normal hemoglobin, third from right, has separated into its A and A_2 constituents. At left is normal fetal hemoglobin F, obtained from an umbilical cord.

before they can be passed on even once. With proper treatment, however, almost 70 per cent of the carriers of the gene for retinoblastoma survive, become able to reproduce and therefore to transmit the defect to half their children.

More dramatic, if genetically less clear-cut, instances are afforded by advances in the control of tuberculosis and malaria. A century ago the annual death rate from tuberculosis in industrially advanced countries was close to 500 per 100,000. Improvement in living conditions and, more recently, the advent of antibiotic drugs have reduced the death rate to 7.5 per 100,000 in the U. S. today. A similarly steep decline is under way in the mortality from malaria, which used to afflict a seventh of the earth's population.

Being infectious, tuberculosis and malaria are hazards of the environment. There is good evidence, however, that individual susceptibility, both as to contracting the infection and as to the severity of the disease, is genetically conditioned. (We have already mentioned the protective effect of the gene for sickle-cell anemia. This is probably only one of several forms of genetic resistance to malaria.) As the prevalence of these diseases decreases, so does the threat to susceptible individuals. In other words, the Darwinian fitness of such individuals has increased.

It was pointed out earlier that one effect of civilization is to increase mutation rates and hence the supply of harmful genes. A second effect is to decrease the rate of discrimination against such genes, and consequently the rate of their elimination from human populations by natural selection. In thus disturbing the former genetic equilibrium of inflow and outflow, is man not frustrating natural selection and polluting his genetic pool?

The danger exists and cannot be ignored. But in the present state of knowledge the problem is tremendously complex. If our culture has an ideal, it is the sacredness of human life. A society that refused, on eugenic grounds, to cure children of retinoblastoma would, in our eyes, lose more by moral degradation than it gained genetically. Not so easy, however, is the question whether a person who knows he carries the gene for retinoblastoma, or a similarly deleterious gene, has a right to have children.

Even here the genetic issue is clear, although the moral issue may not be. This is no longer true when we come to genes that are harmful in double dose,

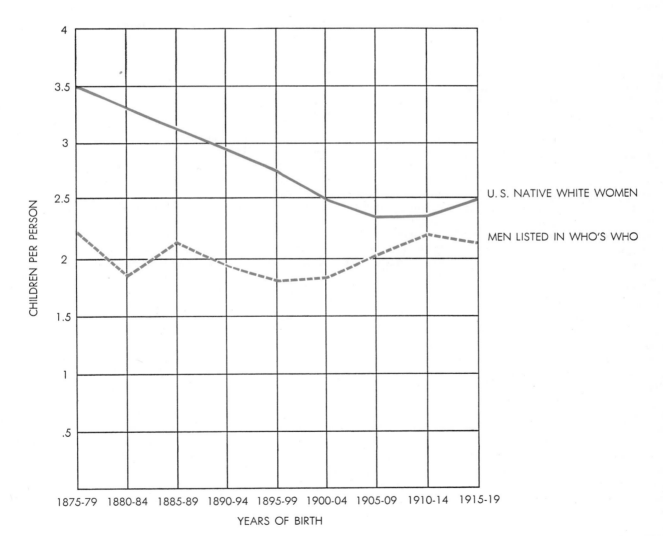

FERTILITY RATE among relatively intelligent people, as represented by a random sample of men listed in *Who's Who in America* for 1956 and 1957, is lower than fertility rate of the U. S. population as a whole, as represented by all native white women. The two fertility rates have recently been moving toward each other. Vertical scale shows average number of children per person; horizontal scale shows approximate birth date of parents. Chart is based upon information collected by Dudley Kirk of the Population Council.

but beneficial in single. If the central African peoples had decided some time ago to breed out the sickle-cell gene, they might have succumbed in much larger numbers to malaria. Fortunately this particular dilemma has been resolved by successful methods of mosquito control. How many other hereditary diseases and malformations are maintained by the advantages their genes confer in heterozygous carriers, we simply do not know.

Conversely, we cannot yet predict the genetic effect of relaxing selection pressure. If, for example, susceptibility to tuberculosis is maintained by recurrent mutations, then the conquest of the disease should increase the concentration of mutant genes as time goes on. On the other hand, if resistance arises from a single dose of genes that make for susceptibility in the double dose, the effects of eradication become much less clear. Other selective forces might then determine the fate of these genes in the population.

In any case, although we cannot see all the consequences, we can be sure that ancient genetic patterns will continue to shift under the shelter of modern medicine. We would not wish it otherwise. It may well be, however, that the social cost of maintaining some genetic variants will be so great that artificial selection against them is ethically, as well as economically, the most acceptable and wisest solution.

If the evolutionary impact of such biological tools as antibiotics and vaccines is still unclear, then computers and rockets, to say nothing of social organizations as a whole, present an even deeper puzzle. There is no doubt that human survival will continue to depend more and more on human intellect and technology. It is idle to argue whether this is good or bad. The point of no return was passed long ago, before anyone knew it was happening.

But to grant that the situation is inevitable is not to ignore the problems it raises. Selection in modern societies does not always encourage characteristics that we regard as desirable. Let us consider one example. Much has been written about the differential fertility that in advanced human societies favors less intelligent over more intelligent people. Studies in several countries have shown that school children from large families tend to score lower on so-called intelligence tests than their classmates with few or no brothers and sisters. Moreover, parents who score lower on these tests have more children on the average than those who get higher marks.

We cannot put our finger on the forces

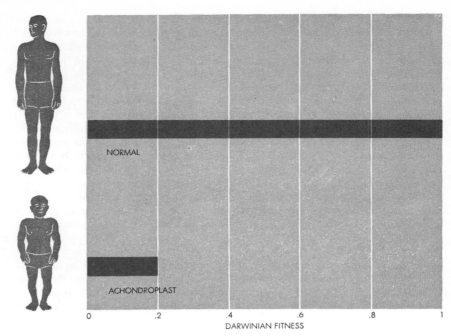

DARWINIAN FITNESS of achondroplastic dwarfs is low. Dwarfs may be healthy, but they have only 20 surviving children to every 100 surviving children of normal parents.

responsible for this presumed selection against intelligence. As a matter of fact, there is some evidence that matters are changing, in the U. S. at least. People included in *Who's Who in America* (assuming that people listed in this directory are on the average more intelligent than people not listed there) had fewer children than the general population during the period from 1875 to 1904. In the next two decades, however, the difference seemed to be disappearing. L. S. Penrose of University College London, one of the outstanding human geneticists, has pointed out that a negative correlation between intelligence and family size may in part be corrected by the relative infertility of low-grade mental defectives. He suggests that selection may thus be working toward maintaining a constant level of genetic conditioning for intelligence in human populations. The evidence presently available is insufficient either to prove or to contradict this hypothesis.

It must also be recognized that in man and other social animals qualities making for successful individuals are not necessarily those most useful to the society as a whole. If there were a gene for altruism, natural selection might well discriminate against it on the individual level, but favor it on the population level. In that case the fate of the gene would be hard to predict.

If this article has asked many more questions than it has answered, the purpose is to suggest that answers be sought with all possible speed. Natural selection is a very remarkable phenomenon. But it does not even guarantee the survival of a species. Most living forms have become extinct without the "softening" influence of civilization, simply by becoming too narrowly specialized. Natural selection is opportunistic; in shaping an organism to fit its surroundings it may leave the organism unable to cope with a change in environment. In this light, man's explosive ability to change his environment may offer as much threat as promise. Technological evolution may have outstripped biological evolution.

Yet man is the only product of biological evolution who knows that he has evolved and is evolving further. He should be able to replace the blind force of natural selection by conscious direction, based on his knowledge of nature and on his values. It is as certain that such direction will be needed as it is questionable whether man is ready to provide it. He is unready because his knowledge of his own nature and its evolution is insufficient; because a vast majority of people are unaware of the necessity of facing the problem; and because there is so wide a gap between the way people actually live and the values and ideals to which they pay lip service.

Mankind Evolving: The Evolution of the Human Species

35

By Theodosius Dobzhansky

Reviewed by Sir Gavin de Beer

*The role of genetics in the evolution of man,
including his future evolution*

Of all the natural sciences that can be brought to bear on the evolution of mankind, which is not quite the same thing as the evolution of man, genetics is among the most important and the author of this book is one of its foremost exponents. His book *Genetics and the Origin of Species* was epoch-making, and the present work is no less important. He begins by using a broad brush to sketch the scope of evolution, including that of man and his culture, and the theories advanced to explain it. Next follows an epitome of the general principles of genetics to which he has himself made such notable contributions, the relative importance of nature and nurture in determining the characters of an organism, the results of observations on identical twins, the integration of genetics and natural selection, the history of man's body as revealed by fossils, and his mental faculties and their antecedents. In a treatment of the problem of race, he shows among other things how the Indian caste system was an attempt to breed varieties of man genetically specialized to perform different functions and trades, whereas ancient China aimed at the converse process of a system of social mobility. The threats of increased mutation rates due to the effects of radiation, and of population increase due to lack of control, come in for careful appraisal; and although these dangers are squarely faced, and self-awareness is recognized as a blessing in giving man the power of imagination but as a curse in accompanying this gift with those of responsibility and freedom, the note on which he ends is not one of despair. Instead his discussion constantly provokes thought, which is obviously the first step along the way to the solution of these problems.

The significance of a hereditary link between the human race and the animal kingdom was already recognized by Darwin in the earliest notebook entries that he made in 1837, within a year of his return to England from the voyage of the *Beagle*. At that time he wrote: "If we choose to let conjecture run wild, then animals, our brethren in pain, disease, death, suffering and famine—our slaves in the most laborious works, our companions in our amusements—they may partake of our origin in one common ancestor—we may be all netted together." It is through genetics that we are all netted together in evolution, although at the time Darwin wrote these words knowledge of genetics amounted to less than nothing. The theory of blending inheritance, all that there then was to go on, is utterly false. It held that offspring struck an average between the characters of their parents and that variation was therefore halved after each generation. With the application of the experimental method to problems of heredity, first by Gregor Mendel and then by Thomas Hunt Morgan and his colleagues, the science of genetics has now been placed on an unassailable basis, and heredity has its particulate genes, just as physics and chemistry have their elemental particles, quanta and atoms. Realization of the implications of the principles of genetics remains, however, astonishingly poor among laymen.

It is still said, for instance, that a son is a chip of the old block. It may be that he resembles his father, but if he does, it is not because he is a detached bit of him, as is commonly imagined. Children are not the products of their parents at all. If they were, it would be impossible to understand why brothers or sisters are not identical; after all, their ancestry is identical. It would be necessary to suppose that all the differences between them were the result of new variations that had arisen during their own lives. Genetics has to account for differences no less than similarities; the problem is as simple—and as fundamental—as that. Children are the products of the germ plasm, the stream of hereditary factors that has flowed through the ancestors containing the genes, of which parents are nothing but the custodians who were themselves formed from the germ plasm of their antecedents. Children are the delayed brothers and sisters of their parents, and from the beginning of the evolution of man on earth it is literally and scientifically true that all men are brothers.

Because of the peculiar mechanism by which germ cells—eggs and sperm—are formed, no child can contain more than half of the genes carried by either parent. The mother is as likely as the father to transmit genes controlling characters that in some instances are shown by neither parent. Furthermore, the same mechanism of germ-cell formation sees to it that the complement of genes received by a child is not identical with that of either parent. There is plenty of room for the possibility that the chip may differ significantly from the old block, and this is what makes it difficult to support the view that the qualities of a useful legislator, say, are bound to appear in his children. For the same reason schemes to establish a sperm bank in which the most distinguished men would have accounts cannot avoid an element of chance. If you breed 10,000 peas or fruit flies, differing in characters controlled by genes that have been analyzed, the proportions in which the offspring will show those characters can be predicted with fair accuracy; when it comes to one child produced by one man and one woman, it is more difficult. Furthermore, as Professor Dobzhansky cogently asks, "Are we ready to agree what the ideal man ought to be?" Besides, there is something more, because there is another notion that is in need of repair. It is the view, still often expressed, that some characters are "innate" and others are "acquired." Nothing would seem to be more innate than that vertebrate animals should have two eyes in their heads. They have had them since the Silurian period, 350 million years ago. Yet if a fish embryo is made to develop in water to which a small quantity of a simple salt such as magnesium chloride has been added, it does not develop a pair of eyes at all but a single eye in the middle of its head like a Cyclops. This is one of the proofs that regardless of how long a time a line of ancestors may have possessed genes that control the development of structures, they cannot produce normal structures if the environment is abnormal. The reason for this is that the development of any character whatever is the result of interaction between the genes inside the organism and the factors of the environment outside it. Conversely, those people who set great store by the action of the environment must be reminded by this same simple experiment that 350 million years of normal environment has done nothing to "fix" the invariable and normal development of characters that one might think had been as irrevocably built in as a pair of eyes.

What all this adds up to is that every character that any plant or animal develops has its basis in the genes (without which it would not develop at all) and is to that extent "inherited"; but because the character is the result of interaction between the genes and the factors of the environment, it is also to that extent "acquired." There is no such thing as a character that owes its existence solely to heredity or solely to environment. All that is inherited by any offspring is a packet of genes with the capacity of reacting in various ways to the environment, and a few of these ways, within a certain latitude of tolerance in a normal environment, are what are regarded as normal. Some of the genes, possessed of what is called a high degree of penetrance, can overcome a wider range of variation in environmental factors than others and show their effects. This is at the base of the old controversy between "nature" and "nurture," opposed to which it is necessary to regard both nature and nurture as co-operating, without our being able to say in any one case exactly how much has been contributed by either.

The extent to which nurture undoubtedly can affect the end product of development is sometimes astonishing, and it is well illustrated by the history of Clarence, a fledgling sparrow less than one day old when it fell out of its nest

and was rescued, nursed and reared by a human foster mother in her home. (The story is told by Clare Kipps in her book *Clarence: The Life of a Sparrow.*) Instead of developing into a hopping, chirruping, timid and characterless little bird, Clarence walked with alternate steps as no sparrow has ever been known to do, invented two new bird songs as a result of listening to its foster mother at the piano, developed a fetish for her hairpins, lay with pleasure on its back, played with playing cards carried in its beak, was quite fearless, scolded, bullied, "acted" and showed devoted affection. Clarence was a little person, with more character than many dogs. He lived more than 12 years. Another sparrow, Timmy, who came to live with Mrs. Kipps under other circumstances, also showed great character but was quite different from Clarence. This surely is one of the most awe-inspiring facts that have come to light, if what was never thought to be anything more than a stupid little creature weighing only a few grams is capable of such a degree of mental development and friendship. Could all sparrows, to say nothing of other passerine birds, become like Clarence and Timmy if they were brought up in similar environments? St. Francis of Assisi would surely have agreed, and Darwin would have rejoiced at being netted together with Clarence and Timmy.

There can be few matters affecting man as a social organism that do not depend for their solution on a scientific appreciation of the nature-nurture problem. Eugenics, as Professor Dobzhansky points out, is, as conceived by some of its exponents, in danger of being a travesty of science through overreaching itself by exaggerating the influence of heredity, and for the opposite reason psychoanalysis is in comparable danger from failure to recognize the part played by heredity. If Freud had appreciated the objectively based principles of genetics and the part heredity plays in psychology, if he had freed himself from his Lamarckian blinkers and the discredited theory of recapitulation, and if he had been less prone to make assumptions about birth traumas, sex drives and Oedipus complexes, there might be less controversy over what was started as a therapeutic technique and has come to be regarded as a pattern of life with ramifications extending into history, sociology and religion.

It is one of the worst injustices of history that Lamarck's name is not used to designate evolution, of which he was the first to put forward a general scheme. Instead "Lamarckism" is used to express concepts such as the supposed inheri-

tance of acquired characters and of the effects of use and disuse of organs, ideas of which he was not the originator and which have been shown to be false. From what has been said above of the relation between heredity and environment in the development of characters, it can readily be seen that the expression "inheritance of acquired characters" has as much meaning as the saying "Caesar and Pompey were very much alike, especially Pompey." It is not surprising that this folk belief should be so old and so persistent because, as the University of Pennsylvania botanist Conway Zirkle has aptly shown, it is based on two propositions each of which by itself is approximately correct. The first is that under the influence of the environment the body of an organism can be made to undergo changes, such as a thickening of the skin where it is subjected to friction or a strengthening of muscles that are in hard use. The second proposition is that like tends to beget like. But when the two propositions are combined into a sort of syllogism, the conclusion is fallacious that parents, after having been modified by the environment, beget offspring that show the same modification in the absence of the environmental factors that originally called it forth. Many people can say that "it stands to reason" that acquired characters should be inherited; but it happens not to stand to fact, as virtually countless experiments show.

An example of the extent to which this fallacy is deep-seated can be seen in the Old Testament story of Jacob and Laban. When Jacob was working for Laban, it was agreed that Jacob could have any brown lambs that were born and any spotted and speckled goats born, whereas all white lambs and unspotted goats belonged to Laban. Jacob thereupon selected (he knew the importance of selection) the most healthy animals and subjected them to visual prenatal impressions by putting them in front of striped patterns of green leaves and white rods just before they conceived, with the result that they "brought forth cattle ringstraked, speckled, and spotted," which of course belonged to Jacob, whereas the weaker, untreated animals produced offspring that remained true to the specification of Laban's property. Another example is the ancient Greek myth of Phaeton driving his father Apollo's chariot with the sun across the sky. Being inexperienced, Phaeton drove the chariot much too near the earth in one place, with the result that the wretched inhabitants were scorched black and thereby became the ancestors of the Negro race. One wonders if Pauline theologians realize that the doctrine of original sin involves the inheritance of an acquired character, for only genes can be inherited and, by the nature of the case, neither Adam nor Eve when they first appeared on the scene possessed the character they are alleged to have transmitted to all their descendants. It is perhaps unkind to drive this last lesson home to its conclusion, but everything known about evolution shows it to be a process that takes place in populations numerous enough to ensure that interchange of genes is widespread and frequent enough to provide a sufficient supply of variation for natural selection to work on. It has been computed that the population of man's ancestors one million years ago was about 125,000 individuals. That was when man was emerging from his prehuman ancestors and no doubt was in many ways very brutal, so that mankind would have started with 125,000 doses of genes predisposing toward behavior that would now be regarded as sinful.

Great as the importance of genetics is in the pageant of evolution because of the part it has played in such continuity as there has been, there are three other actors of no less significance. The first is variation, concerning which Darwin wrote with simple truth that its causes were in his day completely unknown. It is one of the triumphs of genetics that this question can now be answered at a different level by saying that the causes of heritable variation are known; they are the mutation of genes due to fortuitous rearrangement of the contents of the genetic material, and the recombination of genes through sexual reproduction. This results in numbers of possible permutations of such astronomical magnitude that infinitely more variation is potentially possible than is ever realized.

The next actor is adaptation, sometimes called fitness. There is no such thing as adaptation in a vacuum. A plant or animal is adapted in varying degrees to a particular set of environmental conditions—a habitat or place that it is useful to call an ecological niche. The last actor is natural selection. At the time Professor Dobzhansky delivered the lectures that form the subject matter of this book, he had had no opportunity to become familiar with the contents of the manuscript notebooks in which Darwin recorded his thoughts and conclusions soon after his return from the voyage of the *Beagle;* it is only recently that Lady Barlow, Darwin's granddaughter, has provided an authentic version of these notebooks. As a result Professor Dobzhansky, like everyone else, has been slightly misled by the ambiguous

phrasing of the passage in Darwin's autobiography, in which he wrote that it was on reading Thomas Malthus' *An Essay on the Principle of Population* he had at once been struck that favorable variations would tend to be preserved and unfavorable ones to be destroyed. This remark has been generally construed to mean that Darwin derived his theory of natural selection from Malthus. It has always been difficult to understand how Darwin could have been indebted for the key of evolution to Malthus, the Jeremiah who maintained that the social state of man was unimprovable. Darwin's notebooks show that he had thought out for himself the unlimited possibility of variation, the importance of niches in the economy of nature and the principle of natural selection before he ever opened Malthus' book. Darwin began to read Malthus on September 28, 1838, and what he got from it was the realization that natural selection exerts a pressure that forces those individuals who happen to have the requisite characters into the niches and leaves the others outside. Malthus knew nothing of, and did not want to know anything of, unlimited variation, ecological niches or natural selection; all that he supplied to Darwin was the argument, already known to Sir William Petty and Benjamin Franklin, that the reproductive rate unchecked outstrips food supply and that mortality must therefore be high. Nobody but Darwin integrated the facts of extinction, variation, geographical distribution, ecological niches and natural selection into a system that showed how natural selection exerts pressure resulting in adaptation. Professor Dobzhansky has interesting and profound things to say on the nature of creative thought, which, he thinks, may be a greater mystery to the creative poet or scientist than to his biographer.

Natural selection still operates in man and in some respects may become more rigorous, but for the most part its effects are nullified by the evolution of an ethical social system that is the one exclusive feature of man. The evolution of man has been characterized by a process known as pedomorphosis, in which adults resemble their ancestors when their ancestors were young. The principle is the exact opposite of recapitulation, in which it is assumed that the individual organism passes through all the stages of its evolutionary history as it develops from fertilized egg to adult. Pedomorphosis can be shown to have been operative in the evolution of the most successful biological groups, including insects and vertebrates other than man. Professor Dobzhansky agrees

on the importance of pedomorphosis in the emergence of man, but he is concerned to know how it was achieved by natural selection. As I believe I was the first to generalize this subject a third of a century ago, I hope I may be allowed to suggest that the array of variants on which natural selection acts includes not only adult genetic variants but also variants along the time scale of development, some of which may be more juvenile and better adapted than others. The effect of slowing down the rate of bodily development is to allow for such features as more brain growth before the skull sutures close and to make the early postnatal stages so helpless that a prolonged period of parental care is necessary. During this time a character of "authority-acceptance" on the part of the children, as the University of Edinburgh geneticist C. H. Waddington has suggested, confers survival value, because without it the children would inevitably come to grief more than they do. The long period of childhood and parental care consolidated the family as a social unit that tended to become monogamous as woman became uninterruptedly receptive, and it provided a long period of overlap between generations during which experience could be taught. This process, which is not enforced by genetic inheritance, has to be repeated at the start of each generation and is the basis of what Professor Dobzhansky calls superorganic evolution and Sir Julian Huxley calls psychosocial evolution. It is responsible for the origin and maintenance of civilization and culture; man could not live without it. It is vastly more efficient than biological evolution as an instrument to bring about adaptation in man, and the speed with which it works is not only much faster but also is still accelerating. Yet it has not annulled the underlying genetic mechanism of evolution that still determines such matters as the response of the individual to the environment, even if it is the result of civilization.

Nobody would wish for a geneticist dictator even if his name were Plato, but it would do legislators no harm to appreciate the genetic effect of their policies. One cannot help wondering how many of them do, in any country. They might say that there are two cultures, humanities and science, and that there is no time to learn both. This would be no answer. There is only one culture, but most people are not even half-cultured. They should read Professor Dobzhansky's book; they will be surprised how much of it they will understand, so clearly and sympathetically is it written.

36

The Natural History of Aggression

Edited by J. D. Carthy and F. J. Ebling

Reviewed by Anatol Rapoport

*Is warmaking a characteristic
of human beings or of cultures?*

The organization of this book suggests the intent of presenting a comparative study of aggression in the animal world, specifically among social insects (D. I. Wallis), mammals (L. Harrison Matthews), various vertebrates (Konrad Lorenz), primates (K. R. L. Hall) and human beings (Thelma Veness, Cecily de Monchaux and Derek Freeman). In addition to this comparative survey some general topics are treated from different theoretical perspectives, namely aggression between species (James Fisher), physiological aspects of aggression (Arnold Klopper), aggression and mental illness (Denis Hill) and war (Stanislav Andreski, Anthony Storr and John Burton).

The mode of discussion ranges from richly descriptive to highly speculative. In judging a book on a scientific subject by a single author or by authors working in collaboration, one can note the facts presented and the conclusions drawn and then express an opinion on the extent to which the conclusions are justified or significant. In the case of a symposium the reviewer must himself draw conclusions, and on the basis of arguments developed in different theoretical frameworks. In this book, for example, there are two sharp discontinuities in subject matter. One is the discontinuity between the concept of aggression as it pertains to nonhuman species and the concept as it pertains to human beings. The other is the discontinuity between aggression among individuals and aggression among nation-states. The breaks are so sharp that one wonders if it is at all illuminating to place phenomena so different under the same heading.

The discussions collected in the symposium are on firmest ground when they deal with aggression among nonhumans. Here the investigator can ask questions standardized in the biological sciences.

What functions are served by the behavioral patterns listed under aggression? What is the genetic origin of these patterns? What are the triggering mechanisms? What are the concomitant physiological events? Some of the functions of aggression are clearly discernible, for example the defense of nesting territory and the competition for mates. The physiological basis of aggressive behavior has also been systematically investigated. Less is known about the evolution of aggression; behavioral patterns leave no fossils except when they result in artifacts.

Such is the study of aggression as a topic in natural history, and so it is presented in the first half of the book. It is obvious, however, that reviewing such studies was not the sole purpose of the symposium. One purpose clearly was to shed light on aggression as a "problem," not as a topic of natural history. The problem is that human beings are in danger of attacking one another with weapons that are capable of destroying their species. We seek enlightenment on how to cope with the problem of war, and it seems helpful to put the problem in a broader context; hence we define aggression in terms of the harm one organism or group of organisms can inflict on another and we search for instances of such situations. We hope to find features the situations have in common in order to discover their "nature," in particular conditions that are favorable or unfavorable for their occurrence. When we define war as aggression, however, the situations subsumed under the term are no longer necessarily related to one another. Accordingly a discussion of aggression is likely to lead to impasses arising simply from conflicting interpretations of the definition.

A case in point is the distinction between intraspecific and interspecific aggression. In the prologue to this volume the editors point out that predation ought not to be considered aggression. Thus "a hawk swooping on a small bird is no more aggressive than the family butcher engaged in his livelihood." This seems reasonable. But in the process of studying aggression in man we face the necessity of drawing a line between aggressive and nonaggressive killing. Is it aggression when man hunts for sport? Many psychologists will argue that it is. But what if hunting for sport is a manifestation of a predatory drive? Should not the human hunter be absolved from the charge of aggression if the hawk is? Yet Derek Freeman ("Human Aggression in Anthropological Perspective") builds his whole case (to the effect that man is by nature aggressive) on man's predatory instincts.

"The Australopithecinae," he says of the primates believed to be ancestors of man, "are an evolutionary innovation, a primate species that, becoming terrestrial, achieved an unprecedented advance by a predatory and carnivorous adaptation to their new environment, based on an upright stance and the adoption of lethal, manual weapons." If predation is not aggression, then the fact that "man has a carnivorous psychology" (S. L. Washburn, quoted by Freeman) ought not to be relevant to the problem of aggression in man. Nonetheless, Washburn says "it is easy to teach people to kill, and it is hard to develop customs which avoid killing. Many human beings enjoy seeing other human beings suffer, or enjoy the killing of animals...public beatings and tortures are common in many cultures." Freeman concludes: "These human characteristics are seen, in the light of the recent discoveries of palaeo-anthropology, to be phylogenetic; the pervasive aggression and cruelty of historic man, by which he is differentiated from other primates, is explicable, to use the words of Raymond Dart, 'only in terms of his carnivorous and cannibalistic origins.' "

Although man's carnivorous origin is clear, his "cannibalistic origins" are not. If we confine ourselves to man's "carnivorous psychology," we do not really have an adequate explanation of man's cruelty. When one speaks of man's inhumanity to man, one usually refers to intraspecific cruelty. There is no evidence, however, that carnivores exhibit more intense intraspecific aggression than other mammals. Indeed, among the carnivores intraspecific fighting is often highly ritualized and hardly ever lethal. Wolves, for example, are "potentially so dangerous to each other that an elaborate chain of submissive reactions of increasing intensity culminating in the weaker contestant's throwing itself on its back to expose all the vulnerable parts of the body defenseless to the superior who refrains from taking the advantage presented, ensures that intraspecific fighting does not end fatally" (L. Harrison Matthews, "Overt Fighting in Mammals"). Clearly, then, attempts to explain man's inhumanity to man on the basis of his carnivorous origins fail to do the carnivores justice.

The participants in the symposium address themselves to the problem of human aggression in different ways. For example, Stanislav Andreski ("Origins of War") argues that an "innate propensity for fighting" is insufficient to explain the destructiveness of man, pointing out that the extent of damage inflicted by man on himself is made possible only by his use of weapons. This observation is of course incontrovertible, but in itself it only points up the gravity of the war problem. If man has a propensity for fighting and also a capacity for producing weapons of virtually unlimited destructive power, then the two "adaptations" coupled together can certainly ensure the extinction of man.

Andreski goes on, however, to question the "innate propensity for warmaking" (note the shift from "fighting" to "warmaking"). He points out that in order to induce warmaking a great deal of stimulation of martial ardor is needed (playing on vanity, fear of contempt, sexual desire, filial and fraternal attachment, loyalty to the group and so on). If there were an innate propensity, Andreski concludes, "such a stimulation would be unnecessary."

To these arguments Konrad Lorenz replies in a subsequent discussion: "No politician ever could make men really fight, if it were not for very archaic,

instinctive reactions of the crowd on which to play." Evidence in favor of "innate propensities" might also be drawn from the circumstance that "overt expression of aggressive behavior is probably at maximal potential at the start of life" and from the intense manifestation of aggression associated with some forms of mental illness, which can be supposed to involve an impairment of inhibitory mechanisms (Denis Hill, "Aggression and Mental Illness"). In this view innate aggressive tendencies are considered to be latent under a veneer of acquired habits.

We see from these exchanges how difficult it is to put the study of aggression into a unified theoretical perspective. We see how the problem of war can confuse analysis, for example by making "fighting" and "warmaking" appear practically synonymous in spite of the fact that there may be only a remote connection between them. We say that boys fight and also that nations fight. Having identified the two manifestations of aggression, we seek mechanisms common to both types of fighting. There may or may not be such common mechanisms. Or there may once have been common mechanisms underlying both individual aggression and warmaking—mechanisms that no longer exist. Certainly a personal predilection for overt aggression is no longer the mark of the warrior. Indeed, the warrior himself is about to disappear as a component of a nation's warmaking apparatus. He seems to have been replaced by the strategist, the scientist and the technician. It is not obvious that people in these roles have greater innate propensities for fighting than other people. Yet when and if the time comes, their activities will result in more bloodshed than those of the combined hordes of Attila, Genghis Khan and Adolf Hitler.

John Burton ("The Nature of Aggression as Revealed in the Atomic Age") specifically warns against confusing the bases of behavior of individuals and of states: "One of the most common—and as I hope to show, one of the most dangerous—images is that of an international society in which nations each have the attributes of persons within a community. Abnormal psychology, games-theory, value judgments and moral responses then appear to be immediately relevant to international studies. In reality the nation-state is not of this order; if there must be an analogy (and I see no reason why there should be any), then it would be at least as appropriate to use mechanics or electronics as sociology." One could add that

if analogies must be made, they should be made on the basis of inherent structural similarities. Thus the behavior of technological systems may shed more light on the behavior of states than the behavior of individuals or of small groups can.

If we keep this warning in mind, we can avoid the misunderstandings that arise when the problem of aggression is examined in a biological perspective. Indeed, the discontinuities between the behavior of man and of other animals and between the behavior of individuals and of nation-states are seen as necessary consequences of the analysis and can serve to illuminate the problem instead of obscuring it.

To begin with, the comparatively constant, situation-determined patterns of behavior in nonhuman interspecific or intraspecific aggression are reasonably explainable in terms of features established in the process of natural selection. This is in consequence of the survival value conferred on the species by certain aggressive behavior patterns provided with sufficient inhibitory checks to safeguard the species from extensive self-inflicted damage.

Once we proceed to man explanations of this kind no longer apply. The evolution of human behavior in recent millenniums cannot be ascribed to biological natural selection. For one thing, most patterns of human behavior are not transmitted to successive generations by biological mechanisms. For another, cultural evolution is so rapid (compared with biological evolution) that we cannot assume that any culture is in a state of equilibrium either internally or with respect to its environment. Whereas we can reasonably assume that a nonhuman species exists because it is "adapted," we cannot assume that any culture exists because it is adapted. Cultures are too short-lived. Possibly none of them is adapted. In answer to the question "Why, then, are they not extinct?" one can answer comfortably: "They have not had time to become extinct." It is true, as James Fisher points out ("Interspecific Aggression"), that "considering the fate of mammals in the Pleistocene period . . . Homo sapiens has done rather well." The basis for this statement is the fact that man has already existed at least 400,000 years, which is considerably longer than the average life expectancy of a mammalian species in the same general period (about 20,000 years) and even of a bird species (about 40,000 years). On the other hand, it is not safe to bet that as of now our life expectancy as a species exceeds the life expectancy of many other mammalian species.

In short, the concept of adaptation seems of little help in understanding human behavior patterns. If our species is now in a transient phase, all forms of aggressive behavior in man may well be maladaptive. The mobilization of physiological resources by the adrenal hormones may serve as an example. Having ceased to be useful in a civilized environment where threats cannot be dealt with either by physical combat or by flight, adrenal mobilization in response to threat or in preparation for aggression probably only harms the human organism.

Still, we cannot ignore man's biological heritage as a framework within which cultural patterns are accumulated. What is needed, then, is a theory of cultural evolution as comprehensive as the theory of biological evolution. What are the cultural analogues of mutation and selection? One would venture to guess that such a theory would be a "nonequilibrium" theory, analogous to the theory of irreversible processes in thermodynamics rather than to the classical theory that dealt with systems passing through a sequence of equilibrium states. The reason is that cultural systems cannot be explained by some natural-selection process that ensures the persistence of adaptive features and the elimination of maladaptive ones. Nevertheless, some selective process operates, since it is unlikely that cultural systems develop entirely at random. The keystone in a theory of cultural evolution would be the mechanism of selection that directs cultural change.

I suspect that a theory of cultural evolution would have to make full use of a principle unique to human psychology, namely the principle of symbolic displacement (or transformation) of drives. The full meaning of this principle has yet to emerge, but it is possible to give examples of how it may operate. Hunger is normally satisfied by the ingestion of food. Nonhumans seldom overeat to the extent of endangering their lives, but humans frequently do, possibly because with humans the ingestion of food is sometimes a symbolic act instead of a physiological necessity. Moreover, this symbolic act may assume more generalized forms, such as the compulsive acquisition of wealth or the conquest of territory. To take an example more relevant to this discussion, the aggressive drive in nonhumans manifests itself only in thrusts against enemies or rivals who present an immediate and actual threat. Man,

however, by virtue of his ability to manipulate symbols, attaches the label "enemy" to entire categories of things: other animals, other people—even inanimate objects and ideas. Accordingly aggression ceases to be ruled by the situation.

The idea of symbolic displacement is central in psychoanalysis, but it has not yet been investigated by rigorous methods of observation and deduction. Perhaps on the basis of this principle the existence of an "evolutionary momentum" can be demonstrated; such a momentum might serve to explain the monstrous and maladaptive features of man's aggressive behavior without recourse to unresolvable controversies about "human nature."

If one follows the more frequently traveled paths of scientific investigation, seeking correlations among directly observable conditions or events, one naturally looks for environmental determinants of aggression. Such determinants are directly demonstrable in some animals. Lorenz remarks that "animals can be made to behave like men and massacre the fellow-members of their own species. If one crowds a dozen roe deer into a pen in a zoo, the most gory massacre is the result."

Observations of this kind suggest that environmental factors play a central role in aggressive behavior. On the other hand, it is becoming increasingly difficult to give credence to the various purely environmental factors that from time to time have been advanced as the causes of wars. Such factors may well have instigated wars at various times in man's history, but the fact that their virtual disappearance has not led to an abatement of war obviously raises doubts about their importance. At one time wars were fought for territory, for booty, for slaves. It is difficult to explain current wars in these terms. Economic factors have been persistently proposed as causes of wars. Such considerations imply a rational calculation that compares the expected gains and losses of a war. No one today argues that a nuclear war would benefit either side, yet such a war is a distinct possibility.

It is all the more surprising that similar arguments are still advanced. For example, Andreski writes: "In conditions of misery, life, whether one's own or somebody else's, is not valued, and this facilitates greatly warlike propaganda.... Moreover, when there is not enough to satisfy the elementary needs of the population, the struggle for the good things of life becomes so bitter that democratic government...becomes impossible, and despotism re-

mains the only kind of government that can function at all. But absolute power creates the danger that a despot may push his country into war for the sake of satisfying his craving for power and glory."

Such an argument might have seemed plausible with respect to Germany 30 years ago. It scarcely applies to the U.S. today. There is less misery in the U.S. than in most other countries, less domestic despotism than in many other countries, less explicit craving for power and glory than in some other countries. Yet the U.S. is the most military-minded nation of this planet and, whatever else it may be, it is far from unaggressive.

In view of the inadequacy of clear environmental factors (crowdedness, poverty, capitalism, armament lobbies and so on) as explanations of the tendency of a country to engage in warlike acts, one is led to consider "systemic" factors, that is, internal factors inherent in the warmaking systems themselves. The lack of discussion of such considerations (they are mentioned only in passing) is a serious shortcoming of *The Natural History of Aggression.* It seems to me that it is high time to investigate the natural history of the warmaking state (*Status belligerens?*). Whether this object is properly biological is an idle question. If biologists had existed among the protozoa of bygone epochs, they would presumably have argued that metazoa were not proper objects of biological investigation. The concept of the nation-state as a quasi-organism of course goes back to antiquity. Diplomats have traditionally ascribed human patterns of behavior to nation-states. In their pronouncements states have desires and obligations; they "take a serious view," "cannot remain indifferent to," "take appropriate measures" and "pursue their interests." It is easy to dismiss these fantasies as being naïve anthropomorphism. The fact remains that they are taken seriously by men who identify themselves with nation-states. These men make decisions. As a result of these decisions thousands or millions of men engage in coordinated activity. They do so because they must. They must because they have been so conditioned. They function like elements in the nervous system of an animal. Thus the state acts in a coordinated manner, quite like an organism. From the point of view of a generalized biology the nation-state *is* essentially an organism. It behooves us to study this organism, because our lives depend on how it will act.

37

Biology and
the Future of Man

Edited by Philip Handler

Reviewed by Alfred E. Mirsky

*The findings of modern biology
and their implications for man*

Being a biologist, I picked up this book with alacrity. Its 20 chapters and 900 pages present the reader with a survey of virtually the entire sweep of biology. The scope of the presentation is exciting and the sequence in which the topics are ordered is logical. The book begins with a chapter on molecular biology, basic to modern biology. Early chapters take up biochemistry ("The Materials of Life and Their Transformations"), cells and the origins of life. The succeeding chapters, dealing with life at higher levels of biological organization, are concerned with development, physiology, the nervous system, behavior, ecology, heredity and evolution and systematics ("The Diversity of Life"). In all the chapters I have mentioned there are frequent comments on the significance of various lines of investigation for man. The final six chapters are on phases of biology that are directed explicitly to the service of man.

It is fitting that this book should be sponsored by the National Academy of Sciences. The academy is an adviser on science to the Government, and the first step in advising is to inform. The book is accordingly addressed not "to the cognoscenti of the sub-disciplines concerned" but to "reasonably well-read scientists and laymen"—to the "interested non-scientist." To write for such readers was a difficult challenge for the 175 experts who contributed to the book. The challenge must have been equally difficult for Philip Handler, the editor of the book and now the president of the academy.

I found almost every chapter so absorbing that I was impelled to read the book without pausing. This was true even when there were passages that I could not understand, because even the mirage was enticing. There are examples of such passages in the chapter on the nervous system, particularly the sec-

tions on the brain. For anyone but a neurophysiologist far better illustrations are needed for effective communication. Indeed, the illustrations are inadequate in many other chapters. In the section on the kidney the text is excellent but the absence of illustrations makes it just about unintelligible to a reader who does not already know about kidney function. Appropriate illustrations might have doubled or even tripled the cost of the book, but for such a book they would have been worth the cost. An index would also have been well worth the effort.

There are many chapters (for example those on ecology, the diversity of life, digital computers and medicine) that are well suited for the "interested non-scientist" because they are written with enthusiasm and succeed in communicating this enthusiasm along with much fascinating information. Looking for such information, the reader is tempted to browse. If he opens the book at random, he has a fair chance of finding a rewarding section.

One such section deals with the population problem. "The upsurge in the growth of human populations" is described as a major hazard in the future of mankind. I doubt whether any reader of the book will hold a contrary opinion. In this case, however, enthusiasm has led to the following overstatement: "...many of the most tragic ills of human existence *find their origin* in population growth. Hunger, pollution, crime, despoliation of the natural beauty of the planet, irreversible extermination of countless species of plants and animals, overlarge, dirty, overcrowded cities with their paradoxical loneliness, continual erosion of limited natural resources, and the seething unrest which creates the political instability that leads to international conflict and war, *all derive from* the unbridled growth of human popula-

tions." (The italics are mine.) The war in Southeast Asia is surely not due to an upsurge in population. Indeed, it would be difficult to point to wars for which overpopulation was a major cause. Although the other social ills mentioned in the quotation have some connection with the rate of population growth, the connection is only partial. It has been pointed out by Herman Miller, the demographer who heads the population division of the Census Bureau, that "pollution, traffic jams, delinquency and crime are no worse in France, England and Holland than in the United States despite the fact that population density in those countries is between 5 times and 30 times as great as in the United States." What we need, Miller remarks, is a national commitment to use our growing affluence to attack our domestic problems. There is no upsurge of population in Sweden, but there is a water-pollution crisis. Sweden is using its affluence to solve the problem.

The reader is presented with another overstatement concerning population when he is asked in connection with population expansion in the U.S.: "Further, consider the *seemingly impossible burden* of coping with the demand for college education: college enrollments which were 6 million in 1965, will be 8 million in 1970, 10 million in 1975...." (Italics are mine.) Such a reader may know that in Israel, a country far less affluent than the U.S., the number of students in universities rose from 28,520 in 1966 to 40,000 in 1970. The upsurge of population is a hazard, but it must be faced rationally.

If a stationary population is achieved, such a population would be much older than the present one. It would, according to Miller, have an equal number of people under 15 and over 60. There are numerous references to age and population in *Biology and the Future of Man*.

(Without an index, of course, it takes a bit of luck to locate them.) On page 631 one reads: "The reduction in death rate since 1900 has been greatest for relatively young people." On page 763 it is said: "But, life expectancy past the age of 45 has increased only slightly...." On page 912 it is stated: "Increases in life expectancy past the age of 45 have remained smaller...." On page 631, however, there is a table (taken from U.S. Public Health Service Publication No. 600, "The Facts of Life and Death") giving the average remaining lifetime in years at specified ages between 1900–1902 and 1963. Inspection of the table shows that the statements I have just quoted are incorrect. For those of age five the expectancy in 1900–1902 was 82 percent of what it became in 1963. For people of age 45 the corresponding figure is 84 percent; for those of age 60 it is 83.7 percent; age 65, 82.8 percent; age 70, 81.5 percent; age 75, 80.5 percent, and age 80, 82.8 percent. The significance of these figures for the future of man calls for an extended discussion, particularly if there is to be a change in the age structure of the population when a stationary state is achieved.

This brings up another passage (page 917): "...the need for support of research which will benefit the health of the newborn and of young productive people in general competes for the personnel and material resources required for research on aging." This may well be the present state of affairs when our affluent society is expending so much of its resources on war and preparation for war, but if research on early environmental influences and research on the aging process must "compete" with each other for funds, the future is surely dim even for an affluent society.

Throughout the book there are, as there should be, references to genetics. Halfway through the book, in the chapter "Heredity and Evolution," there is this perceptive statement: "Transmission genetics [the genetics of heredity] is no longer the most exciting or the central part of genetics. That role is now played by molecular, cellular, and developmental genetics." These aspects of genetics are presented in the early chapters. Some of the topics covered are the chemical structure of genes, how genes are replicated, the nature of gene action, the way genes determine the synthesis of enzymes and other proteins, the control and regulation of gene activity by what are in the broadest sense environmental factors, and the role of variable patterns of gene activity in development and differentiation. An acquaintance

with these topics is required for a discussion of the interaction of heredity and environment—a major theme of the book.

I found these four chapters to be clearly written and on the whole excellent. Since my own scientific background lies in this field, I asked several "reasonably well-read scientists [nonbiologists] and laymen" to read these chapters. The report I received was that they were difficult and not fully understandable. I then went over the chapters again, and I could see why there was a failure to communicate some of the fundamentals of modern biology. Chapter 2 and Chapter 3 "are...presented in the language of chemistry," which is obviously difficult for many readers, and in Chapter 4 and Chapter 6 some assumptions are made about what was covered in the preceding chapters.

As we come to the succeeding chapters, let us see something of the role played by genetics. In the chapter on physiology there is an excellent section on insect endocrinology. Here is an account of how cells in the insect brain, which responds to changing conditions inside and outside the animal, secrete a hormone that stimulates a second endocrine organ, the prothoracic gland, to release a steroid hormone, ecdysone, that acts on various tissues of the body. Ecdysone is effective because it activates certain genes. This well-studied case shows how gene activation enables the organism to adapt to a change in the environment. In a later chapter, on the nervous system, genetics enters in quite a different way as the following pertinent questions are raised: "If the connections of the nervous system are largely specified genetically, how do functional modifications occur in the brain? The environment continuously produces modifications in the behavior of the organism. How is the modifiability of behavior consistent with a rigidly wired brain?" The genetics referred to here is transmission genetics, which tends to be rigid. In cellular and developmental genetics, on the other hand, the constellation of genes is regarded as plastic, and as the environment changes, batteries of genes are activated or repressed. Beginnings have already been made in the application of this kind of genetics to the investigation of the nervous system of higher animals.

Following the chapter on the nervous system comes one on the biology of behavior. Reading it goes far to explain why this branch of biology has attracted so many new workers in recent years and also the interest of many reasonably well-read scientists and laymen. It seems

likely that many of the older biological disciplines will in time focus more definitely on behavior, particularly on human behavior. The genetics of behavior was founded about 1925; by 1940 Robert C. Tryon's classical work on the inheritance of maze-learning ability in rats was published, and in 1960 there appeared John L. Fuller and W. Robert Thompson's *Behavior Genetics*. Throughout this period transmission genetics was "the central part of genetics," and it was accordingly central for behavior genetics. The inheritance of behavior is well reported in this chapter.

The more recent cellular and developmental genetics, however, are not adequately presented, so that the reader is unable to appreciate the significance for behavior of the newer genetics. Thus one would not know by reading the interesting section on the endocrine system and behavior that the remarkable behavioral effects of estrogenic and androgenic hormones are in many, if not all, instances due to the activation of genes by these steroid hormones. The section on the development of behavior gives some striking examples of the importance of early experience in the development of later behavioral capacities, a field that has been "the subject of a massive experimental assault in recent years." The experiments described will whet the appetite of the reader for further information, and more information along these lines is in fact given in the final chapter. Nonetheless, a reader of the accounts in both chapters would have been greatly helped if the discussion had been linked to what had been presented in the chapter on the biology of development, because there it was shown that "early experience" is responsible for the pattern of gene activation that occurs in development.

In the final chapter ("Biology and the Future of Man") there are several discussions concerning the future of genetic systems. The section on "guarding the genetic quality of man" deals with defective genes: how to recognize them before birth, the ways of coping with them medically and the role of genetic counseling. In the final section of this chapter there is a discussion of the genetic factors concerned with man's mental and behavioral traits, and some proposals for the future are made.

It is interesting that this section begins in the same way that Plato introduces the idea of eugenics in *The Republic*. Plato proposed, and it is also proposed here, that there should be selective breeding of man. The following passage is from Francis Macdonald

Cornford's translation:

How are we to get the best results? You must tell me, Glaucon, because I see you keep sporting dogs and a great many game birds at your house; and there is something about their mating and breeding that you must have noticed.

What is that?

In the first place, though they may all be of good stock, are there not some that turn out to be better than the rest?

There are.

And do you breed from all indiscriminately? Are you not careful to breed from the best so far as you can?

Yes.

And from those in their prime, rather than the very young or the very old?

Yes.

Otherwise, the stock of your birds or dogs would deteriorate very much, wouldn't it?

It would.

And the same is true of horses or of any animal?

It would be very strange if it were not.

Dear me, said I; we shall need consummate skill in our Rulers, if it is also true of the human race.

The corresponding passage in *Biology and the Future of Man* is: "Even without scientific knowledge of genetics, man created a great variety of genetically different strains of domesticated animals and plants by selecting for desired types and breeding." And later it is said: "Presumably, we could also breed for mental performance, for special properties like spatial perception or verbal capacity, perhaps even for cooperativeness or disruptive behavior, even, conceivably, for high scores in intelligence tests."

Between Plato and *Biology and the Future of Man* the most important writer on eugenics was that remarkable Victorian Francis Galton. His presentation of eugenics and the presentation in this book are markedly similar (although the word eugenics is not used in the book).

Galton linked eugenics and evolution in what became virtually a religion for him and his followers in the eugenic societies of Britain and America. The final sentences of *Biology and the Future of Man* are: "[Man] influences the numbers and genetic constitution of virtually all other living species. Now he can guide his own evolution. In him, Nature has reached beyond the hard regularities of physical phenomena. *Homo sapiens*, the creation of Nature, has transcended her. From a product of circumstances, he has risen to responsibility. At last, he is Man. May he behave so!"

It should be said that the discussion of eugenics in *Biology and the Future of Man* is not marred by Galton's gross underestimate of the importance of environmental factors in the shaping of man's traits or by Galton's deplorable racial antipathies. It is also clearly stated that the eugenic proposals put forward in this book can be implemented only at some indefinite time in the future. Some of the difficulties that would be encountered in the establishing of a eugenics program are discussed.

In the preface to the book it is stated that the changes that can come about in the foreseeable future should be mentioned. Are there possible changes in this time span that concern the genetic systems responsible for the mental and behavioral traits of man? In the chapter on the future of man only transmission genetics is considered, and that leads to eugenics. In my opinion the newer genetics, particularly cellular and developmental genetics, provides a more hopeful outlook. The negative attitude toward this kind of genetics is shown by the following sentence in the final chapter: "Man's capacities are, thus, inextricably linked to his genes whose molecular nature is now understood to a very high degree, but which presently lie *outside his control*." (Italics are mine.) In actuality numerous papers on the control of gene activity are published every month. For example, it was recent-

ly shown that when vitamin D is ingested, it is modified in the liver and then reaches the intestinal epithelium, where it activates certain genes and so induces the synthesis of an enzyme that enables the cell to absorb calcium. I have already referred to the role of steroid hormones as controllers of gene activity. The significance of the newer genetics for the development of behavior has recently been well stated by Benson E. Ginsburg of the University of Connecticut: "The developing individual, on this view, has a far wider genetic repertoire than will be activated during his developmental history.... Where environmental events, including external stimulation, alterations in hormone level, vitamins...impinge to alter behavior, they do so, in the sense that we have been discussing, only if they are capable of activating or suppressing existing genetic systems, and only at those times when these become labile.... The genetic potentials for the development of particular neural and behavioral capacities are far broader than those that will be exhibited by a given individual. The activation and/or suppression of these potentials in favor of others occurs as a physiological-genetic process in which particular genes are 'turned on' or off at given stages in development."

As more is learned about factors controlling the genetic systems of higher organisms man's genes will no longer "lie outside his control." That may reasonably be expected to happen in the foreseeable future. It remains to be seen what the attitude toward eugenics will be at that time.

None of these comments alters the fact that *Biology and the Future of Man* represents a great step forward in communication between workers in science and citizens concerned with science—and ultimately all citizens should be concerned with science. In my view the book should be renewed regularly. Five years from now would not be too soon.

38

Prenatal Diagnosis of Genetic Disease

by Theodore Friedmann
November 1971

New techniques are making it possible to detect hereditary diseases early in pregnancy. To what extent is the control of such births justified on biological and social grounds?

More than 1,600 human diseases caused by defects in the content or the expression of the genetic information in DNA have been identified. Some of these diseases are very rare; others, such as cystic fibrosis and sickle-cell anemia, are relatively common and are responsible for much illness and death. It has been estimated that more than 25 percent of the hospitalizations of children are for illnesses with a major genetic component. Thanks to new techniques of biochemistry and cell biology, we are learning a great deal about the biochemical mechanisms that lead from a genetic defect to clinical disease. Particularly important has been the discovery that cells from patients can be grown and studied in tissue culture in artificial nutrient media, and that these cells often continue to express the abnormal function of a mutant gene. As a result genetic manipulative techniques are being developed through which man may acquire the ability to control aspects of his own evolution, to eliminate disease and even to improve his genetic makeup. Another application of these techniques is prenatal genetic diagnosis.

The ability to establish the diagnosis of genetic disease prior to birth came through studies of the fluid that bathes the developing fetus within the amniotic cavity: a sac surrounding the fetus that is lined by two layers of cells (the chorion and the amnion) and is filled with fluid derived mainly from fetal urine and fetal respiratory secretions. Suspended in the fluid are viable cells shed from the fetal skin and respiratory tract, and perhaps from the fetally derived lining of the cavity itself. Amniocentesis, the removal of fluid from the amniotic cavity by needle puncture, became useful and important in the early 1960's for the detection of unborn infants who ran the risk of Rh incompatibility. When an Rh-negative mother carries an Rh-positive fetus, the mother may become sensitized to the "foreign" red blood cells from the fetus, and the antibodies that develop may in later pregnancies cross the placenta, cleave to the fetus's red blood cells and cause the destruction of red cells, severe anemia, brain damage and even death [see "The Prevention of 'Rhesus Babies,'" by C. A. Clarke; SCIENTIFIC AMERICAN Offprint 1126]. Obstetricians discovered that they could estimate the degree of blood destruction by measuring the concentration of hemoglobin breakdown products in the amniotic fluid.

During amniocentesis for Rh disease it became clear that much useful information could be obtained by examining cells in the amniotic fluid. In 1949 Murray Barr of Canada had discovered that nerve cells from female cats were distinguishable from those of the male by the presence in the female cells of a darkly staining piece of chromosomal material on the nuclear membrane. These "Barr bodies" were then found to characterize female cells in many other mammals, including human females. Mary Lyon of England subsequently found that early in mammalian embryogenesis one of the two X chromosomes in female cells (male cells have only one X chromosome and a Y chromosome) randomly becomes condensed and inactive. In the unusual instances where cells have more than two X chromosomes all except one are condensed. In male cells condensation does not take place. The altered physical properties of these condensed chromosomes give rise to their staining characteristics.

Since amniotic-fluid cells are mostly fetal in origin, investigators turned to them as an unprecedentedly valuable material for detecting the kinds of genetic disease that are caused by mutations on the X chromosome and that therefore affect only males. The best-known of the "X-linked" diseases is the bleeding disorder hemophilia. In this disease a deficiency of one of the protein factors required for clotting results in prolonged and intractable bleeding, particularly at sites of traumatic injury.

An ovum from a female carrier of hemophilia will have either a normal X chromosome or a defective one. After fertilization half of all the resulting males will receive as their only X chromosome the one carrying the mutant gene. Since there is no normal copy of the gene from the father such males will express the defect fully. (The father must pass his Y chromosome in order for the fetus to be male.) The other males will be normal, since they have by chance received the normal X chromosome from the mother. Therefore detection of a female fetus *in utero* by the presence of Barr bodies in a pregnancy in which there is a risk of hemophilia rules out the possibility of disease, although 50 percent of the females will be carriers. A male fetus, however, may be either affected or normal.

Predictions can also be made on the genetic constitution of the fetus in the case of diseases associated with an abnormal number of chromosomes or arrangement of chromosomes. In 1959 the French geneticist Jérôme Lejeune discovered that patients with mongolism (now usually called Down's syndrome) have no mutant or defective gene but rather carry an extra chromosome that in itself is probably normal. We now know that most cases of Down's syndrome are caused by a defect in the separation of chromosomes, called nondisjunction, in the developing egg resulting in the formation of ova with two No. 21 chromosomes instead of the usual one.

When such an egg is fertilized by a normal sperm, the result is an embryo carrying three normal No. 21 chromosomes. This "trisomy" of chromosome No. 21 causes Down's syndrome. An important feature of this kind of Down's syndrome is its increased incidence with advanced maternal age. A pregnant woman 40 years old is more than 10 times as likely to have an affected infant as one 25 years old. The disease is the single most common chromosomal aberration found in live-born infants.

In a rarer type of Down's syndrome the extra chromosome No. 21 is translocated onto another chromosome. A healthy carrier mother has only 45 chromosomes instead of the usual 46, but the total amount of genetic information is normal. During the formation of the ovum, however, segregation of chromosomes can give rise to an ovum carrying the translocated No. 21 plus the free No. 21. Fertilization of such an ovum leads to an embryo with an apparently normal chromosome number, but with an extra chromosome No. 21. The abnormalities in this kind of Down's syndrome are similar to those in the nondisjunction type.

Parallel with developments in cell bi-ology have been advances in our knowledge of the flow of genetic information from DNA through RNA to protein. The precise biochemical defects involved in several hundred human disorders have been discovered, and this is due largely to the realization that tissue-culture cells from patients often continue to show the biochemical defect characteristic of a given disease. Such culture methods have most often used skin cells, but recently geneticists have learned that amniotic-fluid cells can also be cultured and used diagnostically.

One disease that illustrates the usefulness of these methods is the Lesch-Nyhan syndrome, a severe neurological disease of males characterized by mental retardation, involuntary writhing motions called choreoathetosis and compulsive self-mutilation of the lips and fingertips by biting. In the healthy carrier mother one of the X chromosomes carries a defective gene for the enzyme hypoxanthine-guanine phosphoribosyl transferase (HGPRT), which is required for the conversion of the bases hypoxanthine and guanine into nucleotides for incorporation into new RNA and DNA by the "reutilization" pathway. Most

body cells can function normally without this enzyme, since there is another pathway for nucleotide synthesis. The function of cells in the basal ganglia of the brain, however, is severely impaired without the HGPRT pathway.

To determine whether or not a male fetus carries a defective HGPRT gene, amniotic-fluid cells in tissue culture can be labeled with radioactive hypoxanthine and then exposed to X-ray film. Normal cells, having incorporated the radioactive precursor, will appear densely labeled in this autoradiographic method, whereas Lesch-Nyhan cells will remain free of radioactivity. Alternatively cells can be homogenized and the enzyme assayed directly.

Many of the diseases that are associated with enzyme deficiencies show autosomal recessive inheritance: the defective gene lies on one of the 22 pairs of non-sex chromosomes (autosomes), and two mutant copies of the gene, one from each parent, are passed on to the offspring. The offspring are thus homozygous for the recessive gene and exhibit the disease; the parents are heterozygous carriers. In many instances where a single mutant copy of the gene is present about half of the normal amount of

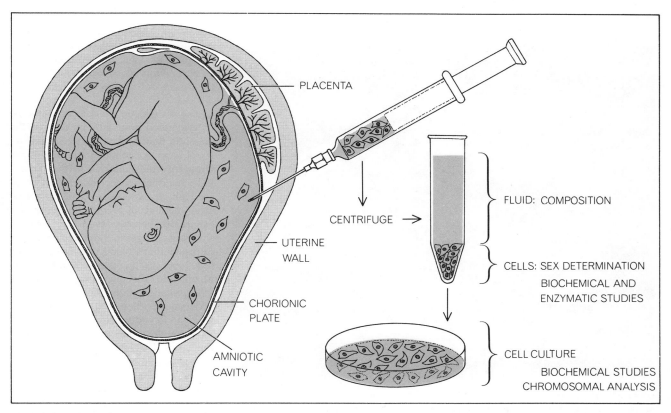

SAMPLE OF FLUID surrounding the fetus is taken by inserting a sterile needle into the amniotic cavity and withdrawing a small amount of fluid. The process is called amniocentesis. The fluid, derived mostly from fetal urine and secretions, contains fetal cells (*not drawn to scale*). Care must be taken not to puncture the placenta or the fetus. The sample is centrifuged to separate cells and fluid. A variety of tests can be made. Optimum time for the amniotic tap for genetic diagnosis is about the 16th week of gestation.

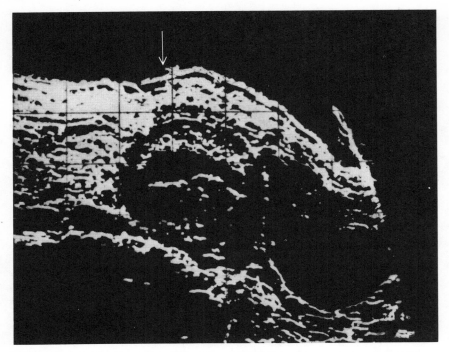

LOCATION AND SIZE of the placenta can be determined by ultrasonic scanning. Bursts of high-frequency sound waves are emitted from a probe moved along the surface of the abdomen. Echoes returned from tissue interfaces within the body are displayed on a storage oscilloscope. The technique is simple, safe and rapid. These sonograms were made at the 18th week of gestation to locate the placenta before amniocentesis. The placenta appears as a crescent-shaped dotted area. The dark area directly below it is part of the amniotic cavity. Scattered echoes within the cavity are from the fetus. The dark shape on the right is the urinary bladder. The scan was made longitudinally from above the navel (*left*) to the pubic area (*right*). The arrow is at the site of the transverse scan shown below.

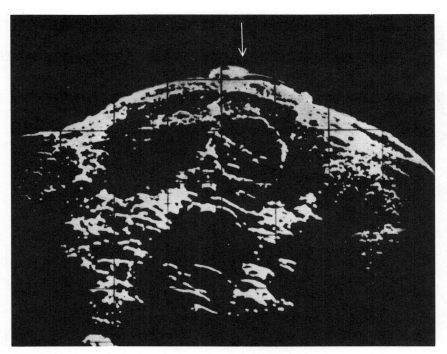

OVAL SHAPE to the right of center is formed by echoes from the fetal head. Above it and to the left is a section of the placenta. The dark area below the placenta is part of the amniotic cavity. The patient's left and right sides respectively are on the left and right of the photograph. The arrow is at the site of the scan in the top illustration. Both scans are necessary in order to locate the placenta precisely. The sonograms were prepared by Mitsunao Kobayashi of the Downstate Medical Center of the State University of New York.

the gene product is made, which is often enough to protect against the disease. This is not the case, however, when the mutant gene is dominant.

One particularly devastating autosomal recessive disease is Tay-Sachs disease, which causes blindness, severe mental retardation and death, usually before three or four years of age. It is most common in Jews of northern European origin (Ashkenazy Jews). In 1969 John O'Brien and his colleagues at the School of Medicine of the University of California at San Diego discovered that in Tay-Sachs disease a mutation leads to a defective form of the enzyme hexosaminidase A, which normally splits the terminal sugar from a lipid-polysaccharide complex called GM_2 ganglioside. There results a massive accumulation of the undegraded ganglioside in nerve cells throughout the body. The enzyme deficiency is detectable in fetal amniotic cells, and O'Brien's group has followed 20 pregnancies in women known to be carriers. Seven affected fetuses were detected, and in all seven cases the women chose to terminate the pregnancy through abortion.

Some diseases in the fetus manifest themselves not by defects in amniotic-fluid cells but rather in abnormal concentrations of metabolites in the fluid itself. For example, fetuses with Hurler's disease (in which cells accumulate mucopolysaccharides, resulting in retardation and skeletal deformities) excrete large amounts of heparitin sulfate with their urine into the amniotic fluid.

Some 40 genetic diseases can now be diagnosed prenatally by tests on the amniotic fluid and its cells. Several referral centers, including the one at the University of California at San Diego, have facilities for performing all or almost all of these tests. It is likely that other methods of prenatal diagnosis will eventually become available, such as studying changes in the enzyme patterns in the mother's blood or even detecting fetal cells in the mother's circulation. Meanwhile the increased availability (and probable automation) of assay procedures, including chromosome analysis, will lead to widespread prenatal diagnosis through amniocentesis in the next few years. This fact compels us to reflect on several important questions.

The most obvious question concerns the safety of the procedure itself. For prenatal diagnostic purposes the optimum time to perform amniocentesis seems to be around the 16th week of gestation. By that time enough amniotic fluid has accumulated for a sample to be

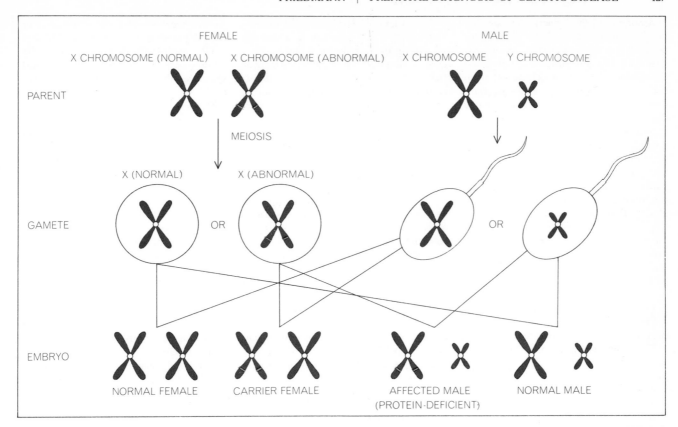

HEMOPHILIA is transmitted by mothers who have a defective gene for a clotting protein in one of their X chromosomes. Female offspring do not develop the disease because they receive at least one X chromosome that is not defective, but half of them like their mother will be carriers. A male offspring has a 50 percent chance of getting the defective gene and being afflicted with the disease.

easily obtained by needle puncture. The fetus is small and not likely to be traumatized, and sufficient time is still available to grow amniotic cells, perform the diagnostic procedures and proceed with a therapeutic abortion if that is desired. In the hands of the relatively small number of experienced individuals now performing amniocentesis the procedure does not seem to present much danger of traumatic injury to the mother or the fetus. The fetal parts can be manipulated away from the site of the needle puncture, and the placenta can be located by ultrasonic methods. One may expect traumatic complications to increase temporarily as less experienced physicians with insufficient specialized training begin to perform amniocentesis. Since any diagnostic procedure with a small but irreducible rate of complications is justifiably used only if the conditions being searched for lead to disease or damage much more frequently than the diagnostic procedure itself, it is important that these questions of safety be answered.

A more vexing problem concerns the possibility of developmental damage to the fetus through interference with the fetal environment, perhaps as a conse-

quence of removal of fluid and its metabolites or through changes in pressure within the uterus. To detect this kind of damage would require a long-term developmental and intellectual evaluation or infants who had experienced amniocentesis. The National Institute of Child Health and Human Development is now undertaking such studies through a newly organized Amniocentesis Registry, which will collect and evaluate long-term effects of the procedure on fetus and mother. Preliminary claims for the safety of amniocentesis have already been made, but since experience with the procedure is still limited, we must be prepared for the possibility that some untoward effects on the fetus will become evident as the number of amniotic taps increases.

If we assume that the procedure will prove to be relatively safe, we can ask how and for what purpose we want to use such methods of prenatal genetic diagnosis. Some have suggested that prenatal genetic screening through amniocentesis may become a routine part of prenatal care—similar to tests on the mother for syphilis, diabetes and high blood pressure—as an effort to detect most fetal diseases and malformations

before birth. This possibility seems remote. The problem of creating facilities to evaluate the three million births per year in the U.S. are of course immense, and many local and regional centers would have to be established. More important is the probability that there is almost certain to be a risk inherent in amniocentesis greater than the probability of detecting an abnormal fetus in an unselected population. This objection will obviously need to be modified if less hazardous methods of obtaining fetal genetic information are developed.

The most obvious purpose of such procedures is to reduce or eliminate the occurrence of genetic diseases that impose a devastating emotional burden on parents and often cause suffering and death in affected children. At present the only genetic diseases that might be detected *in utero* are those in which tissue-culture cells in the laboratory express the genetic abnormality of the disease, or those in which biochemical abnormalities are present in urine and other excretions and might therefore appear in the amniotic fluid. So far most developmental abnormalities, such as congenital heart disease, cannot be detected before birth.

Among the 1,600 genetic diseases that now are recognized, there will almost certainly be many that will not be expressed in the cells or the fluid obtained by amniocentesis. It is believed that all cells in the body, regardless of their function in differentiated tissues, carry the same genetic information. Any individual cell is therefore theoretically capable of performing functions of all other kinds of cells in that organism. We also know, however, that only some kinds of cells can conduct specialized functions such as the making of hemoglobin. If methods could not be found to activate or uncover the genes for hemoglobin in the skin or amniotic-fluid cells of patients with genetic forms of anemia, it might not be possible to detect these diseases in the uterus.

One factor that hinders the development of effective programs for the prevention of genetic diseases is the difficulty of identifying the pregnancies that are at risk. One of the clearest current indications for amniocentesis is advanced maternal age, since that is associated with the greatly increased risk of Down's syndrome. It has been estimated that if all pregnancies in women 35 years of age or older were evaluated by *in utero* detection methods, the rate of occurrence of this disease would be reduced to half the present level if selective abortion were practiced. Such age criteria, however, do not apply in many genetic disorders.

The other common indication for amniocentesis is a pregnancy in a woman who has previously borne a child with a genetic disease; this is called retrospective detection. If the disease is a dominant one such as Huntington's chorea, the risk of disease to the fetus is 50 percent. Monitoring subsequent pregnancies could readily detect all cases except those due to new mutations. Selective abortion on affected fetuses could virtually eliminate the disease. Unfortunately screening methods for Huntington's chorea and other dominant diseases are not available. If the disease is a recessive one, the potential effect of retrospective detection and selective abortion is much less impressive. We can expect to find only a small number of new cases, since the initial cases are all missed and subsequent pregnancies carry only a 25 percent probability of producing an affected child. If we assume a reproductive goal of two normal children per family, the number of new cases detected would at best be only 34 percent of the total. The effect of such programs on individual families known to have a history of genetic abnormality can nonetheless be great.

If prenatal diagnosis and selective abortion were coupled with extensive screening programs to find heterozygous carriers, profound reductions might be achieved in the incidence of some recessive diseases. If the screening program could detect each family in which both parents were carriers, the monitoring of all pregnancies in only those families would result in the detection of virtually all new cases of a recessive disease, and selective abortion for affected fetuses could be practiced. It is possible that with such a regime only cases caused by mutations would occur. Programs of this kind would necessarily be elaborate and expensive, but geneticists have already undertaken programs to detect and prevent new cases of Tay-Sachs disease. Since the frequency of the gene for Tay-Sachs disease among Ashkenazy Jews is 10 times that of the general population, marriages among Jews are being screened by blood tests of both partners. In families where both husband and wife are found to be carriers it is planned to monitor all pregnancies and to offer abortions in cases where the fetus is found to be affected.

Cost-benefit analyses have shown that detection programs for Tay-Sachs disease and Down's syndrome alone would result in very large savings for individual families and for society as a whole if affected fetuses were aborted instead of being born and ultimately institutionalized at state expense. Four thousand infants with Down's syndrome are born each year in the U.S., and lifetime institutional care for each one costs approximately $250,000. Such analyses, however, seldom define what they consider the benefit. Is it only black figures in the ledger instead of red? Economic considerations are undeniably important, but it seems a dangerous precedent to justify screening and selective abortion programs solely on the basis of comparing their cost with the economic burden to families and to society. One could argue cogently that we should be more willing to spend money for the elimination of disease even if it proves to be uneconomical.

Recently some geneticists, notably Arno G. Motulsky of the University of Washington School of Medicine and James V. Neel of the University of Michigan, have become concerned with the possibility that large-scale genetic manipulations such as prenatal detection and abortion might lead to detrimental changes in the quality and the diversity of the human gene pool. Such changes might be the inadvertent result of programs to eliminate disease or the deliberate consequence of eugenic programs to eliminate certain undesirable genes from the population.

Motulsky and Neel have recently shown that programs of prenatal detection and selective abortion might

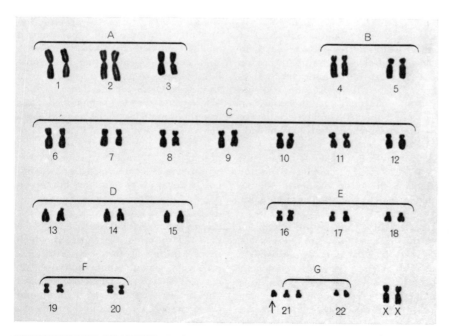

CHROMOSOMAL ANALYSIS of cells obtained by amniocentesis can determine if the developing embryo has Down's syndrome. This karyotype prepared by O. W. Jones shows that the girl has an extra No. 21 chromosome and will have the stigmata of mongolism.

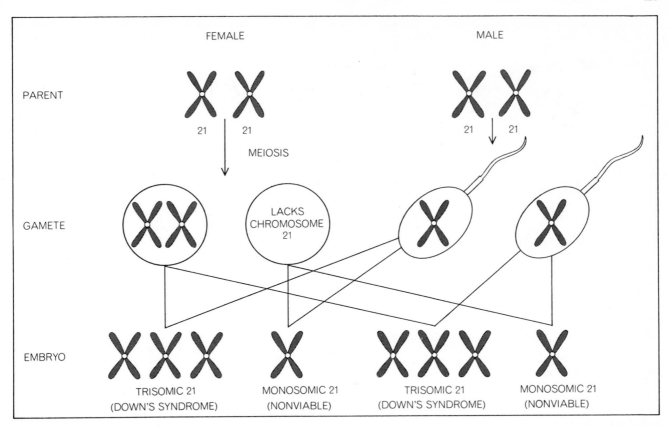

FEMALE   MALE

PARENT

21   21   21   21

MEIOSIS

GAMETE

LACKS
CHROMOSOME
21

EMBRYO

TRISOMIC 21   MONOSOMIC 21   TRISOMIC 21   MONOSOMIC 21
(DOWN'S SYNDROME)   (NONVIABLE)   (DOWN'S SYNDROME)   (NONVIABLE)

DOWN'S SYNDROME, or mongolism, results when chromosomes fail to separate (nondisjunction) during meiosis, giving rise to some ova with two No. 21 chromosomes. When the ovum with the extra chromosome is fertilized, the embryo develops abnormally.

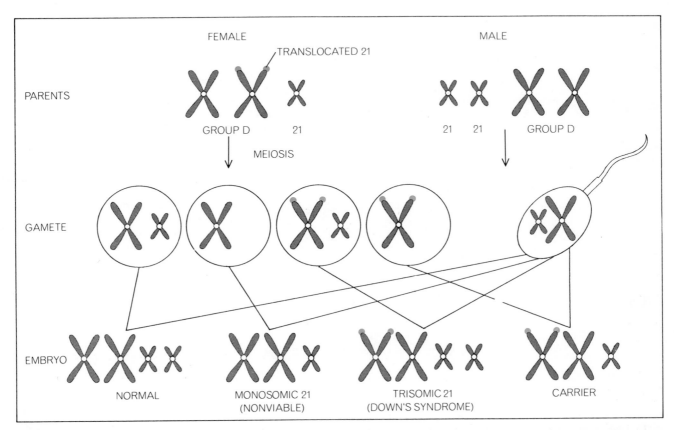

FEMALE ─ TRANSLOCATED 21   MALE

PARENTS

GROUP D   21   21   21   GROUP D

MEIOSIS

GAMETE

EMBRYO

NORMAL   MONOSOMIC 21   TRISOMIC 21   CARRIER
                (NONVIABLE)   (DOWN'S SYNDROME)

TRANSLOCATION of a No. 21 chromosome to another chromosome can also result in Down's syndrome if the ovum with the extra chromosome is fertilized. Fewer than 5 percent of the cases of Down's syndrome are produced by the translocation mechanism.

NUCLEOTIDE SYNTHESIS by cells of the body can occur via two pathways: a *de novo* route and a reutilization route. In the latter the enzyme hypoxanthine-guanine phosphoribosyl transferase (HGPRT) catalyzes the attachment of ribose phosphate onto hypoxanthine and guanine. Most body cells can produce enough of the nucleotide, guanylic acid, by the *de novo* route, so that their function is not impaired. The basal ganglia of the brain, however, require the HGPRT-mediated pathway, and when the enzyme is missing, their function is severely impaired. This result is the Lesch-Nyhan syndrome, a fatal neurological disease.

TAY-SACHS DISEASE, which leads to blindness, severe retardation and early death in infants, is caused by the accumulation of the ganglioside GM_2 in nerve cells. The ganglioside is a complex molecule composed of a lipid fraction, ceramide, linked to a polysaccharide containing glucose, galactose, N-acetyl galactosamine and N-acetyl neuraminic acid (sialic acid). Lack of the enzyme hexosaminidase *A*, which participates in cleaving the terminal sugar N-acetyl galactosamine from the GM_2 ganglioside at the site indicated by the arrow, results in accumulation of the GM_2 ganglioside in nerve cells throughout the body.

bring about unexpected increases in the frequency of genes for some diseases. As an illustration let us assume that in the future each family will have two normal children and will compensate for fetuses lost through abortion. Under these conditions the prevention of natural gene loss through death or nonreproducibility of the affected homozygotes could lead to an increase over many generations of 50 percent in the gene frequency. For cystic fibrosis this means that over 50 generations the frequency of carriers in a population would increase from its present 5 percent to a new equilibrium level of 7.5 percent. Motulsky considers that, in view of the long time required, the change is minimal and probably of no real concern, particularly when it is compared with the effect on gene frequencies of a program of premarital counseling and the prevention of mating between heterozygous carriers. If any selective advantage exists for the heterozygote and persists in the future, as seems to be the case with sickle-cell anemia and cystic fibrosis, the frequency of carriers might rise over many generations to a startling level of 50 percent. Every second person would be a carrier.

Another startling effect could occur in X-linked diseases such as hemophilia, where no distinction can yet be made between affected and normal males *in utero*. If abortion of all male fetuses in carrier mothers were to become widespread, the result could be a 50 percent increase in the gene frequency *with each generation*.

The directed elimination of genes by selective abortion after prenatal detection is certainly feasible and, as Motulsky shows, is probably not deleterious in most instances. The gene responsible for a dominant disease such as Huntington's chorea could be virtually eliminated with a modest detection and abortion program, although that is not yet possible since biochemical tests for this disease and other dominant diseases are not available. It is unlikely that the loss of such a gene would in any way be injurious to the species. The elimination of genes for recessive diseases, however, would require not only much more elaborate screening programs for large segments of the population but also the abortion of all unaffected heterozygous fetuses. It is difficult to see how this could ever be justified.

Geneticists realize that genetic diversity is important for ensuring the adaptability, and therefore the survival, of a species in the face of continually changing evolutionary selective pres-

 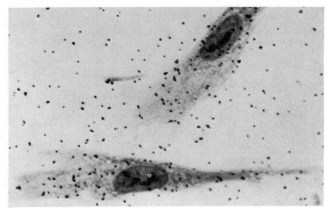

AUTORADIOGRAPHIC METHOD is used to determine if fetal cells contain the enzyme HGPRT. Lack of the enzyme results in the fatal Lesch-Nyhan disease. The fetal cells are grown in a tissue culture and then exposed to radioactive hypoxanthine. The cells are washed with acid and methanol to remove any free hypoxanthine.

The washed cells are placed in contact with a film that is sensitive to radioactivity. Normal cells (*left*) are able to incorporate hypoxanthine and become radioactive. They turn out black on the developed film. Mutant cells deficient in the HGPRT enzyme cannot take up the hypoxanthine and darken the film very little (*right*).

sures. Presumably the human species is no exception. This is not to say that our present gene pool is an optimum one, and it is certain that the evolution of our gene pool is continuing even now. Although one might argue that some changes can be made in our gene pool that are evolutionarily neutral or even advantageous, we must question our ability to use this capacity to even partially direct our genetic future with sufficient wisdom and foresight.

Until now prenatal diagnosis combined with selective abortion has been applied mostly in cases where there has been little or no doubt about the inevitability of disease with a demonstrated genetic abnormality. We are now, however, beginning to understand more about the role of normal genetic variation in man, and about the existence of aberrations that are not so closely associated with disease. Several recent clinical situations have emphasized the uncertainties in the relationship between the existence of a genetic abnormality and the development of clinical disease.

A chromosomal abnormality, the *XYY* syndrome, has recently been described in which some men have an extra *Y* chromosome. Clinical studies have suggested that such men are statistically more likely to develop aggressive antisocial behavior than normal *XY* males. Some of the affected men are criminals but most are not, and most important of all we have no firm evidence that it is the extra chromosome that is directly responsible for the suspected tendency toward criminal behavior.

In another instance a normal parent carrying a translocation of material from a No. 3 chromosome to another chromosome has given birth to a child with apparently the identical chromosomal abnormality but with severe mental retardation. The detection in fetal cells of this kind of translocation would therefore not have helped in determining if the fetus were destined to be severely retarded or of normal intelligence. These findings illustrate the fact that in some cases our knowledge of the mechanism by which a defective gene leads to the

development of human clinical disease is inadequate. We may also recall that some genes may confer a selective advantage on heterozygous carriers. Heterozygotes for sickle-cell anemia are less susceptible to infection with malaria. It is probable that other genes that are detrimental under some conditions are of value to the species. Knowledge of such challenges to our diagnostic and prognostic accuracy may make it increasingly difficult to provide information on which prospective parents can make informed and intelligent decisions.

Some fear that in a society where abortion is becoming acceptable, increasingly arbitrary standards may be applied in the making of decisions on the fitness or desirability of a given fetus. In present circumstances it is not difficult to imagine the emergence of pressures to set standards for desirability in genetically determined human characteristics. At the moment it is not at all clear how these standards might be arrived at, and whose standards they might be. Neel

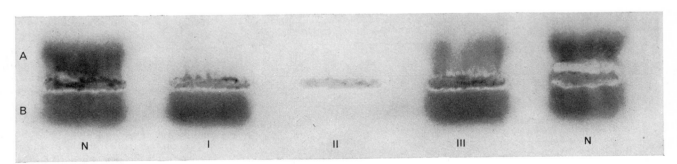

STARCH-GEL ELECTROPHORESIS is used to separate two similar enzymes, hexosaminidase *A* and hexosaminidase *B*. This example, prepared by John O'Brien of the University of California at San Diego, shows that normal individuals (*N*) have both the *A* and the *B* isozymes. Patients with Tay-Sachs disease (*I*) lack the *A* enzyme, and patients with Sandhoff's disease (*II*) lack both forms of the enzyme. A deficiency of the enzyme hexosaminidase *A* (shown in *III*) results in a disease known as juvenile GM$_2$ gangliosidosis.

DISORDER	DEFECTIVE ENZYME OR METABOLIC DERANGEMENT
ASSOCIATED WITH MENTAL RETARDATION	
CHROMOSOMAL ABNORMALITIES (DOWN'S SYNDROME, TURNER'S SYNDROME, XYY, ETC.)	EXCESS OR DEFICIENCY OF TOTAL GENETIC INFORMATION
ARGINOSUCCINIC ACIDURIA	ARGINOSUCCINASE
CITRULLINEMIA	ARGINOSUCCINATE SYNTHETASE
FUCOSIDOSIS	ALPHA-FUCOSIDASE
GALACTOSEMIA	GALACTOSE-1-PHOSPHATE URIDYL TRANSFERASE
GAUCHER'S DISEASE INFANTILE TYPE ADULT TYPE	ABSENT CEREBROSIDASE DEFICIENT CEREBROSIDASE
GENERALIZED GANGLIOSIDOSIS	ABSENT BETA-GALACTOSIDASE
JUVENILE GM$_1$ GANGLIOSIDOSIS	DEFICIENT BETA-GALACTOSIDASE
JUVENILE GM$_2$ GANGLIOSIDOSIS	DEFICIENCY OF HEXOSAMINIDASE A
GLYCOGEN STORAGE DISEASE TYPE 2	ALPHA-1-4 GLUCOSIDASE
HUNTER'S DISEASE	INCREASED AMNIOTIC FLUID HEPARITIN SULFATE
HURLER'S DISEASE	INCREASED AMNIOTIC FLUID HEPARITIN SULFATE
I-CELL DISEASE	MULTIPLE LYSOMAL HYDROLASES
ISOVALERIC ACIDEMIA	ISOVALERYL CoA DEHYDROGENASE
LESCH-NYHAN SYNDROME	HYPOXANTHINE-GUANINE PHOSPHORIBOSE TRANSFERASE
MAPLE SYRUP URINE DISEASE	ALPHA-KETO ISOCAPROATE DECARBOXYLASE
METACHROMATIC LEUCODYSTROPHY LATE INFANTILE TYPE JUVENILE AND ADULT TYPES	ABSENT ARYLSULFATASE A DEFICIENT ARYLSULFATASE A
METHYLMALONIC ACIDEMIA	METHYLMALONYL CoA CARBONYL MUTASE
NIEMANN-PICK DISEASE	SPHINGOMYELINASE
REFSUM'S DISEASE	PHYTANIC ACID ALPHA-OXIDASE
SANDHOFF'S DISEASE	HEXOSAMINIDASE A AND B
SANFILIPPO DISEASE	INCREASED AMNIOTIC FLUID HEPARITIN SULFATE
TAY-SACHS DISEASE	HEXOSAMINIDASE A
WOLMAN'S DISEASE	ACID LIPASE
POSSIBLY ASSOCIATED WITH MENTAL RETARDATION	
CYSTATHIONINURIA	CYSTATHIONASE
HOMOCYSTINURIA	CYSTATHIONINE SYNTHASE
NOT ASSOCIATED WITH MENTAL RETARDATION	
ADRENOGENITAL SYNDROME	INCREASED AMNIOTIC FLUID CORTICO STEROIDS
CYSTINOSIS	INCREASED CELLULAR CYSTINE
FABRY'S DISEASE	ALPHA-GALACTOSIDASE
HYPERVALINEMIA	VALINE TRANSAMINASE
OROTIC ACIDURIA	OROTIDYLIC PYROPHOSPHORYLASE AND OROTIDYLIC DECARBOXYLASE

GENETIC DISEASES that at present can be detected prenatally by studies of fetal cells and amniotic fluid are listed. Most of the diseases result in severe mental retardation.

has pointed out that condemning many of today's infants to famine and inadequate development does not display greater respect for the quality of human life than is found in primitive societies that practice infanticide with undesired or defective newborn infants. Others have questioned the moral justification for making these life-death decisions. Through recent upheavals in our social, legal and religious institutions we are now faced with the dilemma of assigning to the fetus certain rights. In several instances damages have been awarded on behalf of fetuses in criminal and tort suits. At the same time abortion laws have been liberalized to the point of suggesting that early fetuses do not have the right to life if the mother wants to abort a pregnancy. Prenatal genetic diagnosis seemed at first no different from most other new diagnostic methods. Now we see that we are faced with problems of assigning values to individuals with given genetic characteristics and designing programs directed against them. Until now most of these characteristics have been associated with severe clinical disease. Now we are not always certain what the existence of genetic anomalies will mean to the health of an individual. These uncertainties could result in an accentuation of the conflict in our society between personal choice and governmental control, which could possibly come in the form of selected programs of compulsory screening and mandatory abortion for some conditions that are deemed socially intolerable. The obviously dangerous extensions of such a practice would impinge so drastically on our individual liberties as to make them unacceptable and morally unjustifiable.

Intriguing developments in our legal concepts of the unborn child seem imminent, since there are certain to be legal tests of the liability of parents and others for offspring born with genetically determined handicaps that are predictable. Such "wrongful life" suits have already been brought on behalf of illegitimate infants and some infants born with severe developmental defects due to prenatal infection with syphilis and German measles. Similar suits involving genetic diseases will soon test the concept that we—as parents, physicians and human beings—have obligations to the unborn to protect them from the likelihood of genetically determined defects. One may hope that advances in other social institutions will at the same time help us to resolve our individual and societal attitudes toward life, born and unborn.

Science and the Citizen
March 1973

The Abortion Decision

The U.S. now has what is in principle the world's most permissive legal policy on abortion. The procedure will henceforth be regulated on the basis of medical standards and practices, rather than according to socioreligious principles enforced by criminal law. Abortion will nevertheless not become a primary method of fertility control, although its availability as a backup procedure could have a beneficial effect on contraceptive practices. These are among the conclusions reached by legal and medical specialists in the wake of the Supreme Court's January decisions striking down almost all provisions of most of the state laws prohibiting and regulating abortion.

The decisions relied primarily on the right of privacy implied by the Constitution and on a finding that an unviable fetus is not a "person" within the meaning of the 14th Amendment. The Court held that abortion is so safe in the first three months of pregnancy that states may not interfere at all with a decision by a woman and her physician at that stage. In the second and third trimesters states may regulate the practice of abortion, but only in ways "reasonably related to maternal health." Only after the fetus is viable—has the capability of surviving outside the womb—may a state prohibit abortion. Significantly, the Court held that viability comes after 24 to 28 weeks of pregnancy, and it said that abortion must be allowed even after that "when it is necessary to preserve the life or health of the mother." ("Health" specifically includes mental health.) No state law complies completely with the Court's guidelines. Even New York's law permits abortion after 24 weeks only to preserve a woman's life, not her health; Alaska and Hawaii have residency requirements, which the Court disallowed. Moreover, health-code provisions (such as New York City's) that regulate abortions in the first trimester are now presumably unconstitutional. The extent to which the practice can be restricted later in pregnancy remains somewhat unclear. It will probably be tested by the promulgation and enforcement of a wide variety of state and local regulations that will be contested in the courts.

Some proponents of liberalized abortion indicated that they would now work for the complete elimination of all criminal legislation on the subject, holding that abortion should be treated like any other medical procedure and regulated by the medical profession, civil law and health codes. Others indicated they would be satisfied with laws such as New York's if they are modified to include the preservation of maternal health as a reason for abortion after viability.

Although abortion is now legal until late in pregnancy, the procedure is still far from generally available, and proponents of liberalized abortion plan to remedy that lack. Planned Parenthood–World Population announced that it would set up more abortion clinics and run a nationwide referral service. The National Association for the Repeal of Abortion Laws will hold regional workshops for physicians to promote safe abortion methods and advise on how to establish abortion clinics. Christopher Tietze, associate director of the biomedical division of the Population Council, estimated on the basis of New York's experience since 1970 that facilities should be available to provide abortions for some 1.6 million women a year in the U.S. It is now incumbent on the community to make abortions available to all at a fair price, he said.

Tietze pointed out that the Court's decision puts the U.S. well ahead of many northern European countries that have been considered relatively liberal but that still require approval of an abortion by either a medical board or more than one physician. In a legal sense, in authorizing abortion the U.S. now is more liberal than Japan, the U.S.S.R. and other countries of eastern Europe, which limit abortion on demand to the first trimester; on the other hand, it is easier to obtain an early abortion in those countries because more facilities are available.

In spite of the decision, Tietze said, he does not expect a large increase in the number of late-pregnancy abortions in the U.S. He cited the results of a study of abortion in New York. The number of late abortions decreased significantly in the period from mid-1971 to mid-1972 compared with the year before, the first in which legal abortion became generally available. He attributed the decline to the steady increase in facilities during the two years and to women's increasing awareness that early abortion is a great deal safer than late abortion, which, he said, is an indication of a "social failure," and is justifiable primarily by the development of heart or kidney disease in a woman or by an indication that the fetus is defective. In this connection he pointed to recent advances in the analysis of fetal chromosomes for evidence of certain congenital defects; such evidence can now presumably be discovered and adduced in support of abortion in the last trimester, since it certainly can be held to threaten a woman's mental health.

Along with most other students of the subject, Tietze does not think abortion should be a primary method of fertility control. The availability of abortion as a secondary method can be important, however. It means that "good but not perfect" methods of contraception—such as oral contraceptives that may be somewhat safer than the most effective ones—can be prescribed with confidence, with early abortion as a backup. A statistical study he made in 1969 showed that in-hospital abortion produces about the same low fatality rate as use of the most effective oral contraceptive method; the combination of "moderately effective" contraception and in-hospital abortion results in a much lower fatality rate.

Human Food Production as a Process in the Biosphere

by Lester R. Brown
September 1970

Human population growth is mainly the result of increases in food production. This relation raises the question: How many people can the biosphere support without impairment of its overall operation?

Throughout most of man's existence his numbers have been limited by the supply of food. For the first two million years or so he lived as a predator, a herbivore and a scavenger. Under such circumstances the biosphere could not support a human population of more than 10 million, a population smaller than that of London or Afghanistan today. Then, with his domestication of plants and animals some 10,000 years ago, man began to shape the biosphere to his own ends.

As primitive techniques of crop production and animal husbandry became more efficient the earth's food-producing capacity expanded, permitting increases in man's numbers. Population growth in turn exerted pressure on food supply, compelling man to further alter the biosphere in order to meet his food needs. Population growth and advances in food production have thus tended to be mutually reinforcing.

It took two million years for the human population to reach the one-billion mark, but the fourth billion now being added will require only 15 years: from 1960 to 1975. The enormous increase in the demand for food that is generated by this expansion in man's numbers, together with rising incomes, is beginning to have disturbing consequences. New signs of stress on the biosphere are reported almost daily. The continuing expansion of land under the plow and the evolution of a chemically oriented modern agriculture are producing ominous alterations in the biosphere not just on a local scale but, for the first time in history, on a global scale as well. The natural cycles of energy and the chemical elements are clearly being affected by man's efforts to expand his food supply.

Given the steadily advancing demand for food, further intervention in the biosphere for the expansion of the food supply is inevitable. Such intervention, however, can no longer be undertaken by an individual or a nation without consideration of the impact on the biosphere as a whole. The decision by a government to dam a river, by a farmer to use DDT on his crops or by a married couple to have another child, thereby increasing the demand for food, has repercussions for all mankind.

The revolutionary change in man's role from hunter and gatherer to tiller and herdsman took place in circumstances that are not well known, but some of the earliest evidence of agriculture is found in the hills and grassy plains of the Fertile Crescent in western Asia. The cultivation of food plants and the domestication of animals were aided there by the presence of wild wheat, barley, sheep, goats, pigs, cattle and horses. From the beginnings of agriculture man naturally favored above all other species those plants and animals that had been most useful to him in the wild. As a result of this favoritism he has altered the composition of the earth's plant and animal populations. Today his crops, replacing the original cover of grass or forest, occupy some three billion acres. This amounts to about 10 percent of the earth's total land surface and a considerably larger fraction of the land capable of supporting vegetation, that is, the area excluding deserts, polar regions and higher elevations. Two-thirds of the cultivated cropland is planted to cereals. The area planted to wheat alone is 600 million acres—nearly a million square miles, or an area equivalent to the U.S. east of the Mississippi. As for the influence of animal husbandry on the earth's animal populations, Hereford and Black Angus cattle roam the Great Plains, once the home of an estimated 30 to 40 million buffalo; in Australia the kangaroo has given way to European cattle; in Asia the domesticated water buffalo has multiplied in the major river valleys.

Clearly the food-producing enterprise has altered not only the relative abundance of plant and animal species but also their global distribution. The linkage of the Old and the New World in the 15th century set in motion an exchange of crops among various parts of the world that continues today. This exchange greatly increased the earth's capacity to sustain human populations, partly because some of the crops trans-

EXPERIMENTAL FARM in Brazil, one of thousands around the world where improvements in agricultural technology are pioneered, is seen as an image on an infrared-sensitive film in the aerial photograph on the opposite page. The reflectance of vegetation at near-infrared wavelengths of .7 to .9 micron registers on the film in false shades of red that are proportional to the intensity of the energy. The most reflective, and reddest, areas (*bottom*) are land still uncleared of forest cover. Most of the tilled fields, although irregular in shape, are contour-plowed. Regular patterns (*left and bottom right*) are citrus-orchard rows. The photograph was taken by a National Aeronautics and Space Administration mission in cooperation with the Brazilian government in a joint study of the assessment of agricultural resources by remote sensing. The farm is some 80 miles northwest of São Paulo.

ported elsewhere turned out to be better suited there than to their area of origin. Perhaps the classic example is the introduction of the potato from South America into northern Europe, where it greatly augmented the food supply, permitting marked increases in population. This was most clearly apparent in Ireland, where the population increased rapidly for several decades on the strength of the food supply represented by the potato. Only when the potato-blight organism (*Phytophthora infestans*) devastated the potato crop was population growth checked in Ireland.

The soybean, now the leading source of vegetable oil and principal farm export of the U.S., was introduced from China several decades ago. Grain sorghum, the second-ranking feed grain in the U.S. (after corn), came from Africa as a food store in the early slave ships. In the U.S.S.R. today the principal source of vegetable oil is the sunflower, a plant that originated on the southern Great Plains of the U.S. Corn, unknown in the Old World before Columbus, is now grown on every continent. On the other hand, North America is indebted to the Old World for all its livestock and poultry species with the exception of the turkey.

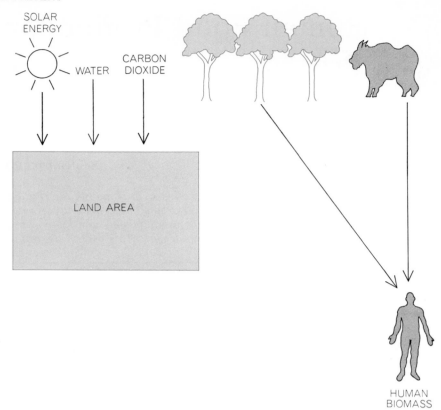

IMPACT OF THE AGRICULTURAL REVOLUTION on the human population is outlined in these two diagrams. The diagram at left shows the state of affairs before the invention of agriculture: the plants and animals supported by photosynthesis on the total land area could support a human population of only about 10 million. The diagram at right shows

To man's accomplishments in exploiting the plants and animals that natural evolution has provided, and in improving them through selective breeding over the millenniums, he has added in this century the creation of remarkably productive new breeds, thanks to the discoveries of genetics. Genetics has made possible the development of cereals and other plant species that are more tolerant to cold, more resistant to drought, less susceptible to disease, more responsive to fertilizer, higher in yield and richer in protein. The story of hybrid corn is only one of many spectacular examples. The breeding of short-season corn varieties has extended the northern limit of this crop some 500 miles.

Plant breeders recently achieved a historic breakthrough in the development of new high-yielding varieties of wheat and rice for tropical and subtropical regions. These wheats and rices, bred by Rockefeller Foundation and Ford Foundation scientists in Mexico and the Philippines, are distinguished by several characteristics. Most important, they are short-statured and stiff-strawed, and are highly responsive to chemical fertilizer. They also mature earlier. The first of the high-yielding rices, IR-8, matures in 120

days as against 150 to 180 days for other varieties.

Another significant advance incorporated into the new strains is the reduced sensitivity of their seed to photoperiod (length of day). This is partly the result of their cosmopolitan ancestry: they were developed from seed collections all over the world. The biological clocks of traditional varieties of cereals were keyed to specific seasonal cycles, and these cereals could be planted only at a certain time of the year, in the case of rice say at the onset of the monsoon season. The new wheats, which are quite flexible in terms of both seasonal and latitudinal variations in length of day, are now being grown in developing countries as far north as Turkey and as far south as Paraguay.

The combination of earlier maturity and reduced sensitivity to day length creates new opportunities for multiple cropping in tropical and subtropical regions where water supplies are adequate, enabling farmers to harvest two, three and occasionally even four crops per year. Workers at the International Rice Research Institute in the Philippines regularly harvest three crops of rice per

year. Each acre they plant yields six tons annually, roughly three times the average yield of corn, the highest-yielding cereal in the U.S. Thousands of farmers in northern India are now alternating a crop of early-maturing winter wheat with a summer crop of rice, greatly increasing the productivity of their land. These new opportunities for farming land more intensively lessen the pressure for bringing marginal land under cultivation, thus helping to conserve precious topsoil. At the same time they increase the use of agricultural chemicals, creating environmental stresses more akin to those in the advanced countries.

The new dwarf wheats and rices are far more efficient than the traditional varieties in their use of land, water, fertilizer and labor. The new opportunities for multiple cropping permit conversion of far more of the available solar energy into food. The new strains are not the solution to the food problem, but they are removing the threat of massive famine in the short run. They are buying time for the stabilization of population, which is ultimately the only solution to the food crisis. This "green revolution"

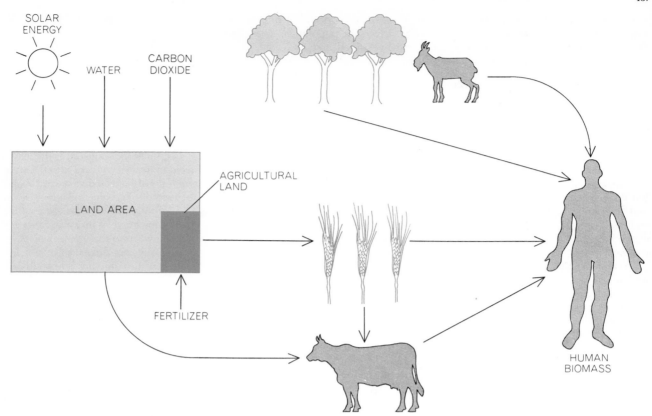

the state of affairs after the invention of agriculture. The 10 percent of the land now under the plow, watered and fertilized by man, is the primary support for a human population of 3.5 billion. Some of the agricultural produce is consumed directly by man; some is consumed indirectly by first being fed to domestic animals. Some of the food for domestic animals, however, comes from land not under the plow (*curved arrow at bottom left*). Man also obtains some food from sources other than agriculture, such as fishing.

may affect the well-being of more people in a shorter period of time than any technological advance in history.

The progress of man's expansion of food production is reflected in the way crop yields have traditionally been calculated. Today the output of cereals is expressed in yield per acre, but in early civilizations it was calculated as a ratio of the grain produced to that required for seed. On this basis the current ratio is perhaps highest in the U.S. corn belt, where farmers realize a four-hundred-fold return on the hybrid corn seed they plant. The ratio for rice is also quite high, but the ratio for wheat, the third of the principal cereals, is much lower, possibly 30 to one on a global basis.

The results of man's efforts to increase the productivity of domestic animals are equally impressive. When the ancestors of our present chickens were domesticated, they laid a clutch of about 15 eggs once a year. Hens in the U.S. today average 220 eggs per year, and the figure is rising steadily as a result of continuing advances in breeding and feeding. When cattle were originally domesticated, they probably did not produce more than 600 pounds of milk per year, barely enough for a calf. (It is roughly the average amount produced by cows in India today.) The 13 million dairy cows in the U.S. today average 9,000 pounds of milk yearly, outproducing their ancestors 15 to one.

Most such advances in the productivity of plant and animal species are recent. Throughout most of history man's efforts to meet his food needs have been directed primarily toward bringing more land under cultivation, spreading agriculture from valley to valley and continent to continent. He has also, however, invented techniques to raise the productivity of land already under cultivation, particularly in this century, when the decreasing availability of new lands for expansion has compelled him to turn to a more intensive agriculture. These techniques involve altering the biosphere's cycles of energy, water, nitrogen and minerals.

Modern agriculture depends heavily on four technologies: mechanization, irrigation, fertilization and the chemical control of weeds and insects. Each of these technologies has made an important contribution to the earth's increased capacity for sustaining human populations, and each has perturbed the cycles of the biosphere.

At least as early as 3000 B.C. the farmers of the Middle East learned to harness draft animals to help them till the soil. Harnessing animals much stronger than himself enabled man to greatly augment his own limited muscle power. It also enabled him to convert roughage (indigestible by humans) into a usable form of energy and thus to free some of his energy for pursuits other than the quest for food. The invention of the internal-combustion engine and the tractor 5,000 years later provided a much greater breakthrough. It now became possible to substitute petroleum (the product of the photosynthesis of aeons ago) for oats, corn and hay grown as feed for draft animals. The replacement of horses by the tractor not only provided the farmer with several times as much power but also released 70 million acres in the U.S. that had been devoted to raising feed for horses.

In the highly mechanized agriculture of today the expenditure of fossil fuel energy per acre is often substantially greater than the energy yield embodied in the food produced. This deficit in the output is of no immediate consequence, because the system is drawing on energy in the bank. When fossil fuels become scarcer, man will have to turn to some other source of motive energy for agriculture: perhaps nuclear energy or some means, other than photosynthesis, of harnessing solar energy. For the present and for the purposes of agriculture the energy budget of the biosphere is still favorable: the supply of solar energy—both the energy stored in fossil fuels and that taken up daily and converted into food energy by crops—enables an advanced nation to be fed with only 5 percent of the population directly employed in agriculture.

The combination of draft animals and mechanical power has given man an enormous capacity for altering the earth's surface by bringing additional land under the plow (not all of it suited for cultivation). In addition, in the poorer countries his expanding need for fuel has forced him to cut forests far in excess of their ability to renew themselves. The areas largely stripped of forest include mainland China and the subcontinent of India and Pakistan, where much of the population must now use cow dung for fuel. Although statistics are not available, the proportion of mankind using cow dung as fuel to prepare meals may

far exceed the proportion using natural gas. Livestock populations providing draft power, food and fuel tend to increase along with human populations, and in many poor countries the needs of livestock for forage far exceed its self-renewal, gradually denuding the countryside of grass cover.

As population pressure builds, not only is more land brought under the plow but also the land remaining is less suited to cultivation. Once valleys are filled, farmers begin to move up hillsides, creating serious soil-erosion problems. As the natural cover that retards runoff is reduced and soil structure deteriorates, floods and droughts become more severe.

Over most of the earth the thin layer of topsoil producing most of man's food is measured in inches. Denuding the land of its year-round natural cover of grass or forest exposes the thin mantle of life-sustaining soil to rapid erosion by wind and water. Much of the soil ultimately washes into the sea, and some of it is lifted into the atmosphere. Man's actions are causing the topsoil to be removed faster than it is formed. This unstable relationship between man and the land from which he derives his subsistence obviously cannot continue indefinitely.

Robert R. Brooks of Williams College, an economist who spent several years in India, gives a wry description of the process occurring in the state of Rajasthan, where tens of thousands of acres of rural land are being abandoned yearly because of the loss of topsoil: "Overgrazing by goats destroys the desert plants which might otherwise hold the soil in place. Goatherds equipped with sickles attached to 20-foot poles strip the leaves of trees to float downward into the waiting mouths of famished goats and sheep. The trees die and the soil blows away 200 miles to New Delhi, where it comes to rest in the lungs of its inhabitants and on the shiny cars of foreign diplomats."

Soil erosion not only results in a loss of soil but also impairs irrigation systems. This is illustrated in the Mangla irrigation reservoir, recently built in the foothills of the Himalayas in West Pakistan as part of the Indus River irrigation system. On the basis of feasibility studies indicating that the reservoir could be expected to have a lifetime of at least 100 years, $600 million was invested in the construction of the reservoir. Denuding and erosion of the soil in the watershed, however, accompanying a rapid growth of population in the area, has already washed so much soil into the reservoir that it is now expected to be completely filled with silt within 50 years.

A historic example of the effects of man's abuse of the soil is all too plainly visible in North Africa, which once was the fertile granary of the Roman Empire and now is largely a desert or near-desert whose people are fed with the aid of food imports from the U.S. In the U.S. itself the "dust bowl" experience of the 1930's remains a vivid lesson on the folly of overplowing. More recently the U.S.S.R. repeated this error, bringing 100 million acres of virgin soil under the plow only to discover that the region's rainfall was too scanty to sustain continuous cultivation. Once moisture reserves in the soil were depleted the soil began to blow.

Soil erosion is one of the most pressing and most difficult problems threatening the future of the biosphere. Each year it is forcing the abandonment of millions of acres of cropland in Asia, the Middle East, North Africa and Central America. Nature's geological cycle continuously produces topsoil, but its pace is far too slow to be useful to man. Someone once defined soil as rock on its way to the sea. Soil is produced by the weathering of rock and the process takes several centuries to form an inch of topsoil. Man is managing to destroy the topsoil

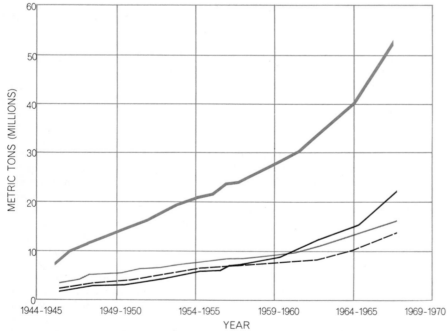

FERTILIZER CONSUMPTION has increased more than fivefold since the end of World War II. The top line in the graph (*color*) shows the tonnage of all kinds of fertilizers combined. The lines below show the tonnages of the three major types: nitrogen (*black*), now the leader, phosphate (*gray*) and potash (*broken line*). Figures, from the most recent report by the UN Food and Agriculture Organization, omit fertilizer consumption in China.

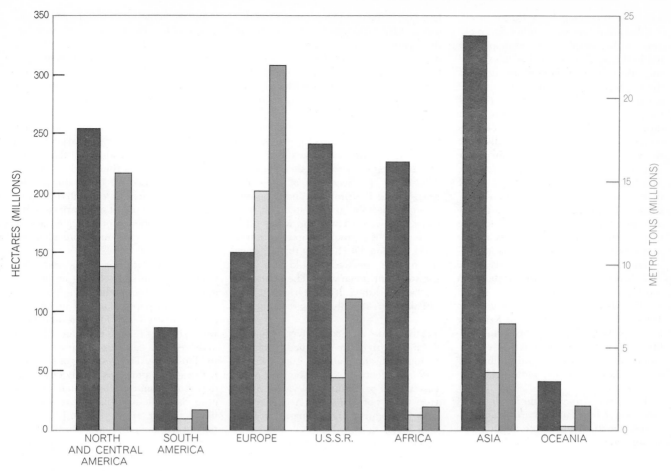

TONS OF FERTILIZER used in seven world areas are compared with the amount of agricultural land in each area. Two tonnages are shown in each instance: the amount used in 1962–1963 (*light color*) and the amount used in 1967–1968 (*solid color*). The great- est use of fertilizer occurs in Europe, the least fertilized area is Africa and the greatest percentage increase in the period was in Australia and New Zealand. Figures, from the Food and Agricul- ture Organization, omit China, North Korea and North Vietnam.

in some areas of the world in a fraction of this time. The only possible remedy is to find ways to conserve the topsoil more effectively.

The dust-bowl era in the U.S. ended with the widespread adoption of con- servation practices by farmers. Twenty million acres were fallowed to accumu- late moisture and thousands of miles of windbreaks were planted across the Great Plains. Fallow land was alternated with strips of wheat ("strip-cropping") to reduce the blowing of soil while the land was idle. The densely populated coun- tries of Asia, however, are in no position to adopt such tactics. Their food needs are so pressing that they cannot afford to take large areas out of cultivation; moreover, they do not yet have the finan- cial resources or the technical skills for the immense projects in reforestation, controlled grazing of cattle, terracing, contour farming and systematic manage- ment of watersheds that would be re- quired to preserve their soil.

The significance of wind erosion goes

far beyond the mere loss of topsoil. As other authors in this issue have observed, a continuing increase in particulate mat- ter in the atmosphere could affect the earth's climate by reducing the amount of incoming solar energy. This particu- late matter comes not only from the technological activities of the richer countries but also from wind erosion in the poorer countries. The poorer coun- tries do not have the resources for un- dertaking the necessary effort to arrest and reverse this trend. Should it be es- tablished that an increasing amount of particulate matter in the atmosphere is changing the climate, the richer coun- tries would have still another reason to provide massive capital and technical as- sistance to the poor countries, joining with them to confront this common threat to mankind.

Irrigation, which agricultural man be- gan to practice at least as early as 6,000 years ago, even earlier than he harnessed animal power, has played its

great role in increasing food production by bringing into profitable cultivation vast areas that would otherwise be un- usable or only marginally productive. Most of the world's irrigated land is in Asia, where it is devoted primarily to the production of rice. In Africa the Volta River of Ghana and the Nile are dammed for irrigation and power pur- poses. The Colorado River system of the U.S. is used extensively for irrigation in the Southwest, as are scores of rivers elsewhere. Still to be exploited for irri- gation are the Mekong of southeastern Asia and the Amazon.

During the past few years there has been an important new irrigation devel- opment in Asia: the widespread installa- tion of small-scale irrigation systems on individual farms. In Pakistan and India, where in many places the water table is close to the surface, hundreds of thou- sands of tube wells with pumps have been installed in recent years. Interest- ingly, this development came about partly as an answer to a problem that had been presented by irrigation itself.

Like many of man's other interventions in the biosphere, his reshaping of the hydrologic cycle has had unwanted side effects. One of them is the raising of the water table by the diversion of river water onto the land. Over a period of time the percolation of irrigation water downward and the accumulation of this water underground may gradually raise the water table until it is within a few feet or even a few inches of the surface. This not only inhibits the growth of plant roots by waterlogging but also results in the surface soil's becoming salty as water evaporates through it, leaving a concentrated deposit of salts in the upper few inches. Such a situation developed in West Pakistan after its fertile plain had been irrigated with water from the Indus for a century. During a visit by President Ayub to Washington in 1961 he appealed to President Kennedy for help: West Pakistan was losing 60,-000 acres of fertile cropland per year because of waterlogging and salinity as its population was expanding 2.5 percent yearly.

This same sequence, the diversion of river water into land for irrigation, followed eventually by waterlogging and salinity and the abandonment of land,

had been repeated many times throughout history. The result was invariably the decline, and sometimes the disappearance, of the civilizations thus intervening in the hydrologic cycle. The remains of civilizations buried in the deserts of the Middle East attest to early experiences similar to those of contemporary Pakistan. These civilizations, however, had no one to turn to for foreign aid. An interdisciplinary U.S. team led by Roger Revelle, then Science Adviser to the Secretary of the Interior, studied the problem and proposed among other things a system of tube wells that would lower the water table by tapping the ground water for intensive irrigation. Discharging this water on the surface, the wells would also wash the soil's salt downward. The stratagem worked, and the salty, waterlogged land of Pakistan is steadily being reclaimed.

Other side effects of river irrigation are not so easily remedied. Such irrigation has brought about a great increase in the incidence of schistosomiasis, a disease that is particularly prevalent in the river valleys of Africa and Asia. The disease is produced by the parasitic larva of a blood fluke, which is harbored by aquatic snails and burrows into the flesh

of people standing in water or in water-soaked fields. The Chinese call schistosomiasis "snail fever"; it might also be called the poor man's emphysema, because, like emphysema, this extremely debilitating disease is environmentally induced through conditions created by man. The snails and the fluke thrive in perennial irrigation systems, where they are in close proximity to large human populations. The incidence of the disease is rising rapidly as the world's large rivers are harnessed for irrigation, and today schistosomiasis is estimated to afflict 250 million people. It now surpasses malaria, the incidence of which is declining, as the world's most prevalent infectious disease.

As a necessity for food production water is of course becoming an increasingly crucial commodity. The projected increases in population and in food requirements will call for more and more water, forcing man to consider still more massive and complex interventions in the biosphere. The desalting of seawater for irrigation purposes is only one major departure from traditional practices. Another is a Russian plan to reverse the flow of four rivers currently flowing northward and emptying into the Arctic Ocean. These rivers would be diverted southward into the semiarid lands of southern Russia, greatly enlarging the irrigated area of the U.S.S.R. Some climatologists are concerned, however, that the shutting off of the flow of relatively warm water from these four rivers would have far-reaching implications for not only the climate of the Arctic but also the climatic system of the entire earth.

The growing competition for scarce water supplies among states and among various uses in the western U.S. is also forcing consideration of heroic plans. For example, a detailed engineering proposal exists for the diversion of the Yukon River in Alaska southward across Canada into the western U.S. to meet the growing need for water for both agricultural and industrial purposes. The effort would cost an estimated $100 billion.

Representing an even greater intervention in the biosphere is the prospect that man may one day consciously alter the earth's climatic patterns, shifting some of the rain now falling on the oceans to the land. Among the steps needed for the realization of such a scheme are the construction of a comprehensive model of the earth's climatic system and the development of a computational facility capable of simulating

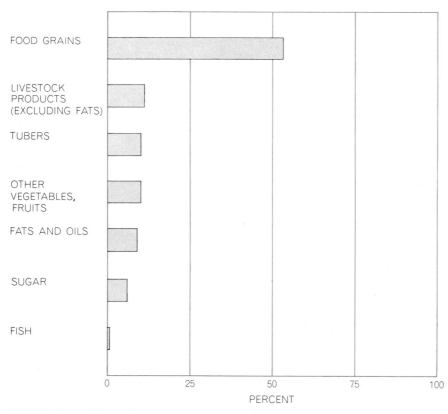

FOOD GRAINS

LIVESTOCK PRODUCTS (EXCLUDING FATS)

TUBERS

OTHER VEGETABLES, FRUITS

FATS AND OILS

SUGAR

FISH

0   25   50   75   100

PERCENT

WORLDWIDE FOOD ENERGY comes in different amounts from different products. Cereals outstrip other foodstuffs; wheat and rice each supply a fifth of mankind's food energy.

and manipulating the model. The required information includes data on temperatures, humidity, precipitation, the movement of air masses, ocean currents and many other factors that enter into the weather. Earth-orbiting satellites will doubtless be able to collect much of this information, and the present generation of advanced computers appears to be capable of carrying out the necessary experiments on the model. For the implementation of the findings, that is, for the useful control of rainfall, there will of course be a further requirement: the project will have to be managed by a global and supranational agency if it is not to lead to weather wars among nations working at cross purposes. Some commercial firms are already in the business of rainmaking, and they are operating on an international basis.

The third great technology that man has introduced to increase food production is the use of chemical fertilizers. We owe the foundation for this development to Justus von Liebig of Germany, who early in the 19th century determined the specific requirements of nitrogen, phosphorus, potassium and other nutrients for plant growth. Chemical fertilizers did not come into widespread use, however, until this century, when the pressure of population and the disappearance of new frontiers compelled farmers to substitute fertilizer for the expansion of cropland to meet growing food needs. One of the first countries to intensify its agriculture, largely by the use of fertilizers, was Japan, whose output of food per acre has steadily risen (except for wartime interruptions) since the turn of the century. The output per acre of a few other countries, including the Netherlands, Denmark and Sweden, began to rise at about the same time. The U.S., richly endowed with vast farmlands, did not turn to the heavy use of fertilizer· and other intensive measures until about 1940. Since then its yields per acre, assisted by new varieties of grain highly responsive to fertilizer, have also shown remarkable gains. Yields of corn, the production of which exceeds that of all other cereals combined in the U.S., have nearly tripled over the past three decades.

Experience has demonstrated that in areas of high rainfall the application of chemical fertilizers in conjunction with other inputs and practices can double, triple or even quadruple the productivity of intensively farmed soils. Such levels of productivity are achieved in Japan and the Netherlands, where farmers ap-

ply up to 300 pounds of plant nutrients per acre per year. The use of chemical fertilizers is estimated to account for at least a fourth of man's total food supply. The world's. farmers are currently applying 60 million metric tons of plant nutrients per year, an average of nearly 45 pounds per acre for the three billion acres of cropland. Such application, however, is unevenly distributed. Some poor countries do not yet benefit from the use of fertilizer in any significant amounts. If global projections of population and income growth materialize, the production of fertilizer over the remaining three decades of this century must almost triple to satisfy food demands.

Can the projected demand for fertilizer be met? The key ingredient is nitrogen, and fortunately man has learned how to speed up the fixation phase of the nitrogen cycle [see "The Nitrogen Cycle," by C. C. Delwiche, SCIENTIFIC AMERICAN Offprint 1194]. In nature the nitrogen ot the air is fixed in the soil by certain microorganisms, such as those present in the root nodules of leguminous plants. Chemists have now devised various ways of incorporating nitrogen from the air into inorganic compounds and making it available in the form of nitrogen fertilizers. These chemical processes produce the fertilizer much more rapidly and economically

than the growing of leguminous-plant sources such as clover, alfalfa or soybeans. More than 25 million tons ot nitrogen fertilizer is now being synthesized and added to the earth's soil annually.

The other principal ingredients of chemical fertilizer are the minerals potassium and phosphorus. Unlike nitrogen, these elements are not replenished· by comparatively fast natural cycles. Potassium presents no immediate problem; the rich potash fields of Canada alone are estimated to contain enough potassium to supply mankind's needs for centuries to come. The reserves of phosphorus, however, are not nearly so plentiful as those of potassium. Every year 3.5 million tons of phosphorus washes into the sea, where it remains as sediment on the ocean floor. Eventually it will be thrust above the ocean surface again by geologic uplift, but man cannot wait that long. Phosphorus may be one of the first necessities that will prompt man to begin to mine the ocean bed.

The great expansion of the use of fertilizers in this century has benefited mankind enormously, but the benefits are not unalloyed. The runoff of chemical fertilizers into rivers, lakes and underground waters creates two important hazards. One is the chemical pollution

EXPERIMENTAL PLANTINGS at the International Rice Research Institute in the Philippine Republic are seen in an aerial photograph. IR-8, a high-yield rice, was bred here.

RUINED FARM in the "dust bowl" area of the U.S. in the 1930's is seen in an aerial photograph. The farm is near Union in Terry County, Tex. The wind has eroded the powdery, drought-parched topsoil and formed drifts among the buildings and across the fields.

of drinking water. In certain areas in Illinois and California the nitrate content of well water has risen to a toxic level. Excessive nitrate can cause the physiological disorder methemoglobinemia, which reduces the blood's oxygen-carrying capacity and can be particularly dangerous to children under five. This hazard is of only local dimensions and can be countered by finding alternative sources of drinking water. A much more extensive hazard, profound in its effects on the biosphere, is the now well-known .phenomenon called eutrophication.

Inorganic nitrates and phosphates discharged into lakes and other bodies of fresh water provide a rich medium for the growth of algae; the massive growth of the algae in turn depletes the water of oxygen and thus kills off the fish life. In the end the eutrophication, or overfertilization, of the lake slowly brings about its death as a body of fresh water, converting it into a swamp. Lake Erie is a prime example of this process now under way.

How much of the now widespread eutrophication of fresh waters is attributable to agricultural fertilization and how much to other causes remains an open question. Undoubtedly the runoff of nitrates and phosphates from farmlands plays a large part. There are also other important contributors, however. Considerable amounts of phosphate, coming mainly from detergents, are discharged into rivers and lakes from sewers carrying municipal and industrial wastes. And there is reason to believe that in some rivers and lakes most of the nitrate may come not from fertilizers but from the internal-combustion engine. It is estimated that in the state of New Jersey, which has heavy automobile traffic, nitrous oxide products of gasoline combustion, picked up and deposited by rainfall, contribute as much as 20 pounds of nitrogen per acre per year to the land. Some of this nitrogen washes into the many rivers and lakes of New Jersey and its adjoining states. A way must be found to deal with the eutrophication problem because even in the short run it can have damaging effects, affecting as it does the supply of potable water, the cycles of aquatic life and consequently man's food supply.

Recent findings have presented us with a related problem in connection with the fourth technology supporting man's present high level of food production: the chemical control of diseases, insects and weeds. It is now clear that the use of DDT and other chlorinated hydrocarbons as pesticides and herbicides is beginning to threaten many species of animal life, possibly including man. DDT today is found in the tissues of animals over a global range of life forms and geography from penguins in Antarctica to children in the villages of Thailand. There is strong evidence that it is actually on the way to extinguishing some animal species, notably predatory birds such as the bald eagle and the peregrine falcon, whose capacity for using calcium is so impaired by DDT that the shells of their eggs are too thin to avoid breakage in the nest before the fledglings hatch. Carnivores are particularly likely to concentrate DDT in their tissues because they feed on herbivores that have already concentrated it from large quantities of vegetation. Concentrations of DDT in mothers' milk in the U.S. now exceed the tolerance levels established for foodstuffs by the Food and Drug Administration.

It is ironic that less than a generation after 1948, when Paul Hermann Müller of Switzerland received a Nobel prize for the discovery of DDT, the use of the insecticide is being banned by law in many countries. This illustrates how little man knows about the effects of his intervening in the biosphere. Up to now he has been using the biosphere as a laboratory, sometimes with unhappy results.

Several new approaches to the problem of controlling pests are now being explored. Chemists are searching for pesticides that will be degradable, instead of long-lasting, after being deposited on vegetation or in the soil, and that will be aimed at specific pests rather than acting as broad-spectrum poisons for many forms of life. Much hope is placed in techniques of biological control, such as are exemplified in the mass sterilization (by irradiation) of male screwworm flies, a pest of cattle that used to cost U.S. livestock producers $100 million per year. The release of 125 million irradiated male screwworm flies weekly in the U.S. and in adjoining areas of Mexico (in a cooperative effort with the Mexican government) is holding the fly population to a negligible level. Efforts are now under way to get rid of the Mexican fruit fly and the pink cotton bollworm in California by the same method.

Successes are also being achieved in breeding resistance to insect pests in various crops. A strain of wheat has been developed that is resistant to the Hessian fly; resistance to the corn borer and the corn earworm has been bred into strains of corn, and work is in progress on a strain of alfalfa that resists aphids and leafhoppers. Another promising approach, which already has a considerable history, is the development of insect parasites, ranging from bacteria and viruses to wasps that lay their eggs in other insects. The fact remains, however, that the biological control of pests is still in its infancy.

I have here briefly reviewed the major agricultural technologies evolved to meet man's increasing food needs, the problems arising from them and some possible solutions. What is the present balance sheet on the satisfaction of human food needs? Although man's food supply has expanded several hundredfold since the invention of agriculture, two-thirds of mankind is still hungry and malnourished much of the time. On the credit side a third of mankind, living largely in North America, Europe, Australia and Japan, has achieved an adequate food supply, and for the remaining two-thirds the threat of large-scale famine has recently been removed, at least for the immediate future. In spite of rapid population growth in the developing countries since World War II, their peoples have been spared from massive famine (except in Biafra in 1969–1970) by huge exports of food from the developed countries. As a result of two consecutive monsoon failures in India, a fifth of the total U.S. wheat crop was shipped to India in both 1966 and 1967, feeding 60 million Indians for two years.

Although the threat of outright famine has been more or less eliminated for the time being, human nutrition on the global scale is still in a sorry state. Malnutrition, particularly protein deficiency, exacts an enormous toll from the physical and mental development of the young in the poorer countries. This was dramatically illustrated when India held tryouts in 1968 to select a team to represent it in the Olympic games that year. Not a single Indian athlete, male or female, met the minimum standards for qualifying to compete in any of the 36 track and field events in Mexico City. No doubt this was partly due to the lack of support for athletics in India, but poor nutrition was certainly also a large factor. The young people of Japan today are visible examples of what a change can be brought about by improvement in nutrition. Well-nourished from infancy, Japanese teen-agers are on the average some two inches taller than their elders.

Protein is as crucial for children's mental development as for their physical development. This was strikingly shown in a recent study extending over several years in Mexico: children who had been severely undernourished before the age of five were found to average 13 points lower in I.Q. than a carefully selected control group. Unfortunately no amount of feeding or education in later life can repair the setbacks to development caused by undernourishment in the early years. Protein shortages in the poor countries today are depreciating human resources for at least a generation to come.

Protein constitutes the main key to human health and vigor, and the key to the protein diet at present is held by grain consumed either directly or indirectly (in the form of meat, milk and eggs). Cereals, occupying more than 70 percent of the world's cropland, provide 52 percent of man's direct energy intake. Eleven percent is supplied by livestock products such as meat, milk and eggs, 10 percent by potatoes and other tubers, 10 percent by fruits and vegetables, 9 percent by animal fats and vegetable oils, 7 percent by sugar and 1 percent by fish. As in the case of the total quantity of the individual diet, however, the composition of the diet varies greatly around the world. The difference is most marked in the per capita use of grain consumed directly and indirectly.

The two billion people living in the poor countries consume an average of about 360 pounds of grain per year, or about a pound per day. With only one pound per day, nearly all must be consumed directly to meet minimal energy requirements; little remains for feeding to livestock, which may convert only a tenth of their feed intake into meat or other edible human food. The average American, in contrast, consumes more than 1,600 pounds of grain per year. He eats only about 150 pounds of this directly in the form of bread, breakfast cereal and so on; the rest is consumed indirectly in the form of meat, milk and eggs. In short, he enjoys the luxury of the highly inefficient animal conversion of grain into tastier and somewhat more nutritious proteins.

Thus the average North American currently makes about four times as great a demand on the earth's agricultural ecosystem as someone living in one of the poor countries. As the income levels in these countries rise, so will their demand for a richer diet of animal products. For the increasing world population at the end of the century, which is expected to be twice the 3.5 billion of today, the world production of grain would have to be doubled merely to maintain present consumption levels. This increase, combined with the projected improvement in diet associated with gains in income over the next three decades, could nearly triple the demand for grain, requiring that the food supply increase more over the next three decades than it has in the 10,000 years since agriculture began.

There are ways in which this pressure can be eased somewhat. One is the breeding of higher protein content in grains and other crops, making them nutritionally more acceptable as alternatives to livestock products. Another is the development of vegetable substitutes for animal products, such as are already available in the form of oleomargarine, soybean oil, imitation meats and other replacements (about 65 percent of the whipped toppings and 35 percent of the coffee whiteners now sold in U.S. supermarkets are nondairy products). Pressures on the agricultural ecosystem would thus drive high-income man one step down in the food chain to a level of more efficient consumption of what could be produced by agriculture.

What is clearly needed today is a cooperative effort—more specifically, a world environmental agency—to monitor, investigate and regulate man's interventions in the environment, including those made in his quest for more food. Since many of his efforts to enlarge his food supply have a global impact, they can only be dealt with in the context of a global institution. The health of the biosphere can no longer be separated from our modes of political organization. Whatever measures are taken, there is growing doubt that the agricultural ecosystem will be able to accommodate both the anticipated increase of the human population to seven billion by the end of the century and the universal desire of the world's hungry for a better diet. The central question is no longer "Can we produce enough food?" but "What are the environmental consequences of attempting to do so?"

40

Toxic Substances and Ecological Cycles

by George M. Woodwell
March 1967

Radioactive elements or pesticides such as DDT that are released in the environment may enter meteorological and biological cycles that distribute them and can concentrate them to dangerous levels

The vastness of the earth has fostered a tradition of unconcern about the release of toxic wastes into the environment. Billowing clouds of smoke are diluted to apparent nothingness; discarded chemicals are flushed away in rivers; insecticides "disappear" after they have done their job; even the massive quantities of radioactive debris of nuclear explosions are diluted in the apparently infinite volume of the environment. Such pollutants are indeed diluted to traces—to levels infinitesimal by ordinary standards, measured as parts per billion or less in air, soil and water. Some pollutants do disappear; they are immobilized or decay to harmless substances. Others last, sometimes in toxic form, for long periods. We have learned in recent years that dilution of persistent pollutants even to trace levels detectable only by refined techniques is no guarantee of safety. Nature has ways of concentrating substances that are frequently surprising and occasionally disastrous.

We have had dramatic examples of one of the hazards in the dense smogs that blanket our cities with increasing frequency. What is less widely realized is that there are global, long-term ecological processes that concentrate toxic substances, sometimes hundreds of thousands of times above levels in the environment. These processes include not only patterns of air and water circulation but also a complex series of biological mechanisms. Over the past decade detailed studies of the distribution of

both radioactive debris and pesticides have revealed patterns that have surprised even biologists long familiar with the unpredictability of nature.

Major contributions to knowledge of these patterns have come from studies of radioactive fallout. The incident that triggered worldwide interest in large-scale radioactive pollution was the hydrogen-bomb test at Bikini in 1954 known as "Project Bravo." This was the test that inadvertently dropped radioactive fallout on several Pacific islands and on the Japanese fishing vessel *Lucky Dragon*. Several thousand square miles of the Pacific were contaminated with fallout radiation that would have been lethal to man. Japanese and U.S. oceanographic vessels surveying the region found that the radioactive debris had been spread by wind and water, and, more disturbing, it was being passed rapidly along food chains from small plants to small marine organisms that ate them to larger animals (including the tuna, a staple of the Japanese diet).

The U.S. Atomic Energy Commission and agencies of other nations, particularly Britain and the U.S.S.R., mounted a large international research program, costing many millions of dollars, to learn the details of the movement of such debris over the earth and to explore its hazards. Although these studies have been focused primarily on radioactive materials, they have produced a great deal of basic information

about pollutants in general. The radioactive substances serve as tracers to show the transport and concentration of materials by wind and water and the biological mechanisms that are characteristic of natural communities.

One series of investigations traced the worldwide movement of particles in the air. The tracer in this case was strontium 90, a fission product released into the earth's atmosphere in large quantities by nuclear-bomb tests. Two reports in 1962 —one by S. Laurence Kulp and Arthur R. Schulert of Columbia University and the other by a United Nations committee— furnished a detailed picture of the travels of strontium 90. The isotope was concentrated on the ground between the latitudes of 30 and 60 degrees in both hemispheres, but concentrations were five to 10 times greater in the Northern Hemisphere, where most of the bomb tests were conducted.

It is apparently in the middle latitudes

FOREST COMMUNITY is an integrated array of plants and animals that accumulates and reuses nutrients in stable cycles, as indicated schematically in black. DDT participates in parallel cycles (*color*). The author measured DDT residues in a New Brunswick forest in which four pounds per acre of DDT had been applied over seven years. (Studies have shown about half of this landed in the forest, the remainder dispersing in the atmosphere.) Three years after the spraying, residues of DDT were as shown (in pounds per acre).

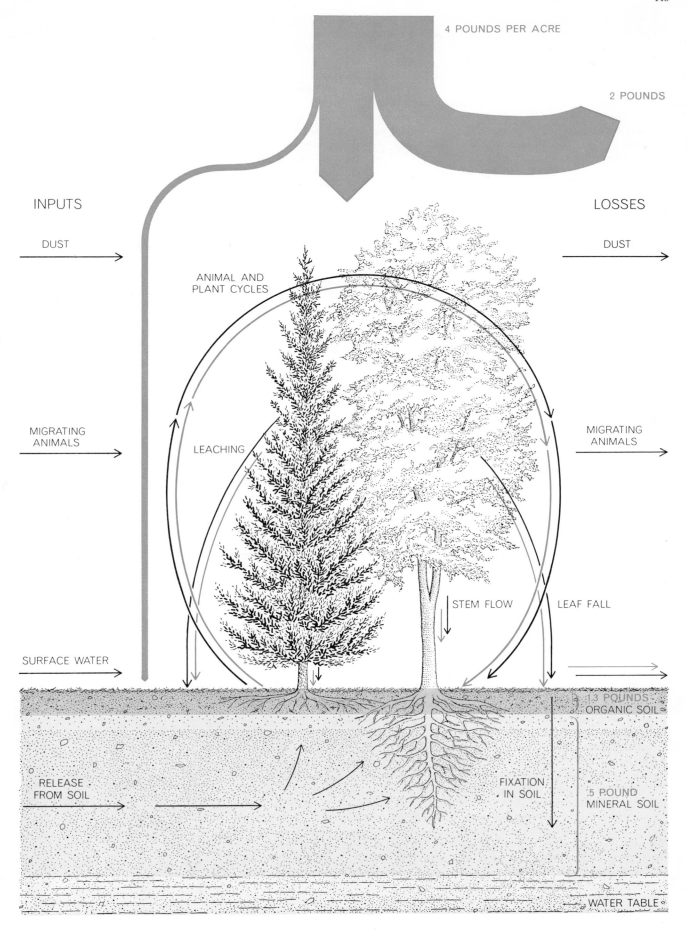

4 POUNDS PER ACRE

2 POUNDS

INPUTS

DUST →

MIGRATING
ANIMALS →

SURFACE WATER →

RELEASE
FROM SOIL

LOSSES

DUST →

MIGRATING
ANIMALS →

ANIMAL AND
PLANT CYCLES

LEACHING

STEM FLOW   LEAF FALL

13 POUNDS
ORGANIC SOIL

FIXATION
IN SOIL

5 POUND
MINERAL SOIL

WATER TABLE

that exchanges occur between the air of upper elevations (the stratosphere) and that of lower elevations (the troposphere). The larger tests have injected debris into the stratosphere; there it remains for relatively long periods, being carried back into the troposphere and to the ground in the middle latitudes in late winter or spring. The mean "half-time" of the particles' residence in the stratosphere (that is, the time for half of a given injection to fall out) is from three months to five years, depending on many factors, including the height of the injection, the size of the particles, the latitude of injection and the time of year. Debris injected into the troposphere has a mean half-time of residence ranging from a few days to about a month. Once airborne, the particles may travel rapidly and far. The time for one circuit around the earth in the middle latitudes varies from 25 days to less than 15. (Following two recent bomb tests in China fallout was detected at the Brookhaven National Laboratory on Long Island respectively nine and 14 days after the tests.)

Numerous studies have shown further that precipitation (rain and snowfall) plays an important role in determining where fallout will be deposited. Lyle T. Alexander of the Soil Conservation Service and Edward P. Hardy, Jr., of the AEC found in an extensive study in Clallam County, Washington, that the amount of fallout was directly proportional to the total annual rainfall.

It is reasonable to assume that the findings about the movement and fallout of radioactive debris also apply to other particles of similar size in the air. This conclusion is supported by a recent report by Donald F. Gatz and A. Nelson Dingle of the University of Michigan, who showed that the concentration of pollen in precipitation follows the same pattern as that of radioactive fallout. This observation is particularly meaningful because pollen is not injected into the troposphere by a nuclear explosion; it is picked up in air currents from plants close to the ground. There is little question that dust and other particles, including small crystals of pesticides, also follow these patterns.

From these and other studies it is clear that various substances released into the air are carried widely around the world and may be deposited in concentrated form far from the original source. Similarly, most bodies of water—especially the oceans—have surface currents that may move materials five to 10 miles a day. Much higher rates, of course, are found in such major oceanic currents as

the Gulf Stream. These currents are one more physical mechanism that can distribute pollutants widely over the earth.

The research programs of the AEC and other organizations have explored not only the pathways of air and water transport but also the pathways along which pollutants are distributed in plant and animal communities. In this connection we must examine what we mean by a "community."

Biologists define communities broadly to include all species, not just man. A natural community is an aggregation of a great many different kinds of organisms, all mutually interdependent. The basic conditions for the integration of a community are determined by physical characteristics of the environment such as climate and soil. Thus a sand dune supports one kind of community, a freshwater lake another, a high mountain still another. Within each type of environment there develops a complex of organisms that in the course of evolution becomes a balanced, self-sustaining biological system.

Such a system has a structure of interrelations that endows the entire community with a predictable developmental pattern, called "succession," that leads toward stability and enables the community to make the best use of its physical environment. This entails the development of cycles through which the community as a whole shares certain resources, such as mineral nutrients and energy. For example, there are a number of different inputs of nutrient elements into such a system. The principal input is from the decay of primary minerals in the soil. There are also certain losses, mainly through the leaching of substances into the underlying water table. Ecologists view the cycles in the system as mechanisms that have evolved to conserve the elements essential for the survival of the organisms making up the community.

One of the most important of these cycles is the movement of nutrients and energy from one organism to another along the pathways that are sometimes called food chains. Such chains start with plants, which use the sun's energy to synthesize organic matter; animals eat the plants; other animals eat these herbivores, and carnivores in turn may constitute additional levels feeding on the herbivores and on one another. If the lower orders in the chain are to survive and endure, there must be a feedback of nutrients. This is provided by decay organisms (mainly microorganisms) that break down organic debris

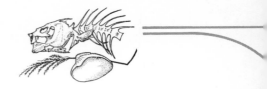

ORGANIC DEBRIS
MARSH **13 POUNDS PER ACRE**
BOTTOM **.3 POUND PER ACRE**

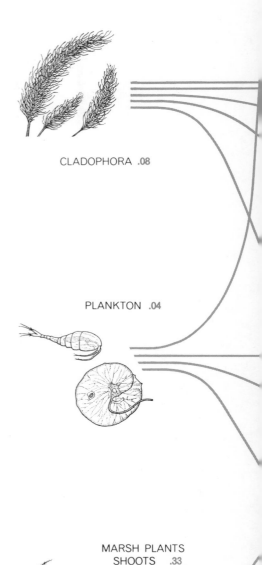

CLADOPHORA .08

PLANKTON .04

MARSH PLANTS
SHOOTS   .33
ROOTS   2.80

FOOD WEB is a complex network through which energy passes from plants to herbivores and on to carnivores within a biologi-

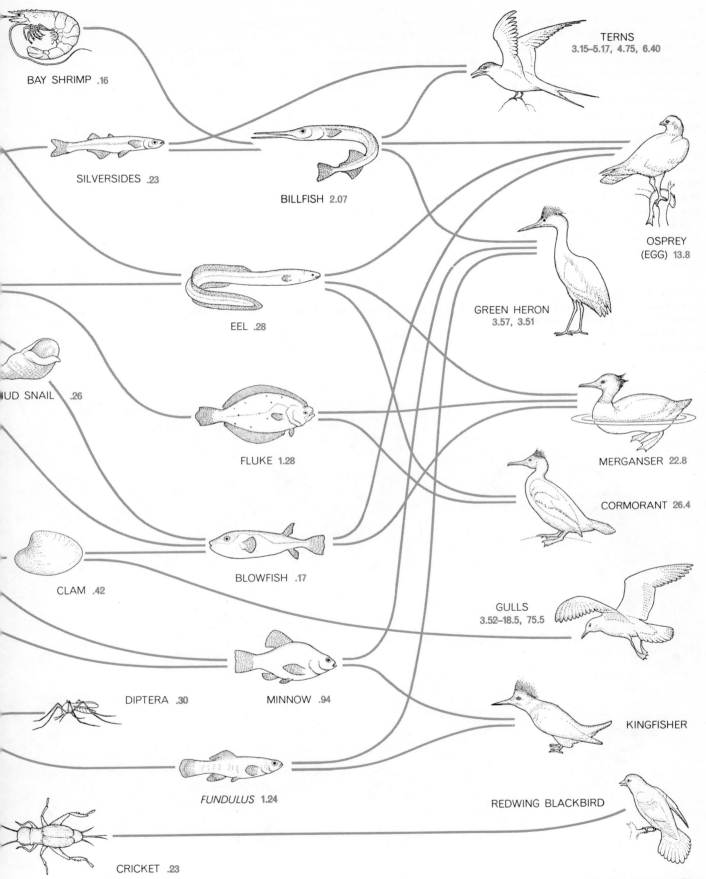

BAY SHRIMP .16

TERNS
3.15–5.17, 4.75, 6.40

SILVERSIDES .23

BILLFISH 2.07

OSPREY
(EGG) 13.8

EEL .28

GREEN HERON
3.57, 3.51

UD SNAIL .26

FLUKE 1.28

MERGANSER 22.8

CORMORANT 26.4

CLAM .42

BLOWFISH .17

GULLS
3.52–18.5, 75.5

DIPTERA .30

MINNOW .94

KINGFISHER

FUNDULUS 1.24

REDWING BLACKBIRD

CRICKET .23

cal community. This web showing some of the plants and animals in a Long Island estuary and along the nearby shore was developed by Dennis Puleston of the Brookhaven National Laboratory. Numbers indicate residues of DDT and its derivatives (in parts per million, wet weight, whole-body basis) found in the course of a study made by the author with Charles F. Wurster, Jr., and Peter A. Isaacson.

into the substances used by plants. It is also obvious that the community will not survive if essential links in the chain are eliminated; therefore the preying of one level on another must be limited.

Ecologists estimate that such a food chain allows the transmission of roughly 10 percent of the energy entering one level to the next level above it, that is, each level can pass on 10 percent of the energy it receives from below without suffering a loss of population that would imperil its survival. The simplest version of a system of this kind takes the form of a pyramid, each successively higher population receiving about a tenth of the energy received at the level below it.

Actually nature seldom builds communities with so simple a structure. Almost invariably the energy is not passed along in a neatly ordered chain but is spread about to a great variety of organisms through a sprawling, complex web of pathways [*see illustration on preceding two pages*]. The more mature the

community, the more diverse its makeup and the more complicated its web. In a natural ecosystem the network may consist of thousands of pathways.

This complexity is one of the principal factors we must consider in investigating how toxic substances may be distributed and concentrated in living communities. Other important basic factors lie in the nature of the metabolic process. For example, of the energy a population of organisms receives as food, usually less than 50 percent goes into the construction of new tissue, the rest being spent for respiration. This circumstance acts as a concentrating mechanism: a substance not involved in respiration and not excreted efficiently may be concentrated in the tissues twofold or more when passed from one population to another.

Let us consider three types of pathway for toxic substances that involve man as the ultimate consumer. The three examples, based on studies of ra-

dioactive substances, illustrate the complexity and variety of pollution problems.

The first and simplest case is that of strontium 90. Similar to calcium in chemical behavior, this element is concentrated in bone. It is a long-lived radioactive isotope and is a hazard because its energetic beta radiation can damage the mechanisms involved in the manufacture of blood cells in the bone marrow. In the long run the irradiation may produce certain types of cancer. The route of strontium 90 from air to man is rather direct: we ingest it in leafy vegetables, which absorbed it from the soil or received it as fallout from the air, or in milk and other dairy products from cows that have fed on contaminated vegetation. Fortunately strontium is not usually concentrated in man's food by an extensive food chain. Since it lodges chiefly in bone, it is not concentrated in passing from animal to animal in the same ways other radioactive substances may be (unless the predator eats bones!).

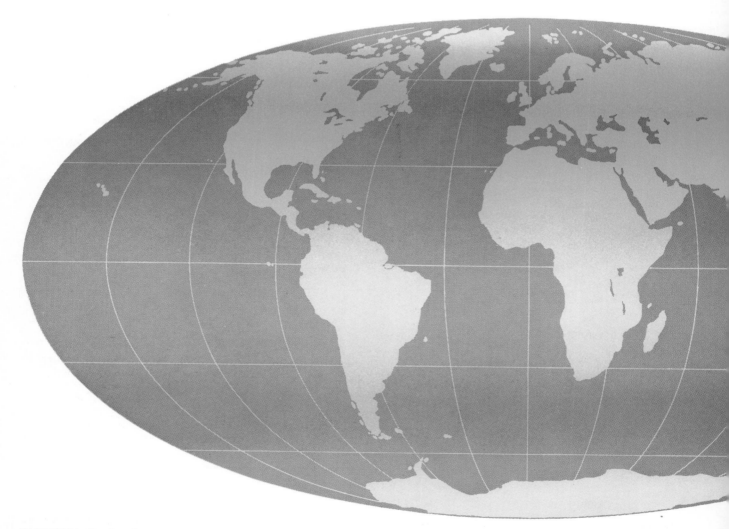

FALLOUT is distributed around the earth by meteorological processes. Deposits of strontium 90, for instance, are concentrated between 30 and 60 degrees north, as shown by depth of color on the map and by the curve (*right*). Points on the chart represent individual samples. The data are from a study made in 1963 and 1964 by Robert J. List and colleagues in several U.S. agencies. Such

Quite different is the case of the radioactive isotope cesium 137. This isotope, also a fission product, has a long-lived radioactivity (its half-life is about 30 years) and emits penetrating gamma rays. Because it behaves chemically like potassium, an essential constituent of all cells, it becomes widely distributed once it enters the body. Consequently it is passed along to meat-eating animals, and under certain circumstances it can accumulate in a chain of carnivores.

A study in Alaska by Wayne C. Hanson, H. E. Palmer and B. I. Griffin of the AEC's Pacific-Northwest Laboratory showed that the concentration factor for cesium 137 may be two or three for one step in a food chain. The first link of the chain in this case was lichens growing in the Alaskan forest and tundra. The lichens collected cesium 137 from fallout in rain. Certain caribou in Alaska live mainly on lichens during the winter, and caribou meat in turn is the principal diet of Eskimos in the same areas. The investigators found that caribou had accumulated about 15 micromicrocuries of cesium radioactivity per gram of tissue in their bodies. The Eskimos who fed on these caribou had a concentration twice as high (about 30 micromicrocuries per gram of tissue) after eating many pounds of caribou meat in the course of a season. Wolves and foxes that ate caribou sometimes contained three times the concentration in the flesh of the caribou. It is easy to see that in a longer chain, involving not just two animals but several, the concentration of a substance that was not excreted or metabolized could be increased to high levels.

A third case is that of iodine 131, another gamma ray emitter. Again the chain to man is short and simple: The contaminant (from fallout) comes to man mainly through cows' milk, and thus the chain involves only grass, cattle, milk and man. The danger of iodine 131 lies in the fact that iodine is concentrated in the thyroid gland. Although iodine 131 is short-lived (its half-life is only about eight days), its quick and localized concentration in the thyroid can cause damage. For instance, a research team from the Brookhaven National Laboratory headed by Robert Conard has discovered that children on Rongelap Atoll who were exposed to fallout from the 1954 bomb test later developed thyroid nodules.

The investigations of the iodine 131 hazard yielded two lessons that have an important bearing on the problem of pesticides and other toxic substances released in the environment. In the first place we have had a demonstration that the hazard of the toxic substance itself often tends to be underestimated. This was shown to be true of the exposure of the thyroid to radiation. Thyroid tumors were found in children who had been treated years before for enlarged thymus glands with doses of X rays that had been considered safe. As a result of this discovery and studies of the effects of iodine 131, the Federal Radiation Council in 1961 issued a new guide reducing the permissible limit of exposure to ionizing radiation to less than a tenth of what had previously been accepted. Not the least significant aspect of this lesson is the fact that the toxic effects of such a hazard may not appear until long after the exposure; on Rongelap Atoll 10 years passed before the thyroid abnormalities showed up in the children who had been exposed.

The second lesson is that, even when the pathways are well understood, it is almost impossible to predict just where toxic substances released into the environment will reach dangerous levels. Even in the case of the simple pathway followed by iodine 131 the eventual destination of the substance and its effects on people are complicated by a great many variables: the area of the cow's pasture (the smaller the area, the less fallout the cow will pick up); the amount and timing of rains on the pasture (which on the one hand may bring down fallout but on the other may wash it off the forage); the extent to which the cow is given stored, uncontaminated feed; the amount of iodine the cow secretes in its milk; the amount of milk in the diet of the individual consumer, and so on.

If it is difficult to estimate the nature and extent of the hazards from radioactive fallout, which have been investigated in great detail for more than a decade by an international research program, it must be said that we are in a poor position indeed to estimate the hazards from pesticides. So far the

LATITUDE

STRONTIUM 90 (MILLICURIES PER SQUARE MILE)

studies have not been made for pesticides but it appears that DDT may also be carried in air and deposited in precipitation.

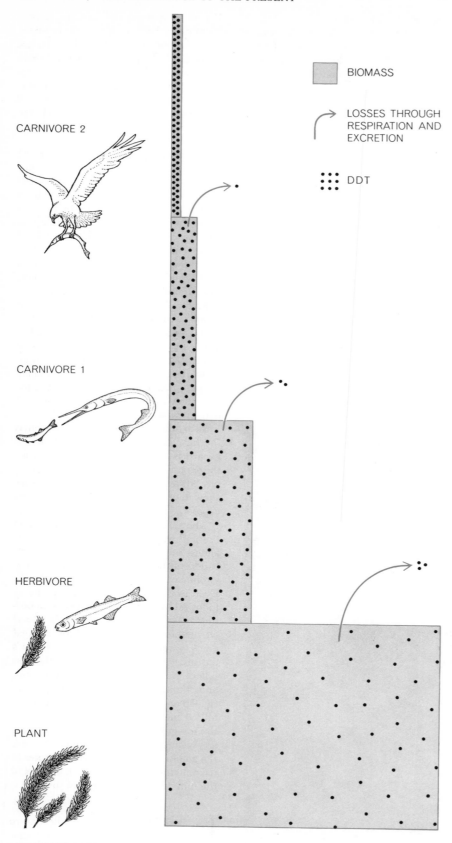

CARNIVORE 2

CARNIVORE 1

HERBIVORE

PLANT

BIOMASS

LOSSES THROUGH
RESPIRATION AND
EXCRETION

DDT

CONCENTRATION of DDT residues being passed along a simple food chain is indicated schematically in this diagram. As "biomass," or living material, is transferred from one link to another along such a chain, usually more than half of it is consumed in respiration or is excreted (*arrows*); the remainder forms new biomass. The losses of DDT residues along the chain, on the other hand, are small in proportion to the amount that is transferred from one link to the next. For this reason high concentrations occur in the carnivores.

amount of research effort given to the ecological effects of these poisons has been comparatively small, although it is increasing rapidly. Much has been learned, however, about the movement and distribution of pesticides in the environment, thanks in part to the clues supplied by the studies of radioactive fallout.

Our chief tool in the pesticide inquiry is DDT. There are many reasons for focusing on DDT: it is long-lasting, it is now comparatively easy to detect, it is by far the most widely used pesticide and it is toxic to a broad spectrum of animals, including man. Introduced only a quarter-century ago and spectacularly successful during World War II in controlling body lice and therefore typhus, DDT quickly became a universal weapon in agriculture and in public health campaigns against disease-carriers. Not surprisingly, by this time DDT has thoroughly permeated our environment. It is found in the air of cities, in wildlife all over North America and in remote corners of the earth, even in Adélie penguins and skua gulls (both carnivores) in the Antarctic. It is also found the world over in the fatty tissue of man. It is fair to say that there are probably few populations in the world that are not contaminated to some extent with DDT.

We now have a considerable amount of evidence that DDT is spread over the earth by wind and water in much the same patterns as radioactive fallout. This seems to be true in spite of the fact that DDT is not injected high into the atmosphere by an explosion. When DDT is sprayed in the air, some fraction of it is picked up by air currents as pollen is, circulated through the lower troposphere and deposited on the ground by rainfall. I found in tests in Maine and New Brunswick, where DDT has been sprayed from airplanes to control the spruce budworm in forests, that even in the open, away from trees, about 50 percent of the DDT does not fall to the ground. Instead it is probably dispersed as small crystals in the air. This is true even on days when the air is still and when the low-flying planes release the spray only 50 to 100 feet above treetop level. Other mechanisms besides air movement can carry DDT for great distances around the world. Migrating fish and birds can transport it thousands of miles. So also do oceanic currents. DDT has only a low solubility in water (the upper limit is about one part per billion), but as algae and other organisms in the water absorb the substance in fats, where it is highly soluble, they make room for more DDT to be dissolved into the water. Accordingly water that never contains more than a trace of DDT can continuously transfer it from deposits on the bottom to organisms.

DDT is an extremely stable compound that breaks down very slowly in the environment. Hence with repeated spraying the residues in the soil or water basins accumulate. Working with Frederic T. Martin of the University of Maine, I found that in a New Brunswick forest where spraying had been discontinued in 1958 the DDT content of the soil increased from half a pound per acre to 1.8 pounds per acre in the three years between 1958 and 1961. Apparently the DDT residues were carried to the ground very slowly on foliage and decayed very little. The conclusion is that DDT has a long half-life in the trees and soil of a forest, certainly in the range of tens of years.

LOCATION		ORGANISM	TISSUE	CONCENTRATION (PARTS PER MILLION)
U.S. (AVERAGE)		MAN	FAT	11
ALASKA (ESKIMO)				2.8
ENGLAND				2.2
WEST GERMANY				2.3
FRANCE				5.2
CANADA				5.3
HUNGARY				12.4
ISRAEL				19.2
INDIA				12.8-31.0
U.S.	CALIFORNIA	PLANKTON		5.3
	CALIFORNIA	BASS	EDIBLE FLESH	4-138
	CALIFORNIA	GREBES	VISCERAL FAT	UP TO 1,600
	MONTANA	ROBIN	WHOLE BODY	6.8-13.9
	WISCONSIN	CRUSTACEA		.41
	WISCONSIN	CHUB	WHOLE BODY	4.52
	WISCONSIN	GULL	BRAIN	20.8
	MISSOURI	BALD EAGLE	EGGS	1.1-5.6
	CONNECTICUT	OSPREY	EGGS	6.5
	FLORIDA	DOLPHIN	BLUBBER	ABOUT 220
CANADA		WOODCOCK	WHOLE BODY	1.7
ANTARCTICA		PENGUIN	FAT	.015-.18
ANTARCTICA		SEAL	FAT	.042-.12
SCOTLAND		EAGLE	EGGS	1.18
NEW ZEALAND		TROUT	WHOLE BODY	.6-.8

DDT RESIDUES, which include the derivatives DDD and DDE as well as DDT itself, have apparently entered most food webs. These data were selected from hundreds of reports that show DDT has a worldwide distribution, with the highest concentrations in carnivorous birds.

Doubtless there are many places in the world where reservoirs of DDT are accumulating. With my colleagues Charles F. Wurster, Jr., and Peter A. Isaacson of the State University of New York at Stony Brook, I recently sampled a marsh along the south shore of Long Island that had been sprayed with DDT for 20 years to control mosquitoes. We found that the DDT residues in the upper layer of mud in this marsh ranged up to 32 pounds per acre!

We learned further that plant and animal life in the area constituted a chain that concentrated the DDT in spectacular fashion. At the lowest level the plankton in the water contained .04 part per million of DDT; minnows contained one part per million, and a carnivorous scavenging bird (a ring-billed gull) contained about 75 parts per million in its tissues (on a whole-body, wet-weight basis). Some of the carnivorous animals in this community had concentrated DDT by a factor of more than 1,000 over the organisms at the base of the ladder.

A further tenfold increase in the concentrations along this food web would in all likelihood result in the death of many of the organisms in it. It would then be impossible to discover why they had disappeared. The damage from DDT concentration is particularly serious in the higher carnivores. The mere fact that conspicuous mortality is not observed is no assurance of safety. Comparatively low concentrations may inhibit reproduction and thus cause the species to fade away.

That DDT is a serious ecological hazard was recognized from the beginning of its use. In 1946 Clarence Cottam and Elmer Higgins of the U.S. Fish and Wildlife Service warned in the *Journal of Economic Entomology* that the pesticide was a potential menace to mammals, birds, fishes and other wildlife and that special care should be taken to avoid its application to streams, lakes and coastal bays because of the sensitivity of fishes and crabs. Because of the wide distribution of DDT the effects of the substance on a species of animal can be more damaging than hunting or the elimination of a habitat (through an operation such as dredging marshes). DDT affects the entire species rather than a single population and may well wipe out the species by eliminating reproduction.

Within the past five years, with the development of improved techniques for detecting the presence of pesticide residues in animals and the environment, ecologists have been able to measure the extent of the hazards presented by DDT and other persistent general poisons. The picture that is emerging is not a comforting one. Pesticide residues have now accumulated to levels that are catastrophic for certain animal populations, particularly carnivorous birds. Furthermore, it has been clear for many years that because of their shotgun effect these weapons not only attack the pests but also destroy predators and competitors that normally tend to limit proliferation of the pests. Under exposure to pesticides the pests tend to develop new strains that are resistant to the chemicals. The result is an escalating chemical warfare that is self-defeating and has secondary effects whose costs are only beginning to be measured. One of the costs is wildlife, notably carnivorous and scavenging birds such as hawks and eagles. There are others: destruction of food webs aggravates pollution problems, particularly in bodies of water that receive mineral nutrients in sewage or in water draining from heavily fertilized agricultural lands. The plant populations, no longer consumed by animals, fall to the bottom to decay anaerobically, producing hydrogen sulfide and other noxious gases, further degrading the environment.

The accumulation of persistent toxic substances in the ecological cycles of the earth is a problem to which mankind will have to pay increasing attention. It affects many elements of society, not only in the necessity for concern about the disposal of wastes but also in the need for a revolution in pest control. We must learn to use pesticides that have a short half-life in the environment—better yet, to use pest-control techniques that do not require applications of general poisons. What has been learned about the dangers in polluting ecological cycles is ample proof that there is no longer safety in the vastness of the earth.

Science and the Citizen
September 1970

The Side Effects of Man

Pollution, broadly defined as the unwanted side effects of human activity, is effecting global changes in the environment and causing a deterioration of the biosphere. The precise nature of these processes is obscure, however, and the amount of damage inflicted and the rate of increase in man's demands on the environment are still uncertain because of a lack of sufficient information. These are the overall conclusions of a group of scientists and other professional people who conducted a Study of Critical Environmental Problems during July. The study, sponsored by the Massachusetts Institute of Technology and directed by Carroll L. Wilson of M.I.T., was designed to focus attention on some of the issues that will be considered by the United Nations Conference on the Human Environment in 1972. It concentrated on broad problems of worldwide significance: on the indirect effects of pollution through changes in climate, ocean ecology and large terrestrial ecosystems rather than the direct local and regional effects of pollution. Its participants came from such disciplines as meteorology, atmospheric chemistry, oceanography, biology, ecology, geology, physics, engineering, economics, social sciences and the law. Their findings and recommendations were summarized in a preliminary report at the end of the study session and will be published later this year.

The major problems considered were the climatic effects of increasing loads of carbon dioxide and particles in the atmosphere (specifically emissions from supersonic aircraft) and the ecological effects of persistent pesticides, heavy metals, oil in the oceans and accumulations of nutrients in waterways. The group did not consider the management of radioactive wastes but called for an independent study of the subject.

A projected 18 percent increase by the year 2000 in atmospheric carbon dioxide from the burning of fossil fuels could raise the earth's average surface temperature half a degree Celsius, the study concluded; a doubling of the carbon dioxide might raise the temperature two degrees, leading to long-term warming of the planet. The direct climatic change in this century will probably be small, the group reported, but the long-term consequences may be profound. Careful estimates of fuel combustion, monitoring of atmospheric carbon dioxide and studies of its movement through the total biomass, the atmosphere and the oceans are required, and better computer models of worldwide atmospheric patterns should be developed. The level of fine particles in the atmosphere is increasing as man's activities release sulfates, nitrates and hydrocarbons, the group noted. The particles both reflect and absorb radiation, and not enough is known about their optical properties for one to say whether they tend to warm or cool the earth's surface. Again the group called for more research and monitoring.

Fine particles, carbon dioxide and water vapor will be introduced into the stratosphere by supersonic transports, according to the report. The carbon dioxide should not affect the climate, but a possible doubling of the fine-particle load and a 10 percent global stratospheric increase in water vapor could make a significant difference, raising the temperature of the stratosphere and increasing cloudiness. Expressing "genuine concern," the participants urged that "uncertainties about SST contamination and its effects be resolved before large-scale operation of SST's begins."

Pesticides have broad ecological effects, according to the report, because the reduction of one pest population may be accompanied by damage to a predator population that in turn allows the proliferation of new pests. Toxic, persistent pesticides such as DDT create special problems. The participants recommended "drastic reduction in the use of DDT as soon as possible." Taking account of the heavy dependence on DDT in many developing countries, they urged that subsidies be made available to enable such countries to switch to more expensive nonpersistent pesticides and biological controls. Like DDT, mercury and many other heavy metals are concentrated by marine and land organisms and are highly toxic. The use of mercury in pesticides should be drastically curtailed and industrial wastes should be better controlled.

A million and a half tons of oil are spread on the ocean every year and perhaps two or three times as much may be leaked away on land. The group recommended extensive research on the effects of oil in the ocean, restrictions on sources of oil spills and studies of the possibility of recycling oil used for lubrication.

Eutrophication of waters—enrichment through overfertilization with nitrogen and phosphorus—is having a broad ecological effect, the group found. The pollutants come largely from municipal wastes and from runoff from agricultural land. Detergents, which in the U.S. provide about 75 percent of the phosphorus in waste water, should be reformulated to eliminate the phosphorus, and nutrients should be reclaimed and recycled from sewage plants and feedlots.

Until recently, the report concluded, men have been absorbed with the "first-order effects of science and technology: the goods and services produced." The side effects were taken in stride. Now a shift in values is discernible: control of the side effects is getting a higher priority. Society will have to "make a more thorough and imaginative use of its resources of science and technology, its organizational skills and its financial resources" to achieve a balance between production and side effects. This will require new institutions for assessing the effects of new technologies and materials, monitoring the distribution of pollutants, identifying options and educating the public on those options.

Science and the Citizen
March 1969

Pollution by Fertilizer

Man's injection of excess nitrogen into the biosphere not only is seriously polluting rivers and lakes but also has greatly increased the frequency of a rare form of poisoning among both humans and domestic animals. Reporting at a symposium on pollution during the annual meeting of the American Association for the Advancement of Science, Barry Commoner of Washington University noted these results of the rise in nitrogen production in the U.S. during the past 25 years. Nitrogen from sewage, a reflection of the nation's population growth, has increased no more than 70 percent in that time, but the oxides of nitrogen produced by power plant fumes and automobile exhaust have increased by 300 percent and the use of nitrogen fertilizers by 1,400 percent. The last two processes add some 10 million tons of nitrogen compounds to the environment each year, more nitrogen than is cycled annually within the U.S. by all the processes of nature combined.

The excess quickly appears in the

form of nitrate in ground water, entering rivers and lakes to nourish algal "blooms" that reduce the oxygen content of the water to the point where processes of self-purification are halted. A measure of the quantities involved is provided in a recent Federal Water Pollution Commission study of Lake Erie, which estimates that municipal sewage annually contributes 90 million pounds of nitrogen and fertilizer runoff from surrounding farmlands 75 million pounds of nitrogen to the lake yearly.

Concentration of nitrate in ground water also affects wells and other potable water supplies. The maximum public health limit on nitrate concentration in drinking water is 10 parts per million. Already the water in a quarter of the shallow wells in Illinois exceeds this limit, as do many wells in southern California. Excess nitrate concentration in the water of one Minnesota town has forced complete replacement of the water system.

The danger to health from nitrate-polluted water arises not from the nitrate, which is relatively innocuous, but from the fact that certain intestinal bacteria convert nitrate (NO_3) into nitrite (NO_2). Nitrite combines with hemoglobin and destroys its oxygen-transporting properties. Commoner notes that polluted water is not the only source of danger. Poisoning from an overabundance of nitrate in foodstuffs has been reported in Europe; children under the age of three months are particularly vulnerable. One French pediatrician has set the maximum permissible concentration of nitrate in foodstuffs at 300 parts per million. A recent study of commercial baby foods, Commoner points out, found 444 parts of nitrate per million in wax beans, 977 in beets and 1,373 in spinach.

Noting that it is at least theoretically possible to halt nitrate pollution from municipal and industrial wastes, Commoner cites the painful dilemma presented by fertilizers: high agricultural yields and thus the whole of the farm economy depend on fertilizers, yet it is physically impossible to prevent the escape of nitrates from field to water table. To impose limitations on the use of fertilizers would be to reduce food supplies at a time of mounting worldwide needs, as well as to engender fierce opposition from farmers and the chemical industry. To fail to do so exposes the environment to steady degradation. "Science can reveal the depths of this crisis," Commoner concludes, "but only social action can resolve it."

Science and the Citizen
May 1969

Silent Epidemic

Although lead pigments were eliminated from interior paints in the U.S. some 20 years ago, multiple layers of lead-based paint still cover the walls and woodwork in many old houses and apartments. Therefore lead poisoning, once an occupational hazard for painters, is now primarily a disease of small children: toddlers between one and five who live in slum housing and nibble steadily at the paint that flakes off dilapidated walls and can be gnawed off peeling windowsills. At a conference at Rockefeller University in March participants estimated that lead poisoning in children is much more prevalent than is generally assumed, but they pointed out that the "silent epidemic" could be eliminated by aggressive medical, social and legal action.

The habit of eating nonfood substances (known as pica, from the Latin name for the magpie, a scavenger) is common in young children. A few small chips of old paint can contain more than 100 milligrams of lead, according to J. Julian Chisolm, Jr., of the Johns Hopkins University School of Medicine; the safe long-term daily intake of lead is less than half a milligram, and so a child who eats two or three paint chips a day for three months can accumulate a potentially lethal dose. Lead poisoning often goes unrecognized. The acute symptoms in small children are like those of many ailments: stomach ache, nausea, lassitude, anemia, convulsions. Often there are merely behavioral manifestations: fits that simulate epilepsy, hyperactive behavior or mental retardation. A urine test (for a metabolite that accumulates in the presence of lead poisoning) and a blood test are required to establish the diagnosis.

The mortality from the severe brain disease that can arise from lead poisoning used to be about 66 percent, Chisolm said. In the 1950's this was reduced to about 30 percent by the advent of chelating agents, drugs that combine strongly with the lead atom, removing it from the proteins to which it tends to bind (see "Chelation in Medicine," by Jack Schubert; SCIENTIFIC AMERICAN, May, 1966). Still, severe permanent brain damage occurs in more than a quarter of those who survive, and reex-posure to lead poisoning increases the incidence to almost 100 percent.

Mass screening for lead poisoning can be undertaken on the basis of the urine test, spectrophotometry of hair samples or blood tests. None of these measures is simple, however, and experts at the conference urged that preventive measures be instituted instead: the eradication of slum housing or at least the removal or covering of dangerous painted surfaces.

Science and the Citizen
June 1969

Legal Remedy

In the first action by a state to end the use of DDT, Michigan has moved to cancel permission for the sale of products containing the pesticide at the end of June. The State Agriculture Commission, which had stopped the sale of DDT for mosquito control a year ago, took the new action on the basis of a recommendation from the state university's agricultural experiment station. A major consideration was apparently concern for commercial and sport fishing in Lake Michigan, into which much of the surface water in the state eventually drains. High concentrations of DDT have been reported in the fat of whitefish, trout, perch and salmon.

DDT, like other chlorinated hydrocarbons, is a persistent chemical, not readily broken down. It accumulates in soil and water and is concentrated as it moves up the aquatic food chain from algae to increasingly large fishes and carnivorous birds (see "Toxic Substances and Ecological Cycles," by George M. Woodwell; SCIENTIFIC AMERICAN Offprint 1066]. Both its persistence and its lethal effect across a broad spectrum of animal life have spurred the development of newer pesticides that are more specific in their effect and less long-lasting, and now DDT is coming under increasing attack. In Sweden a two-year moratorium on the use of DDT and a ban on some other chlorinated hydrocarbons will go into effect in 1970. A trial one-year moratorium is in force in Arizona. The Wisconsin Department of Natural Resources has been holding intensive hearings on a citizens' petition to declare DDT a pollutant and end its use. Legislation to the same effect is

Science and the Citizen
September 1970

Mercury and Mud

Tiny amounts of mercury in the human body can produce kidney damage, muscular tremors, irritability and depression. Larger amounts can be fatal. Until recently, however, the managers of chemical companies and other industrial enterprises that were losing as much as 50 pounds of mercury a day from their plants had no major cause for concern. It was assumed that any of the heavy metal lost during manufacturing cycles would ultimately sink to the bottom of a stream or lake and would lie harmlessly and inertly in the mud. As any chemist knows, the safest place to keep mercury is under water, where it cannot evaporate into the air and enter the body.

In the past few months manufacturers and the public have learned once again that the web of nature is fine-spun and that distorting it can have unexpected effects. It appears that mercury and mercuric chloride escaping from factories producing chlorine, paper, mercury lamps, batteries, electrical appliances and other products do not lie inertly in the mud. The mercury has been entering the food chain. According to findings by Arne Jernelöv of the University of Stockholm and John M. Wood of the University of Illinois, anaerobic bacteria dwelling in mud take up the inorganic mercury and convert it into organic dimethyl mercury, which they release. Dimethyl mercury is volatile, that is, it diffuses from the mud into the water. Wood believes the anaerobes methylate mercury in order to avoid poisoning. "They clean their environment," he says, "at the expense of ours." Since dimethyl mercury passes easily through membranes, active fishes such as the pike pick up large amounts through their gills. Dimethyl mercury also rises through the food chain from microorganisms to smaller fishes to larger fishes. Once dimethyl mercury has been ingested by a fish, Wood believes, it is converted to monomethyl mercury, the form of organic mercury found when fish are examined for contamination.

As a result of this sequence of events, and perhaps others as well, lakes and streams have been widely polluted with mercury. Since the first reports of contamination in March, mercury has been detected in the waters of at least 17 states. A number of shipments of fish have been found to be contaminated with mercury, and their interstate transportation has been prohibited by the Food and Drug Administration. The Department of Justice has brought suit against several companies, and some concerns have already reduced the loss of mercury from their plants. No cases of mercury poisoning from polluted waters have yet been reported among human beings. The only victims so far, postmortem examinations have shown, have been fish-eating bald eagles.

Science and the Citizen
July 1970

The Ecology of War

War is always destructive of the environment, but in Vietnam war is being waged directly against it. The tactics of chemical defoliation and crop destruction are having a profound effect on the country's ecology, according to two biologists who visited Vietnam last year. In their report, published in *Science*, Gordon H. Orians of the University of Washington and E. W. Pfeiffer of the University of Montana urge the American Association for the Advancement of Science to help set up an international research program on the long-term effects of the military use of herbicides.

Orians and Pfeiffer interviewed military personnel, flew on spraying missions, surveyed defoliated areas from the air and by boat, talked with plantation owners, agricultural experts and scientists and studied records and photographs. The defoliation program, they write, was begun in 1962 and was stepped up sharply in 1966. Defoliation is now considered a potent weapon in guerrilla warfare, and "it is to be expected that in any future wars of this nature more extensive use will be made of it."

In forests, where most spraying operations are conducted in an effort to reduce concealment, a significant fraction of mature trees are killed by a single application; almost complete kills can be expected if spraying is repeated often. Orians and Pfeiffer estimate that from 20 to 25 percent of Vietnam's forests have been sprayed more than once. The mangrove forests characteristic of the river deltas southeast of Saigon are particularly susceptible to defoliation; one application kills most of the trees. Orians and Pfeiffer toured a large mangrove area and found it almost completely barren; the forest may never become completely reestablished, they report. As for upland forests, they cite earlier studies to the effect that two or three spray applications may kill about half of the commercially valuable timber. (The timber can be harvested, but then there is another complication: so much of it is studded with shrapnel that damage to saw blades has become a serious problem for lumber mills.)

Most of the spraying is directed against forest and brushland with two preparations called White and Orange, in which the active chemicals are 2,4-D and 2,4,5-T. Another agent, called Blue, in which the active chemical is cacodylic acid, an arsenic compound, is applied to cropland in mountainous parts of the country generally under the control of the National Liberation Front (Vietcong). U.S. officers consider this "resource denial" program successful because many captured soldiers from the sprayed areas are seriously undernourished. The authors remark that any such food shortage may well affect children, women and old people more than it does soldiers.

Military officials and some independent studies have suggested that herbicides do not often do damage beyond intended target areas. Orians and Pfeiffer disagree. In several instances they observed damage to fruit trees and other crops that could be traced to defoliation attacks or to the jettisoning of chemicals nearby. It was difficult to establish the extent of this damage, they observe, because claims for damages are discouraged by local officials. Orians and Pfeiffer did find that damage to rubber trees, one of South Vietnam's major resources, has been extensive. It has presumably all been accidental, caused by vaporized defoliant that is blown by the wind into plantations from nearby target areas, since permission to spray rubber plantations is said never to be granted. According to the Rubber Research Institute of Vietnam, repeated defoliation threatens the existence of rubber culture in the country.

As for the effect of herbicides on animal populations, the authors conclude that it may be primarily through the destruction of habitat, although there may also be direct toxic effects. In the defoliated mangrove areas, Orians and Pfeiffer found no local birds that live on insects or berries, and the number of fish-eating birds was smaller than expected. They cite a recent report on the production of birth defects by 2,4-D and 2,4,5-T, and they point out that U.S. manufacturers of these agents and the arsenic herbicide include warnings on their labels regarding possible toxic effects on humans and domestic animals.

Moving beyond defoliation, Orians and Pfeiffer mention other environmental effects: the pockmarking of Vietnam with bomb craters (2.6 million of them in 1968, they calculate), the upsetting of human ecology through destruction of villages and forced urbanization in Saigon, the sharp increase in air pollution and the promotion of forest fires. Not all animals have suffered from the war, however. Tigers seem to have benefited. "In the past 24 years they have learned to associate the sounds of gunfire with the presence of dead and wounded human beings in the vicinity. As a result, tigers rapidly move toward gunfire and apparently consume large numbers of battle casualties."

LETTERS TO THE EDITOR

June 1967

Sirs:

The article "Toxic Substances and Ecological Cycles" by George M. Woodwell in your March issue deals first with the distribution and lethal effects of radioactive fallout from the testing of hydrogen bombs. The author then states that "if it is difficult to estimate the nature and extent of the hazards from radioactive fallout ... we are in a poor position indeed to estimate the hazards from pesticides.... Our chief tool in the pesticide inquiry is DDT.... It is toxic to a broad spectrum of animals, including man." At this point the reader may well be prepared to equate DDT with strontium 90.

The toxicology of DDT and other pesticides is reviewed in a recent article (*Proceedings of the Royal Society*, Series B, Vol. 167, No. 101; February 21, 1967) by W. J. Hayes, who has studied the subject in depth for a number of years. He states that DDT has been consumed by human subjects at the rate of .5 milligram per kilogram of body weight per day for more than 600 days without any clinical effect. The largest nonfatal single dose was 285 milligrams per kilogram, part of which was vomited, and the median single dose with a clinical effect was 16 milligrams per kilogram. Of considerable interest is the observation that "workers who have been employed in the formulation of DDT since 1945 or even earlier...remain well while absorbing doses that for some are equivalent to 35 mg" per man per day. Hayes states that this is a dosage that is between 200 and 1,000 times as great as the exposure of people who eat "ordinary restaurant meals." Clearly the statement that DDT is toxic to man needs quantitative explanation.

What does the term "toxic to man" mean? Is it the effect of DDT on an isolated experimental subject or on human beings as a species? How does the term apply to human beings in India, where the use of DDT has been the principal factor in reducing the incidence of malaria from 100 million cases a year to less than 100,000 (P. C. C. Garnham, *loc. cit.* p. 134)? The main effect of pesticides is to increase the number of human beings; this increase exceeds all other factors in producing changes in ecology.

THOMAS H. JUKES

University of California
Berkeley, Calif.

Sirs:

As a manufacturer of DDT, I read George M. Woodwell's article "Toxic Substances and Ecological Cycles" with great interest and, I admit, some bias. While I have no quarrel with the mass of data he presents on the concentration of DDT in various organisms in the ecological cycle, I feel exception should be taken to his statement that DDT "is toxic to a broad spectrum of animals, including man." Indeed, his very next sentence, recalling DDT's "spectacularly successful [use] during World War II in controlling body lice and therefore typhus," offers evidence to the contrary, since hundreds of thousands of soldiers and civilians were dusted with large quantities of DDT without ill effect....

In view of the widespread public "belief" that DDT is toxic to humans, which Dr. Woodwell apparently shares, the paucity of supporting clinical evidence can only be considered surprising. During 1966 the Toxicology Laboratory of the Pesticides Program of the U.S. Public Health Service in Atlanta, Ga., undertook a clinical study of men with intensive occupational exposure to DDT. The group studied consisted of employees at the Torrance, Calif., plant of the Montrose Chemical Corporation of California. This plant has manufactured DDT continuously and exclusively since it was built in 1947, during which time it has produced almost 900 million pounds of DDT technical, as well as converting much of this to DDT dusts and liquid formulations.

From a group of more than 60 volunteers with over five years of heavy exposure to DDT, 35 were chosen who had been employed between 11 and 19 years and ranged in age from 30 to 63. In addition to analysis of their blood, urine and fatty tissue for pesticides (DDT, DDE, DDD, BHC and Heptachlor) they underwent complete physical examinations, routine clinical laboratory tests and chest X rays. High concentrations of isomers and metabolites of DDT were found in their fat (ranging from 30 to 647 parts per million) as well as in their urine and blood. Based on their storage of DDT in fat and excretion of DDA in urine, the average daily intake of DDT is estimated at 17 to 18 milligrams per man per day compared with an average of .04 milligram per man per day for the general population. In spite of these high levels of DDT, the overall clinical findings did not reveal any ill effects attributable to DDT and did "not differ significantly from those one might expect from a group of similar age and socioeconomic status with no occupational exposure to DDT."

During the 20 years our plant has operated we have not had a single case of occupational disease attributable to DDT, our employee turnover rate is well below that for the chemical industry in Southern California as a whole and our industrial accident rate is likewise below that for the State of California.

While no one would propose that DDT be sprayed indiscriminately or be prescribed as an elixir to assure a long healthy life, there is substantial clinical evidence that man can ingest considerable quantities over a long period of time without ill effects.

I have made no mention of the beneficial effects of DDT: lives saved, countless millions once debilitated by malaria enabled to perform useful work, forests preserved, crops protected, and so on. These facts are sometimes forgotten. True, the ecological process is changed, but change is part of life. The very fact that man's life-span has been extended by chlorination of his water supply, by vaccination and by chemicals such as DDT has resulted in a changed ecology. As Dr. Woodwell points out, we face a problem with many facets and all factors must be weighed before charting a course. It does not help to have scare words such as "toxic to man" thrown into the reasoning process.

Samuel Rotrosen

Montrose Chemical Corporation
    of California
Newark, N.J.

Sirs:

Messrs. Jukes and Rotrosen are correct in their contention that DDT's toxicity to man is low relative to other pesticides. It is, nonetheless, "toxic" not only to insects but, as I wrote, "to a broad spectrum of animals, including man." Its toxicology is far from simple and a discussion of it was beyond the scope of my article. DDT is a nerve toxin and clinical symptoms are correlated most closely with residues in the brain, not with those in fat. Residues may be stored in the fat of mammals for long periods and at comparatively high concentrations without obvious harm, as Mr. Rotrosen has indicated, but there is good reason to believe residues stored in fat are released when fat is mobilized during starvation or illness, increasing the danger of toxicity. DDT can be used safely in clothing against lice because in crystalline or powdered form it is not readily absorbed, either through the skin or the gut. Dissolved in oil, it is absorbed much more readily and the hazards of exposure are greater.

The point of the article, however, was not that current levels of DDT in human fat are toxic (there is reason for intensive interest in this, but no evidence that current levels are dangerous) but that the persistence of biologically active substances such as DDT that are distributed freely and in large quantities in the environment adds another important dimension to the hazards, including direct hazards both to man and to other organisms that are important to man. Messrs. Jukes and Rotrosen reflect what has become the classical approach to hazards from toxic substances, perpetuated by agencies treating public health, namely that the only important consideration is a direct, acute hazard to man. If man is protected, the rest of the environment will take care of itself. This attractively simple assumption breaks down when we find residues of substances such as DDT accumulating to levels that steadily degrade the environment. . . .

G. M. Woodwell

Brookhaven National Laboratory
Upton, N.Y.

The History of the Human Population

by Ansley J. Coale
September 1974

Until some 200 years ago the size of the human population remained fairly stable because high birth rates were balanced by high death rates. The great demographic transition came when death rates fell

In designating 1974 World Population Year the United Nations has given expression to worldwide interest in the rapid rate of population increase and to apprehension about the consequences of continued rapid growth. Much less attention is given to the growth of the population in the past, to the process by which a few thousand wanderers a million years ago became billions of residents of cities, towns and villages today. An understanding of this process is essential if one would evaluate the present circumstances and future prospects of the human population.

Any numerical description of the development of the human population cannot avoid conjecture, simply because there has never been a census of all the people in the world. Even today there are national populations that have not been enumerated, and where censuses have been taken they are not always reliable. Recent censuses of the U.S., for example, have undercounted the population by between 2 and 3 percent; some other censuses, such as the one taken in Nigeria in 1963, are evidently gross overcounts. Moreover, in many instances the extent of the error cannot be estimated with any precision.

If the size of the population today is imperfectly known, that of the past is even more uncertain. The first series of censuses taken at regular intervals of no more than 10 years was begun by Sweden in 1750; the U.S. has made decennial enumerations since 1790, as have France and England since 1800. The census became common in the more developed countries only in the 19th century, and it has spread slowly to other parts of the world. India's population has been enumerated at decennial intervals since 1871, and a number of Latin American populations have been counted, mostly at irregular intervals, since late in the 19th century. The first comprehensive census of Russia was conducted in 1897, and only four more have been made since then. The population of most of tropical Africa remained uncounted until after World War II. A conspicuous source of uncertainty in the population of the world today is the poorly known size of the population of China, where the most recent enumeration was made in 1953 and was of untested accuracy.

As one considers earlier periods the margin of error increases. The earliest date for which the global population can be calculated with an uncertainty of only, say, 20 percent is the middle of the 18th century. The next-earliest time for which useful data are available is the beginning of the Christian era, when Rome collected information bearing on the number of people in various parts of the empire. At about the same time imperial records provide some data on the population of China, and historians have made a tenuous estimate of the population of India in that period. By employing this information and by making a crude allowance for the number of people in other regions one can estimate the population of the world at the time of Augustus within a factor of two.

For still earlier periods the population must be estimated indirectly from calculations of the number of people who could subsist under the social and technological institutions presumed to prevail at the time. Anthropologists and historians have estimated, for example, that before the introduction of agriculture the world could have supported a hunting-and-gathering culture of between five and 10 million people.

From guesses such as these for the earlier periods and from somewhat more reliable data for more recent times a general outline of the growth of the human population can be constructed [*see illustrations on next page*]. Perhaps the most uncertain figure of all in these calculations is the size of the initial population, when man first appeared about a million years ago. As the human species gradually became distinct from its hominid predecessors there was presumably an original gene pool of some thousands or hundreds of thousands of individuals. The next date at which the population

RUBBING OF A GRAVESTONE records the death of a mother and her child in 18th-century Massachusetts. The inscription reads (with emended punctuation and orthography): "In Memory of Mrs. Naomi, Wife of Mr. Ritchard, Woolworth, who died August 22d, 1760, aged 39 Years; also Joseph, their Son, died the Same Day aged 6 days." It is probable that both mother and son died as a result of some crisis attendant on childbirth, in the case of the mother perhaps from puerperal fever. Such deaths were very common throughout most of man's history; the high death rate they contributed to demanded that the birth rate also be high merely to sustain the population. A decline in the death rate, which had an important effect on the survival of infants and children, began in most parts of Europe and America in the decades following the events recorded on this gravestone. The figures at the top of the stone are a scythe and an hourglass, traditional symbols of mortality; a crowing cock, which probably represents an admonition to vigilance, and an object whose identity is uncertain but that may be a candle with snuffer, another commonplace figure in the imagery of death. The stone is at Longmeadow, Mass., and has been attributed to Aaron Bliss. The rubbing is reproduced from *Early New England Gravestone Rubbings,* by Edmund Vincent Gillon, Jr., published by Dover Publications, Inc. Surveys of gravestones are among the methods by which demographers measure historical populations.

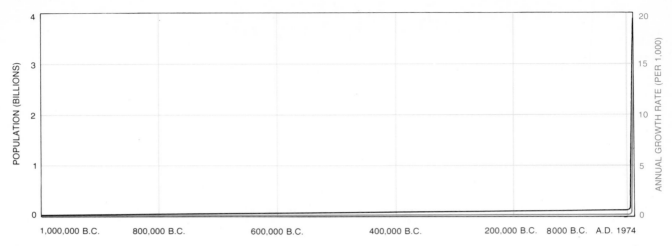

OVERVIEW OF THE HUMAN POPULATION, from the emergence of man about a million years ago to the present, emphasizes the dichotomous nature of man's history. At this level of detail the growth curve approximates one where the size of the population (*black*) and the annual rate of increase (*color*) are constant for almost the entire period, then rise vertically in the most recent years.

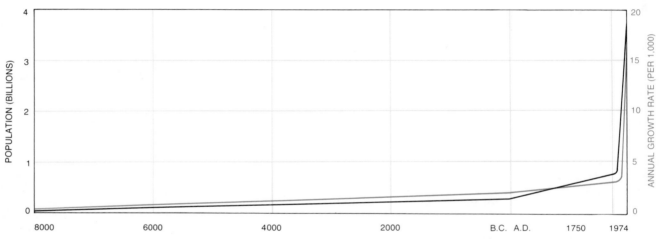

INTRODUCTION OF AGRICULTURE some 10,000 years ago marks the beginning of a period that represents about 1 percent of that considered in the illustration at the top of the page. Even in this much briefer time span, however, the rate of population increase was modest throughout most of the period, and the gain during the past few centuries again appears to be almost vertical.

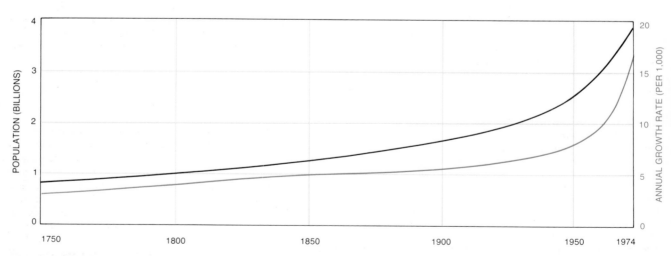

PERIOD SINCE 1750 is characterized by rapid and rapidly accelerating growth in the size of the world population. This period represents only about .02 percent of man's history, yet 80 percent of the increase in human numbers has occurred during it. Moreover, within this period the rate of increase has climbed most dramatically in very recent times: it has doubled in the past 25 years.

can be estimated is at the initiation of agriculture and the domestication of animals, which is generally believed to have begun about 8000 B.C. The median of several estimates of the ultimate size of the hunting-and-gathering cultures that preceded the introduction of agriculture is eight million. Thus whatever the size of the initial human population, the rate of growth during man's first 990,000 years (about 99 percent of his history) was exceedingly small. Even if one assumed that in the beginning the population was two—Adam and Eve—the annual rate of increase during this first long interval was only about 15 additional persons per million of population.

After the establishment of agriculture the growth of the population accelerated somewhat. The eight million of 8000 B.C. became by A.D. 1 about 300 million (the midpoint of a range of informed guesses of from 200 million to 400 million). This increase represents an annual growth rate of 360 per million, or, as it is usually expressed, .36 per 1,000.

From A.D. 1 to 1750 the population increased by about 500 million to some 800 million (the median of a range estimated by John D. Durand of the University of Pennsylvania). It was at this time that the extraordinary modern acceleration of population growth began. The average annual growth rate from A.D. 1 to 1750 was .56 per 1,000; from 1750 to 1800 it was 4.4 per 1,000, bringing the population at the end of this 50-year interval to about a billion. By 1850 there were 1.3 billion people in the world, and by 1900 there were 1.7 billion, yielding growth rates in the respective 50-year intervals of 5.2 and 5.4 per 1,000. (These totals too are based on estimates made by Durand.)

By 1950, according to the UN, the world population was 2.5 billion, indicating an annual growth rate during the first half of the 20th century of 7.9 per 1,000. From 1950 to 1974 the growth rate more than doubled, to 17.1 per 1,000, producing the present world population of 3.9 billion. The median value of several projections made by the UN in 1973 indicates that by 2000 the population will be 6.4 billion, an increase that implies an annual growth rate during the next 25 years of 19 per 1,000.

It is evident even from this brief description that the history of the population can be readily divided into two periods: a very long era of slow growth and a very brief period of rapid growth. An understanding of the development of the population during these two phases can be derived from a few simple mathematical relations involving the absolute size of the population, the growth rate and the factors that determine the growth rate.

Persistent growth at any proportionate rate produces ever increasing increments of growth, and the total, even at a relatively modest rate of increase, surpasses any designated finite limit in a surprisingly short time. An increasing population doubles in size during an interval equal to 693 divided by the annual rate of increase, expressed in additional persons per 1,000 population [see illustration on page 464]. Thus in the period from A.D. 1 to 1750, when the growth rate was .56 per 1,000, the population doubled about every 1,200 years; in the next few decades, when a growth rate of about 20 per 1,000 is anticipated, the population will double in 34.7 years.

The cumulative effect of a small number of doublings is a surprise to common sense. One well-known illustration of this phenomenon is the legend of the king who offered his daughter in marriage to anyone who could supply a grain of wheat for the first square of a chessboard, two grains for the second square and so on. To comply with this request for all 64 squares would require a mountain of grain many times larger than today's worldwide wheat production.

In accordance with the same law of geometric progression, the human population has reached its present size through comparatively few doublings. Even if we again assume that humanity began with a hypothetical Adam and Eve, the population has doubled only 31 times, or an average of about once every 30,000 years. This is another way of saying that the peopling of the world has been accomplished with a very low rate of increase, when that rate is averaged over the entire history of the species. The average annual rate is about .02 additional persons per 1,000. Even when only the more rapid growth of the past 2,000 years is considered, the average rate is modest. Since A.D. 1 the population has doubled no more than four times, or about once every 500 years, which implies an annual rate of 1.4 persons per 1,000.

In the context of these long-term averages the rate of growth today seems all the more extraordinary, yet the source of this exceptional proliferation is in the conventional mathematics of geometric series. The population of the world increases to the extent that births exceed deaths; the growth rate is the difference between the birth rate and the death rate. Another way of stating the relation is that the average rate of increase, over a long period, is dependent on the ratio of the sizes of successive generations. This ratio is approximately equal to the average number of daughters born to women who pass through the span of fertile years multiplied by the proportion of women surviving to the mean age of childbearing. This product specifies the average number of daughters born during the lifetime of a newborn female, after making allowance for those women whose biological fertility is abnormal and for those who die before reaching the age of childbearing. When the product is 1—signifying one daughter per woman, under the prevailing conditions of fertility and mortality—successive generations are the same average size. When the product is 2, the population doubles with each generation, or about every 28 years.

The fertility of a population can also be measured by the number of offspring, both sons and daughters, born per woman during a lifetime of childbearing; this number is called the total fertility rate. Mortality is summarized by the average age at death, or the average duration of life, which is expressed as the expectation of life at birth. In 1973 the total fertility rate of American women was 1.94; the expectation of life at birth was 75 years. Thus women experiencing 1973 birth rates at each age would bear an average of 1.94 children, and women experiencing 1973 death rates at each age would have an average duration of life of 75 years.

When the average life span is short, the proportion of women surviving to the mean age of reproduction is small. In fact, among populations for which there are adequate data there is a close relation between these two numbers, and we can with some confidence estimate the proportion of women surviving to become mothers from the average duration of life. Another predictable characteristic of the human population is the ratio of male births to female births; for any large sample it is always about 1.05 to 1.

Because of these constant relations in the population it is possible to calculate all the combinations of female life expectancy and total fertility that will yield any specified growth rate. Of particular interest are the conditions producing zero population growth, since during most of the past million years the population has approached zero growth [see illustration on page 463]. In a static population the average duration of life is the reciprocal of the birth rate. Expressed another way, in a population of constant size the birth rate is the number of births per person-year lived and the average duration of life is the number of person-years lived per birth.

There are many combinations of fertility and mortality that will just maintain a population at fixed size. Consider a static population in which the average duration of female life is 70 years. Given this mortality rate, the proportion of women surviving to the mean age of childbearing is 93.8 percent. Because the size of the population is to remain constant the average number of daughters born per woman must be 1/.938, or 1.066; since there are 1.05 male births for each female birth, the total fertility rate must be 2.05 × 1.066, or 2.19. The birth rate in such a population is 1/70, or 14.3 per 1,000 population.

If the average duration of female life is 20 years, as it probably was at times during the premodern period, then 31.6 percent of the women survive to the mean age of childbearing and those who live to the age of menopause have an average of 6.5 children; the birth rate under these circumstances is 50 per 1,000. (It should be pointed out that there is no inconsistency in the survival of many women to menopause in a population in which the average age at death is 20 years. When the death rate is high, the average age at death is not at all a typical age at death. When the life expectancy in a static population is 20 years, for example, about half the deaths occur before age five, about a fourth occur after age 50, and only about 6.5 percent occur in the 10-year span centered on the mean age at death.)

The importance of these relations is that they express the possible combinations of fertility and mortality that must have characterized the human population during each era of its history. If some other combination of fertility and mortality had been maintained for more than a few generations (as has happened during the past two centuries), the population would have expanded or contracted dramatically.

These combinations also determine the most extreme fertility and mortality rates possible in a static population. One limit is set by the minimum feasible mortality. When the average life expectancy is 75 years, 97.3 percent of all women survive to the mean age of reproduction, and it is necessary for them to have only 2.1 children to maintain the population; this represents a birth rate of 13.3 per 1,000. Any further reduction in mortality might raise the average duration of life to 80 years or more, but it would not significantly change the proportion of women surviving to childbearing age, nor would it much reduce the number of births per woman required to maintain the population. The other limit is imposed by fertility. When the life expectancy falls to 15 years, only 23.9 percent of all women live to have children, and those who do must have an average of 8.6 in order to prevent a decline in population. Although it is certainly biologically possible for a woman to bear more than eight or nine children, no sizable populations have been observed with

CENSUS TALLY SHEET from the first enumeration of the U.S. population was employed in one of the earliest attempts to keep a current and regularly revised account of the size and distribution of a national population. Sweden, in 1750, was the first nation to institute a periodic census; the U.S. followed in 1790, when this schedule for a New York City neighborhood was filled out. The columns record the number of free white males 16 years old and older, free white males under 16 years old, free white females, other free persons and slaves. In the bottom half of the column appears the name of Alexander Hamilton.

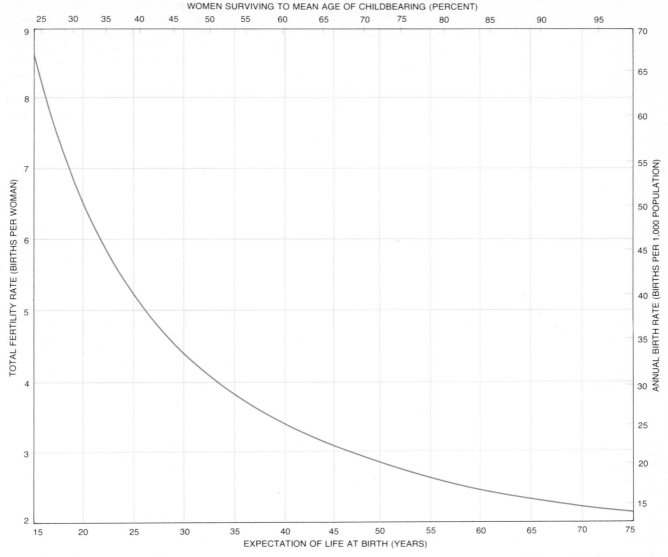

WOMEN SURVIVING TO MEAN AGE OF CHILDBEARING (PERCENT)

TOTAL FERTILITY RATE (BIRTHS PER WOMAN)

ANNUAL BIRTH RATE (BIRTHS PER 1,000 POPULATION)

EXPECTATION OF LIFE AT BIRTH (YEARS)

POPULATION IN EQUILIBRIUM can be maintained at constant size by many combinations of fertility and mortality. The total fertility rate is the number of children born per woman to a hypothetical group of women subject in each year of their lives to annual birth rates prevailing at a specified moment. Analogously, the expectation of life at birth is the average life span of a hypothetical group of people subject at each age to the death rates prevailing at a specified time. When the population is neither growing nor declining, two other demographic measures can be derived from these data: the birth rate and the proportion of women surviving to the mean age of childbearing. Some combination of these rates that approximates the conditions of zero growth must have prevailed during most of man's history. If the birth rate was 50 per 1,000, for example, then the average life span must have been 20 years, about a third of all women must have lived to childbearing age and those who survived must have had an average of 6.5 children.

total fertility much higher than eight births per woman.

Accurate records of human fertility and mortality are even more meager than records of numbers of people. Today fewer than half of the world population live in areas where vital statistics are reliably recorded; in most of Asia, almost all of Africa and much of Latin America, for example, the registration of births and deaths is inadequate. Precise information about fertility and mortality is therefore limited to the recent experience of the more developed countries, beginning in the 18th century in Scandinavia, the 19th century in most of the rest of Europe and the 20th century in Japan and the U.S. Much has been inferred about the present vital rates of underdeveloped countries from the age composition recorded in censuses, from the rate of population increase between censuses and from retrospective information collected in censuses and demographic surveys. For past populations, however, valid data on births and deaths are very rarely available, and they must therefore be derived by analyzing the forces that affect fertility and mortality.

Differences in fertility can be attributed to two factors: the differential exposure of women of childbearing age to the risk of childbirth through cohabitation with a sexual partner, and differences in the rate at which conceptions and live births occur among women who are cohabiting. In many populations the only socially sanctioned cohabitation is that between married couples, and thus the laws and customs governing the formation and dissolution of marriages influence fertility. A conspicuous example is the pattern of late marriage common until a generation ago in many Western European nations. For many years before World War II in Germany, Scandinavia, the Low Countries and Britain the average age of first marriage for women

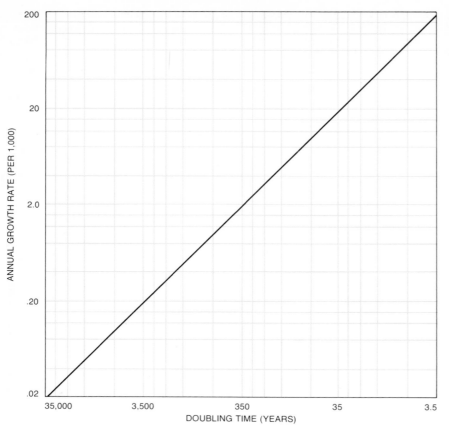

DOUBLING TIME for a population is calculated by dividing the annual growth rate, in additional persons per 1,000 population, into the number 693. Until about 10,000 years ago the growth rate was .02 or less, and at least 35,000 years were required for the population to double. The rate today approaches 20 per 1,000, and the population could double in the next 35 years. Sustained growth has extreme consequences: 10 doublings, which would require 350 years at the present rate, would produce a population of more than four trillion.

was between 24 and 28, and from 1 to 30 percent remained unmarried at age 50. As a result the proportion of women of reproductive age who by being married were exposed to the risk of childbearing was less than half, and in some cases, such as Ireland, was as low as a third.

A much different nuptial custom that may also reduce fertility is common in areas of Asia and North Africa. Women are married at age 17 or 18, but the average age of the married male population is often eight or nine years greater than that of the married women. The fertility of some of the women is probably reduced by marriage to much older men, often widowers. Marriages are made by arrangement with the bride's parents, in many cases requiring the payment of a bride price, and older men are more likely to have the property or the prestige needed to claim the more desirable young women. Still another social influence on fertility is found in India, where Hinduism forbids the remarriage of widows. Although the prohibition has not always been scrupulously observed, it has

doubtless reduced Indian fertility below what it might otherwise have been.

Among cohabiting couples fertility is obviously influenced by whether or not measures are employed to avoid having children. Louis Henry of the Institut National d'Études Démographiques has defined "natural fertility" as the fertility of couples who do not modify their behavior according to the number of children already born. Natural fertility thus defined is far from uniform: it is affected by custom, health and nutrition. Breast-feeding, for example, prolongs the period of postpartum amenorrhea and thereby postpones the resumption of ovulation following childbirth. In some populations low fertility can be attributed to pathological sterility associated with widespread gonorrheal infection. Finally, fertility may be influenced by diet, as has been suggested by the work of Rose E. Frisch and her colleagues at Harvard University. Age at menarche appears to be determined at least in part by the fat content of the body and is hence related to diet. Furthermore, among women past

the age of menarche a sufficient reduction in weight relative to height causes amenorrhea. In populations with meager diets fertility may therefore be depressed. Because of the severe caloric drain of pregnancy and breast-feeding, it is probable that nursing prolongs amenorrhea more effectively in populations where the average body fat is near the threshold needed for a regular reproductive cycle.

The most conspicuous source of differences in fertility among cohabiting couples today is the deliberate control of fertility by contraception and induced abortion. In some modern societies very low fertility rates have been obtained: the total fertility rate has fallen as low as 1.5 (in Czechoslovakia in 1930, in Austria in 1937 and in West Germany in 1973).

The prevalence of birth-control practices is known from the direct evidence of fertility surveys for only a few populations, and for those only during the past two or three decades. (The International Statistical Institute has begun a World Fertility Survey that should illuminate present practices but not those of the past.) Indications that fertility was deliberately controlled in past societies must be inferred from such clues as the cessation of childbearing earlier among women who married early than among those who married late. Evidence of this kind, together with the observation of a large reduction in the fertility of all married women, indicates that birth control was common in the 17th century among such groups as the bourgeoisie of Geneva and the peers of France. Norman Himes, in his *Medical History of Contraception*, has shown that prescriptions for the avoidance of birth, ranging from magical and wholly ineffective procedures to quite practical techniques, have been known in many societies at least since classical Greek times. A doctoral dissertation at Harvard University by Basim Musallam has demonstrated that *coitus interruptus*, a contraceptive method that compares in effectiveness with the condom and the diaphragm, was common enough in the medieval Islamic world to be the subject of explicit provisions in seven prominent schools of law. On the other hand, analysis of parish registers in western Europe from the 17th and 18th centuries and observations in less developed countries today suggest that effective birth-control practices are not common in most rural, premodern societies.

Large fluctuations in fertility, and in mortality as well, are not inconsistent with the long period of near-zero growth that characterizes most of the history of the population. Although the arithmetic of growth leaves no room for a rate of increase very different from zero in the long run, short-term variations were probably frequent and of considerable extent. In actuality the population that from our perspective appears to have been almost static for hundreds of thousands of years may well have experienced brief periods of rapid growth, during which it expanded severalfold, and then suffered catastrophic setbacks. The preagricultural population, for example, must have been vulnerable to changes in climate, such as periods of glaciation, and to the disappearance of species of prey. Once the cultivation of crops had become established the population could have been periodically decimated by epidemics and by the destruction of crops through drought, disease or insect infestation. Moreover, at all times the population has been subject to reduction by man's own violence through individual depredation and organized warfare.

Because earlier populations never expanded to fill the world with numbers comparable to the billions of the 20th century, we must conclude that sustained high fertility was always accompanied by high average mortality. Similarly, sustained low fertility must have been compensated for by low mortality; any societies that persisted in low fertility while mortality remained high must have vanished.

In the conventional outline of human prehistory it is assumed that at each earlier date the average duration of life was shorter, on the principle that early man faced greater hazards than his descendants. It is commonly supposed, for example, that hunters and gatherers had higher mortality than settled agriculturists. The greater population attained by the agriculturists is correctly attributed to an enhanced supply of food, but the appealing inference that reduced mortality was responsible for this acceleration of growth is not necessarily justified.

The advent of agriculture produced only a small increment in the growth rate; if this increment had been caused by a decline in mortality, the change in the average life expectancy would have been hardly noticeable. If in the hunting-and-gathering society the average number of births per woman was 6.5, for example, the average duration of life must have been 20 years. If the fertility of the early cultivators remained the same as that of their predecessors, then the in-

crease in the life span required to produce the observed acceleration of growth is merely .2 year. The increase in life expectancy, from 20 to 20.2 years, would not have been perceptible.

If one assumes that preagricultural man had substantially higher mortality than the early cultivators, it must also be assumed that the hunters and gatherers had much higher fertility. If the earlier culture had an average age at death of 15 instead of 20, for example, then its fertility must have been 8.6 births per woman rather than 6.5. Such a change is not inconceivable; the complete reorganization of life represented

by the adoption of agriculture could certainly be expected to influence both fertility and mortality. There is reason to suspect, however, that both vital rates increased rather than decreased [see illustration on next page].

Both disease and unpredictable famine might have increased the death rate of the first cultivators. Village life, by bringing comparatively large numbers into proximity, may have provided a basis for the transmission of pathogens and may have created reservoirs of endemic disease. Moreover, the greater density of agricultural populations may have led to greater contamination of food, soil and

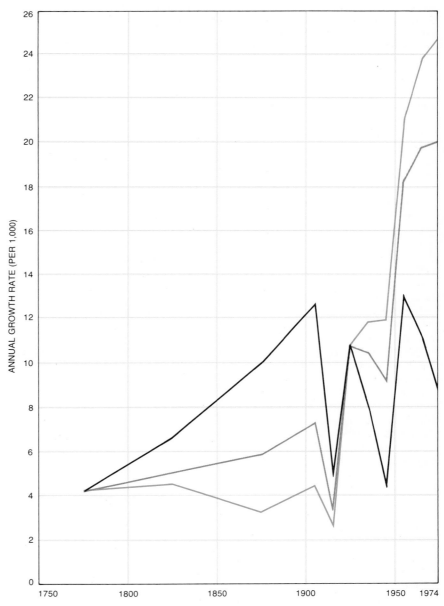

DEVELOPED AND UNDERDEVELOPED NATIONS have different population histories. From the 18th century until after World War I the growth rate in the developed countries (*black*) exceeded that in the underdeveloped ones (*color*). Since the 1920's growth in underdeveloped regions has predominated, and since 1950 the gap has become large. Future trends (*black and color*) will be determined largely by events in the underdeveloped nations.

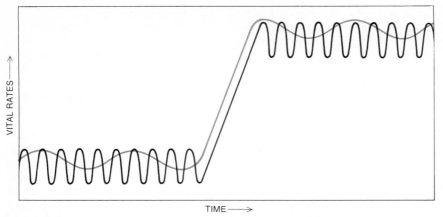

NEOLITHIC REVOLUTION had demographic consequences whose net effect was a slight increase in the rate of population growth. One reconstruction of these events suggests that the death rate (*black*) increased as a result of greater susceptibility to disease in village life, and perhaps also because agriculture is vulnerable to climatic crises. If the death rate did increase, then it is certain that the birth rate (*color*) also rose, and by a slightly greater margin. Both vital rates must have fluctuated from year to year, the death rate somewhat more than the birth rate. Even after the transition difference between the rates was small.

water. Greater density and the more or less total reliance on crops may also have made agriculturists extremely vulnerable to crop failure, whereas the hunting-and-gathering culture may have been more resistant to adversity.

If mortality did increase on the introduction of agriculture, then it is certain that fertility also rose, and by a slightly larger margin. The supposition that both vital rates did increase is supported by observations of the fertility rates of contemporary peoples who maintain themselves by hunting and gathering, such as the Kung tribe of the Kalahari Desert in southwestern Africa. Nancy Howell of the University of Toronto, analyzing observations made by her and by her colleague Richard Borshay Lee, has found that Kung women have long intervals between births and moderate overall fertility. A possible explanation, suggested by the work of Rose Frisch, is that the Kung diet yields a body composition low enough in fat to cause irregular ovulation. Interbirth intervals may be further prolonged by protracted breast-feeding combined with low body weight. If such conditions were common among preagricultural societies, the cultivation of crops could have increased fertility by increasing body weight and possibly by promoting the earlier weaning of infants so that mothers could work in the fields.

Unfortunately these speculations on the demographic events that may have accompanied the Neolithic revolution cannot be adequately tested by direct evidence. Until relatively recent times the only available indicators of mortality rates were tombstone inscriptions and the age-related characteristics of skeletons. Because the sample of deaths obtained in these ways may not be representative, it is not possible to reliably estimate for early periods such statistics as the average duration of life.

The accelerated growth in the world population that began in the 18th century is more readily understood if the areas classified by the UN as "more developed" and "less developed" are considered separately.

A general description, if not a full explanation, of the changing rates of increase in the more developed areas since the 18th century is provided by what demographers call the demographic transition. The changes in fertility and mortality that constitute the demographic transition are in general expected to accompany a nation's progression from a largely rural, agrarian and at least partly illiterate society to a primarily urban, industrial and literate one. Virtually all the populations classified by the UN as more developed have undergone demographic changes of this kind, although the timing and extent of the changes vary considerably.

The demographic experience common to all the more developed countries includes a major reduction in both fertility and mortality at some time during the past 200 years. In the 18th century the average duration of life was no more than 35 years, and in many of the nations that are now counted among the more developed it must have been much less. Today, almost without exception, the average life expectancy in these nations is 70 years or more. Two hundred years ago the number of births per woman ranged from more than 7.5 in some of the now more developed areas, such as the American colonies and probably Russia, to no more than 4.5 in Sweden and probably in England and Wales. In 1973 only Ireland among the more developed countries had a fertility rate that would produce more than three children per woman, and in most of the wealthier nations total fertility was below 2.5. Thus virtually all the more developed nations have, during the past two centuries, doubled the average life expectancy and halved the total fertility rate.

If the decline in fertility and mortality had been simultaneous, the growth in the population of the developed countries since 1750 might have been modest. Indeed, that was the experience of France, where the birth rate as well as the death rate began to decline before the end of the 18th century. As a consequence the increase in the French population was much less than that of most other European nations. The combined population of the developed countries experienced extraordinary growth after 1750, however, a growth that accelerated until early in the 20th century. The reason for the increase in numbers is that the decline in mortality has in almost all cases preceded the decline in fertility, often by many years [see illustration on opposite page].

The decline in fertility in the U.S., as in France, began early; it appears to have been under way by the beginning of the 19th century. Because of early marriage, however, fertility in the U.S. had been very high, so that the excess of births over deaths was still quite large. In most of the other more developed countries the birth rate did not begin to fall until late in the 19th century or early in the 20th.

Another universal feature of the transition is a change in the stability of the vital rates. In the premodern era the high birth rate was relatively constant, but the death rate fluctuated from year to year, reflecting the effects of epidemics and variations in the food supply. In those countries that have completed the demographic transition this pattern is reversed: the death rate remains constant but fertility varies considerably.

The causes of the event that began the demographic transition—the decline in mortality in the late 18th century—are a matter of controversy to social and medical historians. According to one school of thought, until the middle of the 19th century medical innovations in England could not account for the reduction of the English death rate; the principal factor proposed instead is an improvement in the average diet. Others argue that protection from smallpox through inoculation with cowpox serum, a procedure introduced late in the 18th century, was sufficient to markedly reduce the death rate. They propose that the further decline in mortality in the early 19th century may have been brought about by improvements in personal hygiene.

A third hypothesis is that before the 18th century fortuitous periods of low mortality were not exceptional, but that they were followed by periods of very severe mortality caused by major epidemics. According to this view, the late 18th century was a normal period of respite, and improved conditions early in the 19th century averted the next cycle of epidemics, which would other-

wise have produced a recurrence of high mortality rates.

Whatever the cause of the initial decline in the death rate, there is no doubt that subsequent improvements in sanitation, public health and medicine made possible further reductions during the 19th century; indeed, the process continues today. It is equally clear that the reduction in mortality was dependent on the increased availability of food and other material resources. This rise in living standards was in turn brought about by the extension of cultivation, particularly in the Western Hemisphere, by increased productivity in both agriculture and industry and by the development of efficient trade and transportation.

The decline in the birth rate that eventually followed the decline in the death rate in the more developed countries was, with the exception of late-19th-cen-

tury Ireland, almost entirely a decline in the fertility of married couples and can be attributed directly to the practice of contraception and abortion. The reduction in fertility was not a result of the invention of new contraceptive techniques, however. Among selected Americans married before 1910, English couples interviewed in the 1930's and couples surveyed in France and several eastern European nations after World War II, the principal method of birth control was *coitus interruptus*, a technique that had always been available. The birth rate declined because the perceived benefits and liabilities of having more children had changed, and perhaps also because the couples' view of the propriety of preventing births had been modified.

Reduced fertility can be considered one of the consequences of the charac-

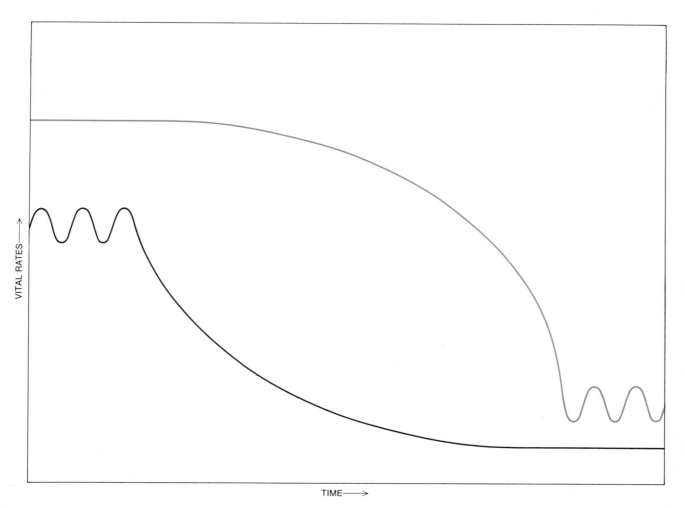

THE DEMOGRAPHIC TRANSITION, represented schematically here, is the central event in the recent history of the human population. It begins with a decline in the death rate (*black*), precipitated by advances in medicine (particularly in public health), nutrition or both. Some years later the birth rate (*color*) also declines, primarily because of changes in the perceived value of having children. Before the transition the birth rate is constant but the death rate varies; afterward the death rate is constant but the birth

rate fluctuates. The demographic transition usually accompanies the modernization of nations; it began in Europe and the U.S. late in the 18th century and early in the 19th, but in the underdeveloped nations it began only much later, often in the 20th century. In the developed countries the transition is now substantially complete, but in much of the rest of the world only mortality has been reduced; the fertility rate remains high. In the interim between the drop in mortality and fertility population has increased rapidly.

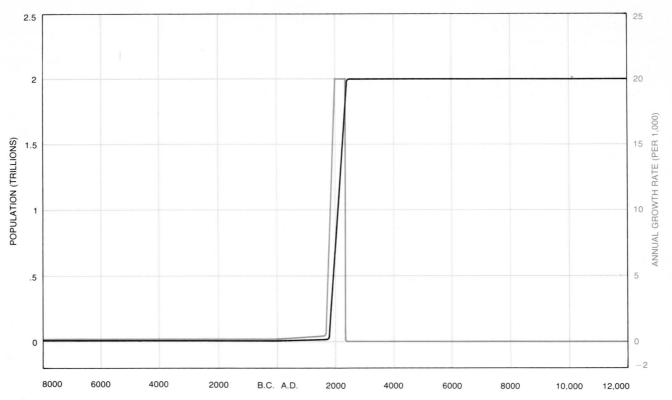

RETURN TO NEAR-ZERO GROWTH does not necessarily imply a low future population. If the rate of increase (*color*) were to remain at its present level until the year 2300, then immediately drop to zero, the average growth rate over the next 10,000 years would be as low as it has been during the past 10,000. Population, however (*black*), would reach two trillion, 500 times the present one.

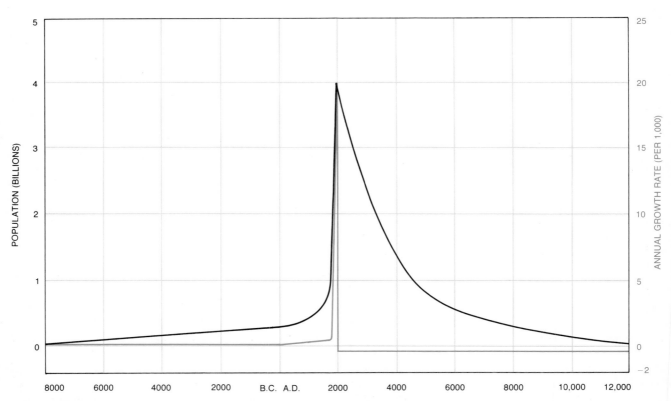

IMMEDIATE REDUCTION of the growth rate to —.2 would result in a slow decline, eventually returning the world population to its level of 10,000 years ago: about eight million, or 1/500th of the present population. Under these circumstances too the rate of change in the size of the population during the next 10,000 years would differ from zero no more than it did during the past 10,000.

teristics by which the more developed countries are defined. In an urban, industrial society the family is no longer the main locus of economic activity, nor are children the expected means of support in old age. In an agrarian, preindustrial society, on the other hand, the family is a basic economic unit and sons are a form of social security. Moreover, in the less developed countries the costs of raising and educating a child are minimal; indeed, a child may contribute to the welfare of the family from an early age. In the industrial society child labor is prohibited, education is compulsory and it often extends through adolescence. These conditions conspire to discourage couples in the more developed countries from having large families, whereas in long-established agrarian societies social norms supporting childbearing tend to be perpetuated.

In the less developed countries the estimated rate of population growth was virtually zero until about 200 years ago, when a moderate rate of increase, about four per 1,000, was apparently induced by a reduction in mortality [see illustration on page 465]. The cause of this reduced death rate is uncertain. Durand has suggested that the interchange of staple foods between regions that had previously been isolated might have contributed to population growth in Asia and in Europe as well. In particular the introduction of the potato into Europe and of maize and the sweet potato into China have been cited as possible contributing factors.

Since the aggregate population of the less developed countries includes many large areas that have not been reliably enumerated, a description of the historical course of population growth in these countries is subject to much uncertainty. A slight reduction in the average rate of increase in the latter half of the 19th century, for example, can be attributed entirely to an estimated zero rate of growth in China, and that estimate is based on uncertain data. There is no doubt, however, that in the poorer nations rapid growth began in the 1920's, 1930's and 1940's, and that since World War II the population increase has accelerated dramatically.

The enormous recent growth of the populations of the less developed nations can be interpreted in terms of the demographic transition, but some parts of the process have been more rapid and more extreme than they were in the industrial nations; moreover, the transition is not yet complete, and its future course cannot be predicted. Mortality has dropped precipitously, but fertility has so far remained unchanged or declined only moderately. In the combined populations of the less developed countries the number of births per woman is about 5.5, and the average duration of life is more than 50 years, yielding an annual growth rate of about 25 per 1,000. Since World War II mortality in the less developed countries has fallen much more quickly than it did in 19th-century Europe, largely because modern technology, and particularly medical technology, can be imported more rapidly today than it could be discovered and developed 100 years ago. Insecticides, antibiotics and public health measures that were unknown during the European demographic transition are now commonplace in the less developed countries.

According to estimates prepared by the UN, the average duration of life in the less developed areas has risen from 32 to 50 years during the past three decades, an increase of 56 percent. During the same period the birth rate is estimated to have declined by no more than 7 to 8 percent. The actual fall in fertility is in fact even less, by about 4 percent, since demographic changes have reduced the proportion of women in the childbearing years. (Although the fertility of the less developed countries as a group remains very high, there are some countries where the birth rate has fallen significantly—by from 25 to 50 percent— and very rapidly. They include Hong Kong, Singapore, Taiwan, South Korea, West Malaysia, Barbados, Chile, Cuba, Jamaica, Trinidad and Tobago, Puerto Rico and Mauritius. According to reports from travelers, there has also been a decline in fertility in China, particularly in the cities.)

The present rapid growth in the world population is a result of a high rate of increase in the less developed areas and a moderate rate in the rest of the world. According to projections prepared by the UN, more than 90 percent of the increase in population to be anticipated by 2000 will be contributed by the less developed nations, even though a large reduction in fertility in these countries is expected in the next 25 years. The future course of the world's population depends largely on demographic trends in these countries.

The events of the demographic transition provide no sure way of calculating when or how quickly fertility will decline in the less developed nations. The experience of the industrial world is not a satisfactory basis for prediction. The history of the Western population during the past 200 years suggests that vital rates normally fall as a concomitant of modernization, but it provides no checklist of advances in literacy, mortality reduction and urbanization that would enable one to estimate when fertility will fall. In the more developed world there are instances of large reductions in fertility in populations that were still rural, mostly illiterate and still subject to moderately high mortality, as in the Garonne valley in southwestern France before 1850. In other instances fertility did not decline until after education was almost universal, the population was mostly urban and agriculture had become the occupation of a small minority, as in England and Wales.

The present rate of world population increase—20 per 1,000—is almost certainly without precedent, and it is hundreds of times greater than the rate that has been the norm for most of man's history. Without doubt this period of growth will be a transitory episode in the history of the population. If the present rate were to be maintained, the population would double approximately every 35 years, it would be multiplied by 1,000 every 350 years and by a million every 700 years. The consequences of sustained growth at this pace are clearly impossible: in less than 700 years there would be one person for every square foot on the surface of the earth; in less than 1,200 years the human population would outweigh the earth; in less than 6,000 years the mass of humanity would form a sphere expanding at the speed of light. Considering more realistic limits for the future, if the present population is not multiplied by a factor greater than 500 and thus does not exceed two trillion, and if it does not fall below the estimated population of preagricultural society, then the rate of increase or decrease during the next 10,000 years must fall as close to zero as it was during the past 10,000 years [see illustrations on opposite page].

Arithmetic makes a return to a growth rate near zero inevitable before many generations have passed. What is uncertain is not that the future rate of growth will be about zero but how large the future population will be and what combination of fertility and mortality will sustain it. The possibilities range from more than eight children per woman and a life that lasts an average of 15 years, to slightly more than two children per woman and a life span that surpasses 75 years.

EPILOGUE

When we compare the length of just one individual's life with the life span of our genus and species, we can quickly grasp the immensity of the human evolutionary time dimension. Yet it has only been over the relatively short period of the last hundred years we have moved from a biblical time frame to another with the development of evolutionary theory and the scientific study of human paleontology. Over the last thirty years the human population has nearly doubled to levels of density and size that must have been inconceivable even during Darwin's lifetime. At one end of the spectrum of our knowledge and adaptation, we have been able to design a space ship that can put humans on the moon and at another end we are almost ready to program changes in the DNA of our genomes. These and the many other remarkable developments in our knowledge about ourselves and our environment might be comforting—even inspiring—if we were not also faced with the specters of starvation, disease, and the threat of massive nuclear warfare.

How we adapt to these imminent problems and maintain our humanity in the process is one of the greatest challenges of this century, and probably of the next as well. It is increasingly clear that we need new kinds of holistic and integrative perspectives of man to help us avoid some of the harsh and possibly catastrophic outcomes of our population growth, impact on the world's ecological resources, and capacity for nuclear agression. Our future course may still be within the realm of our decision-making capacities. If time and chance are with us, we can move to understand ourselves not just within an objective scientific framework but within a subjective humanistic framework as well. We must meld our scientific and humanistic traditions together in a highly effective manner in order to adapt to the world we have evolved. Just as it is impossible to turn biological evolution backward, it is difficult to do so with social developments. We are too dependent on science and technology to throw them out and return to some primitive state; instead, we need to know how to make more intelligent use of them. We need a science and a technology that are first and foremost human.

We can start by recognizing the "pseudo," or "pop," science that permeates too much of our thinking and creates vague and invalid generalizations. We must recognize that reductionistic methodology when applied to humanity may result in too great an objectification and dehumanization of our complexity. We should begin to place as much emphasis on the development of a *synthetic method* as we have upon the experimental and reductionistic* methodology.

Once a synthetic method has been developed, we must use it to integrate and synthesize our knowledge of the neurological and bioevolutionary sciences of man with the social and psychological sciences. With this new kind of unity we might well develop a whole new kind of insight into human nature. It is my hope that, by describing the issues and the current state of the bioanthropological sciences, this book will have supplied some of the knowledge and theory necessary for the emerging science of man to deal effectively and humanely with the vital issues of today and tomorrow.

---

*By this I mean we should stop hoping to find answers purely by isolating and reducing the scope of the problem as much of modern science advocates. Rather we need to expend more of our efforts on effectively synthesizing what we know.

SUGGESTED READINGS

Acsádi, Gy. and J. Nemeskéri. 1970. *History of Human Life Span and Mortality.* Budapest: Akadémiai Kiadó.

Alland, A. 1971. *Human Diversity.* New York: Columbia Univ. Press.

Alland, A. 1972. *The Human Imperative.* New York: Columbia Univ. Press.

Allison, A. C. 1956. Sickle cells and evolution. *Scientific American,* Aug., 87.

Alpers, M. and D. C. Gajdusek. 1965. Changing patterns of kuru. *Amer. J. Trop. Med. Hyg.* 14:852–76.

Altmann, S. A., ed. 1967. *Social Communication among Primates.* Chicago: Univ. of Chicago Press.

Angel, J. L. 1972. Ecology and population in the Eastern Mediterranean. *World Archaeol.* 4(1):88–105.

Bajema, C. J. 1971. *Natural Selection in Human Populations.* New York: John Wiley.

Baker, P. 1969. Human adaptation to high altitude. *Science* 163:1149–56.

Baker, P. T. and J. S. Weiner, eds. 1966. *The Biology of Human Adaptability.* Oxford: Oxford Univ. Press.

Bassett, C. A. L. 1965. Electrical effects in bone. *Scientific American,* Oct., 18.

Benzer, S. 1973. Genetic dissection of behavior. *Scientific American,* Dec., 24.

Binford, S. R. and L. R. Binford. 1969. Stone tools and human behavior. *Scientific American,* April, 71.

Birdsell, J. B. 1972. *Human Evolution: An Introduction to the New Physical Anthropology.* Chicago: Rand McNally.

Bishop, W. W. and J. A. Miller, eds. 1972. *Calibration of Hominoid Evolution.* Edinburgh: Scottish Academic Press.

A Reader in Human Biology. Boston: Allyn and Bacon.

Blumberg, B. S. 1970. Australia antigen and hepatitis. *Amer. J. Phys. Anthropol.* 32(2):305–8.

Bowlby, J. 1969. *Attachment and Loss,* Vol. 1. New York: Basic Books.

Boyd, W. C. 1950. *Genetics and the Races of Man.* Boston: Little, Brown.

Boyle, M. and H. V. Vallois. 1957. *Fossil Men.* New York: Dryden Press.

Brace, C. L. 1967. *The Stages of Human Evolution.* Englewood Cliffs, N.J.: Prentice-Hall.

Brace, C. L. and M. F. Ashley Montagu. 1965. *Man's Evolution: An Introduction to Physical Anthropology.* New York: Macmillan.

Brace, C. L., H. Nelson, and N. Korn. 1971. *Atlas of Fossil Man.* New York: Holt, Rinehart and Winston.

Brachet, J. 1961. The living cell. *Scientific American,* Sept., 50.

Brothwell, D. R. 1971. Paleodemography. In *Biological Aspects of Demography,* Vol. 10 of Symp. S.S.H.B., ed. W. Brass, pp. 111–30.

Brothwell, D. R. 1972. Paleodemography of earlier British populations. *World Archaeol.* 4(1):75–87.

Brothwell, D. R. 1973. *Digging Up Bones.* London: British Museum (Natural History).

Buettner-Janusch, J. 1966. *Origins of man.* New York: John Wiley.

Burnet, F. M. 1962. *Natural History of Infectious Disease.* 3rd ed. Cambridge: Cambridge Univ. Press.

Campbell, B. G. 1965. The nomenclature of the Hominidae. *Occasional Papers* 22. Royal Anthropological Institute of Great Britain and Ireland.

Campbell, B. G. 1966. *Human Evolution: An Introduction to Man's Adaptations.* Chicago: Aldine-Atherton.

Cavalli-Sforza, L. L. and W. Bodmer. 1971. *The Genetics of Human Populations.* San Francisco: W. H. Freeman and Company.

Chance, N. A. 1966. *The Eskimo of North Alaska.* New York: Holt, Rinehart & Winston.

Chapple, E. D. 1970. *Culture and Biological Man: Explorations in Behavioral Anthropology.* New York: Holt, Rinehart and Winston.

Chomsky, N. 1965. *Aspects of the Theory of Syntax.* Cambridge: MIT Press.

Chomsky, N. 1968. *Language and the Mind.* New York: Harcourt Brace Jovanovich.

Chomsky, N. 1971. *Chomsky: Selected Readings,* ed. J. P. B. Allen and P. Van Buren. London: Oxford Univ. Press.

Clegg, J. 1968. *The Study of Man.* New York: American Elsevier.

Cohen, Y. A. 1974b. *Man in Adaptation: The Cultural Present.* Chicago: Aldine-Atherton.

Cohen, Y. A. 1971. *Man in Adaptation: The Institutional Framework.* Chicago: Aldine-Atherton.

Cohen, Y. A. 1974a. *Man in Adaptation: The Biosocial Background.* 2nd ed. Chicago: Aldine-Atherton.

Colbert, E. H. 1961. *Evolution of the Vertebrates.* New York: Science Editions.

Comas, J. 1960. *Manual of Physical Anthropology.* Springfield, Ill.: Charles C. Thomas.

Coon, C. S. 1962. *The Origin of Races.* New York: Alfred A. Knopf.

Coon, C. S. 1965. *The Living Races of Man.* New York: Alfred A. Knopf.

Crick, F. H. C. 1962. The genetic code. *Scientific American,* Oct., 66.

Crow, J. F. 1959. Ionizing radiation and evolution. *Scientific American,* Sept., 138.

Crow, J. F. 1962. Mechanisms and trends in human evolution. In *Evolution and Man's Progress,* ed. H. Hoagland and R. Burhoe, pp. 6–21. New York: Columbia Univ. Press.

Darlington, C. D. 1969. *The Evolution of Man and Society.* New York: Simon and Schuster.

Darwin, C. 1859. *Origin of Species.* London: John Murray.

Darwin, C. 1871. *The Descent of Man.* London: John Murray.

Day, M. 1965. *Guide to Fossil Man.* New York: World Publishing.

Day, M. H., and B. A. Wood. 1968. Functional affinities of the Olduvai hominid 8 talus. *Man* 3:440–455.

DeVore, I., ed. 1965. *Primate Behavior: Field Studies of Monkeys and Apes.* New York: Holt, Rinehart and Winston.

Dobzhansky, T. 1950. The genetic basis of evolution. *Scientific American,* Jan., 32.

Dobzhansky, T. 1962. *Mankind Evolving.* New Haven: Yale Univ. Press.

Dobzhansky, T. 1971. *Genetics of the Evolutionary Process.* New York: Columbia Univ. Press.

Dolhinow, P. and V. Sarich, eds. 1971. *Background to Man: Readings in Physical Anthropology.* New York: Little, Brown.

Dubos, R. 1965. *Man Adapting.* New Haven: Yale Univ. Press.

Eckhardt, R. B. 1972. Population genetics and human origins. *Scientific American,* Jan., 72.

Edey, M. A. and the Editors of Time-Life Books, eds. 1972. *The Missing Link.* New York: Time-Life Books.

Edwards, R. G. 1966. Mammalian eggs in the laboratory. *Scientific American,* Aug., 72.

Eimerl, S., I. DeVore, and the Editors of Time-Life Books. 1965. *The Primates.* Life Nature Library. New York: Time-Life Books.

Eiseley, L. C. 1956. Charles Darwin. *Scientific American,* Feb., 62.

Eiseley, L. C. 1959a. Charles Lyell. *Scientific American,* Aug., 98.

Eiseley, L. C. 1959b. Alfred Russel Wallace. *Scientific American,* Feb., 70.

Eiseley, L. C. 1961. *Darwin's Century.* New York: Anchor.

Fernstrom, J. D. and R. J. Wurtman. 1974. Nutrition and the brain. *Scientific American,* Feb., 84.

Fisher, R. A. 1958. *The Genetical Theory of Natural Selection.* 2nd rev. ed. New York: Dover.

Frieden, E. 1972. The chemical elements of life. *Scientific American,* July, 52.

Gardiner, R. A. and B. T. Gardiner. 1969. Teaching sign language to a chimpanzee. *Science* 169:664–72.

Garn, S. M. 1970. *Human Races.* rev. ed. Springfield, Ill.: Charles C Thomas.

Gazzaniga, M. S. 1967. The split brain in man. *Scientific American,* Aug., 24.

Geschwind, N. 1965. Disconnection syndromes in animals and man. *Brain* 88:237–94, 585–644.

Glass, H. B. 1953. The genetics of the Dunkers. *Scientific American,* Aug., 76.

Glasse, R. 1967. Cannibalism in the kuru region of New Guinea. *Trans. N.Y. Acad. Sci.* 29:748–54.

Gray, G. W. 1953. Human Growth. *Scientific American,* Oct., 65.

Hanna, J. M. 1970. A comparison of laboratory and field studies of cold response. *Am. J. Phys. Anthro.* 32(2):227–31.

Harlow, H. F. and M. K. Harlow. 1949. Learning to think. *Scientific American,* Aug., 36.

Harlow, H. F. and M. K. Harlow. 1962. Social deprivation in monkeys. *Scientific American,* Nov., 136.

Harrison, G. A., J. S. Weiner, J. M. Tanner, and N. A. Barnicot. 1964. *Human Biology.* Oxford: Oxford Univ. Press.

Harrison, R. J. and W. Montagna. 1969. *Man.* New York: Appleton-Century-Crofts.

Hayflick, L. 1968. Aging and human cells. *Scientific American,* March, 32.

Hiernaux, J. 1968. La diversité humaine en Afrique subsaharienne. Brussels: *Editions de l'Institut de Sociologie Université Libre de Bruxelles.*

Hockett, C. F. 1960. The Origin of Speech. *Scientific American,* Sept., 88.

Hockett, C. F. 1973. *Man's Place in Nature.* New York: McGraw-Hill.

Hoebel, E. A. 1966. *Anthropology: The Study of Man.* 3rd ed. New York: McGraw-Hill.

Hoff, C. J. 1968. Demography and research with high altitude populations. *Pa. State Univ. Occas. Pap. Anthropol.* 1:65–89.

Holland, J. J. 1974. Slow inapparent and recurrent viruses. *Scientific American,* Feb., 32.

Hong, S. K. and H. Rahn. 1967. The diving women of Korea and Japan. *Scientific American,* May, 34.

Howell, F. C. and the Editors of Time-Life Books. 1965. *Early Man.* Life Nature Library. New York: Time-Life Books.

Howells, W. W. 1960. The distribution of man. *Scientific American,* Sept., 112.

Howells, W. W. 1966. *Homo erectus. Scientific American,* Nov., 46.

Howells, W. W. 1967. *Mankind in the Making.* New York: Doubleday.

Howells, W. W. 1973. *Evolution of the Genus Homo.* Reading, Mass: Addison-Wesley.

Howells, W. W., ed. 1962. *Ideas on Human Evolution: Selected Essays 1949-1961.* Cambridge: Harvard Univ. Press.

Hrdlicka, A. 1930. *The Skeletal Remains of Early Man.* Smithsonian Misc. Coll. 83.

Hulse, F. S. 1971. *The Human Species: An Introduction to Physical Anthropology.* New York: Random House.

Huxley, J. S. 1942. *Evolution, the Modern Synthesis.* London: Allen & Unwin.

Huxley, J. S. 1956. World population. *Scientific American,* March, 64.

Huxley, T. 1863. *Evidence as to Man's Place in Nature.* London: Williams & Morgate.

Irving, L. 1966. Adaptations to cold. *Scientific American,* Jan., 94.

Jay, P. C., ed. 1968. *Primate Studies in Adaptation and Variability.* New York: Holt, Rinehart and Winston.

Johnson, R. 1972. *Aggression in Man and Animals.* Philadelphia: W. J. Saunders.

Johnston, F. E. 1973. *Microevolution of Human Populations.* Englewood Cliffs, N.Y.: Prentice-Hall.

Jolly, A. 1972. *The Evolution of Primate Behavior.* New York: Macmillan.

Jouvet, M. 1967. The states of sleep. *Scientific American,* Feb., 62.

Katz, S. H. 1972a. Biological factors in population control. In *Population Growth: Anthropological Implications,* ed. B. Spooner, pp. 351–69. Cambridge: MIT Press.

Katz, S. H. 1972b. Change on top of the world. *Expeditions* 15:15–21, Fall

Katz, S. H. 1972c. Unity and diversity of man from the point of view of social and cultural anthropology. In *Seminar on the Unity and Diversity of Man.* Paris: Fondation Royaumont. Also, in *The Unity of Man,* Paris, in press.

Katz, S. H. 1973a. Evolutionary perspectives on purpose and man. *Zygon, J. Rel. Sci.* 8(3–4):325–40, Sept.–Dec.

Katz, S. H. 1973b. Genetic adaptation in 20th century man. *Genetics and Human Evolution,* ed. M. Crawford and P. Workman. Chapter 18. Albuquerque: Univ. of New Mexico Press.

Katz, S. H. and E. Foulks. 1973. An ecosystems approach to health in the Arctic. *Second International Symposium on Circumpolar Health. Acta Sociomed. Scand. Sup.* 6:185–94.

Katz, S. H., M. L. Hediger, and L. A. Valleroy. 1974. Traditional maize processing techniques in the New World. *Science* 184:765–773.

Kosambi, D. D. 1967. Living prehistory in India. *Scientific American,* Feb., 104.

Krogman, W. M. 1962. *The Skeleton in Forensic Medicine.* Springfield, Ill.: A. H. Thomas.

Krogman, W. M. 1972. *Child Growth.* Ann Arbor: Univ. of Michigan Press.

Kummer, H. 1971. *Primate Societies.* Chicago: Aldine-Atherton.

Langer, W. L. 1972. Checks on population growth: 1750–1850. *Scientific American,* Feb., 92.

Lasker, G. W. 1973. *Physical Anthropology.* New York: Holt, Rinehart and Winston.

Laughlin, W. S. 1963. Eskimos and Aleuts: their origins and evolution. *Science* 142(3593):633–45.

Laughlin, W. S. and R. H. Osborne, eds. 1967. *Human Variation and Origins.* Readings from Scientific American. San Francisco: W. H. Freeman and Company.

Lawick-Goodall, J. van. 1971. *In the Shadow of Man.* Boston: Houghton Mifflin.

Leader, R. W. 1967. The kinship of animal and human diseases. *Scientific American,* Jan., 110.

LeGros Clark, W. E. 1964. *The Fossil Evidence for Human Evolution.* rev. ed. Chicago: Univ. of Chicago Press.

LeGros Clark, W. E. 1967. *Man-Apes or Ape-Men?* New York: Holt, Rinehart and Winston.

Lenneberg, E. H. 1967. *The Biological Foundations of Language.* New York: John Wiley.

Lenning, E. P. and T. C. Patterson. 1967. Early man in South America. *Scientific American,* Nov., 44.

Lerner, J. M. 1968. *Heredity, Evolution, and Society.* San Francisco: W. H. Freeman and Company.

Levine, S. 1971. Stress and behavior. *Scientific American,* Jan., 26.

Levi-Strauss, C. 1969. *The Elementary Structures of Kinship.* Toronto: Beacon Press.

Levi-Strauss, C. 1970. *The Raw and the Cooked.* New York: Harper & Row.

Levi-Strauss, C. 1973. *From Honey to Ashes*. New York: Harper & Row.

Lieberman, P. and E. S. Crelin. 1971. On the Speech of Neanderthal man. *Linguistic Inquiry* 2:203–222.

Livingstone, F. B. 1963. Blood groups and ancestry: a test case from the New Guinea highlands. *Curr. Anthropol.* 4:541–42.

Livingstone, F. B. and J. N. Spuhler. 1965. Cultural determinants in natural selection. *Internat. Soc. Sci. J.* 17:118–20.

Loomis, W. F. 1967. Skin pigment regulation and vitamin D synthesis. *Science.* 157:501–6.

Lovejoy, A. O. 1936. *The Great Chain of Being*. Cambridge: Harvard Univ. Press.

Lovejoy, C. O., K. G. Heiple, and A. H. Burstein. 1973. The gait of the Australopithecus. *Amer. J. Phys. Anthropol.* 38(3):757–79, May.

Luria, A. R. 1970. The Functional organization of the brain. *Scientific American*, March, 66.

MacArthur, R. and J. Connell. 1967. *The Biology of Populations*. New York: John Wiley.

McCracken, R. D. 1971. Lactase deficiency: an example of dietary evolution. *C. A.* 12:479–517.

MacNeish, R. S. 1964. The origins of New World civilization. *Scientific American*, Nov., 29.

Malefijt, A. de W. 1968. Homo Monstrosus. *Scientific American*, Oct., 112.

Mann, A. *The Demography of the Australopithecus*. University of Pennsylvania Publications in Anthropology, No. 1. Philadelphia: Univ. of Pennsylvania Press, in press.

Marples, M. J. 1969. Life on the human skin. *Scientific American*, Jan., 108.

Mayr, E. 1963. *Animal Species and Evolution*. Cambridge: Harvard Univ. Press.

Mazia, D. 1974. The cell cycle. *Scientific American*, Jan., 54.

Mirsky, A. E. 1968. The discovery of DNA. *Scientific American*, June, 78.

Monod, J. 1971. *Chance and Necessity: An Essay on the Natural Philosophy of Modern Biology*, trans. A. Winehouse. New York: Alfred A. Knopf.

Montagna, W. 1965. The Skin. *Scientific American*, Feb., 56.

Montagu, F. M. A., ed. 1964. *The Concept of Race*. New York: The Free Press.

Moore R. and the Editors of Time-Life Books. 1962. *Evolution*. Life Nature Library. New York: Time-Life Books.

Morris, L. N., ed. 1971. *Human Populations, Genetic Variation, and Evolution*. San Francisco: Chandler.

Movius, H. L. 1944. Early man and Pleistocene stratigraphy in Southern and Eastern Asia. *Papers Peabody Mus. Amer. Archaeology and Ethnology* 19:1–125.

Muller, H. J. 1963. Genetic progress by voluntarily conducted germinal choice. In *Man and His Future*, ed. G. Wolstenhome. Boston: Little, Brown.

Mulvaney, D. J. 1966. The prehistory of the Australian aborigine. *Scientific American*, March, 84.

Napier, J. R. 1962. The evolution of the hand. *Scientific American*, Dec., 56.

Napier, J. R. 1967. The antiquity of human walking. *Scientific American*, April, 56.

Napier, J. R., ed. 1963. *The Primates*. Symposia 10, Zoological Soc. of London.

Napier, J. R. and P. H. Napier. 1967. *A Handbook of Living Primates*. New York: Academic Press.

Newell, N. D. 1963. Crises in the history of life. *Scientific American*, Feb., 76.

Newman, M. T. 1958. Man in the heights. *Nat. Hist.* 67:9–19.

Newman, M. T. 1962. Ecology and nutritional stress in man. *Amer. J. Phys. Anthropol.* 64(11):22–34.

Oakley, K. P. 1966. *Frameworks for Dating Fossil Man.* 2nd ed. Chicago: Aldine-Atherton.

Osborne, R. H. and F. V. deGeorge. 1959. *Genetic Basis of Morphological Variation*. Cambridge: Harvard Univ. Press.

Penrose, L. S. 1969. Dermatoglyphics. *Scientific American.* Dec., 72.

Pfeiffer, J. 1972. *The Emergence of Man*. rev. ed. New York: Harper & Row.

Pilbeam, D. R. 1970. *The Evolution of Man*. London: Thames & Hudson.

Pilbeam, D. R. 1972. *The Ascent of Man*. New York: Macmillan.

Pirie, N. W. 1967. Orthodox and unorthodox methods of meeting world food needs. *Scientific American*, Feb., 27.

Premack, D. 1971. Language in chimpanzees? *Science* 172:808–22.

The Primary Production of the Biosphere. 1973. A Symposium Given at the 2nd Congress of the American Institute of Biological Sciences, Miami, Florida, October 24, 1971. *Human Ecol.* 1(4):301–94, Sept.

Reisfeld, R. A. and B. D. Kahan. 1972. Markers of biological individuality. *Scientific American*, June, 28.

Rivinus, H. and S. Katz. 1971. Evolution, newborn behavior and maternal attachment. *Commun. Contemp. Psychiat.* 1:95–104, Nov./Dec.

Romer, A. S. 1965. *Vertebrate Paleontology*. 2nd ed. Chicago: Univ. of Chicago Press.

Schaller, G. B. 1963. *The Mountain Gorilla: Ecology and Behavior*. Chicago: Univ. of Chicago Press.

Schultz, A. H. 1969. *The Life of Primates*. New York: Universe Books.

Shapiro, I. 1974. Subclinical lead exposure in Philadelphia school children. *N. Engl. J. Med.*, 31 Jan.

Shock, N. W. 1962. The physiology of aging. *Scientific American*, Jan, 100.

Simons, E. L. 1964. The early relatives of man. *Scientific American*, July, 50.

Simons, E. L. and P. C. Ettel. 1970. Gigantopithecus. *Scientific American*, Jan., 76.

Simons, E. L. 1972. *Primate Evolution*. New York: Macmillan.

Sinclair, D. 1969. *Human Growth After Birth*. New York: Oxford.

Smith, J. M. 1969. *The Theory of Evolution*. 2nd ed. New York: Pelican.

Solheim, II, W. G. 1972. An earlier agricultural revolution. *Scientific American*, April, 34.

Steegmann, A. T. 1970. Cold adaptation and the human face. *Amer. J. Phys. Anthropol.* 32(2):243–50.

Stern, C. and E. R. Sherwood. 1966. *The Origin of Genetics*. A Mendel Source Book. San Francisco: W. H. Freeman and Company.

Tanner, J. M. 1961. *Growth at Adolescence*. 2nd ed. Oxford: Blackwell Sci. Pub.

Tanner, J. M. 1968. Earlier maturation in man. *Scientific American*, Jan., 21.

Tanner, J. M., ed. 1960. *Human Growth*. New York: Pergamon.

Tazieff, H. 1970. Afar triangle. *Scientific American*, Feb., 32.

Thoma, A. 1966. L'occipital de L'homme mindelien de Vertesszöllös. *L'Anthropologie* 70:495–534.

Tobias, P. V. 1970. *The Brain in Hominid Evolution*. New York: Columbia Univ. Press.

Töró, I., E. Szabady, J. Nemeskéri, and O. G. Eiben, eds. 1972. *Advances in the Biology of Human Populations*. Budapest: Akadémiai Kiadó.

Turnbull, C. M. 1963. The lesson of the pygmies. *Scientific American*, Jan., 28.

UNESCO. 1969. *Race and Science: the Race Question in Modern Science*. New York: Columbia Univ. Press.

Waddington, C. H. 1953. How do cells differentiate? *Scientific American*, Sept., 108.

Washburn, S. L. 1960. Tools and human evolution. *Scientific American*, Sept., 62.

Washburn, S. L., ed. 1961. *Social Life of Early Man*. Chicago: Aldine-Atherton.

Washburn, S. L., ed. 1963. *Classification and Human Evolution*. Chicago: Aldine-Atherton.

Washburn, S. L. and P. C. Dolhinow, eds. 1972. *Perspectives on Human Evolution 2*. New York: Holt, Rinehart and Winston.

Washburn, S. L. and P. C. Jay, eds. 1968. *Perspectives on Human Evolution 1*. New York: Holt, Rinehart and Winston.

Washburn, S. L. and R. Moore. 1974. *Ape Into Man: A Study of Human Evolution*. Boston: Little, Brown.

Watson, J. D. 1970. *Molecular Biology of the Gene*. rev. ed. New York: W. A. Benjamin.

Weidenreich, F. 1947. Facts and speculations concerning the origin of *Homo sapiens*. *American Anthropologist* 49:187–203.

Weiner, J. S. 1971. *The Natural History of Man*. New York: Universe Books.

Weisenphel, S. L. 1967. Sickle cell trait in human biology and cultural evolution. *Science* 157:1134–40.

Weiss, J. M. 1972. Psychological factors in stress and disease. *Scientific American*, June, 104.

Wheat, J. B. 1967. A paleo-Indian bison kill. *Scientific American*, Jan., 44.

Williams, R. J. 1959. *Biochemical Individuality*. New York: John Wiley.

Wilson, E. O. 1972. Animal communication. *Scientific American*, Sept., 52.

Yanofsky, C. 1967. Gene structure and protein structure. *Scientific American*, May, 80.

Young, J. Z. 1973. *An Introduction to the Study of Man*. Oxford: Oxford Univ. Press.

Young, V. R. and M. S. Scrimshaw. 1971. The Physiology of Starvation. *Scientific American*, Oct., 14.

BIBLIOGRAPHIES

I THE EVOLUTIONARY ROOTS AND POTENTIALS OF THE HUMAN SPECIES

1. The Earliest Apes

A Critical Reappraisal of Tertiary Primates. Elwyn L. Simons in *Genetic and Evolutionary Biology of the Primates: Vol. I*, edited by John Beuttner-Janusch. Academic Press Inc., 1963.

New Fossil Apes from Egypt and the Initial Differentiation of Hominoidea. E. L. Simons in *Nature*, Vol. 205, No. 4967, pages 135–139; January 9, 1965.

Origins of Man: Physical Anthropology. John Buettner-Janusch. John Wiley & Sons, Inc., 1966.

2. The Antiquity of Human Walking

The Ape-Men. Robert Broom in *Scientific American*; November, 1949.

The Foot and the Shoe. J. R. Napier in *Physiotherapy*, Vol. 43, No. 3, pages 65–74; March, 1957.

A Hominid Toe Bone from Bed 1, Olduvai Gorge, Tanzania. M. H. Day and J. R. Napier in *Nature*, Vol. 211, No. 5052, pages 929–930; August 27, 1966.

3. Tools and Human Evolution

Cerebral Cortex of Man. Wilder Penfield and Theodore Rasmussen. Macmillan Company, 1950.

The Evolution of Man, edited by Sol Tax. University of Chicago Press, 1960.

The Evolution of Man's Capacity for Culture. Arranged by J. N. Spuhler. Wayne State University Press, 1959.

Human Ecology during the Pleistocene and Later Times in Africa South of the Sahara. J. Desmond Clark in *Current Anthropology*, Vol. I, pages 307–324; 1960.

4. Homo Erectus

Mankind in the Making. William W. Howells. Doubleday & Company, Inc., revised edition in press.

The Nomenclature of the Hominidae. Bernard G. Campbell. Occasional Paper No. 22, Royal Anthropological Institute of Great Britain and Ireland, 1965.

The Taxonomic Evolution of Fossil Hominids. Ernst Mayr in *Classification and Human Evolution*, edited by Sherwood L. Washburn. Viking Fund Publications in Anthropology, No. 37, 1963.

5. The Casts of Fossil Hominid Brains

The Evolution of the Primate Brain: Some Aspects of Quantitative Relationships. R. L. Holloway in *Brain Research*, Vol. 7, pages 121–172; 1968.

Australopithecine Endocasts, Brain Evolution in the Hominoidea, and a Model of Hominid Evolution. R. L. Holloway in *The Functional and Evolutionary Biology of Primates*, edited by R. Tuttle. Aldine Press, 1972.

Evolution of Primate Brains: A Comparative Anatomical Investigation. H. Stephan in *The Functional and Evolutionary Biology of Primates*, edited by R. Tuttle. Aldine Press, 1972.

6. The Social Life of Baboons

BEHAVIOR AND EVOLUTION. Edited by Anne Roe and George Gaylord Simpson. Yale University Press, 1958.

A STUDY OF BEHAVIOUR OF THE CHACMA BABOON, PAPIO URSINUS. Niels Bolwig in *Behaviour*, Vol. 14, No. 1–2, pages 136–163; 1959.

7. The Omnivorous Chimpanzee

BABOON ECOLOGY AND HUMAN EVOLUTION. Irven DeVore and S. L. Washburn in *African Ecology and Human Evolution*, edited by F. Clark Howell and François Bourlière. Wenner-Gren Foundation for Anthropological Research, Inc., 1963.

ONE OBSERVED CASE OF HUNTING BEHAVIOR AMONG WILD CHIMPANZEES LIVING IN THE SAVANNA WOODLAND OF WESTERN TANZANIA. M. Kawabe in *Primates*, Vol. 7, pages 393–396; 1966.

THE BEHAVIOUR OF FREE-LIVING CHIMPANZEES IN THE GOMBE STREAM RESERVE. Jane van Lawick-Goodall in *Animal Behaviour Monographs*, Vol. 1, Part 3, pages 161–311; 1968.

THE PREDATORY BEHAVIOR OF WILD CHIMPANZEES. G. Teleki. Bucknell University Press, in press.

8. Teaching Language to an Ape

SYNTACTIC STRUCTURES. Noam Chomsky. Mouton & Co., 1957.

THE GENESIS OF LANGUAGE. Edited by F. Smith and G. A. Miller. The M.I.T. Press, 1966.

BEHAVIOR OF NONHUMAN PRIMATES: VOLS. III–IV. Edited by Fred Stollnitz and Allan M. Schrier. Academic Press, 1971.

LANGUAGE IN CHIMPANZEE? David Premack in *Science*, Vol. 172, No. 3985, pages 808–822; May 21, 1971.

A FIRST LANGUAGE: THE EARLY STAGES. Roger Brown. Harvard University Press, in press.

10. Language and the Brain

CEREBRAL DOMINANCE AND ITS RELATION TO PSYCHOLOGICAL FUNCTION. O. L. Zangwill. Oliver and Boyd, 1960.

DISCONNEXION SYNDROMES IN ANIMALS AND MAN: PART I. Norman Geschwind in *Brain*, Vol. 88, Part 2, pages 237–294; June, 1965.

DISCONNEXION SYNDROMES IN ANIMALS AND MAN: PART II. Norman Geschwind in *Brain*, Vol. 88, Part 3, pages 585–644; September, 1965.

HUMAN BRAIN: LEFT-RIGHT ASYMMETRIES IN TEMPORAL SPEECH REGION. Norman Geschwind and Walter Levitsky in *Science*, Vol. 161, No. 3837, pages 186–187; July 12, 1968.

TRAUMATIC APHASIA: ITS SYNDROMES, PSYCHOLOGY AND TREATMENT. A. R. Luria. Mouton & Co., 1970.

Later References provided by the Author:

HUMAN BRAIN: MORPHOLOGICAL DIFFERENCES IN THE HEMISPHERES DEMONSTRABLE BY CAROTID ARTERIOGRAPHY. M. Lemay and S. Culebras in *New England Journal of Medicine*, Vol. 287, pages 168–170; 1972.

THE LANGUAGE CAPABILITY OF NEANDERTHAL MAN. M. Lemay in *American Journal of Physical Anthropology;* 1973.

THE DEVELOPMENT OF THE BRAIN AND THE EVOLUTION OF LANGUAGE. N. Geschwind in *Monograph Series on Language and Linguistics*, Vol. 17, pages 155–169; 1964.

II EVOLUTIONARY THEORY AND ITS APPLICATION TO THE HUMAN SPECIES

11. The Origin of Darwinism

EVOLUTION, OLD AND NEW. Samuel Butler. E. P. Dutton & Company, 1914.

LECTURES ON PHYSIOLOGY, ZOOLOGY, AND THE NATURAL HISTORY OF MAN. W. Lawrence. Printed for J. Callow, 1819.

THE NATURAL HISTORY OF MAN. James Cowles Prichard. H. Baillière, 1845.

RESEARCHES INTO THE PHYSICAL HISTORY OF MANKIND. James Cowles Prichard. Sherwood, Gilbert & Piper, 1836.

ZOONOMIA. Erasmus Darwin. Printed by T. & J. Swords, 1796.

12. Charles Lyell

CHARLES DARWIN, EDWARD BLYTH AND THE THEORY OF NATURAL SELECTION. Loren C. Eiseley in *Proceedings of the American Philosophical Society*, Vol. 103, No. 1, pages 94–158; February 28, 1959.

CHARLES LYELL AND MODERN GEOLOGY. T. G. Bonney. Macmillan & Co., 1895.

DARWIN'S CENTURY. Loren C. Eiseley. Doubleday & Co., Inc., 1958.

LIFE, LETTERS AND JOURNALS OF SIR CHARLES LYELL, BART. Edited by his sister-in-law, Mrs. Lyell. John Murray, 1881.

PRINCIPLES OF GEOLOGY. Charles Lyell. John Murray, 1830.

13. The Genetic Basis of Evolution

GENETICS AND THE ORIGIN OF SPECIES. Th. Dobzhansky. Columbia University Press, 1937.

14. The Genetic Code: III

THE GENETIC CODE, VOL. XXXI: 1966 COLD SPRING HARBOR SYMPOSIA ON QUANTITATIVE BIOLOGY. Cold Spring Harbor Laboratory of Quantitative Biology, in press.

MOLECULAR BIOLOGY OF THE GENE. James D. Watson. W. A. Benjamin, Inc., 1965.

RNA CODEWORDS AND PROTEIN SYNTHESIS, VII: ON THE GENERAL NATURE OF THE RNA CODE. M. Nirenberg, P. Leder, M. Bernfield, R. Brimacombe, J. Trupin, F. Rottman and C. O'Neal in Proceedings of the National Academy of Sciences, Vol. 53, No. 5, pages 1161–1168; May, 1965.

STUDIES ON POLYNUCLEOTIDES, LVI: FURTHER SYNTHESES, IN VITRO, OF COPOLYPEPTIDES CONTAINING TWO AMINO ACIDS IN ALTERNATING SEQUENCE DEPENDENT UPON DNA-LIKE POLYMERS CONTAINING TWO NUCLEOTIDES IN ALTERNATING SEQUENCE. D. S. Jones, S. Nishimura and H. G. Khorana in Journal of Molecular Biology, Vol. 16, No. 2, pages 454–472; April, 1966.

15. The Mapping of Human Chromosomes

PROBABLE ASSIGNMENT OF THE DUFFY BLOOD GROUP LOCUS TO CHROMOSOME 1 IN MAN. Roger P. Donahue, Wilma B. Bias, James H. Renwick and Victor A. McKusick in Proceedings of the National Academy of Sciences of the United States of America, Vol. 61, No. 3, pages 949–955; November, 1968.

LINKAGE BETWEEN HUMAN LACTATE DEHYDROGENASE A AND B AND PEPTIDASE B. F. H. Ruddle, V. M. Chapman, T. R. Chen and R. J. Klebe in Nature, Vol. 227, No. 5255, pages 251–257; July 18, 1970.

MENDELIAN INHERITANCE IN MAN: CATALOGS OF AUTOSOMAL DOMINANT, AUTOSOMAL RECESSIVE, AND X-LINKED PHENOTYPES. Victor A. McKusick. The Johns Hopkins Press, 1971.

16. Ionizing Radiation and Evolution

THE CAUSES OF EVOLUTION. J. B. S. Haldane. Harper & Brothers, 1932.

THE DARWINIAN AND MODERN CONCEPTIONS OF NATURAL SELECTION. H. J. Muller in Proceedings of the American Philosophical Society, Vol. 93, No. 6, pages 459–479; December 29, 1949.

EVOLUTION, GENETICS AND MAN. Theodosius Dobzhansky. John Wiley & Sons, Inc., 1955.

GENETICS, PALEONTOLOGY AND EVOLUTION. Edited by Glenn L. Jepsen, Ernst Mayr and George Gaylord Simpson. Princeton University Press, 1949.

RADIATION AND THE ORIGIN OF THE GENE. Carl Sagan in Evolution, Vol. 11, No. 1, pages 40–55; March, 1957.

17. Genetic Load

OUR LOAD OF MUTATIONS. H. J. Muller in The American Journal of Human Genetics, Vol. 2, No. 2, pages 111–176; June, 1950.

A MOLECULAR APPROACH TO THE STUDY OF GENIC HETEROZYGOSITY IN NATURAL POPULATIONS. J. L. Hubby and R. C. Lewontin in Genetics, Vol. 54, No. 2, pages 577–609; August, 1966.

THE FATE OF X-RAY INDUCED CHROMOSOMAL REARRANGEMENTS INTRODUCED INTO LABORATORY POPULATIONS OF DROSOPHILA MELANOGASTER. Edwin Vann in The American Naturalist, Vol. 100, No. 914, pages 425–449; September–October, 1966.

THREE KINDS OF GENETIC VARIABILITY IN YEAST POPULATIONS. Christopher Wills in Proceedings of the National Academy of Sciences of the United States of America, Vol. 61, No. 3, pages 937–944; November, 1968.

Later Reference provided by the author:

HOW GENET BACKGROUND MASKS SINGLE-GENE HETEROSIS IN DROSOPHILA. Christopher Wills and Lois Nichols in Proceedings of the National Academy of Sciences of the United States of America, Vol. 69, pages 323–325.

18. Genetic Drift in an Italian Population

FREQUENCIES OF PEDIGREES OF CONSANGUINEOUS MARRIAGES AND MATING STRUCTURE OF THE POPULATION. I. Barrai, L. L. Cavalli-Sforza and A. Moroni in Annals of Human Genetics, Vol. 25, Part 4, pages 347–377; May, 1962.

THE PROBABILITY OF CONSANGUINEOUS MARRIAGES. L. L. Cavalli-Sforza, M. Kimura and I. Barrai in Genetics, Vol. 54, No. 1, Part 1, pages 37–60; July, 1966.

EXPERIMENTS WITH AN ARTIFICIAL POPULATION. L. L. Cavalli-Sforza and G. Zei in Proceedings of the International Congress of Human Genetics, edited by James F. Crow and James V. Neel. The Johns Hopkins Press, 1967.

III   RACE AND INDIVIDUALITY

19.   The Distribution of Man

HUMAN ANCESTRY FROM A GENETICAL POINT OF VIEW. Reginald Ruggles Gates. Harvard University Press, 1948.

MANKIND IN THE MAKING. William White Howells. Doubleday & Company, Inc., 1959.

RACES: A STUDY OF THE PROBLEMS OF RACE FORMATION IN MAN. Carleton S. Coon, Stanley M. Garn and Joseph B. Birdsell. Charles C. Thomas, 1950.

THE STORY OF MAN. Carleton Stevens Coon. Alfred A. Knopf, Inc., 1954.

21.   Intelligence and Race

INTRODUCTION TO QUANTITATIVE GENETICS. D. S. Falconer. Oliver and Boyd, 1960.

INTELLIGENCE AND SOCIAL MOBILITY. Cyril Burt in *The British Journal of Statistical Psychology*, Vol. 14, Part 1, pages 3–24; May, 1961.

MONOZYGOTIC TWINS BROUGHT UP APART AND BROUGHT UP TOGETHER: AN INVESTIGATION INTO THE GENETIC AND ENVIRONMENTAL CAUSES OF VARIATION IN PERSONALITY. James Shields. Oxford University Press, 1962.

GENETICS AND INTELLIGENCE: A REVIEW. L. Erlenmeyer-Kimling and Lissy F. Jarvik in *Science*, Vol. 142, No. 3598, pages 1477–1479; December 13, 1963.

HOW MUCH CAN WE BOOST IQ AND SCHOLASTIC ACHIEVEMENT? Arthur R. Jensen in *Harvard Educational Review*, Vol. 39, No. 1, pages 1–123; Winter, 1969.

DISCUSSION: HOW MUCH CAN WE BOOST IQ AND SCHOLASTIC ACHIEVEMENT? *Harvard Educational Review*, Vol. 39, No. 2, pages 273–356; Spring, 1969.

22.   Growing Up

GROWTH AT ADOLESCENCE. J. M. Tanner. Blackwell Scientific Publications, 1962.

HUMAN DEVELOPMENT. Edited by Frank Falkner. W. B. Saunders Company, 1966.

HUMAN GROWTH: BODY COMPOSITION, CELL GROWTH, ENERGY, AND INTELLIGENCE. Edited by Donald B. Cheek. Lea & Febiger, 1968.

EFFECT OF HUMAN GROWTH HORMONE TREATMENT FOR 1 TO 7 YEARS ON GROWTH OF 100 CHILDREN, WITH GROWTH HORMONE DEFICIENCY, LOW BIRTHWEIGHT, INHERITED SMALLNESS, TURNER'S SYNDROME, AND OTHER COMPLAINTS. J. M. Tanner, R. H. Whitehouse, P. C. R. Hughes and F. P. Vince in *Archives of Disease in Childhood*, Vol. 46, No. 250, pages 745–782; December, 1971.

MAN AND WOMAN, BOY AND GIRL: DIFFERENTIATION AND DIMORPHISM OF GENDER IDENTITY. John Money and Anke A. Ehrhardt. The Johns Hopkins University Press, 1972.

23.   Deprivation Dwarfism

GROWTH FAILURE IN MATERNAL DEPRIVATION. Robert Gray Patton and Lytt I. Gardner. Charles C. Thomas, Publisher, 1963.

EMOTIONAL DEPRIVATION AND GROWTH RETARDATION SIMULATING IDIOPATHIC HYPOPITUITARISM, II: ENDOCRINOLOGIC EVALUATION OF THE SYNDROME. G. F. Powell, J. A. Brasel, S. Raiti and R. M. Blizzard in *The New England Journal of Medicine*, Vol. 267, No. 23, pages 1279–1283; June 8, 1967.

SHORT STATURE ASSOCIATED WITH MATERNAL DEPRIVATION SYNDROME: DISORDERED FAMILY ENVIRONMENT AS CAUSE OF SO-CALLED IDIOPATHIC HYPOPITUITARISM. Robert Gray Patton and Lytt I. Gardner in *Endocrine and Genetic Diseases of Childhood*, edited by L. I. Gardner. W. B. Saunders Company, 1969.

GROWTH HORMONE IN NEWBORN INFANTS DURING SLEEP-WAKE PERIODS. Bennett A. Shaywitz, Jordan Finkelstein, Leon Hellman and Elliot D. Weitzman in *Pediatrics*, Vol. 48, No. 1, pages 103–109; July, 1971.

24.   Getting Old

CHEMICAL ASPECTS OF AGING AND THE EFFECT OF DIET UPON AGING. C. M. McCay in *Cowdry's Problems of Aging*, edited by A. I. Lansing. Williams & Wilkins Company, 1952.

AGING: THE BIOLOGY OF SENESCENCE. Alexander Comfort. Holt, Rinehart and Winston, Inc., 1964.

BEHAVIOR AND ADAPTATION IN LATE LIFE. Edited by Ewald W. Busse and Eric Pfeiffer. Little, Brown and Company, 1969.

THE IMMUNOLOGIC THEORY OF AGING. Roy A. Walford. Munksgaard, Copenhagen, 1969.

SOCIAL IMPLICATIONS OF A PROLONGED LIFE-SPAN. Bernice L. Neugarten in *The Gerontologist*, Vol. 12, No. 4, page 323, pages 438–440; Winter, 1972.

IV ADAPTATION AND ADAPTABILITY

25. Sickle Cells and Evolution

SICKLE-CELL ANEMIA. George W. Gray in *Scientific American*, Vol. 185, No. 2, pages 56–59; August, 1951.

PROTECTION AFFORDED BY SICKLE-CELL TRAITS AGAINST SUBTERTIAN MALARIAL INFECTION. A. C. Allison in *British Medical Journal*, Vol. 1, pages 290–301; February, 1954.

26. Lactose and Lactase

A RACIAL DIFFERENCE IN INCIDENCE OF LACTASE DEFICIENCY. Theodore M. Bayless and Norton S. Rosensweig in *The Journal of the American Medical Association*, Vol. 197, No. 12, pages 968–972; September 19, 1966.

MILK. Stuart Patton in *Scientific American*, Vol. 221, No. 1, pages 58–68; July, 1969.

PRIMARY ADULT LACTOSE INTOLERANCE AND THE MILKING HABIT: A PROBLEM IN BIOLOGIC AND CULTURAL INTERRELATIONS. II. A CULTURAL HISTORICAL HYPOTHESIS. Frederick J. Simoons in *The American Journal of Digestive Diseases*, Vol. 15, No. 8, pages 695–710; August, 1970.

LACTASE DEFICIENCY: AN EXAMPLE OF DIETARY EVOLUTION. R. D. McCracken in *Current Anthropology*, Vol. 12, No. 4–5, pages 479–517; October–December, 1971.

MEMORIAL LECTURE: LACTOSE AND LACTASE—A HISTORICAL PERSPECTIVE. Norman Kretchmer in *Gastroenterology*, Vol. 61, No. 6, pages 805–813; December, 1971.

27. The Black Death

THE BLACK DEATH. G. G. Coulton. Ernest Benn Limited, 1929.

THE BLACK DEATH: A CHRONICLE OF THE PLAGUE. Compiled by Johannes Nohl. George Allen & Unwin Ltd., 1926.

THE BLIGHT OF PESTILENCE ON EARLY MODERN CIVILIZATION. Lynn Thorndike in *The American Historical Review*, Vol. 32, No. 3, pages 455–474; April, 1927.

THE BUBONIC PLAGUE AND ENGLAND. Charles F. Mullett. University of Kentucky Press, 1956.

PLAGUE AND PESTILENCE IN LITERATURE AND ART. Raymond Crawfurd. Oxford University Press, 1914.

Later references provided by the Author:
THE BLACK DEATH. George Deaux. London, 1969.
THE BLACK DEATH. Philip Ziegler.

28. Adaptations to Cold

BODY INSULATION OF SOME ARCTIC AND TROPICAL MAMMALS AND BIRDS. P. F. Scholander, Vladimir Walters, Raymond Hock and Laurence Irving in *The Biological Bulletin*, Vol. 99, No. 2, pages 225–236; October, 1950.

BODY TEMPERATURES OF ARCTIC AND SUBARCTIC BIRDS AND MAMMALS. Laurence Irving and John Krog in *Journal of Applied Physiology*, Vol. 6, No. 11, pages 667–680; May, 1954.

EFFECT OF TEMPERATURE ON SENSITIVITY OF THE FINGER. Laurence Irving in *Journal of Applied Physiology*, Vol. 18, No. 6, pages 1201–1205; November, 1963.

METABOLISM AND INSULATION OF SWINE AS BARE-SKINNED MAMMALS. Laurence Irving, Leonard J. Peyton and Mildred Monson in *Journal of Applied Physiology*, Vol. 9, No. 3, pages 421–426; November, 1956.

PHYSIOLOGICAL INSULATION OF SWINE AS BARE-SKINNED MAMMALS. Laurence Irving in *Journal of Applied Physiology*, Vol. 9, No. 3, pages 414–420; November, 1956.

TERRESTRIAL ANIMALS IN COLD: INTRODUCTION. Laurence Irving in *Handbook of Physiology, Section 4: Adaptation to the Environment.* American Physiological Society, 1964.

29. The Physiology of High Altitude

EFFECTS OF ALTITUDE ON BROWN FAT AND METABOLISM OF THE DEER MOUSE, *Peromyscus*. Jane C. Roberts, Raymond J. Hock and Robert E. Smith in *Federation Proceedings*, Vol. 28, No. 3, pages 1065–1072; May–June, 1969.

PHYSIOLOGICAL RESPONSES OF DEER MICE TO VARIOUS NATIVE ALTITUDES. R. J. Hock in *The Physiological Effects of High Altitude: Proceedings of a Symposium Held at Interlaken, September 18–22, 1962,* edited by W. H. Weihe. Pergamon Press, 1964.

HUMAN ADAPTATION TO HIGH ALTITUDE. Paul T. Baker in *Science*, Vol. 163, No. 3872, pages 1149–1156; March 14, 1969.

30. The Skin

ADVANCES IN THE BIOLOGY OF SKIN, Vol. V: WOUND HEALING. William Montagna and Rupert E. Billingham. Pergamon Press, 1964.

THE BIOLOGY OF HAIR GROWTH. Edited by William Montagna and Richard A. Ellis. Academic Press, 1958.

FINGER PRINTS, PALMS AND SOLES: AN INTRODUCTION TO DERMATOGLYPHICS. Harold Cummins and Charles Midlo. Dover Publications, Inc., 1961.

HUMAN PERSPIRATION. Yas. Kuno. Charles C. Thomas, Publisher, 1956.

PHYSIOLOGY AND BIOCHEMISTRY OF THE SKIN. Stephen Rothman. The University of Chicago Press, 1954.

THE STRUCTURE AND FUNCTION OF SKIN. William Montagna. Academic Press, 1962.

31. The Multiple Sclerosis Problem

THE FREQUENCY AND GEOGRAPHIC DISTRIBUTION OF MULTIPLE SCLEROSIS AS INDICATED BY MORTALITY STATISTICS AND MORBIDITY SURVEYS IN THE UNITED STATES AND CANADA. Leonard T. Kurland in *The American Journal of Hygiene*, Vol. 55, No. 3, pages 457–476; May, 1952.

MULTIPLE SCLEROSIS IN ISRAEL. Milton Alter, Lipman Halpern, Leonard T. Kurland, Bernard Bornstein, Uri Leibowitz and Joseph Silberstein in *Archives of Neurology*, Vol. 7, No. 4, pages 253–263; October, 1962.

THE PREVALENCE OF MULTIPLE SCLEROSIS IN AUSTRALIA. John M. Sutherland, John H. Tyrer and Mervyn J. Eadie in *Brain: A Journal of Neurology*, Vol. 85, Part I, pages 149–164; 1962.

MULTIPLE SCLEROSIS: A REAPPRAISAL. Douglas McAlpine, Charles E. Lumsden and E. D. Acheson. E. & S. Livingstone Ltd, 1968.

32. The Flow of Energy in A Hunting Society

THE NETSILIK ESKIMOS: SOCIAL LIFE AND SPIRITUAL CULTURE. Knud Rasmussen in *Report of the Fifth Thule Expedition, 1921–24, No. 8.* Copenhagen: Gyldendalake Boghandel, 1931.

THE ESKIMOS: THEIR ENVIRONMENT AND FOLKWAYS. Edward Moffat Weyer, Jr. Yale University Press, 1932.

MAN THE HUNTER. Edited by Richard B. Lee and Irven DeVore. Aldine Publishing Company, 1969.

33. The Flow of Energy in an Agricultural Society

ECOLOGICAL ENERGETICS. John Phillipson. Edward Arnold Publishers, 1966.

PERSPECTIVES IN ECOLOGICAL THEORY. Ramón Margalef. The University of Chicago Press, 1968.

PIGS FOR THE ANCESTORS: RITUAL IN THE ECOLOGY OF A NEW GUINEA PEOPLE. Roy A. Rappaport. Yale University Press, 1968.

ENVIRONMENT, POWER, AND SOCIETY. Howard T. Odum. Wiley-Interscience, 1971.

V   THE CHALLENGE OF THE PRESENT

34. The Present Evolution of Man

EVOLUTION, GENETICS AND MAN. Theodosius Dobzhansky. John Wiley & Sons, Inc., 1955.

MIRROR FOR MAN. Clyde Kluckhohn. McGraw-Hill Book Co., Inc., 1949.

RADIATION, GENES AND MAN. Bruce Wallace and Theodosius Dobzhansky. Henry Holt & Co., Inc., 1959.

38. Prenatal Diagnosis of Genetic Disease

WHO SHALL LIVE? MAN'S CONTROL OVER BIRTH AND DEATH. American Friends Service Committee. Hill and Wang, 1970.

WHO SHALL LIVE? MEDICINE TECHNOLOGY ETHICS. Edited by Kenneth Vaux. Fortress Press, 1970.

ON THE NATURE OF MEN. Jérôme Lejeune in *The American Journal of Human Genetics*, Vol. 22, No. 2, pages 121–128; March, 1970.

PRENATAL GENETIC DIAGNOSIS. Aubrey Milunsky, John W. Littlefield, Julian N. Kanfer, Edwin H. Kolodny, Vivian E. Shih and Leonard Atkins in *The New England Journal of Medicine*, Vol. 283, No. 25, pages 1370–1381, December 17, 1970; Vol. 283, No. 26, pages 1441–1447, December 24, 1970; Vol. 283, No. 27, pages 1498–1504, December 31, 1970.

SYMPOSIUM ON INTRAUTERINE DIAGNOSIS. Edited by Daniel Bergsma in *Birth Defects: Original Article Series*, Vol. 7, No. 5, pages 1–36; April, 1971.

39. Human Food Production as a Process in the Biosphere

MALNUTRITION AND NATIONAL DEVELOPMENT. Alan D. Berg in *Foreign Affairs*, Vol. 46, No. 1, pages 126–136; October, 1967.

ON THE SHRED OF A CLOUD. Rolf Edberg. Translated by Sven Ahmån. The University of Alabama Press, 1969.

POLITICS AND ENVIRONMENT: A READER IN ECOLOGICAL CRISIS. Edited by Walt Anderson. Goodyear Publishing Company, Inc., 1970.

POPULATION, RESOURCES, ENVIRONMENT: ISSUES IN HUMAN ECOLOGY. Paul R. Ehrlich and Anne H. Ehrlich. W. H. Freeman and Company, 1970.

SEEDS OF CHANGE: THE GREEN REVOLUTION AND DEVELOPMENT IN THE 1970's. Lester R. Brown. Praeger Publishers, 1970.

40. Toxic Substances and Ecological Cycles

ENVIRONMENTAL RADIOACTIVITY. Merril Eisenbud. McGraw-Hill Book Company, Inc., 1963.

PESTICIDES AND THE LIVING LANDSCAPE. Robert L. Rudd. University of Wisconsin Press, 1964.

REPORT OF THE UNITED NATIONS SCIENTIFIC COMMITTEE ON THE EFFECTS OF ATOMIC RADIATION. Official Records of the General Assembly, 13th Session, Supplement No. 17, 1958; 17th Session, Supplement No. 16, 1962; 19th Session, Supplement No. 14, 1964.

41. The Prospects for a Stationary World Population

REFLECTIONS ON THE DEMOGRAPHIC CONDITIONS NEEDED TO ESTABLISH A U.S. STATIONARY POPULATION GROWTH. Tomas Frejka in *Population Studies*, Vol. 22, No. 3, pages 379–397; 1968.

UN TAUX D'ACCROISSMENT NUL POUR LES PAYS EN VOIE DE DEVELOPPEMENT EN L'AN 2000: REVE OU REALITE? Jean Pichat-Bourgeois and Si-Ahmed Taleb in *Population*, No. 5, pages 957–974; September–October, 1970.

THE GROWTH AND STRUCTURE OF HUMAN POPULATIONS: A MATHEMATICAL INVESTIGATION. Ansley J. Coale. Princeton University Press, 1972.

POPULATION AND THE AMERICAN FUTURE. United States Commission on Population Growth and the American Future, 1972.

INDEX